CHEQUERED PAST,
UNCERTAIN FUTURE

CHEQUERED PAST, UNCERTAIN FUTURE
The History of Pakistan

TAHIR KAMRAN

REAKTION BOOKS

For Ian Talbot

Published by
Reaktion Books Ltd
Unit 32, Waterside
44–48 Wharf Road
London N1 7UX, UK
www.reaktionbooks.co.uk

First published 2024
Copyright © Tahir Kamran 2024

All rights reserved

No part of this publication may be reproduced, stored in a retrieval system, or transmitted, in any form or by any means, electronic, mechanical, photocopying, recording or otherwise, without the prior permission of the publishers

Printed and bound in Great Britain by TJ Books Ltd, Padstow, Cornwall

A catalogue record for this book is available from the British Library

ISBN 978 1 78914 913 5

CONTENTS

Introduction by Ian Talbot 7

1
From Prehistory to the Early Modern Era,
3800 BCE to 1707 CE 13

2
British Rule and the Rise of
Muslim Nationalism 46

3
Bloodied Partition and the Punjab's Bifurcation, 1947 82

4
Multiple Challenges, Limited Options: Making Sense
of the Early Problems 103

5
The Faltering Years of a Nascent State, 1947–58 134

6
Praetorianism Unbound (Ayub Khan's Rule), 1958–69 161

7
Praetorianism under General Yahya Khan and East Pakistan's
Separation, 1969–71 194

8
The Era of Populism: Zulfiqar Ali Bhutto, 1971–7 218

9
Piety and Praetorianism:
General Zia ul Haq's Reign, 1977–88 246

10
The Rule of the Troika and the Onset of 'Establishmentarian Democracy', 1988–99 *291*

11
Pervez Musharraf: An Autocrat Re-Engineering Politics, 1999–2008 *337*

12
A Decade of Uncertainty, 2008–18 *377*

13
Imran Khan Takes Charge *420*

14
Regime Change and a Year of Uncertainty, 2022–3 *461*

Epilogue *481*

REFERENCES *493*
BIBLIOGRAPHY *543*
ACKNOWLEDGEMENTS *553*
PHOTO ACKNOWLEDGEMENTS *555*
INDEX *557*

Introduction

by Ian Talbot

This volume's title reflects Pakistan's post-independence struggles to secure sustainable political development. Turmoil punctuated by increasing military intervention has dominated the landscape. Political failings have gone hand in hand with cycles of economic boom and bust and a failure to undertake structural reforms. Growth has stalled under successive regimes, contributing to foreign-exchange crises that have made the country reliant on foreign aid, IMF bailouts and the remittances sent home by Pakistani diasporic communities. For many decades, sovereignty has been traded for such assistance. In recent times, China, the so-called 'game changer', has replaced the United States as the main source of development aid, which is desperately required because Pakistan has failed to get its own house in order.

In a timely manner, the publication of *Chequered Past, Uncertain Future* coincides with another crisis moment in Pakistan's political and economic development, which follows Imran Khan's ousting from power in April 2022 and the subsequent economic and political fallout. The crisis has brought into sharp focus the long-standing tensions in civil–military relations and Pakistan's economic vulnerability. The latter has been worsened by the Ukraine conflict, the supply-chain shocks that have followed the COVID-19 pandemic and the exceptional 2022 monsoon flooding. The concluding chapters of the volume provide a detailed narrative description of the unfolding events that have polarized political life and led to clashes between Pakistan's key institutions. Readers will immediately discern familiar patterns at play in the current turmoil. To name but three: political engineering by the military; the presence of a zero-sum-game approach to politics that hampers democratic consolidation; and pervasive conspiracy theories regarding the influence of the United States. There are changes as well as continuities. Khan's boldness in taking on the military reflects the confidence brought by the appeal of Pakistan's Tehrik-i-Insaf's (PTI – Pakistan's Movement for Justice) – through adroit social media – first to the 'youth bulge' whose urban element is better educated and informed than ever before and second to a politically active diaspora. Indeed, it could be argued that Imran Khan has effectively copied from Narendra Modi's populist playbook in acquiring financial, lobbying and media support through courting Pakistanis living in the USA and the UK.

Initially, Imran Khan's ability to reach out to Pakistani youth and the hope of his addressing mounting structural problems attracted the establishment's attention, the so-called 'Project Imran'. Without PTI political activists' unprecedented attacks on military installations on 9 May 2023 there was still a way back for him, despite the feathers he had ruffled following the vote of no confidence.

The imbalances in the civil–military relationship form a major focus of the book. The author provides sufficient empirical data to move beyond a simplistic military–civilian dichotomy. The volume dissects authoritarianism, whether of Nawaz Sharif in the later 1990s, Imran Khan in the early 2020s or Zulfiqar Ali Bhutto half a century earlier. The evidence points to the fact that civilian leaders could just as readily muzzle the press, or implicate opponents in false cases, as could any military regime. Earlier chapters reveal the conditions for the emergence of a political culture of clientelism and opportunism that have, in successive generations, ensured military rulers the backing of a 'Martial Law B team', or 'King's Party'. The volume stands on the shoulders of earlier scholars in revealing the creep of military influence into ever wider areas of Pakistan's institutional, administrative and economic life. The more recent term 'hybrid regime' has been coined for the continuing existence of military influence over civilian governments when the Army has formally retired to its barracks.

The book further identifies the absence of the rule of law and the persistence of dynastic politics as key elements of political instability. Allied to all of these is the construction of a unitary identity around Islam and Urdu to the detriment of an acceptance of Pakistan's inherent pluralism. Pakistan's emergence as an ideological state is always associated with the Zia era; the volume reveals, however, its long-standing roots. Islam flowered in the early 1950s because of the efforts of political activists and religious scholars who had migrated to Pakistan, despite their earlier pan-Islamic opposition to the struggle to achieve a Muslim territorial homeland. Just as simple civilian–military dichotomies are dissolved, so too are easy binaries between 'secularists' and Islamists. Liaquat Ali Khan and Zulfiqar Ali Bhutto could both be seen as creating the conditions for the later institutionalized Islamization of the reviled Zia regime, the former with respect to the legacy of the adoption of the Objectives Resolution on 12 March 1949 by the Constituent Assembly. In 1974, Bhutto completed the exclusionary response to the Ahmadis, which was rooted in the activism of the Majlis-i-Ahrar in the late colonial era.

The volume interestingly provides a more nuanced account than that of many authors with respect to the Yahya regime's 'blame' for the 1971 breakup of Pakistan (see Chapter Seven). The exception is, of course, the launching of the brutal military crackdown in East Pakistan on 25 March 1970. The language dimension of Bengali separatism is traced back to the attitudes in favour of Urdu expressed by Pakistan's founding father, Muhammad Ali Jinnah. The 1956 Constitution's adoption of Bengali as an official language was too little too late. The Bengali language already had its martyrs, and there was a growing sense in the eastern wing that West Pakistan was treating East Bengal as a colony with respect to economic development. The previous year, One Unit had been introduced, which was seen in East Bengal as an attempt to prevent through inter-wing parity the majority Bengali population implementing its outlook in national politics. Along with its negative impact on national cohesion, One Unit further encouraged the development of a military–bureaucratic combination in what has been termed a 'creeping coup'.

The limited representation of Bengalis in the Pakistan Army (just 5 per cent of the officer corps) was a further alienating factor following Ayub Khan's October 1958 coup. His regime's attempts at Pakistanization and the widening economic gap between the two wings were additional factors in the growing tensions. Bengalis were under-represented both in the Central Secretariat and on the commissions of enquiry that littered the Ayub years. This meant not only that Bengali interests went unheard, but that the regime's awareness of conditions in the eastern wing was hampered. Even so, the Awami League did not adopt a secessionist approach until repression gave it little choice; the result was a highly polarized conflict.

It seemed few lessons had been learned when Bhutto overturned the promise of the 1973 Constitution by refusing to allow a rival party (the National Awami Party) to wield power in Baluchistan. While the background to the dismissal of Ataullah Mengal's government remains controversial, the consequences of tribal insurgency and escalated military conflict only intensified nationalist demands. Moreover, they provided the context for the discredited military to return to centre stage.

Zia ul Haq's rule (1977–88) strengthened presidential authority and the Army's entrenched political and economic role. Tahir Kamran does not pull any punches in his judgement of General Zia in Chapter Nine. The Army now saw itself as safeguarding not only Pakistan's territorial borders but the state-sanctioned ideology. Many of the mosque schools that mushroomed in this era were highly sectarian in scope as well as being committed to a trans-national jihadist outlook. The 1988 Restoration of Democracy only partially reversed Zia's narrowing of space for pluralism and tolerance. Other rulers, both civilian and military, damaged institutions, acted arbitrarily and stunted prospects for democracy. Zia's rule was especially damaging because of both its longevity and its severity. Most importantly, Zia's lingering legacy created conditions for the social acceptance of militancy.

Chequered Past, Uncertain Future traces the complex international, regional and local sectarian influences in the rise of militancy in contemporary Pakistan. The detail again dispels simplistic understandings that confuse Islamic piety and conservatism with militancy. These developments were greatly assisted by the United States' need for Pakistan's support in the struggle against the Soviet occupation of Afghanistan. The role of the Army again comes into play, with its doctrine of strategic depth in Afghanistan and the use of Islamic proxies in low-intensity conflict in India-occupied Kashmir. Successive chapters chronologically examine these processes at work, with the devil often being in the detail. The seeds were also being sown for Islamic extremists to turn their weapons on their erstwhile Inter Services Intelligence (ISI) and army patrons, although the bitter harvest would only be reaped in the wake of 9/11.

Kamran not only reinforces well-established narratives but introduces material that may be unfamiliar to the reader. In Chapter Twelve, there is a discussion of the Waziristan-based Pashtun Tahafuz movement, which has been ignored by many reporters and researchers due to military restrictions. Yet it shares with Imran Khan's Pakistan Tehreek-e-Insaf a youth-led, social-media-savvy politics that is highly critical of the status quo formed by existing political elites and the military establishment.

The volume is not solely confined to political history. There is discussion in Chapter Thirteen of the important reforestation programme designed to mitigate the effects of climate change. In Chapter Eleven, cultural issues are discussed in an interesting section on representation of Pakistani identity after 9/11, and early in Chapter Four reference is made to the Progressive Writers' Movement.

Despite this book's achievements, there are also some unanswered questions. During his time in office, was there a gulf between Imran Khan's rhetoric and the delivery of welfare for the masses? Did the Army and civilian leaders genuinely believe in a potentially existential Indian threat and thereby respond in the ways that have contributed to the narrowing of the public sphere or has the threat perception been exaggerated to shape state policy in their interest? If the former is the case, another question arises: what are the ways in which Pakistan can cease being a victim of its geography?

Kamran does not, however, just serve up a cold dish of political and economic failure. The reader is made aware that Pakistan's chequered history was not preordained. The state's development took its current form because of the political choices made by civilian and military elites. Zulfiqar Ali Bhutto's increasing authoritarianism, for example, resulted in a missed transformative moment with respect to both civil–military relations and centre–state relations. There were similarly missed opportunities for democratic consolidation during the formative decade of the 1950s and the democratic interlude of the 1990s. The break-up of Pakistan could have been avoided if different choices had been made. This book points to the potential for a transformed Pakistan not only in these pivotal moments but importantly through a general commitment to the rebalancing of civil–military relations and the removal of social inequalities.

Pakistan's contemporary crisis is more serious than any previously experienced due to its multidimensional character, which involves a clash of institutions, political turmoil and the threat of a sovereign-default economic crisis. It occurs to the backdrop of climate change, which could provide an existential threat not just to Pakistan but to much of South Asia. Twenty-first-century global economic and environmental conditions create a call for increased regional cooperation if Pakistan is to move beyond its crisis-ridden state.

Indeed, a question must be raised: could there ever be a fully consolidated Pakistani democracy with a reset in civilian–military relations without some degree of normalization between the 'distant' neighbours of Pakistan and India? The replacement of a strategic-centric approach to national security with a human-centric one surely requires a normalization of relations with New Delhi. A Modi victory in the 2024 Indian elections is not, at the time of writing, as certain as once thought. It is not inconceivable that the current minister of foreign affairs and chairman of the Pakistan People's Party, Bilawal Bhutto Zardari, might be prime minister. Could Rahul Gandhi and Bilawal deliver on the hopes raised in 1988 by Rajiv Gandhi and Benazir Bhutto and secure a peace dividend for the subcontinent?

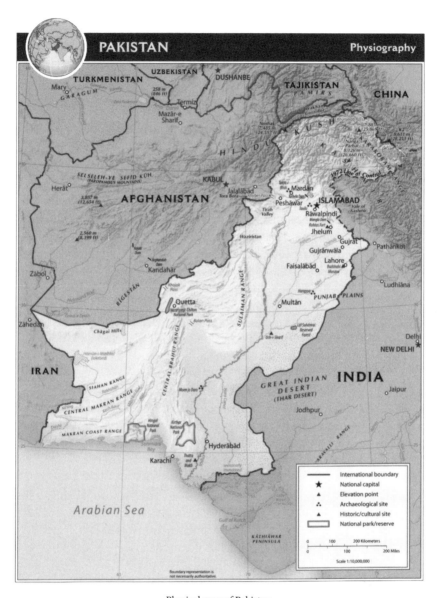

Physical map of Pakistan.

1

From Prehistory to the Early Modern Era,

3800 BCE to 1707 CE

Since the 1980s, Pakistan's early history has been excluded from textbooks, and the national narrative of the country's history has focused on Muhammad bin Qasim's arrival in Sindh in 711 CE. This approach has removed the Indus Valley civilization, as well as later incarnations such as Taxila, Hakra-Gagger and Kot Diji, from the curriculum, which raises a serious question: what essential context is missing from the discourse surrounding Pakistan's history?[1] The Arab conquest of Sindh cannot be fully understood without acknowledging the region's previous history; starting with this event is too spontaneous and makes little sense to serious historians.

Another issue that has complicated Pakistan's history is its conflation with the history of Muslim rule in India. Since 1206 CE, the centre of Muslim political power was located in Delhi and Agra, both areas within India, and their role in the evolution of South Asian Muslim culture cannot be refuted. One might question the idea of equating a language with a cultural symbol and how well this concept applies. Take, for example, Urdu, which evolved and played a significant role in the cultural identity of Muslims. This, in turn, is said to have influenced the formation of Pakistan. Urdu's journey and development can be traced through its different phases in cities like Hyderabad, Lucknow and Delhi.[2] The Doab (which literally means land between the two rivers) region situated between the Ganga and Jumna rivers also played a crucial role in fostering a cultural ethos of North Indian Muslims, making it the locus of a cultural and political crystallization of Muslim identity.

A history of Pakistan should therefore focus on the geographical regions that make up the country rather than linking it up with the Arabian Peninsula. These areas have been on the periphery of the empire systems that Muslims built in the subcontinent from the thirteenth century to the nineteenth, which has created a disconnect between geography and history. The importance of geography as a determinant of Pakistan's history has always been contested. The country is a plural polity underpinned by multifarious sociocultural layers. The deepest layer is Turko-Persian, which made its cultural mark from the twelfth century onwards and which is an important constituent of Pakistani culture and societal make-up. Forms of language and abstract concepts, such as Sufism in its diverse manifestations, are deeply rooted in the epistemological and cultural heritage influenced by the Turko-Persian tradition. Finally, the impact of colonial modernity brought by the British in the early nineteenth century had a distinctive and profound influence on the development of Pakistani nationalism. While nationalism and colonial influence were not exclusive to Pakistan, the way in which these forces intertwined in the region created a remarkably complex and intricate phenomenon. This complexity arises from the unique historical, cultural and political context of what is now Pakistan, making it an idiosyncratic case within the broader global narrative of nationalism and colonialism. Countless influences from various regions have contributed to the make-up of the landscape's socio-political entity.

Given the complex composition of Pakistan's society, this book aims to shed light on the country's rich past, which has often been denied or overlooked. Acknowledging and exploring its complexities is essential in order to gain a better understanding of Pakistan's history and cultural heritage. The denial of this past is symptomatic of an approach that has contributed to the problems of nation-building by rejecting pluralism.

The Formation of the Indus Basin's Physical Features and Natural Environment

Earth is commonly believed to have formed around 4.6 billion years ago. However, radioactive dating has revealed that the oldest rocks on Earth are approximately 4.3 billion years old and belong to the Archean age (4 billion to 2.5 billion years ago). It was during this time that the earliest forms of life, such as algae and bacteria, appeared. While life evolved and diversified, the Earth's surface, or 'crust', underwent constant changes.[3]

Evidence of marine life from the Cambrian period, dating back to 570 million years ago, has been discovered in rocks within the Himalayas that contain fossils. These range across Pakistan's neighbouring countries and the Salt Range, situated in northern Punjab. This indicates that the rocks were once sea sediments, and these mountain ranges were once part of the Tethys Sea, which is believed to have spanned from the Mediterranean to China.[4]

Over time, the Himalayas underwent a process where significant quantities of fragmented rock and alluvial deposits were transported by glaciers and rivers, giving rise to the Siwalik Hills along the base of the mountain range.[5] The rivers and streams from the Himalayas carried and deposited sediment in the regions beyond the Siwalik Hills on an ongoing basis, eventually filling up the Tethys Sea, which varied in depth from 2,000 to 6,000 metres (6,560–19,685 ft).[6] This process occurred during the Pleistocene epoch, which spans from approximately 2.6 million to 11,700 years ago. It resulted in the formation of the extensive alluvial basins of the Indus and Ganga-Brahmaputra rivers.[7]

Our Early Ancestors

In 1932 a fossil ape called *Ramapithecus* was unearthed in the Siwalik Hills, within sediments dating back to the earlier Miocene period, which spans from 16 to 25 million years ago. It was once wrongly thought to represent an intermediate species in the evolution of mankind, but it is now understood to be a female *Sivapithecus*, fossil skeletons of both having been found since in Pakistan and other countries.[8] Our ancestral line evolved within Africa, and while the fossil ape *Kenyapithecus* (dated to 14 million years ago) found in Kenya was thought to belong to the main pre-hominid line, it belonged to an offshoot of hominid evolution that we cannot count among our ancestors. Unlike hominids, *Kenyapithecus* could not walk erect on two legs, and thus was not a biped.[9] Human evolution continued, and hominids underwent a phase of hunting for survival and manufacturing tools from stones and flints to protect themselves from the perils of nature. They initially lived in caves before eventually building huts for shelter, and this evolutionary process led to the era of proto-civilization. According to the British archaeologist Mortimer Wheeler, 'civilization, in a minimum sense of the term, is the art of living in towns, with all that the condition implies in respect of social skills and discipline.'[10]

The onward march of evolution made humans food producers, the builders of houses and villages, and the creators of pots, pans, clothing and polished stone tools and weapons. Security and availability of food led to a sudden growth in human population. Those who lived in river valleys were able to develop settled life further as their fields were fertilized every year by river silt. For others, however, continued cultivation made their lands barren, forcing them to move to new territories, which resulted in discord between settled and semi-nomadic peoples.[11] In Western Asia, during this period of struggle and movement, a new material was discovered: metal. This material, first discovered in the form of copper, could be beaten and expanded when hot, which facilitated the production of better tools. When copper was mixed with tin, a new metal was discovered: bronze. However, copper was not available everywhere and required special skill to work with. As a result, the search for the metal and its mining and transportation led to trade, and its working led to the training and employment of skilled labourers.[12]

Both of these developments were possible because of a surplus of food. For convenience, two occupations of people, traders and smiths, were freed from agricultural labour. Their concentration in selected places increased the populations in these areas, and so villages, over time, developed into cities. However, a city must rely on the products of many villages. Cities became centres of industry, trade and commerce and gradually extended their influence and control over villages, making the simple life of early villagers more complex. This led to the rise of kingdoms and international trade and commerce.¹³ Businesses needed systems for counting, which led to writing. People thus became literate, and began to transcribe their own experiences, embodying thought and passing it on to posterity. All these developments took place in the ancient Orient, and the regions that later constituted Pakistan were active participants. In the wake of this evolution, those areas entered the Bronze Age.

Baluchi Village Culture

The Bronze Age influenced the earlier nomadic life and small villages, which eventually led to the rise of the Indus Valley civilization. However, due to the Baluchistan plateau's topography, characterized by hills and deserts, essential resources necessary for city growth were scarce. The small river valleys enclosed by hills could only support village cultures, or, at best, towns with limited economic strength that tended to be localized. All these cultures are grouped under the term 'Baluchi village cultures'.

Baluchistan forms a component of an extensive plateau system that extends alongside the Iranian uplands to the west and converges with the central Afghan massif to the north. This expansive, mountainous and arid region is delineated by the Indus Valley to the east, the Tigris and Euphrates valleys to the west, the Oxus Valley to the northeast and the cis-Caspian settlements to the northwest.¹⁴ The (proto-)Baluchi people's frequent mobility and trade activities from one valley to another helped to diffuse technical knowledge, leading to cultural infiltration. Baluchistan benefited from such activities and absorbed many elements of the Bronze Age civilization that thrived given the region's resources, however limited.¹⁵

The Baluchi village cultures are typically situated in small river valleys, hemmed in by hills and connected by passes. Coastal traffic due to the valleys' proximity to the Arabian Sea could have had an impact, except in the cases of Zhob and Quetta. The primary cultural influence came from northern Iran through Kandahar and Quetta, then branched off to the northeast via the Zhob Valley or to the south through Kalat into the Nal-Hingol Valley.

South Iranian cultures flowed along the slopes of the Zagros Mountains and, passing through Bampur, reached Shahi Tump in the Dasht Valley. That cultural stream extended further north along the coastal Makran Range to Kulli in south-central Baluchistan, Lasbela and onwards to the mouth of the Indus. The influence of southern Iranian cultures is reflected in the buff-coloured painted pottery found in south Baluchistan, while the northern influence is evident in the red pottery of the north.¹⁶

The Indus Civilization

The Indus civilization is often referred to as a product of the Bronze Age, representing the mature phase of earlier village cultures found in sites such as Amri. The Pakistani historian Yehya Amjad suggests that the citadel of Kot Diji represents centralized authority, and the city's widely scattered ruins indicate an intermediate phase of urban growth.[17] However, the existence of a mature civilization is most evident at Mohenjo Daro ('Mound of the Dead'), located near the Indus riverbanks in the Larkana District of Sindh, and at Harappa, which is situated on an old bed of the River Ravi in the Sahiwal District of the Punjab. These two cities are around 644 kilometres (400 mi.) apart in two sub-zones of the Indus, but both share the homogeneous features of a common culture. Although the civilization was initially associated with these two cities, it is now known to have been widespread, with its core centred around the Indus River system. As a result, it is referred to as the Indus Valley civilization.

During the period 3800–3200 BCE, two primarily Neolithic cultures existed in the Indus basin. The first, marked by Kechi Beg pottery, was discovered in the northeastern region of Baluchistan and southern Khyber Pakhtunkhwa, while the other, characterized by Hakra ware, is found in the Punjab region of Pakistan. Kechi Beg pottery is associated with the Indus Valley civilization and is typically dated to around 3300 to 2800 BCE. Hakra pottery has been dated to an identical time frame. These communities were primarily agricultural and pastoral with small settlements.[18]

Around 3200 BCE, a notable transformation occurred when three distinct cultures emerged, spanning the entire Indus basin. These cultures were characterized by their distinctive pottery styles, often named after the specific archaeological sites where the styles were first identified. Among these cultures, the Kot Diji culture stood out as the largest, encompassing regions such as Khyber Pakhtunkhwa, the Punjab and northern Sindh. The Sothi Siswal culture established settlements in northern Rajasthan, the Punjab and Haryana, while the Amri Nal culture thrived in Baluchistan and central and southern Sindh, with extensions into Gujarat. These three cultures existed from approximately 3200 to 2600 BCE, with the Kot Diji culture continuing to exist independently in its northwestern territory until after 2000 BCE. The Kulli culture, previously believed to have been earlier, is now assigned to the period of the Indus civilization between 2600 and 2000 BCE.[19] Some scholars consider the Damb Sadaat culture to be an Early Indus culture, but it likely belongs more to the Helmand region in Afghanistan and Iran.

The early Indus cultures may have had different pottery styles, but they shared several features. One significant development was the use of oxen as draft animals, which was made possible through castration. Castrated oxen could also function as pack animals. Cart ruts found in Harappa and terracotta models of carts and bulls in Jalilpur suggest that oxen were also used for ploughing.[20] Mehrgarh in the plains below Quetta is known to have cultivated barley and wheat, which were also found at Rehman Dheri and Kalibangan during the Early Indus period.[21] Sorghum

Mohenjo Daro ('Mound of the Dead').

millet, a summer crop, was reported at Rohira in the Punjab, but there is no other evidence of its presence in the Indus basin before 2000 BCE. Cotton was likely grown, although there is no direct evidence for it during this period. Balakot yielded a species of vetches, while dates and grapes were found at Rohira. Ovens, including tandoors, were used during the Early Indus phase.[22] The vertical wheel, which enabled the use of carts and heavy transport vehicles, was a significant innovation. Wheel-made pottery was the most common craft product and dominated all three Early Indus cultures.[23] The chert stone was the chief material for tools; chert flakes and blades comprised the bulk of the normal toolkit, with some bone tools added. At Kot Diji, the production of fine flint blades sourced from the nearby Rohri or Sukkur hills in northern Sindh marked a transition to Chalcolithic technology that combined the use of stone and copper. Progress in copper-smelting is evident from the remains of a workshop discovered at Nal in Baluchistan, while precious metals were also worked to create ornaments.[24] Such advancements resulted in a significant increase in the number of settlements, which were larger and more permanent than those of the preceding Hakra-ware culture in the Punjab. Houses were built with mud-bricks, and stone was used in foundations and lower levels of walls where available. The use of fired bricks was not yet present. The estimated size of Harappa during the Kot Diji period was 40 hectares (98 ac), with an average settlement size of 4.5 hectares (11 ac) among the 291 early Indus sites studied. Thirty-four settlements exceeded 10 hectares (25 ac), approaching the size of small townships, although the urban revolution had not yet fully arrived.[25]

The extent of social differentiation during the early Indus period was rather limited. The Indian historian Irfan Habib suggests that seals, which were probably used as symbols of ownership claims, were rather rare.[26] Nonetheless, there have been reports of six small stone seals discovered in the Kunal region, believed to date back to the latter stages of the early Indus period. Additionally, small terracotta seals have emerged from the excavations at Nausharo in Sindh. In contrast, substantial residences and opulent palaces were notably scarce. Furthermore, there is no evidence of any monumental structures that could have served as the dwelling of a ruler. While defensive walls have been unearthed at various sites, such as Kot Diji, Kalibangan, Kohtras Buthi in western Sindh and Rehman Dheri, they evoke an image of small principalities rather than the presence of formidable, centralized states.

Funerary rites were an important aspect of religion during the Early Indus period. In the Amri Nal culture area, at sites such as Nal and Damb Buthi in Baluchistan and Surkotada and Nagwada in Gujarat, burials were fractional, which suggests that the dead were left exposed, and their bones were later collected and buried along with pots. At the Kot Diji sites of Periano Ghundai and Mughal Ghundai (northeast Baluchistan), by contrast, the dead seem to have been cremated first and then their bones collected and put in pots to be buried. No straightforward extended burial is firmly attributable to the early Indus period.

Of the three early Indus cultures considered here (Kot Diji, Sothi Siswal and Amri Nal), only the Kot Diji culture survived the onset of the Indus civilization, in a substantial area covering much of Khyber Pakhtunkhwa and the northwestern Punjab. Remains of this phase (*c.* 2600–2000 BCE) have been found at sites including Rehman Dheri, Gumla and Tarakai Qila, and Sarai Khola in the northwestern Punjab, largely corresponding to the period of the Indus civilization. While showing some influence of the Indus civilization, they do not have any of its characteristic features, such as writing, baked bricks, distinctive pottery and so on. In the mature Indus period, numerous small Sothi Siswal villages in the Ghaggar Valley seem to have existed, while in central Baluchistan, a local culture named after the type-site Kulli established itself on the periphery of the Indus civilization.

The Onset of the Indus Civilization

Harappa – also known as Haryuppa in Sanskrit, which means 'a city with golden pillars'[27] – is located in the Sahiwal District of the West Punjab, Pakistan. Although it had long been recognized as an extensive site situated on the Ravi River, its true significance as a major city of an early great civilization was not fully understood until the discovery of Mohenjo Daro, located near the banks of the Indus in the Larkana District of Sindh, by R. D. Banerji in 1922. Sir John Marshall, the director general of the Archaeological Survey of India, coined the term 'Indus civilization' to describe the culture discovered at Harappa and Mohenjo Daro. The term was fitting since it referred to the geographical context of the Indus River and the presence of cities. According to the *Oxford English Dictionary*, 'to civilize' is 'to bring out of a state of barbarism, to instruct in the arts of life; to enlighten and refine'.[28] Harappa and Mohenjo Daro were key sites that provided defining cultural markers for identifying other settlements as part of the Indus (or 'Mature Indus') civilization. These markers include:

1. Wheel-made pottery of a distinctive kind: baked to a red colour, thick-walled, heavy, sometimes coated with red slip. Some pots were painted black; and there were certain popular motifs painted in black on the pottery, such as the peepal leaf, intersecting circles and the peacock.
2. The Indus script, especially appearing on seals, with characters that show practically no regional variations.
3. Baked bricks, as well as sun-dried mud-bricks of standard size, with sides in the ratio of 1:2:4.
4. Standard weights, based apparently on a unit of 13.63 grams (½ oz).
5. A tendency to lay out straight roads (meeting others at right angles) in urban and semi-urban settlements, and to pay considerable attention to drainage.
6. Citadels built adjacent to, but separate from, the towns.
7. Masonry wells and tanks.
8. Supine burial of the dead, aligned north–south, usually in out-of-town cemeteries.[29]

While not all of these features were present in every settlement, pottery and bricks are the most recognizable markers of the Indus civilization. The settlements associated with this civilization are found in a contiguous zone that covers the Punjab plains and parts of Baluchistan, as well as the Indian states of the Punjab, Haryana, northwestern Uttar Pradesh, northern Rajasthan and Gujarat.

Since societies that emerged here exhibited cultural uniformity across a large region, civilization likely did not originate independently in different regions simultaneously. Instead, it is suggested that civilization spread from a smaller core area to achieve the uniformity observed across the larger region over time. The exact location of this core area is uncertain because no excavated site of an early Indus culture has shown the main features of the Indus civilization originating from within itself, except for Harappa and Nausharo, which show cultural overlap with Kot Diji and Indus. The initial site of the Indus civilization likely lay within Kot Diji, which covers the Punjab and northern and central Sindh. The diffusion of the Indus civilization could only have been achieved through political expansion, since uniformity in units of measure, town planning and writing elsewhere would not have arisen spontaneously.[30]

Cities and Towns

Mohenjo Daro and Harappa span 200 and 150 hectares (494 and 370 ac) of land, respectively, indicating a peak population of approximately 85,000 and 65,000 inhabitants. Adjacent to these two major sites is Ganweriwala, located in the southern Punjab by the dry Hakra River, which covers around 80 hectares (197 ac), but has yet to be excavated. The planning of Indus cities is mostly inferred from Mohenjo Daro and Harappa, both of which were carefully designed. Mohenjo Daro, like other large Indus settlements, was built on a raised platform, or acropolis, constructed with mud-brick walls.[31] Additional platforms were built for blocks of houses in the Lower Town. These platforms, which were initially 10 metres (32 ft) high, were later extended or raised to ensure the houses remained above flood level. Mohenjo Daro had wide, unpaved roads that were planned before house construction began. The city's main street in the acropolis was 6 metres (20 ft) wide, while the First Street in the Lower Town was more than 10 metres wide.[32] The broad streets in the city were designed to meet at right angles, with the lanes intersecting them. The broad streets were not encroached upon or built upon during most of the city's existence.

After laying out the roads and building platforms, construction began in both the acropolis and the main town. The buildings were mostly made of mud-brick, but they were raised on foundation walls of fired brick. The

Archaeological site of Harappa.

houses were uniformly rectangular in plan but varied in size and were arranged around courtyards. Each house had a single entrance, often hidden from the outside, and one in every three houses had a fired-brick-lined well near the entrance. Close to the wells, many houses also had bathing cells. Larger houses appeared to have served as residences for the master's family, as well as for slaves, servants or sub-families within a joint family. Some houses had brick-made privies, and the presence of discarded materials from crafting activities found in several houses suggests that these dwellings may have also accommodated the living quarters of artisans.

As the houses were built, a remarkably careful drainage system was laid out throughout the city. Waste water from each house flowed into a cesspit that connected to a drain running alongside the road. The drains along the main roads were sometimes covered and had corbelled burnt-brick roofing, almost 2 metres (6 ft) high to enable cleaners to enter them. However, all drains ultimately ended in soak-pits by the roadside, which might have overflowed from time to time. Despite such limitations, the drainage system of Mohenjo Daro stands unique among the Bronze Age cities of the world.[33] Mohenjo Daro is estimated to have contained 2,000–3,000 houses and some seven hundred wells, but these figures may have to be raised, as the occupied area is now thought to have been much larger. Still, even with a population of 85,000 or so, Mohenjo Daro was one of the great cities of the world.[34]

Harappa, although slightly smaller than Mohenjo Daro, was built in a similar manner. It was constructed over a Kot Diji settlement and had an acropolis known as the citadel, which was situated on a massive platform. The citadel was held by a retaining mud-brick wall with a facing of fired bricks, which not only provided support but served as a defensive structure. The retaining wall rose 10.7 metres (35 ft) from the ground, making it an impressive sight. The citadel had two gateways, northern and western, but the western one was later blocked.

Adjacent to the citadel's northern side, there were several workmen's quarters that were attached to numerous rows of fired-brick floors. These floors had enough space in the centre to hold wooden mortars, which were used to mill wheat and barley. Further north of the workmen's quarters, there was a large structure that stood over a mud-brick platform. This structure was formed from numerous blocks made of bricks on both sides of a central aisle. It is believed that these blocks served as floors for wooden structures that were used for storing grain. Thus, the whole building is interpreted as a great granary. Close to the granary, there were also metal workers' furnaces.

Trade

Trade played a significant role in the Indus civilization and can be divided into three levels: local village–town trade, long-distance trade within the civilization's territory and commerce with other regions. The two large structures identified by Pandit Vats and Mortimer Wheeler as granaries at Harappa and Mohenjo Daro likely stored grain brought by officials as taxes levied on the villages attached to the two towns.[35] The granary at Mohenjo Daro was located within the citadel, while at Harappa it was outside but near the citadel and away from the Lower Town. It is probable that the grain stored was intended for distribution within the citadels. However, for ordinary inhabitants, the grain they needed must have been brought by merchants or grain-carriers using pack oxen, carts, rivercraft or even human backs.

Another source of local trade was the supply of raw materials to urban craft centres. For example, Balakot, Dholavira, Nageshwar and Lothal show evidence of seashell workings. The marine shells were probably sourced from places along the seashore close to these townships. Similarly, agate and cornelian cut into beads at Lothal came from the Ratanpur mines located south of the Narmada River near Bharuch. The large stone workings near Sukkur on both sides of the Indus can only be explained by the significant demand for chert blades from Mohenjo Daro downstream on the Indus River. However, in this case, most of the manufacturing probably took place at the quarries themselves.[36]

The uniformity in style of many artefacts found in various parts of the Indus territory indicates considerable long-distance trade that maintained similar tastes and fashions in manufactured goods across the civilization's different regions. This might have been achieved through the migration of artisans from the core areas, rather than just through the transport of goods. For example, fired bricks found at Kalibangan or Lothal could not have been exported from Harappa and Mohenjo Daro; skilled brick makers must have migrated there to establish these crafts. The identical Indus styles of pottery, particularly the more affordable varieties, must have been made by local potters. This is because the risk of breakage would have rendered long-distance transportation prohibitively expensive. The seals found in the Indus Valley civilization may have been made for individual owners and based on their personal preferences. As a result, they were likely produced locally, yet still display a strong degree of uniformity in the images and characters engraved on them. While early seals at Dholavira lacked inscriptions and only featured pictures, writing later appeared when craftsmen who could cut the Indus characters arrived on the scene.[37]

Having addressed the local perspective, let us now shift our focus to long-distance trade. Raw materials such as agate and cornelian from the Ratanpur mines were transported to other regions, such as Lothal, Kuntasi and Chanhu Daro, for the production of beads. Gold used by Indus metalsmiths likely came from the Indus River and its tributaries in the Himalayas. Other specialized items, such as faience and shell articles, were also clearly products of long-distance trade.[38] The Indus River system facilitated transportation, although downstream movement was far easier than upstream. Land transport between certain areas, such as Harappa and Kalibangan, was possible but likely more expensive than water transport.

Individual merchants likely conducted most long-distance commerce, as evidenced by the numerous seal impressions found at a warehouse in Lothal. Each seal was placed on reed mats or cloth tied to the mouth of a jar containing merchandise, with none of the seals matching those found at Lothal. It is believed that every merchant or mercantile family had a seal bearing an emblem and name, often of religious significance. Seals were also used as amulets and were regularly carried by their owners.[39]

The absence of coins in the Indus Valley civilization raises questions about how goods were bought and sold. Uniformity in weights suggests that many goods were priced according to mass, but materials that could have served as money are unknown. Some transactions may have been conducted using particular measures of grain or numbers of beads or shells as a medium of payment, but the use of seals as tokens for goods is also a possibility.[40]

The trade of the Indus civilization beyond its borders is a subject of great importance. Although there is no credible evidence of any trade with Neolithic south India, the mature Indus settlement at Daimabad boasts a limited survival of seals and Indus writing, which suggests that earlier commercial links might have existed with at least the upper Godavari basin.[41] Moving further north to Kayatha, near Ujjain in Madhya Pradesh, the type-site of a culture that could date back to 2400 BCE, three caches were discovered. Two of them contained cornelian and agate beads, while the third contained steatite micro-beads that could have come from workshops in the Indus territories.

In the north, the Neolithic culture of Kashmir during its ceramic phase (2500–2000 BCE) was almost contemporary with the Indus civilization, and it is possible that the Indus lapidaries obtained their jade from Kashmir. The Indus civilization likely drew its silver from the mines in the Panjshir Valley in northern Afghanistan. This is highly probable because the valley was situated on the navigable route that connected the Indus basin with Shortughai, a colony on the Oxus River in northeastern Afghanistan. Carbon dating of pottery, mud-bricks, houses and artefacts at Shortughai within the 2865–1975 BCE period indicates that their creation followed the Mature Indus models. The people at Shortughai partly sustained themselves by cultivation, but their primary occupation was the making of lapis lazuli beads. This semi-precious stone almost certainly came from the celebrated mines at Sar-i Sang on the upper reaches of the Kokcha River, which converges with the Oxus, where craftsmen also cut agate and cornelian beads, most likely receiving their raw materials from the Indus basin. Shortughai served as the entrepôt where agate and cornelian were exchanged with lapis lazuli.[42]

An Indus seal of the Namazga culture was found datable to 3200–2900 BCE at Altyn Depe in Turkmenistan. The etched cornelian beads and ivory also found there were most probably transported by Indus merchants. Furthermore, evidence of caravans led by Central Asian merchants into the Indus basin comes from the possible remains of Bactrian camels found at Mohenjo Daro and Harappa. Some of the shells worked at Shahr-i Sokhta (Sistan in Iran) might have come from the Indus coastal settlements.[43] Mature Indus seals have been found at Susa and the Elamite site of Tepe Yahya in central Iran, suggesting the presence of Indus merchants there. However, what was precisely traded remains unclear.

Finally, we come to links with West Asia, which were maintained by sea rather than across the overland route. Before the discovery of monsoon winds as a propeller to carry sailing ships across the Arabian Sea, primary sea traffic was along the coast, which ships and their crews stayed close to and depended heavily on for supplies from the ports located at intermediate stages in their voyage. This might explain the presence of Indus settlements as far west on the Makran (Baluchistan) coast as Sotkakoh and the fortified settlement of Sutkagen-dor, the latter being close to the Pakistan–Iran frontier.[44] Across the Gulf of Oman, opposite Sutkagen-dor, lies the site of Ras al-Junayz in Oman, which was known to the Sumerians at that time as Magan.[45] Many Indus imports, such as large pottery jars, alabaster vases, etched cornelian beads, metal artefacts and ivory-work, have been found at Ras al-Junayz and elsewhere in Oman. Copper and steatite seals represent the presence of Indus merchants, but it is clear that Indus artisans also travelled to the region.

Oman, or 'Magan', possessed its own distinct culture, including a unique style of pottery. However, excavations at certain sites have revealed the presence of Indus pottery made from locally sourced materials, as well as seals and metal artefacts produced in the Indus fashion.[46] Ships from Indus ports would sail northwestwards to enter the Persian Gulf, making their way to the region known to the Sumerians as 'Dilmun', which encompassed the islands of Bahrain and Faylakah, as well as the nearby Arabian coast. Dilmun had its own culture, but many of its seals, which were of local design, bore Indus characters, indicating the presence of Indus merchants operating within the community. Conversely, a Dilmun seal discovered at Lothal indicates that Dilmun merchants also traded at the port.[47] Unfortunately, little information exists regarding the goods that the Indus territories received in return from Mesopotamia. Nevertheless, the beard and robe decoration on the stone statue of the 'Priest King' found at Mohenjo Daro display strong similarities to Mesopotamian fashion, suggesting a familiarity with Mesopotamian culture. Furthermore, a young woman buried in Harappa in the Sumerian style, wrapped in reed matting within a wooden-lidded coffin, provides evidence of the presence of a Mesopotamian community within the city.

The End of the Indus Civilization

According to Irfan Habib, 'The end of the Indus civilization remains as much a puzzle as its beginning. Just as many of its essential features lack precedents in the preceding early Indus cultures, many also seem to disappear with similar suddenness at its end.'[48] Strangely, the cities and towns gradually disappeared due to floods or external aggression (or both) soon after 2000 BCE, with places like Mohenjo Daro, Harappa and Lothal showing signs of administrative deterioration. In Mohenjo Daro, for example, private constructions encroached upon roads, the drainage system deteriorated and houses were haphazardly divided and subdivided. These factors lead us to believe that while a sense of governance may have been lost, the citizens remained in the city. Moreover, signs of the 'Late Indus' or 'Post-Indus' cultures have yet been traced through the Indus basin. The Indian historian D. N. Jha suggests that man-made alterations in the course of the Indus and Ravi rivers caused the desiccation of the countryside around Harappa, making it impossible to produce food for urban centres. Excavations have revealed that Mohenjo Daro and Chanhu Daro flooded more than once, with traces of several phases of catastrophic flooding being detected there.[49] However, the suggestion that there was a flood with the volume and force to overwhelm towns in the Punjab, Sindh and Gujarat simultaneously strains credulity. In the phase of decline, no settlement shows evidence of town planning with regard to roads or drainage, and fired bricks occur only rarely. Indus writing disappears as inscribed seals and graffiti on potsherds almost vanish. The figures of sacred animals and deities on seals and tablets disappear altogether, even in Gujarat, where seals with Indus characters continued to be made for some time. The characteristic terracotta figurines, especially those of the Indus Mother Goddess, disappear, and there are sharp changes in burial practices, indicating a radical change in religious beliefs. Some crafts, such as steatite-cutting and stoneware manufacture, or the deliberate alloying of copper with tin to make bronze, fade or disappear altogether. The Indus weights are no longer in use, and finally, the characteristic Indus pottery is replaced by markedly coarser forms. The change is so complete and pervasive that both non-urban conditions and illiteracy staged a comeback. Surviving features from the Indus civilization in succeeding cultures were of a minor and secondary nature.[50] The flourishing of the Indus civilization was likely due to the initial conquest by a core state within the Indus basin, and the ability of the Indus state to impose heavy tribute on rural communities was essential for the existence of the Indus cities. If this ability was weakened by internal dissension within the ruling class or a shift in armed power, the cities, constituting the core, would no longer be able to obtain the tribute on which their prosperity depended. The administrative deterioration noticed in Mohenjo Daro, Harappa and Lothal is consistent with this situation: the signs of violence found in Mohenjo Daro suggest an external agent for the destruction of the weakened Indus empire.[51]

It is challenging to speculate as to who created the Indus civilization, which had much in common with ancient civilizations in Iran and Mesopotamia and also a distinctive character of its own. The Indus people were the first to establish the unity of the Indus, utilize technical knowledge of the ancient world and develop a civilization rooted in the Indus pattern. They also established trade relations with neighbouring countries, imported and exported commodities and spread their influence far and wide. Indus-style seals have been found as far west as Mesopotamia and as far as the Bahrain islands.

The decline of the Indus civilization did not bring an end to their way of life. The organized system that maintained the urban civilization was dismantled, but villages continued to exist. However, they were cut off from their source of inspiration and control, and the main bond of common cultural life was lost. The disintegration of urban organization can already be seen in the last period of the cities, and it spelled disaster for this rich civilization.[52] Evidence suggests the impingement of a semi-nomadic culture on the settled populace: urbanization merged with rural culture, leaving the field open for a new civilization. The unity of the Indus was destroyed, and a rich heritage was lost.

Aryans and the Vedic Tradition

The Indus Valley civilization, which had flourished for centuries, experienced a decline in the second millennium BCE and had nearly disintegrated by 1500 BCE. This decline coincided with the migration of the Aryans into the northwest of India. According to the American Indologist Wendy Doniger, during the five hundred years between 2000 and 1500 BCE the Indus Valley civilization was diminishing, while another culture was emerging to preserve its poetry. The Vedas, which signify this cultural shift, emerged as a result.[53]

The Aryans, also known as the Indo-Aryans, had resided in Bactria and the northern Iranian plateau for some time. However, by approximately 1500 BCE they had migrated into northern India through the passes in the Hindu Kush Mountains, most likely entering via the Khyber Pass. Initially they roamed across the plains of the Punjab searching for pastures, since cattle-breeding was their primary occupation. Eventually they settled in small village communities in forest clearings and gradually took up agriculture, which had been the primary economy of the earlier Indus Valley people.[54] Hence there was a transition from a herding-based economy to an agricultural one.

It was during this period that the hymns of the Rig Veda, the earliest examples of Vedic literature, were memorized and collected (*ved* in Sanskrit means 'to know'), marking the earliest literary source from areas of the Indus Valley. Some parts of the Rig Veda were originally composed before 1000 BCE, while the remaining Vedic literature, including the Sama, Yajur and Atharva Vedas, dates from a later period. Any historical reconstruction of Aryan life and institutions is primarily based on Vedic literature. While the Ramayana and Mahabharata epics describe events that took place between approximately 1000 and 700 BCE, the versions that have survived date from the first half of the first millennium CE. During the Rig Vedic period, the Aryans had spread to the Punjab and Delhi regions but had not yet begun to move eastwards. The region was much wetter and was covered in forests, unlike today's vast plains and deserts. In the first few centuries, Aryan expansion was slow, and stone, bronze and copper axes were used for clearing the woodland, with iron being introduced only around 800 BCE. Excavations at Hastinapur show that iron implements were familiar by about 700 BCE, and this led to an acceleration in the process of expansion.[55]

The hymns of the Rig Veda mention many of the Aryan tribes, especially in inter-tribal conflicts such as the Battle of the Ten Kings. However, wars were not limited to inter-tribal fighting, as the Aryans also had to contend with the indigenous people of northern India, who were of non-Aryan origin and were viewed with contempt by the Aryans. The enemies are described as Panis and Dasas.[56] The Panis were problematic because they were cattle thieves, and cattle were the main source of wealth for the Aryans. The fight with the Dasas was more protracted, as they were well settled on the land. Eventually, the Aryans emerged victorious, as evidenced by the fact that the word *dasa* later came to mean a slave. The Dasas were considered inferior due to their darker complexion, flat features and different language and living habits.[57] Ahmed Hassan Dani notes that the Dasas were described as black-skinned and flat-nosed (*anash*), and that they spoke an unintelligible tongue (*mridhra-vach*). They were also considered 'riteless, indifferent to gods, without devotion, not performing sacrifices, lawless, following strange customs and reviling (Vedic) gods'.[58]

The Aryans were semi-nomadic pastoralists who relied mainly on cattle for their livelihoods. Initially, cattle-rearing remained their primary occupation, with cows being a measure of value and a precious commodity. Among the other animals they reared, horses held the highest status. Horses were essential for movement and speed in war, and they drew the chariots of both men and gods. When the Aryans first arrived in the Indus Valley, they were divided into three social classes: the aristocracy or warriors, the priests and the common people.[59] There was no consciousness of caste and professions were not hereditary. There were no rules restricting marriages within these classes or taboos as to whom one could eat with: the three divisions merely facilitated social and economic organization. However, the

Aryans began to treat the Dasas as beyond the social pale, and they were condemned to a lowly status. This was likely due to fear of the Dasas and a concern that assimilation with them would lead to a loss of Aryan identity. Hence, the Dasas gradually became known as 'slaves' and later became the Shudras, marking a rudimentary step towards the caste system.[60] An initial administrative system was introduced, with the king serving as the pivot. The tribal kingdom (*rashtra*) consisted of tribes (*jana*), tribal units (*vish*) and villages (*grama*), with the family (*kula*) serving as the nucleus. The eldest male member served as its head (*kulapa*). The king was supported by a court of the tribe's elders and village headmen. Two officers – the chief priest (*purohita*) and the military commander (*senani*) – were closer to the king. The *purohita* combined the functions of priest, astrologer and advisor, while the *senani* was responsible for military command. Spies and messengers completed the king's entourage.[61]

The Gandhara Civilization

The historical region of Gandhara is located in northwestern Pakistan and encompasses the Vale of Peshawar, as well as the lower valleys of the Kābul and Swat rivers. The Gandhara civilization existed from the middle of the first millennium BCE to the beginning of the second millennium CE.[62] Throughout ancient times, Gandhara was a trade hub and a point of cultural convergence between India, Central Asia and the Middle East. It is believed that Gandhara was a triangular tract of land measuring about 100 kilometres (62 mi.) from east to west and 70 kilometres (43 mi.) from north to south. It was primarily situated to the west of the Indus River and bounded to the north by the Hindu Kush Mountains. The extent of Gandhara proper included the Peshawar Valley, as well as the hills of Swat, Dir, Buner and Bajaur – all of which lie within the northern boundaries of Pakistan.[63]

The name 'Gandhara' has several possible meanings, but the most widely accepted theory relates it to the word *qand* or *gand*, which means 'fragrance', and *har*, which means 'lands'. Thus, in its simplest form, Gandhara is the 'Land of Fragrance'.[64] Another more geographically supported theory is that the word *qand/gand* is derived from *kun*, which means 'well' or 'pool of water'. The word *gand* appears in many other place names associated with water, such as Gand-ao or Gand-ab (Pool of Water) and Gand-Dheri (Water Mound). Tashkand (Stone-Walled Pool) and Yarkand (Oasis City) are also associated names, leading some to believe that the area could have been known as the 'Land of the Lake(s)'.[65]

Around 75 CE, one of the tribes in Gandhara, the Kushan (Kuṣāṇa), gained control of the region under the leadership of Kujula Kadphises. Kujula was the one who united the Yuezhi confederation in Bactria during the first century CE and became the first Kushan emperor. The Kushan Empire started as a Central Asian kingdom and expanded into Afghanistan and

northwestern India in the early centuries CE. The main cities of Gandhara were Purushapura (now Peshawar), Takshashila (or Taxila) and Pushkalavati. The latter remained the capital of Gandhara until the second century CE, when the capital was moved to Peshawar.[66] An important Buddhist shrine, Kanishka Stupa, helped to make the city a centre of pilgrimage until the seventh century. What may have been the tallest building in the world at the time was built by King Kanishka to house Buddhist relics just outside the present-day Ganj Gate of the old city of Peshawar. Taxila (meaning 'cloven rock' in Sanskrit) is an important archaeological site located in the modern-day city of the same name in the Punjab, Pakistan. It dates back more than 3,000 years and was the main centre of Gandhara. Alexander of Macedon was attracted to Taxila, and Taxila's Raja Ombhi welcomed him in the hopes of using him against his enemy, Raja Porus.[67] This resulted in the Battle of Hydaspes. Alexander went on to Persia, leaving behind sizeable Greek populations in every region he set foot in, including Gandhara. The ancient Taxila University was one of the oldest universities in the world,

Hunza Valley, Gilgit Baltistan.

with several renowned learned personalities associated with it across different disciplines.[68] Nalanda, one of the world's first residential universities, located in ancient Magadha, India (modern-day Bihar), was renowned for its history and academic excellence. In contrast, Taxila operated under informal conditions. During the fifth century CE, the White Huns – also known as the Hephthalites, a nomadic Central Asian people who played a significant role in the history of Central Asia and India during the fifth and sixth centuries CE – made several incursions into the Indian subcontinent, and one of the most notable events associated with their invasion was the sack and burning of Taxila, which they destroyed in 600 CE. This occurred as part of the broader military incursions by the White Huns into the Gupta Empire, a powerful Indian dynasty of that time. The exact details of the destruction of Taxila are not fully documented in historical records, and different sources provide varying accounts. However, it is generally accepted that the White Huns, as part of their military campaign, caused significant

Stupa at Jaulian monastery, Taxila.

damage to the city. They likely sacked and set fire to various parts of it, leading to the destruction of its buildings and infrastructure. The White Huns' attacks played a role in the decline of the Gupta Empire and the disruption of established political and cultural centres in northern India during that period. They are believed to have originated in the region of modern-day Afghanistan and were of Turkic or Mongolic origin.[69]

In 316 BCE, King Chandragupta of Magadha moved in and conquered the Indus Valley, annexing Gandhara and naming Taxila a provincial capital of his newly formed Mauryan Empire. His son Bindusara succeeded him, and he was then succeeded by his own son, Ashoka, a former governor of Taxila. After waging a spate of bloody wars, Ashoka propagated the spread of Buddhism, building multiple monasteries and orchestrating the dissemination of the edicts of his 'Dharm' across the subcontinent. One of these is the grand Dharmarajika monastery east of the River Tamra at Taxila, famous for its stupa, and it is said that Ashoka buried several relics of Buddha there.[70] Mankiyala, Dharmarajika and Sanchi are said to be contemporary stupas.

In 184 BCE, the Greeks invaded Gandhara again under King Demetrius, who built a new city, Bhir Mound, opposite the river. Now it is known as Sirkap. The kingdom of Demetrius consisted of Gandhara, Arachosia, the Punjab and a section of the Ganges Valley. The gradual takeover of the Punjab by the nomadic Scythians of Central Asia began around 110 BCE, and they eventually took over Taxila. In the first quarter of the first century CE, the Parthians took over the Greek kingdoms in Gandhara and the Punjab.[71]

The Kushans migrated to Gandhara around the first century CE from Central Asia and Afghanistan. The tribe selected Peshawar as its seat of power and later expanded east into the heartland of India to establish the Kushan Empire, which lasted until the third century CE. In 80 CE, the Kushans wrested control of Gandhara from the Scytho-Parthians. The main city at Taxila was rebuilt at another site and given a new name: Sirsukh. It became a hub of Buddhist activity and hosted pilgrims from Central Asia and China. The Kushan era is considered a golden age in the history of this region, with Taxila, Swat and Charsadda becoming three important centres for culture, trade and learning.[72] However, a quick succession of rule by the Sassanian Empire, the Kidarites and finally the White Huns resulted in the region constantly being raided, invaded or in some way or another mired in turmoil. In about 241 CE, the rulers of the area were defeated by the Sassanians of Persia under the kingship of Shapur I, and Gandhara became annexed to the Persian Empire.[73]

The Kidarites successfully maintained the region and continued the cultural legacy of the Kushans until the mid-fifth century CE, when the White Huns, or Hephthalites, arrived and invaded the area. At this point, Buddhism and the Gandhara culture were already in decline, but the invasion caused further destruction. The White Huns adopted the Shivite faith, a strand of Hinduism, causing the cultural relevance of Buddhism to fade rapidly. During the invasions, the religious character of the region shifted towards Hinduism as the White Huns sought alliances with the Hindu Gupta Empire against the Sassanids. This change in religion led to a significant decline in Buddhism, which had been the centre of social life in the region for centuries. The White Huns' alliance with the Gupta Empire against the

Dharmarajika stupa and monastery, Taxila.

Sassanians significantly contributed to the decline of Buddhist culture. As a result, Buddhism gradually shifted northward into China, while Hinduism gained prominence in the region, leading to the dispersion of Buddhist communities. Importantly, despite the rule of various major powers during this era, they all demonstrated deep respect for Buddhism and the Indo-Greek artistic tradition, which had evolved in the region after Alexander's invasion of India. However, the following centuries were marked by constant invasions from the northwest, especially Muslim conquests, which caused the remnants of the older cultures to fall into obscurity.

The Emergence of Turko-Afghan Rule

Common understanding of India's past is based on two mistaken assumptions: first, that the Brahmanical texts describe the existing society; and second, that India's 'timelessness' means that colonial or contemporary village and caste organization is a guide to its historical past.[74] However, a closer look at medieval history refutes these claims. The periods of the Delhi sultans and the Mughals accelerated patterns of change that were already in place. During these centuries, the agricultural frontier expanded, commercial networks were created, technology evolved and political and religious institutions substantially changed. Therefore, it is these societal changes, rather than stagnation, that formed the prelude to the colonial era, argue the historians Thomas and Barbara Metcalf.[75] It is also misleading to describe Muslim rulers as 'foreign', or to refer to this era as the period of 'Muslim' rule. This exaggerates the differences between states ruled by Muslims and those ruled by non-Muslims and obscures the participation of non-Muslims in the Muslim-led polities.[76] As the American historian Richard M. Eaton argues,

> It was between the eleventh and eighteenth centuries, after all, that India witnessed, among other things, the disappearance of Buddhism, the appearance of Sikhism, the growth of the world's largest Muslim society, the transformation of vast tracts of land from jungle to fields of grain and the integration of tribal clans into the Hindu social order as castes.[77]

Eaton also states that this era saw the subcontinent become the world's first industrial powerhouse, owing to its export of manufactured textiles.[78]

The five Turko-Afghan dynasties that ruled India from 1206 to 1526 are collectively referred to as the Delhi sultanate.[79] During the late thirteenth and fourteenth centuries, its 28 rulers dominated political life in the north, with occasional incursions into the south. The Turks and Afghans launched military campaigns mostly to secure access to the agricultural surplus of the countryside, much like other states, including that of the

Rajput raja Prithviraj Chauhan.[80] They had fragmented political authority, with subordinates assigned a share of the land revenue of a specific area as compensation. The Delhi sultans offered scope for individual achievement, particularly through military prowess, without religious discrimination. Any periodization of the history of the subcontinent based solely on the religion of the rulers tends to gloss over fundamental similarities.[81] The Turks and Afghans were invaders, but they were assimilated into the local culture and society. Categories such as 'yavana', meaning 'Ionian', used to describe the Greek invaders who followed Alexander of Macedon a millennium before, or 'mlecca', meaning 'barbarians', for aliens to the settled Indic civilization, were used to describe them.

The military and economic institutions under the Delhi sultans were not inherently 'Islamic' in nature, since they did not derive their legitimacy from religious leadership or Islamic knowledge. Rather, the sultans' legitimacy stemmed from their military leadership and governing abilities. While they did patronize the religious and learned, they did not claim to be religious leaders themselves. Peter Hardy, a British historian, refers to the sultans as 'pious policemen' who collaborated with 'pious lawyers'.[82] Muslim rulers supported not only the learned legal scholars, or *ulema*, but the moral guides and spiritual intermediaries of the Muslim community, the Sufi sheikhs. Both the ulema and Sufi sheikhs had become integral to community life among Muslims since the eleventh century. Similarly, Hindu rulers, including both warrior rajas and lesser lords, patronized Brahmins, who were skilled in both ritual and legal learning from the sacred Sanskrit texts. Brahmins played a crucial role in temple cults, where devotional piety (*bhakti*) thrived during the sultanate era.[83]

Amir Khusrau: The Cultural Icon

During the sultanate rule, Amir Khusrau (1253–1325) emerged as a cultural icon of northern India. Multiple sociocultural strands seem to have converged in his persona: he was a poet, a musician, a courtier, a Sufi, a scholar and a historian. Moreover, he epitomized the amalgamation of Hindu–Muslim cultures, occupying a unique position in thirteenth-century India.[84] At that time, Muslims considered Khurasan as their homeland and remained indifferent to Indian culture and religion, but Khusrau, in contrast, considered India as his homeland and was drawn to its culture and beauty, which he regarded as superior to that of Bukhara, Khwarizm and Baghdad. Proud of both Indian and Turkic cultures, his writings signify the synthesis of the two. Khusrau wrote his poetry extensively in Persian, remarking that it was far superior to the language used in Khurasan, Sistan and Adharba'ijan. He was the first to express his patriotic love and passion for India in poetry. Khusrau lived through the dominion of seven rulers and was attached longest to the court of Alau din Khilji, where he completed his famous literary project *Khamsa*, five masnawis dedicated to Alaus-Din Khilji, which was praised by critics such as Jami.[85]

While some may argue that Amir Khusrau used Hindi language extensively in his poetry, the Pakistani Canadian academic Aziz Ahmad dispels this idea, arguing that only the verses in the introduction of his diwan, the 'Ghurrat al-kamal', can be considered genuine work in Hindi.[86] However, Khusrau's extensive study and knowledge of languages such as Persian, Arabic, Turkish and Hindi enabled him to experiment with different styles of poetry and prose, and he is often credited with a new genre of the historical epic.

To what extent can Khusrau be credited with laying the foundations of the Urdu language? His importance in the history of Urdu literature is due to his writings in Hindvi, an earlier language form that interspersed Urdu and Hindi. *Khaliq Bari* is often cited as a prime example of Khusrau's literary works. This composition, traditionally attributed to Khusrau, was primarily designed as a bilingual dictionary for educational use. It featured verses that elucidated the meanings of words in Arabic and Persian, along with their corresponding Urdu equivalents. *Khaliq Bari* not only set a precedent but paved the way for a plethora of similar works, giving rise to a widely popular genre known as *nisaab nama*. While the researcher and poet Hafiz Mehmood Sherani refused to admit that *Khaliq Bari* was Khusrau's creation, Jamil Jalbi, a Pakistani linguist, and the Indian literary critic Gopi Chand Narang consider it to be so. However, the Pakistani author Tabassum Kashmiri argues that rather than debating whether or not Khusrau wrote a lot of Hindvi poetry, we should instead consider him one of the leading icons of the cultural heritage of the subcontinent.[87]

Khusrau stands as an exemplary embodiment of the rich interplay between Hindu and Muslim cultures, showcasing the profound diversity that characterized this coexistence. This cultural pluralism found its roots in the inspirational currents of the Bhakti movement.[88] Thus Khusrau can be seen as the person who laid the foundation of Muslim identity by accepting and absorbing the culture of north India, or Hind. Scholar of Urdu literature and Khusrau's biographer Waheed Mirza explains that before Khusrau the tradition of Persian language was vague, but in him we can see how the discrete Hindu and Muslim cultures accepted and absorbed each other.[89] Khusrau's synthesis of Turko-Persian and indigenous cultural strains became manifest in his persona.[90] Therefore, he can be seen as a symbol of the cultural diversity and social inclusivity that Pakistan aspired to embody. Regrettably, in today's Pakistan, his impact is largely superficial. Yet Khusrau's significance as a cultural icon is so profound that he deserves a place among the revered founding figures of Pakistan, symbolizing the essence of the nation's cultural heritage.

Muslim dynasties, despite their institutional similarities with non-Muslim states, also charted new directions in the Indian subcontinent. For more than six hundred years, beginning with the establishment of the first Turkic dynasty in Delhi by the Mamluk ruler Qutbu'd-din Aibak in 1206, Persian was the language of the Muslim ruling elite. As participants in a Persian-speaking culture that extended into Central and Southwest Asia, these dynasties served as a conduit for introducing innovations in ruling institutions, as well as distinctive cultural traditions in law, political theory and literary and religious styles.[91] They also brought practical innovations in mounted warfare, cropping patterns and irrigation techniques, such as the widespread 'Persian' wheel, and fostered urban growth and road networks that encouraged trade within the region and beyond.

Arabic-speaking Muslims had already established a kingdom in Sindh in the lower Indus Valley in 711 when Muhammad bin Qasim defeated Raja Dahir. This was part of the Umayyad dynasty's expansion project based in Damascus. Muslims of Arabian descent had migrated and settled along the Malabar coast of the southwest by the eighth century, where they intermarried and sustained distinctive cultural forms forged from their Arab ties and local setting, linking 'al-Hind' to seaborne trade routes.[92]

From roughly 1200 to 1500, the movement of goods and peoples through Indian Ocean ports, as well as overland through the Persian-speaking territories, constituted an 'Islamic world system'.[93] Participation in these ruling and trading networks did not necessitate that an individual be Muslim. However, Muslim political expansion facilitated the success of the entire network.

Another pattern that featured early in the sultanate period was the enduring ethnic and linguistic pluralism that both the ruling elites and the ruled assimilated. The rulers were not only of Turkish heritage but Afghan, Persian and native-born, as well as immigrants from afar. Among the best known was Ibn Battuta, a Berber Maghrebi scholar and explorer who travelled extensively in the lands of Afro-Eurasia, largely in the Muslim world.[94] Ibn Battuta's profound knowledge of Arabic/Islamic law served as the cornerstone of his abilities, empowering him to embark on extensive travels and secure positions at various royal courts. Ibn Battuta served the Tughlaq dynasty of fourteenth-century India as chief judge of Delhi, and his memoirs are a testimony to the cosmopolitan vitality and variety he experienced.

The majority of subjects over whom the Delhi sultans ruled followed religions other than Islam. The question of whether they should be considered *zimmi*, or 'protected people', entitled to their own laws and customs, was up for debate. In principle, they were required to pay a poll tax (*jizya*) but were not subject to military conscription. Laws were generally administered according to the law of the parties involved or, if they differed, according to the defendant's law. For most Muslims, this meant following Hanafi law, which was shared with Central and Southwest Asia. However, for those in the south with ties to Arabia via the Indian Ocean,

Maliki law was used. Administrative law on matters such as taxes had its own codes separate from Sharia norms based on classical Arabic texts of jurisprudence. The Indian historian Athar Abbas Rizvi is of the view that although Brahmins were correctly exempted from paying *jizya* by early Turkic sultans, Sultan Firoz Shah Tughluq wrongly imposed it on them.[95] Despite these differences, the pluralism of the society led to a creative and vibrant cultural life.[96]

The sultans of Delhi and the Mughals who followed them were primarily concerned with expanding their territories rather than converting people to Islam. This is evident when considering the fact that India's Muslim population remained small in areas of Muslim rule. Converts were thought to have been attracted to the Sufi message of egalitarianism and social equality as a means of escaping the hierarchical discrimination of Brahman-dominated caste in the society. However, there is no clear correlation between areas of Brahmanical influence and those of substantial conversion to Islam. Furthermore, the extent of Brahmanical influence in the pre-colonial period is disputed.[97]

In areas undergoing settlement, Sufis played a crucial role in incorporating people into larger cultural and civilizational structures. Sufis were granted forested land, which they cleared, and acted as mediators between worldly and divine powers. This process could be evidenced in the West Punjab and East Bengal, two regions with largely Muslim populations.[98] Another driving force behind conversion was the desire of individuals or families to move up the social hierarchy. Intermarriage and the influence of charismatic teachers also contributed to the growth of the Muslim population.[99] By the late nineteenth century, the Muslim population of British India accounted for roughly one-quarter of the whole.

Historians have raised objections to accounts of forced mass conversions and systematic destruction of non-Muslim holy places by Muslim rulers.[100] Some historians have misinterpreted the contents of Muslim court histories because they took them too literally. These histories were actually written in a particular literary style or convention, which may not always reflect events exactly as they happened. So, historians who don't recognize this literary aspect might misunderstand the true context and meaning of these historical accounts. While it is true that non-Muslim temples and places of worship were destroyed in certain situations, such as during raids on areas outside one's own territories for plunder, these instances were not as widespread as previously thought. Mahmud Ghaznawi, for example, raided Sindh and Gujarat in search of riches to secure booty for his cosmopolitan court in Ghazna, much like Indian rulers who took vanquished idols as symbols of their victory along with their booty. Some sultans who established permanent courts in north India also destroyed temples during the initial phase of conquest to mark their triumph. The Quwwat-ul-Islam Mosque, built near the Qutb Minar in Delhi in the early twelfth century, utilized elements of earlier structures that had been destroyed.[101] This practice of 'recycling' elements from earlier structures was common around the Mediterranean and in India; it was sometimes a declaration of power, and sometimes simply an expedient use of abandoned debris.[102]

Muslim spiritual and religious life in the subcontinent evolved alongside the religious life of other groups, resulting in cultural hybridity. The Bhakti movement, for example, demonstrated this cultural hybridity, as different groups interacted with one another's expressions of their respective traditions. The most enduring cultural pattern for Muslims during the rule of the Delhi sultans was Sufi devotionalism, which can be described as Islamic mysticism or asceticism. Sufism helps Muslims attain nearness to Allah by way of direct personal experience of God through belief and practice. The four principles of Repentance, Sincerity, Remembrance and Love outline the fundamental stages and states of the spiritual novice's transformative journey, emphasizing the importance of embracing human limitations and God's limitless love.[103] In the Indian context, Sufism is pervasive in discourse and institutions. Sufi adherents follow Sharia law and emphasize 'inner realization of the divine presence, the practice of moral and physical disciplines, and the need to submit to the authority of charismatic chains of saintly authority'.[104] The founders of the most important Sufi lineages, such as Chishti, Suhrawardi, Qadiri and Naqshbandi, were of Central and West Asian origin, but they blended well with the epistemic and cultural ethos of the subcontinent. The earliest Sufi of eminence to settle in India was Ali Usman Hujweri, also known as Data Ganj Baksh (d. 1088), the author of the celebrated treatise on Sufism entitled *Kashf al-Mahjub*. Sufi teachings were enriched and stimulated by the presence and competition of similar holy men of the Indic *bhakti* traditions of devotion, spiritual disciplines and sophisticated monistic philosophies, and *bhakti* devotion and worship, in turn, flourished as well.

The Mughal period (1526–1857) was a time of significant political, economic and social changes that transformed India. The first six Mughal emperors, Babur, Humayun, Akbar, Jahangir, Shah Jahan and Aurangzeb, were known for their intellectual and political prowess.[105] In total, nineteen Mughal kings ruled the empire, and the period from Akbar to Shah Jahan is regarded as the peak period of the Mughal dynasty, not only in politics but in cultural development. Cultural life flourished, fuelled by internal pluralism and regional cross-fertilization. Mughal miniature painting and architecture – rooted in Persia but transformed in the Indian environment – left a lasting cultural legacy. The Sanskrit *ayurveda* and Arabic *yunani tibb* medical systems interacted, enriching each other. Music and Vaishnavite (believers of the Hindu deity Vaishnu) devotionalism, as seen in the work of poets such as Sur and Tulsidas, flourished.

Shaikh Ahmad Sirhindi, also known as Mujaddid Alif Sani (1564–1624), was a prominent figure in the Mughal period. He propagated puritanical

Mausoleum of Shah Rukn-e Alam, an eminent 13th- and 14th-century Sufi saint who represented Suhrawardiya Order. He is buried in Multan (present-day Pakistani Punjab).

religious thought and criticized Mughal cultural policies, which led to his imprisonment in the fort of Gwalior by Jahangir. His cosmological and philosophical thought had a profound impact on the subcontinent and Central Asia. His ideology stood in contrast to the prevailing syncretic tendencies of the Mughal court, which sought to blend elements of various religious traditions, including Hinduism and Islam. Shaikh Ahmad Sirhindi was a staunch advocate of orthodox Sunni Islam, and he believed in the strict adherence to Sharia (Islamic law) as outlined in the Qur'an and Hadith. He was critical of what he perceived as the syncretic and heterodox practices of some Mughal rulers and the integration of Hindu customs into Islamic rituals.

Shaikh Ahmad Sirhindi's ideology was marked by several key principles. Foremost among them was his unwavering commitment to Tawhid, the absolute monotheism of Islam. He stressed the importance of preserving the pure concept of monotheism and vehemently opposed any syncretism or blending of beliefs that could dilute this fundamental tenet. Additionally, Shaikh Ahmad Sirhindi was a staunch critic of Hindu influences seeping into Islamic practices and beliefs, including his reservations about certain Sufi practices that he believed had been influenced by Hindu mysticism. His vision extended to advocating for the reform and purification of Islamic practices, with a strong emphasis on adhering to the original teachings of Islam as outlined in the Qur'an and Hadith, while eliminating any innovations or heterodox elements. Finally, while he critiqued certain aspects of

Sufism, he did not outright reject it. Instead, he called for a more orthodox and less syncretic form of Sufism that remained faithful to Islamic principles. His efforts contributed to the preservation and propagation of traditional Islamic beliefs and practices in the Indian subcontinent during a period of significant cultural and religious interaction. In the Pakistani textbooks, he is regarded as the first architect of Pakistani ideology.[106]

The Mughal period was not stagnant but rather flexible and open to change.[107] With the arrival of European trading companies, new techniques of shipbuilding, horticulture and art were incorporated into the wider culture, illustrating the openness and eclecticism of the era. The Mughal institutions were also flexible and open, as is evident in the adoption of the term 'early modern' by many historians, emphasizing the range of transformations that began in the 1500s across Eurasia. John Richards, an American historian of Mughal India, has identified several of these unprecedented worldwide processes of change, starting with the creation of global sea passages that linked the entire world for the first time.[108] The intensification of monetization, the expansion of textile production, population growth and the spread of the agricultural frontier were some such changes. The Mughal Empire was a centralized state that experienced technological diffusion, particularly in relation to gunpowder, leading to new levels of bureaucratic control.[109]

Contrary to orientalist views and recent Hindu nationalism, Hindu beliefs and institutions were not repressed during the Mughal period. New patterns of worship emerged: Vaishnavite and Shaivite – two Hindu sects, worshipping two different deities, Shiva and Vaishnu. Islamic thought and practice were transformed within the framework of Sufi devotionalism. The Mughal regime was Muslim-led, but participation was defined by loyalty rather than religious affiliation. The regimes were 'Muslim' in that they were led by Muslims, who patronized learned and holy Muslim leaders (among others) and justified their existence in Islamic terms. Non-Muslim elites were central to the functioning of the regime, and there were no mass pogroms or forced conversions. Overall, the Mughal period was a time of significant change and development in India, with a rich cultural legacy that continues to influence the region to this day.

The question of whether the Delhi sultanate and Mughal regimes were 'foreign' is often raised by Hindu nationalists. While it is true that these dynasties were founded by individuals from outside of South Asia, cultural spheres extended beyond current borders. Those within Central Asian circuits, or ocean-borne trading networks east and west, had more in common with each other than with putatively 'national' groupings. It is also worth considering what 'foreign' meant in an era before modern states and passports, and how long it takes for individuals of different origins to be accepted as 'natural' in any given place. Indigenous symbolic systems and institutions were themselves changing in interaction with those of the erstwhile outsiders. The fact that Hindus and Muslims eventually saw themselves as distinct religious communities, even two nations, is central to the modern history of the subcontinent. However, despite continuities in terminology, past communities were very different from those that incorporated individuals of diverse regions and religions. The contrasting image of self-conscious 'horizontal' communities of Hindus and Muslims, like the image of pre-colonial India as a land of self-sufficient villages and rigid caste hierarchies, reads characteristics of colonial society into the pre-colonial past.[110]

One Hindu Kayastha memoirist, Bhimsen Saxena, provides a cogent perspective on Aurangzeb as a ruler. In his final decades of service, he acted as auditor and inspector for a Rajput noble. Writing at the end of Aurangzeb's life, Bhimsen gives us a 'grass-roots' view of what he sees as imperial failure. Bhimsen and many others claimed generations of loyalty to the Mughal regime, priding themselves on their devotion, courage and mastery of Indo-Persian courtly culture.[111] However, as Bhimsen followed his master into the futile battles against the rebellious *zamindars* and chiefs, he despaired at the difference between earlier Mughal rulers and the later Aurangzeb:

> When the aim of the ruling sovereign is the happiness of the people, the country prospers, the peasants are at ease, and people live in peace. The fear of the king's order seizes the hearts of high and low. Now that the last age has come, nobody has an honest desire; the Emperor, seized with a passion for capturing forts, has given up attending to the happiness of the subjects. The nobles have turned aside from giving good counsel.[112]

Bhimsen offers a sociological analysis of the disorder witnessed under Aurangzeb's rule. He identifies the upstart *zamindars*, local lineage heads and chieftains who controlled the peasantry and possessed local knowledge, as key players. During the prosperous seventeenth century, *zamindars* accumulated enough resources and wealth to secure recognition, including rank and office, from the Mughal authorities. After Aurangzeb's death, they fomented resistance against imperial authority, sometimes coalescing to form communities that mounted an enduring challenge to Mughal rule.[113] The Marathas of the Deccan, the Sikhs in the Punjab and the Jats in southeast Delhi were among the most prominent of these communities.

A second fault line marks the established princely rulers who accepted Mughal power but kept authority within their own domains, rendering tribute but refusing subjection to Mughal administration. These territories were typically located in inaccessible or peripheral areas.[114] Some chiefs simply ceased to deliver tribute, and others increasingly resisted Mughal demands from the strength of their forts. To some extent, the Rajputs, who held full control of their desert homeland even while serving the empire, fit this category. By the late seventeenth century, two of the most important Rajput houses were in rebellion.[115]

Derawar Fort, which was built in the 9th century CE by Rai Jajja Bhati, a Hindu Rajput ruler of the Bhati clan.

The third fault line was that of provincial governors, appointed by the emperor as administrators for areas where they had hardly any pre-existing local connections.[116] They acted autonomously, paying lip service to Mughal authority while breaking away from it. In 1724, the imperial prime minister, Nizamu'l Mulk, withdrew to Hyderabad, ceased to participate in imperial projects and even fought against Mughal troops to assert his autonomy.[117] In the early eighteenth century, significant political transformations were under way in the Indian subcontinent. The provinces of Awadh and Bengal, during the 1720s, saw the emergence of independent political entities. This shift in power was marked by the actions of local governors who adopted the prestigious title of nawab.

These nawabs didn't stop at mere titles; they also took control of administrative affairs by appointing their own officials and handpicking successors. While the emperor confirmed these successors until the 1730s, this was merely a formality. By the middle of the century, these once-appointed governors had effectively transformed into the formidable heads of dynasties in their own right. This shift in authority marked a profound change in the political landscape of Awadh and Bengal, where local leaders now held sway over their regions, independent of central authority. As rulers of quasi-independent states, 'they diverted to themselves revenues formerly sent to Delhi, engaged in diplomatic and military activity and withdrew from attendance at court. From appointed Mughal officials, these erstwhile governors had become by mid-century the heads of dynasties of their own.'[118]

The Mughal fault lines, particularly those that involved chiefs and *zamindars*, have often been seen as expressions of the Hindu struggle against foreign rule. Later in the nineteenth century, Indian nationalists such as Rao Bahadur Mahadev Govind Ranade (1842–1901) viewed Shivaji I, a prominent Indian ruler (1674–80) and a member of the Bhonsle Maratha clan, and his successors through an anachronistic lens, portraying them as a nation challenging foreign domination, in the context of their opposition to British rule. Shivaji played a pivotal role in shaping the destiny of the Indian subcontinent during the seventeenth century. He established his own sovereign realm amid the waning Adilshahi sultanate of Bijapur. This achievement marked the birth of the Maratha Empire in the south of the subcontinent. In addition to his rise to power, Shivaji also became a formidable adversary to the Mughal Empire. His staunch opposition to the Mughals further underscored his commitment to preserving and expanding his realm, setting the stage for exclusionary vision in India's history. Bal Gangadhar Tilak, the leader of the Indian National Congress's (INC) extremist wing, elevated Shivaji to a symbol of Hindu rule in 1896.

In the 1930s and '40s, as the divide between Hindus and Muslims grew in the lead-up to independence, Shivaji became a symbol of Hindu resistance to Muslim dominance. Similarly, Sikh resistance to Mughal rule has been interpreted as being driven by ideology, but the rebels formed alliances based on expediency, rather than a shared religious belief. For instance, during the reign of Aurangzeb, when Rajput rajas of Marwar and Mewar rebelled, Prince Akbar was sent to suppress them, but he instead joined their ranks. He even reached out to Shivaji's son and successor before ultimately failing and fleeing for his life. The Marathas were active participants in Mughal factional rivalries, paying lip service to Mughal power while often making deals to share access to contested tracts of land.

In 1736 Nadir Shah became the ruler of Persia after Shah Tahmasp, the last ruler of the Safavid dynasty, died. Nadir Shah, a member of the Afshar tribe of Khurasan, established the Afsharid dynasty when he became king of Persia. Before ascending to the throne, Nadir Shah captured and influenced many regions near the Mughal and Safavid spheres of influence. The diplomatic relations between the Mughal and Safavid empires began deteriorating as Nadir Shah ascended to the throne. The Mughal emperor stopped exchanging ambassadors with the Persian court, which Nadir Shah considered a great insult.

Nadir Shah invaded India in 1739, for two reasons. First, he sought to take revenge for the insults inflicted by the Mughals. Second, he was motivated by his ambitions and the rumours of India's wealth, which excited him and made him eager to attack. The Persian ruler's invasion of India left the most destructive and tumultuous mark on Mughal history. He brutally killed 20,000 to 30,000 citizens (men, women and children) of Delhi in about six hours, destroying the entire city. It was a demonstration of the most inhumane treatment ever witnessed in Indian history. After Nadir Shah's invasion and sack of Delhi, the Mughal Empire was so weakened that it was unable to regain its strength and fight against its other enemies. This was an opportune time for the British to establish their paramountcy over northern India. Ahmad Shah Abdali's incessant attacks dealt the final blow to Mughal rule.

After Delhi was ransacked, a requiem of what the city went through was articulated through a genre of Urdu poetry called *shehr-e-ashoob*. This genre of Urdu poetry was composed by many poets, including Mir Taqi Mir, and reflects the pathos and tragic feelings that emerged from witnessing the sad state of the city following its destruction. This legacy continued, and we can see glimpses of it in Mirza Muhammad Rafi Sauda's poetry from 1857.[119] It is a treasure trove that depicts the stark realities of that time.

AT THE OUTSET of this chapter, it was clear that the history of Pakistan is a reflection of its sociocultural plurality, drawing on traditions and customs that have developed since the Indus Valley civilization, particularly in town planning, trade and commerce. However, the impact of Buddhism and the Graeco-Persian model of governance during the Gandhara civilization, followed by the arrival of the Aryans and their contribution through the Rig Vedas and warrior culture, added complexity to the region's sociocultural dispensation. This synthesis was further articulated through the Bhakti stalwarts. The advent of Turko-Persian rule brought new dimensions of Sufism, literary genres, governance, architecture, language, food and dress, making the society of Hindustan more nuanced. Therefore, the history of Pakistan cannot be confined to the traditional narrative that starts with Muhammad bin Qasim's arrival in Sindh. It is a multi-layered and complex history that demands a more sophisticated analysis.

2

British Rule and the Rise of Muslim Nationalism

The emergence of Muslim nationalism was one of the many facets of the wider Indian nationalist movement that emerged in the late nineteenth and early twentieth centuries. Muslims in India were a minority group, and their distinct cultural, religious and political identity played a crucial role in shaping their nationalist aspirations. The Aligarh movement, which began in the late nineteenth century, was a significant force in shaping Muslim nationalism in India. It was led by Sir Syed Ahmed Khan, who aimed to modernize Muslim society by promoting education and social reform.

One of the key features of Muslim nationalism was its emphasis on the preservation and promotion of Muslim identity in the face of British colonialism and Hindu majoritarianism. The All-India Muslim League, founded in 1906, was the primary political vehicle for Muslim nationalism in India. Its leaders, such as Muhammad Ali Jinnah, advocated for the creation of a separate Muslim state in the Indian subcontinent.

The Muslim League's demand for a separate Muslim state was based on the belief that Muslims could not achieve their political, economic and cultural aspirations within a Hindu-majority India. This demand was met with resistance from the INC, also known as the Congress or Congress Party, and other non-Muslim nationalist groups who believed in a united, secular India. However, the demand for a separate Muslim state gained momentum in the early decades of the twentieth century, culminating in the Lahore Resolution of 1940, which called for the creation of an independent Muslim state in the northwestern and northeastern regions of India.

Muslim nationalism in India was a complex and multifaceted phenomenon that emerged in response to British colonialism, Hindu majoritarianism and the broader Indian nationalist movement. It was driven by a desire to preserve and promote Muslim identity and achieve political, economic and cultural aspirations within the Indian subcontinent. The demand for a separate Muslim state eventually led to the partition of India and Pakistan in 1947, marking a significant moment in the history of the subcontinent.

The Coming of the East India Company

Starting in the late fifteenth century, European states such as Portugal, Spain, the Netherlands, France, Denmark and Britain initiated conquests around the world, primarily focused on trade in spices, textiles and chinaware. Christian proselytizing frequently followed in their wake. The British East India Company was granted a royal charter by Queen Elizabeth I on 31 December 1600, with the aim of providing trade privileges in India.[1] The royal charter gave the newly created Honourable East India Company (HEIC) a 21-year monopoly on all trade in the East Indies. Over time, the Company's commercial trading venture transformed into a virtual ruling authority in India, acquiring auxiliary governmental and military functions until its dissolution in 1858.

The Company's operations were based on the 'factory' system, which originated in medieval Europe. When ships returned to Europe, agents known as 'factors' were left behind at trading posts to negotiate with local merchants for the sale of current stocks of goods and the procurement of return cargoes for the next year's voyage. The British East India Company's first factory in Bengal was established at Hooghly in 1651, which later moved to Calcutta in 1690.[2] The steady decline of the Mughal Empire from the early eighteenth century created a power vacuum in the Indian subcontinent. As a result, the region became highly volatile and vulnerable to external pressure. The Dutch, French and British, as well as powerful regional rulers such as the Marathas in central and western India, the nizam of Hyderabad, Haidar Ali and Tipu Sultan in Mysore and the nawabs of Bengal, were engaged in economic, political and military rivalries. A common practice was for Europeans to fight proxy wars.

Company business was overseen by a central administration in London, consisting of 24 elected members of the Court of Directors. The directors were accountable to the Company shareholders, who regularly met at the General Court of Proprietors. In India, the Company was led by one governor and 24 directors who made up the Court of Directors. They were appointed by and reported to the Court of Proprietors. The Court of Directors had ten committees reporting to it. The Company established several enclaves along India's western and eastern coastline, including Masulipatnam (1611), Surat (1613), Madras (1839, with work on Fort St George commencing in 1640, now known as Chennai), Bombay (1661, now Mumbai) and Calcutta (Kolkata, 1690). The last three settlements became the Company's primary trading ports.

The appointment of Warren Hastings (1732–1818) as the first governor general of India marked a period of enlightened harmony in Anglo-Indian society.[3] Indian laws, literature and sacred texts were translated into English, and there was a profound interest in oriental studies. Intermarriage between British and local peoples was common. That practice was prevalent among

Sir Syed Ahmed Khan (1817–1898).

the Scottish, who in relative percentage comprised half of the Company's members.

However, Hastings shared the spotlight of imperial success with Robert Clive (1725–1774), a keystone figure in British history. Both Clive and Hastings were smeared by severe corruption within the Company, which led to the pauperization of Bengal. Clive played a crucial role in the Bengal conquest and established the Company's hold on India, overthrowing the nawab of Bengal, Siraj-ud-Daulah, and installing a puppet, Mir Jaffar, after the Battle of Plassey in 1757.[4] If not for Clive, one might speculate that there would have been no British Empire.

The British paramountcy was further consolidated after the Battle of Buxar against Mir Kasim in 1764.[5] From 1773 the British assumed Diwani rights (the rights to collect agricultural revenue tax in Bengal). Their control over Bengal was effectively consolidated in the 1770s when Hastings brought the nawab's administrative offices from Murshidabad to Calcutta under his oversight.

According to the British historian P. J. Marshall,

In what was to be the most constructive period of his administration, from 1772 to 1774, Hastings detached the machinery of the central government from the nawab's court and brought it to the British settlement in Calcutta under direct British control, remodelled the administration of justice throughout Bengal, and began a series of experiments aimed at bringing the collection of taxation under effective supervision.[6]

Around the same time, the British parliament began regulating the East India Company through successive India Acts, bringing Bengal under the indirect control of the British government. Over the next eight decades, a series of wars, treaties and annexations extended the dominion of the Company across the subcontinent, subjugating most of India to the political aspirations of British officials and merchants. During the Carnatic Wars, spanning from 1746 to 1763, British and French forces forged alliances with competing regional powers, each vying for supremacy in the rich tapestry of India. It was amid these tumultuous conflicts that the British, operating through the formidable East India Company, ascended to a position of unparalleled prominence. Their ascendancy began in the 1760s, as they gradually outmanoeuvred and subdued their French counterparts, ultimately securing their dominion by the late 1790s.

The British forces secured victories in Bengal and exerted their influence on the Mughal emperor, gaining political control over Bengal, one of the richest Mughal provinces. In 1765, the British East India Company received from Mughal emperor Shah Alam II (r. 1759–1806) the agricultural revenue rights (Diwani) for Bengal province, resulting in their headquarters being established in Calcutta. The British hailed Robert Clive, who was the linchpin of the conquest of Bengal.

Bengal's conquest by the British paved the way for their expansion of control over the rest of India, Ceylon (modern-day Sri Lanka) and Burma (Myanmar) through a combination of wars and treaties with regional rulers, all of which benefited British interests. While attempts were made to extend British control over Afghanistan, these efforts met with little success. Some notable examples of the wars fought by the British include those against Mysore (1767–99), the Marathas (1775–1819), the Sikhs in the Punjab (1849), the princely state of Awadh (1856) and the Afghan tribes beyond India's northwest frontier (1839–80). Subsidiary alliances were formed with the Princely States to enable indirect rule. Dutch Ceylon and the Kandyan kingdom were brought under British administrative control in 1802 and 1817, respectively.

The East India Company employed 'military fiscalism' and profit maximization, utilizing its revenues from land tax to finance Britain's imperial wars and its trade with China.[7] Initially, the task of maintaining law and order was entrusted to the de facto puppet nawab Mir Jaffar, but after the disastrous Bengal famine (1770–72), stemming from revenue exploitation and corruption among East India Company officers, the British parliament forced the Company to assume direct responsibility for Indian governance, albeit under parliamentary oversight. Lord North's Regulating Act of 1773 and Pitt's India Act of 1784 were intended to bring the company's administration under the oversight of the parliament through a Board of Control.[8]

The East India Company's governmental focus was economic, and the colonized territory was divided into revenue districts. The systems varied, ranging from the Permanent Settlement in Bengal, whereby property rights were vested in gentleman-farmer intermediaries (*zamindars*), with contributions fixed in perpetuity, to more direct arrangements in Madras and parts of Bombay presidencies (Ryotwari), Awadh and the Northwest Provinces (Mahalwari). Under the Mahalwari system, the land revenue was collected from the farmers by the village headmen on behalf of the whole village, ostensibly to protect village-level autonomy. The Mahalwari system was introduced by Holt Mackenzie in 1822. The Ryotwari system, on the other hand, involved farmers paying land revenue directly to the state, with the tax subject to alteration with each new settlement operation. The Indian scientist Ramkrishna Mukherjee deliberates on the Mahalwari system, whereby *mahals*, or estates, were created in the inhabited parts of the country, and the proprietors of a *mahal* (these being held either individually or by several proprietors conjointly) were made responsible in their persons and property for the payment of the sum assessed by the government on the *mahal*.[9] This system was devised by Captain Alexander Read and Sir Thomas Munro at the end of the eighteenth century, with Munro introducing it during his tenure as governor of Madras (1820–27). The *zamindari* system was initiated by the East India Company in 1793, during Lord Cornwallis's tenure as governor general. One main feature of the Permanent Settlement was that the rajas and *talukdars* were recognized as *zamindars*.[10] They were responsible for collecting revenue from peasants and paying it to the Company, and the revenue demand was permanently fixed. However, this often led to absentee property ownership, with rural estates left to managers (*munshis*) while the landowners enjoyed luxurious urban lives, visiting their properties once or at most twice a year. This situation put the peasantry at a disadvantage, and mounting hardships eventually led to retaliation.

A Militant Response (Jihad) from the Peasantry

These developments triggered a strong response through the Faraizi movement, spearheaded by Haji Shariatullah from the Faridpur District in East Bengal. Shariatullah, who had spent about twenty years primarily in Mecca before returning to Bengal in 1820, stirred the dormant spirit of Bengali Muslims. Influenced by the equalitarian doctrines of Muhammad bin

Abdul Wahab, the founder of the Wahabi movement in Arabia, Shariatullah started the Faraizi movement in 1819–20. The movement exhorted Muslims in Bengal to give up un-Islamic practices and to fulfil their duties as Muslims. It was spread widely in the districts of Dhaka, Faridpur, Barisal, Mymensingh and Comilla, with large numbers of peasants who were pestered and exploited by *zamindars* rallying around him.[11] According to Hafiz Malik, a Pakistani American political scientist, Shariatullah's reformation bound the Muslim peasantry together, while its levelling aspect alarmed the landlords. He introduced the titles of *ustad* (teacher) and *shagird* (student) instead of *pir* (master) and *murid* (disciple), and the relationship between *ustad* and *shagird* was more flexible than *pir* and *murid*.[12]

After Shariatullah's death, his son Muhsin ud Din Ahmad, better known as Dudu Miyan, assumed charge of the movement. Though he did not attain the levels of scholarship achieved by his father, he became a powerful leader of the peasant movements against colonial indigo planters and wealthy landlords.[13] Dudu Miyan set up his own administrative system with each village constituting a unit to be administered by a *khalifa* (leader) appointed by him.[14] Thus he created a state within the British-ruled state and became a powerful voice of the oppressed peasantry against their oppressive landlords.[15]

In 1838 Dudu Miyan called upon his followers not to pay revenue to the *zamindars*. Indigo planters were frequently attacked and plantations looted. In retaliation, landlords and indigo planters tried to contain him by instituting cases against him. Though he was arrested several times, he was always released: he had become so popular with the peasantry that courts seldom found a witness against him.[16] At the time of the cataclysmic events of the uprising in 1857, the British government arrested Dudu Miyan as a precaution and kept him in Alipore Jail, Calcutta. He was released in 1859 but rearrested shortly after and finally freed in 1860. In 1862 he fell seriously ill and died in Dhaka at the age of 42 or 43.

After the death of Dudu Miyan, his second son, Abdul Ghafoor (1864–1884), known as Naya Miyan, took over the Faraizi movement. However, due to his young age, three individuals from the older generation managed the movement until the 1870s. In 1874 Naya Miyan became actively involved with the movement, coinciding with a pivotal moment in the conflict between Bengal farmers and landlords. Tenant farmers demanded written leases that would grant them legal occupancy rights to the land, but landlords refused and instead asked tenants to pay a cess, further escalating the conflict. This situation persisted until 1879, when the peasants emerged victorious with the assistance of sympathetic British officers, marking the beginning of a period of cooperation with the government.

After Naya Miyan's death in 1884, his youngest brother, Syed Ud Din Ahmed (1855–1906), succeeded him. Under Syed Ud Din, the Faraizi movement became solely focused on religious goals, rather than significant economic and political aspirations. Their cordial relations with the British were recognized in 1899 when the government granted the title of Khan Bahadur to Syed Ud Din. This marked the end of the Faraizi movement's militant phase.

Around the same period when the Faraizi movement was just beginning to emerge, there was another revivalist movement led by Titu Mir (1782–1831), who became prominent in the 1820s. Titu Mir, a disciple of Syed Ahmed Barelwi, drew inspiration from the Tarikah i-Muhammadiyah, a revivalist movement that advocated a return to the pure Islamic practices of the past and promoted jihad against non-Muslims. He primarily preached his ideas in rural areas of West Bengal and strongly criticized popular Islam, considering it to be a collection of heretical beliefs. Titu Mir urged his followers to embrace equality among fellow Muslims and adopt a distinctive dress code as a symbol of their religious dedication. He also voiced opposition against Hinduism and the landlord class, which garnered significant support from the local peasantry.

Despite successfully gaining control over three districts, Titu Mir's movement met its demise in 1831 when he confronted the British authorities. This confrontation led to a decisive military campaign by the British, resulting in the complete suppression of the movement. However, even with the British implementing stringent measures, the spirit of Muslim dissent in the region could not be entirely extinguished. This enduring spirit found expression through figures like Maulana Karamat Ali, who continued to advocate for puritanical Islam in Bengal, ensuring that the flame of resistance persisted amid the challenges.

Nevertheless, it appeared that armed struggle ended with Titu Mir. Over time, Muslim activism shifted its focus from economic and political concerns to a more religious orientation. However, the movement with the most enduring legacy was Jihad Tehrik, spearheaded by Sayyid Ahmad. Ayesha Jalal, a Pakistani American historian, regards it as the only genuine jihad in the subcontinent aimed at establishing the supremacy of the Islamic faith, marking a significant chapter in the history of Muslims in the region.[17]

Syed Ahmed, a Hindustani born in Rae Bareilly near Lucknow in the United Provinces (now Uttar Pradesh), was a devout follower of Shah Waliullah. He found the demise of Muslim rule in Delhi and Lahore unbearable and was opposed to both the British and the Sikhs. He believed that fighting against Sikhs would give him a better chance of success to establish Sharia-based Islamic rule. Despite this, the British did not impede his journey via Sindh to Peshawar, or that of the numerous fighters he enlisted in Uttar Pradesh and Bihar.[18] One of Syed Ahmed's recruiting pamphlets, issued in north India in the mid-1820s, alleged that the Sikh nation had long held sway in Lahore and other places, and that their oppressions had exceeded all bounds. The pamphlet claimed that thousands

Lahore Museum, opened in 1894.

of Mohammedans had been unjustly killed, that the call to prayer from the mosques was no longer allowed and that the killing of cows had been entirely prohibited.[19]

Recruits, arms and donations were raised in several Indian cities, and towards the end of 1826, a jihad commenced in the tribal areas around Peshawar. For a while, Yusufzai, Khattak and other Pashtun tribesmen responded fervently to Syed Ahmed's call, and Peshawar was vacated by the maharaja's Pashtun governor. However, an army led by Maharaja Ranjit Singh's French commanders, Allard and Ventura, played a vital role in retrieving Peshawar. Ranjit Singh made effective use of money and clan rivalries to establish his own political writ. In the summer of 1830, troops led by Prince Sher Singh, Hari Singh Nalwa and Allard won a major battle against Syed Ahmed and his companions. However, in a reversal of earlier clashes between Jihadist soldiers and Sikh bands, the maharaja's regiments were ambushed by determined Pashtun bands, and some battles were daringly won by the jihadists. What eventually proved fatal for Syed Ahmed's bid was Pashtun resentment of Hindustani jihadists. According to Olaf Caroe (1892–1981), a keen student of Pashtun history and a future British governor of the Northwest Frontier Province (NWFP), the people were greatly incensed when Ahmed was accused – as many say, unjustly – of assigning maidens one by one to his needy Hindustani followers.[20] In May 1831 a Sikh party led by Prince Sher Singh surprised and killed an isolated Syed Ahmed and Shah Ismael (1791–1831) at Balakot.[21]

During the time of early British rule, the colonial authorities invested considerable energy and resources in indigo dye production for export

– albeit less directly than they did opium. Most of the indigo cultivators were Europeans. Initially, they had to rely on government support to boost their production and trade. However, by 1802, they had amassed sufficient capital, acquired through trade and banking institutions known as 'agency houses', to finance their endeavours independently. There was a blue era in early nineteenth-century fashion and attire for the European war, and thus, due to the high demand at home, massive European companies heavily dominated the indigo industry. However, the economic depression of the late 1820s expanded to India, and as a result, all the main agency firms failed between 1830 and 1833.[22] Between 1830 and 1860, peasant indigo production became entirely unproductive, necessitating the state's support through various coercive means. Apart from the potential use of direct force, the main incentive for small peasants to engage in indigo production before 1830 was the cash advance they received as part of the arrangement. During this period, the demand for indigo became increasingly unpopular among peasants, especially in comparison to other industries like jute and rice, which were in higher demand and more profitable by the mid-1850s.[23] Financing for indigo production and trade became available once more between 1835 and 1840, but it was adversely affected by the downturn of London's stock market in the 1840s and its subsequent collapse during the depression of 1847–8.[24]

Large-Scale Knowledge Projects

To gain a better understanding of Bengal and the surrounding areas, in order to devise a suitable control strategy, the British undertook extensive knowledge projects such as the Asiatic Society of Bengal (established in 1784) to encourage 'oriental' studies. Warren Hastings, supervised by Muiz ud Din, allowed the opening of the Calcutta Madrasa in 1780, making it the earliest state-managed educational institution under British rule in India. The Madrasa trained individuals in Persian, Arabic and Muslim law (*fiqh*) for appointment to lower positions in government offices and courts of justice, primarily as interpreters of Muslim law. Additionally, it provided employment opportunities for the discontented Muslim aristocracy of Bengal, serving as a gesture of conciliation. However, Ainuddin Shiqdar, the collector for 24-Parganas (a district in West Bengal – the name is derived from the number of parganas or divisions contained in the zamindari of Calcutta, which was ceded to the East India Company by Mir Jafar in 1757), assumed control of the Madrasa in 1790 amid widespread allegations of fund misappropriation and student indiscipline. After an investigation, the headteacher, Muiz ud Din, was removed in 1791, and management was handed over to a three-member committee, with the chairman of the board of revenue serving as the convenor. Captain Ayron, a retired British army officer, was appointed as the first secretary of the Madrasa Management Committee in 1819 to improve its administration; the committee became defunct in 1842. Aloys Sprenger (1813–1893) was appointed principal in 1850 to rescue the Madrasa from ongoing deterioration.[25] Several other European principals followed him, with the last in the series being A. H. Harley, who held office during 1910–11. However, what concerns us here is Fort William College, which had far-reaching influence on Muslim literati of the nineteenth century and beyond.

In 1798, Lord Wellesley arrived in India as governor general with a vision for the Company's rule in India that was magisterial and imperial. He believed that the young men appointed to the Company's Civil Service should be trained not just as agents of a commercial concern but as 'ministers and officers of a powerful sovereign'.[26] To achieve this, he established Fort William College on 10 July 1800 without seeking permission from the Court of Directors.[27] Wellesley believed that the college should impart a broad knowledge of 'those branches of literature and science' that were included in the education of persons 'destined for high office in Europe'.[28] As rulers of an alien race, young officers needed 'an intimate acquaintance with the history, languages, customs, laws and religions of India'.[29] The spectrum of Fort William College was far wider than that of the Calcutta Madrasa, which later catered only to those seeking religious instruction.

Wellesley saw the college as a necessary tool to shape the moral character of the young officers, providing them with the virtues of 'industry, prudence, integrity and religious sensibility' to help them steer clear of the 'temptations and corruption' they would face in India due to the climate and the 'peculiar depravity' of the Indian people.[30] To make his vision a reality, he built a residential college where the young men's lives could be closely monitored and properly nurtured. He recruited a staff of eight to ten European faculty who could teach Indian languages as well as the European curriculum. A clergyman of the Anglican faith was appointed as vice-provost, and fifty *munshis* were employed to teach Indian subjects.

The term *munshi* originally referred to individuals who worked as contractors, writers or secretaries and evolved to include native language instructors in the Mughal Empire of India. Four departments were established at Fort William College: Sanskrit–Bengali, Arabic, Persian and Hindustani (Urdu). Each department had a European professor, a chief *munshi*, a second *munshi* and a subordinate *munshi*.[31] One of the subordinate *munshis* was Mir Aman, the writer of *Bagh o Bahar* (The Garden and the Spring), which the Indian linguist Sisir Kumar Das calls 'the rising star of Urdu prose'.[32] Although *Bagh o Bahar* is a translation of Meer Ata Hussain Tehseen's *Nau Tarz-e-Murassa*, it's a fascinating narrative and stands entirely on its own. Its significance may be appreciated with reference to the fact that it has immensely influenced Urdu writers in succeeding generations and has directed later Urdu prose.[33]

Under John Hay Gilchrist's leadership, Fort William College became a centre for Urdu prose, with writers from Delhi and Lucknow crafting a simple style that British officers and merchants could understand.[34] One of Gilchrist's pupils was the missionary Henry Martyn, who translated the New Testament, Psalms and Book of Common Prayer into Urdu and Persian. By the early nineteenth century, Urdu replaced Persian as the administrative language of the growing colonial bureaucracy, thanks in part to the efforts of Gilchrist and Fort William College. Urdu became a cultural expression of Muslim nationalism and a principal cause leading to the establishment of Pakistan. Fort William College was not only a centre of research but a publication unit, producing works in diverse indigenous languages. The college compiled and printed dictionaries, and its policy of publishing extensively in the living languages of India led to the realization of the lack of quality textbooks, which resulted in the establishment of the School Book Society in 1810.[35] Fort William College introduced the Western system of punctuation to the Indian writing style and played a significant role in the development of printing in Indian languages. However, financial difficulties led to cuts in faculty size and salaries, and the college's academic life deteriorated. In 1830, on the day of its thirtieth anniversary, the college's professorships were abolished, and lectures were discontinued. Despite its decline, Fort William College's impact on Urdu and the promotion of indigenous languages in India cannot be underestimated.[36]

The Clapham Sect, or 'The Saints', a group of wealthy and philanthropic Evangelical Christians, was brought together by John Venn, the rector of Holy Trinity Church in Clapham, London, between 1790 and 1830.[37] Notable members included William Wilberforce, Henry Thornton, James Stephen and Zachary Macaulay. They were strong advocates for the abolition of slavery and also worked towards prison reform, the prevention of cruel sports and the suspension of game laws and the lottery.[38] Despite being politically conservative and appealing to the rich, the Claphamites believed in philanthropic benevolence from above and the preservation of the ranks and orders within society. The Macaulays, following in the footsteps of Edmund Burke, were devoutly carrying on the traditions of their predecessors, with a driving moral force that defined and set the stage for the staunchly conservative and stultifying Victorian period that followed.[39]

However, this period was also marked by the rise of Christian evangelical fundamentalism, with missionaries seeing it as their divine duty to bring enlightenment to the benighted 'heathens' of the realm, and to Christianize British colonies. This approach was ethnocentric and ruthless, and followed a 'might makes right' mentality. Charles Grant, a former Company director and recent convert, joined the group and recommended the introduction of English education in India as well as making English the official language of the Company for local affairs. However, his recommendations and methods were not accepted by the British parliament, and the offer of spiritual illumination was neither desired nor accepted by the native population of India.[40] The fervent proselytizing by Christian missionaries served as one of the sparks for the Indian Uprising in 1857, catalysing many Indians to fight back against impositions by the British.[41]

Lord William Bentinck's tenure as governor general in India from 1829 to 1836 is often remembered for social reforms such as the abolition of Sati in 1829, the suppression of Thugi and the suppression of infanticide. He managed to do this by crafting laws and organizing their proper enforcement. However, the decision to introduce English as a medium of higher education instead of Persian, based on the advice of his council member Thomas Babington Macaulay, had a lasting cultural impact on the Muslim community. The Muslim literati, whose cultural capital was tied to classical Persian knowledge, felt devalued. Nevertheless, the relegation of Persian led to the flourishing of Urdu as a court language and medium of instruction in northern India and, from 1854 onwards, in the Punjab. As will be discussed later, Urdu became the cultural insignia for the Muslims, serving as a marker of their identity as a nation.[42]

Despite these shortcomings, some social and religious changes introduced during Bentinck's tenure had a positive impact, such as improved education and aid to lepers and the poor. Social legislation rooting out the practices of Thugi, infanticide and Sati were also widely welcomed. British colonial settlements gradually expanded from the subcontinent's coastal fringes to inland areas, marking the transition from mercantile to political/industrial colonization.[43] Throughout India, cash-cropping centres, industrial factories and military cantonments were established along the fertile River Ganges plains. Bengal's alluvial soil meant high yields and revenues, while the black cotton soil in Bombay, along with the new Suez Canal constructed in the 1860s, contributed to its emergence as a major industrial and commercial centre in the late nineteenth century.[44]

The 1857 War of Independence and the Muslim Response

The 1857 War of Independence, often referred to as a spontaneous revolt of the sepoys triggered by the incident of the greased Enfield cartridge, was in fact a complex interplay of various conflicting circumstances. The uprising was influenced by the zealous efforts of Christian missionaries to convert locals; the land-tax reform scheme, which caused impoverishment among Indian farmers; and unregulated moneylenders. Additionally, policy decisions such as Lord Dalhousie's 'Doctrine of Lapse' and the Widow Remarriage Act added to the already volatile situation.[45] This episode marked a significant event in Anglo-Indian relations, with severe repercussions for both parties. The uprising, which lasted about eighteen months, was characterized by fierce fighting on both sides that raged along the Ganges, beginning in Meerut and culminating in Delhi. Despite being able to overcome the rebels through strategic alliances with various princely states, the British were shaken to their core by the uprising.

As noted by the British historian Percival Spear, the uprising was a shock to British complacency and a blow to its self-confidence.[46] The British Army underwent a complete restructuring, with a large increase in non-native troops. The Army also shifted its reliance from troops of different regions, castes and language groups to those who had never wavered in their loyalty, such as the Sikhs and Ghurkhas. Although the British referred to the uprising as a 'mutiny', attempting to downplay the significance and number of people involved, the truth is that many individuals held grievances and participated in the rebellion. The peasants tried to remain neutral, but the princes, who rose in revolt against the Widow Remarriage laws, joined out of fear of suffering the same fate. During the revolt, both the *talukdars*, who were local landlords of Awadh, and some of the most prominent leaders took part. Additionally, dispossessed tax collectors from the region were also involved. The 1857 war was not a spontaneous revolt but a complex interplay of various factors that led to one of the most significant episodes in Anglo-Indian relations.

The catastrophic conclusion of the 1857 mutiny forced the Muslim intelligentsia to confront a pressing question: how to steer their co-religionists away from the 'fatal shroud of complacent self-esteem' that threatened to engulf them in a new political era.[47] Two contrasting responses emerged: the 'traditionalist'/literalist and 'modernist' approaches.[48] Both aimed for 'ameliorative change' among the Muslims, albeit in different ways.[49] Syed Ahmed Khan was a key figure among the modernists who worked tirelessly to convince his fellow Muslims to abandon the oppressive edifice of centuries of 'sterile' scholasticism, blind imitation and the intransigence of the religious specialists.[50] He sought to reinterpret the foundational texts of Islam in the light of liberal rationality, as seen in his exegesis of the Quran, known as 'Tafsir ul Quran'.[51] Other Muslim bridge-builders included Abd al-Latif, Syed Amir Ali and Maulvi Chiragh Ali, who worked towards a rapprochement between Islam and the nineteenth-century Western-dominated world.[52] The first of the two Muslim movements, the traditionalists, who trained at the Dar ul Ulum Deoband, established in 1867, adopted a more literal exegesis of the religious text, thereby prioritizing religious tradition.[53] They aimed to revive Islam in its original form by emphasizing renewal and a steadfast commitment to the teachings of the Prophet. This endeavour was influenced by the ideologies of the theologian Shah Walliullah (1703–1762) and scholar Shah Abdul Aziz (1746–1824). The literalists – Deobandis and Ahl-i-Hadith – professed the revival of Islam in its pristine form through what Barbara Metcalf terms 'tajdid': 'the process of renewal and specifically commitment to the ways of the Prophet'.[54] They sought to eliminate deviationist accretions in their belief system, as they believed that only then could the past glory of the Muslims be restored.

The dissolution of the Mughal Empire led to a period of contemplation for Muslim India, where distinct historical currents – indigenous

Indian Muslim, Mughal and British – initially appeared to be in conflict. However, the dynamic forces of history ultimately compelled them to intersect and forge symbols of hope for Indian Muslims in the nineteenth century. Key figures in this convergence included Sir Syed Ahmed Khan, Mirza Asadullah Khan Ghalib and Maulana Shibli Naumani.[55] Sir Syed Ahmed Khan was a modernist, while Shibli leaned towards Muslim tradition. Despite their differing opinions, both offered hope to Muslim South Asia and created institutions that had an impact on Muslim society.

Ghalib (1797–1869), a man of profound complexity, grappled with the contradictions inherent in his upbringing as a traditional Muslim within the diverse tapestry of Mughal India. Despite these conflicting forces, he eventually accepted the dominance of British rule. Through his personal experiences, he managed to harmonize these historical currents within himself, emerging as the preeminent symbol of Muslim culture in nineteenth-century India. His poetry and correspondence offer a glimpse into the intricate and multifaceted nature of Indian, Turkish, Persian and modernist cultural influences that shaped his world view. Particularly noteworthy are his letters, known as *Khatoot-i-Ghalib*. Crafted in a modern prose style, they stand as paragons of Urdu prose, not only revealing the literary prowess of the man but shedding light on the dark realities of 1857. Ghalib, an eyewitness to the mistreatment inflicted by both colonial powers and local rulers, unflinchingly documented the tumultuous events of that era: 'Just as it is very difficult to resist a torrential flood with mere sticks, so each of the allies of the British was rendered helpless. These allies decided to sit in mourning inside the comfort of their homes. You may count me among these mourners as well.'[56] 'They ransacked the [Haveli] of Hakeem Ahsan Ullah Khan, an advocate of the British. The Haveli was as adorned as the palace of mirrors in China. They set the room adjacent to the reception hall on fire.'[57] After defeating these Marathas, colonials treated them very badly and inflicted all types of atrocities on the people. They compelled people to leave the city. The cultural life of Delhi became decadent. About this decay, Ghalib says: 'Think about my tattered condition. I want to pen down a lot but what should I write? Can I actually write something, and would it even be enough? It is true that you and I are alive. None of us should say anything more about this situation.'[58]

The Victorian Period: The High Noon of Imperialism

The cataclysmic events of 1857 marked the beginning of the end for the British East India Company and the start of British rule in India, with the country becoming a direct possession of the Crown. The Industrial Revolution was in full swing during Queen Victoria's reign, which began in 1837, and had a significant impact on India, particularly in the areas of steamship, railway and telegraph development.

The British East India Company no longer held control over India's vested interests; a designated viceroy was now responsible for governing the country. Lord Canning was the first to hold this position. The Royal Title Act of 1876 led to the crowning of Victoria as empress of India, and the Delhi Durbar held under the direction of Lord Lytton sealed the fate of the empire.

Despite the infrastructural improvements brought about by the Industrial Revolution, life for the average Indian worsened due to two key factors. First, the railways subsidized by taxes on the natives allowed for cheaper and further travel, but profits from ticket prices were returned directly to government coffers, creating an inequitable trade. Industrial goods from London, Lancashire and Manchester were being carried across India, and Indian goods could not compete. Raw materials were drawn from India, processed in Britain and resold to the native population, which led to a vicious circle of economic impoverishment.

Second, greed and poor government policy during times of deadly famine led to a series of outbreaks of cholera, bubonic plague, typhoid fever, malaria, leprosy and dysentery.[59] The Great Indian Famine of 1876-8 was the worst instance, with an estimated death toll of more than 10 million people. Two years prior, Lord Northbrook's enlightened leadership during the Bihar famine of 1873-4 had prevented many deaths. These famines and plagues disproportionately affected India's native population, with little regard for nationality, religion or caste. One may wonder if this horror was allowed to take place as a reprisal for the recent Indian Uprising of 1857.[60] There were so many dead that they could not be buried or cremated.[61]

The rapid urbanization and commercialization of agriculture in the context of mass poverty caused these calamities, and similar occurrences happened in European countries undergoing sudden industrialization. Bombay witnessed an outbreak of bubonic plague in 1898, and Calcutta riots were caused by the typical poor government response to the crisis. More than 1 million people lost their lives in the subsequent plague epidemic of 1899-1900, and Benjamin Disraeli's ignominious policies and Lord Lytton's questionable ones were directly responsible for the catastrophe.

The Imperial Splendour of the Victorian Era

The British Raj, born from imperial aspirations and post-mutiny pacification, was a complex entity consisting of British India and Princely India. Some argue that the British Empire simply plundered India, while others, like Lord Curzon, believed it was a necessary exercise of power during the 'Great Game' to counter powers such as Russia, Germany, Italy, France and the Ottoman Empire.[62] Queen Victoria's 1858 proclamation addressed Indian concerns and promised change, but many promises were not kept, such as the new land settlement scheme. Britain's power depended on

India, with a large standing army consisting of native Indian troops, as well as the highly influential and elitist Indian Civil Service (ICS), a handful of 'heaven-born' souls in a land of millions. The Delhi Durbar in 1877 was a display of imperial power and a political statement of loyalty to the Crown. The Durbar was not only a display of imperial splendour and power but a political statement guaranteeing the princes their right to existence and protection in exchange for their loyalty to the Crown. While the British previously viewed Indians with contempt, events of 1857 tempered this feeling with suspicion, fear and hatred. As Swapna Banerjee so astutely points out: 'The relationship between British officials and native Indians was hierarchical and charged with racial arrogance.'[63] 'Recorded evidence of the kind of behaviour meted out to the Indian servants and the "negative" qualities attributed to them indiscriminately point to the unequal and racialized character of the relationship.'[64] No longer would the local wet nurses be employed to breastfeed future generations of the colonial masters. Social norms were defined afresh. Maintaining a certain degree of separation between those in authority and the general population was deemed essential during British colonial rule in India. The British administration was resolute in retaining the subcontinent as the linchpin of their empire, a sentiment vividly articulated by Lord Curzon in 1901, who prophetically recognized that the loss of India would equate to the unravelling of the British Empire. The resulting dynamic between British officials and the local Indian populace was often marked by a defined social stratum imbued with racial hubris.

Officially, the governance of India was overseen by the Secretary of State for India, based in London. Nevertheless, it was widely understood that the practical aspects of governing India were conducted on Indian soil, with the Civil Service serving as the principal instrument of the administrative machinery. This approach underscored the pivotal role played by the ICS in the day-to-day governance of the subcontinent, even as ultimate authority rested with the secretary of state across the seas in Britain.

The bureaucratic control established by the British colonial administration in India, often referred to as the 'steel frame' of administration, was a meticulously structured and highly efficient system that wielded immense influence over the subcontinent. This administrative framework, characterized by its hierarchical structure and stringent regulations, played a pivotal role in consolidating British rule and exerting control over India's vast and diverse landscape. Comprising primarily British officers, the ICS was at the core of this system, and its members were meticulously trained to uphold and perpetuate British interests. The 'steel frame' was instrumental not only in maintaining law and order but in executing policies, collecting revenue and overseeing a wide array of government functions. While it facilitated effective governance from the British perspective, this system also faced criticism for being distant and insensitive to the needs and aspirations of the Indian population. Nevertheless, there is no denying its impact in shaping the course of India's history during the colonial era.

The British colonial administration's firm and often oppressive control over India provoked a significant reaction from the Indian populace. While early indications of this response began to emerge as early as the 1820s, it was not until the latter part of the nineteenth century that it coalesced into a more organized and visible form. At the forefront of this organized response was the Hindu middle class, often referred to as the *bhadralok*, which played a pivotal role in driving a reform movement that catalysed what became known as the Bengal Renaissance. A key figurehead and champion of this reformist wave hailed from Bengal, Raja Ram Mohan Roy.[65]

These developments sparked deep concerns within the Muslim Ashraf, the elite and genteel class of Muslims. Their primary apprehension stemmed from the tendency of certain influential figures, such as Aurobindo Ghose, Bankim Chandra Chatterjee and Vivekananda, to equate India exclusively with Hinduism in its most puritanical form. According to these thinkers, the pre-Muslim Indian history represented a pure and unadulterated expression of Hinduism, often referred to as 'Sanatam Dharam'.[66] In essence, these intellectuals believed that a revival of Hinduism was taking place, driven by the Bengal Renaissance. However, this resurgence was not mirrored within the Muslim Ashraf, the members of which chose to maintain a distinct separation from the increasing politicization of the Hindu community, which eventually led to the formation of the INC in 1885.

The Articulation of the Nationalistic Impulse

The India Office was a pivotal institution within the framework of British colonial administration in India, and its actions led to the emergence of a massive bureaucratic state in the country. Established as part of the comprehensive administrative reforms introduced in the aftermath of the 1857 uprising, the Office played a central role in the governance of British India and served multiple functions of paramount importance. First, it acted as the administrative nerve centre that facilitated communication and coordination between the British government in London and the viceroyalty in India. This was crucial for ensuring that the policies and directives from London were effectively implemented on the Indian subcontinent.

Second, the India Office played a critical role in managing India's financial affairs. It oversaw the allocation and distribution of funds for various departments and projects, including sanitation, health, education, forestry, the military, policing and finance. This financial oversight was vital in sustaining the colonial machinery and supporting the development and maintenance of infrastructure and services in India.

Third, the India Office contributed to the creation and implementation of key administrative structures and policies in India. It played a significant part in the establishment of the ICS, which provided a cadre of British officers who administered and governed different regions of India. Moreover, it helped in transforming the designation of the colonial head from 'governor general' to 'viceroy', reflecting the expanded authority and symbolic significance of the position.

Overall, the India Office was the linchpin that connected the British colonial apparatus in India to the decision-makers and resources in London. Its functions encompassed financial management, policy formulation and administrative coordination, making it a vital institution in the complex machinery of British rule in India. Additionally, large-scale investments were made by the Office in national projects, such as a railway system that facilitated imperial trade and resource extraction.

To support governance, the British government also undertook state-sponsored knowledge projects, including a statistical survey of India by W. W. Hunter in 1869, the Census of India in 1871, the Survey of India in 1878 and the Linguistic Survey of India in 1898. Alongside this, Indian society was officially 'ordered' into immutable religious (such as Hindu and Muslim) categories, caste and tribal groups.

From the 1880s, organized but varied forms of nationalist resistance to colonial rule emerged, aimed at gaining greater Indian representation in government. The INC (founded in 1885 by Octavian Hume, a British citizen) led the way, with the Muslim Ashraf opting to stay away from becoming part of the Congress at the behest of reformer Sir Syed Ahmed Khan.[67] Khan encouraged Muslims to invest in modern education and set up the Muhammadan Anglo-Oriental College in Aligarh in 1867.

Simultaneously, in 1867, the Hindi–Urdu controversy erupted as the British government contemplated acquiescing to the Hindu communities of the United Provinces and Bihar. Their demand was to transition the official language from the Perso-Arabic script to Devanagari and embrace Hindi as the secondary official language, a request firmly asserted by the Hindu populace. This controversy galvanized the Muslim opinion on the path to nationhood.[68] An account of Syed Ahmed Khan's conversations with the commissioner of Benares in 1867 along with a translation of his letter dated 29 April 1870 foretell that the Hindu attempt to replace Urdu with Hindi would strike at the root of Hindu–Muslim unity.[69]

Following an examination of the inception of the nationalist movement, which was predominantly characterized by its Hindu and Bengali roots, it becomes evident that the successors of Ram Mohan Roy were primarily figures associated with Hindu social and religious reform movements.[70] In 1867 Hindu nationalism began to garner significant support among influential circles. During this year, Raj Narain Bose, who happened to be Sri Aurobindo's maternal grandfather, inaugurated the Hindu Mela, an annual gathering that continued from 1867 to 1880. It is worth noting that during these gatherings Rabindranath Tagore composed two delightful songs. Furthermore, the National Society was established in 1870 with the aim of fostering unity and nurturing a sense of national identity among Hindus.[71] When objections were raised over the use of the word 'national' for a Hindu organization, the *National Paper*, an organ of the Hindu Mela,[72] responded, 'We do not understand why our correspondent takes exception to the Hindus [sic] who certainly form a nation by themselves, and as such a society established by them can very properly be called a national society.'[73]

In those times, and even into subsequent periods, the term 'Bengali' distinctly denoted the Hindu populace of Bengal, while the Muslim community of Bengal was consistently identified as 'Muslims'. The only other substantial Muslim population was found in the Punjab, yet when Bengalis mentioned the 'Punjabis', they invariably alluded to the Sikhs, whose martial exploits resonated deeply within the hearts of Bengali nationalists. They also drew inspiration from the struggles of the Marathas and Rajputs against the Muslim rulers. Notably, Bankim Chandra Chatterjee, renowned as the author of *Ananda Math*, crafted numerous historical novels that portrayed Rajput princes as paragons of chivalry, but, with a sole exception, depicted Muslims as vanquished antagonists.[74] These novels were translated into all Indian languages, and their effects on readers are not hard to imagine as communal antagonism grew. Bankim's novels were based on military officer and writer James Tod's (1782–1835) book *Annals and Antiquities of Rajasthan*, which sustained the Hindu revivalist movement to a degree not typically appreciated.[75]

Tagore wrote poems on Rajput, Sikh and Maratha heroes, but apart from the single poem on the Taj Mahal, where he had to mention Shah Jahan, no figure of Muslim India stirred his imagination enough to inspire a verse. As a result, the Bengali language that developed during the nineteenth century produced a predominantly 'Hindu' literature. This separatist trend was also evident with respect to Persian, which had been extensively cultivated by Hindus in Bengal until the early nineteenth century.[76]

Ramesh Chandra Majumdar, a prominent Indian nationalist historian, offers an insightful perspective, elucidating that such a situation prevailed due to the fact that Muslims constituted a minority in these regions, and, in Bengal specifically, they lagged significantly behind Hindus in intellectual pursuits. Nonetheless, challenges surfaced in the Hindi-speaking regions, where Urdu had historically held sway as the dominant language:

> In the early nineteenth century, Hindustani, or the language of Upper India, essentially signified Urdu. It is difficult to determine when Hindus began to protest against Urdu, but beginning in 1869, Hindus began organizing meetings to mobilize public opinion and appeal to the government to replace Urdu, a Muslim language, with Hindi. In Bihar, then a part of Bengal, orders were issued to replace Urdu with Hindi written in Nagri characters, but persistent

attempts were made to ignore the order, which was only enforced in 1881 after peremptory orders were issued by Sir Ashley Eden, the Lt.-Governor (1831–1887).[77]

Rise of Muslim Nationalism

The origins of Muslim nationalism in northern India, where Muslims were a minority, can be traced back to the post-1857 reform period. Initially, this nationalist sentiment was manifested through reforms, but it eventually gave rise to exclusionary attitudes in the late nineteenth century. This exclusionism developed alongside the growth of nationalism, resulting in communal animosity and sectarian tensions within communities, leading to the fragmentation of what was once a pluralistic society. Specific social identities, such as caste, kinship and tribal affiliations, solidified, hindering social mobility across groups. The British exacerbated these social divisions through various methods, including conducting a census in 1872, producing settlement reports and writing Indian history in a way that intensified religious and communal hostilities. Consequently, South Asian society became divided into distinct socio-religious categories that continue to persist in urban areas today.

In British India, the middle class was divided along communal lines, challenging the commonly held belief that the middle class is primarily driven by material interests. Religion became the focal point of political action in the late nineteenth century, leading to social reform approaches centred around religious ideology and ethos. For the middle classes of various religious communities in north India, religious ideology served as their primary identity marker. As a result, the middle classes in South Asia were unable to transcend religious or communal differences, as religious adherence became even more deeply rooted among them.

The social regimentation imposed by the colonial regime resulted in the development of a class hierarchy following modernist lines evident across urban areas. Regarding the reform process among the Muslims of northern India, it is worth noting that the reformers who emerged at the turn of the nineteenth and twentieth centuries were influenced by three factors: socio-cultural traditions embedded in history; religion, and its reinterpretation within a theological framework; and modernity, drawing on the principles of the Enlightenment. Most of these reformers positioned themselves within the Muslim tradition and sought to initiate change from within that socio-epistemic framework. Allama Muhammad Iqbal (1877–1938), an eminent Muslim scholar and poet, was a significant synthesizer of these three strands of thought. However, his engagement with pan-Islamism makes it difficult to fit him into the framework of Muslim nationalism in South Asia. Nevertheless, Iqbal emphasized the importance of enlightenment, religious tradition and history as the principal components of his thought (*fikr*). This can also be said of the Islamic scholar Shibli Naumani and Syed Ameer Ali, a jurist and historian.

It's remarkable to discover that an Englishman, Octavian Hume, played a pivotal role in the genesis of the INC and the broader national movement in India. In an address delivered to the graduating class of Calcutta University, Hume made the momentous announcement of the INC's establishment. This assembly, consisting of lawyers and other luminaries, convened for the inaugural meeting on 28 December 1885. The paramount aim of the INC was to endow Indians with a greater sense of autonomy in shaping their own destiny.

While the Congress had secular foundations, younger members increasingly drew on a glorious pre-Islamic Hindu past and demanded self-rule (*swaraj*), which led to the Swadeshi movement following Bengal's partition in 1905 under the viceroyalty of Lord Curzon.[78] This partition was seen as a device to quell the spread of Indian nationalism, and it sparked widespread protests and boycotts and the burning of British products, as well as the promotion of indigenous goods. Unfortunately, these boycotts led to significant suffering for poorer Muslim communities, and the use of Hindu imagery by protesters alienated Muslims on the whole.[79]

Muslim leaders founded the Muslim League in 1906 in response to the exclusion of Muslims from Congress's nationalist vision. Historians such as Syed Razi Wasti suggest that the British may have played a role in the formation of the Muslim League to offset Congress's political standing. In 1905, 35 Muslim notables, led by Sir Agha Khan, met with Viceroy Lord Minto and demanded a separate electorate to ensure Muslim representation. This demand was granted in 1909 under the Minto–Morley reforms.[80]

Following the Muslim League's formation in Dhaka, the evolution of Muslim nationalism in India underwent four distinct phases before culminating in the establishment of Pakistan. The first phase began with the Muslim League's pledge to ensure Muslim loyalty to the British, which was rewarded with a separate electorate under the Minto–Morley reform of 1909. However, this phase ended in 1911 when the Muslim League leadership felt betrayed by the British unilateral annulment of the Partition of Bengal, which put Muslim interests in jeopardy. Additionally, British actions that violated Muslim sensibilities, such as demolishing part of a mosque in Cawnpore and supporting Italy in its campaign in Tripoli, further alienated Muslims.

It is important to note that Muslim nationalism in India drew inspiration from pan-Islamism, which made it inherently different from nationalism in the West. The first phase of Indian Muslim nationalism ended in 1911–12, during which time Muhammad Ali Jinnah emerged as the representative of Indian Muslims. Jinnah, a staunch nationalist and protégé of a prominent Indian nationalist leader and the first Asian to be elected to the British parliament, Dadabhai Neroji (1825–1917), and Gopal

Muhammad Iqbal
(1877–1938).

Krishna Gokhale (1866–1915), a distinguished Indian freedom fighter and social reformer, drew intellectual influence from Edmund Burke and John Morley.[81]

Jinnah's Transformation: Nationalist to Separatist

In old Karachi lies the house where Muhammad Ali Jinnah, the founder of Pakistan, later to be referred to as Quaid-e-Azam ('the great leader'), was born. The exact date of his birth is uncertain: some sources record it as 20 October 1875, while Jinnah himself claimed to have been born on Christmas Day in 1876. If the latter is true, he would have been seven days old when Queen Victoria was proclaimed Kaisar-i-Hind (Empress of India) in 1876.[82]

Jinnah's ancestors were Muslims, but like many Muslim families in India, they descended from Hindu roots. They migrated to the Kathiawar Peninsula from the Multan area before eventually settling in Karachi. Jinnah attended several schools in Karachi and Bombay, including the Sindh Madrasah High School and the Christian Missionary Society High School.

In the year 1892, a significant event in Jinnah's life occurred: his departure for England. This journey was not driven by mere wanderlust; it was a pragmatic decision born out of the need to address the financial challenges his family faced. At that time, his father's business had encountered substantial losses, and the weight of familial responsibility fell upon Jinnah's shoulders. Initially, he took up a position as an employee within a firm, a role that was intended to support his father's ailing business. However, it quickly became apparent that this job was in discord with his inherent disposition and ambitions.

Recognizing that his true calling lay elsewhere, Jinnah made the momentous choice to pursue a legal education. He enrolled at Lincoln's Inn, where he embarked on a journey of legal scholarship and rigorous training. Eventually, his dedication and diligence led to his being called to the Bar.

But it was not merely the study of law that captivated Jinnah during his time in England. He found himself drawn to the world of politics, an arena where he could channel his passion for public service and advocacy. His interest in governance and the democratic process led him to frequent the House of Commons, where he would attentively listen to the debates taking place within the hallowed chambers of the British parliament. During his time in England, his young wife, whom his parents had arranged for him to marry, passed away.[83]

Quaid-e-Azam Muhammad Ali Jinnah, 1946.

In essence, Jinnah's sojourn in England not only saw him acquire legal expertise but was the germination of his political aspirations. This pivotal period of his life laid the foundation for his future endeavours, as he would later return to India and emerge as a towering figure in the struggle for independence, ultimately playing a central role in the creation of Pakistan.

The evolution of Quaid-e-Azam Muhammad Ali Jinnah's political views from being a vocal advocate of Hindu–Muslim unity to a firm proponent of the partition of India and the creation of Pakistan remains one of the most fascinating questions of the Muslim freedom movement in British India. In 1916, Jinnah played a crucial role in facilitating the signing of a comprehensive constitutional scheme between the All-India Muslim League, which he had joined in 1913, and the INC, which he had become a part of in 1906. This historical event marked a significant milestone in Jinnah's political career and served as a stepping stone towards his ultimate goal of achieving a separate homeland for Indian Muslims.[84] The Lucknow Pact was a historic agreement that sought to safeguard the interests of both Hindus and Muslims in British India. One of its most contentious issues was the demand for separate electorates for Muslims in legislative bodies. However, despite the complexity of the negotiations, the pact served as a testament to the possibility of resolving constitutional and political differences between the two communities. It demonstrated that Muslim and Hindu leaders, represented by the Muslim League and the Congress, could come together and find a mutually agreeable solution to their long-standing disputes.[85]

Jinnah's contributions to this historic agreement were widely recognized, and he was hailed not only as an ambassador of Hindu–Muslim unity but as an embodied symbol of it. His contemporary Sarojini Naidu, a poet-politician, even published a collection of his speeches under the title *Mohomed Ali Jinnah: An Ambassador of Unity* in 1917.[86] Jinnah's shift towards advocating for a separate Muslim state in India is a topic of ongoing debate and analysis. However, his earlier efforts towards promoting Hindu–Muslim unity, such as his involvement in the Lucknow Pact, demonstrate his unwavering commitment to finding a peaceful and just solution to the constitutional and political challenges faced by India.[87]

At a session of the Muslim League in Lahore on 22 March 1940, Jinnah declared that the differences between Hindus and Muslims in India were too great to ignore. The next day, the League adopted a resolution calling for the creation of independent and sovereign states for Muslims in areas where they were the majority. This led to the eventual partition of India. During the 1945–6 elections, Jinnah reiterated that Pakistan was intended only for areas with a Muslim majority seeking independence.[88] At the Muslim League Legislator's Convention in April 1946, it was decided that a sovereign independent state should be created by constituting the zones comprising Bengal, Assam, the Punjab, the Northwest Frontier Province,

Sindh and Baluchistan. Jinnah's demand for Pakistan was not a bargaining chip in the constitutional struggle, as some British authorities and more recently Ayesha Jalal has claimed. Rather, he had firmly committed himself to Pakistan, as noted by Stanley Wolpert, and closed the door on any prospects of a united India. Jinnah had transformed himself into Pakistan's great leader, and there was no going back.[89]

The enigma of Jinnah's transformation from an advocate of Hindu–Muslim unity and an Indian nationalist to a proponent of Pakistan as a separate nation state raises questions. What led to this drastic shift in his thinking and approach to India's communal-constitutional problem? Multiple factors contributed to this transformation, and although they shall be discussed here separately, they often interconnect and overlap.[90]

Muslims and Hindus, although living in close proximity to each other in cities and villages, remained largely separate. The Hindu caste system discouraged natural ties of the neighbourhood or locality, and each community had its own culture, traditions and norms that were irreconcilable. Even past attempts by Muslim rulers, such as Emperor Akbar's 'synthesis', failed to bridge the gap. After the fall of the Mughal Empire and the arrival of the British, these sociocultural divisions became increasingly hostile, which led to significant conflict during British rule.[91]

Jinnah believed that the British introduction of representative government in India labelled the Muslims as a minority community and subordinated their communal interests to national interests. In a 1940 article for the magazine *Time and Tide*, he made it clear that the Muslim League was opposed to federal objectives that would lead to majority communal rule disguised as democracy. However, the system of representative

Muhammad Ali Jinnah and Mahatma Gandhi, 1944.

government made majority communal rule inevitable, which went against the Muslim League's objectives. Initially, the British were hesitant to introduce representative government, and Lord Curzon ruled out representative institutions in India during a debate on the Indian Councils Bill of 1892, claiming that it was 'alien to the Indian mind'.[92] The British rulers acknowledged the significant socio-religious differences between Muslims and Hindus, and recognized that at play was not merely a difference in faith but something that encompassed all aspects of social life, tradition and history, that is, communal tethers. This realization prompted the Act of 1909, which provided separate electorates for the Muslims.

Initially, Jinnah was against separate electorates, but he eventually realized that the Muslim community's interests needed protection in a system based on numbers, which would favour the Hindu majority. The Congress agreed to separate electorates in 1916, but they reneged when India received its first measure of transfer of power in 1919. The Nehru Report of 1928 rejected the principle of separate electorates and called for joint mixed electorates.[93] Despite Jinnah's efforts to persuade the Congress (and the Hindu Mahasabha) to help 'seven crores of Mussalmans to march along with us in the struggle for freedom', he was unsuccessful.

Jinnah's 'Fourteen Points' demanded separate electorates and a federal Constitution with residuary powers vested in the provinces to protect Muslim-majority provinces against Hindu domination. Despite Mohan Das Karamchand Gandhi's promise of representations for the rights of the minorities (specifically of the Muslims) at the Round Table Conference in 1931, Jinnah and the Muslims were not satisfied and felt compelled to demand a separate state, especially after the distressing Congress rule of the provinces from 1937 to 1939.[94]

Jinnah attempted to reconcile with the Congress in the 1936–7 elections, aiming to unite for India's freedom. However, Nehru, the newly elected INC president, rejected the idea and refused to acknowledge the Muslim League as a political party. Despite Jinnah's attempts to form a coalition government in the UP Assembly, Nehru's arrogance cost both parties and led to the League's resurgence. Congress rule, with policies such as the Wardha Scheme and Vande Mataram, confirmed to Muslims that a 'Hindu raj' had arrived before a British departure. The Wardha Scheme, also known as the Basic Education Scheme, was a proposal for educational reform in India put forward by Mahatma Gandhi in the 1930s. Its nature was rooted in the principles of basic education and self-reliance. The scheme aimed to provide education that was more practical, relevant to the needs of rural India, and focused on character-building and vocational skills. It advocated the use of indigenous languages and crafts in education, emphasizing the development of a strong moral and ethical foundation in students. The scheme was inspired by Gandhi's belief in the importance of integrating traditional Indian values and culture into education.[95]

'Vande Mataram' is a patriotic slogan and song that was popularized during the Indian freedom struggle. Its literal English translation is 'I praise thee, Mother.' The phrase has Hindu connotations because it is taken from Bankim Chandra Chatterjee's novel *Anandamath*, where it is used in the context of worshipping the Motherland as a deity. In this sense, it can be seen as an expression of reverence for the land of India, which has a spiritual and cultural significance in Hinduism. During the freedom movement, 'Vande Mataram' became a rallying cry for Indian nationalists, including those of Hindu background, who viewed India's struggle for independence as a sacred mission. That obviously made Muslims uncomfortable.

Jinnah sought Gandhi's involvement but was met with disdain; he had no choice but to break ties with Congress and Indian nationalism.[96] In 1916 Jinnah was a prominent leader among both Hindus and Muslims, but Gandhi's non-cooperation movement in 1920 weakened his position. The non-cooperation movement was a peaceful protest against British colonial rule in India. It involved Indians refusing to cooperate with British authorities, boycotting British goods and engaging in acts of civil disobedience to demand independence.[97] Jinnah, as a constitutionalist, opposed the movement and left the Congress to focus on the Muslim League. Despite attempts to find common ground, such as the Delhi Muslim Proposal and the Fourteen Points, he was unsuccessful in accommodating Muslim interests within the Congress.[98] The Round Table Conference in London failed to produce any meaningful results as Gandhi, the Congress's sole representative, refused to cooperate. Even during Jinnah's self-imposed exile in London from 1931 to 1935, he persisted in trying to resolve the Hindu–Muslim issue, but Nehru's indifference and hostility thwarted his efforts. According to the Indian scholar and lawyer A. G. Noorani, Nehru's treatment of Jinnah was unbecoming of a political leader and driven by a dislike that bordered on hate. Gandhi's condescending attitude towards Jinnah also contributed to the latter's eventual split with the Congress. These slights, neglect and perceived anti-Muslim sentiment all contributed to Jinnah's transformation and his eventual leadership of the Muslim separatist movement.[99] It is apt now to look at the Swadeshi movement and its peculiar trajectory, and the development of communal antagonism in Indian politics.

The Politics of Communalism

The Swadeshi movement of the early twentieth century in India was a key proponent of economic nationalism, Indian modernity and independence from British rule. Although it officially ended in 1908, its ideals and principles continued to gain traction among the Indian populace. One of its main objectives was to revive traditional arts and crafts, including hand-spun fabric, which Gandhi fervently promoted during his later political career.

Another important aspect was the revival of Indian spiritual traditions, which Rabindranath Tagore, the renowned Bengali laureate and cultural icon, exemplified through his teaching experiments from 1901 onwards. These efforts eventually led to protests and agitation against British colonial rule, which influenced the government to incorporate a small number of Indian voters in the Central and Provincial Legislative Councils through the Indian Councils Acts of 1892 and 1909. However, separate council electorates for Muslims were introduced in 1909 under pressure from the Muslim League, setting a precedent for separate representation. Despite these efforts, Indian demands for self-government remained unrecognized when the First World War broke out in 1914, which historians such as Ramachandra Guha see as the main factor behind the eventual end of British rule in India in 1947. However, it was Gandhi who became the decisive figure in India's anti-imperialist struggle after his return to India in 1914. Trained as a barrister in England, Gandhi mobilized civil resistance during his time in South Africa, leading a series of non-violent agrarian protests.[100]

The second phase of Muslim nationalism in India began with rapprochement between the Muslim League and Congress, and the relationship between the two largest communities started to mend. This rapprochement culminated in the Lucknow Pact of 1916, where Muhammad Ali Jinnah earned the title of an ambassador of Hindu–Muslim unity.[101] In the pact, Muslims generously conceded weightage to Congress in provinces where they constituted the majority, leading them to lose their majority in the Punjab. Similarly, Muslims were accorded the same weightage in minority provinces such as United Provinces/Uttar Pradesh, Madras and Bombay, but despite the weightage they remained a minority in those provinces. Holistically, both parties agreed on the principal clauses of the future Constitution, which they envisaged after the First World War.

During the war, all classes of Indians cooperated with the British, and even Gandhi participated in a recruitment drive urging Gujarati peasants to win independence by joining the army. However, after the war ended, the Indians felt that the Rowlatt Committee's report, published in the summer of 1918, was a poor reward for the sacrifices that Indians made in both men and money to support the British cause.[102] The committee recommended that in the event of the government being faced with anarchical and revolutionary movements, it could deprive a man of his liberty and intern him for a long period. The government argued that the Rowlatt Act was not as drastic as it was made out to be, since action could be taken against an individual only after receiving a report from a judicial officer. Even after action had been taken, the government had to submit the matter within a month to an investigating authority consisting of three officers. However, this explanation was deemed insufficient by the general populace, who read the Rowlatt Report alongside the Montagu–Chelmsford Report, which promised responsible government by measured stages. The two reports were seen as a betrayal by the British, and this sense of betrayal was compounded when the tragedy of Amritsar occurred on 13 April 1919.[103]

The disturbances in Amritsar began after the deportation of two prominent nationalist leaders. During the riots, some banks were attacked and a handful of Europeans lost their lives, but the severity of the situation escalated dramatically when General Dyer took drastic and horrifying action to stifle the anarchy.

In the infamous Jallianwala Bagh massacre, General Dyer ordered his troops to open fire on a densely packed crowd that had gathered in the Jallianwala Bagh public garden in Amritsar. The extent of this brutality was staggering. This tragic incident stands as a dark chapter in India's struggle for independence, underscoring the ruthless and excessive measures taken by the British colonial authorities to suppress dissent. According to official figures, 379 people were killed and at least 1,200 were wounded.[104] In the aftermath of the massacre, the response from the British colonial authorities was deeply troubling. The provincial government, shockingly, approved of General Dyer's actions. The severity of their stance became evident as they resorted to further measures to assert control.

On the day after the massacre, aerial bombings were carried out in Gujranwala, where riots had taken place in response to the violence in Jallianwala Bagh. Terror was instilled among the population. Subsequently, martial law was imposed and remained in effect until 9 June, during which time several orders were issued to humiliate and subjugate the Indian population.

The Hunter Committee, established by the British government to investigate the incident, and which published its report in 1920, uncovered disturbing details of the oppressive measures taken. Indians were subjected to degrading acts, such as being made to crawl when passing through streets where Europeans resided. For instance, at Gujranwala, they were even required to offer their salaams (greetings) to any commissioned officer they encountered.

Public flogging was employed as a punitive measure for relatively minor offences, including contravening the curfew order, failing to salaam a commissioned officer, showing disrespect to a European, taking a commandeered car without permission or refusing to sell milk, among other similar transgressions. These actions were indicative of the extreme measures taken by the colonial authorities to suppress and subdue the Indian population, adding to the enduring legacy of the Jallianwala Bagh massacre as a symbol of British colonial brutality during the period of the Indian independence struggle.[105] The period following the Jallianwala Bagh incident marked a profoundly significant phase in India's political history, characterized as it was by intensified dissent and oppressive rule imposed by the British colonial authorities. In the wake of the massacre, Indians experienced a harsh and authoritarian response from the colonial government, which escalated tensions and served as a catalyst for the burgeoning Indian nationalist movement, eventually inspiring the country on its quest for freedom from British colonial rule.

The Khilafat movement, coupled with the non-cooperation movement, marked the climax of communal bonhomie, with the extra geographical dimension of Muslim nationalism demonstrated through the movement's launch to show solidarity with Turks who had joined hands with Germany against the Allied Powers.[106] This development was significant, as it transformed the religious scholars' entry into politics, creating an agitational mode of voicing dissent. Ironically, when this movement was in full swing, Gandhi was given an elevated status as the unanimously acclaimed leader of both communities, with support from both the Indian National Congress and Indian Muslims.

Gandhi's movement was based on a spiritual, economic nationalism built around the idea of the self-sufficient village, rejecting foreign manufacturers and adopting homespun cloth (*khadi*). His Dandi march against the Salt Tax in 1930 and other civil disobedience strategies based on everyday life resonated strongly with ordinary Indians, and had a far wider base, including women, than the INC, which placed great pressure upon the colonial government.[107] However, on 4 February 1922, the Chauri Chaura incident occurred. This violent episode saw a large crowd of protesters participating in the non-cooperation/Khilafat movement led by Gandhi gather in the town of Chauri Chaura in Uttar Pradesh. Tensions escalated, leading to clashes between the police and the demonstrators. In a moment of extreme violence, the protesters set fire to a police station, resulting in the deaths of 22 police officers. This incident deeply troubled Gandhi, who was committed to non-violence as a means of achieving independence. In response to the violence at Chauri Chaura, he called off the non-cooperation/Khilafat movement as he believed that the movement had taken an undesirable turn. The incident drove a wedge of dissension into the unified movement, and the two communities embarked on their separate course to realize their destiny – that is, *swaraj* and *azadi*.[108] *Swaraj* is a Hindi term that means 'self-rule' or 'self-governance'. In the context of India's independence movement, it was a central concept advocated by Gandhi. *Swaraj* represented the idea of Indians governing themselves and achieving political and economic independence from British colonial rule. Gandhi's vision of *swaraj* emphasized not just political freedom but also self-reliance, community empowerment, and moral and ethical principles in governance.[109]

The third phase of India's political history, spanning from 1922 to 1940, was characterized by the Muslim struggle for constitutional guarantees in relation to Hindus. During this period, a multitude of proposals, commissions, reports, pacts, discussions and public demonstrations took place, each reflecting varying degrees of political intensity. Although caste dynamics held immense significance in Indian politics, Gandhi endeavoured to integrate the 'untouchables' into the political mainstream. To achieve this, he reached out to Bhimrao Ramji Ambedkar, a prominent leader of the Dalits (formerly known as untouchables) and the law minister of the government of India from 1947 to 1951. Ambedkar played a pivotal role in drafting the Indian Constitution and was widely recognized as the unchallenged leader and sole representative of the untouchable community.[110] Gandhi's outreach to Ambedkar aimed to unite caste Hindus and untouchables in their quest for freedom. Furthermore, Gandhi recognized that if the untouchables aligned themselves with the Muslim community, it would challenge the INC's claim to be the sole representative of all Indians. However, it is important to note that there was neither a clear and concrete policy nor a substantial part of the social reform process initiated by Gandhi specifically focused on improving the social conditions or addressing the grievances of the untouchables concerning discrimination. Gandhi's distinctive approach to politics revolved around the use of symbolism to convey powerful messages and principles. He often employed symbolic acts, gestures and practices to emphasize key ideas, such as non-violence, civil disobedience and self-reliance. For example, his use of the spinning wheel (*charkha*) symbolized self-sufficiency and the economic independence of India. Additionally, his choice of clothing, such as the simple dhoti and shawl, represented his commitment to simplicity and rejection of British colonial attire. These symbols became powerful tools for communication and mobilization, allowing Gandhi to connect with and inspire people on a deep and emotional level, transcending mere political rhetoric. He started to live with the untouchables, calling them Harijan, and published his own weekly magazine with the same title. *Harijan*, released from 1933 to 1948, advocated for the uplift of Dalits and marginalized communities, promoted non-violence and civil disobedience as tools for social and political change, offered political commentary on India and the world, emphasized spiritual and ethical principles like truth and simplicity, and encouraged community-building efforts, particularly at the grass-roots level. It played a crucial role in disseminating Gandhi's ideas for social justice and an independent, morally grounded India.

All these attempts were focused on ensuring internal cohesion within the communities, but cleavage between Hindus and Muslims widened. In 1930, Gandhi and Congress declared full independence (*purna swaraj*) as their goal, but the colonial administration refused all such demands, which were also unacceptable to the Muslim League leadership.

Muhammad Iqbal's Allahabad address in 1930 provided the context for the construction of Pakistan's national narrative and is considered the most decisive step towards its creation.[111] In his speech, Iqbal argued that India was not a social unity but rather a continent of human groups belonging to different races, speaking different languages and professing different religions.[112] He believed that the creation of a state based on the unity of language, race, history, religion and identity of economic interest was the only way to secure a constitutional structure in India, given the country's infinite variety in climates, races, languages and social systems.

Iqbal proposed the amalgamation of certain regions into a distinct, integrated state, and envisioned the consolidated northwest Indian Muslim states as the 'final destiny' of the Muslim nation in India. Iqbal stated: 'I would like to see the Punjab North West Frontier Province, Sindh and Baluchistan amalgamated into the single state.' He further declared that whether India had 'self-government within the British Empire [or] without the British Empire, the formation of the consolidated northwest Indian Moslem's states appears to me to be the final destiny of the Moslem, at least of northwest India.'[113] He emphasized the importance of centralizing Islam in a specified territory, as the life of Islam in the country depended on its cultural force. Iqbal firmly believed in the principle of one nation and one state and argued that the Muslims of India were the only Indian people who could accurately be described as a nation in the modern sense of the word.[114]

Generally, due to the Allahabad address, Iqbal is considered to be the architect of the state of Pakistan (in a conceptual sense), despite the fact that he did not mention the word 'Pakistan'. This assumption is at best partially correct. First of all, Iqbal is silent about the fate of the Moslems of East Bengal, who were more numerous than the northwestern Muslims. Whether this was an oversight or deliberate omission is not clear. Similarly, with regard to the defence of the subcontinent, Iqbal was ambiguous to say the least:

> I am sure that the scheme of a neutral Indian army based on a federated India will intensify Moslem patriotic feeling, and finally set at rest the suspicion, if any, of Indian Moslems joining Moslems from beyond the frontier in the event of an invasion ... thus processing full opportunity of development within the body politic of India, the north-western Moslems will prove the best defenders of India against foreign invasion, be that invasion one of ideas or one of bayonets.[115]

In Lahore, the issue over the sacred site Masjid Shahid Ganj, which had a disputed history, strained the relations between Sikhs and Muslims.[116] These political wranglings vitiated the situation and made inter-community settlement even more tenuous. In 1935 the Government of India Act, which fell short of nationalist aspirations for dominion status, granted greater autonomy with free provincial elections, laying the groundwork for India's future federalist Constitution. Congress, after winning elections in seven provinces between 1937 and 1939, adopted symbols from

Hindu mythology, causing resentment among Muslims, as evidenced by the findings of the Pirpur report (1938).[117] Living under Congress rule fostered inclusivity among politically active Muslims, setting the stage for the Lahore Resolution in March 1940, which articulated the distinct political aspirations and demands of the Muslim community within the broader struggle for independence. This Act also introduced separate electorates for Muslims led by the Muslim League and reserved seats for 'backward' and 'untouchable' castes under Ambedkar's leadership. In the 1937 elections held in eleven provinces, Congress secured significant victories, while the Muslim League faced marginalization within a majority-rule system.[118]

Hence, the evolutionary process in Muslim nationalism entered a phase that was defined by the demand of separatism. Options of a composite sense of belonging were exhausted. When Britain dragged India into the Second World War without consulting its recently elected governments, Congress members resigned in protest. Meanwhile, the Muslim League remained loyal to the colonial government for tactical reasons, and in 1940 declared its demand for a separate, independent state named Pakistan. As various events unfolded, the idea of a separate state that, according to Ayesha Jalal, was merely a bargaining chip steadily inched towards its practical realization. All political engagement between the triumvirate

'Dominion of India', front cover of *The Hindu*, 15 August 1947.

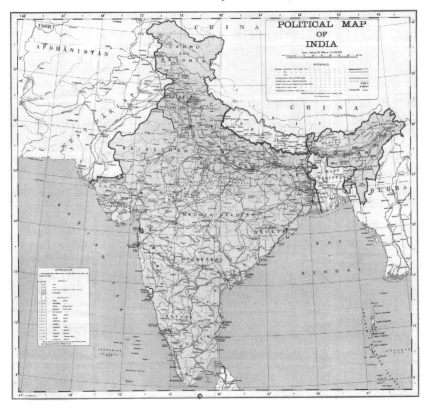

Political map of India, 1944, showing East and West Pakistan.

(the British, Congress and the Muslim League), from the Cripps Mission (1942) to Gandhi–Jinnah talks (1944), C. R. Formula (1944), the Wavell Plan (1945), the Simla Conference (1945) or finally the Cabinet Mission (1946), had a common objective: how to keep India together. The idea of separatism, by then, had sunk in with the Muslim masses. In only seven years, Jinnah became the most significant political figure in the entire subcontinent. Besides him, every stakeholder in Indian politics espoused a proposition to keep India united. Jinnah's political eminence was stamped in the elections of 1946, which endorses the veracity of Jalal's assertion that Jinnah was the sole spokesman of the Muslim community. Indian soldiers joined the war effort, but Gandhi and Congress leaders continued their civil disobedience and were jailed for lengthy periods. The 1940s were marked by industrial strikes, naval mutinies and riots in the face of a colonial state seemingly indifferent to Indian concerns. The 1943 Bengal famine saw 2 million people die of starvation and disease, in part due to an inadequate response from a colonial government preoccupied with the threat of Japanese forces invading India. After the war, Indian independence was announced in 1946. At midnight on 15 August 1947, the republics of Pakistan and India were born amid a bloodbath of sectarian violence and one of the largest displacements of population in history, as Muslims from India moved across the border to Pakistan, and Hindus and Sikhs there moved to India. In 1948, Ceylon and Burma were declared free nations.

THE INDIAN NATIONALIST struggle and the Pakistan movement differed in their methods and attitudes towards colonialism, with profound long-term effects that are often overlooked by scholars. These differences led to the two successor states of the British Raj following separate trajectories. India gained independence through sustained anti-colonial struggle, while Pakistan pursued a path of separatism, steeped in religious exclusion.

Both the Congress Party and the Muslim League were founded with the premise of cultivating cordiality between the natives and the British government. While Muslim stalwarts like Sir Syed Ahmed Khan were initially hesitant about Muslims joining the INC, Muslim gravitation towards the party remained a strong possibility. However, the influence of prominent Hindu writers and thinkers such as Bankim Chandra Chatterjee, Swami Vivekananda and Aurobindo Ghose soon began to permeate the inner sanctum of the party, leading to the exclusion of Muslims.

The partition of Bengal in 1905 radicalized both the INC leadership and its rank and file, marking a significant difference between the Muslims and the party. The Congress went all out against Lord Curzon's decision to divide Bengal, and the Swadeshi movement encouraged people to boycott foreign goods and use locally manufactured products. This laid the foundation on which Indian nationalism, championed by the Congress, evolved and culminated in the establishment of the postcolonial state of India.

However, the Congress's assertive political stance left Muslims feeling cornered and eroded the party's long-standing commitment to a liberal political ethos, especially following Gokhale's passing in 1915. The Muslim apprehension of Hindu dominance deepened over time, prompting their pursuit of concessions from the British government to curb unilateral Hindu actions.

While temporary reconciliations, such as the Lucknow Pact and the Khilafat movement, may have momentarily eased communal tensions, Muslim leaders consistently sought legal and constitutional safeguards against Hindu hegemony. Jinnah, in particular, advocated for these guarantees, especially if India was to adopt the Westminster model of democracy.

Thus, the two political communities had divergent sets of objectives and used starkly different methods to achieve their desired results. The Muslim League leadership went for a mediated settlement, engaging both the British and the Congress instead of alienating one for the other. However, the Congress, given its massive popular support, was not willing to strike any deal with either the British or the Muslim League. Pakistan's genesis diverged from the typical anti-colonial struggles that led to the formation of many postcolonial nations. Instead of primarily seeking liberation from colonial rule, Pakistan's birth was driven by a desire to evade Hindu majoritarianism. This unique origin story has posed challenges for academics attempting to articulate Pakistan's distinct postcolonial identity, contributing to its ongoing struggle in defining itself.

3

Bloodied Partition and the Punjab's Bifurcation, 1947

The creation of Pakistan in August 1947 also saw the Partition of Bengal and the Punjab. The division of these regions was marked by communal turbulence causing large-scale massacre and migration. The Colonial Punjab, given its geo-strategic importance and status as the 'granary of India', was at the epicentre of violence that occurred across northern India. The Partition of the Punjab, with all the tragedy it entailed, is riddled with complexity and conflicting interpretations. These persist even three-quarters of a century after its occurrence. This chapter looks afresh at the crucial period from March to August 1947, utilizing primary material drawn from the Mountbatten archives.[1] The objective is to comprehend the increasing prevalence of communalism in the province, the reactions of the British authorities to it and how much the actions of local political leaders were influenced by the All-India leadership's demands.

The traditional narratives connect communal divisions to the introduction of separate electorates in 1909, which holds true for a broader perspective of the whole of India. However, the Punjab had a distinct political path due to the British government's desire to promote unity among Hindus, Sikhs and Muslims in the rural regions of the province. Such social cohesion would secure the stability of the 'sword arm' and 'granary' of British India. From 1857 onwards the British sought to co-opt the rural power holders. That bond was cemented when the Punjab became the main recruitment area for the Indian Army from the 1880s onwards.[2] Thus, while in the urban setting of the Punjab there were similarities with developments in, for example, Uttar Pradesh, as a result of the impact of competitive religious revivalisms,[3] in the countryside the British engineered cross-community alliances through electoral division of the population along the lines of 'agriculturalist' and 'non-agriculturalist'. This terminology lies at the heart of the 1900 Punjab Alienation of Land Act, which served to ensure rural stability by preventing the expropriation of landowners by urban moneylenders.[4] The result was that two types of politics emerged in the colonial Punjab. In the towns there was emphasis on religious community, whereas in the countryside cross-allegiances irrespective of religion had been the mainstay of politics.[5]

The advent of the Unionist Party in 1923 provided the political articulation to the rural interest group with unequivocal support from the British. The Unionist Party remained at the helm in the Punjab for a quarter of a century until 2 March 1947. It drew support from the rural Punjab, cutting across religious and caste as well as kinship allegiances. The political elite of all three communities had conjoined under the banner of the Unionist Party. Here it is pertinent to mention its agenda as a party. The Unionist Party of the Punjab, also known as the Punjab Unionist Party (PUP), was formed as a coalition of influential landlords and aristocrats in the Punjab region. Its main agenda was to safeguard the interests of the landowning elite and promote unity among different religious and ethnic communities:

Protection of Landlords: The Unionist Party primarily represented the interests of large landowners, and their agenda focused on maintaining the privileges and rights of the landed gentry in the Punjab province.

Communal Harmony: The party aimed to foster communal harmony and promote cooperation among different religious and ethnic groups in the Punjab. It sought to create a united front against the growing influence of the Indian National Congress and the Muslim League.

Autonomy for Punjab: The Unionist Party advocated for a significant degree of provincial autonomy for the Punjab region within a federal framework. It aimed to protect and promote the cultural, economic and political interests of the province.[6]

Given the political arithmetic of the colonial Punjab, the Unionist Party was able to predominate up to the 1946 provincial elections. During that period the urban-based parties were marginalized. The territorial integrity of the Punjab remained the priority to such an extent that the only proposal for a possible redrawing of the Punjab boundaries was put forward in 1932 by Geoffrey Corbett, chief secretary of the Punjab. He suggested to the minority commission in the Second Round Table Conference (1931) that the Ambala Division excluding the Simla District be separated from the Punjab and attached to the United Provinces. By doing so, Muslims would have a decisive majority with 63 per cent of population, which Corbett thought would guarantee stability and peace in the Punjab.[7] That scheme did not find favour with the minority commission as it was considered detrimental to bring about such a change in the geography of the province given that it might have caused a communal imbalance. Sikh representatives at the round table conference such as Sampuran Singh and Ujjal Singh, in a bid to counteract Corbett's suggestion, proposed that Multan and Rawalpindi divisions be separated from the Punjab and attached to the NWFP.[8] Subsequently, however, both did not press the point and instead proposed 30 per cent representation for the Sikhs in the forthcoming Punjab Assembly.

Nonetheless, the Muslim League's demand for Pakistan starting from 1940 did prompt Sikhs to reassess their position, leading to deliberations about potential territorial restructuring that would result in the establishment of an entity referred to as 'Azad Punjab'. Master Tara Singh was its main protagonist.[9] The same demand was raised by the Sikh All Parties Committee in a Memorandum, handed over to Sir S. Cripps on 31 March 1942.[10] Like other proposals, that too fizzled out, as dividing the Punjab in accordance with the wishes of Sikhs involved practical hazards for the British. Suffice it to say, the voices raised for cutting the Punjab asunder remained peripheral until the fall of the Khizr Ministry on 2 March 1947.

The Unionist Party leader Khizr Hayat Khan Tiwana had been under mounting pressure from 1944 onwards.[11] He sought support from the British to offset the mounting Muslim League campaign. While British officials in the Punjab were personally favourable to the Unionist cause, the view from New Delhi was less favourable. This was because of the desire for an All-India settlement between the Muslim League and the Congress and the feeling that the Unionists could not be allowed to stand in its way. With the end of the war, the Unionist Party's usefulness to the British further diminished. Ian Talbot states that 'although Wavell and Mountbatten still found Khizr personally charming and certainly much better company than Jinnah, his views were dismissed as irrelevant and anachronistic.'[12] His call that the Punjab should remain undivided proved to be a cry in the wilderness. Unionist stalwarts such as Pirs and Sajjaada Nashins, with their sprawling *jagirs* (large landholdings) and the overriding influence they wielded over multitudes of their *murids* (disciples), were gradually switching sides and joining the Muslim League en masse.[13] A dynamic body like the Muslim Student Federation reached out to every nook and corner of the rural Punjab and disseminated the consciousness of religious differentiation among the villagers. Slogans like *Muslim hai to Muslim League mein Aa* (Join the Ranks of Muslim League if You Are a Muslim) and *Pakistan ka Matlab Kia La illah ha ill lallah* (The Meaning of Pakistan Is *La illah ha ill lallah*) aided the League in gaining mass appeal for the demand for a separate Muslim state. Thereby, the League moved from political insignificance in 1937 to a position of incredible strength in 1946. The party's phenomenal success, polling 75.26 per cent of the votes against the Unionists, who managed to obtain only 26.61 per cent of the votes in the 1946 elections, bore testimony to its soaring popularity among the Muslim community.[14]

By securing 75 out of 86 Muslim seats, the Muslim League emerged as the single largest party in the Punjab Legislative Assembly. Quite conversely, the Unionist Party, which had won 96 seats previously, now could bag no more than a paltry eighteen seats.[15] The rump Unionist Party nevertheless formed a coalition with Congress and the Akalis.[16]

Khizr found the premiership of the province no less than a bed of thorns. The Muslim League's call for a province-wide strike on the very day the ministry was sworn in did not augur well for the future of the new dispensation. Merely two days had elapsed when the traitor's day was observed, to the utter embarrassment of Khizr.[17] However, despite all the hazards he managed to ward off direct action of the Muslim League and successfully preserved peace in the Punjab. Khizr's political outlook, articulated in his 'instinctive and pragmatic consociationalism',[18] ran out of relevance for the British, particularly in the context of their political expediencies at the All-India level. Even at the Punjab level, the agreement between the League and the Panthic Party was considered more vital for the stability of the province.[19] As such possibility could not be realized, the Khizr ministry was the solitary option for the British, which they accepted with gritted teeth. Nevertheless, Khizr's loyalty towards the British did not falter. He even went to the extent of suggesting 'that in the last resort the Punjab should be declared a dominion and maintain direct relations with the crown after the British departure'.[20] He kept on disseminating that idea with unflinching doggedness. However, with bellicose organizations like the Rashtriya Swayam Sevak Sangh (RSS), the Muslim League National Guards and the Sikh Akali Fauj flouting the law recurrently, the situation in the province was precariously poised.

The fall of the Khizr ministry was hastened when on 24 January 1947 the ban was clamped on the Muslim League National Guards and the RSS. The Muslim League leadership, in retaliation, resorted to direct action in the Punjab. Processions were taken out in utter disregard of the prohibition by the government on such activity. Without demur Punjab Muslim League leaders Mian Iftikhar ud Din, Mumtaz Mohammad Khan Daultana and Sardar Shaukat Hayat Khan courted arrest, leading to strikes in Lahore and other major cities. The situation vitiated to such an extent that Khizr was unnerved and 'forced to come to terms with the League by lifting the ban on the processions and meetings'.[21] He finally resigned, bringing an era of Unionist rule to a close.

The end of the Khizr ministry marked a crucial turning point in Punjab politics. In this section we will both explain the reasons and assess their significance. Controversy surrounds the introduction of governor's rule, rather than the swearing in of a purely Muslim League ministry following Khizr's resignation. Can this be seen as a hindrance to cooperation between Punjabi politicians which might have prevented the bloodletting that accompanied the British departure? Or is it rather a question of their inability to agree because of local power rivalries, or having their hands tied by the All-India leaderships?

Khizr's resignation occurred against the backdrop of both the Muslim League's mounting Direct Action campaign against him and British prime minister Clement Attlee's announcement on 20 February 1947 stating the

British intention of transferring power in the Indian subcontinent by June 1948. Punjab governor Evan Jenkins reported to the viceroy Lord Wavell on 3 March.[22] Khizr's anxiety about his position was increased by the Muslim League agitation and rose still further by the UK government's announcement on 20 February. The announcement shook Khizr severely, and after an attempt to 'laugh it off' on 21 February he became increasingly gloomy.[23]

Khizr's exit raised the political stakes in the key province of the Punjab. It raised for the Sikhs especially the alarming prospect of Muslim raj (rule) in their spiritual homeland. The fall of the Unionist ministry as such removed the barrier to communal violence overwhelming the Punjab. The province's descent into violence began with the riots in Lahore and Amritsar in early March and these spread quickly to the Multan Division.

Politicians of the Punjab and National Leadership Constraints on a Local Settlement

Khizr was under no illusions even when he was in office regarding the declining popularity of his ministry, particularly among the Punjab Muslims. He stated quite succinctly to Jenkins that 'in the Punjab, parliamentary majorities mean very little and ... what matters is the strength of the "sanctions" behind a Ministry.' If that ambiguous allusion is rephrased in simpler terms one can easily get to the point Khizr was making. In the words of Jenkins himself, he meant that 'no Punjab ministry can be stable unless it commands not merely a majority in the Assembly but a majority in the major communities in the Province as a whole.'[24] Therefore, he had already made up his mind to relinquish power in any case although he might have contemplated continuing until April or May.[25] However, parliamentary majority notwithstanding, Khizr could not even see the budget session through that was scheduled on 3 March. The leading Hindu and Sikh figures in his coalition government, Bhim Sen Sacher and Swaran Singh, were simply shocked to know of Khizr's intentions. They wanted him to continue through with the budget session as previously proposed.[26] What seemed imminent in the prevailing political polarization was the enforcement of Section 93 whereby all the discretionary powers would be vested in the governor.

Khizr was also in favour of biding a little more time instead of tendering immediate resignation. He knew, as did Jenkins, that Iftikhar Hussain Khan Mamdot would be unable to form a ministry. He was aware of the ignorance of Muslim League leadership about the strength of Hindu and Sikh feelings against them. In such an atmosphere of ill will, a political impasse was imminent. In that case Section 93 would be the only option, but it 'might prove awkward indeed'.[27] Mamdot wished to act as a 'bridge' between the Muslim League and the non-Muslims, which did not seem possible either.

Jenkins, while briefing Wavell about the prevailing uncertainty, stated on 3 March:

> He (Khizr) did not feel that the unnatural coalition ministry could continue for very long and he was not disposed to lead the Congress and the Panthic Sikhs during the Budget Session only to make it clear to them immediately afterwards that he intended to break the Ministry. He felt that if he attempted to act as a 'bridge', he could do nothing effective, and in the meantime communal relations would inevitably worsen.[28]

Given the prevailing situation after Khizr's resignation, Jenkins strongly desired that Mamdot assume power and establish a government. However, he was aware of the serious consequences it might entail such as an early Section 93 situation in the Government of India Act 1935, which gave discretionary power to the governor.[29] He thought that undiluted Muslim rule as the League was envisaging would not last for more than a few weeks. He was fully cognizant of the fact that the only government that could keep the Punjab steady until June 1948 had to represent a large section of all the major communities or at least the vast majority of the Muslims and the Sikhs.

Jenkins held meetings with the leaders of all three communities, with some hope of putting together a multi-communal ministry. However, his meetings with Sachar and Swaran Singh were not at all promising. Both made no secret of their unwillingness to cooperate with the Muslim League and espoused Section 93 instead. They entertained serious doubts about how the League might behave towards the minorities if it came to power. Sachar did not show any inclination to lend support to Mamdot. Swaran Singh was even more categorical. He went to the extent of saying, 'The Sikhs have no plan of being treated as serfs under Muslim Masters and felt that they were strong enough to defend themselves.'[30] A statement to the same effect was issued subsequently by Baldev Singh in his letter to Wavell: 'the Sikhs cannot and will not join any Ministry if it is now formed by the Muslim League.'[31]

In such a state of political uncertainty, Jenkins knew that 'unless the Muslim League leaders could deal with minorities as Punjabis negotiating with the Punjabis', they would hardly make any progress.[32] Besides, Jenkins desperately wanted the ministry to be formed well in time so that the budget could be passed. Mamdot did not give any assurances during his conversation with Jenkins on 3 March. Even Baldev Singh, a moderate among the Sikh leadership, made no bones about the unacceptability of the League Ministry in the Punjab.[33] In a despatch to Lord Wavell, he denounced the League in strong words:

We have built up a Coalition there (the Punjab), after much labour and great care. It was an inter-communal Ministry, held up as a model by the highest personages. The League had not been kept out as it was falsely stated in its quarters. On the contrary, it was asked to join, and the invitation was always there. It remained out because of its deliberate design to dominate the province and to this neither Sikhs nor Unionists and Congress agree. It was for such an exclusive communal domination that the present move was made. The proof, if any needed, their intentions were not clean when they seek our collaboration, was their refusal to collaborate in the coalition. For that reason, the Sikhs cannot and will not join any Ministry if it is now formed by the Muslim League.[34]

Khizr was spot on when once he described himself along with his Unionist Muslim colleagues as 'acting as a buffer' between the League and the minority communities.[35] Immediately after that buffer was removed communal frenzy broke loose. On 3 March, the incident involving Tara Singh wielding a sword on the steps of the Punjab Assembly building was a response to the Muslim League's call for the partition of the Punjab. This act of intimidation sparked the already volatile atmosphere of communal hostility. The Punjab's partition was deemed inimical to the material as well as religious interests of the Sikh community. The situation deteriorated further when 'the Panthic Party passed a resolution that it would fight Pakistan to the last drop of its blood'.[36] The anti-Pakistan demonstration by Hindu and Sikh students in Anarkali Bazaar in Lahore added further venom to the mutual alienation among the communities.[37] Widespread rioting was the upshot of all these aggressive overtones, which spread out to Amritsar within a week. Four thousand Muslim shops were burned down in the walled city. That act of aggression evoked a sharp response in the Western Punjab, particularly in Multan and Rawalpindi divisions, where scattered Hindu and Sikh communities had fallen victim to vicious attacks from the Muslims.[38] There, the minority formed, in Donald L. Horowitz's terms, 'unprotected segments of strong groups'.[39] The death count was 3,000, whereas 40,000, mostly Sikhs, had to seek shelter in the refugee camps.[40] The figures of the casualties in the month of March revealed that 2,090 people died and 1,142 were seriously injured.[41] In the three districts of Attock, Rawalpindi and Jhelum property losses amounted to between 40 and 50 crores of rupees (or 400–500 million rupees).[42] The Rawalpindi massacre, as it had been referred to in official correspondence, left behind a legacy of distrust and hatred, which, along with the fall of Khizr ministry, sealed the fate of the united Punjab.

Communal disturbances were not confined only to the northwestern or the central districts. Violence also erupted towards the end of March and continued well into April in the southeastern district of Gurgaon. Initially the trouble began at Hodal, a small town at the southern end of the district, but it soon spread into other parts of Gurgaon. A dispute over the theft of a buffalo led to a pitched battle between Ahirs and Meos on communal lines. A large area on the border of the Gurgaon District and Alwar State was badly affected and many villages, both Hindu and Muslim, were burnt to ashes. The total death toll in the district was around one hundred. After a few days 36 dead bodies of Meos were found in a nallah near a village named Dharu Hera. There was also some evidence of Alwar state aiding Ahirs against the Meos, forcing the Punjab government to turn to the Political Department to intervene. Order was eventually restored only after three battalions were sent to Gurgaon District.[43]

Ironically, Muslim League leaders like Ghazanfar Ali Khan and Feroze Khan Noon were quite complacent about the rural massacre. Ghazanfar Ali instead suggested (a) a general election and since he expected winning all the Muslim seats therefore (b) the formation of a purely Muslim League government.[44] Jenkins was certainly not amused to learn that League leaders, instead of worrying about somehow harnessing the Frankenstein monster of communalism and anarchy, were more interested in forming a ministry. Mumtaz Daultana, while touring Attock, 'told the people in at least one village that if they could stick it out for a fortnight or three weeks, all the proceedings against them would be withdrawn, and the officials who have suppressed the disturbances would be given a hot time'.[45] Even Jinnah and Liaquat Ali Khan were quite bitter and complained to Mountbatten that he was in fact instructing Jenkins to 'reject Mamdot's request to be allowed to form a predominantly Muslim League Ministry'.[46] They maintained that Mountbatten was yielding to the threat of force by the Sikhs. Jinnah's assertion reflected the urgency on the part of the All-India Muslim League to put together a ministry in the Punjab that unequivocally followed the central leadership's agenda.

Such circumstances were hardly conducive for the League to form a government as they could precipitate a non-Muslim rebellion and could trigger extreme violence in the central and eastern Punjab. Mamdot nevertheless demanded the 'immediate appointment of... Ministry with support of 90 members of Assembly including Muslim League 80, other Muslims 3, Scheduled Castes 4, Indian Christians 2 and European 1'.[47] He did not provide any names of his Muslim League supporters nor of those outside the party who would lend him support in the Assembly on 'all questions of confidence'.[48] A ministry so formed was likely to be dominated by one community and this seemed extremely perilous to Jenkins in the given circumstances. He was not in favour of installing solely a Muslim League Ministry, as it would be a 'fraud on Constitution and instrument of instruction'.[49] Jenkins urged Mamdot more than once 'to renew his efforts to negotiate with other communities', but this advice was ignored.[50] Meanwhile, Jenkins, after obtaining the viceroy's concurrence on 5 March, had 'made the proclamation under section 93 having first prorogued (the) Assembly'.[51] He also knew full well that in case Mamdot succeeded in forming a ministry, there would be dire consequences. 'There would then be immediate Sikh rising with Hindu support. Police, troops, and I [Jenkins] would immediately be involved on Muslim side in what would in fact be civil war for possession of the Punjab.'[52] Already communal frenzy was at its worst in many districts, and thus there were ominous prospects for the Punjab. In these circumstances there was 'no alternative to a Section 93 administration'.[53]

Mamdot's resignation from the Security Committee that Jenkins constituted to help oversee law and order in the Punjab also reflected the League's indifference to the state of anarchy that the province had been plunged into. Mamdot resigned as a protest to the search carried out by the law enforcement agencies in the vicinity of Misri Shah in Lahore. Such defiance hardly helped to stem the rising tide of violence.[54]

The difficulties for the Punjab administration mounted because of communal polarization, which affected its functioning. According to correspondence, several irrigation engineers in Mianwali District, including one British officer, practically packed up at the first sign of danger. General attempts 'to get Muslim officials substituted for non-Muslims and vice versa' became the order of the day.[55] Not only the Civil Service but the Army was subjected to communal polarization. Jenkins had to exhort the politicians: 'we do not run the police or the Army on communal lines, and it is most dangerous to suggest a communal distribution of our resources.'[56]

Demand for Partition, the B. S. Rau Scheme and Notional Divide

After the Rawalpindi massacre, Hindus and Sikhs were irreconcilable. They were intent on a partition of the Punjab. The resolution of the Congress Working Committee on 8 March was a confirmation of their resolve to see the Punjab divided into Muslim and non-Muslim provinces. It was stated in the resolution:

> These tragic events have demonstrated that there can be no settlement of the problem of the Punjab by violence and coercion and no arrangement based on coercion can last. Therefore, it is necessary to find a way out which involves the least amount of compulsion. This would necessitate the division of the Punjab into two provinces, so that the predominantly Muslim parts may be separated from the predominantly non-Muslim parts.[57]

The demand of non-Muslims became more and more vociferous with every passing day. Communal cleansing in Multan and Rawalpindi divisions and the nonchalant attitude of the League leadership over the huge loss of human life and property accentuated the fissures among the three communities. Non-Muslim notables in a letter to Nehru stated, 'recent happenings in North Western Panjab have very rudely shaken the confidence of the Hindu and the Sikh minorities in the belief that there will be any fair deal for them at the hands of the Muslims in the future.'[58] Baldev Singh also reiterated the same demand for 'a division of the Punjab and the creation of a new province embracing the contiguous area where non-Muslims form a clear majority as a whole and have larger property interests.'[59] On 16 April the Working Committee of the Shiromani Akali Dal (SAD) adopted the resolution in which on behalf of the Nationalist Hindus and the Sikhs of the Punjab it put forward a demand for the Punjab's partition into two provinces. It further said, 'for the redistribution of the provincial boundaries a boundary commission should be set up.'[60] While demarcating the provincial boundaries, SAD asked that the following criteria be observed: population, landed property and revenue, and historical places and traditions of the various communities.

SAD also called for proper arrangements for the exchange of population and property.[61] Furthermore, special arrangements for the protection, honour, integrity and sanctity of the historically religious places were solicited. It appealed to 'all the Panthic Organizations and workers to unite and solidly stand behind this demand.'[62]

Jinnah demanded that the entire province of the Punjab be included in the future Pakistan, which was contrary to the wishes of Jenkins and the non-Muslims, who were advocating for the partition of the Punjab. However, Mountbatten termed Jinnah's demand merely as a counterblast to the article published in the *Hindustan Times* on 9 March.[63] Nevertheless tension kept on mounting as no amicable solution was in sight. Nehru suggested to Mountbatten on 24 March the idea of 'temporary partition (primarily in order to end Section 93) into three areas, the first predominantly Muslim, the second predominantly Hindu and the third a mixed area.'[64] Nehru also proposed separate ministers to be appointed for each area, all under one governor. He emphasized that this dispensation would be strictly provisional.

Sir B. N. Rau also propounded a scheme for regional ministries ostensibly to end Section 93 in the Punjab. The very idea of national partition seemed to have emanated from that scheme.[65] Interestingly, Nehru's suggestions reflected Rau's scheme. Both the schemes had striking similarities. Rau suggested that 'the Governor (acting under Section 59 of 1935 Act) should substitute a Regional for a Subject wise allocation of posts in the government.'[66] Hence the province, for administrative purposes, was to be divided into two regions, Muslim and non-Muslim. In the form of the viceroy's Conference Paper No. 7, it was presented on 31 March and the Lahore Division was mentioned as a 'joint territory'. Subjects like education, agriculture and local self-government would be called 'Regional

Subjects' as two regions 'may have divergent interests and needs.' Others like finance and irrigation, 'as to which their interests and needs cannot be divided may be called Joint Subjects'.[67] The governor would have two sets of ministers, Muslims and non-Muslims, to advise him on the regional subjects whereas both sets of ministers would advise him on the joint subjects. The portfolios of the prime minister and the deputy prime minister for the province were deemed very important. Interestingly, if the prime minister were one of the ministers from one region, the deputy prime minister had to be from another region. However, the province would have a single legislature – 'when legislation relating exclusively to regional subjects is under consideration, the members representing constituencies of the other region should abstain from voting'.[68] Sir B. N. Rau prescribed a similar procedure to be adopted in connection with the central government. Further reference to Rau's suggestion regarding the central government is, however, beyond the scope of this chapter. Suffice it to say, Rau thought that his plan was not useful enough if implemented only in the Punjab. In that eventuality the Muslim League would ask for fresh elections that would result in their obtaining a small majority. However, it would eventually lead to much bloodshed. The League's objection would not hold only if, in his view, 'the plan were also put into operation at the centre'.[69]

Rau's scheme drew considerable attention at the highest level. However, Jenkins was unimpressed. In a letter to G.E.B. Abell, he denunciated the plan as unworkable after scrutinizing it from three aspects: its political acceptability, its administrative working and the timing of its introduction. In his view, it would not be acceptable to Muslims and Hindus as both were tied to a High Command. Muslims would not accept any partition of the Punjab 'beyond what would be involved in the surrender of the non-Punjabi-speaking districts of the Ambala division'.[70] Sikhs could accept such a plan with substantial modifications but in that case it was likely to be rejected by the Muslims and 'officially accepted by the Punjab Congress on behalf of the Hindus with many vocal dissensions'.[71] Jenkins's critique seemed more tenable with respect to the aspect of its administrative working. He thought any plan calling for the division of the Punjab into Eastern and Western impracticable 'because the Lahore Division will be the final *casus belli* and must be kept wholly or in part out of the two main regions'.[72] Therefore, the Lahore Division would be kept in the Central Region while the Amritsar District was to be transferred to the Eastern Region. The Lahore Division or 'Central Region' would have to have its own ministers and as much autonomy as the other regions.[73] A few more hazards that would make the administration intolerably cumbersome were the division of the budget into four parts, division of the revenue and the confusion cropping up in a department like education.[74] Similarly, Jenkins found the prime minister's task under the plan virtually impossible because of the existing communal polarization.

The only solution in Jenkins's view rested with the Muslim League and Congress High Commands. If they allowed their Punjabi followers to negotiate on their own, then a way out of the imbroglio could be hoped for and settlement on the Union idea would become a possibility. The other option was partition, which could provide a long-term solution but could only be imposed by force. Undivided Punjab had always been preferred by Jenkins as partition would result in conflicting territorial claims of the Muslims and Sikhs.[75] The Muslim League claimed most of the Punjab. It was ready only to reluctantly surrender Ambala, whereas Sikhs wanted Chenab as the western boundary.[76] The leadership of the Punjab League was told by the All-India Muslim League Council in no uncertain terms to avoid any negotiations that could jeopardize the demand for Pakistan. According to Talbot, Jinnah was unwilling to take the risk of securing peace in the Punjab, as he believed that the region's problems could only be resolved through a political detente at the centre.[77] The unfolding of subsequent events eventually convinced Jenkins about the inevitability of the partition despite its gruesome implications. He wrote to the viceroy on 15 June, arguing 'unity means ruin of one kind, and partition ruin of another; if there is to be ruin anyway, partition seems the simpler and perhaps the less bloody form of it.'[78] The idea of holding a referendum to ascertain the will of all the parties regarding the partition of the Punjab was floated mainly by Mountbatten but was subsequently dropped. Jenkins was unenthusiastic as it seemed to him 'in any circumstances a doubtful expedient in the Punjab, where the voters are entirely in the hands or at the mercy of the party leaders'. A referendum, according to Jenkins, 'could not be on [the] simple issue of adherence to Pakistan or Hindustan as in NWFP but would have to be based on partition to which no question can at present be framed that could be answered in an unqualified "yes" or "no".'

In those trying circumstances, Mountbatten thought it prudent to secure the All-India leadership's consent on partition, which in fact was the raison d'être for the 3 June Plan. In that plan the provincial legislative assemblies of Bengal and the Punjab were to meet in two parts, one representing the Muslim-majority districts and the other the rest of the province. The members of the two parts of each legislative assembly sitting separately were supposed to cast their votes 'whether or not the province should be partitioned'.[79] If a simple majority of either side voted in favour of a partition, the province would be divided accordingly. For the purpose of the final partition of these provinces, the governor general was authorized to set up a boundary commission. On 4 June, Mountbatten in a press conference brought forward the date of transfer of power to 15 August 1947, instead of June 1948. That step is the focus of great historiographical controversy. Some writers have called it an 'ill-judged decision' that intensified communal hostilities. However, violence was already endemic in parts of the Punjab by this juncture. The Partition Plan could be seen as a response to

Lord Mountbatten with wife Edwina and Gandhi in the garden of the Viceroy's House, New Delhi, 1947.

this fact, rather than a precipitating factor. The Muslim League accepted the Partition Plan on 9 June by passing a resolution whereby full authority was vested in the president of the All-India Muslim League 'to accept the fundamental principles of the plan as a compromise, although it cannot agree to the partition of Bengal and the Punjab or give its consent to such partition it has to consider H.M.G's plan for the transfer of power as a whole'.[80] The Congress Working Committee also accepted the plan on 15 June though it had reservations about the status of the NWFP. A day earlier, the Working Committee of the Shiromani Akali Dal and the Panthic Pratinidhi board jointly gave their assent. They, however, emphasized that 'in the absence of a provision of transfer of population and property, the very purpose of partition would be defeated.'[81]

The Sikhs claimed that the division of the Punjab should be 'on the basis of the division of the total area of the province into half and half, or, 49,544 out of 99,089 square miles'. Baldev Singh considered the non-Muslim claim on the divisions of Lahore, Ambala and Jullundur as 'incontrovertible'.[82] The total area of the three divisions was 119,000 square kilometres (45,945 sq. mi.) whereas the total population was 17.3 million, of which the non-Muslim proportion was 9,956 and the population of the Sikhs just over 3 million. If the Punjab was divided on that basis, around 80 per cent of the Sikhs and Nankana Sahib would form the part of that area. Total revenue incurred from that area was PKR 24,228,998 and non-Muslims' share was PKR 16,434,704; the Sikhs paid PKR 8,365,969. Thus, on the basis of population and revenue payments, these three divisions constituted, in the reckoning of Sikh leaders, 'a pre-eminently non-Muslim area'.[83] Credit for the higher revenue was given to the Sikh Jats, described as the most desirable of the 'Colonists' and responsible for making the wilderness of the Western Punjab's colony districts blossom like a rose. As Baldev Singh stated, 'it is as if the energy of the virgin soil of the Bar has passed into his veins and made him almost a part of the forces of nature which he has conquered.'[84] Therefore, as compensation, out of two districts, Montgomery and Lyallpur, one was demanded.

As the plan was enshrined in paragraph 9, the wishes of the people would be ascertained before setting up any partition machinery. The national boundary for the Punjab had already been set up based on the 1941 census. Thereby, West Punjab was to be constituted by the Muslim-majority areas comprising Lahore Division (excluding Amritsar District), and Rawalpindi and Multan divisions, and the non-Muslim areas of Ambala and Jullundur divisions, and Amritsar District would be the East Punjab. Therefore, members of western and eastern sections of the Punjab Legislative Assembly met on 23 June and at the joint session, held at Lahore, 91 members voted in favour of the new Constituent Assembly and 77 for the existing Constituent Assembly. The Western Punjab section of the Punjab Assembly voted against partition of the province by 69 to 27 votes, while the East Punjab section, meeting separately, decided in favour of partition of the Punjab by 50 to 22 votes. Hence, as Tan Tai Yong states, 'by the decision of the Legislative Assembly, the die was thus cast for the partition of Punjab'.[85]

British Responses: The Machinery of Partition

Section 9 of the Indian Independence Act 1947 vested special powers in the governors of the provinces of the Punjab and Bengal 'for dividing between the new Dominions and between the new provinces to be constituted under this Act, the powers, rights, property and duties and liabilities of the governor general in Council or as the case may be'.[86] Thus the Punjab Partition Committee was constituted on 17 June. Besides the governor it consisted of four members. Two of the members would be the nominees of the Muslim League, one of the Congress and one the Panthic Party.[87] Mian Mumtaz Daultana and Mr Zahid Hussain were the League's nominees, whereas Dr Gopi Chand Bhargava was nominated by the Congress and Swaran Singh represented the Panthic Patry.[88] The parties were given full liberty regarding the choice of their nominee whether from within or outside the Punjab. It was agreed that the governor would preside over the meetings of the Partition Committee. Issues were to be settled not by votes but by setting up 'an agreed machinery for the settlement of disputes'.[89] A Steering Committee was constituted comprising Mr Sachdev and Syed Yaqub Shah, who would form the nucleus of the Partition Committee Secretariat.[90] Four expert committees were also formed 'on the principle that the proper advisors on official matters were the persons actually responsible for the administration of those matters'.[91] The four expert committees were Financial Assets and Liabilities; Physical Assets (irrigation and electric systems, roads and bridges and so on); Services and Records; and Use of Institutions of Provincial Importance.[92]

The Partition Committee started working regularly from 1 July. However, Jenkins was dissatisfied with its progress. During the first fortnight, the Committee had managed to take decisions on the distribution of the ICS personnel between the two provinces. However, some disputes cropped up in due course and the Partition Council at the Centre was asked to intercede. The matters specifically in dispute were twofold: whether the East Punjab government should plan to move to Shimla, and do so if the national boundary was confirmed on 15 August; and whether the staff for disputed districts should be selected and posted on some joint basis, on the assumption that the national boundary was confirmed on 15 August.[93] The Partition Council agreed as to the first issue and left the second one for the viceroy to decide. To settle those disputes Mountbatten visited Lahore on Sunday, 20 July, and met with the Punjab Partition Committee. Two important decisions emerged from that meeting which merit mention here. In the case of the Radcliffe Boundary Commission placing Lahore in West Punjab, 'the remnants of the East Punjab government' were advised to leave Lahore 'by midnight 14/15 August and vice versa.' The posting of the officers would also continue based on the notional partition except in the case of the deputy commissioners and superintendents of police in the districts of Gurdaspur, Amritsar and Lahore.[94]

The Punjab Partition Committee had a huge task ahead of it: the division of the administrative machinery within a short span of time. Despite enormous difficulties Jenkins pushed the process forward and vexed issues were settled by prompt decision-making. In the case of stalemate Mountbatten himself took the responsibility of its expeditious resolution. The systematic handling of every problem first by the Expert Committee then by the Steering Committee and finally by the Partition Committee made that cumbersome process not only possible but smooth and transparent. Only three problems were referred to the Partition Council at the Centre: Lahore as the centre of both the governments (the Eastern and Western Punjab), the posting of the officers in three disputed districts, and the decision of Punjab University. However, some cases in which differences were substantial were referred to the Arbitral Tribunal by 31 December 1947 and the final decision was reached within three months.[95] In a meeting of the Partition Council held on 17 July, the 'Punjab Boundary Force' was formed to check the border clashes in the Punjab after its partition. The details given were as follows:

a) It was supposed to deal with disturbances about the two dominions on or after 15th August.
b) Major General T. W. 'Pete' Rees was appointed Joint Commander of the Punjab Boundary Forces operating in the designated areas in the Punjab. The chain of control from the two Dominion governments was through the Joint Defence Council 93 and Supreme Commander, General Auchinleck.
c) The troops were to take position by 7 or 8 August at the latest.
d) The law governing the use of the troops in aid of the civil authority would remain enforced even after 15 August.[96]

After detailed and protracted discussions between Evan Jenkins, commander-in-chief, and the Punjab Partition Committee, Sialkot, Gujranwala, Sheikhupura, Lyallpur, Montgomery, Lahore, Amritsar, Gurdaspur, Hoshiarpur, Jullundur and Ferozepur were declared disturbed areas. Hence the total area assigned to the Punjab Boundary Force (PBF) was about 97,125 square kilometres (37,500 sq. mi.), which included 26 towns and approximately 17,000 villages.[97] The PBF consisted of two brigades of the 4th Indian Division – 11 Brigade covered Jullundur, Hoshiarpur and Ludhiana districts whereas the districts of Amritsar and Gurdaspur were assigned to 5 Brigade. Similarly, 14 Paratroop was to manage Lahore, Sialkot, Gujranwala, Lyallpur and Sheikhupura districts; 43 Lorried Infantry was responsible for Ferozepur and Montgomery District; and 114 Infantry was specified for Lahore city only. The total strength of the PBF was seventeen battalions of infantry; a cavalry regiment; and engineer, signal and medical units. It was 23,000 strong.[98]

For two divisions of the PBF, it proved to be a daunting task to control such a huge area, especially when communal bitterness was at its peak. The situation in certain towns showed some improvement; however, the rural parts within the area of PBF were by no means peaceful. Rather the disturbances spread to the places outside PBF's jurisdiction. According to one report, for example, '70 per cent of the major attacks on the railway trains have occurred outside the Punjab Boundary Force area.'[99] Therefore, in a special meeting of the Joint Defence Council held in Lahore on 29 August 1947 it was unanimously decided that 'as the task allotted to the Punjab Boundary Force for helping to maintain law and order in the disputed areas has now grown out of all proportion to the responsibilities placed upon it, this Force should be abolished with effect from midnight 31st August/1st September.'[100] Hence, the force was indeed abolished.

The Punjab Boundary Commission and Award

The Punjab Boundary Commission was constituted by the announcement of the governor general on 30 June 1947 under Section 9 of the 3 June Plan. The members of the commission were four judges of the Indian High Court. Mr Justice Din Muhammad and Mr Justice Mohammad Munir represented Muslims; Mr Justice Mehar Chand Mahajan and Mr Justice Teja Singh represented Hindus and Sikhs respectively.[101] Sir Cyril Radcliffe was appointed as its chairman. At the time he was vice chairman of the General Council of the English Bar. The secretary of state recommended his name as a man of 'great legal abilities, right personality and wide administrative experience'.[102]

Radcliffe arrived in India on 8 July and had only five weeks to make the most difficult decision of his life. Another fact compounding the difficulty was his ignorance of India or Indian politics; he 'had absolutely no local knowledge of the territories he was to divide'.[103] His little knowledge of local conditions and inexperience in this sort of arbitration helped in creating an impression of Radcliffe's impartiality, which was painstakingly projected by the viceroy himself. Such impartiality was an important consideration for the venture that Radcliffe was meant to undertake. In a situation where members of the commission represented the communal interests of the parties to whom they owed their allegiance, Radcliffe was left 'with a considerable role to play in the deliberation process'.[104] In the event of disagreement between the representatives of the Congress and the Muslim League, the chairman had the discretion of a casting vote, which made his role extremely critical. The terms of reference of the commission as set out in the announcement of 30 June aimed at demarcating 'the boundaries of the two parts of the Punjab based on ascertaining the contiguous majority areas of Muslims and non-Muslims. In doing so, it will also consider other factors.'[105] The date stipulated for the commission to arrive at a decision was 15 August.

The public sittings of the Punjab Boundary Commission were held in Lahore from 21 July to 31 July. The INC, the Muslim League and the Akali Dal were the main parties that made representations before the commission through their counsels, M. L. Seetalvad, Sir Chaudhry Zafarullah and Harnam Singh respectively. Several other interest groups and parties also argued their respective cases before the commission. As Radcliffe was also chairman of the Bengal Boundary Commission, whose proceedings were taking place simultaneously with the proceedings of the Punjab Boundary Commission, he therefore could not attend the public sittings himself. However, he decided to keep himself abreast of the proceedings daily. When members of the commission entered upon discussions with the aim of reaching an agreed decision on the demarcation of the boundaries, the divergence of opinion among them was just baffling for Radcliffe. Particularly, when it came to the extensive but disputed areas in which the boundary must be drawn, differences of opinion as to the significance of the term 'other factors', which we were directed by our terms of reference to take into account, and as to weight and the value to be attached to those factors, made it impossible to arrive at any agreed line.[106]

In such circumstances when an agreed solution seemed remote, the onus fell entirely on Radcliffe's shoulders to make a final decision. According to the final award, West Punjab got an area of 163,000 square kilometres (63,000 sq. mi.) and a population of 16 million, including 4 million non-Muslims. East Punjab got an area of around 96,000 square kilometres (37,000 sq. mi.) and a population of 12.5 million, of which 4.4 million were Muslims. West Punjab had 25 per cent of the non-Muslim population whereas Muslims constituted slightly more than 35 per cent of East Punjab's population.[107]

Delimiting a boundary in the Punjab was an extremely complex task. However, 'the truly debatable ground in the end proved to lie in and around the area between the Beas and Sutlej rivers on the one hand and the river Ravi on the other.'[108] Drawing a boundary line in that area proved even more tenuous because of the canal systems, 'so vital to the life of the Punjab but developed only under the conception of a single administration'.[109] The same could be said about the systems of road and rail communication, which had been planned on similar lines. Radcliffe was also cognizant of 'the stubborn geographical fact of the respective situations of Lahore and Amritsar' and the claims to each or both the cities that Muslims and the non-Muslims had forcefully maintained.[110] The areas east of Sutlej and particularly in the angle of the Beas and Sutlej rivers with Muslim majorities proved to be an acid test for Radcliffe as an arbiter. Radcliffe thought it rather detrimental to the interests of both the states if a strip on the far side of the Sutlej was included in the Western Punjab. According to Tan Tai Yong, the disputed and debatable areas comprised the districts of Lahore, Amritsar, Gurdaspur, Hoshiarpur and Jullundur in the central Punjab.[111] Radcliffe saw disruption of the railway communications and water systems if the Muslim-majority areas on the Sutlej were awarded to West Punjab. Concurrently the intake of certain canals like Dipalpur canal, dependent on Ferozepore head works but serving areas in the West Punjab, made the task of demarcation of the boundary even more tedious. To Radcliffe, some arrangement for joint control of such canals was the only workable proposition.[112] He did not find it possible 'to preserve undivided the irrigation system of the Upper Bari Doab Canal', springing from Madhopur and spread across to the neighbourhood of Lahore. To mitigate the consequences of this severance, he resorted to making minor adjustments to the Lahore–Amritsar district boundary. Similarly, the Mandi Hydro-Electric Scheme supplying power to Kangra, Gurdaspur, Amritsar, Lahore,

Jullundur, Ludhiana, Ferozepore, Sheikhupura and Lyallpur could not be preserved under one territorial jurisdiction. Given that drawing the boundary line could not avoid disruption to unitary services like canal irrigation, railways and electric power transmission, Radcliffe saw agreement between the two states for some joint control of those valuable assets as the only viable solution.[113] In such cases the 'other factors' were brought in as the more important mean rather than the principal of majority contiguous areas, to ascertain the future of the territories and assets, particularly those lying on the east of the Sutlej. The term 'other factors' had not been clearly defined, therefore it gave rise to myriad controversies and conflicting interpretations. Radcliffe gave precedence to 'other factors' over the communal criterion, particularly in the cases of Lahore, Amritsar and Gurdaspur.

The Lahore District, with all its *tehsils* (*tehsil* is revenue subdivision in India and Pakistan), had a Muslim majority. However, the awarded boundary diagonally sliced away the southeast of Kasur Tehsil and gave it to East Punjab – the 'other factors' and mainly the consideration of minimizing disruptions to railways, canal systems and communication networks being the reason for this decision. The Amritsar District had 53.5 per cent of the non-Muslim population, with its northern *tehsil* of Ajnala having a clear Muslim majority. Nevertheless, the whole of Amritsar District was allotted to East Punjab.[114] However, another example of inconsistency on the part of the Boundary Commission was the Gurdaspur District, which also was subjected to the criterion of the 'other factors' while determining its future. In that district Muslims formed a majority by a very narrow margin as their population was 50.2 per cent. Its four *tehsils*, Gurdaspur, Shakargarh, Pathankot and Batala, had a Muslim-majority population but regardless of that fact all of them but Shakargarh were given over to India. Shakargarh, though, became a part of Sialkot District in the West Punjab – but a sizable part of it was sliced away and given to East Punjab.[115]

The award of almost the whole of Gurdaspur District to East Punjab generated a controversy that had far-reaching implications. In Pakistan it has been believed with conviction that Gurdaspur was allotted to India to provide it with access to Jammu and Kashmir. Mountbatten is usually incriminated; it is said he exerted pressure on Radcliffe because the former was not pleased with Jinnah, who refused to entertain his wish of becoming Pakistan's first governor general. However, the impact of the Gurdaspur award on the Kashmir issue is beyond the scope of this book. Suffice it to say that Radcliffe deployed multiple factors in determining the boundary line: communal, irrigation, communication and, most significantly, 'other factors'.[116] That inconsistency evoked sharp criticism among many people and the press. It was 'self-contradictory, anomalous and arbitrary' according to the *Hindustan Standard* of Delhi and 'territorial murder, a biased decision' and an 'act of shameful partiality' according to *Dawn*.[117] Radcliffe himself was cognizant of the impending criticism that the award would be likely to evoke. While concluding his report, he stated: 'I am conscious too that the award cannot go far towards satisfying sentiments and aspirations deeply held on either side but directly in conflict as to their bearing on the placing of the boundary.'[118]

Only political arrangements and not the boundary line drawn under the terms of reference of the commission, Radcliffe thought, could have 'gratified to the full the sentiments and aspirations' of the communities, with which he was not at all concerned.[119] Nevertheless Radcliffe is a much-maligned figure, particularly by the three communities, as each one of them felt slighted and cheated.

The Punjab experienced unprecedented turbulence and communal polarization in the months preceding its partition. From the fall of the Khizr ministry and promulgation of Section 93, the Punjab became simply ungovernable. Massive killings because of religious differences were a routine phenomenon. Even Jenkins, an administrator of commendable repute and with vast knowledge of the province, was at a loss to come to grips with the ever-deteriorating situation. He thought a coalition ministry representing all three communities could present a workable proposition. However, cobbling together such a ministry remained his unfulfilled desire. He resisted Mamdot's bid to form a single-party ministry and, in those circumstances, he was fully justified, as doing so could have triggered a civil war in the Punjab as communal sentiments were running very high. The central command of the League and the Congress, according to Jenkins, were mainly responsible for impeding political rapprochement at the provincial level. Here too Jenkins was spot on. Provincial interests were sacrificed for the gain at All-India level. The onus of the worsening situation in the Punjab can be placed not only on the central leadership of the League and Congress but on the viceroy, who prioritized settlement of the issues at the central rather than at the provincial level.

The Congress leadership held the British government responsible for the prevailing violence and chaos in the final six months of the Raj. According to Nehru, British district administrators were deemed ineffective in dealing with the severe and distressing situation. He highlighted that all the districts experiencing violence were under the supervision of British deputy commissioners and superintendents of police. However, that argument can be inverted: the administration of all such districts plagued with violence had been entrusted to the British officers, who performed their duties under trying circumstances, including knowing their own lives were under threat. Mountbatten and Radcliffe both incur sharp criticism in Pakistan because of their supposed role in the award in which injustice was perpetrated on Pakistan. Assigning the task of partitioning the Punjab and Bengal to someone like Radcliffe could not assuage expectations of the competing claims of Muslims and non-Muslims. One must not lose sight of the fact that dividing the Punjab was undoubtedly the most daunting task assigned to the Boundary Commission. The Punjab under the British was not conducive to partition; however, communal polarization made it imperative to draw a dividing line. The decision of the Boundary Commission regarding the award of Gurdaspur and Ferozepur districts to East Punjab in consideration of 'other factors' can be termed highly inexpedient to say the least. The partition of the Punjab – with all the killings, rape, looting and plunder that it entailed – engendered so much pathos that it still rankles in the collective memory of the people on both sides of the divide. The following poem by renowned Punjabi laureate Amrita Pritam is one illustration of it.

> (Today, I call Waris Shah,
> 'Speak from inside your grave'
> And turn, today,
> the book of love's next affectionate page)
> (Once, one daughter of Punjab cried;
> you wrote a wailing saga
> Today, a million daughters,
> cry to you, Waris Shah)
>
> (Rise! O' narrator of the grieving;
> rise! look at your Punjab
> Today, fields are lined with corpses,
> and blood fills the Chenab)
> (This fertile land is sprouting,
> venom from every pore
> The sky is turning red
> from endless cries of gore).

4
Multiple Challenges, Limited Options: Making Sense of the Early Problems

> The light, smeared and spotted, this night-bitten dawn
> This isn't surely the dawn we waited for so eagerly
> This isn't surely the dawn with whose desire cradled in our hearts
> We had set out, friends all, hoping
> We should somewhere find the final destination.
>
> Faiz Ahmed, Colours of my Heart[1]

The colonial legacy still resonates in the political culture of Pakistan. Literary theorist Rajeswari Sunder Rajan's assertion is accurate when she says, 'Colonialism is not simply a matter of legacy but of active, immediate and constitutive determinants.'[2] Certain Western academics, according to political scientist Inayat Ullah, contend that postcolonial societies might not have witnessed the emergence of democracy had it not been for colonial intervention.[3] According to some scholars, certain societies in South and West Asia, such as Nepal, Thailand and Iran, would have not been able to develop democratic institutions independently. Despite not having undergone colonialism directly, these countries have been ruled by absolute monarchs or authoritarian leaders, which suggests that their internal dynamics have hindered democratic development. In contrast, some former British colonies, such as Jamaica, have managed to establish stable democracies under colonial rule. However, it is worth noting that 'the relationship between colonialism and democracy is complex and cannot be reduced to a simple formula.'[4] Some scholars from the postcolonial world, particularly those from India, hold a different view. They argue that if not for colonialism, postcolonial societies would have been able to develop their own modernity and democratic institutions. According to this perspective, colonialism not only disrupted existing political systems but suppressed local cultures and knowledge systems that would have proved crucial for democratic development. Therefore, these scholars contend that the lack of democracy in the postcolonial world is not due to inherent cultural or social factors, but rather to the legacy of colonialism.

The impact of colonialism on the democratization of colonized states and societies is complex, with both favourable and unfavourable forces at play. The interaction of these forces with local conditions could either foster or stifle democracy.[5] Ayesha Jalal provides further insight into the differences brought about by the colonial period. She argues that the British attempt to expand imperial control through rule-bound institutions based on Western concepts of contractual law and impersonal sovereignty, rather than on the personal patronage of rulers, was unprecedented in the subcontinent. Consequently, the political unity created in a calculated manner and frozen in the rationality of bureaucratic institutions could not reflect or capture the internal dynamics of a society accustomed to direct personalized rule.[6]

Personalized and direct rule in Pakistan had a significant impact on the bureaucratic apparatus, which played a key role in reinforcing the centralized administrative structure of the country. As a result, Pakistan relied heavily on the 'colonial state's methods of bureaucratic control and centralization' to maintain order and stability. This approach not only perpetuated the legacy of colonialism but limited the scope for democratic governance and public participation. The bureaucracy, being a powerful institution, often acted as a gatekeeper, monopolizing access to resources and decision-making and further undermining the democratic aspirations of the people.[7] The India Act of 1935 strengthened the existing bureaucratic structure of the British Raj, which was later adapted to serve as the constitutional framework for Pakistan. While the Westminster model of parliamentary democracy called for a separation between bureaucracy and the elected representatives, the bureaucratic authoritarianism inherent in the colonial state persisted. As a result, establishing the supremacy of the legislative branch over the executive proved to be a daunting task from the outset.

The Pakistani political elite were reluctant to undertake a radical reorganization of the administrative structure inherited from the colonial era, which would have empowered elected bodies. Instead, they formed alliances of convenience with the bureaucracy to maintain administrative continuity and tackle the massive dislocation and law and order problems that arose following the partition of the subcontinent. This pragmatic approach meant that the bureaucracy retained considerable power and influence, which hindered the growth of democratic institutions and processes. Therefore, despite the adoption of a parliamentary system, the balance of power remained heavily skewed in favour of the bureaucracy and the executive branch, rather than the legislative. The legacy of colonialism and the challenges of nation-building in the aftermath of partition further complicated the task of democratic consolidation in Pakistan.[8]

Asma Barlas reflects on the democratic experiences of Pakistan and India, lamenting the former's failure to establish robust democratic institutions despite acquiring nearly identical administrative structures from the British Raj.[9] However, the alternative view attributes Pakistan's overdeveloped state structure to colonial practices aimed at maintaining law and order rather than facilitating popular representation.[10] Similarly, Khalid bin Sayeed's term 'viceregalism' underscores the continuity between colonial and postcolonial dispensations in Pakistan.[11] The arbitrary methods enforced (by the British) in the areas that became Pakistan included measures such as preventive detention, the prohibition of political actions perceived as prejudicial to public order and control of the press. These measures originated from colonial technology of control and precluded the spread of representative institutions. Additionally, Pakistan re-enacted emergency powers from the 1935 Government of India Act, enabling the centre to dissolve provincial governments. The Public and Representatives Office (Disqualification) Act, also known as PRODA, promulgated in 1949 by Liaquat Ali Khan's ministry, reflected the paranoia of Pakistani political leaders, which later became a pervasive feature of the country's politics.

All these rather stringent measures were indicative of the grave security concerns of the British regarding northwestern India. With the sole exception of East Bengal, the rest of the Pakistani areas were conquered by the British for strategic reasons rather than in pursuance of economic interests, as was the case of southern or eastern India. Among the territories constituting Pakistan, Sindh was the first to fall to the British, in 1843. That 'act of imperial private enterprise' was conceived and subsequently realized by Charles Napier by displacing Sindh's Talpur rulers. Similarly stiff resistance from the Khalsa Army at Chillianwalla (in the Gujrat district) notwithstanding, the British annexed the whole of the Punjab in 1849. The main motive behind the annexation of the Punjab was indeed defence-related. British paternalism began with the Board of Administration, with the Lawrence brothers (Henry and John) and Mansel, an expert in revenue administration.[12] Immediately after the annexation, a force of 8,000 policemen was raised to keep tabs on the troublemakers. Besides, the district administrators were fully invested with both administrative and judicial powers. They were also supposed 'to win allegiance of the rural population by their example of hard work and fairmindedness'.[13]

The region that would eventually become Pakistan has a long and rich history, having served as a gateway for successive waves of invaders from the northwest for centuries. During the reign of Ranjit Singh, the Northwest Frontier was integrated with the Punjab, where it remained a part of the province until the early twentieth century.

In 1901, the settled districts of the trans-Indus region were carved out into a separate province from the Punjab. However, NWFP remained a minor province until 1930–32, when it was granted devolved powers under the system of diarchy established by the 1919 Government of India Act. Despite these reforms, the province remained relatively powerless, since the governor exercised significant authority and frequently banned demonstrations and processions.

This authoritarian approach meant that the people of NWFP had little say in their own governance and remained marginalized from mainstream politics. The lack of meaningful representation and the suppression of dissent contributed to a sense of alienation and disenfranchisement that was to have significant consequences in the years to come.

In the latter half of the nineteenth century, the British perceived a security threat from the imperial designs of Russia and began to transform the Punjab into a military stronghold. The cantonments, strategic roads, railways, hill-top forts and the imposing double-decker iron bridge spanning the narrow Indus gorge at Attock all bear witness to the strategic importance of the Punjab to the British.[14] During the Indian Uprising in 1857, the Punjab played a pivotal role in the restoration of British authority in the Gangetic plain, which was experiencing widespread revolt and rebellion at the time. The British military's suppression of the uprising was made possible in large part by the deployment of troops and resources from the Punjab. The experience of quelling the rebellion further solidified the Punjab's reputation as a key strategic asset for the British in South Asia.

The militarization of the Punjab had far-reaching consequences for the region's social, economic and political development. The concentration of military power in the region contributed to the growth of a distinct martial culture, which prioritized loyalty, discipline and obedience to authority. The deployment of troops and the construction of military infrastructure also spurred urbanization and economic growth in certain parts of the Punjab, while exacerbating social and economic inequalities in others.

The British thus began to view the landed elite of the Punjab as their allies, relying on them to supply soldiers to the imperial military machine as needed. The 'Punjabization' of the Indian Army, which began in the 1870s, was based on the social-Darwinist theory of 'martial castes'.[15] However, it was mainly driven by the practical considerations of the region's stability after the 1857 uprising and its proximity to the frontier, where a potential Russian invasion was feared.[16] The people of the Punjab, and particularly those inhabiting the northwestern districts of Jhelum, Chakwal, Rawalpindi and Attock, were deemed ideally suited to army recruitment. By 1875, one-third of the Indian Army consisted of Punjabis, and this had increased to three-fifths by 1914.[17] As mentioned in Chapter Three, landlords played a crucial role in recruiting soldiers for the British Indian Army. This gave rise to a symbiotic relationship between the landholding class and the armed forces, which had a profound impact on the social and political landscape of the areas that would become Pakistan in 1947. By co-opting local landlords, the military and political elites of the time not only hindered the development of democratic institutions but perpetuated a culture of clientelism.

This nexus between landlords and the military has remained a defining feature of Pakistani politics since its inception. It has impeded the growth of democratic institutions and blocked attempts to implement socio-economic reforms that would challenge the dominant interests of the landed class. Even after the country gained independence, the military's close ties to the landed elites have continued to exert a powerful influence on the country's politics. The effects of this relationship can be seen in the persistence of social and economic inequalities, as well as in the uneven distribution of power and resources. Landlords and military elites have often worked in tandem to preserve their privileged status, leaving little room for the emergence of alternative power structures or the promotion of inclusive development. Despite periodic attempts at reform, the nexus between landlords and the military remains a formidable obstacle to the realization of a more equitable and democratic Pakistan.

The region of the NWFP (now Khyber Pakhtunkhwa) was of significant importance to the British due to its strategic location near Afghanistan, where the British had ongoing imperial conflicts with Russia in the nineteenth century. Similarly, British interests also turned towards Baluchistan due to its proximity to Afghanistan. Starting in 1854, Britain steadily increased its influence in Baluchistan, eventually granting Kalat and its feudatories the status of protected states. In 1872, a clear boundary line was defined between Iran and Baluchistan through a geographical reconfiguration. The importance of Quetta, a cantonment, increased when, in 1876, the khan of Kalat signed a treaty that allowed British troops to be stationed there, making it a crucial location for military operations during the Second Afghan War (1878–80). As a result, shortly thereafter, the khan of Kalat ceded the entire Quetta district to the British.[18] Furthermore, during the Second Afghan War, the British assumed control over the strategically crucial regions of Sibi and Pishin. This expansion continued throughout the remaining years of the nineteenth century, with the pivotal Bolan Pass coming under British suzerainty in 1883. Additionally, the areas traversed by the Mushkaf-Bolan and Noshki Railways were passed over to the British in 1894 and 1903, respectively, which further solidified their grip on the region.[19]

Imperial expansion had a lasting impact on postcolonial Baluchistan. The precedence of executive and military interests over democratic institutions has far stronger reverberation in Baluchistan than in any other province of Pakistan. The power of administrative machinery was enhanced beyond measure by striking an alliance with the local sardars. While it was not a common occurrence in Baluchistan, the presence of strategic imperatives and a society less focused on equality compared to the Frontier allowed this phenomenon to flourish more extensively in the region. This was achieved by strengthening the sardars' authority through the formalization of the tribal council's power, known as the *jirga*.[20] Thus democracy was confined only to the municipality of Quetta until the creation of Pakistan. The Shahi Jirga, comprising 54 sardars and five members of the Quetta municipality, took the decision to join Pakistan.

In the unfolding narrative of this chapter, the distinctive character of Pakistan emerges, revealing its intrinsic nature as a multicultural, pluralistic, and geographically diverse entity. In the ensuing section, our focus will shift to explore whether this rich tapestry of plurality and diversity finds resonance within the realm of Pakistani literature.

The Partition, the Literati and the Construction of Pakistani Identity

The post-partition era saw the emergence of a remarkable cohort of Pakistani literary luminaries, including Faiz Ahmed Faiz, Noon Meem Rashid, Majieed Amjid, Nasir Kazmi and Munir Niazi among poets, and Intizar Hussain, Ashfaq Ahmed, Abdullah Hussain and Khadija Mastoor among writers.[21] These visionary artists were steeped in a rich and diverse literary tradition that had taken shape in the pre-partition landscape of India, reflecting a nuanced cross-cultural ethos that permeated their work.[22]

Regarded by many as a quintessential masterpiece of its genre, 'Gadariya' (The Shepherd), a short story penned by Ashfaq Ahmed (1925–2004) in 1953, continues to captivate readers with its timeless appeal.[23] 'Gadariya' is a testament to the pluralistic and humanistic values that characterize Muslim Sufism, as seen through the eyes of the eponymous protagonist – a Hindu teacher who selflessly imparts his knowledge of Persian to a young Muslim boy, while also displaying deep reverence for the teachings of the Quran and the revered Prophet Muhammad (peace be upon him). In a similar vein, Ahmed's novel *Khel Tamasha* (Games and Spectacle) also embodies this cross-cultural ethos, showcasing the author's nuanced understanding of the complexities of Pakistani society.[24] The narrative arc of this story spans multiple decades and geographic locations, beginning in a small village in the East Punjab just prior to partition, and culminating in Afghanistan during the 1980s, where the protagonist eventually meets his demise and is laid to rest.

Interestingly, during this same period, a group of writers associated with the Anjuman Taraqqi Pasand Musannifeen (Progressive Writers' Association) offered a contrasting interpretation of the partition experience, challenging conventional notions and prompting readers to reconsider the underlying socio-political dynamics at play.[25] Through the pages of its Lahore-based magazine, *Savera*, the progressive writers of this period sought to expose the brutal reality of the communal hatred that partition had unleashed, which resulted in widespread massacres, pogroms and displacement. Rather than celebrating partition as a momentous event that marked the end of colonial rule, these writers viewed it through an anti-imperialist lens, recognizing it as a ploy designed to weaken the Indian people. Their literary impulse was thus imbued with a sense of dissatisfaction and frustration at the emergence of Pakistan, which they believed had only served to divide the subcontinent and its people. Despite this, some members of the progressive writers' movement, such as the renowned poet Faiz (1911–1984), viewed partition as a necessary sacrifice for India's eventual freedom, even as they expressed horror and anguish at the violent events that accompanied it. Faiz's poignant poem 'Subh-i-Azadi' (The Dawn of Freedom) stands as a testament to this deep-seated sense of frustration and grief at the bloodshed that marred Pakistan's birth in August 1947.[26] While the movement was a powerful force in shaping the literary landscape of Pakistan, it was not without its critics. Among them were writers such as Muhammad Hasan Askari (1919–1978) and Intizar Hussain (1923–2016), who, despite harbouring ambivalent views towards India's partition, were reluctant to align themselves with the progressive writers. Even the celebrated writer Saadat Hasan Manto (1912–1955), whose short stories were a damning critique of partition and the violence it engendered, kept himself apart from the movement. Askari, for his part, celebrated the birth of Pakistan as a new country and chafed at the progressive writers' tendency to link it to imperialist machinations. He sought to carve out a distinct identity for Pakistani literature but struggled to clearly define it. Ironically, his efforts to do so resulted in the assertion of a geographically unbound Muslim identity as a distinctly Pakistani one. Naseem Hijazi (1914–1996), who wrote fictional narratives glorifying Muslim conquerors, emerged as the most prominent and popular exponent of this Islamic Pakistani identity. While contemporaries Qudratullah Shahab, Jamil-ud Din Aali and Hafeez Jalandhari came close to realizing what Askari had proposed, none could truly be considered his followers. According to the critic, academic and poet Khawaja Muhammad Zakariya, Askari's legacy was ultimately stymied by his own vacillation regarding the contours of Pakistani literature, despite his impressive erudition and body of scholarship.[27] Thus the establishment of an independent identity for Pakistani literature proved to be a challenging task. Askari's hostile stance towards the West and Western knowledge systems rendered his ideas and thoughts somewhat obscure, even appearing cynical at times. Aamer Hussein astutely observes that Askari's call for an imagined nativist perspective or a sort of magic realism received little traction.[28]

Intizar Hussain is a distinctive case. He emerged as the most influential Urdu laureate in fiction, demonstrating his mastery of both the novel and short-story forms. His work is particularly significant for its profound questioning of partition and the galvanizing impact it had on the literary consciousness of later Pakistani writers. Hussain's writing is widely believed to be infused with a nostalgia that transcends both temporal and spatial boundaries, and which some regard as the central trait of his fiction. He invokes the traditions of *daastan* (a long, narrative story), mythological tales and magic realism, synthesizing these divergent literary streams to create a genre unique to himself. This convergence of myriad sociocultural strands constitutes the South Asian Muslim consciousness, which differs fundamentally from the rest of the Muslim world.

While the work of the playwrights Imtiaz Ali Taj (1900–1970), Rafi Peerzada (1898–1974) and Shaukat Siddiqui (1923–2006) may not have been as profound as that of Intizar Hussain, they were all deeply engaged with the effects of partition. However, their exploratory focus failed to address sociocultural themes of local relevance. In his conversation with Muhammad Umar Memon in 1974, Hussain revealed the significance of partition for him and other literary artists. He equated partition with the Prophet's *hijrat* (the migration he undertook from Mecca to Medina to create a new state and society).

The *hijrat*, a central event in the history of Muslims, occupies a unique place in the collective consciousness of the community. Hussain, in his reflection on partition, drew a parallel between this event and the experience of contemporary Muslims. For Hussain, the *hijrat* was not just a physical migration, but a transformative process that occurred on both external and internal planes, leading to a profound creative experience. Partition, in his view, was a moment of great creativity, as it allowed for the re-enactment of the Prophet's migration from Mecca to Medina and gave rise to a powerful creative force. Hussain believed that partition was not simply a geographic relocation, but a spiritual and cultural transformation from the old to the new, as the Muslims of the subcontinent embarked on a journey of self-discovery and self-definition. While playwrights such as Taj, Peerzada and Siddiqui also grappled with the effects of partition in their work, none was able to match Hussain's depth of engagement or his ability to synthesize diverse literary traditions and cultural themes.[29] Mushtaq Ahmed Yusufi (1923–2018), a celebrated humourist of the past half-century found resonance in partition in his writings that spoke to the realities of contemporary Pakistan. His literary masterpiece, the novel *Aab-i-Gum* (Disappeared Water), published in 1990, positions him at the intersection of the period under scrutiny in this study.[30] In the book, nostalgia emerges as the driving force behind the lives of those who experienced partition, casting a melancholic spell over the reader. The soul-searching experience of nostalgia, accompanied by the agony it inflicts on the main protagonist, makes *Aab-i-Gum* one of the most enduring contributions to Urdu literature. Even though his autobiographical final book, *Shaam-e-Shaire-Yaaraan* (Evening with Poet Friends), was considered his weakest, Yusufi spent the 1990s and 2000s delivering prose pieces at various public events. Recordings of most of these readings are now accessible on YouTube, which is a testament to how good prose can find an audience regardless of its medium.[31]

Mukhtar Masood wrote significant books that were partly autobiographical but mostly focused on nostalgia for the Muslim past, such as *Awaz-i-Dost* (The Voice of a Friend, 1973), *Safar-i-Naseeb* (Destiny's Journey, 1981) and *Loh-i-Ayam* (A Record of Ages Gone By, 1997). But his last book, *Harf-i-Shauq* (Word of Fondness), published posthumously in 2018, delves into his pre-partition memories of Aligarh University, where he was a student, and thus epitomizes the nostalgia for the pre-partition era.[32] Besides identity, however, another issue confronted Pakistani decision-makers: sovereignty.

The Issue of Sovereignty

The issue of sovereignty was significant and complex for Pakistan. One of the earliest threats to Pakistan's sovereignty came from the Indian Independence Bill, which assumed that Pakistan would be a seceding state under the government of the Indian National Congress.[33] The Muslim League vehemently opposed the proposal of having one governor general for both India and Pakistan, as they feared that it would encourage more secessionist movements within Pakistan during times of crisis. Moreover, due to the incomplete transfer of armed forces, Pakistan would not be considered a sovereign nation if it had the same governor general as India. This was because the governor general at the time of partition was given unlimited powers to ensure the proper implementation of the partition process. According to Ayesha Jalal, this resulted in 'the governor-general having broader powers than those typically given to a governor-general of a dominion'.[34]

Quaid-e-Azam Muhammad Ali Jinnah (heretofore Jinnah) had asked that the independence bill should clearly state that the governor general would not act on his ministers' counsel.[35] However, Congress rebutted this. It wanted to pre-empt the equal importance given to both sovereign states' governors general in matters of arbitration when it came to the division of resources. Jinnah was convinced that only a separate governor general would effectively contest Pakistan's case without giving in to the pressure of the union government of independent India. While drawing on Mountbatten's correspondence with J. B. Kripalani, Yasser Latif Hamdani reveals in his book on Jinnah this little-known fact about his counter-proposal asking for 'a Super Governor General with arbitral powers sitting in Delhi overseeing the division of assets between the two proposed dominions'.[36] The writer highlights an intriguing proposal made by Jinnah, which was to convene the constituent assemblies of both Pakistan and India simultaneously in New Delhi. According to Ayesha Jalal, 'this proposal could have potentially established friendly relations between the two dominions. However, it was rejected by Congress, which did not want the Pakistan Constituent Assembly to be in close proximity to New Delhi.'[37]

The Government of India Act 1935 granted extensive authority to the governor general across all government functions, establishing a position of immense power and authoritarian control. Consequently, upon India's attainment of independence, the governor general's office emerged as the epicentre of authority. This is why Jinnah opposed the notion of a singular governor general presiding over both India and Pakistan. His opposition stemmed from the fact that the Indian Independence Bill was constructed on the foundation of the 1935 Act. Until alternative constitutions were devised by the constituent assemblies of both nations, the 1935 Act continued to serve as the legal framework for both countries. Jalal emphasizes that Jinnah's resistance was rooted in his apprehension that having 'a common governor-general for both nations would hinder Pakistan from attaining full sovereignty, given the extensive discretionary powers vested in the governor-general under the 1935 Act'.[38] Thus, the bill would have compromised the sovereignty of Pakistan.

Jinnah, recognizing the extensive powers vested in the governor general by the Government of India Act 1935, concluded that he could not trust anyone other than himself within the Muslim League leadership to hold that office. However, there is an opposing perspective on this matter. Hamdani suggests that Jinnah had expressed a desire to retire to Bombay and leave the governance of Pakistan in the hands of individuals such as Liaquat Ali Khan and Zafrullah Khan. Jinnah intended the governor general to be represented by Nawab Hamidullah Khan of Bhopal (1896–1960).[39] However, the nawab of Bhopal decided to remain in India. Therefore, Jinnah assumed the charge of governor general; he informed Mountbatten of his decision on 2 July 1947 and asked him to assume the office of India's governor general on the Congress's invitation. Mountbatten wrote in his report that Jinnah was concerned that 'unless there ... [was] a steadying influence he was afraid of what the Congress might do to Pakistan'.[40] Jalal has rightly contended that Jinnah was not a man driven by his 'megalomania', as Mountbatten thought.[41] Jinnah was an astute and visionary statesman who understood the machinations of the Congress, but he was also aware of the weaknesses of those around him. He seized a historic moment to ensure that the project he had spearheaded was not derailed or aborted. Through his foresight and acumen, Jinnah prevented any attempts to deny Pakistan its sovereign status and rights. It was his leadership from August 1947 until his death in 1948 that guaranteed Pakistan's sustainability and consolidation as an independent and sovereign state.

Early Problems

The British ruled the Indian subcontinent as a unified economic entity, with a single tariff, free trade and an integrated system of currency, credit, railways and telegraphs. However, they did not pay attention to balanced development of various geographically peripheral regions, which was particularly ironic in a subcontinent that was geographically, culturally and religiously diverse. The British model of centralized control fostered mutual alienation among the populace, rather than integration. The British were primarily concerned with their imperial interests, and not in planned development.[42] The colonial state focused all its attention on developing ports in the megalopolises of Calcutta, Bombay and Madras, which were industrial hubs located in India. Pakistan, on the other hand, was left with very little industry. Its agricultural products were transported to India's industrial centres for manufacturing and value addition before being exported. The commercial houses and banks controlling the integrated economy of the subcontinent had their headquarters in those megacities.[43]

Pakistan was a unique country, composed of two equally important parts separated by 1,930 kilometres (1,200 mi.) of Indian territory. According to the 1961 census, East Pakistan had a population of 51 million, while West Pakistan had a population of 43 million, making up a total populace of 94 million. East Pakistan was only one-sixth of the area of West Pakistan, but it had a larger population. East Pakistan had a subtropical climate with an average rainfall of 223 centimetres (88 in.) per year, while West Pakistan was situated north of the tropics and had an average rainfall of 30 centimetres (12 in.) per year. East Pakistan was prone to huge cyclones, torrential rains and devastation, but its fertile soil and extremely humid climate produced luxuriant vegetation, with rice and jute being the main crops. West Pakistan had deserts and barren hills that could not support large populations, and its agriculture depended on artificial irrigation. The high mountains in the north were the point of origin for the rivers flowing down to the Arabian Sea, and the areas irrigated by the canals from those rivers were fertile. The main crops were wheat, cotton, sugar cane, rice, maize and tobacco, with some parts of West Pakistan dotted with orange and mango orchards.

At the time of partition, East Pakistan was dealt a severe blow when Calcutta, where more than 90 per cent of the industrial units of united India were located, became part of India. East Pakistan had only 5 per cent of the industrial workers of undivided Bengal on the eve of partition. Industries, banks, insurance companies, commercial houses, import and export firms, communication centres, power stations and educational institutions were all located in Calcutta. East Pakistan produced nearly 75 per cent of jute with all its best varieties. However, not a single jute mill existed in East Pakistan, and almost all the jute produced there had to be transported to Calcutta to be manufactured into hessian and other jute products. The well-being of farmers in East Pakistan hinged on the price of jute, a factor significantly influenced by conditions in the Calcutta market. Back in 1947, East Pakistan had just one port, Chittagong, with a limited capacity of half a million tons. It took several years to increase its capacity, particularly to accommodate the growing traffic directed towards it. In the intervening period, hardly any outlet for jute and other products from East Pakistan existed, except Calcutta.

In West Pakistan, the most important cash crop was cotton. West Pakistan produced 40 per cent of the raw cotton crop in undivided India, which included some of the best medium staples of cotton of the American type. The cotton textile industry was the biggest industry in undivided

India, but at the time of partition, 380 of its 394 cotton mills were in India and just fourteen were in Pakistan. The raw cotton produced in West Pakistan was transported by railway to industrial centres such as Bombay and Ahmedabad, which in return supplied cloth to Pakistan. All said and done, the relationship between Pakistan and India at partition was that of a supplier of raw materials and an industrial producer.

In West Pakistan, agriculture was the primary source of employment for the majority of the population, with over 60 per cent of the total national income of PKR 18.6 billion in 1949–50 coming from this sector. The per capita income was PKR 237, which was slightly less than U.S.$50, or less than £25. However, education and health services were insufficient: 87 per cent of the population lived in rural areas, and only 16 per cent of the populace was literate.

In the summer of 1947, severe floods devastated the Chittagong and Noakhali districts of East Pakistan, submerging 1,295 square kilometres (500 sq. mi.) of land and destroying the rice crops. Consequently, 100,000 tons of food grains were needed by the end of the year, with the memory of the 1943 Bengal famine still fresh in people's minds. Khwaja Nazimuddin, the chief minister of East Pakistan, came to Karachi on 25 August 1947 to ensure supplies. Although West Pakistan had a rice surplus, procurement and transportation difficulties arose due to a shortage of coal in some branches of the railway system and scarce shipping.

By January 1948, a wheat shortage had emerged in West Pakistan, largely due to the massive upheaval of the refugee movement, and no surpluses were available from the outside world. The intensity of floods exacerbated the situation, with 1.4 million hectares (3.5 million ac) severely affected in West Pakistan and 600,000 tons of the autumn crop destroyed. The newly established state was grappling with these issues.

Communication

Not only were East Pakistan and West Pakistan separated by 1,930 kilometres of land, but by 4,828 kilometres (3,000 mi.) of sea. Telecommunication between the two wings was an urgent necessity. Work on the establishment of Radio Pakistan, and the acquisition of a transmitter of sufficient power, had started in 1947.[44] When Pakistan was formed in 1947, Karachi had an international airport that connected the country to the outside world, but Dhaka did not have any direct international air links. To bridge this gap, it was necessary to establish a domestic air service between the two wings of the country. This is where Orient Airways stepped in. The airline was originally registered in Calcutta on 23 October 1946, and it shifted its headquarters to Karachi after partition. The initial investment for the airline was provided by the Ispahani, Adamjee and Arag groups. Mirza Ahmad Ispahani was appointed as the first chairman of the airline, and Air Vice

Marshal O. K. Carter was hired as the general manager. In February 1947, Orient Airways acquired four Douglas DC-3s from Temple, Texas; in May, it obtained its operating licence, and by June, operations had begun.[45] At the start, the airline operated out of Isphani House on McLeod Road in Karachi, but due to a lack of technical facilities, it remained in Calcutta until such facilities were developed in Karachi. Once relocated, Orient Airways' main office was at Karachi airport. Its designated route was Kolkata–Sittwe (then known as Akyab)–Yangon (Myanmar), which marked the first postwar international operation flown by an airline registered in the British Raj.

Orient Airways played a critical role in facilitating relief operations and transportation of people between Delhi and Karachi, the respective capitals of India and Pakistan, with the help of chartered British Overseas Airways Corporation (BOAC) aircraft. Following this, the airline shifted its base to Pakistan and established a crucial link between Karachi and Dhaka. Although initially equipped with only four DC-3s, three crew and twelve mechanics, Orient Airways managed to restart its scheduled operations on the Karachi–Lahore–Peshawar, Karachi–Quetta–Lahore and Karachi–Delhi–Calcutta–Dhaka routes. By the end of 1949, it had procured ten DC-3s and three Convair 240s to serve these routes. As the demand for air travel grew, Orient Airways realized that it needed to increase its capacity, which led to the merger of the airline with others to form Pakistan International Airlines on 11 March 1955.[46]

In 1948, another private company, Pak Airways, was founded, due to the initiative of Malik Ghulam Muhammad, the finance minister. Ghulam Muhammad tried hard to extract a contribution from the nizam of Hyderabad – who, according to some, was the richest man in the world at that time – to finance Pak Air. Despite initial reluctance from the nizam, Ghulam Muhammad's persistence paid off: Pak Air's financial worries were taken care of. However, the company was poorly managed. It went into liquidation in 1949 after a series of crashes in which many notable lives were lost, including Major General Iftikhar Khan and Brigadier Sher Khan. Also with them was Qazi Musa, brother of Baluchistan Muslim League leader Qazi Isa and uncle of Qazi Faiz Isa, who later became Chief Justice of Pakistan. The plane was flying from Lahore to Karachi but crashed 105 kilometres (65 mi.) short of its intended destination.[47]

The British initiated the construction of the Assam Bengal railway in 1891 in response to the request of British tea planters who had invested in tea cultivation. Tea export at least cost-necessitated the development of the Chittagong port and Assam Bengal Railway. After Pakistan came into being, this railway was split up between Pakistan and India. East Bengal (East Pakistan) inherited 2,606 kilometres (1,620 mi.) of railway line, which was named the Eastern Bengal Railway (EBR).[48] On 1 February 1961, the East Bengal Railway was renamed the Pakistan Eastern Railway. The most pressing issue in East Pakistan at the time was the establishment of a solid foundation for communication and power. The railway tracks and rolling stock in East Pakistan had deteriorated significantly due to the heavy movement of military personnel and supplies from the Burma front during the Second World War, requiring extensive replacements. The shortage of coal was a significant obstacle to the railways' smooth operation. Inland water transport, which played a key role in East Pakistan's economy, was disorganized. West Pakistan had a slightly better position, with the Northwestern Railway being able to manage the mass movement of refugees despite the disorganization caused by disturbances in the Punjab and neighbouring areas. While the Karachi port needed repairs and expansion, it was sufficiently large for immediate needs. The network of roads in West Pakistan was the most developed in the subcontinent, partially for strategic reasons, but the scarcity of stone and challenging terrain in East Pakistan made road construction difficult and expensive.[49]

Electric Power

At the time of partition, both wings of Pakistan were plagued by electricity shortages. In West Punjab in Pakistan, a large area had relied on electricity from the Mandi Hydroelectric Works in East Punjab, which became part of India after partition. This left Pakistan without a dependable source of electricity in that region. The total installed capacity in the country was 75,028 kilowatts, but a lack of repairs and competent staff led to a decline in power generation capacity. In East Pakistan, the situation was even more dire, with a capacity of only 15,600 kilowatts. The Karnafuli Hydroelectric Project, which was supposed to alleviate the shortage, was not fully functional. The Karnafuli Hydropower Station was completed in 1962 and became the only hydropower plant in East Bengal, located about 50 kilometres (31 mi.) from Chittagong. This plant was constructed as part of the 'Karnafuli Multipurpose Project', one of the biggest water resources development projects in East Pakistan (now Bangladesh), which was started in 1957 with the help of the United States Agency for International Development (USAID).[50] To address the electricity shortage in West Pakistan, the Warsak Project was initiated in the Northwest Frontier Province. This project was a result of the cooperative effort between the Pakistani and Canadian governments. The construction of the first phase started in 1951, and by 1960–61, four generating units, each with 40-megawatt capacities, were commissioned. The Warsak Power Station is considered a monument to the friendship between Canada and Pakistan.[51] The immediate aftermath of partition exacerbated the challenges of generating electric power due to the reliance on thermal power, for which machinery had to be imported from Europe. However, the delivery of such orders was delayed by post-war reconstruction efforts in Europe. Pakistan's oil and mineral resources were yet untapped, compounding the challenge.[52]

Pakistan faced enormous challenges from the moment of its inception due to the trauma of partition. Few nations have begun their independent lives under such dire circumstances. Until 1940, most Muslims had not anticipated the possibility that British rule would soon end. Political activity was therefore primarily aimed at mounting a defence against rising Hindu influence. There was no time to debate the structure of the new state or its policies. The movement to create Pakistan between 1940 and 1947 gathered momentum, but the complications and risks of partition were unforeseen. Political leaders did not plan how to address the challenges of refugee resettlement, the shortage of administrative personnel and the maintenance of law and order, all of which arose from the mass migration. While Pakistan's creation was the outcome of the tireless struggle of Indian Muslims, the immediate aftermath of partition was characterized by significant difficulties.

Rehabilitation of Refugees

The partition of India resulted in massive migration and bloodshed, which has been extensively documented. Feeding and settling the millions who migrated was a daunting task, as was protecting the lives and properties of the Hindus and Sikhs who were leaving Pakistan. According to estimates, around 6.5 million Muslim refugees entered Pakistan, while 5.5 million Hindus and Sikhs left Pakistan, leaving behind all property that could not be easily transferred.[53] It is also reported that around 500,000 Muslims lost their lives or were abducted during this period. The mass migration resulting from the partition of India created an enormous law and order problem that was difficult to manage. Sir Robert Francis Mudie, the governor of the Punjab, expressed great concern about the lack of administrative personnel to deal with the situation. The government in the Punjab had inexperienced ministers and civil servants who were unable to adapt to the situation, and in their efforts to maintain law and order, the provincial government was becoming increasingly unpopular.[54] The entire machinery was redirected towards settling the refugees, leaving many other important tasks unattended. Attempts to recruit officers on an ad hoc basis were met with resistance from the bureaucratic establishment, which was heavily influenced by the centralized system of the British Raj. This bureaucracy was set in its ways: it believed that traditional methods were the only way to tackle the problems at hand.

To address the issue of rehabilitating refugees in West Punjab, Mian Iftikhar Uddin, the minister for refugee rehabilitation, suggested that land reform was the most appropriate solution. However, his proposal faced fierce opposition from politicians such as Chief Minister Iftikhar Hussain Khan Mamdot, Finance Minister Mian Mumtaz Muhammad Khan Daultana and Revenue Minister Sardar Shaukat Hayat Khan. Ultimately, Mian Iftikhar Uddin was forced to resign from the cabinet due to his

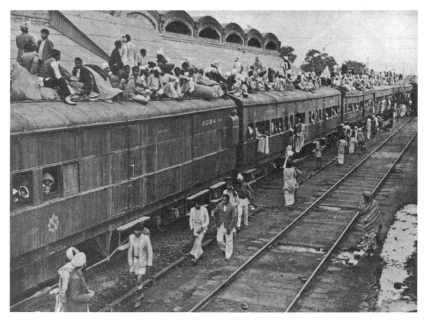

Refugees migrating from India to Pakistan, 1947.

disappointment and frustration with the lack of progress in implementing his proposed solution.[55] The situation in Sindh was similar, where the Sindhi landlords were reluctant to rehabilitate the refugees, and the provincial governments did not comply with the central government's directives on settlement. To address this issue, the central government established its own Ministry of Refugees and Rehabilitation, with the task of evacuating, feeding and settling refugees overseen primarily by two officers, E. V. Moss and Brigadier F. F. Stevens, who directed all refugee movements with the assistance of the Pakistan Army.

To deal with the crisis in a systematic manner, the Government of India (Second Amendment) Act 1948 was passed, and on 27 August 1948 Quaid-e-Azam Muhammad Ali Jinnah, the governor general of Pakistan, issued a proclamation declaring a state of emergency in Pakistan. The proclamation acknowledged the grave circumstances arising from the mass movement of peoples to and from Pakistan, which was threatening the country's economic life.

In East Pakistan, while the refugee problem was not as acute as it was in West Pakistan, the task of setting up the administrative machinery proved to be a significant challenge. The under-representation of East Bengalis in the administrative services was a major hurdle. Following partition, most key positions of administration were occupied by Punjabi- or Urdu-speaking civil servants, leaving East Bengalis marginalized. Prior to partition, only one Muslim officer from East Bengal had served in the entire Indian Civil Service.

The representation of Muslims in government services was disproportionate to their numerical strength. Out of the 1,157 officers in the Indian Civil Service and Indian Police Service, only 101 were Muslims, and out of these, 95 chose to join Pakistan. In other services, the number of officers who opted for Pakistan was relatively small, particularly in higher positions. To address this shortfall, 36 British officers were hired or retained on contract.[56] In some instances, the number of personnel opting for Pakistan in the lower cadres exceeded the country's needs and placed a strain on its scarce economic resources. Furthermore, the majority of those who opted for Pakistan were stationed in Indian areas, presenting yet another challenge for the newly formed nation. In fact, the transfer of these officials from India to Pakistan was not an easy task. An unfortunate incident occurred on 8 August 1947, when a train carrying Pakistani government personnel from Delhi to Karachi was derailed near Bhatinda due to a bomb explosion, resulting in the death of four individuals and injuries to twenty others.[57] Because of the train attack, the transportation of personnel had to be halted, and the Pakistani government resorted to hiring 26 BOAC planes for the evacuation of its employees from Delhi to Karachi. This operation, dubbed 'Operation Pakistan', commenced on 4 September 1947, and transported around 7,000 government employees. Furthermore, more than 17,000 employees and their families travelled by sea via Bombay. The process of transferring administrative personnel continued until December 1947.[58]

Financial Problems

Pakistan was primarily an agricultural economy, with limited industrial development in all of its regions. In contrast to the 394 textile mills present, only a mere fourteen textile mills were located within Pakistan's borders, and none of the 106 jute mills were within the new country. The number of registered factories in Pakistan totalled 14,677, with a meagre inheritance of 1,414, which amounted to just 9.6 per cent of the total. Furthermore, a significant portion of these inherited factories – 41.2 per cent of the total – consisted of small-scale establishments.[59] The industrial units in Pakistan were primarily focused on the processing of agricultural raw materials and operated on a seasonal basis. Owing to their location in Indian areas, assets were not shared fairly with Pakistan, and the new nation had to accept whatever it was offered, resulting in significant losses during the transfer.

The division of financial assets and liabilities between India and Pakistan was a complicated process, further exacerbated by disagreements over Pakistan's balance, including a cash balance of PKR 4 billion (equivalent to £925 million) and a public debt of PKR 18 billion. These factors compounded the economic challenges faced by Pakistan in its early years, hindering its ability to establish a strong economic foundation.[60] As of 14 August 1947, an agreement regarding the division of financial assets and liabilities between India and Pakistan had not been reached. Consequently, arbitration was sought to resolve the dispute and Pakistan received a provisional allocation of PKR 200 million and £28 million, which constituted a portion of its share in the cash and sterling balances, respectively.[61] Three months after the initial arbitration, direct negotiations between Pakistan and India resumed, resulting in a comprehensive agreement reached in December 1947. As a result, all references to arbitration were withdrawn. Pakistan's share of the financial assets was determined as follows: a cash balance of PKR 750 million, with the PKR 200 million previously drawn being subtracted; a sterling balance of £165 million, with the £28 million previously drawn being subtracted; public debt amounting to 17.5 per cent of the total, payable to India in Indian rupees in fifty equal instalments, with an initial moratorium of four years; and one-third of the military stores. The division of sixteen ordnance factories proved to be challenging, and India agreed to pay PKR 60 million towards the establishment of necessary enterprises. However, the Indian government refused to release the cash balances owed to Pakistan, citing concerns that the funds could be used in the ongoing conflict in Kashmir.[62] Eventually, it released the cash balances primarily because of the decision of the board of directors of the Reserve Bank of India on 14 January 1948. Gandhi's fast-unto-death also had some effect on the decision.

During its first fiscal year, Pakistan's available finances were insufficient to pay even one month's salary to its employees. The country faced a severe shortage of funds, not only to cover its routine expenses but for the rehabilitation of refugees and the upkeep of the armed forces. Despite its efforts to secure financial assistance from commonwealth countries, Muslim countries and the United States, Pakistan was unable to generate the necessary funds. Fortunately, the financial crisis was averted by a timely loan of PKR 200 million from the Hyderabad state in October 1947. This loan provided much-needed relief to Pakistan, enabling it to address its immediate financial challenges and lay the groundwork for a more stable economic future.[63]

Despite the issues faced by Pakistan in its early years, the situation began to improve from December 1947 onwards. In fact, Pakistan's first budget ended with a surplus, indicating positive economic progress. Another important development was the establishment of the State Bank of Pakistan in July 1948, which took over the responsibility of handling currency from the Reserve Bank of India. This move allowed Pakistan to have greater control over its monetary policy and to manage its economic affairs more effectively and independently. These developments were important steps towards building a more stable and prosperous Pakistan, despite the significant challenges that lay ahead.

Armed Forces

The original plan of the British was to keep the Indian Army and Pakistan Army under one British leader.[64] However, this proposal was met with resistance from Jinnah, who insisted on the creation of independent armed forces. On 7 April 1947, Liaquat Ali Khan submitted a note to Lord Mountbatten outlining specific demands related to the division of the armed forces of undivided India. Initially hesitant, the British eventually agreed to the Muslim League's proposal for separate armed forces for Pakistan. Jinnah was adamant that the All-India Muslim League would not assume power without control over a separate, predominantly Muslim army of appreciable strength. The process of creating a separate military began in July, with the formation of an Armed Forces Reconstitution Committee, chaired by Sir Claude Auchinleck, the commander-in-chief. Four subcommittees were established to oversee the Army, the Navy, the Air Force and the division of financial assets. Auchinleck was designated as the supreme commander, responsible to the Joint Defence Council, which comprised Mountbatten as chairman, Liaquat Ali Khan and Baldev Singh as defence ministers of Pakistan and India, respectively, and Auchinleck himself. This complex arrangement allowed for the creation of separate armed forces and set the stage for the development of the military institutions that continue to play a critical role in the defence of Pakistan today.[65] However, the council had no operational control over the forces of either dominion other than the Punjab Boundary Force. Initially, 1 April 1948 was the deadline for the division of armed forces, but it was preponed to 1 December 1947.[66]

After Pakistan gained independence, it inherited an army composed mainly of Muslim units stationed within its borders, with General Sir Frank Messervy as the first commander-in-chief. However, there was still a need to transfer Muslim-majority units stationed outside of Pakistan's territorial limits, as well as voluntary transfers from Muslim-minority units. The process of dividing military stores was also complex: the Joint Defence Council allocated one-third of the stores to Pakistan, but most of these were located in Indian territory.

Upon the inception of Pakistan's nascent armed forces, a stark disparity in their capabilities relative to their Indian counterparts became evident. In this context, Stephen P. Cohen has expounded on the distribution of military assets between India and Pakistan. Pakistan found itself in possession of a mere six armoured regiments, juxtaposed with India's formidable fourteen. Similarly, Pakistan's allotment comprised eight artillery regiments in contrast to India's commanding forty, and a meagre eight infantry regiments vis-à-vis India's robust complement of 21.[67]

Among the fixed installations accorded to Pakistan were the prestigious Staff College, strategically situated in Quetta, and the Royal Indian Army Service Corps School, situated at Kakul. Additionally, Pakistan secured several miscellaneous facilities and regimental training centres. Notably, it also inherited vital naval facilities at Karachi and Chittagong, alongside the antiquated defensive infrastructure located in the Northwest Frontier.

The initial blueprint for Pakistan's armed forces envisioned an army comprising 150,000 soldiers, led by a corps of 4,000 officers. However, in reality, only 2,500 officers were available at the outset. Following the proclamation of Pakistan as a sovereign nation on 14–15 August 1947, the stark discrepancy in senior leadership became apparent. At that juncture, Pakistan could boast of only a solitary major general, flanked by two brigadiers and six colonels, while the requisite complement called for thirteen generals, forty brigadiers and 53 colonels. This glaring void was partially bridged by the recruitment of approximately five hundred contracted British officers, with 355 already stationed within Pakistan and an additional 129 freshly enlisted from England. Among them was Major General Walter Joseph Cawthorne, an Australian-born British officer who founded Inter Services Intelligence (ISI) in 1948.[68] He headed the agency from January to June 1948. Moreover, the initial stewardship of the newly formed Army was entrusted to British generals, Sir Francis Messervy and Sir Douglas Gracey. It was not until January 1951, with the appointment of Ayub Khan, that Pakistan witnessed the elevation of its first Pakistani commander-in-chief (C-in-C).[69]

By 14 August 1947, the allocated stores were still pending, and India was not willing to release them. India accused Auchinleck of being pro-Pakistan and forced him to resign, resulting in the closure of the supreme command headquarters on 1 December. India promised to hand over Pakistan's due share of stores, but Pakistan only received a small portion of what was allocated to them. Out of Pakistan's share, it received only 23,225 out of 160,000 tons of ordnance stores, 74 out of 1,461 soft vehicles, none of the 249 armoured vehicles (which included tanks), none of the 40,000–60,000 tons of ammunition and only 1,128 out of 172,667 tons of engineering stores, including machinery. This left Pakistan at a significant disadvantage, since it had to rely on imports to build up its armed forces.[70] Despite being allocated a portion of military stores by the Joint Defence Council, Pakistan received mostly damaged and unserviceable items. As a result, it had to turn to other sources to acquire military equipment. However, Pakistan's efforts to secure military aid from other countries were largely unsuccessful. One factor was Pakistan's preference to obtain arms and ammunition on credit, which was unappealing to potential suppliers, but even when Pakistan was able to pay up front, few countries were willing to sell arms, due to the ongoing conflict in Kashmir.[71]

The formation of the Punjab Boundary Force (PBF) on 1 August 1947, consisting of mixed units with a high percentage of British officers, caused a stir. Its primary objective was to maintain law and order in the regions of the Punjab where communal unrest had erupted. The PBF was commanded by Major General T. W. Rees, and it had a strength of 55,000 soldiers.[72] However, the PBF failed to contain the communal violence, leading to widespread demand for its immediate disbandment. The PBF was disbanded on 31 August. It was replaced by area headquarters in each of the two Punjabs, which had more localized control and were better suited to addressing the communal tensions in the region. It is important to note that the PBF operated under the direct command of the supreme commander, with no authority given to the two dominions.[73]

Pakistan achieved independence on 14 August 1947, and by 1 December 1947 it had established its own independent armed forces under its own control. This was accomplished four months ahead of schedule. However, the process of organizing and consolidating the armed forces continued until early 1953. The first commander-in-chief of the Pakistani Armed Forces, General Muhammad Ayub Khan, assumed his position in January 1951. Commodore Muhammad Siddique Chaudhry took over as the naval chief in February 1953, while Air Marshal Asghar Khan became the first air chief in July 1957.[74]

Calcutta and the Fate of Bengal

From the announcement of the partition plan on 3 June 1947 to the transfer of power to the newly formed Union of India and Pakistan on 15 August of the same year, a total of 72 days had passed. While some of those days were spent sorting out major issues and establishing the partition machinery, the effective period of work was limited to the two months prescribed by Sardar Vallabhbhai Patel, first Indian home minister. Within this short period, an extensive list of problems had to be solved and countless administrative tasks had to be completed. However, the Dominion of India faced fewer and less challenging problems than Pakistan did.

The government of India in Delhi was already well established and, aside from ceasing to exercise jurisdiction over Pakistan, was expected to continue functioning in much the same way as before. Moreover, the number of British and Muslim officials who would leave its service was not large enough to require major reorganization. Diplomatic and trade missions established abroad became the responsibility of the Union of India. Meanwhile, control over the currency, banking system and various economic and financial institutions remained under the jurisdiction of the government of India. The Indian railways, ports, post and telegraph formed an integrated communication system overseen from Delhi, connecting different regions of the subcontinent. Additionally, most government-owned industrial facilities and research institutions were situated within the Indian Union. Delhi housed the central government archives and records, while Calcutta was home to the Imperial Library. The Army, Air Force and Navy headquarters were located near the Department of Defence in Delhi, and the majority of ordnance factories and military store depots were situated within the Indian Dominion. The reorganization and division of the armed forces posed fewer challenges for India compared to Pakistan.[75]

In Calcutta, there was a noticeable movement advocating for an independent Bengal, which had the potential to destabilize Pakistan. The chief minister of Bengal, Hossain Shaheed Suhrawardy, along with Sarat Chandra Bose, proposed a plan for a sovereign united Bengal that was also supported by the British governor and European stakeholders in the jute industry. Jute mills were located in and around Calcutta, where wealth had flowed for two centuries. Gandhi met with Bose, Suhrawardy and other leaders, including Abul Hashim, secretary of the Bengal Muslim League, who surprisingly supported a united Bengal on the basis of 'common language, common culture and common history'. However, Gandhi insisted that any government action must have the cooperation of at least two-thirds of the Hindu minority in the executive and legislature. This demand contradicted Gandhi's earlier opposition to the two-nation theory of Jinnah, as the Hindus in Bengal were far more advanced educationally, economically and politically than the Muslim majority. Despite this, Gandhi wanted an admission by the Muslim League that Bengal had a common culture.

Suhrawardy's proposal for a sovereign united Bengal was rooted in the recognition of the fundamental unity shared by the people of Bengal, irrespective of their religious affiliations. As the Muslims in Bengal were the majority, the proposal held significant potential to undermine the two-nation theory on which the Muslim League's vision of Pakistan rested. If the Bengal Muslim League were to renounce the two-nation theory, with Jinnah's approval, it would effectively dismantle the entire plan for Pakistan that was founded on this theory.[76]

During a conference on 20 May attended by leaders such as Sarat Chandra Bose, Suhrawardy and others, a tentative agreement for a sovereign united Bengal was drawn up. However, ultimately nothing came of it. A strong faction of Hindus, led by Hindu Mahasabha leader Shyamaprasad Mukherji, vehemently opposed the proposal for a united Bengal. Meanwhile, Gandhi persistently advocated for Hindu rule over the entire subcontinent, even before the formation of Pakistan, leading the Muslim League to adopt a stronger stance in its demand for a fully fledged Pakistan. In response, Jinnah denounced the partition of the provinces of Bengal and the Punjab and called for a corridor to link East and West Pakistan, causing a stir in the Indian press. Gandhi's anti-Pakistan campaign became increasingly aggressive, with him proclaiming on 31 May at a prayer meeting, 'Even if the whole of India burns, we shall not surrender Pakistan.' Such language was uncharacteristic of the apostle of peace and nonviolence.

The partition of the Punjab and Bengal was highly controversial, since it would cut across populated areas and impact millions, as well as disrupt the integrated economy and communication systems. The Punjab also had an extensive irrigation and hydroelectric system, which further complicated matters. Hasty and arbitrary boundary lines could result in significant economic injury and hardships for villagers. Despite the complexity of the task, it had to be completed quickly due to the deal between Mountbatten and Congress leaders for a quick transfer of power.[77]

The fate of Calcutta was the most crucial issue in Bengal. As the province's capital and centre of industry, commerce and education, as well as its only major port, it was vital to the region's economy. The Muslim peasantry of Bengal had toiled for centuries to build the wealth of the city. The Congress leaders were determined to keep Calcutta in India, while the Muslim League saw it as crucial to Pakistan's economic viability. The governor of Bengal suggested making it a free port, but this idea was rejected by Mountbatten.[78]

Muslims, who formed only one-quarter of Calcutta's population, had a strong claim to the city and its hinterland. East Bengal, which contributed the bulk of the city's resources and workforce, was a Muslim-majority area, and Scheduled Castes (historically disadvantaged and marginalized communities, particularly those from the lower strata of the caste system), who allied with the Muslim League, made up a large section of Calcutta's population. If a free plebiscite were held, Pakistan would likely win. Mountbatten knew the importance of Calcutta to the Muslim League and expressed concern at a staff meeting about its future. A plebiscite might give the 'wrong answer', so he did not lay down a procedure for self-determination.[79] It is evident that Mountbatten was not impartial: his preference for India was revealed through a secret agreement with the Congress leaders to retain Calcutta. This fact was later disclosed by the Congress leader Sardar Patel, who shared that the Congress had made it a condition of partition that Calcutta should not be included in Pakistan. Patel reiterated the city's significance to India, stating that losing Calcutta would be equivalent to losing India itself, since it played a vital role in India's economic and political landscape.[80] Clearly, this condition could only have been negotiated with Mountbatten. On 2 July 1947, Ismay presented Mountbatten's initial partition plan to the British government in London to seek its approval. The plan stipulated that 'Eastern Bengal and West Punjab were to be allocated to Pakistan and Western Bengal (including Calcutta) and the Eastern Punjab were to go to India. The Boundary Commission, with a British chairman and one Hindu and one Muslim as members, would demarcate the borders.'[81] The deliberate exclusion of the Muslim League from Mountbatten's plan to transfer Calcutta to India, a pivotal aspect of his partition proposal, becomes more comprehensible when viewed in context. Mountbatten recognized that if the Congress Party's stance on Calcutta's fate was openly integrated into the partition plan, the Muslim League would vehemently reject it. Instead, the Muslim League was led to believe that the ultimate decision on this matter would be made by the boundary commission.

These details shed light on Nehru's reluctance to entrust the United Nations with the boundary demarcation and Mountbatten's dismissal of Quaid-e-Azam's suggestion to involve three British law lords in the boundary commission. Additionally, these facts clarify why the fate of Calcutta became public knowledge several days before Radcliffe issued his award. A leak had occurred, revealing that Calcutta was slated to be assigned to India. Ian Stephens, who served as the editor of *The Statesman* at that time, reported on the timing of Radcliffe's award and the leak regarding Calcutta's disposition.[82]

When tasked with the assignment of Calcutta, Sir Cyril Radcliffe confronted two pivotal questions that held significant ramifications for the Indian subcontinent's partition in 1947. His decision-making process was influenced by several factors, and it is imperative to understand the rationale behind his choices. First, Radcliffe grappled with the dilemma of determining which newly formed state, either India or Pakistan, should lay claim to Calcutta. This question carried profound implications, as Calcutta was a major cultural, economic and political centre in British India. Its strategic location and historical significance made it a desirable asset for both nations. In his final decision, Radcliffe opted to assign Calcutta to India. This choice can be attributed to several reasons:

1 **Demographics**: Calcutta had a diverse population, including significant Hindu and Muslim communities. Radcliffe might have considered the demographic composition of the city and the surrounding areas. Assigning it to India, with its predominantly Hindu population, may have been seen as a way to maintain a certain religious balance in the two newly formed nations.
2 **Economic importance**: Calcutta was the economic hub of the region, hosting numerous industries and businesses. Radcliffe's decision might have been influenced by the economic interests of the respective nations. India's larger economy and industrial base could have made it a more viable choice for the city's administration.
3 **Historical ties**: Calcutta had been a significant part of British India and had historical ties to the Indian nationalist movement. These ties and its cultural importance to India could have factored into Radcliffe's decision.

Additionally, Radcliffe had to address the issue of dividing districts in the vicinity of Calcutta between India and Pakistan. He chose to assign the Muslim-majority districts of Murshidabad and Nadia to India. This decision, while contributing to India's demographic majority in Calcutta, resulted in territorial and population losses for East Bengal (which became part of Pakistan).

Furthermore, Radcliffe's decision to allocate the Chittagong Hill Tracts to Pakistan deserves mention. This choice was likely influenced by the proximity of these regions to the predominantly Muslim district of Chittagong, aligning with the principle of grouping contiguous areas with similar demographics. It is worth noting too that Radcliffe's decision to assign Calcutta to India was made without a detailed explanation provided in his final report, leaving room for speculation and debate. Nevertheless, his choices were undoubtedly shaped by a complex interplay of demographic, economic and historical factors, with the goal of achieving a somewhat balanced partition of the subcontinent.[83]

The Accession of Princely States

The issue of asserting control over princely states led to disputes, especially with the accession of Junagarh. Junagarh was the fifth-largest princely state in terms of revenue, encompassing an area of 8,643 square kilometres (3,337 sq. mi.). Despite being ruled by a Muslim leader, the majority of its population, roughly 80 percent, was non-Muslim. The state had a total population of 700,000, including residents in its subordinate territories like Mangrol and various sub-districts in the Kathiawar region, along with the state of Manavadar.[84] The areas of Junagarh, Manavadar, Mangrol and Babriawad taluka (sub-district) were not contiguous with Pakistan, despite the fact that, in September 1947, the nawabs of Junagarh and Manavadar declared their accession to Pakistan. However, the rulers of Mangrol and the landlords of Babriawad taluka, who lacked independent constitutional status, chose to accede to India. The Indian government strongly objected to Junagarh's accession, arguing that it was in blatant disregard of geographic contiguity and contrary to the wishes of the people.[85] To counter the nawab's rule, the Indian government created a provisional government led Mahatma Gandhi's nephew Samaldas Gandhi and raised an army to overthrow the nawab.

Pakistan proposed a plebiscite in Junagarh under the joint auspices of India and Pakistan, but India rejected the proposal and instead used force to annex Junagarh's three principalities. The state government of Junagarh, unable to resist Indian force and facing financial collapse, invited the Indian government to take control.

In December, a plebiscite was held, and the overwhelming majority of people (approximately 99.95 per cent) chose to join India instead of Pakistan. The propaganda campaign against the nawab and the formation of a provisional government helped to sway public opinion towards India, leading to the plebiscite's result in India's favour.[86] On 10 November 1947, the Indian government imposed an economic blockade on Junagarh and invaded it with regular army units, resulting in the state's conquest. The nawab and his family fled to Karachi before the army arrived. Pakistan was unable to retaliate due to a lack of military resources and was forced to watch helplessly as events unfolded. However, Pakistan condemned the Indian aggression and raised the issue at the UN, arguing that it was a violation of international law. India arranged a plebiscite in Junagarh under its own auspices, which Pakistan refused to accept and dismissed as spurious. However, Pakistan's objections were not acknowledged at any forum. The plebiscite resulted in an overwhelming vote in India's favour.

The next contentious issue was the Hyderabad state. It was ruled by a Muslim, the nizam, and had a non-Muslim majority. Hyderabad was supposedly the most developed state, but to South Asian Muslims it looked like a legatee of the Mughal tradition. With a total area of 212,000 square kilometres (82,000 sq. mi.) and a population of 16 million, its annual revenue was PKR 260 million, and it had its own currency and stamps.[87] It enjoyed a unique status with complete internal autonomy, and the nizam, officially designated as Britain's faithful ally, had the distinction of the title 'The Exalted Highness'.[88]

As India approached independence in 1947, the nizam of Hyderabad made the choice to abstain from aligning with either of the newly emerging dominions, with the aspiration of preserving a degree of independence for his state. Nevertheless, India employed assertive diplomatic measures to undermine his ambitions and ultimately compelled the nizam to enter into a Standstill Agreement on 29 November 1947. The main provision of the agreement was to maintain the status quo in terms of essential services and communication between Hyderabad and India. Specifically, it allowed for the continuation of services like postal, telegraphic and transportation links between the two. This agreement was intended to prevent any disruption in these critical services while negotiations were ongoing regarding the future relationship between Hyderabad and India.

India particularly resented the nizam's loan of PKR 200 million to Pakistan and his refusal to ban the Anjuman Ittehad-ul-Muslimeen, a political party that was campaigning against accession to India. India resorted to an economic blockade of the state, which impacted food supplies – an utter violation of the provisions of the Standstill Agreement.[89] India also rejected the nizam's offer to refer the differences to arbitration. Then, the nizam proposed a plebiscite under the auspices of some impartial organization on the question of the state either acceding to India or remaining independent. However, the proposal was rejected outright by India. On 24 August 1948, Hyderabad filed a complaint to the Security Council, but on 13 September, the Indian Army invaded the state, occupying it completely within four days.[90] The council did not hear the complaint, which is still gathering dust somewhere in its archives.

At the birth of Pakistan, the expectation 'had always been that Muslim majority (states) provinces that were contiguous to Pakistan would accede to it. India, which also had a small area that abutted Kashmir, had similar hopes, with Nehru, himself a Kashmiri pandit, seeing the state as an integral part of the Indian union.'[91] According to the census report of 1941, Kashmir's total population was 4,021,616, out of which 3,101,247 citizens were Muslims, comprising 77 per cent of the population. This gave Muslims a clear majority in the areas of the Kashmir province and the Frontier districts.[92] Jammu and Udhampur were the only districts where non-Muslims were in a slight majority. Kashmir had been ruled by the Dogra family since 1846, when the Treaty of Amritsar was concluded between Gulab Singh and the British and Kashmir was handed over to the ruler for PKR 7.5 million.[93] At the time of the partition of India, Hari Singh was Kashmir's maharaja and final Dogra monarch.

The two major routes connecting Kashmir to British India passed through territories that went to Pakistan: the Rawalpindi–Murree–Baramula–Srinagar Road, which followed the Jhelum River for part of the way, and the Sialkot–Jammu–Srinagar Road, which crossed the 2,743-metre-high (9,000 ft) Banihal Pass in the Pir Panjal Range. In the north, the Indus Valley provided a connection for Gilgit to the area that would become Pakistan. The criticality of these links between Kashmir, India and Pakistan was to be borne out as the drama of partition unfolded. Ayesha Jalal is of the opinion that 'in the all-too-frequent exchanges of words and bullets, a great deal of objective ground has been lost, figuratively as well as literally. To attempt to apportion blame simply to strike a sympathetic chord in one or the other camp would be an exercise in historiographical futility.'[94] In such a circumstance, according to Jalal, steering a middle course 'might be an even more hazardous option, but it might at least help dispel some of the clouds that have dulled any understanding of the wide-ranging impact of the Kashmir dispute on internal developments in Pakistan'.[95]

The accession of the princely state of Chitral to Pakistan marked a significant turning point in the regional dynamics of South Asia, particularly due to its unique geographical location and historical connections. Situated at the crossroads of China, Russia and Afghanistan, Chitral held strategic importance as a point of confluence in the region. Its historical ties with Kashmir dating back to 1854 added complexity to the situation.

Chitral's decision to join Pakistan in the wake of partition triggered a dispute that reverberated through the region. This dispute was also influenced by the intricate web of political and ethnic factors in play. The accession of Chitral had implications for the broader regional balance of power and raised questions about the alignment of princely states in the aftermath of colonial rule.

The dispute surrounding Chitral's accession to Pakistan became a focal point for discussions and negotiations among various stakeholders, including India, Pakistan and the local populations of Chitral.[96] The disquiet between the two dominions was compounded when the Boundary

Commission made the decision to award Gurdaspur, a district with a slight Muslim majority, to India. Importantly, Gurdaspur had just one *tehsil* with a non-Muslim majority, Pathankot, which provided a vital link between Kashmir and India. This enabled India to despatch its troops to the predominantly Muslim state of Kashmir, with Mountbatten as its accomplice, to procure a controversial letter of accession from Maharaja Hari Singh.

It is crucial to recognize and acknowledge the significant and instrumental role played by V. P. Menon, a senior civil servant and constitutional advisor to the government of India, whose diplomatic skills and negotiations were pivotal in securing the accession of Jammu and Kashmir to India, a decision that had far-reaching consequences for the region's history and geopolitics.[97]

Concomitantly, the situation inside the state had gone from bad to worse because the Muslim dissidents were demanding the abolition of Dogra rule. To quell this uprising, Hari Singh ordered his troops to launch a crackdown, which gave rise to several accounts of persecution and mass murders of Muslims in Poonch. Several Kashmiri Muslim families who settled in the Rawalpindi and Jhelum districts of the Punjab had been natives of Poonch. On top of that, there was a colony of Afridi tribesmen in Poonch. The dislocated populace of that area told of the massacre of Muslims by Dogra troops in harrowing detail. Some were undoubtedly exaggerated, but passions were stirred in both the Punjab and NWFP. As Jalal states, 'The tribesmen, attracted by opportunities to loot and plunder afforded by the withdrawal of British rule, swung into action under the noble pretext of saving their Muslim brethren.'[98] While it is difficult to establish the understandings, if any, given to the tribesmen by the Pakistani government, it is almost an established fact that the incursions were actively encouraged by government officials in NWFP. Khan Abdul Qayyum Khan, the Muslim League chief minister of the NWFP, who himself was from Poonch, oversaw the whole campaign.[99] It was at Qayyum's behest that petrol was supplied, grain rations were provided and transportation was made available to tribal volunteers.[100] Jalal contends that 'by assisting the comings and goings of armed tribesmen from the Kashmir border, the government inadvertently contributed to the already considerable law and order problem in Western Punjab and the North-West Frontier Province.'[101] One cannot help but draw the conclusion that the Pakistani government, in cahoots with the Frontier ministry, was actively fanning the flames of communal sentiments that provided the stimulus for the tribesmen to invade Kashmir. The Pakistani government refrained from officially committing the Army in Kashmir, primarily because of the severe shortage of arms and ammunition, not because it was the 'preferred course of action'.[102] Pakistani military officers, ostensibly on leave from the Army, were certainly fighting alongside the Azad Forces, a conglomerate of Kashmiri Muslims and Pathan tribesmen. The Pakistan Army regulars who were believed to be part of the Azad Forces were no more than 5 per cent of the total force. The Azad Forces relied greatly on supplies and equipment from the Pakistan Army depot, and their commander-in-chief was in fact Pakistan Army officer Colonel Muhammad Akbar, who went under the pseudonym of General Tariq. He had been in very close contact with Qayyum Khan throughout the campaign.

The facts furnished above controvert the Pakistani claim that it was not involved in the actual fighting in Kashmir. The reluctance of the Pakistani Army command to commit itself wholeheartedly in the Kashmir war is an understudied fact. They wanted a ceasefire, but they also wanted the tribesmen to remain engaged in the campaign. So long as 'they stuck to the tactics deployed against British troops, they would cause continual embarrassment and a steady toll of casualties'.[103] This situation led to a sense of uncertainty, which resulted in a division among the senior ranks of the Pakistani Army. Some advocated for direct intervention in Kashmir, while others opposed such a course of action. The top brass did not harbour any intention of waging all-out war against India, but they pressed the Pakistani government to make 'sorties in foreign armaments markets'.[104] Arms and ammunition, the necessary accoutrement for the Army, needed to be secured in order to bolster the defence establishment, whose leadership was in two minds regarding the plausibility of a military solution of the Kashmir issue.

The adventure in Kashmir cost the two dominions heavily, but the drain on Pakistani resources was more tangible, and the consequences for its internal political configuration more severe than those for India. The fact remains, however, that the rebels threatened to capture Srinagar and make the accession a fait accompli. At this point, Hari Singh acceded to India, accepting the condition that doing so would subsequently be ratified by the people of Kashmir through a referendum.[105] It also should be highlighted here that Nehru, at Mountbatten's bidding, referred the dispute to the UN in December 1947, and accepted a Security Council resolution that called for a plebiscite to be held subject to the withdrawal of all troops from Kashmir.[106] All this notwithstanding, the hostilities between India and Pakistan with respect to Jammu and Kashmir continued throughout 1948. The formal ceasefire took effect on 1 January 1949, marking the de facto division of the state between India and Pakistan. It was to be divided permanently to become the oldest unresolved conflict before the UN, with the western territory under Pakistani control, and two-thirds of Jammu and Kashmir under Indian occupation, including Srinagar.

Indian governance in the former princely state of Kashmir rested on two key pillars: first, the province's special status within the Indian Constitution, safeguarded by Article 370. This article limited the central government's authority to specific areas such as foreign affairs, defence, currency and communications. Second, the National Conference, led by the charismatic Sheikh Abdullah, enjoyed significant popularity. However, Sheikh Abdullah's aspirations for greater autonomy and self-rule faced challenges in the 1950s owing to the rise of Hindu communalism, which constrained Prime Minister Nehru's ability to act freely. Consequently, Sheikh Abdullah was arrested and subsequently detained for nearly two decades. During this time, a compliant Provincial Assembly formally voted for the state's merger with India in 1956.

The Kashmir dispute became a matter of vigorous contention at the United Nations, with Pakistan actively opposing it. Despite the UN General Assembly's persistent efforts to pass a Security Council resolution on the issue, the Soviet Union used its veto power to prevent its passage.

Water Dispute

In the undivided Punjab, agriculture relied entirely on the unified system of irrigation, which consisted of six rivers and thirty canals. The Punjab Partition Committee faced a daunting task in resolving the water issue. The committee declared that the authorized share of the various canals to which the two zones (East Punjab and West Punjab) were entitled could not be changed.[107] The Muslim League representatives, who were not members of the Partition Committee, did not demand clearer assurances for an equitable share of water resources. When Cyril Radcliffe partitioned India, he assigned the major headworks (Madhopur Headworks and Ferozepur control points of the upper Bari Doab canals) that controlled the waters flowing into West Punjab and the Bahawalpur state to Indian Punjab, but he also promised to respect the existing share of water. However, on 1 April 1948, when the arbitral tribunal was dissolved, India cut off water supplies to the Dipalpur canal in West Pakistan. This affected 671,778 hectares (1.66 million ac) of land, which was 5.5 per cent of the sown area of West Pakistan at a crucial time in the agricultural year – the sowing of the Kharif crop. The Muslim League representatives did not use their influence to obtain a more favourable outcome, and the situation remained unresolved until a Pakistani delegation went to Delhi in May 1948 to negotiate. India maintained that Pakistan had no right to the waters, which Pakistan refused to accept. The deadlock was finally broken on 4 May when both sides agreed to a joint statement that outlined their respective claims and allowed for the water to be restored on a cash-payment basis. However, the issue of proprietary rights in the waters of the rivers remained contentious, and the construction of new canals and the raising of the capacity of the Bhakra Dam led to a reduction in water supplies to Pakistan's canals.[108] In light of this situation, a Pakistani delegation was sent to Delhi in May 1948 to resolve the water dispute. Pakistan was compelled to reject India's precondition that it had no rights to the waters. Nonetheless, on 4 May, a joint statement was issued that acknowledged the respective claims of East and

West Punjab and restored the water supply for cash payment. Both sides agreed to continue the dialogue while examining the legal and logistical issues. Although water was made available for Dipalpur, the Bahawalpur canals remained dry. In July, negotiations resumed, but India's claim that the proprietary rights of the rivers' waters were vested in the East Punjab government created another complication.[109] The issue of sharing Indus River water between India and Pakistan remained unresolved for several years, despite negotiations. Finally, in September 1953, the president of the World Bank, Eugene R. Black, stepped in to arbitrate. However, it took a few more years before a resolution was reached through the Indus Water Basin Treaty, which was finally concluded in September 1960. As part of the treaty, the Indus Waters Commission was established on a permanent basis, and the waters of the Indus, Jhelum and Chenab were assigned to Pakistan. To facilitate the transfer of water to areas previously irrigated by the eastern Ravi, Sutlej and Beas rivers, 644 kilometres (400 mi.) of canals were dug out – a project financed by international sources.

After partition, Pakistan faced numerous challenges, with limited resources and options to overcome them. The political leadership was ill-prepared for the magnitude of issues that arose, such as the rehabilitation of refugees, economic handicaps and inadequate infrastructure. These factors made the situation quite daunting for the Pakistani leadership. In hindsight, it is clear that the majority of Muslim League leaders did not anticipate the difficulties that would arise immediately after the establishment of Pakistan. Tensions with India that had arisen from the partition process exacerbated the situation. The accession of princely states resulted in negative feelings on both sides, and the Kashmir dispute had brought Pakistan and India to the brink of war, causing the former to become a security state where the Army wielded unprecedented power at the expense of democratic forces. The ascension of a military–bureaucratic oligarchy to a position of substantial power, surpassing the authority of democratic institutions, has engendered a multifaceted predicament. One key consequence of this power shift is the diversion of critical resources and attention away from the vital task of fortifying democratic institutions. Instead, what we witness is a pronounced preference for executive responses, where the executive branch, typically helmed by a head of state or government, becomes the central locus of decision-making and policy execution.

5
The Faltering Years of a Nascent State, 1947–58

In a culturally and ethnically diverse country such as Pakistan, maintaining political stability is of utmost importance. Given Pakistan's pluralistic nature, a democratic system with a bottom-up approach is essential to ensure the country's territorial and political integrity. The fair distribution of economic and environmental resources such as water and gas among the provinces can only be achieved through democratic means. Pakistan was initially established as a parliamentary democracy modelled on the Westminster system. However, the country's political system has also been shaped by religious ideology, creating a persistent contradiction in its polity that has hindered its transition to democracy. While there is no single cause for Pakistan's struggle to embrace democracy fully, the failure of politicians to forge consensus on important issues has certainly played a role.

One key challenge has been striking a balance between colonial legacy and the realities of postcolonial Pakistan. This requires broad consensus across the political spectrum to facilitate the reforms necessary to nurture democracy in the new state. Unfortunately, mistrust and dissension among political leaders have led to delays in constitutional framing and in the implementation of necessary administrative reforms. As a result, policies formulated by state institutions have failed to reflect the aspirations of the people – a pattern that is perpetuated to this day.

This chapter delves into the colonial context of Pakistan, and the ways in which the military–bureaucratic oligarchy has manipulated political events to its advantage. Additionally, it explores the politics of religious groups and factions, which have exacerbated regional tensions. One issue in particular, the question of the national language, has contributed to these regional dissensions. Although the 1956 Constitution attempted to address this problem, it was implemented too late to make a significant impact.

A Nation State Embedded in Religious Ideology

The growth of democracy in Pakistan has been hindered by ideological confusion. Despite being a Western/modernist construct, Pakistan was ascribed an Islamic rationale, resulting in a novel connotation of nationalism that is a theoretical quandary of immense proportion. The founding fathers of Pakistan failed to come up with a creative synthesis between local administrative–legislative structures and the Western notion of democracy that is informed by the ideals of the enlightenment. As a result, Muslims in India appropriated the concept of democracy without resolving the core issue of territoriality and the sanctity that nationalism accords it, which runs counter to the concept of umma as projected in Islamic political thought.

The Objectives Resolution, passed on 12 March 1949, was a significant step towards this state of ambivalence since it allowed excessive space for the religious element in the social and political setting of Pakistan. Justice Muhammad Munir argues in his book *From Jinnah to Zia* that this would likely not have occurred if Jinnah had remained alive.[1] Jinnah's absence led to an increased religious influence in the state, further complicating the already confusing ideology of Pakistan.

The Objectives Resolution, which was passed by the Muslim League prime minister Liaquat Ali Khan, declared that Pakistan's future would be based on the principles of Islam. However, the resolution's first clause, 'Sovereignty lies with Allah', caused concern among Hindu representatives in the Constituent Assembly from East Bengal, who feared that they would be treated as second-class citizens. Despite reservations being expressed, the resolution was hastily passed without due consideration. Joginder Nath Mandal, the Hindu president of the Constituent Assembly and Pakistan's first law minister, was so dismayed by his colleagues' disregard for the rights of minorities that he resigned and left the country. He felt that Pakistan was not the nation envisioned by Jinnah and that minorities were suffocated and threatened in the country, contrary to the security that Jinnah had promised. The pluralistic and secular spirit of democracy was severely distorted, which led to political instability and authoritarianism, which in turn fostered religious fundamentalism and sectarianism in the 1980s and '90s. After 9/11, these problems became so acute that they posed an existential threat to the state. Pakistan's immensely centralized state structure, inherited from the British, failed to reflect its political and cultural diversity, and the ruling elite could not reinvent it to serve the people's needs. The Objectives Resolution legitimized religious fundamentalism as the glue meant to bind the disparate units of the country together, while also providing an ideological underpinning to the centralized state structure. This led to the suppression of regional voices and aspirations. However, from the 1970s onwards, religious political parties were able to maintain their electoral base only in certain regional pockets, because they had no answers for the people's socio-economic needs. The notion that Deobandi ulema (Islamic scholars) were opposed to the creation of Pakistan is a common misperception among the liberal section of Pakistani society. As Ishtiaq Hussain Qureshi argues in his book *Ulema in Politics*, Deobandi opinion on the creation of Pakistan was actually divided.[2] Abul Kalam Azad, Abul Hassan Nadvi and Hussain Ahmed Madni were opposed to the idea of Pakistan, whereas Shabbir Usmani, Zafar Ahmad Ansari, Mufti Muhammad Shafi and Jamal Mian were strong supporters of a separate state for Indian Muslims. These *maulanas* (religious clerics) and religious parties remained influential political voices in Pakistan's history. Jamiat Ulema-e-Islam and Jamaat-e-Islami emerged as the main proponents of religious politics in post-1949 Pakistan. However, it was during the 1980s, under the patronage of General Zia ul Haq, that they were thrust onto the centre stage of Pakistani politics. The Afghan Jihad, resisting the Soviet occupation from 1979 to 1989, was pivotal for the Middle East and South Asia. It boosted Mujahideen prominence and laid the foundation for groups like Al-Qaeda. Supported by Saudi Arabia and the United States, it fuelled a diverse Mujahideen resistance. This conflict also influenced Islamic seminaries, promoting puritanical Islam in Pakistan and Afghanistan, indirectly funded by the United States. The Afghan Jihad led to the rise of extremist ideologies with fighters like Osama bin Laden, and its aftermath contributed to the Taliban's emergence and Al-Qaeda's global terrorism. In summary, it shaped global geopolitics and radical Islamist ideologies, with Saudi and U.S. support, leaving a lasting impact on world affairs. This led to a rise in sectarianism and suicide bombings, as Islamist groups with differing ideologies engaged in violent conflict.

Such a situation, characterized by unilateralism and religious extremism, hindered the establishment of democracy in Pakistan, and gave rise to fissiparous tendencies brewing up in smaller provinces, posing a continuous threat to the federal structure of the state. Furthermore, the social and cultural plurality necessary for civil society to flourish was condemned by those in power.

After Pakistan's creation, many ulema from East Punjab, the United Provinces and Bihar migrated to Pakistan. Seminaries upholding the puritanical version of Islam were relocated to major Pakistani cities, such as Khair-ul-Madaris in Multan, Jamia Salafia, Faisalabad and Madrissa Banori Town in Karachi, with the optimism that Pakistan would become an Islamic state. Many of them subscribed to the Deobandi denomination.[3] The religious leaders' influence on the government and state officials was evident in the Objectives Resolution, which had a tangible impact on state policy. This resolution included declarations such as 'sovereignty rests with Allah' and 'He delegates sovereignty to the people', which contradict the principles of democracy.[4] Besides, such clauses provided a sufficient niche to the clerics in the realm of statecraft and politics because of their supposed expertise on the ecclesiastical commands of Allah. The Anti-Qadiani movement in 1953 was the corollary of the religious activism spearheaded by the ulema.[5] Almost twenty years later, the movement culminated in their denunciation as non-Muslims in 1974.[6] Besides, it also provided a background to the policy of Islamization subsequently pursued by General Zia ul Haq, which was punctuated with statutory laws such as the Hudood Ordinance, or blasphemy law during the Nawaz Sharif era. The repercussions that unfolded from the 1980s onwards were the astronomical rise in sectarianism and militancy, exemplified by suicide bombing and targeted killing.

In 1949, an often-overlooked historical development occurred, which has eluded the scrutiny of most historians and political theorists: the establishment of an entity known as the Majlis-i-Tahafuz-i-Khatam-i-Nabuwwat or the Assembly to Safeguard the Finality of Prophethood. This assembly operated as a subsidiary organization of the Majlis-i-Ahrar-Islam, a religious Muslim political party that was founded in 1929 and vehemently opposed the creation of Pakistan. During the 1946 elections, the Majlis-i-Ahrar had actively protested against the Muslim League, articulating a manifesto that outrightly rejected the notion of a separate state. However, they were decisively defeated in these elections. Following the establishment of Pakistan, the leadership of the party opted for a more subdued presence within the newly formed nation.

For the next two years Majlis-i-Ahrar stayed in the shadows, but, in 1949, rebranded as Majlis-i-Tahfuz-i-Khatam-i-Nabuwwat (MTKN), it re-emerged. Following Jinnah's demise, the version of Islam that gained currency in Pakistan sprouted from the exclusionary and puritanical interpretation propagated by the MTKN. The MTKN was founded by Ahrar leaders in a small town of the Punjab, Toba Tek Singh, in January 1949. Its fundamental aim was to cast the followers of the Ahmadi sect, the followers of Mirza Ghulam Ahmed, out of the pale of Islam.[7] The MTKN orchestrated the anti-Ahmadi movement, which mounted a challenge to the state authorities in 1953 and exerted extreme pressure on the Nazimuddin government, but failed to achieve its objectives. However, it did launch the political careers of several religious leaders who previously held no prominence. This event had significant and far-reaching consequences in South Asian politics and is considered the most historically influential outcome of the rise of the MTKN – the emergence of the religious right in Pakistani politics and the gradual exclusion of various progressive, leftist and centrist political groups. Meanwhile, as the anti-Ahmadi movement gained momentum, the Pakistani state was grappling with an acute wheat crisis in 1952–3, a major challenge for the central government that distracted them from addressing the challenge posed by the MTKN.[8] This challenge, along with those of other religio-political groups, would prove so severe that it led to the downfall of both the central government and the Punjab government, dealing a catastrophic blow to the state of Pakistan.[9]

The downfall of the governments, causing political instability, was contrary to what the founder of Pakistan envisioned when he spoke on 11 August 1947 while addressing the Constituent Assembly. The crux of the speech is encapsulated in a few sentences:

Mazar-e-Quaid, mausoleum of Muhammad Ali Jinnah, Karachi.

Now I think you should keep in front of us as our ideal, and you will find that in course of time Hindus would cease to be Hindus and Muslims would cease to be Muslims, not in the religious sense, because that is the personal faith of each individual, but in the political sense as citizens of the State.[10]

The idea that Islam would serve as the cornerstone of Pakistan had been pivotal to the argument for a separate state since March 1940, marking the beginning of a serious push towards independence. However, just days before Pakistan's formation, its leader, Jinnah, put forth an inclusive agenda for the new country. As a political visionary, he sought to reconcile the inherent contradiction that came with founding a nation state on the basis of religious identity. Unfortunately, Jinnah's death just over a year later in September 1948 meant that his vision would remain unfulfilled. The Pakistan that emerged in 1949 was not what Jinnah had envisaged, just as modern India does not fully embody the ideals of its founding inspiration, Gandhi. This is a prevailing trend in contemporary South Asian politics – that the visions of the founding fathers have been compromised and overtaken by subsequent generations.[11]

Civil–Military Oligarchy and Inept Politicians

From the very beginning, democracy was severely hindered by the self-serving attitudes of the ruling elite in Pakistan. The Muslim League leadership itself was a major obstacle to the smooth development of democracy. Democratic norms were not practised within the party, and it eventually became a tool for the oligarchs who held power. Furthermore, most of the party's leaders in West Pakistan belonged to the landed aristocracy, and thus did not represent the common people. The leaders also failed to agree on the fundamental rules of the game, leading to the Muslim League's division into various factions. Iftikhar Hussain Khan Mamdot and Mumtaz Daultana led their own factions and were at odds with each other. In such a situation, the Muslim League's political cadre was unable to grow into a strong political force. As the Pakistani political scientist Hasan Askari Rizvi argues, 'the Muslim League failed to reinvent itself as a nationalist party that could lead the nation towards democracy, stability and prosperity.'[12]

The Muslim League could not develop the 'procedures of internal discussion and collective leadership'.[13] Its political outreach extended to the key Muslim-majority provinces of Bengal and the Punjab after 1937, but many Muslim leaders only joined the party when the creation of Pakistan seemed inevitable.[14] Rizvi notes that the Unionist Ministry in the Punjab is a good example of this trend. They opposed the Muslim League until early 1947, when they withdrew from the political scene after realizing that their efforts would not succeed. Some of their members joined the Muslim League during 1945–6, while others remained silent observers.[15]

Several political leaders who occupied positions of immense significance joined the ranks of the Muslim League between 1944 and 1947, but their experience of working with the party's rank and file was extremely limited. Instead of advancing the party's cause, they invested their energies in pursuing their personal political aspirations, without any regard for the harm they caused along the way. As Keith Callard observed about Pakistani politicians in the 1950s,

> a large number of leading persons ... with their political dependents, form loose agreements to achieve power and to maintain it. Consequently, rigid adherence to a policy or a measure is likely to make a politician less available for office. Those who lacked fixed ideas but who controlled legislators, money, or influence tended to prosper.[16]

Callard's assertion alludes to the establishment pulling political strings from the very outset. Successive governments in early postcolonial Pakistan opposed the growth of a healthy opposition and repressed dissenting voices using three methods. First, they resorted to brutal measures to suppress opposition, including the frequent use of punitive measures such as arresting opposition members and imprisoning them. Public meetings and processions were also prohibited. To further restrain opposition, the Public and Representative Office (Disqualification) Act, commonly referred to as PRODA, was introduced in 1949. This Act authorized the government to bar individuals found guilty of misconduct in any public office or representative capacity from public life for a specified period of time. The governor general or provincial governor could refer charges of misconduct against any person in public office to a special tribunal. During the five years of PRODA's existence, seven cases were referred to the tribunal, resulting in convictions of four political leaders: Ayub Khuhro, Kazi Fazlullah, Ghulam Nabi Khan Pathan and Hamid ul Haq. The tribunal made adverse remarks against Ghulam Ali Talpur, but did not convict him, and proceedings against Mumtaz Daultana could not be completed.[17]

Second, financial and material favours were extended to garner political support. Import permits and different sorts of licences were issued for political purposes. Politicians sold those permits to businessmen and made huge amounts of money. Similarly, in the rural areas, licences to keep arms were issued on the recommendation of district-level leaders of the party in power. The Pakistani British political activist Tariq Ali makes an important point here. He maintains, 'As governments changed rapidly and ministers were replaced with monotonous regularity, the Civil Service became responsible for granting import and export licenses, government loans and route permits for private bus companies, and by this distribution of patronage it acquired great political influence.'[18]

Third, ministerial positions were offered to those meant to be wooed in the ranks of the party in power. In 1958, 'when Ayub-Mirza declared martial law, 26 out of 80 members were holding ministerial posts. That pattern of political patronage continues even until today.'[19]

While it is commonly believed that Jinnah's early death was a tragic event that prevented Pakistan's democracy from flourishing, historical evidence suggests otherwise. The allocation of executive powers to the governor general, following the Westminster democratic model, was highly unusual and resulted in the prime minister having little actual power.[20] Moreover, Jinnah favoured bureaucrats over his fellow politicians, which strengthened non-political elements in Pakistan, further diminishing the role of the political cadres of the Muslim League. In the 1950s, a bureaucratic–military oligarchy emerged and made all the major decisions, preventing the evolution of strong political cadres and delaying the establishment of a constitution and free and fair elections. Constitution-making and elections would have threatened the unchecked powers of the bureaucracy, which was represented by figures such as Malik Ghulam Muhammad, Chaudhry Muhammad Ali and Iskandar Mirza. This trio, along with General Ayub Khan, guided Pakistan through the 1950s, which can rightly be called a decade of bureaucratic, rather than democratic or civilian, rule. Nevertheless, it is important to recognize that this oligarchic rule was dominated by military leaders and West Pakistani feudal politicians, with bureaucrats holding the most significant power. The Pakistani social scientist Hamza Alavi's concept of the 'overdeveloped state' is pertinent in understanding the impact of the two colonial institutions and their role in impeding efforts to bring political stability to the country.[21]

Pakistani autocrats, whether civilian or military, have always sought a pliable judiciary, making it impossible for the Pakistani courts to be independent and pro-people. From the days of Justice Munir to Justice Qazi Faiz Isa, Pakistani courts have often validated the arbitrary acts of Army generals, usurping power to the detriment of constitutional rule. However, Justice Rustum Kyani, Justice Cornelius and Justice Durab Patel were exceptions who had the courage to stand firm in the face of such indiscretion. Unfortunately, the majority of judges found no crises of conscience in taking oaths under the Provisional Constitutional Orders, as repeated during successive authoritarian regimes.

Moving from institutional hindrances to democratization to the ideological context, it is essential to reiterate that ambivalence about the role of religion in public and political life has caused conceptual and ideological confusion among the literati. Pakistan, conceived as a nation state for the Muslims of India, became an 'ideological' polity with religion as the fundamental rationale for its existence. However, this amalgamation of modernity (democracy as a Western construct) and tradition (articulated in Islam steeped in its primordial/literalist context) has provided a justification for clerics to challenge the writ of the state in the name of religion. The literalist version of Islam propagated in South Asia since the last quarter of the nineteenth century is an ahistoricized version, reconstructed in the later part of the nineteenth century, and it seems to be frozen in time. The continuous mention of Pakistan, as the national narrative proclaims it, having been founded in the name of Islam has given clerics a free hand to destabilize the political process, which they have done with impunity. They also prevent such 'audacities' as reinterpretation of Islam through the prism of local tradition and perceive them as *bidah* (deviation). One could say that such tendencies flourished slowly but steadily over time, with the first stride in that direction being taken immediately after the birth of Pakistan. Before proceeding any further, the problems of governance that confronted Pakistan in the 1950s must be scrutinized.

Governance, in simple terms, is a process by which decisions are made and implemented. Political theorists study governance at international, national and local levels. In recent years, good governance has been regarded as a yardstick of economic development, particularly in underdeveloped economies. However, according to a few analysts, good governance is a phenomenon that democracy often poses a hurdle to achieving. China and Singapore are often cited as examples to illustrate this point. Therefore, in the case of Pakistan, decision-making in the field of economy is best left to apolitical actors, specifically economic experts who have no vested interests in Pakistani politics. These experts can act as neutral advisors, solely focused on maximizing economic growth and development for the country. This chapter aims to explore the dynamics of governance at the national level by highlighting the roles of political as well as apolitical actors involved in the formulation and implementation of decisions made in the 1950s.

In postcolonial states like Pakistan, instruments of governance were defined by the state, primarily due to Alavi's concept of the 'overdeveloped state'.[22] Theoretical features of good governance, such as the participation of all stakeholders, transparent and consensus-orientated decision-making, accountability, rule of law and minimizing corruption while incorporating marginalized groups, can hardly be observed in the fractured political fibre of Pakistan. Problems of governance can only be understood by studying the genealogy of democracy in the country, which was under-representative or undemocratic, so far as the state structure was concerned.

With the overdeveloped state structure, the prescribed aims and objectives of good governance – accountability, transparency, minimal role of the state in the economic activity and, most of all, the rule of law – could not be achieved. To realize good governance, it is essential that the policies of the state reflect the free will of the people. Unfortunately, democracy has not been able to take root smoothly in Pakistan, thus making good governance an unrealized dream. The growing defence expenditure and the virtual immunity of the Army from any measure of accountability, coupled with its continuous interference in the affairs of the state, pose a significant obstacle to the realization of democracy and thus of good governance. In addition, the state's monopoly on the decision-making process and policy implementation is another factor that hinders progress towards achieving this goal. The situation is further exacerbated when the state bureaucracy wields power without any accountability to the people.

Impediments in the Evolution of Democracy

Pakistan has had a tumultuous history with only a few brief periods of democratic rule during its 77-year existence. Parliamentary democracy has collapsed four times, largely due to mismanagement, an imbalanced institutional structure and the growing political ambitions of military leaders. As Ian Talbot notes, Pakistan's political history has been marked by 'a fruitless search for stability with frequent changes of government and regime'.[23] Talbot also mentions the experiments that the state of Pakistan made during the first two decades of its existence, with 'two constituent assemblies, one constitutional commission and three constitutions'.[24]

Despite efforts, Pakistan has yet to achieve long-lasting political stability and a sustainable democratic system. When examining the country's democracy, it is essential to consider the colonial perspective, which was reinforced by a rigid bureaucratic structure. It was, in the words of Mohammad Waseem, 'bureaucratic paternalism' that was central to the British imperial project in the subcontinent. Procedural safeguards were put in place to preclude 'any infringement of the bureaucrats' monopoly over the articulation of public interests by the non-officials'.[25] In essence, the British civil servants who established the controlling mechanism in colonial India were always inclined to restrain the representative institutions, despite their nascent form. The same mechanism was inherited by Pakistan, where politicians and the representative form of government were viewed as corrupt, inefficient, irrational and uninformed. Therefore, the colonial legacy and its impact on the post-independence era should be the first aspect to be explored.

Another key issue is the relationship between Islam and the state of Pakistan, which has been projected with extraordinary zeal. Any alternative interpretation of Pakistan's genesis is regarded as taboo, making academic review or debate on the issue challenging. Scholars such as Abdul Majid Sindhi, Ahmed Hasan Dani and Aitzaz Ahsan have attempted to explain the genesis of Pakistan in terms of civilization, emphasizing it as a fountainhead of the Indus Valley civilization, which differentiates Pakistan from India. In other words, instead of religion, they foregrounded civilization as the key difference between the two nations. However, this theory has not gained much traction in academia, largely because the state did not endorse it.

Pakistan was conceptualized as an ideological state with an Islamic character, which created political ambivalence but also provided ample space for clerics in the country's political arena. This ambivalence was further compounded when parliamentary democracy was deemed a prerequisite for the sustainability of the Pakistani state. Hence, parliamentary democracy would operate within the ideological framework of Islam, which some quarters portrayed as a distinct code of life, with its unique system of government denouncing democracy as an alien system. Fortunately, such a view did not gain popular support. However, the democratic experience predicated on Islamic ideology has led to cultural and social (and sectarian) fissures in Pakistani society, which is inherently pluralistic, and this will be further explored below.

To emphasize ideology as the reason for Pakistan's creation, a new discourse was introduced into the study and discussion of the country's history which highlighted the concept of Muslim separatism from Hindus as a primary construct. Ishtiaq Hussain Qureshi, Sheikh Muhammad Ikram and Khurshid Kamal Aziz led the charge in providing a separatist perspective to South Asian history. In their scholarly efforts, they centred their arguments on three key variables: Islam, Urdu and the divergence of the Hindu world view.[26] Hence Islam as an identity marker was accorded extraordinary salience in the struggle for Pakistan (from 1937 onwards[27]) by the League leadership and thereby Islam became a rallying cry for the Muslims of various hues vis-à-vis the composite nationalism of the INC. As a result, the notion of the two-nation theory, which was based on religious exclusivism, gained complete legitimacy. This ideological orientation was used as a pretext by the ruling oligarchy in Pakistan to undermine the democratic dispensation. As Pakistan's political history clearly shows, the relationship between democracy and religious ideology is fundamentally antithetical, yet this paradoxical combination is pursued without any realization that it is bound to fail. This is precisely why Pakistan's historical realities are complex and messy, and they do not lend themselves to simplistic theories put forth by Islamic ideologues or political scientists who seek to fit them into ideal categories of the postcolonial state.[28] The paradoxical situation in Pakistan is that the modern nation state is associated with an ideology that is seemingly incompatible with it. This mismatch has not only hindered the development of democratic institutions but impeded the smooth functioning of the state apparatus. From the very beginning, Pakistan was dominated by the centripetal forces of the 'establishment', which consisted of the civil bureaucracy and the military, as an overdeveloped state structure. The establishment has always sought to maintain a strong power centre, often at the expense of provincial and regional actors who have been relegated to the periphery of Pakistani politics. This has resulted in friction between the Punjab and the smaller provinces, with the establishment being perceived as having a 'centrist' orientation. The same approach has also led to integration problems, particularly in East Pakistan. Sindh and Baluchistan have also not accepted the centrist approach. The establishment, dominated by Punjabi bureaucrats and Army generals, has popularized expressions such as 'the Punjabization of Pakistan'. These political and administrative arrangements deserve scrutiny and academic attention.

According to some political analysts, the democratization of Pakistan's state and society did not occur simultaneously. The political culture needed to instigate societal change and control over the state was underdeveloped. As a result, the state exercised its control over society, and the representatives of the people could not act as a supervisory body over the arbitrary functioning of the state. These issues require further examination.

Before delving into these questions, it is essential to provide some basic facts about Pakistan. As of 1994, the country's population was estimated at 128 million, with an annual growth rate of almost 3 per cent, one of the highest in the world. Pakistan is located west of India and east of the Persian Gulf, spanning more than 2 million square kilometres (803,943 sq. mi.). Its strategic proximity to Russia and China has made it of great international interest, particularly during the Cold War era. Despite its size and economy, Pakistan's geopolitical position has warranted significant attention.[29] According to some analysts, Pakistan's unique geographical location plays a crucial role in shaping its foreign policy and diplomatic relations with other nations. Given its close proximity to China, India, Russia and the Gulf region, Pakistan's strategic importance is heightened, which in turn requires a more significant role for the military and establishment in policy formulation.[30] Pakistan is considered an emerging middle-income country with a rapidly changing socio-economic landscape. While agriculture has historically been the mainstay of the economy, its contribution has been gradually declining.[31] Nevertheless, it still remains a crucial sector, accounting for 25 per cent of the total area of the country. This is largely due to the extensive canal irrigation networks – among the largest in the world – which enable the cultivation of various crops and support the livelihoods of millions of people.

Pakistani society is deeply rooted in patriarchal social and cultural norms, which are reinforced by the state and religious-political groups, alongside strong Islamic values. While the puritanical religious traditions of Deobandi and Ahl-e-Hadith are gaining ground, Islam in Pakistan is far from being monolithic or homogeneous.[32] Rather, it encompasses various sectarian and mystic traditions. However, sectarianism has become a major social issue in the country, with both local and international dimensions. Additionally, the concept of *biraderi*, or kinship groups, holds great importance as a social institution and locus of political authority, especially in central Punjab and to some extent in Sindh. While patrilineal descent is a central component of *biraderi*, other factors such as bonds of marriage, reciprocal obligation and common political interests also play a significant role in shaping these groups. Among the peasant proprietors of the Punjab, *biraderi* solidarity is particularly strong, although tribal and landed elites also use it for political mobilization.[33] The Pakistani political landscape is characterized by unequal power relationships in rural areas, which are primarily shaped by the prevalent feudal system. Scholars argue that this system has a more significant impact on power politics than either Islam or *biraderi*. Feudalism is a root cause of the significant social and economic disparity between the landed aristocracy and the rural masses. The landed elite derived their legitimacy from the strategic alliances formed by the Muslim League with the big *zamindars* in the 1946 elections. Since then, the landed elite have become the most critical source of political authority, alongside the unelected pillars of the state.

'Centralization' as an Administrative Tool

Pakistan's political history has been shaped by charismatic figures, viewed as personifications of 'the world spirit' in Hegelian terms. One such figure was Muhammad Ali Jinnah, the founder of Pakistan. Jinnah's centrality to Pakistani politics, however, came at the expense of political and constitutional institutions. His decision to prioritize the office of the governor general over the premiership had enduring repercussions for the nation. In fact, Jinnah's vested power elevated him to an unprecedented level. When he first assumed the role, 'he immediately applied for powers under the ninth schedule rather than Part II of the 1935 Act.' This gave him dictatorial powers that no constitutional governor general representing the king had ever wielded before.[34] As the founder of the newly formed republic, he enjoyed unchallenged acceptance and authority, superseding any constitutional or legislative body. The Muslim newspaper *Dawn* made this point clear in one of its editorials, stating, 'Regardless of the constitutional powers held by a Dominion's Governor General, Quaid-e-Azam's position is not subject to legal or formal limitations.'[35] Khalid bin Sayeed shed light on Jinnah's revered persona, describing him as the Quaid-e-Azam, or the Great Leader, of the national movement. In a remarkable feat, Jinnah achieved the creation of Pakistan within a mere seven years, something no other Muslim leader had even dreamt of. Muslims, especially in northern India, regarded him as a successor to the great Mughal emperors such as Babur and Aurangzeb. After the announcement of the partition scheme on 3 June 1947, Muslims in New Delhi hailed him as the emperor of Pakistan. Even years after his death, *Dawn* wrote: 'The populace had already begun to greet the Quaid-e-Azam as Shahinshah-e-Pakistan [the emperor of Pakistan].' Such was his reputation that, if Jinnah had desired it, 80 million willing hands would have rejoiced to put a crown upon his head.[36]

The people of Pakistan yearned for a leader who embodied the all-powerful king, or *shahinshah*, similar to the great Mughals of the past who were seen as the wellspring of all powers. In their political vocabulary and comprehension, such a leader could restore the past glory of the Muslims, which had vanished since the eighteenth century. The vast majority of the populace was not well versed in the concept of democracy or representative government. This lack of understanding posed a significant obstacle to the establishment of democratic governance. Despite this, Jinnah remained a staunch constitutionalist and envisioned a model of parliamentary democracy for the newly founded state, following the path of Westminster. While the people of Pakistan yearned for a king-like figure, Jinnah remained committed to establishing a democratic order that would uphold the principles of the Constitution. There was some controversy surrounding Jinnah's assumption of the role of governor general. His pursuit of the position caused concern in England, given that he was an active politician. The dispassionate analysis may lead us to believe that the constitutional theory of a governor general in a dominion was that he represented the king and had the same relationship to the government's ministers as the king had to his ministers in the United Kingdom.[37] While it was recognized that a dominion had the right to recommend someone for the role, having an active party politician in the position who intended to continue their political leadership after assuming the office was an innovation that fundamentally altered the nature of the dominion bond.

Moreover, Jinnah's rule appeared to be headed towards a thinly veiled dictatorship, making his demand for the office of governor general all the more concerning. His motive for seeking the position likely stemmed from the prestige it held in the eyes of the masses he led. Historically, as Khalid bin Sayeed contends, the viceroy as governor general had been the supreme executive ruler, with his ministers serving merely as members of his Executive Council. The man on the street was likely to continue to view the governor general as more important than the prime minister owing to the familiar conflation of the former with power.[38]

In the years that followed, the governor general wielded executive powers that overshadowed the prime minister, reducing the latter to a mere figurehead. This had a detrimental impact on the growth of parliamentary democracy in Pakistan. The governor general derived his authority from the Indian Independence Act, which vested him with unlimited powers to amend the Constitution through a simple decree. However, this provision was intended to be transitional and to help find quick solutions to the pressing issues facing the newly founded state. These powers were only supposed to last for seven and a half months, until 31 March 1948. Under the Government of India Act 1935, the governor general had the authority to appoint and dismiss ministers, as well as to make decisions related to defence, ecclesiastical and external affairs and the administration of tribal areas. The specific functions and powers vested in the governor general were numerous: maintenance of law and order, the safeguarding of the financial stability and credit of the federal government, the safeguarding of the rights and interest of minorities, the prevention of commercial discrimination and action that would subject goods of United Kingdom or Burmese origin imported into India to discriminatory or penal treatment, the protections of the rights of Indian states, and so on.[39] Ironically, the span of these discretionary powers was extended by another year.

This practice continued in subsequent years, as individuals acting in the name of Jinnah regularly invoked these powers, often disregarding the role of the Cabinet and the Constituent Assembly and encroaching upon their legitimate functions and powers. Hamza Alavi has noted that this practice persisted without any challenge to the wielders' authority, allowing it to become a regular occurrence. As a result, the growth of parliamentary democracy was stunted, and the executive branch was able to maintain its dominance over other branches of government.[40] Alavi challenges the widely held belief that Jinnah was fully in control of the state's affairs. According to him, Jinnah was actually very ill by the time of partition and was in no condition to manage the crisis-ridden affairs of the newly formed state. He was physically weak and could not pull himself together due to the incompetence of his colleagues, whom he had grown to despise and criticize publicly.[41] In these circumstances, all the crucial decisions, including constitutional amendments, were being made in Jinnah's name, despite his declining health. When some members of the Constituent Assembly expressed their concerns about being bypassed on matters of great importance, Prime Minister Liaquat Ali Khan addressed the assembly, stating that 'under the present constitution, the man who has been vested with all powers is the governor general. He can do whatever he likes.'[42]

Three reasons can be cited for the bureaucracy's seizure of power: Jinnah's fatal illness, which left a power vacuum that the bureaucrats were quick to fill; the mediocrity and incompetence of leaders other than Jinnah, who were unable to effectively steer the new country; and the Muslim League's inability to unite the diverse political and ethnic entities of the country. During the pre-independence period, the core leadership of the Muslim League, with the exception of Jinnah, came from Muslim-minority provinces, particularly United Provinces and Bihar. This was primarily because the Krishak Praja Party and the Unionist Party dominated politics in Bengal and the Punjab until the end of the colonial era, leaving little room for the Muslim League to operate. After independence, the central leadership of the Muslim League found itself without an electoral base. Despite this, the party continued to assert itself as a unifying national party.[43] Furthermore, its leadership started equating the party with the nation: 'if you destroy the League, you destroy Pakistan.'[44] Jinnah went so far as to suggest that no other political party was necessary besides the Muslim League. Despite the Muslim League's lack of a representative institutional framework, the party's top leadership heavily relied on bureaucracy to formulate and execute policies.[45]

The Muslim League's inability to become an integrative force in a culturally diverse and ethnically plural society and state was due in large part to its exclusionary approach. The League's leadership relied on Islam and Urdu as symbols to create unity among disparate groups and factions, but these instruments of homogeneity proved to be counterproductive, especially in Bengal. Instead of bringing people together, they created division and resentment. The political scientist Tahir Amin has argued that Jinnah sought to build a strong nation based on the principle of 'one nation, one culture, one language'. However, this vision was not shared by all, and it ultimately failed to take root in a society as diverse as Pakistan's.[46] This perspective appears to be relevant to and indicative of the centrist ideology that prevailed in the early days of Pakistan's formation. Undoubtedly, the slogan of Islam was extensively used for political mobilization throughout the country. Mosques and shrines served as political platforms where clerics and spiritual leaders urged the public to support the Muslim League's call for a separate homeland for Muslims.

The Pakistani central government had a significant number of officers from the minority provinces, just like the leaders of the Muslim League. Eventually, Punjabis also gained representation in the prestigious Civil Service. As a result, the alliance between the Muhajirs and Punjabis became a key tool for centralization within the state apparatus.[47] That centralization was forged ostensibly to ward off the 'perceived' security threats, mostly on the part of the ruling elite. Omar Noman highlights the major consequences of Pakistan's perceived vulnerability to external threats: on the one hand, this perception led Pakistan to join military alliances under the American umbrella as a means of protecting itself against potential Indian military intervention; on the other hand, it contributed to the accumulation of power by Jinnah and other central authorities, without any meaningful basis of representation. Noman argues that a powerful central government *could* have helped to bind diverse elements into a cohesive national framework. However, the concentration of power in the hands of an unrepresentative central government ultimately proved divisive and undermined efforts to establish a truly democratic and inclusive political system.[48]

In an effort to counter the Bengali majority in East Pakistan, the 1954 provincial elections were nullified, and Iskander Mirza was appointed as governor of the province. Shortly thereafter, the provinces of the Punjab, Sindh and Northwest Frontier, along with Baluchistan and tribal areas, were merged into a single entity called West Pakistan in 1955. Lahore became the capital of this new province. The creation of West Pakistan aimed to balance the representation of the two regions, thereby denying the Bengalis their majority in the national parliament. Those who spoke out against the One Unit policy were met with stern measures by the governor general, Malik Ghulam Muhammad, who was known for his bureaucratic approach. In November 1954, Abdul Sattar Pirzada's Sindh ministry was dismissed by Ghulam Muhammad due to their opposition to One Unit, and a similar fate befell the NWFP ministry. When Feroze Khan Noon raised concerns about some aspects of the policy, Ghulam Muhammad intervened in Punjab politics as well. These measures were deeply divisive and undermined the democratic foundations of Pakistan's political system. They contributed to growing tensions between East and West Pakistan and ultimately paved the way for the country's eventual dissolution. Regarding the political marginalization of the Bengalis, the ruling elite of Pakistan, with the bureaucrats at the forefront, displayed apathy towards the protests and appeals of the Bengalis against the centralizing policies. However, things took a turn for the worse. Before delving into the details, it is pertinent to examine the rise of bureaucracy and its strengthening grip on power.

The power bestowed upon the bureaucracy did not occur through an overt coup, but rather implicitly. Given the numerous challenges Pakistan faced, certain institutional changes were implemented, which granted the bureaucracy a degree of autonomy from political leadership. The most noteworthy of these changes was the subordination of the entire bureaucracy under the newly established post of secretary general. Hamza asserts that Jinnah may have created this post, possibly on the advice of the first appointee himself. The rationale was that a person 'controlling the entire government machinery working directly under Jinnah as governor general was needed for speedy decisions'.[49]

Chaudhry Muhammad Ali, a capable Punjabi officer with significant experience in the finance department of the government of India, was appointed as the first secretary general. In this position, Ali had direct access to all federal secretaries and files. To institutionalize his role and position, he established a 'Planning Committee' with the secretaries of all ministries as members. The Planning Committee allowed the entire state apparatus to function as a unified machine under a single leader, the secretary general. As a result, the structure of the state was no longer fragmented but rather internally cohesive. Effectively serving as a parallel cabinet of bureaucrats, the planning committee had a bureaucrat functioning as a de facto 'prime minister'. This mechanism bypassed the cabinet, reducing its proceedings to meaningless formalities. Major issues were decided in advance by the Planning Committee, and the cabinet acted as a mere rubber stamp, at best making minor adjustments to bureaucratic decisions. In some cases, significant decisions were not even referred to the cabinet, operating on the principle that ignorance was bliss.[50]

In many respects, the actions of the bureaucrats represented a continuation of the colonial legacy in which political leaders were looked down upon. This attitude was evident during the Constituent Assembly debates of 1956, and it became an integral part of the training and upbringing of Pakistani civil servants. Provincial ministers frequently complained about several officers who refused to comply with their orders due to the ministers' inability to hold them accountable. Given the overwhelming power of the military–bureaucratic oligarchy, the ministers were often powerless to effect change. However, it is important to note that the lack of effective political leadership also contributed to the country's political turmoil. Jinnah himself prevented any potential rivals from emerging, resulting in a spineless and short-sighted political leadership that had a negative impact on the Muslim League's organizational structure. Consequently, democracy in Pakistan was built on a precarious and shifting foundation.

When Ghulam Muhammad dismissed Prime Minister Khawaja Nazimuddin in April 1953, it marked the first public demonstration of the bureaucracy's power behind the parliamentary facade. Ghulam Muhammad, a bureaucrat from the Indian Audit and Account service, assumed the role of governor general after the assassination of Liaquat Ali Khan in 1951. The significance of his dismissal of the prime minister lay in its ability to highlight the lack of effective links between the prime minister, party institutions and parliament.[51] The abrupt departure of Nazimuddin

Liaquat Ali Khan with U.S. president Harry S. Truman, Washington, DC, 1950.

did not have any negative consequences for the governor general, but it did spark a delayed response from politicians. In 1954, the assembly tried to limit the governor general's power by revoking the PRODA legislation that Liaquat Ali Khan had introduced in 1949 to control politicians. However, this move proved to be overly ambitious, and on 24 October 1954, the governor general dissolved the Constituent Assembly.

Over the next four years, Pakistan's political system was held hostage by the Civil Service, which, in collusion with the military, regulated and controlled the crucial decision-making process. In 1956 Iskandar Mirza took over as governor general, and his tenure was marked by political intrigues and conspiracies that ultimately led to military rule in 1958. According to Omar Noman, during this period, Khan Sahib, a former INC leader who had opposed the creation of Pakistan, was appointed chief minister of West Pakistan. However, some members of the Muslim League leadership disapproved of his appointment and questioned his loyalty to the country. In response, President Mirza encouraged Khan Sahib to form a new party called the Republican Party, which was quickly embraced by members of Pakistan's Civil Service and led to defections from the Muslim League.

In a matter of months, the Republican Party allied with Suhrawardy's Awami League and ousted the Muslim League from the centre. However, the alliance was short-lived, and the Republican Party soon joined forces with the Muslim League to oppose the Awami League. As a result, a series of unstable governments were formed, with the legislature serving mainly to validate decisions made outside of it. Political parties were reduced to bickering factions controlled by the executive, and their power within the legislature was significantly diminished.[52]

One significant factor that contributed to the failure of democracy in Pakistan was the delay in constitution-making. This can be attributed to the Muslim League's slow approach to constitutional issues. During the period from 1948 to 1954, the Constituent Assembly convened for only sixteen days per year on average to draft a constitution. This lack of urgency was further underscored by the fact that attendance at these sessions averaged only 46 members.[53]

After a prolonged delay of nine years, a constitution was finally drafted and promulgated on 23 March 1956. The Constitution of 1956 was a lengthy and detailed document, comprising 234 articles divided into thirteen parts and six schedules. The federal structure was provided for with the principle of parity between East Pakistan and West Pakistan, despite East Pakistan having a majority. However, it failed to recognize the plurality that Pakistan represented.

The Constitution of 1956 established a parliamentary form of government, where executive authority was vested in a cabinet presided over by the prime minister, and was collectively responsible to the legislature. The Constitution established a unicameral legislature, the National Assembly, which ensured equality between the two wings of Pakistan. The governor general was replaced by a president, who was elected by the Electoral College of Pakistan, composed of members of the National Assembly and Provincial Assembly. The Constitution provided for democratic rights and freedoms such as freedom of speech and expression, assembly and association, movement and profession, but with the usual qualifications. Civil rights, such as the right to life, liberty and property, were granted, again with the usual qualifications and safeguards. The executive was empowered to enforce fundamental rights, while the courts were tasked with determining if a law was repugnant to any provisions of the fundamental rights. The Constitution accorded Urdu and Bengali the status of national languages.[54]

The Contested Status of Urdu as a National Language

Language has played a significant role in shaping the political landscape of and identity in South Asia. In the colonial era, Muslim separatism in India was closely linked to the Urdu–Hindi controversy, which began in Banaras in 1867. The Urdu–Hindi controversy was a linguistic and cultural dispute that emerged in India in the years after the 1857 uprising. It revolved around the choice of language for government jobs, particularly in the British-administered regions of north India. This controversy had a significant connection with job opportunities during this time. As noted by

Waseem in his book *Politics and State in Pakistan*, Muslim leaders in Uttar Pradesh, starting with Sir Syed Ahmed Khan, began emphasizing the need to protect their rights through collective representations to the government. They advocated for the promotion of Urdu in court proceedings and in government jobs, as it was seen as crucial for the socio-economic advancement of the Muslim community. This was particularly significant against the backdrop of communal strife, as the language controversy further exacerbated tensions between two major religious communities. This linguistic and cultural dispute played a role in shaping the politics and aspirations of various communities, particularly the Muslim leadership, who sought to safeguard their rights and interests in the changing landscape of British colonial rule. This highlights the complex interplay between language, politics and communalism in the region's history.[55] The emergence of the Urdu Defence Association, at the behest of Mohsin-ul-Mulk, solidified Urdu as a significant symbol of Muslim identity. However, Ayesha Jalal believes that the All-India Muslim League downplayed the linguistic particularities of Muslims in the majority provinces. After asserting a distinct Muslim political identity, the League aimed to reinforce religious ties using the Urdu language at a supra-regional level.[56] Following the creation of Pakistan, Urdu was promoted as a means to advance the ambitions of centrist forces, which ultimately led to smaller provinces developing strong reservations towards it. Ian Talbot argues that 'the efforts to strengthen Urdu as a tool to foster a shared national identity in Pakistan eventually had an adverse effect. This was particularly evident in East Bengal, where the imposition of Urdu as the sole official language caused widespread resentment, ultimately contributing to the region's secession from Pakistan.'[57]

Although Urdu is considered the primary language in Pakistan, the country boasts a rich and diverse cultural heritage expressed through a variety of languages and dialects. These languages not only serve as cultural symbols of the regions where they are spoken but have political significance. Unfortunately, Pakistan has witnessed several instances of ethnic and linguistic conflicts that have resulted in bloodshed – for example, the 1952 riots in East Bengal and the deadly riots in June 1972 following the Urdu–Sindhi controversy.

The leadership of the Muslim League, which played a significant role in the creation of Pakistan, came mainly from the regions of Uttar Pradesh and Bihar, where Muslim separatism had taken root during colonial times. Urdu, with its Persian script, was deemed a crucial symbol of Muslim and Pakistani identity. Since the Urdu–Hindi controversy in United Provinces/Uttar Pradesh in the late nineteenth century, the Muslim Ashraaf had used Urdu as a means to unite the ethnically and culturally diverse Muslim community.

When Pakistan was founded as a multi-ethnic and multicultural state, Punjabis, Sindhis, Pathans, Muhajirs, Baluchis and Bengalis constituted major segments of the population. The fact that Bengalis formed the majority sent shockwaves through the West Pakistani ruling elite, consisting of Muslim League politicians, bureaucrats and military officers. As a result, Urdu was employed as a unifying symbol of the state at the expense of other languages, including Bengali.

At the first educational conference held in November–December 1947, the policy of making Urdu the lingua franca of Pakistan and teaching it as a compulsory language was established. However, this policy of using Urdu as a tool for integration backfired and led to violent responses, particularly in East Bengal (1948–52) and Karachi (1972), resulting in the loss of numerous lives.[58]

The issue of language became increasingly contentious when Jinnah, during his official visit to East Bengal, made a strongly worded statement accusing foreign-funded agents of trying to disrupt and sabotage Pakistan. He warned the people of East Bengal to be vigilant and not to fall for attractive slogans that claimed the government was out to destroy their language. He went on to declare that Urdu would be the only state language of Pakistan: 'Without one state language, no nation can remain tied up solidly together and function. Look at the history of other countries.'[59] However, this decision was met with opposition in East Bengal and ultimately contributed to the region's secession from Pakistan. 'The use of Urdu as the sole official language of Pakistan was seen as a means of imposing a dominant West Pakistani culture on the rest of the country, disregarding the linguistic diversity of its people. As a result, it sparked linguistic and ethnic conflicts, leading to violent riots and bloodshed.'[60]

The statement made by Jinnah on his official tour of East Bengal caused a significant uproar among the Bengali educated classes. Despite this reaction, Jinnah did not back down from his position on the language issue. In fact, he reiterated his stance while addressing the convocation at Dhaka University three days later. He stated, 'The state language must be Urdu, a language nurtured by a hundred million Muslims of the subcontinent, a language understood throughout Pakistan, and a language that embodies the best of Islamic culture and Muslim tradition and is closest to the language used in other Islamic countries.'[61] When the Bengali bourgeoisie expressed their reservations about Jinnah's unequivocal support for Urdu as the national language and criticized his invalidation of a resolution from the East Bengal Assembly demanding national status for Bengali, it revealed the growing discontent in East Pakistan towards the West Pakistani ruling elite. The Bengalis felt their linguistic and cultural identity was being marginalized and that the West Pakistanis were trying to impose their language and culture on them. This led to a growing demand 'for greater autonomy and recognition of Bengali language rights, ultimately culminating in the Bengali Language Movement of 1952'.[62] However, Jinnah and Prime Minister Liaquat Ali Khan both disregarded these concerns as manifestations of provincialism, which they believed was a curse that Pakistanis needed to guard against. In February 1948 Liaquat Ali Khan rejected a motion in the Constituent Assembly seeking equal status for Bengali and Urdu, stating that Pakistan had been created because of the demand of 100 million Muslims in the subcontinent and that Urdu was the language of the nation.[63] Furthermore, attempts were made by a Language Committee appointed by the East Bengal government to change the character of the Bengali language because its script had to be de-Sanskritized. Hence the proposal to change the script into the *Nastaliq* Perso-Arabic script met with the vociferous condemnation by Bengali students, in particular.[64]

The anthropologist Alyssa Ayres argues that the annual observance of the origins of Bangladeshi national consciousness is not focused on issues related to bureaucratic under-representation or any other statist questions, but rather on language. Bangladeshis mark the commemoration of 'Ekushe', which means '21' in Bengali, on 21 February 1952. This day is significant as it marks the sacrifice of four Bangladeshis who gave their lives in 1952 protesting for the Bengali language to be used as a medium for conducting administrative business. It is astonishing that the language spoken by 56 per cent of the population was not granted national status.[65] Ayres highlights the sensitivity of the people of East Bengal towards the Bengali language and its significance by tracing the origins of their discontent back to early October 1947, when the Rashtra Bhasa Sangram Parishad (State Language Committee of Action) was formed. The committee's goal was 'to protest the exclusion of Bengali language from the new official forms, currency notes, stamps and coins of the new Pakistan'.[66]

The Army in Politics

After independence, the Pakistan Army was initially weak and poorly organized. Its commander-in-chief was General Sir Frank Walter Messervy, who was followed by General Douglas Gracey until 1951. During this period, the Army remained an apolitical institution, much like it had been before partition. Aqil Shah argues that unlike the armies of Turkey, Algeria and Indonesia, the Pakistan Army did not participate in a war of liberation. As a result, it was not a 'national liberation army' or a 'postliberation army', but rather an 'ex-colonial army'.[67] Most Pakistani officers received their training from institutions such as the China Royal Military Academy and Sandhurst. Starting in 1932, they were also trained at Dehra Dun, where the focus was on military-technical subjects such as drill, fortifications, military history and geography.[68] Informal socialization in army messes among senior and junior officers discouraged political discussion. This tradition persisted in military training institutions after 1947, including the Command and Staff College in Quetta for mid-level officers. These institutions focused solely on military professional curricula and training regimens, with no emphasis on politics.

In January 1951 General Ayub Khan became the first Pakistani commander-in-chief. Upon taking charge, he emphasized the need for the military to avoid any active involvement in party politics or the propagation of political views. He stated that the military must see itself as a servant of Pakistan, regardless of which party is in power. This stance reflected the apolitical tradition of the Pakistan Army, which had been inherited from the British Indian Army. 'The emphasis remained on military professional curricula and training regimens, with no political indoctrination.'[69] But Ayub Khan's resolution did not last very long: the Army became increasingly involved in the country's politics, due to several factors, as enumerated by Hasan Askari Rizvi.[70] The precarious existence of Pakistan from the outset, due to politicians' inability to establish an effective government and the country's confrontation with communal riots, undefined borders, strained relations with India, war in Kashmir and the maintenance of law and order in the early years, drew the Army into politics. Additionally, the weak social base of the political leadership meant that the governing power could not muster the necessary organized political support for the sustenance of political institutions. The Army's high standard of training, experience in two world wars, discipline, cohesiveness and organizational skills made it arguably the most organized national institution, and its personnel had experience running training institutes and ordinance factories, as well as a knowledge of modern technology and managerial expertise that could benefit civilian sectors as well. Lastly, the Army commanded the respect of the common people, since its personnel were regarded as patriotic and dedicated to the nation's cause. However, the Army's increasing involvement in politics was facilitated by these factors.[71]

When calamities such as floods or cyclones hit any part of Pakistan, the Army and Air Force undertook relief operations. The Army's fight against locust attacks in Khyber Pakhtunkhwa and Sindh in 1951–2 was commendable.[72] Similarly, the Pakistan Army played a decisive role in dealing with the problem of salinity in Sindh in 1958. It also conducted Operation Wild Boar near the Indian border in 1962. In East Pakistan, the Army launched several operations to tackle crucial issues afflicting the region, such as smuggling and food shortage. These included Operation Jute (1952–3), Operation Service First (1956) and Operation Close Door (1957–8).[73]

The Pakistani Army played a vital role in supporting various governments during periods of intense political agitation, student unrest and labour strikes. Whenever religious or ethnic violence escalated beyond the control of the civil administration from 1947 to 1958, the Army provided all possible assistance. The Army's experiences included Karachi riots (1949), Dhaka riots (1950), language riots in East Pakistan (1952), anti-Ahmadi riots in the Punjab (1953) and labour disputes in East Pakistan.

Malik Ghulam Muhammad, 1950.

The Army's first taste of civil administration occurred in 1953, following the outbreak of anti-Ahmadi riots in the Punjab. According to Rizvi, this was a turning point in the military's top brass's thinking.[74] Unfortunately, political leaders were so preoccupied with power politics that they had no time to reinforce the civilian supremacy inherited from the British. Instead, they looked to the Army's leaders for support. There was a significant difference in the consistency of civilian and military leadership. Pakistan had six prime ministers from 1951 to 1958, while in that time there was one commander-in-chief for the Army, General Ayub Khan, who received two extensions. His extended stay in office allowed him to observe the polarization in Pakistani politics and consolidate his own position in the Army.

A close examination of Pakistan's first decade suggests that the anti-Ahmadi movement of 1953 was a decisive moment when General Ayub Khan began harbouring the ambition to establish military rule in Pakistan. On the civilian side, he was confident of support from his long-time comrade Major General Iskander Mirza. Humayun Mirza believes that Ayub Khan seriously began to entertain political ambitions after Malik Ghulam Muhammad dismissed Khawaja Nazimuddin as prime minister.[75]

According to available sources, the top military officers wielded significant influence over the political leadership, who often followed their advice or commands. The decision to accept military aid from the United States and join the SEATO and the Bagdad Pact (later CENTO) was primarily taken by the military high command, with the political leadership acquiescing to it. Ayub Khan's biographers claim that he took the initiative to negotiate the military aid programme with the United States, since he believed that American support was crucial to sustain Pakistan.

Major General Iskander Mirza, later Pakistan's first president, belonged to the political service of colonial India but was trained at Sandhurst, where he became friends with Ayub Khan. Liaquat Ali Khan, who served as both prime minister and defence minister, delegated many of his day-to-day responsibilities to Mirza. According to Ayub Khan's private secretary, the prime minister's focus was primarily on consolidating his party's position and attending to parliamentary matters, leaving little time to address defence issues, which had traditionally been under the prime minister's purview.[76]

It is evident that in the early years of Pakistan's history, the civilian government was gradually losing control over defence matters to the military. The defence budget was driven not only by the Indian threat but by the need to protect the strategically vulnerable northwestern frontiers. As a result, Pakistan's defence expenditures were higher than those of the undivided government of India.[77] Pakistan was clearly on the pathway to what Ayesha Jalal has termed a political economy of defence, rather than of development.[78] This was yet another factor in the failure to consolidate democracy.

Economic Development

During the initial decade of its independence, Pakistan's economic policy was underpinned by a triad of crucial objectives. First, the nation sought to embark on a path of robust economic development and industrialization, driven by the desire to diminish its historical reliance on agriculture, which had hitherto dominated the regional landscape. Industrialization, perceived as a conduit for job creation, enhanced productivity and offered an elevated standard of living for its populace, which stood as a paramount ambition.

Second, poverty alleviation loomed large on Pakistan's economic agenda. In earnest efforts to reduce income disparities and uplift living conditions, the government aimed to provide improved access to fundamental services such as education, healthcare and housing. These pursuits were bolstered by the implementation of social welfare programmes and the introduction of land reforms to grapple with issues of inequality. Lastly, a cornerstone of Pakistan's economic strategy was to strengthen national self-reliance. The nation aspired to attain self-sufficiency across a spectrum of economic sectors, encompassing agriculture and industry. This objective was intricately tied to the overarching goal of achieving greater economic independence while diminishing reliance on foreign aid and imports. Recognized as indispensable for safeguarding national sovereignty and ensuring long-term economic stability, this pursuit was etched into the core of Pakistan's early economic policies.

These objectives found expression in various economic plans and policies, with the first five-year plan (1955–60) being a notable milestone in this journey. However, the translation of these aspirations into reality encountered multifaceted challenges. The policy's emphasis on developing import-substituting industries, for instance, necessitated the importation of machinery due to the absence of a domestic capital goods sector. Moreover, the limited investment in human resource development led to neglect in critical sectors like education and healthcare, revealing the intricate complexities and evolving nature of Pakistan's economic landscape during this formative period.[79]

At the time of independence, there were few large-scale industries in the areas that became Pakistan. During the colonial period, industrialization was concentrated around port cities in India, leaving areas such as Sindh and the Punjab to provide raw materials for Indian industries. This led to a situation where, on the eve of independence, only one of the top 57 Indian companies was owned by a Muslim. Overall, during this period, Pakistan faced significant challenges in developing its economy in the aftermath of independence, including a lack of infrastructure and investment in human capital.[80]

Different regions in the subcontinent were economically interconnected, with one area supplying raw materials to another for industrial production such as East Bengal and its provision of jute to the jute industry in West Bengal.

During this period, a new economic group known as the 'mercantile capitalists' emerged in Pakistan, and its activities played a pivotal role in the country's economic development. This group benefited greatly from the Korean War bonanza in 1949, and subsequently invested the profits in various industries. This injection of capital provided a significant boost to Pakistan's economy in the early 1950s. S. Akbar Zaidi discusses how, in the mid- to late 1950s, Pakistan's industrialization process was largely steered by the bureaucratic machinery, which played a pivotal role in establishing industrial units across the country. Specifically, state-owned institutions like the Pakistan Industrial Credit and Investment Corporation (PICIC) and Pakistan Industrial Development Corporation (PIDC) played an essential role in promoting industrial development in key sectors, while a trade policy was also implemented to support a specific type of industrialization process. Overall, it was a combination of strategic government interventions and bureaucratic expertise that enabled Pakistan to successfully establish itself as a key player in the region's industrial landscape.[81]

According to Zaidi, Pakistan's industrialization process was largely led and assisted by the bureaucracy, with civil servants playing a crucial role in establishing and promoting key industries. However, his emphasis on the centrality of bureaucrats in this process discounts the contributions of other powerful actors such as feudal landowners, sardars and tribal leaders.[82]

One could argue that the bureaucrats' control over economic resources and decision-making processes further entrenched their power within the state apparatus, potentially leading to imbalances of power and influence. Therefore, while the bureaucracy undoubtedly played a significant role in Pakistan's industrialization, it is important to consider the broader social and political context within which this process unfolded. The first decade of Pakistan's political history was characterized by instability, indecision on the part of the ruling oligarchy, governance issues and a delay in the constitution-making process. After Pakistan's inception, the country faced a significant challenge due to the inability of the Muslim League to adapt to the new circumstances. Instead of embracing the nation's cultural and socio-political diversity, there was a preference for a centralized governance system. Unfortunately, the Muslim League's failure to undergo a transformation post-partition exacerbated the political turmoil. Internal disputes within the party became a lasting issue, creating a political void subsequently occupied by a bureaucratic military oligarchy. The absence of political consensus extended the constitution-making process to a lengthy nine years, in stark contrast to India's swift accomplishment of this task within just two and a half years.

As a result, democratic institutions were not nurtured, and the powerful section ruling the country propagated the view that democracy was not consistent with the genius of the Pakistani populace. This line of thinking crystallized divisive tendencies in society. During this period, politics revolved around a few bureaucrats and one general, while politicians were relegated to secondary roles. These circumstances culminated in the imposition of martial law in 1958, which seems, in hindsight, a natural corollary.

6

Praetorianism Unbound (Ayub Khan's Rule), 1958–69

Pakistan's early years marked a period of exceptional challenges, unparalleled in contemporary history. Despite a relentless pursuit of political stability spanning over a decade, achieving this goal proved to be a formidable task for the nation's leadership. Notably, a convergence of the bureaucratic and military sectors gave rise to an oligarchic power structure, effectively sidelining the country's political leaders. The demise of Muhammad Ali Jinnah in April 1948 marked a turning point as a group of non-political figures from the bureaucracy and the military consolidated their authority over the government apparatus, employing ruthless measures to suppress any dissent or divisive movements. This group of individuals, including Malik Ghulam Muhammad, Chaudhry Muhammad Ali, Iskander Mirza and General Ayub Khan, orchestrated their ascent to power, solidifying an undeserved grip on Pakistan's political landscape.

However, with the implicit support of Ayub Khan, the shrewd and astute Iskander Mirza pushed Malik Ghulam Muhammad and Chaudhry Muhammad Ali into political anonymity. As a result, the political foundation of the country became as unstable as shifting sands, making it impossible for any government to establish a firm footing. Ironically, Prime Minister Ibrahim Ismael Chundrigar (1897–1960) lasted only two months in office, becoming the sixth prime minister of Pakistan when he was appointed on 17 October 1957. He resigned after a vote of no confidence was passed against him on 11 December 1957.

The case of Malik Feroze Khan Noon (1893–1970) was no different.[1] Feroz Khan Noon's close ties with Iskander Mirza positioned him as a pivotal figure in the formation of the Republican Party in the Punjab, where he assumed the role of its president. Riding on the Republican Party's platform, Noon secured the position of Pakistan's prime minister on 16 December 1957. Initially, President Iskander Mirza lent his support to Noon's government. However, the dynamic shifted when Noon, in a move that posed a direct challenge to the Iskander–Ayub partnership, proposed holding early elections in 1959, a proposition deemed unacceptable by both Mirza and Ayub. This proposal, would it come to fruition, threatened to disrupt their plans of consolidating control over Pakistan, making Noon's dismissal from office a necessary step in their eyes. Noon's tenure as prime minister concluded when martial law was promulgated in Pakistan on 7 October 1958. Ian Talbot's observations on the situation are particularly fitting. He notes that prime ministers came and went with alarming frequency as power gradually shifted from Karachi to Army Headquarters in Rawalpindi, akin to a revolving door of leadership.[2] Talbot's assertion captures the fluidity of the political turmoil with precision. Indeed, with every passing day, the Pakistani state inched closer to martial rule. The kaleidoscopic politics of Pakistan during the 1950s were characterized by frequent and sudden shifts in political loyalties, which resulted in a highly unstable political climate. Despite increasing control by the ruling oligarchy, pressure mounted incrementally throughout 1957 and 1958 to hold the elections mandated by the 1956 Constitution. Projections suggested that if elections were held, the ruling oligarchy would be dealt a blow, since the Awami League was expected to win the polls in East Pakistan and the Muslim League under Qayyum Khan was predicted to have a solid majority in West Pakistan.

The potential outcome of these elections held the promise of establishing a democratically elected government in Pakistan, a nation firmly committed to a robust alliance with the United States. Nonetheless, one unmistakable truth loomed: President Iskander Mirza's exit from power was on the horizon, as neither political party could tolerate his ongoing presence. This inexorable development, a pivotal episode in Pakistan's political history, went largely unnoticed by observers at the time.[3]

Iskander Mirza and his wife, 1957.

Therefore, Mirza and the members of the oligarchy had no alternative but to take proactive measures, leading to the dissolution of parliament and the suspension of the Constitution. In taking this action, Mirza effectively thwarted the politicians' electoral strategy. The Karachi daily newspaper *Dawn* celebrated this turn of events as a remarkable upheaval, viewing it as a providential response and marvelling at a rational transition, 'that brought forth a complete change of both system and regime without any strife or bitterness'.[4] Similarly, G. W. Chaudhary paid a tribute that reflected his deep admiration for Ayub Khan. He wrote,

> No Muslim ruler, since the fall of the Mughal Empire, governed over a larger area in the Indian subcontinent for a longer period or more effectively than Field Marshal Mohammed Ayub Khan did in undivided Pakistan from 27 October 1958 to 25 March 1969. Under Ayub's leadership, Pakistan was regarded as a model for developing countries. His political innovation, Basic Democracy, was praised by many, including historian Arnold Toynbee, as a viable alternative to both Western democracy and communist systems.[5]

On 7 October 1958, President Mirza declared martial law, thereby dismantling the constitutional government apparatus. The impending general elections could have produced a new political leadership that would not be easily swayed, which jeopardized the political manipulation of the governor general and, after 1956, President Mirza. Although martial law was declared, it was not a typical military coup.[6] As a result, Pakistan found itself in a political dead end that lasted almost eleven years under Ayub Khan's rule, followed by another two years and eight months under Yahya Khan. During Ayub's tenure, the two opposing principles of economic modernization and political conservatism clashed, creating a contradictory state policy. Ayub centralized power in himself, believing in absolute control over the state structure. Analyst of Pakistan's politics Khalid Mahmud accurately points out that the rise of the civil–military bureaucracy as a 'power-centre' and the subsequent era of 'controlled democracy' after Ayub's 1958 coup dealt a fatal blow to the notion of autonomous provinces forming a federation in the country harboured by various political leaders.[7]

It is worth noting that at the time when Mirza–Ayub established the civilian–oligarchic rule, there had already been 47 coups in the post-Second World War world by 1959, with six of them occurring in developing countries, while France experienced one in 1958.[8] The central reason for such events is usually attributed to the postcolonial teething pains of these countries, which secured their independence after the Second World War. However, according to Shuja Nawaz, this argument is not entirely plausible if one considers some thirty coups in South and Central America. Nawaz argues that many countries stumble on their way to nationhood and stable polities due to their lack of fully developed political systems. Therefore, the interaction of military and political leaders and their respective ambitions and inclinations may well account for some of these interventions.[9] Iskander Mirza's justification for his actions included criticism of the 1956 Constitution, which he deemed unworkable due to dangerous compromises that could lead to the disintegration of the country. Mirza proposed to form a committee of 'patriotic' individuals to examine the country's problems and develop a new constitution to be presented in a referendum. Since the constitution under which he was elected had been abrogated, Mirza acknowledged that he could not claim the office of president and instead declared his authority to be a 'revolution'. According to General Ayub, the chief justice of Pakistan endorsed Mirza's continued tenure in office.[10]

However, Ayub deposed him and assumed power in the third week of October, and thus held supreme authority over the nation.[11] Before delving into his policy of centralization and its repercussions, it is important to examine his background as a military officer, before he developed political aspirations and ascended to autocratic rule to ultimately wield unfettered power.

Contextualizing the Military–Civilian Relationship

The Pakistan Army inherited a 'great tradition of loyalty, sense of duty, patriotism and complete subordination to civil authority'.[12] But this tradition was not without some degree of flexibility. In October 1947, as Indian troops began their occupation of Kashmir, Jinnah flew to Lahore to address the Kashmir issue. As the supreme civilian authority in the newly founded state, he ordered the Pakistani Army to enter Kashmir. However, the orders were defied, as Hector Bolitho, an author from New Zealand, documents, and 'Field Marshal Sir Claud Auchinleck flew to Lahore at an hour's notice and reasoned with Quaid.' Auchinleck explained that the presence of Indian troops in Kashmir was justified because the Maharaja Hari Singh had acceded, and any action by the Pakistan Army would force him to withdraw all British officers, including the commander-in-chief of India and Pakistan. As a result, the desperate move was abandoned.[13] In light of this precarious situation, Jinnah issued a directive to his acting commander-in-chief, General Sid Douglas Gracey, instructing him to deploy Pakistani troops to Kashmir. Instead of following the orders from civilian authorities, Gracey chose to contact Auchinleck.[14] The events that unfolded in Kashmir further challenge Ayub's claim of 'subordination to the civilian authority'. This meant that the decision to send troops into Kashmir was not in the hands of the civilian authority, but rather in the hands of the British officers. Therefore, the notion of civilian supremacy during colonial rule was merely a facade, and Ayub's claim that it existed in Pakistan's history stands contradicted.

The British Empire often assigned soldiers to political roles in its colonies, including India. The last two viceroys of India, Lord Wavell and Louis Mountbatten, both from the armed forces, had a reputation for giving orders to politicians and even imprisoning them if necessary. This behaviour of senior officers was not lost on Indian officers serving in the British Indian Army. It provides context for understanding Ayub Khan's conduct towards civilian leaders during his time as general officer commanding (GOC) in East Bengal from January 1948 to November 1949. His dealings with Chief Minister Khawaja Nazimuddin and other politicians reflected the typical mindset of a British colonial officer.[15] Shuja Nawaz states that Ayub told American Consul General Raleigh A. Gibson that

> he had been talking to the leading politicians of Pakistan, and had told them that they must make up their minds to go whole-heartedly with the West ... He stated that the Pakistan Army will not allow the politicians to get out of hand, and the same is true regarding the people of Pakistan.[16]

Ayub Khan assumed the position of commander-in-chief in the Pakistan armed forces in January 1951. Major General Iskander Mirza, a civil servant of the Indian Political Service and a fellow Sandhurst graduate, was serving as the defence secretary at the time. Mirza's mindset, as described by Kalim Siddiqui, was that of a 'political intriguer'.[17] After attaining the rank of colonel, he resigned his commission and joined the Indian Political Service in August 1926, which was composed of equal parts ICS and the Indian Army.[18] Mirza had long experience as a British political agent on the Northwest Frontier. Ayub Khan, however, was a simple soldier who did not expect to reach the rank of brigadier in the British Indian Army.[19] A typical soldier, Khan had a tendency to view issues in a simplistic manner with clear distinctions between right and wrong. This quality was essential for soldiers in order to prevent them from being plagued by doubts in the midst of battle. Khan grasped a fundamental truth: Pakistan's survival hinged on the presence of a highly skilled, adequately equipped and expertly led military force. His vision did not extend beyond this crucial point.[20]

The majority of Muslim officers in the British Army were the offspring of feudal lords who supported the Raj. At first, the colonial system offered financial assistance to the poor relations of the British aristocracy. Later, this privilege was extended to the sons of loyal natives. It is worth noting that there was a significant difference between Hindu and Muslim officers in the British Indian Army. Hindu officers remained connected to the national struggle led by the Indian National Congress, while Muslim officers merely observed Jinnah's campaign. Muslim leader of the INC and India's first minister for education Abul Kalam Azad recalls that wherever Congress leaders went, they were greeted by members of the Hindu armed forces, both non-commissioned and commissioned officers.[21] Muslim officers were not as bold as their Hindu counterparts in the British Indian Army. Muslim army personnel, like their civilian counterparts, were uncertain about the outcome of the political struggle and were hesitant to take risks in case Jinnah's efforts were unsuccessful.

Ayub Khan's Formative Years

Ayub Khan, a member of the Tarin tribe and a native speaker of Hindko, a Punjabi dialect spoken in the northern Punjab and the Hazara Division of Khyber Pakhtunkhwa, was born on 14 May 1906 in the scenic village of Rehana in Haripur, which is now a district of Khyber Pakhtunkhwa. His father, Mir Dad Khan, was a Risaldar major in Hodson's Horse, a cavalry regiment in the British Indian Army. Despite having limited means, with his military pension and land, Mir Dad Khan supported his large family, as Ayub Khan notes in his memoirs *Friends Not Masters*.[22] After losing his first wife, who had given him four children, he remarried, and Ayub became the first child of his second wife.

Ayub's father had a strong religious inclination: he wanted Ayub to memorize the Quran, but Ayub's reluctance to do so led to his early departure from religious instruction. Instead, he was sent to a school in a nearby village, where he made steady progress in his studies. His father was pleased with his progress and subsequently sent him to Mohammadan Anglo Oriental College in Aligarh, a prestigious educational institution for north Indian Muslims, where he continued his education.[23]

In his autobiography, Ayub recounts how his time at Aligarh taught him the importance of internalizing and understanding different perspectives. He also worked on improving his Urdu pronunciation, and developed a Muslim nationalist outlook and modernist approach to Islam that would shape his social and religious policies as a leader.

In July 1926, Ayub went to England to attend Sandhurst, where he quickly made a name for himself as the first overseas cadet to be promoted to corporal. After serving in the 1st/14th Punjab Regiment, he was appointed as a staff officer at Army headquarters in Delhi. During the Second World War, he fought in Burma as second in command of the 1st Assam Regiment before being transferred to the Khyber Pass, where he received his first command position.

However, it was Ayub's role as an advisory officer to Major General Thomas Wynford Rees (1898–1959), a Welsh officer in the British Indian Army from the First through the Second World War, that altered his views on soldiers intervening in politics. The Punjab Boundary Force was created to protect the population of the twelve border areas of partitioned Punjab during the transfer of power, but it was hopelessly inadequate, and the communal atmosphere infected the police and the force itself. The mass

Khyber Pass.

migrations resulted in uncontrollable mayhem, forcing the Joint Defence Council to disband the Boundary Force in Lahore on 29 August 1947.

Shortly after Ayub's return to West Pakistan, General Gracey's term as Pakistan's commander-in-chief expired. Gracey had hoped for an extension, but his controversial refusal to obey Jinnah's order to send troops into Kashmir in October 1947 had dashed those dreams. Ayub was appointed as the first Pakistani commander-in-chief of the Army in January 1951. His rapid promotion was partly due to luck, as some distinguished senior officers, including General Akbar Khan, had died in a plane crash. Ayub Khan's rapid promotion to the position of commander-in-chief of the armed forces was a result of his administrative abilities and apparent apolitical stance. However, it is now clear that his manoeuvres were politically motivated, and he had been involved in political intrigue since the days of Malik Ghulam Muhammad. He played a key role in the uncertain chain of events that troubled Pakistan's political landscape in the 1950s. Despite this, he managed to secure an extension as commander-in-chief in 1954 and assumed the position of Pakistan's defence minister while still holding the post of commander-in-chief of the armed forces.[24] Ayub Khan wielded significant power as commander-in-chief, which enabled him to veto any policies that he believed went against the military's interests.

Throughout the 1950s and '60s, Khan emerged as the most powerful figure in Pakistani politics, and his alignment of Pakistan's external and internal policies with U.S. interests played a critical role in consolidating his power. The United States supported the dominance of the military in Pakistan, viewing it as the most capable and forward-looking institution in the country. American military-aid programmes brought military and economic elements closer, further strengthening the military's position in the country.²⁵ Similarly, an American President's Committee concluded that the military officers' corps was a significant bulwark in the fight against communist expansion and infiltration.

It is worth highlighting the regime's external connections, since they influenced the way Ayub's government defended its place in society. The government's self-conception was shaped by the ideological framework of modernization theory, which portrayed the military as agents of modernization in a traditional society. Like most conceptions of self, it was a flattering portrayal.²⁶ Hence the military, with U.S. support, had become the senior partner in its nexus with the civilian bureaucracy, and took over the mantle of ensuring centralization in Pakistan. As the Bangladeshi political scientist Rounaq Jahan states,

> The first cabinet of the Ayub regime did not include any prominent politicians nor did the subsequent cabinets during the martial law period (1958–62). However, with the introduction of the 1962 constitution, the regime had to come to terms with the political elite and included politicians in the cabinet. But even after 1962, none of the key cabinet portfolios such as defence, planning, finance, or home were entrusted to the politicians.²⁷

Ayub's first cabinet consisted of three generals and six civilians, three from West Pakistan and three from East Pakistan, and a 1954 Constitution document was adopted as its political charter. Ayub, a spokesman for the military elite in 1954, circulated his draft constitution among various non-political colleagues, including Iskander Mirza, urging the adoption of a controlled

Ayub Khan (right) with U.S. president Lyndon B. Johnson, Karachi, 1967.

form of democracy with checks and counterchecks. He had drawn up the document in a London hotel. He suggested that certain preliminary steps would have to be taken before such a constitution could be adopted, and that the taking of such preliminary steps should be the immediate aim of Pakistan.[28] He did not, however, elaborate on what those preliminary steps would be.

Two civilians who stood out for their exceptional abilities during Ayub Khan's regime were Manzoor Qadir from the Punjab, known for his independent thinking, and Zulfiqar Ali Bhutto, a passionate young lawyer from Sindh who served as the minister of commerce. During the early years of Ayub's rule, Qadir and Bhutto were instrumental in drafting the constitution that was promulgated by Ayub in 1962.[29] In fact, Qadir convinced Ayub that public opinion was often ill-informed and that political parties were a threat to the stability of any political system. Meanwhile, Bhutto argued that Ayub must retain all power and establish a centralized authoritarian administration. Together, these two men had a significant impact on shaping Ayub's political ideology and governance style.[30] The aspiration for a centralized set-up on the part of military as well as civilian lieutenants of Ayub was realized in the 1962 Constitution.

The Constitution of 1962

In his memoir, Ayub Khan expressed serious doubts about the ingenuity of Chaudhry Muhammad Ali, who was the chief architect of the 1956 Constitution. In Ayub's view, that constitution was completely disconnected from the genius of the Pakistani people.[31] He referred to it as a 'document of despair'.[32] Therefore, he felt a pressing need for a new constitution that was better suited to the people and the country, which he believed were not yet ready for Western-style democracy. As a result, a new text was drafted and circulated, which he described as 'a blending of democracy with discipline'.[33] The 1962 Constitution was characterized by the centralization of power in the hands of Ayub, who became an extremely powerful president of a federal government. This led to the provinces losing their autonomy, making it nearly impossible for their governments to function independently. Additionally, the Constitution only provided one list of subjects, the federal list, which contained 48 items.[34] It included 'such subjects as defence, external affairs, admission and departure of aliens, citizenship, trade and commerce between the provinces and with foreign countries, currency, posts and many similar matters'.[35] The increased powers vested in the president and the restricted role of the legislatures compromised any independence that had thus far been a given for the provinces.[36]

Many analysts equated Ayub Khan with Lyallpur's Ghanta Ghar (the central square of Faisalabad where the eight bazaars converge), a metaphor for the omnipotence accorded to Ayub Khan by the 1962 Constitution.

Justice M. Rustom Kyani among them was the most trenchant, calling it a 'Constitution of the President, by the President, for the President'.[37] The president had exclusive authority to appoint provincial governors as his representatives, whose primary responsibility was to provide him with information on political affairs within their respective provinces. The Provincial Assembly, which was composed of individuals indirectly elected and handpicked by deputy commissioners, served merely as a symbolic entity and lacked any real decision-making power. Its members were 'yesmen' who complied with the government's agenda without any meaningful debate or opposition.[38] Ayub placed unequivocal faith in the bureaucracy for the effective implementation of policies and governance.

The routine decision-making process was delegated to the bureaucracy, and the military maintained a low profile, in order to avoid meddling in civil administration affairs. As a result, there was hardly any deviation from the state structure established by the British. Ayub Khan relied heavily on the steel framework of the civil services, much like the viceroy during the colonial era. Unlike his successor, General Zia ul Haq, Ayub trusted the civil bureaucracy to provide the backbone of his regime. He sought advice from bureaucrats such as Akhtar Hussain, S. M. Yousaf, Fida Hassan, Qudrat Ullah Shahab and Altaf Gauhar, but mostly he made his own decisions.[39] The Pakistani poet Habib Jalib (1928–1993) composed a work on the 1962 Constitution that became widely popularized:

> He whose light shines only in Palaces
> Who seeks only to please the few
> Who moves in the shadow of compromise
> Such a debased tradition, such a dark dawn
> I don't know, I don't own
> Like audacious Mansoor I declare
> I have no dread of the hangman's plank
> Why do you fear the prison wall,
> These acts of cruelty these nights in jail
> I will not accept, I will not condone.[40]

The 1962 Constitution did not allow any room for political parties; instead, it proposed 'a federal system in which the provinces would have a degree of autonomy that is compatible with the unity and interests of Pakistan as a whole'.[41] Article 131 provided legal backing to any action taken in the national interest, but according to Omar Noman's analysis, the regime's collaboration with the establishment of institutions lacked proper political institutionalization. This refers to the legitimacy of the formal structures of public authority, which can only be attained through the consent of the people. Without this consent, the process can prove to be counterproductive, and the institutions may become a symbol of mass alienation rather than a means of neutralizing political tensions. In Ayub Khan's regime, certain sections of society were incorporated while crucial communities were excluded. The regime's structure had a built-in tendency to exclude opposition, which led to political communities resorting to violent means in order to register their protests.[42]

Political Policies

The execution of policies received far greater emphasis than their formulation, with the exclusion of politicians from the political centre stage proving to be a cardinal feature of policy making. The blame for all the malaise in the country was placed squarely on the shoulders of 'unruly' politicians. To keep these politicians at bay and ensure Ayub Khan remained in the president's office, a policy of political exclusion was formulated. This took the form of the Elective Bodies Disqualification Order (EBDO), which authorized newly established tribunals to try politicians for 'misconduct'. Those accused could avoid prosecution by agreeing not to be a candidate for any elective body for a period of seven years. In 1959, approximately 7,000 individuals were relegated to ignominy through the EBDO. Despite the risk, Hussein Shaheed Suhrawardy, Qazi Isa and Sahibzada Hassan Mehmud opted to face trial and were subsequently arrested and prosecuted.[43] Mohammad Waseem singles out Hussain Shaheed Suhrawardy as the only national leader who dared to oppose the EBDO. In late 1960, Suhrawardy formed the National Democratic Front (NDF), which served as a front organization for the political activities of those who had been EBDOed, although it was not a political party in the strictest sense. This strategy aimed to avoid the axe of the Political Parties Act of 1962, which conditionally allowed the revival of parties. However, an amendment soon broadened the definition of parties and curtailed their activities. Nonetheless, the emergence of the NDF had an important consequence: it catalysed the formation of national alliances of opposition parties in Pakistan's political system. Before Ayub's fall from power on 25 March 1969, at least three such alliances were formed: the Combined Opposition Parties (COP), the Pakistan Democratic Movement (PDM) and the Democratic Action Committee (DAC). This marked a new era of national opposition, at a time when almost all political forces felt threatened by attempts to delegitimize political activity itself.[44]

Ayub Khan utilized the media to both defame politicians and tout the accomplishments of his regime, though the latter was met with limited success. On 16 April 1959, a martial-law ordinance authorized the government to take over newspapers that 'published or contained matters likely to endanger the defence, external affairs, or security of Pakistan'. Concurrently, the Public Safety Ordinances, already established to regulate news content, were strictly enforced. On 28 March 1963, the Press and

Muhammad Ali Jinnah with his sister Fatima Jinnah, Karachi, 1948.

Publication Ordinance was enacted with the aim of making the press conform to recognized principles of journalism and patriotism.[45] Subsequently newspapers the *Pakistan Times* and *The Imroz* were seized by the government. The media house Progressive Papers Limited was taken over because of its alleged leftist leanings, and a ban was imposed on the publication of news related to strikes and industrial unrest. That same year, all newspapers were required to publish press releases issued by the central and provincial governments. In an effort to silence dissenting voices, the National Press Trust was established, funded by 24 industrialists and supported by the state. Its objective was to cultivate and promote positive sentiments towards the Ayub regime.

During the 1964–5 election campaign, Radio Pakistan was the only available media, and it adopted a blanket 'blackout' policy on opposition voices. Furthermore, it attempted to minimize the coverage of Fatima Jinnah, Jinnah's sister and the main opposition leader. The combined opposition candidate, Jinnah had emerged from her self-imposed political retirement in 1965 to participate in the presidential election against Ayub Khan. Upon entering the political scene, she accused the government of creating an 'atmosphere laden with fear and reeking with corruption'.[46] She was a vocal advocate for the abolition of the current authoritarian presidential system and the carefully controlled pyramid of successive indirect votes for national and provincial legislatures. She believed that people must be given the right to full and direct franchise, and she sought to restore a parliamentary form of government with a prime minister as its head.[47] Despite winning 35.86 per cent of the Electoral College votes, her media coverage was limited. (Contemporaneously, the Lahore radio station launched a programme called *Massi Mehru* intended to ridicule women's participation in the election.)

The first phase of the election campaign began on 18 September 1964, and continued until the end of October. During this time, Fatima Jinnah travelled to major cities in West Pakistan to rally support. Meanwhile, the ruling political party maintained a discreet silence because no one in the government dared to criticize Jinnah, creating a disconcerting situation for Ayub Khan himself. Partly due to Jinnah's status as a woman and the sister of Quaid-e-Azam, Ayub's acolytes resorted to criticizing her political advisors instead of her directly, but to no avail. Eventually, Ayub decided to take up the challenge and began addressing her in public meetings. His first such meeting was held in Peshawar on 13 October, with the help of the local administration, who amassed a large crowd. However, Ayub lacked Jinnah's charisma and popular appeal, and his inadequate command of Urdu compounded his problems. According to the Pakistani civil servant and author Altaf Gauhar, he quickly learned from his mistakes and began speaking with greater confidence after three or four public meetings.[48]

Fatima Jinnah completed her initial series of public meetings in West Pakistan before proceeding to East Pakistan. There, people felt that their rights had been unjustly stripped away and that the province was being treated as a mere colony of Islamabad. They saw Jinnah as the only hope for change in the oppressive system. In East Pakistan, she garnered full support from the Awami League, led by Sheikh Mujibur Rahman (1920–1975), and drew larger crowds there than in West Pakistan.[49]

In her speeches, Jinnah strongly criticized Ayub Khan, depicting him as an 'interloper and a dictator'. She accused his ministers and governors of being mere puppets with no real power. One minister in particular whom she condemned was Zulfiqar Ali Bhutto, referring to him as an 'inebriate and a philanderer' in her speech at a public rally in Hyderabad. In response, Khan made derogatory remarks about Jinnah's personal life, describing her spinsterhood as 'unnatural' and suggesting that she was surrounded by 'perverts'.[50]

The opposition led by Fatima Jinnah levelled allegations of corruption against Ayub Khan's family, specifically his son Gauhar Ayub Khan, which were widely believed by the public. Gauhar, a retired captain from the Army, had acquired assembly plants from General Motors and renamed them Gandhara Motors. The opposition adopted the slogan 'Gandhara' and used it to devastating effect.[51] From Peshawar to Chittagong, people regarded the name 'Gandhara' as the ultimate symbol of corruption in both Ayub's government and his own family. To counter its impact, Ayub went so far as to obtain a fatwa declaring that a woman could not become the head of a Muslim state. Nevertheless, backed by a consortium of political parties, Jinnah managed to win two of Pakistan's largest cities, Karachi and Dhaka, despite political rigging by the military. Although Khan won the election with 62.43 per cent of the electoral vote, thanks to faithless electors, he had lost the popular vote, and his reputation was further tarnished by the allegations of corruption against his family.[52] This election was a significant blow to Khan's self-confidence.

In a post-election analysis of the voting, the ministry of information identified the segments of the public that held an anti-regime stance. These included the refugees of Karachi, minority communities, industrial labourers and individuals who genuinely believed in civil rights and democracy. During a meeting held by Khan on 17 January, which was attended by, among others, the governors Nawab Amir Muhammad Khan of Kalabagh (of West Pakistan) and Monim Khan (of East Pakistan), he attributed the poor showing to the conduct of officials and individuals who enjoyed the financial patronage of the government.[53]

Scholars and intellectuals faced strict surveillance by the state authorities during Khan's regime and were prohibited from publishing work that

Sheikh Mujibur Rahman, leader of the Awami League and the founding father of Bangladesh, early 1970s.

expressed dissenting views. Faiz Ahmed Faiz, a prominent Pakistani poet and intellectual, stated in 1976 that Khan's government relied not only on coercion and intimidation but on incentives and terror to suppress rebellious voices among the literati and intelligentsia. This led many writers to deviate from their original paths due to fear of reprisal.[54] Social scientist Saadia Toor described these attempts as a strategy for creating the 'Establishment Writer'.[55] The establishment writer was created through the Writers' Guild, which was created by the government to control writers with the implicit motive of restricting free expression and as a thinly disguised attempt by the state to co-opt writers as propagandists. Some who did express criticism, like Safdar Mir (1922-1998), were even exiled to remote areas. The regime also prevented academics and faculty members with overt leftist leanings from being employed in universities.[56]

Notably, Qudrat Ullah Shahab (1917-1986) played a key role in the Guild's creation, along with figures such as Jamil-ud-Din Aali (1925-2015). Through the Writer's Guild, the state provided patronage to the literati, which had a detrimental effect on the intelligentsia and the literature of resistance. Despite this, some voices did speak out against the state's efforts to control writers and poets through covert means. Among them were Josh Malih Abadi (1898-1982) and Habib Jalib.[57]

Ayub Khan's governance was marked by the efficient implementation of policies, but there was little effort to develop these policies through critical thinking. His approach centred on controlling the Civil Service, and this extended to political, social and cultural expressions. Even the judiciary was not exempt from this control. Law reforms had brought the courts under the executive's supervision, a trend that had begun during Ghulam Muhammad's time. At the district level, the judiciary and executive functions were merged in the deputy commissioner's office. The higher judiciary was also subject to control by state functionaries. Judges were evaluated for loyalty to the government through interviews with provincial governors and the president.

Bengali Under-Representation in National Politics

Pakistan's political problems can be traced back to a structural imbalance between the Bengali majority and the dominance of Punjabi-Muhajir elites. During the 1950s, Bengalis negotiated with other power brokers to gain a share of power in the central government. The Constitution of 1956 provided a framework to accommodate different groups and factions – to some extent – but it was far from ideal. Despite their frustration with the military–bureaucratic oligarchy, Bengalis remained hopeful for a democratic dispensation that would include them as partners. However, their hopes were dashed when Iskander Mirza's coup in 1959 disrupted the political process. As a result, the military–bureaucratic oligarchy was further

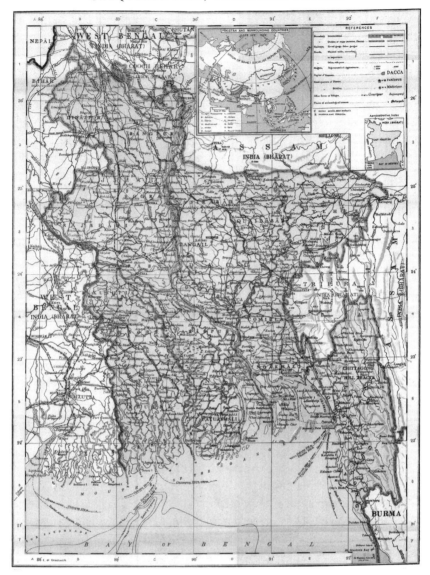

Map of East Pakistan, 1962.

strengthened at the expense of Bengalis, who were under-represented in the government and military throughout Ayub's regime in the 1960s.

In 1966, the mainstream political parties in East Pakistan became fed up with the authoritarian rule of the government and put forth the notion that there were two distinct nations within Pakistan. This call was intended to be a wake-up for the ruling oligarchy and the president, but both dismissed it without much concern. In response, a national conference was organized in Lahore in February of that year, where opposition parties gathered to discuss their differences and find common ground. However, the central issue at the conference was the Tashkent Declaration, which most of the assembled politicians saw as Ayub Khan's unnecessary surrender to India.[58] A more pressing issue at the conference was the lack of representation for politicians from the eastern wing of Pakistan. Out of the seven hundred attendees, only 21 were from East Pakistan, led by Sheikh Mujibur Rahman of the Awami League. At the conference, Rahman presented his controversial six-point plan, which outlined a political and economic programme for East Pakistan. The six points demanded a federal and parliamentary government; universal adult suffrage with legislative representation based on population distribution; foreign-affairs and defence responsibilities to be held by the federal government only; separate currencies and fiscal accounts for each wing; taxation at the provincial level with constitutionally guaranteed grants funding the federal government, each federal unit controlling its own foreign-exchange earnings; and the ability for each unit to raise its own militia or paramilitary forces.[59]

The Punjabi elite, who had dominated the controlling power structures since the 1950s, had assumed the persona of the colonizer. They considered the Bengalis to be inferior, dark-skinned, weak, lesser men of short stature, not fit to rub shoulders with the manly martial races that they imagined themselves to be.[60] Thus the Punjabi elite marginalized the Bengalis from the key organizations of the state apparatus. In 1955, in the higher ranks of the central secretariat, not even one out of nineteen secretaries was Bengali, and at the joint-secretary level, only three out of 41 were Bengalis.[61] Among Army officers, only fourteen out of 908 were Bengali officers; in the Navy, they numbered seven out of six hundred officers; and in the Air Force, sixty out of a total of seven hundred officers.[62]

A System of Basic Democracies

During Ayub Khan's regime, which lasted for over a decade, the institutional structure of the country – which was in its early stages in the 1950s – was significantly redefined with two primary goals in mind. First, the self-perpetuation of the government in the corridors of power, and second, the establishment of a 'direct relationship between the bureaucracy and the rural elite (feudal lords)' by creating a 'network of allies for the government based on access to state resources'. This led to a tangible shift in power dynamics and a consolidation of power within the ruling elites, further marginalizing those without access to resources and political patronage.[63] This new restructuring was 'a particular form of representational dictatorship' based on a system of basic democracies introduced in October 1959.[64] The country, therefore, was divided into 80,000 geographical units, with each constituency comprising an average of 1,000 electorates.

The Basic Democracy (BD) system introduced a four-tiered structure of local government, with BD members being elected through direct adult franchise. At the grass-roots level, two-thirds of Rural Union Councils or Urban Town and Union Committees were comprised of BD members, while the remaining one-third was composed of nominated non-official members appointed by the government. These councils/committees were led by an elected chairman from within their ranks. The Thana or Tehsil Council, one tier above, was chaired by the local *tehsildar*, and half of its members were chairmen from the local Union Councils or Town and Union Committees, while the other half were *thana-/tehsil*-level government officers. The District Council, the third tier, was chaired by the deputy commissioner, and half of its members came from district-level government officers of development departments, while the other half consisted of unofficial members. Only half of the unofficial members, or one-quarter of the total membership, were represented by chairmen of the District Union Councils/Town and Union Committees (that is, elected BD members). At the highest level, the Divisional Council was chaired by the divisional commissioner, and its membership requirement was the same as that of the District Council, except for the inclusion of all deputy commissioners in the division as government officers.[65]

The new electoral system in Pakistan divided the country into small constituencies, effectively ensuring that the elected BD members from rural areas remained under the control of *tehsildars* and deputy commissioners. This meant that the Rural Union Councils were vulnerable to manipulation and coercion by local officialdom, which allowed Ayub Khan to outmanoeuvre potential urban hostility. The hope was that the rural areas would remain passive and not pose a threat to his regime. The first election of the basic democrats was held on 26 December 1959, and two and a half months later, on 14 February 1960, despite the absence of a proper constitution, they managed to 'elect' General Ayub Khan as president, solidifying his new source of power.[66]

The state aimed to legitimize the Ayub regime by bestowing privileges and cultivating new elites. However, this approach inadvertently intensified social, economic and societal tensions.[67] Ayesha Jalal argues that the civil servants played a crucial role in the BD system, since they were responsible for selecting the candidates. This selection process further strengthened the rural elite. The bureaucracy, particularly the Civil Service, was given the privilege of nominating half of the members of the District and Divisional Councils under this new system. It is crucial to provide context by delving into the role, power and privileges of the Civil Service of Pakistan during the 1950s and '60s.[68] It inherited the administrative framework established by the British colonial rulers, commonly referred to as the 'steel frame' of governance.

Under the Ayub Khan regime in Pakistan, the Civil Service assumed a central and influential role. It not only wielded considerable power but enjoyed a wide range of privileges. This bureaucracy held substantial sway in shaping government policies and decisions, effectively acting as a cornerstone of governance and shaping the socio-political landscape of Pakistan. Its administrative control extended across various sectors, and it played a pivotal role in the implementation of both economic and political reforms, which were instrumental in further consolidating its authority.

However, while its influence was intended to promote stability and development, it occasionally gave rise to disparities and social tensions within the nation. This was partly due to the concentration of power and decision-making authority within a relatively small group of individuals, which could lead to policies that favoured certain sections of society over others.

This arrangement, which enhanced civil servants' role, favoured rural politicians since it tipped the balance in their favour. However, this disenfranchised the industrial labourers and intelligentsia, who were the most volatile sections of urban societies. Despite opposition from the urban sections of society, the BD order was incorporated into the 1962 Constitution.[69]

On 6 February 1960 the basic democrats were asked a simple question: 'Do you have confidence in President Ayub Khan?' By securing 95.6 per cent of votes, Ayub Khan legitimized his position as president.[70] Whether the BD system proved advantageous for Pakistan or not, in the United States, Ayub Khan's unique leadership experience received acclaim and admiration. The extensive rural development initiatives implemented during his presidency, particularly in East Pakistan, were lauded in 1968 as a demonstration of Jeffersonian democracy in action by the leaders of the Harvard Advisory Group (HAG) in Dhaka.[71] Even the British historian Arnold Toynbee considered it to be a plausible alternative between the Western democratic system and the communist system, stating that BD suggested 'a possible way in which politically and economically backward countries can arrive at self-government on our Western lines. So, I should say that the Pakistan experiment in so-called basic democracy deserves our sympathy and support and certainly deserves our attention.'[72]

Given the role of HAG on the nation's economic planning during the 1960s, it seems imperative to divert our attention to describe what it was and its significance for Pakistan's economic history. Until 1970, Pakistan's economic development was significantly shaped by foreign economic advisors, particularly from 1960 to 1970. In the 1950s, while foreign assistance in macroeconomic management existed, it played a more catalytic role in economic decision-making. Technical assistance was necessary for establishing the Planning Commission and provincial planning boards and in various sectors. However, as a result of Pakistan's closer economic and political ties with the United States under General Ayub Khan's military regime, foreign advisors became more predominant. The primary source of economic advisory services for Pakistan was HAG, sponsored by the Ford Foundation. In 1954, when the first two Harvard advisors arrived in

Pakistan, the nascent Pakistan Planning Board had only a few professionals on staff. By mid-1965, during the completion of the first five-year plan, the staff had grown to 55. The number of HAG advisors reached its peak at seventeen in January 1965.

Foreign advisors played a leading role in drafting the first five-year plan. However, Zahid Hussain, the chairman of the Board, also contributed significantly by writing the introductory chapters that outlined the social and cultural planning framework and by addressing public administration and land reforms. He edited drafts of other chapters prepared by HAG members. The influence of HAG in Pakistan's planning and economic management processes grew significantly during Ayub's regime, particularly with the arrival of Richard Gilbert in September 1960 as the group's field supervisor. Gilbert, an advocate of government intervention in the economy, played a pivotal role in securing PL480 funding for Pakistan and increasing consortium aid for the second five-year plan. His efforts led to the strengthening of the Planning Commission, the robustness of which served the goals of both the Harvard advisors and President Khan. The advisors aimed to align Pakistan with market-oriented policies, such as liberalization of imports, relaxation of economic regulations and the promotion of private enterprise. For Khan, higher growth and substantial foreign aid were essential to legitimizing his regime, by mitigating development challenges and maintaining defence spending. These policies resulted in a substantial increase in foreign aid to Pakistan from Western countries.

Foreign advisors at the Pakistan Institute of Development Economics (PIDE) focused on gaining experience in a developing country and contributing to the growing field of development economics. Notable advisors at PIDE included Gustav Ranis, John Fei, Richard Porter, Henry Bruton, John Powers, Keith Griffin and Stephen Lewis Jr. PIDE also facilitated the training of young Pakistani economists and promoted their research.

While West Pakistani economists dominated the Planning Commission, East Pakistani economists had a larger presence at PIDE. Dr Nurul Islam's appointment as the first Pakistani Director of PIDE emphasized this difference. However, much of the research published in the *Pakistan Development Review* during the 1960s was conducted by foreign advisors or East Pakistani economists, and West Pakistani economists often felt marginalized. Collaboration between PIDE and the Department of Economics at Quaid-e-Azam University was hindered by turf conflicts, preventing the growth of a collaborative relationship that could have contributed to the development of a top-tier economics centre in Pakistan.[73]

Economic Development or Differential Economic Patronage

Economic development was a key priority for Khan, who believed it could address Pakistan's myriad problems. His comprehensive scheme for economic development was widely praised. However, a closer look at the economic progress made in the 1960s suggests that sustainable economic growth requires political liberalism and stability, which can only be achieved through democracy. Democracy prevents the emergence of monopolies, ensuring that wealth is more equitably distributed. Consequently, the fruits of development benefit not just the elite but the middle and lower echelons of society. Jalal points out that the BD system was beset with politico-economic contradictions, and the measures taken to make the system acceptable to society and to legitimize the regime actually ended up favouring a narrow political constituency. Economic progress was seen as a solution to suppress dissent, but it resulted in differential economic favouritism: the assumption that rapid economic growth would benefit all society proved to be inaccurate.[74]

The economic development efforts by Khan's regime were globally seen as a remarkable success story, with impressive growth indicators reflecting its progress. During the second five-year plan, the large-scale manufacturing sector achieved an unparalleled growth rate of 16.2 per cent, the highest in the world. Although the rate slowed to 7.7 per cent during the third five-year plan, it still performed well by international standards. Even the agricultural sector, which had long been considered the 'sick man' of economic development in the 1960s, achieved a respectable growth rate of 3.8 per cent.

The achievements of the second five-year plan were largely credited to a strategic shift towards embracing market mechanisms and employing fiscal and monetary policies, as opposed to relying on direct controls over prices, profits and resource allocation. The plan placed significant emphasis on the execution of the industrial development programme, primarily leaning on private enterprise for its implementation. However, despite the notable growth indicators, Pakistan's economic progress during Ayub Khan's administration was marred by the emergence of political and economic contradictions stemming from the BD system. This period of economic growth was accompanied by a form of selective economic favouritism, which primarily benefited a narrowly defined political constituency.[75]

The Ayub government implemented various policy measures to improve the investment climate and boost the morale of the private sector. Fiscal incentives were provided to investors, while trade unions were banned and anyone inciting labour strikes faced up to two years' imprisonment. The government also began dismantling direct controls on foreign exchange and investment sanctions, leading to a significant increase in capital inflow from 2.5 per cent of GNP in the mid-1950s to around 7 per cent in the mid-1960s. Instead of import substitution, the market for manufactured goods was made available by expanding domestic demand. However, during the third five-year-plan, which began after the 1965 war with India, things started to go wrong. All foreign aid to Pakistan was suspended, and even when it resumed a year later, it was significantly lower than the third plan had anticipated. A large amount of foreign exchange was also allocated for defence purposes, further worsening the state of the economy. Moreover, severe droughts in 1965 and 1967 led to the need for food imports, which put additional pressure on Pakistan's foreign-exchange reserves.[76]

The economic policies adopted by Ayub's government to accclerate economic growth also resulted in significant political and economic tensions. The tensions escalated into widespread political unrest in the winter of 1968, with mass protests organized by students, industrial workers and lawyers in urban areas. The demonstrations were triggered by rising prices of consumer goods and fuelled by growing resentment over increasing inequalities in Pakistan. Ayub's development strategy was blamed for exacerbating these inequalities, not just among different income groups but between different regions of the country.

In response to these tensions, the government had to abandon its focus on manufacturing capital goods and instead prioritize export-orientated consumer goods industries. However, this change of direction had limited success due to constraints on foreign exchange and other economic challenges, such as droughts. The deceleration of economic growth, coupled with an increase in the prices of everyday goods, led to the reintroduction of regulatory measures. These circumstances collectively exerted a stifling influence on industrial expansion and played a part in exacerbating the mounting political and economic tensions throughout Ayub's rule.[77]

The Ayub regime's strategy for industrial development, which heavily leaned on private enterprise and foreign investments, faced substantial criticism. Notably, Pakistani economist Akmal Hussain scrutinizes the period during which the two five-year plans were conceived and executed. Hussain highlights that the establishment of consumer goods industries during this time was centred on 'import substitution' and often under the control of foreign monopoly capital. This approach led to the exploitation of impoverished workers, further aggravating social disparities rather than mitigating them. Consequently, it nurtured a West Pakistani elite with government backing.

Critics of Ayub's economic growth strategy pointed out that the apparent economic growth gains came at the cost of addressing underlying structural inequalities and poverty in a meaningful manner.[78] During the Ayub regime, the economic policies implemented primarily favoured Muhajirs and Punjabis, and this was not a mere coincidence.

In terms of per capita income, from 1959 to 1970 there was a modest increase. However, a notable disparity becomes evident when we look at the growth rates in agriculture and large-scale manufacturing – the two sectors in which Muhajirs and Punjabis were most prominently engaged. Agriculture experienced a substantial growth rate of 6.3 per cent during this period, indicating a favourable environment for those involved in this sector. Large-scale manufacturing, on the other hand, showed an even more significant growth rate of 16.9 per cent at the beginning of Ayub's tenure, though this had declined to 9.9 per cent by the end of his rule. This selective economic growth was not coincidental but rather a result of the government's policies and priorities during that era.[79]

The Land Reforms Regulation, enforced on 7 February 1959, was a serious attempt at land reform in West Pakistan, which was dominated by landlords. But Ayub Khan's policy, despite its initial promise, ultimately failed to bring about its intended social and political changes. While it was hailed by many as a 'radical measure', its high ceiling of 202 hectares (500 ac) of irrigated land or 404 hectares (1,000 ac) of unirrigated land was not enforced due to intra-family transfers and numerous other irregularities that severely restricted the amount of land that was resumed. Revenue officials nullified sales to tenants, and landlords still charged rent on land that tenants had purchased. Such anomalies in implementation rendered the reforms ineffective, allowing big landholdings to continue to exist and their owners to retain control over crucial decisions about the fate of the country.

During Ayub Khan's leadership, Pakistan's atomic energy programme garnered substantial backing, marked by the transformation of the Pakistan Atomic Energy Commission (PAEC) into a statutory entity in 1965. In order to strengthen the nuclear power initiative, the National Center for Advanced Studies in Research (PINSTECH) was founded in Nilore, Islamabad. It was equipped with essential facilities, including a 5-megawatt swimming pool research reactor and a sub-critical assembly, as well as other critical tools like neutron generators and cobalt sources. PINSTECH was equipped to address the challenges in nuclear technology that the PAEC faced. It included large laboratories in the fields of electronics, nuclear materials, radioisotope production and application, nuclear physics and radiation chemistry.[80]

The construction of the Karachi Nuclear Power Plant (KANUPP), located 29 kilometres (18 mi.) west of Karachi, marked the country's first foray into atomic power, with a generating capacity of 137,000 kilowatts gross. KANUPP served as a vital solution to Pakistan's growing energy demands and limited supply. Together with PINSTECH, it became a key focus of the country's peaceful nuclear energy efforts. Although the Engineering Research Laboratory (ERL), later renamed the Dr A. Q. Khan Research Laboratory, was established in July 1976 – that is, after Ayub Khan's tenure had ended – his contributions to Pakistan's nuclear programme at policy level cannot be overlooked.[81]

The Misadventure of 1965

The Indo-Pakistani War of 1965 marked a significant escalation of tensions between Pakistan and India, following a series of skirmishes that took place from April to September of that year. The conflict was triggered by Pakistan's launch of Operation Gibraltar, which involved sending Army personnel to infiltrate Jammu and Kashmir and instigate an insurgency against Indian rule. The war was predominantly fought by the land forces of India and Pakistan, mainly in the region of Kashmir and along the shared border. The military engagements involved infantry and armoured units on both sides, with substantial support from air and naval operations. The hostilities between the two countries persisted for several months, causing immense damage and loss of life on both sides. However, the conflict eventually came to a halt after a ceasefire was declared through UNSC Resolution 211, a resolution made possible by diplomatic interventions from the Soviet Union and the United States.

In the wake of the war, the Tashkent Declaration was signed with the objective of re-establishing peace and fostering better relations between Pakistan and India. Regrettably, the declaration fell short of fully realizing its intended objectives, and tensions between the two nations have endured until today.[82]

At the time, the war was viewed internationally in the context of the broader Cold War, and it had significant geopolitical implications for the subcontinent. Prior to the conflict, the United States and the United Kingdom had been crucial allies of both India and Pakistan, supplying them with military hardware and foreign developmental aid. However, during and after the war, both countries felt let down by the perceived lack of support from their Western allies, particularly following the imposition of an American and British embargo on military aid to both sides.

Consequently, India and Pakistan pivoted towards closer relationships with different global powers, with India forging closer ties with the Soviet Union and Pakistan strengthening its relationship with China. This geopolitical realignment had far-reaching consequences for the region, and it significantly impacted the subsequent development of India–Pakistan relations.

Border Disputes and Conflict Dynamics

Pakistan and India have been embroiled in several conflicts since the partition of British India in 1947, with the issue of Kashmir being the most contentious and well known of their disputes. However, there were also other border disagreements, including the Rann of Kutch region, a desolate landscape that spans some 23,000 square kilometres (8,880 sq. mi.) of dried-out salt beds, marshes and sand dunes that are thought to have previously been part of the Arabian Sea. The Rann of Kutch issue initially emerged in 1956, when Pakistan and India engaged in armed conflict over control of the area. However, after a prolonged dispute-resolution process, India ultimately regained control over the region.

Despite this, tensions between Pakistan and India over border disputes have continued to simmer, resulting in several military conflicts and diplomatic stand-offs over the years. The issue of the Rann of Kutch, while not as well known as the Kashmir conflict, serves as an example of the complexity and volatility of the border disputes that continue to divide the nations.[83] In January 1965, Pakistani forces began patrolling territory that was under the control of India, and this eventually led to both countries launching attacks on each other's posts, on 8 April 1965.[84] To gain control of the region, Pakistan launched Operation Desert Hawk, which resulted in the capture of several Indian posts near the Kanjarkot fort border area.[85] In June 1965 the British prime minister, Harold Wilson, successfully negotiated a ceasefire agreement between Pakistan and India, which brought an end to hostilities in the disputed Rann of Kutch region. However, it was not until 1968 that an international tribunal was able to formally settle the territorial dispute.

The tribunal's verdict delineated the marshy salt flats that form the two shallow lakes of the region (the Great Rann and the Little Rann). In the dry season, this land is a salt-covered desert. The tribunal awarded 90 per cent of the Rann of Kutch to India and the remaining 10 per cent (approximately 800 square kilometres (309 sq. mi.) to Pakistan, which primarily comprised the elevated area above water throughout the year. Both Pakistan and India accepted the tribunal's decision, thus ending the territorial dispute and setting the stage for improved diplomatic relations between the two nations.[86]

Following Operation Desert Hawk in the Rann of Kutch, Pakistani leadership believed that the Indian Army was ill-prepared to defend itself against a rapid military campaign in the disputed region of Kashmir, especially since the Indian military had suffered a defeat in the 1962 Sino-Indian War. Although the Indian military was undergoing massive changes in terms of personnel and equipment, Pakistani armed forces had a qualitative edge in air power and armour over India, which they sought to utilize before India completed its defence build-up.

Since its annexation in 1948, Kashmir had been a source of discontentment, with many Kashmiris unhappy about Indian rule, particularly after the incarceration of Kashmiri leader Shaikh Abdullah. Pakistani leadership, including Foreign Minister Zulfiqar Ali Bhutto and Foreign Secretary Aziz Ahmad, saw an opportunity to take action. Major General Akhter Malik, who conceived the idea of Operation Gibraltar, as stated in his planning directive of 17 May 1965, aimed to compel India to 'either come to the negotiating table in a chastened mood or face a growing menace in Kashmir imposing an ever-increasing burden on her economy'.[87]

In December 1964 the idea of provoking a Kashmiri revolt against India was first presented to Ayub Khan, but he dismissed it as 'quixotic' after examining it with Altaf Gauhar. Ayub had previously rejected such a plan as 'amateurish' when he was commander-in-chief. However, in February 1965, it was presented again to the Intelligence Committee of the Cabinet, with General Musa, Bhutto and Aziz Ahmed also in attendance. Ayub listened to the presentation and asked who authorized the Foreign Office and the ISI to draw up such a plan, since it was not their job. He had only asked them to keep an eye on the situation in Kashmir. He realized that they could force the government into a campaign of military action. Despite being a generally cautious man, Ayub ultimately took the risk of implementing the plan in 1965.[88] Gul Hassan and Mahmud Ahmed assert that the Kashmir cell was likely the source of persuasion for Ayub, since the General Headquarters (GHQ) did not support the plan. Interestingly, General Musa Khan was not particularly keen on the plan either. He believed that India would seize the opportunity to escalate the conflict into a larger war by conducting deep raids in the disputed territory.[89]

General Musa Khan, who served as the commander-in-chief of the Pakistani Armed Forces, shared his perspective during a 1978 interview held at the Staff College, Quetta. He expressed his bewilderment over President Ayub Khan's decision-making process, particularly with regard to the pivotal choice over how to deal with Kashmir and the president's risky and daring course of action.

Operation Gibraltar

Pakistan launched a covert operation, named Operation Gibraltar, to ignite a resistance movement in Kashmir by infiltrating its soldiers. However, the plan was soon discovered when the presence of the infiltrators was reported by local Kashmiris, and the operation failed to yield the desired results. According to Gul Hassan, the chief of general staff (CGS) in 1965, General Sher Bahadur viewed Operation Gibraltar as an illegitimate plan, created through the collaboration of the Foreign Office and HQ 12 Division. As a result, there was no formal meeting held in the GHQ to coordinate or resolve the problems that arose during the operation.[90]

On 5 August 1965, an estimated 26,000 to 33,000 Pakistani soldiers reportedly infiltrated the Line of Control disguised as Kashmiri locals and headed to different parts of Kashmir. However, the Indian forces had been alerted by the local population and on 15 August the Indian forces crossed the ceasefire line.[91] Initially, the Indian Army achieved some success, capturing three strategically important mountain positions after a prolonged artillery barrage. However, by the end of August, Pakistan had gained ground in areas such as Tithwal, Uri and Poonch, while India had managed to capture the Haji Pir Pass, which was located 8 kilometres (5 mi.) inside Pakistan-administered Kashmir.[92]

On 1 September at 5 a.m., Pakistan launched a counterattack, dubbed Operation Grand Slam, with the aim of capturing the crucial town of Akhnoor in Jammu. The capture of Akhnoor would effectively sever communication and supply routes to Indian troops. Ayub Khan was of the opinion that 'Hindu morale would not stand more than a couple of hard blows at the right time and place,' although, at that time, Operation Gibraltar was in a slump and India had already captured the Haji Pir Pass. At 3:30 a.m., the entire Chhamb area, the last outpost of Pakistan-controlled Kashmir, came under heavy artillery bombardment.[93] When Pakistan initiated Operation Grand Slam, it caught India's army headquarters off guard, leading to significant initial gains for Pakistani forces as unprepared Indian units suffered heavy losses. In response, India called upon its Air Force to repel the Pakistani offensive. The following day, Pakistan retaliated by launching air attacks on Indian forces and air bases in both Kashmir and the Punjab.

However, India made a strategic decision to broaden the scope of its counterattack, specifically targeting the Pakistani Punjab region. This move compelled the Pakistani Army to divert troops from Operation Grand Slam to protect the homeland. This significant shift marked a turning point in the conflict, as India sought to alleviate pressure on its troops in Kashmir by expanding its operations further south.[94] Consequently, Operation Grand Slam failed to achieve its intended objectives and essentially became a pivotal moment in the war, characterized by India's strategic shift and Pakistan's need to redirect its forces to defend its heartland.

The Kargil sector, a part of the disputed territory, was of significant strategic importance as Pakistan had occupied high ground overlooking Kargil and the Srinagar–Leh Road, which was under Indian control. However, after the launch of a massive anti-infiltration operation by the Indian Army by August 1965 the Pakistani infiltrators were forced to retreat from the area.[95]

India crossed the international border on the western front on 6 September, launching Operation Riddle.[96] On 6 September the 15th Infantry Division of the Indian Army, led by Major General Niranjan Prasad, encountered a massive counterattack by Pakistan near the west bank of the Icchogil (BRB) Canal, which served as the de facto border between India and Pakistan. During the ambush, the general's entourage was targeted, and he was forced to flee his vehicle. Later, the Indian Army made another attempt to cross the Ichhogil Canal, which was successful, and it happened over the bridge in the village of Burki, located east of Lahore. The Battle of Burki took place along the Khalra–Burki–Lahore Road. Pakistan's primary objective was to push the Indian infantry into retreat before their armoured support and supply lines could reinforce them. Additionally, the Pakistani Army sought to regain the territory it had lost in previous engagements. However, the Indian Army's advance brought them dangerously close to Lahore International Airport. It was during this critical phase that Major Aziz Bhatti exhibited extraordinary courage and successfully repelled the Indian advance. Tragically, he paid the ultimate sacrifice and was martyred in the line of duty on 12 September 1965.[97]

The thrust against Lahore was led by the 1st Infantry Division, with support from the three tank regiments of the 2nd Independent Armoured Brigade. They quickly crossed the border and reached the BRB Canal by 6 September. However, the Pakistani Army held the bridges over the canal – or blew up those it could not hold – effectively stalling any further advance on Lahore by the Indians. One unit of the Indian Jat Regiment, 3 Jat, had also crossed the BRB Canal and captured the town of Batapore (Jallo Mur to Pakistan) on the canal's west side. The same day, a counteroffensive consisting of an armoured division and infantry division supported by Pakistan Air Force Sabres forced the Indian 15th Division to withdraw to its starting point.

Although 3 Jat suffered minimal casualties, the higher commanders were misinformed about their capture of Batapore, leading the command to withdraw from Batapore and Dograi to Ghosal-Dial. This move brought extreme disappointment to Lieutenant Colonel Desmond Hayde, commanding officer of 3 Jat. Dograi was eventually recaptured by 3 Jat – but after a much harder battle, due to Pakistani reinforcements – on 21 September in the Battle of Dograi.

On 8 September 1965 a company of 5 Maratha Light Infantry was tasked with reinforcing a Rajasthan Armed Constabulary (RAC) post at Munabao, a strategic hamlet located about 250 kilometres (155 mi.) from Jodhpur. Their mission was straightforward: to hold the post and prevent Pakistani infantry battalions from overrunning it. However, the Indian company could only fend off the intense attack for 24 hours at Maratha Hill (Munabao post). A company of three guards, along with 954 heavy mortar batteries, was ordered to reinforce the RAC post, but did not reach it. The Pakistani Air Force had strafed the entire area and hit a railway train coming from Barmer near Gadra Road railway station with reinforcements. On 10 September Munabao fell to the Pakistan Army, and subsequent attempts to recapture the strategic point were unsuccessful.

In the days following 9 September, both nations' premier formations were routed in unequal battles. India's 1st Armoured Division, considered the 'pride of the Indian Army', launched an offensive towards Sialkot, dividing itself into two prongs. However, the Pakistani 6th Armoured Division forced them back at Chawinda, and they were compelled to withdraw after suffering heavy losses of almost a hundred tanks. The Pakistanis followed up their success by launching Operation Windup, which pushed the Indians back even further. Similarly, Pakistan's 1st Armoured Division launched an offensive towards Khem Karan with the intention of capturing Amritsar and the bridge on River Beas to Jalandhar.

The hostilities in the Rajasthan sector began on 8 September, with the Pakistan Desert Force and the Hur militia (followers of Sanghar-based Pir Pagara) initially placed in a defensive role, which suited them well. The Hurs were familiar with the terrain and local area and possessed many essential desert survival skills that their opponents – and even their comrades in the Pakistan Army – did not have. Fighting mainly as light infantry, the Hurs inflicted many injuries on the Indian forces as they ventured into Sindh. They were also employed as skirmishers, harassing the Indian Line of Control, a task they often undertook on camels. As the battle continued, the Hurs and the Desert Force were increasingly used to attack and capture Indian villages inside Rajasthan.

Ceasefire

The war was heading for a stalemate, with both nations holding territory of the other. On 20 September, the United Nations Security Council unanimously passed a resolution, which noted that its previous two resolutions had gone 'unheeded' and that they now demanded an unconditional ceasefire from both nations within 48 hours. India immediately accepted, while Pakistan waited until 23 September to respond and accept. The ceasefire remained in effect until the start of the Indo-Pakistani War of 1971.

Historian of the Pakistan Army Shuja Nawaz and author of *Pakistani Wars* Tariq Rahman agree that the 1965 war was a costly one. Pakistan had spent PKR 7.6 billion (or U.S.$1.6 billion, approximately £570 million) on its defence establishment since the military takeover in 1958, averaging close to 53 per cent of total government expenditure in the period between 1958 and 1965. Pakistan claimed to have captured territory ranging from 544 square kilometres (210 sq. mi.) (according to Indian sources) to 4,188 square kilometres (1,617 sq. mi.) (according to Pakistani sources). India's matching claims were 1,918 square kilometres (740 sq. mi.), by its own estimate, to 1,155 square kilometres (446 sq. mi.), by Pakistan's estimate. Pakistan claimed to have lost 1,033 men, while India claimed 1,333 killed in action, and both sides claimed victory, when, in fact, both had failed in their military objectives – the immediate effort for both was to put a good face on a difficult situation.[98]

Truce agreement

The United States and the Soviet Union both played significant roles in preventing any further escalation of the conflict between India and Pakistan. Premier Alexei Kosygin led the Soviet Union's diplomatic efforts, hosting peace negotiations in Tashkent, Uzbekistan. The Indian prime minister Lal Bahadur Shastri and the Pakistani president Ayub Khan signed the Tashkent Agreement on 10 January 1966, agreeing to withdraw their forces to pre-August lines by 25 February 1966. Tragically, Shastri had a heart attack and passed away the following day, which led to a wave of sympathy for the INC.

However, many Pakistanis criticized the ceasefire, since they believed that the military had achieved significant gains and that the Tashkent Declaration had surrendered them. This led to protests and student riots, as Pakistanis expressed their dissatisfaction with the agreement. Despite this, the Tashkent Agreement proved to be a crucial step towards reducing tensions between India and Pakistan and preventing further conflict.

Pakistani miscalculations

The Pakistani leadership's belief that the disaffected Kashmiri populace, when presented with the chance offered by the Pakistani offensive, would rise against the Indian administration and lead to a conclusive relinquishment of Kashmir turned out to be unfounded. Instead of a revolt from the Kashmiri people, what ensued was the Indian Army's acquisition of substantial intelligence regarding Operation Gibraltar, leading to the unexpected establishment of a secondary theatre of conflict, which took the Pakistani high command by surprise.

The Pakistani military had initially envisioned the 1965 conflict with India as confined to Kashmir. However, the Indian government confounded their expectations by initiating a second front in the southern sector. As a result, Pakistan was forced to divert troops away from Kashmir to protect Sialkot and Lahore. Additionally, Pakistan's Operation Grand Slam, which aimed to capture Akhnoor – a town that served as a crucial link between Kashmir and the rest of India – failed to yield the intended results. Some critics blamed Ayub Khan's indecisiveness for the failure of the operation. They claimed that although he understood the strategic importance of Akhnoor, he did not want to capture it and provoke an all-out war with India. Despite initial progress, the president replaced the commanding officer, Major General Akhtar Hussain Malik, with General Yahya Khan. This move led to a 24-hour lull in the fighting, which allowed the Indian Army to regroup and successfully oppose a lacklustre attack by the new general. As the Indian chief of staff of the Western Command, Lieutenant General Harbaksh Singh, put it, 'the enemy came to our rescue.'[99] Later, Akhtar Hussain Malik accused Ayub Khan of relieving him of his command at a critical moment in the war.

Reaction to Ayub's Policies

There were two factors at the heart of the precarious situation that prevailed during the concluding phase of the Ayub era. First, the 1965 war highlighted the vulnerability and isolation of East Pakistan, which was left to defend itself during the seventeen-day military campaign. With only one infantry division and a squadron of outdated U.S.-built F-86 Sabre jets, East Pakistan was vastly outnumbered by its adversary. This experience led to demands for an independent defence capability among Bengalis. Despite what is propagated in Pakistani textbooks and media, Operation Gibraltar failed to achieve its desired goal of liberating Kashmir. The war also exposed the vulnerability of the Pakistani armed forces since Indian troops had almost captured Lahore on the eastern border of West Pakistan.

Aziz Bhatti's gallantry saved the Punjab's capital, but the myth of the West Pakistan martial caste's military prowess was undermined, which may have encouraged Bengali enthusiasts to intensify their movement for East Pakistan's autonomy. The war also created economic depression and led to the diversion of resources to the West Pakistan military, widening the economic gap between the two wings.

Second, in January 1968, the Agartala conspiracy case was initiated against 35 individuals, including Sheikh Mujibur Rahman, who were accused of conspiring to secede East Pakistan with the help of India. The case got its name from the alleged meeting of the accused with Indian Army officers in Agartala. However, later revelations suggested that Sheikh Mujibur Rahman had secret discussions with local Indian leaders back in July 1962. This gave the Ayub government some grounds to act against the proponents of provincial autonomy as enshrined in the six-point plan. Nevertheless, the Agartala contacts failed to provide solid evidence of Mujib's involvement in a secessionist conspiracy in East Pakistan. As a result, the trial turned out to be extremely counterproductive, especially in the midst of such a volatile political climate. According to Talbot, it only served to further undermine the government's credibility and fuelled the simmering dissent in East Pakistan.

Mujibur Rahman's imprisonment since May 1966 had already caused resentment among the Bengali bourgeoisie. But when reports of police torture emerged, Mujib and his co-defendants were seen as martyrs. The public hearing provided a perfect platform for Sheikh Mujib to argue for the Awami League's cause. The government's mistakes in the Agartala conspiracy case further undermined its credibility, and the death of one of the defendants in custody ignited protests in East Pakistan. Students led the protests and formed an Action Committee with an eleven-point programme. To calm tensions, Ayub Khan withdrew the case and called for a round-table conference, but Mujib staged a walkout over the issue of provincial autonomy. Thus the conference failed to achieve its intended purpose. The situation continued to deteriorate, providing no hope for Ayub's regime; change of the 'Man on Horseback' seemed imminent.[100]

In West Pakistan, the situation was far from favourable. Despite growing calls for decentralization, the ruling elite, predominantly composed of Punjabis and Muhajirs, remained unresponsive to these demands. In October 1968, the government organized the Decade of Development celebration. However, instead of highlighting the achievements of Ayub Khan's regime, it accentuated the frustration of the urban poor, who were grappling with inflation and the financial burdens of the 1965 war. Ayub Khan had become a symbol of inequality, and Bhutto skilfully leveraged this sentiment to challenge his leadership.

In East Pakistan, the opposition to the regime ran deeper than mere dissatisfaction with Ayub Khan. In January 1969, several opposition parties came together to form the Democratic Action Committee (DAC), with the shared objective of restoring democracy through a mass movement. Concurrently, the Pakistan People's Party (PPP) mobilized disenchanted urban groups and traditional feudal forces in opposition to the ruling regime.

By 1968, Ayub Khan had lost much of his support, with the exception of the military and the Civil Service. His illness in February 1968 and allegations of corruption against his family members further weakened his position. In West Pakistan, Bhutto's PPP called for a 'revolution', and in the East, the Awami League's six points became the opposition's rallying cry.

On 25 March 1969, martial law was proclaimed, with General Agha Mohammad Yahya Khan designated as chief martial-law administrator. The 1962 Constitution was abrogated, and Ayub Khan announced his resignation. Yahya Khan took over the presidency instead of Abdul Jabbar Khan, the speaker of the National Assembly, as specified in the 1962 Constitution. After assuming power, Yahya Khan promised elections based on adult franchise to the National Assembly, which would draft a new constitution. He also held talks with political party leaders.

As Ayub Khan's regime neared collapse, he confided in one of his former ministers, expressing regret:

> I am sorry we have reached this point. Pakistan is a very difficult country structurally. Maybe I pushed it too fast into the modern age. We were not prepared for the changes. To be frank, I have failed. I must admit that clearly. Our laws were designed for a more sophisticated society.[101]

Ayub Khan's presidency marked a pivotal juncture in Pakistan's history, characterized by distinct ideological shifts and unfolding developments. He wholeheartedly prioritized economic reforms while neglecting the political rights of the Pakistani populace. This approach generated inherent contradictions that ultimately contributed to his downfall. Ayub Khan failed to recognize that in the contemporary era, economic liberalization must be complemented by political liberalization and the cultivation of democratic principles.

During Khan's tenure, economic transformation was propelled by industrialization, agricultural improvements and limited land reforms that extended beyond urban centres. Consequently, many regions in West Pakistan became less swayed by vague appeals to Islamic unity. However, the ruling elites, who were not particularly religious, had established an economic and social structure riddled with inequalities. As awareness of these social and economic disparities grew, a significant credibility gap emerged when the ruling elites continued to assert the Islamic nature of Pakistan's political system.

This credibility gap played a pivotal role in the PPP gaining substantial support in relatively prosperous areas such as Lahore and Multan divisions, as well as along the Grand Trunk Road, during the 1970 elections. Ideology typically serves to justify or elucidate the rationale behind a specific social order, and in Pakistan, the ruling elites' lack of religious commitment, coupled with socio-economic disparities, gave rise to a credibility gap that eroded their claims to legitimacy.[102]

7
Praetorianism under General Yahya Khan and East Pakistan's Separation, 1969–71

Yahya Khan is a highly controversial figure in the political history of Pakistan. He has been maligned for his personal oddities as well as his alleged role in the separation of East Pakistan. However, a discourse of history constructed solely around his personality overlooks the nuances and subtleties of the historical process that led to such a momentous event. While Yahya Khan cannot be absolved of his role in effecting this ominous change, it is unjustifiable to solely blame him for the dismemberment of Pakistan, since myriad currents and crosscurrents wove the complex web of the course of history. In this context, Lawrence Ziring's take on Yahya Khan is noteworthy, as it highlights how all major actors of the period were creatures of a historic legacy and a psycho-political milieu that did not lend itself to accommodation and compromise, but rather promoted violent judgements.[1]

Yahya Khan inherited a legacy of extreme political centralization, which brought with it economic and political grievances in East Pakistan. Unfortunately, Yahya possessed neither the political acumen nor insight, energy or will to lead a country that was stuck in a quagmire. However, it is essential to note that the gravity of the situation would have put even the best political minds in a spin. Yahya's regime was not a departure from the past; rather, it was a continuation of the same old story. General Yahya Khan stepped in where Ayub Khan had left off. It was a much-chastened military leadership, although it was clear that Yahya Khan represented a continuation of Ayub Khan's policies.[2] Ayub Khan had to go because he had come to symbolize a hated regime. Before scrutinizing the events that took place during Yahya's regime, it is worthwhile to contextualize his rise to power. Additionally, taking a glimpse at Yahya's early life may help us make sense of his personhood and style of governance.

Agha Muhammad Yahya Khan, born on 4 February 1917 in Chakwal, a district in the northern Punjab, belonged to a Shia Qizilbash family of Persian descent. His family had military links tracing back to the time of Nadir Shah, and there were even some familial connections to the historical figure.[3] Yahya's father, Saadat Ali Khan, was a police officer from Peshawar.

Yahya Khan, c. 1966.

Yahya graduated from Punjab University with good grades before joining the Indian Military Academy at Dehra Dun. He received his commission in the Indian Army in 1938 and served as an officer in the 4th Infantry Division. Shuja Nawaz provides insight into Yahya's character, stating that he belonged to the generation of the British Indian Army that adopted the habits and accent of the British. However, unlike some of his colleagues in both independent Pakistan and India, Yahya was neither a reader nor a deep thinker. His early postings were in Northwest Frontier Province, and he saw himself as a man of action.[4]

During the Second World War, Yahya participated in military action against the Axis powers in North Africa, Iraq and Italy. While on a military campaign, he was captured by Axis forces but managed to escape from the prisoner camp in Italy on his third attempt. After Pakistan's independence, Yahya played a crucial role in reorganizing Pakistan's armed forces and was particularly instrumental in setting up the Pakistan Staff College in Quetta. During the September 1965 war against India, he commanded an infantry division. In 1966 Yahya was promoted to the rank of general and appointed as the commander-in-chief of the Pakistan Army, a position of significant authority.[5] At the age of 34, he became the youngest brigadier in the Army and was appointed to command the 106th Infantry Brigade along the Line of Control in Kashmir. By the age of forty, he had become Pakistan's youngest general. Throughout his career, Yahya Khan consistently achieved new ranks at a young age, making him the youngest officer to reach each rank along the way.[6] Yahya played a key role in integrating U.S.-provided weapons systems in the Pakistan Army, working closely with American military advisors. Additionally, he was tasked with overseeing the construction of Islamabad, Pakistan's new capital. Not only did he serve on the commission that recommended the project, but he went on to become the chairman of the Capital Development Authority responsible for planning and executing the development of the city.[7]

In the midst of rampant unrest and protests, Ayub Khan had no choice but to step down, paving the way for General Yahya Khan to assume power. According to an article in *Time* magazine, Yahya Khan, a stocky and bushy-browed Pathan from a Persian-speaking Qizilbash family, had been the chief of staff of the Army since 1966. Several high-ranking generals were concerned about Ayub Khan's potential willingness to allow the return of parliamentary democracy, despite his own characterization of politicians as 'five cats tied by their tails'.[8] Upon assuming power, Yahya Khan swiftly declared martial law, on 25 March 1969, elevating himself to the position of chief martial law administrator (CMLA). Merely six days later, he also took on the mantle of the presidency, albeit with some speculating that this move may have been influenced by diplomatic pressures. Despite being characterized as 'reluctant' and 'shy', Yahya Khan embraced the dual roles of president and military leader. As he assumed the role of CMLA on that pivotal day in 1969, the international community voiced concerns about the diplomatic protocol involved in recognizing a ruler with a military background. The U.S. government raised the question of 'recognition' of Yahya's regime through diplomatic channels. But when Yahya reluctantly assumed the office of president six days later, diplomatic formalities were resolved. Nevertheless, Yahya retained his position as commander-in-chief of the Army and described himself first as commander-in-chief, then as CMLA and lastly as president.

Yahya abrogated the Constitution and dissolved the National and Provincial Assemblies. He introduced several reforms, including raising the minimum industrial wage by 30 per cent, appointing civilian ministers when soldiers proved unfit and reducing official corruption. Although he had no intention of restoring civilian rule immediately, he pressed ahead with an election and a new constitution. He acknowledged that some Pakistanis opposed these reforms and feared that the dissent would lead to chaos, but he remained committed to his vision for Pakistan's future. Despite the saying that 'a general galloping upon a stallion is slow to dismount,' Yahya did not appear to crave power.[9]

The Martial-Law Administration

When General Yahya Khan took over as CMLA of Pakistan, the situation was worse than in October 1958, when Iskander Mirza proclaimed martial law. Back then, the Pakistani people were fed up with politicians' ineptitude, and the resulting political instability was harming the economy. Thus, when martial law was promulgated, many people breathed a sigh of relief. However, when Yahya seized power eleven years later, the political leaders had restored their reputation to a great extent and regained mass support. Moreover, during the final five months of Ayub's rule, complete erosion of the state's authority had led to anarchy and disorder. Left–right confrontation, regional divisiveness and a lack of consensus on crucial political issues had paralysed the country's politics. These issues, along with the smouldering discontent in East Pakistan, added to the gravity and complexity of the situation.

How did Yahya's regime differ from that of his military predecessor, Ayub Khan? Ayub's government was a civil–military partnership in which some top civil officials were as influential as the generals. This situation was thought to be a major factor in Ayub's downfall. In contrast, Yahya's regime, under the guidance of Major General Syed Ghulam Muhy-ud-Din Pirzada, took care not to make the same mistake. They were careful to keep senior bureaucrats away from Yahya and not give them too much influence. Pirzada was even described as the de facto prime minister and Yahya's own Rasputin, underscoring his power and influence within the government.[10] Under the president's secretariat organization (PSO) were two brigadiers – Rahim, a Punjabi who handled affairs of martial law, and Karim, a Bengali who oversaw civil affairs. These two brigadiers were colloquially referred to as the 'super secretaries'. No secretary of any ministry could access the president without going through them, since they were under the direct control and supervision of the PSO. This led to a comical scenario where top bureaucrats waited in the corridors of the brigadiers and at the office of the all-powerful PSO, rarely having the opportunity to meet the president himself.

When martial law was declared in Pakistan, the country was divided into two zones: Zone A, which covered West Pakistan, and Zone B, comprising East Pakistan. Following the dissolution of One Unit on 1 July 1970, new zones were established in the newly created provinces of the Punjab, Sindh, the Northwest Frontier Province and Baluchistan, with Baluchistan attaining provincial status for the first time. Each zone had a deputy CMLA who acted as its governor until August 1969, after which military officers were assigned to administer sectors and sub-sectors within the zones.

To oversee the administration of these zones, Yahya Khan established a Council of Administration consisting of three deputy CMLAs: Lieutenant General Abdul Hamid Khan, Air Marshal Noor Khan and Admiral S. M. Ahsan. The council was chaired by Yahya Khan himself, with Pirzada serving as its secretary. The council helped to streamline the governance of the country during this turbulent period.[11] The Council of Administration remained operational until 3 August 1969. The Ayub–Mirza regime in 1958 had been prompt in having a civilian cabinet, but the new regime decided to have no such partnership.[12] The Council of Administration controlled the whole administration, central and provincial, through the office of the CMLA. However, on 3 August, Yahya appointed a cabinet that continued to function until February 1970. Even after this, the generals remained the key decision-makers.

Yahya Khan retained control over the critical portfolios of defence and foreign affairs, while General Hamid, the chief of staff, was responsible for managing the Home Ministry. The remaining portfolios were divided between the Air Force and Navy chiefs. Air Marshal Noor Khan took charge of the ministries of education, labour, health and social welfare, while Admiral Ahsan oversaw finance, planning, industry and commerce. Despite concerns about the competence and technical knowledge of those placed in charge, no specialized training or acumen was required for these positions. Whenever a matter related to a specific ministry was to be discussed, the secretary of that ministry was summoned before the council.[13]

Four of the ministers in the cabinet had a background in senior bureaucracy, with two having served as police chiefs of their provinces. The other two ministers were former politicians who had held cabinet posts prior to Ayub Khan's takeover in 1958. The remaining members of the cabinet included a retired major general who had graduated from RMA Sandhurst, as well as a former chief justice of Pakistan. Apart from the two former politicians, all of the other cabinet members had held significant official positions in the past.[14]

Yahya Khan established a National Security Council with Major General Ghulam Umar as its secretary; however, its activities remained limited in scope. As the situation in East Pakistan deteriorated into civil war, the National Security Council became inactive. Despite this, Major General Umar became increasingly close to Yahya Khan over time.

The Policy of Appeasement

In 1963 Major General Wasi-ud-Din, commander of the 10th Division, stationed at Lahore, emphasized the importance of flexibility in addressing the rising discontent in East Pakistan. He suggested that the central government should acknowledge and rectify their mistakes in the eastern wing since partition in 1947 and seek to address the issues with empathy and understanding. He warned against the use of force or repression, as it would not only fail to solve the problems but exacerbate the political situation in the region.[15] The autocratic attitude and extreme centralization policy led to a growing sense of alienation, especially in East Pakistan. Except for a tiny minority in the ruling civil–military oligarchy, large segments of society felt completely disenfranchised. During Ayub Khan's eleven-year rule, they had virtually no say in the decision-making process. (However, this situation was not new and had existed even before 1958.) Sensing the urgency, Yahya Khan adopted a policy of appeasement to placate the Bengalis, in particular. On 28 July 1969, in a broadcast to the nation, he expressed his firm intention to redress Bengali grievances. The first significant step in this direction was the doubling of the Bengali quota in the defence services. At that time, East Pakistan had only seven infantry battalions. Although Yahya's announcement was made with the noblest and most generous intentions, it came about twenty years too late. Major General Khadim Hussain Raja, the general officer commanding 14 Division in East Pakistan, opposed Yahya's intention to raise more pure Bengali battalions, suggesting that the Bengalis were 'too meek'.[16]

Appeasement with Social Reform

Yahya Khan announced his goals to restore law and order, facilitate the installation of a constitutional government and return power to civilian leadership. However, he diverted his time and energy towards unnecessary ventures, some of which resulted in confusion and social conflict. As a result, his administration failed to effectively address the root causes of the country's problems and achieve its stated objectives.[17] Yahya Khan attempted to implement reforms in various sectors without proper planning, resulting in controversies.

> The proposed education policy was particularly contentious, since it called for radical changes such as achieving universal literacy by 1980, nationalizing private educational institutions (including foreign missionary institutions), replacing English with Bengali and Urdu as official languages by 1975, teaching of Islamiyat up to class X, and making significant amendments to the University Ordinance.[18]

The education policy continued to be in effect merely for the sake of appearances, while its essence quickly dissipated.[19]

Yahya Khan recognized the role played by students and workers in the anti-Ayub protests. Workers were agitated because they had been stripped of the right to strike and trade unions were banned. To address their grievances, Air Marshal Noor Khan announced the restoration of the right of collective bargaining. In cases where bilateral negotiations failed, the right to strike and lockout was also restored. The newly drawn-up labour policy made it easier for trade unions to be recognized and provided regulations for their proper functioning. Administrators' power to prosecute unions in a court of law was reduced in cases of default and legal protection was extended to union office-bearers. Additionally, a welfare fund with seed money of PKR 100 million was instituted.

Despite these efforts, the Planning Commission viewed these proposals as too radical. They also believed that the government had enacted new regulations on industrial relations without achieving an agreement between employers and employees on the basic tenets.[20] Hence, the policy failed to address the workers' problems.

The Yahya Khan regime was acutely aware of the pivotal role economic planning and development policies had played in the downfall of the Ayub government. This was primarily due to the stark concentration of wealth in the hands of a privileged few, leaving the masses marginalized and discontented. In a concerted effort to champion social justice and egalitarian principles, the regime implemented a series of measures aimed at curbing the concentration of wealth and the emergence of monopolies and restrictive trade practices. One significant step taken in this direction was the enactment of the Control and Prevention Ordinance in 1970. This marked a departure from the previous economic policy, which had primarily focused on maximizing production. Instead, the new policy prioritized the welfare of society as a whole.

However, despite the earnest proposals put forth by the Planning Commission, the materialization of these initiatives was hampered by a critical obstacle – the lack of adequate funding. This constraint posed a formidable challenge to the regime's efforts to translate its vision of social justice and economic egalitarianism into tangible reality.[21] The establishment of the Equity Participation Fund, headquartered in Dhaka, aimed to provide additional capital resources to small and medium-sized enterprises in the private sector, both in East Pakistan and in the underdeveloped regions of West Pakistan. Additionally, the head office of the Industrial Development Bank was relocated to Dhaka, demonstrating a recognition of the importance of promoting economic development in the eastern wing of the country.

The fourth five-year plan (1970–75) was a clear reflection of the government's desire to undertake a wider distribution of resources and fruits of economic development.[22] The allocation of resources in the new plan reflected an effort to address the historical neglect of East Pakistan. In fact, 52.5 per cent of the total funds were earmarked for East Pakistan, a significant increase from the 36 per cent allotted in the previous five-year plan. However, the political climate was highly polarized by this time. Even before the plan was implemented, there were demands from various political quarters to postpone it, citing the shortcomings of the third five-year plan in addressing the needs of East Pakistan. These critics argued that the previous plan's deficiencies needed to be rectified before a new plan could be introduced.[23]

One point of contention was whether the new plan should be introduced by the elected government after the 1970 elections. Despite this, the military went ahead and implemented the plan, which was eventually disrupted due to insurgency and military actions in East Pakistan.

To combat the growing issues of nepotism, favouritism and corruption within the civil administration, the military enforced several martial-law regulations. The public was urged to launch campaigns against instances of bribery, smuggling, black marketing and any other forms of corruption, with the military authority overseeing these efforts. Yahya also attempted to downsize the higher Civil Service. Under Martial Law Regulation No. 58, 303 class–1/civil officers were suspended on charges of power misuse during the previous eleven years. While these officials were given the opportunity to defend themselves, only a handful were spared, as many were either dismissed or forced to retire. Although bureaucratic influence was reduced, administration remained centralized, with the real power held by the secretariat or CMLA headquarters. Lieutenant General Pirzada held a significant amount of power and influence, and once remarked that the Army would take full credit for everything done during this martial law, unlike the previous martial law within Ayub Khan's regime, where civilians were blamed for everything.[24]

Significant reforms were introduced, including the abolition of the One Unit scheme and the promotion of Baluchistan to provincial status on 1 July 1970. However, these necessary changes had a cost, as they weakened the relationship between the Yahya regime and the Punjabi elite.[25] The abolition of the One Unit scheme resulted in the principle of parity between East Pakistan and West Pakistan becoming null and void. Additionally, during Yahya Khan's tenure, the states of Chitral, Swat, Bahawalpur and Dir were merged with West Pakistan, despite their previous status as (semi-) independent states ruled by princes, who had already acceded to Pakistan.

Upon assuming power, Yahya Khan pledged to hold free and fair elections. To fulfil his promise, he appointed Justice Abd-us-Sattar, the judge of the Supreme Court of Pakistan, as chief election commissioner on 28 July 1969 to prepare 'electoral rolls and delimit constituencies'.[26] Yahya Khan promulgated a legal framework order (LFO) on 30 March 1970. It was meant to provide the guidelines for the general elections and the salient features that the future constitution must embody. They were:

> Pakistan would be a federal republic, known as the Islamic Republic of Pakistan, ensuring its independence, territorial integrity, and national solidarity.
> Islamic ideology would be preserved.
> The head of the state would be a Muslim.
> Democratic principles would be ensured by holding national and provincial elections on the basis of population and adult franchise.

Fundamental rights would be guaranteed.
Independence of judiciary would be secured.
Provinces would have maximum autonomy consistent with independence.[27]

The unbridled powers of the president were the most contentious issue regarding the LFO. The Constitution was only considered valid if it was authenticated by the president,[28] but the president's authority to 'decide any question or doubt as to the interpretation of the LFO' was even more contentious, since it could not be challenged in any court of law, which ran counter to democratic principles. In this regard, Omar Noman's statement that 'Yahya had no intention of surrendering complete power to civilians, hoping to retain a permanent role for the Army in a new constitutional structure', appears to be justified.[29]

The National Assembly was expected to draft a constitution within 120 days, which many felt was a highly insufficient period for such a significant task. The assembly's membership was set at 313, with 169 seats allocated for East Pakistan, 85 for the Punjab, 28 for Sindh, 19 for NWFP, 5 for Baluchistan and 7 for the tribal areas. The distribution of seats for the five provincial assemblies was:

Province	General seats	Women's seats	Total
East Pakistan	300	10	310
Punjab	180	6	186
Sindh	60	2	62
NWFP	40	2	42
Baluchistan	20	1	21

The future constitution was required to include five essential principles: Islamic ideology and a Muslim head of state; periodic elections that are free and transparent, based on universal adult franchise; an independent judiciary and guaranteed fundamental rights of citizens; maximum provincial autonomy within a federal system; and sufficient powers to the central government to ensure the territorial integrity of the country.

It is worth noting that not all the generals were satisfied with the LFO. Some within the junta opposed granting East Pakistan majority representation in the central legislature. Despite this, the LFO was implemented, and both Army officers and politicians had to accept the reality of Yahya's reform programme. However, Bengali politician Maulana Bhashani described the LFO as a 'Trojan Horse' – a subterfuge that would divide East Bengal and perpetuate West Pakistani dominance. Mujib also accepted it with a grain of salt.[30]

The ideology of Islam was emphasized as the *raison d'être* of Pakistan. This viewpoint was passionately advocated by conservative generals such as

Major Generals Sher Ali and Umar, who attempted to popularize the two-nation theory as a means of countering leftist politics, which was deemed un-Islamic, particularly in the 1960s.[31] The LFO also laid down the condition that the head of the state had to be a Muslim.

The LFO was not only a response to growing demands for a return to democracy, but a calculated strategy to maintain military and bureaucratic control over the country. As Ayesha Jalal notes, the LFO was designed to pre-empt a constitutional framework that would challenge the power of the military establishment and its bureaucratic allies. Despite Yahya Khan's promise of free and fair elections, the LFO ensured that the military would retain ultimate authority, regardless of which political party came to power. Jalal argues that the Yahya regime had no intention of ceding power to any political configuration, regardless of whether it was from the eastern or western half of the country, if it threatened the dominance of the military and the bureaucracy. In this way, the LFO was not a genuine attempt to restore democracy but rather a means of maintaining the status quo.[32]

The Elections of 1970

The LFO was a crucial framework for conducting the upcoming elections. Yahya Khan promised to restore civilian rule through a new Constitution, which would grant representation to the National Assembly based on population distribution. As a result, East Pakistan was allocated more seats than West Pakistan. Additionally, Yahya promised elections based on the principle of 'one man, one vote'. However, Shuja Nawaz points out that military intelligence predicted the Awami League would win no more than 46–70 out of 167 seats in East Pakistan, while the PPP was projected to win no more than 20–30 out of the 144 seats allotted to the West. The Yahya regime expected the Qayyum Muslim League to secure seventy seats; the Muslim League (Daultana) expected to win forty seats. Therefore, despite the promise of free and fair elections, the Yahya regime's intentions remained unclear.[33] Based on these estimates, the regime relied on a fragmented parliament that could be easily controlled by the ruling junta.[34] Despite their extensive political experience, numerous seasoned politicians consistently underestimated the comparative electoral prowess of the Awami League and the PPP. Even Mian Mumtaz Daultana's Convention Muslim League rejected an offer of 29 uncontested seats in East Pakistan from Mujib in exchange for post-election cooperation.[35]

Torrential rains in the summer of 1970 caused massive flooding and rural devastation in East Pakistan. Yahya Khan responded by postponing the elections from October to 7 December 1970. However, an even worse disaster struck on 13 November, when a massive cyclone accompanied by tidal waves hit the unprotected underbelly of East Pakistan at night. This disaster claimed more than 200,000 lives and left millions homeless.[36] The absence of government assistance provided an opportunity for Mujib to criticize the Yahya regime as being callous. The catastrophic devastation caused by the cyclone raised concerns about the possibility of postponing the elections. However, Yahya remained steadfast in his decision to hold the elections as scheduled. He appeared confident that a hung parliament would be formed, allowing him to create a compliant civilian government while retaining his presidential powers.[37]

Operation Blitz

Before turning to the elections and their aftermath, it is pertinent to bring Operation Blitz into focus. Lieutenant General Sahibzada Yaqub Khan (1920–2016), martial-law administrator of Zone B, developed a plan codenamed 'Operation Blitz', which was evolved well before the December elections.[38] On 11 December 1970, just four days after the National Assembly elections, Yaqub Khan signed and issued an operational directive. The plan was formulated in consultation with Brigadier M. A. Majid, the director of military operations and the commander of the Eastern Command. It authorized the commander of the Eastern Command to relieve the governor of his duties and take control of the entire civil administration of the province, giving him complete freedom in exercising his powers. The plan aimed to restore law and order in the province.[39]

Brigadier Siddiqi recalls Yaqub stating words to the effect that 'we may have to give him [Mujib and his party men] a whiff of the grapeshot, should they refuse to behave and go berserk.'[40] Despite cultivating an image in the Army as a cultured, sensitive and liberal individual, and even beginning to learn Bengali upon taking command of troops in East Pakistan, Yaqub Khan's strong words were surprising. He had been known as a thoughtful officer and had gained a reputation as one of the few senior officers in the entire subcontinent during the 1965 war who truly understood operational strategy. In fact, he had even gone to the battlefield as an armour advisor to the corps commander, Lieutenant General Bakhtiar Rana.[41] He had developed a bold and innovative strategy to defend the Sialkot front against India, utilizing a 'scheme of manoeuvre' to execute an engulfing armour movement against the Indian forces. He was well versed in military strategy, at least in theory.[42]

The operation could only be implemented based on the 'recommendation of MLA Zone B' with the approval of the CMLA, General Yahya Khan, conveyed through the martial-law headquarters. Operation Blitz was set to commence after the declaration of an emergency in East Pakistan, subject to the following conditions:

a. Open defiance of martial law and/or declaration of 'Independent Bengal', rejection of the Legal Framework Order ending up in a 'mass movement' like the sporadic outbreaks which shook the province in the period January '69–March '69.

b. An anarchist movement sparked off by extremist Naxalite/Communists [Indian separatist movements] or even NAP [National Awami Party of Maulana Bhashani] and other groups of province-wide dimensions.

c. If frustrated in their designs, the majority party [Awami League] may resort to a mass movement for enforcing their will outside the Assembly, to the jeopardy of the integrity of Pakistan.[43]

The operation was designed to be implemented only in the most severe situation where the normal machinery of law and order had collapsed, and the province-wide situation had gone beyond the control of the civil administration, police and the East Pakistan rifles. Yaqub proposed that the operation should be carried out with utmost vigour and determination to make an unmistakable impact and remove any doubts about the kind of martial law being imposed, which was different from the intentionally weakened martial law that people had grown accustomed to. Shock action was, therefore, necessary, and force was permitted to be used without hesitation to achieve the desired effect, which would ultimately save lives. He then outlined the operation's details, specifying who would be detained and who would carry out the actions, using the military operations at Dhaka University in July 1970 for the arrest of political dissidents Manto and Saleem, the student leaders associated with Awami League, as a model. The primary operation was expected to be completed within 24 hours, and everything would be kept secret. Yaqub stated that 'complete censorship would be imposed.'[44]

Within just three months, Yaqub Khan reversed his stance on the effectiveness of this approach, citing the need for additional time and troops on the one hand, and emphasizing that a political solution was the only viable option on the other.[45] When Admiral Ahsan resigned on 1 March, an embattled and isolated Yaqub followed suit four days later via telegram.

Yahya was furious and had contemplated court-martialling Yaqub Khan for failing to follow orders, but instead he was demoted to his previous rank of major general. Rumours spread within the Army that Yaqub had lost his nerve, further fuelled by the appointment of Lieutenant General Tikka Khan, a Janjua Rajput from a village near Kahuta in Rawalpindi district, as Yaqub's replacement.[46] Tikka Khan was known for his strict adherence to orders but lacked the counterbalancing influence that Yaqub had provided. Meanwhile, the 1970 elections, which were held on 7 December and marked the first elections since the creation of Pakistan, did little to restore political normalcy. Despite Yahya's credit for holding the elections, they resulted in a split mandate that only worsened the political turmoil. The Awami League, led by Sheikh Mujibur Rahman, won a resounding victory in East Pakistan, taking 160 out of 162 seats. The remaining two seats were won by Raja Tridev Roy, chief of the Chakma tribe (the largest ethnic group) in the Chittagong hilly tract, and Nurul Amin, who ran as an independent.[47] The Awami League's sweeping victory in the 1970 elections was confined to East Pakistan, since it failed to secure even a single seat from the western wing, despite fielding seven candidates. In East Pakistan, in addition to 160 seats, the party secured all seven seats reserved for women based on East Pakistan's majority. In the aftermath of a devastating cyclone, delayed elections were held in January in the affected areas, and the Awami League secured nine more seats. However, the party's success was limited to East Pakistan, since it received only 0.07 per cent, 0.25 per cent, 0.22 per cent and 1.06 per cent of the votes cast in the Punjab, Sindh, NWFP and Baluchistan, respectively.[48]

In the 1970 elections, the PPP, led by Zulfiqar Ali Bhutto, emerged as the largest party in the Punjab and Sindh, winning 81 National Assembly seats, all from the western wing. Out of 138 total seats in West Pakistan on which the elections were held the PPP secured 62 seats in the Punjab and eighteen in Sindh. The party's tally later increased to 88 with the addition of women's seats and independent candidates who joined their ranks. However, despite their impressive showing in the west, they were unable to pose a significant challenge to Mujib's absolute majority in the National Assembly.[49] Bhutto's political stronghold was primarily in Sindh and the Punjab, as his party managed to secure only one seat from the Northwest Frontier Province. Neither Bhutto nor Mujib were willing to accept each other as the prime minister of Pakistan, exacerbating the already tense political climate in the country. Both leaders refused to compromise on the convening of the National Assembly session, resulting in an impasse that lasted for some time.

Ayub's Muslim League and other older parties were conspicuously absent during the election, since only the most powerful feudal lords managed to retain their seats. The rise of newcomers, driven by fierce nationalism in East Pakistan and a mixture of socialism and youthful contrarian politics in the West, swept away the traditional holders of political power. Unfortunately, Yahya Khan, who was tasked with taking decisive action, only exacerbated the situation. The denial of Sheikh Mujib's legitimate claim to the position of prime minister of Pakistan sparked political unrest in East Pakistan. The coercive policies of the Pakistani state, coupled with Indian intervention, further aggravated the situation, culminating in the 1971 war between India and Pakistan, which ultimately led to the disintegration of Pakistan. According to Waseem, Yahya Khan may have hoped for a hung parliament, which could have allowed the military to act as a broker.[50] In 1970, it became increasingly apparent that the military and the bureaucracy had much greater institutional stakes in the existing state structure than the social groups represented by the Awami League and the PPP.[51]

Military Alliance with the Minority Party

The Awami League's victory in the election came as a surprise to the intelligence services, leading Yahya to assume the role of an arbiter. However, hawkish figures in the Army remained sceptical of Sheikh Mujib, and Bhutto aligned himself with these hawks, even going so far as to threaten to harm party members who planned to attend the inaugural session of the National Assembly on 3 March 1971.[52] During an interview, Bhutto suggested that the separation of East Pakistan might not be an entirely disastrous outcome, since the current state of Pakistan was already unwieldy. He argued that the only way to maintain unity would be to establish a loose constitutional arrangement, which could set a dangerous precedent for West Pakistan, where the Baluch may demand similar treatment. According to Bhutto, a smaller, more manageable and compact Pakistan might be preferable to the current situation.[53]

The Awami League's six-point proposal was a nightmare for Yahya Khan and his advisors. Despite this, they were determined to bring down Mujib and reach a compromise. Yahya and Bhutto made several trips to the East to persuade Mujib to work with them. However, every time Yahya seemed ready to recognize Mujib as the legitimate prime minister, he was dissuaded by his colleagues, who feared that Mujib might use his majority in the assembly to legally secede from Pakistan or diminish the Army's power. Meanwhile, the Army began bringing in new troops disguised as civilians on Pakistan International Airlines flights via Colombo, although the locals quickly noticed them. Fortunately for the military, Bhutto's opposition to the six-point proposal provided a much-needed respite. As a result, Yahya postponed the National Assembly session scheduled for 1 March 1971, citing the absence of the largest political party from West Pakistan at the inaugural session. He claimed that the postponement would give the political leaders more time to work out a settlement, and he set a new date for the session on 25 March 1971. This decision triggered a massive uprising in East Pakistan, and a call for civil disobedience resulted in the complete closure of government offices, businesses, the High Court and banks, and brought transportation to a standstill.[54] As polarization intensified, some hardline Awami Leaguers began calling for independence, and League leaders assumed control. The state's authority had all but collapsed and reprisals were taken against Urdu-speakers and political opponents. Army officers were attacked and humiliated, and non-Bengali residents of East Pakistan found themselves under sporadic attack. Reports of these events circulated, causing fear and panic among West Pakistanis living in the region. The Army, despite facing insults and even suspension of their food supplies by Bengali contractors, maintained discipline and became alienated in their own country.

As Pakistan's national day, 23 March, approached, Yahya and Bhutto were in Dhaka, but discussions with Mujib fell apart. Mujib's forces hoisted the Bangladesh flag over most of East Pakistan, turning Pakistan Day into Resistance Day. The Army had a plan, and when talks failed, they launched Operation Searchlight on the night of 25 March. By 8 p.m. Mujib received news that soldiers of the East Pakistan Regiment (EPR) at Road Number 2 in Dhanmondi had been disarmed by their West Pakistani commanders. He told Bengali journalists that he anticipated the Army's movement that night and expressed concerns about 'selective killing'. He decided to stay but advised other Awami League leaders to leave. Tajuddin left, and eventually became the prime minister of the Bangladeshi government-in-exile in Calcutta. Yahya departed for West Pakistan that evening, leaving Bhutto behind in his hotel room.

The regime's use of 'full-scale military terror' was in defence of a unitary state and viceregal tradition, despite knowing its utilization could ultimately lead to losing half the country. Rather than coming to terms with the democratic desires of the majority Bengali population, the government sought to dispel that population's aspirations.[55] The Awami League was proscribed as a political party and all the prominent leaders, including Mujib, were put behind bars.

The Pakistan Army had approximately 45,000 soldiers stationed in East Pakistan, including a brigade led by Brigadier Jahanzeb Arbab in Dhaka. The Army crackdown began overnight, with a group of Special Services Group (SSG) commandos capturing Mujib, while other leaders were allowed to escape. The commandos destroyed the students' dormitories at Dhaka University, which had been used to house militants who were trained in using armaments with mock weapons. The raid on Dhaka University has been a subject of controversy, with some accusing the Army of attacking unarmed students. However, the Indian American journalist Sarmila Bose contests this version and provides evidence from a recording of Army communications during the attack made by a Bengali and made available to her by the Liberation War Museum in Dhaka. The recording supports the Army's version of a two-way battle, but reveals that it was very unequal, with only .303 rifle fire from the student halls and no evidence of automatic weapons or grenades.[56] The Army's actions during the crackdown included attacks on newspaper offices and printing presses, reportedly in retaliation for articles critical of the military. Bhutto witnessed the military operation for approximately three hours, during which he observed multiple fires and the destruction of *The People* newspaper's office. This local English-language daily had published inflammatory and provocative articles against the Army and West Pakistan. As Bhutto looked out at the chaotic scene, he couldn't help but reflect on the past and contemplate what the future held. Witnessing the death and destruction of his own people before his eyes was heartbreaking.[57]

The Army swiftly took control of all key installations and broadcasting centres in Dhaka, but their efforts were thwarted in Chittagong where the

8th East Bengal Regiment (EBR) rebelled under the leadership of Major Ziaur Rehman, who took over the radio station and broadcasted messages for four days before an air attack destroyed the transmitter. Similar uprisings were witnessed all over the province, leading to firefights and the eventual departure of Bengali officers and soldiers to India. The regime made a crucial mistake by hastily sending foreign journalists in Dhaka away from the city, a decision ordered by Tikka Khan but supported by Roedad Khan, a hawkish civil servant who exercised strict control over the media as the secretary of the ministry of information. As a result, most journalists covered the ensuing events from India. However, three journalists, Michel Laurent, Simon Dring and Arnold Zeitlin, remained in Dhaka and filed reports that were critical and vivid, exposing the military action taking place. Consequently, the propaganda war was already lost. Bhutto left for Karachi the next day and from there, uttered his 'memorable' words: 'Thank God, Pakistan has been saved.'[58] In retrospect, Bhutto believed that the Awami League would have unilaterally declared the independence of Bangladesh if the regime had not acted the next day. However, in his account published in September 1971, Bhutto maintained his support for Army action while also criticizing the brutality of its execution. He believed that the Army should have acted quickly but not brutally, and that the rebels should have been ferreted out individually rather than through mass destruction, which aggravated the problem.[59] Bhutto professed a desire to reinstate democratic governance, but he avoided addressing his own involvement in fuelling the inter-wing conflict that led to the military intervention. He relied on the Army to resolve the crisis and grant him a portion of power in the central government.

The most scathing criticism of the Army's actions came from Lieutenant General Amir Abdullah Khan Niazi, who was appointed as the governor and MLA by Yahya after being promoted over many officers. Niazi had served in the region during the Second World War and had commanded the 5th Punjab Regiment in Dhaka in 1958. In his memoirs, published many years after the events, Niazi stated that General Tikka, who was tasked with disarming Bengali units and individuals and apprehending Bengali leaders, instead pursued a 'scorched-earth' policy. According to Niazi, Tikka instructed his troops to 'want the land and not the people'. In his diary, Major General Rao Farman Ali wrote that 'the green land of East Pakistan will be painted red.'[60]

To fully understand the significance of these comments, it is important to consider the context in which they were made. Lieutenant General Amir Abdullah Khan Niazi made these statements many years after the events took place, and there are some who question his credibility given his own reputation for using strong-arm tactics. Additionally, some officers who served with him claim that he condoned, if not encouraged, the atrocities committed by the Pakistan Army under his command in East Pakistan, raising questions about his own actions during the conflict.[61]

As expected, Lieutenant General Niazi sent Tikka's key officers back to West Pakistan and replaced them with his own appointees. He had requested additional troops for East Pakistan, but the promised reinforcements had not arrived by the start of the military operation. Niazi assembled a new staff around him, including Brigadier Ghulam Jilani Khan, whom he appointed as his chief of staff, replacing El-Edroos, whom Niazi dismissed as a 'drawing room soldier'. Niazi also took action against some officers for their role in the events of the military operation, including Brigadier Arbab, who Niazi states was removed from command and later court-martialled for looting and theft based on the recommendation of Major General Rahim, GOC 14 Division.

The Awami League's preparations appeared to have been effective, as evidenced by the fact that well-trained and well-equipped soldiers from the EPR and EBR defected and took control of the countryside, putting up strong resistance against the Pakistan Army. This left the Army operating in an adversarial atmosphere, struggling to gain control. According to Niazi:

> The Pakistan Army was fighting in and around cantonments and camps and these became their fortresses of power. Their only link with Dhaka and each other was by air. All other communications were cut, blocked, or out of commission. The rest of the country was under the control of the Mukti Bahini [Liberation Army], whose morale was sky high and who had the initiative with them.[62]

Niazi's force, which consisted of 45,000 troops, of which 34,000 were Army personnel and the rest paramilitary, was severely under-equipped. Heavy equipment and tanks could not be brought from the West, and only one squadron of aircraft at Dhaka provided air cover and support. Despite these challenges, Niazi, who was known by the nickname 'Tiger', chose to launch an offensive plan in which troops raced towards the Indian border, took over major towns along the perimeter of East Pakistan, and opened up the communications system within the province. However, this was no easy feat: Niazi faced stiff resistance from the peoples' army under his eponymous opponent, Colonel M.A.G. 'Tiger' Osmany, who had taken over as chief of the Mukti Bahini.[63] He stated that he wished to take the battle to India in hot pursuit but lacked the troops and equipment. Moreover, he stated that General Abdul Hamid Khan forbade him from any such actions.

Operation Searchlight was a prolonged and violent conflict between Bengalis and the Pakistan Army. The militant factions of the Awami League were highly active, and their ranks were further bolstered by the large number of personnel from the East Pakistan Rifles, East Pakistan Regiment and the Bengali Police who deserted, taking their arms with them. The East Pakistani public had also turned against the Pakistan Army, making the situation even more conducive to the guerrillas of Mukti Bahini, who retreated to rural areas whenever the Army launched an operation, where the local population provided refuge. The Indian government saw the political crisis in East Pakistan as an opportunity to weaken their traditional adversary, and their support for Mukti Bahini added to the Pakistan Army's vulnerability.[64]

India played a significant part in altering the nature and course of the civil conflict in East Pakistan. On 30 January 1971 two Indian intelligence agents disguised as Kashmiri freedom fighters hijacked an Indian Airlines plane named Ganga and diverted it to Lahore. The hijackers later destroyed the plane after freeing the passengers. The Pakistani government facilitated the swift repatriation of the passengers to India and constituted a judicial commission, led by a High Court judge, to investigate the incident. The commission's findings concluded that 'Indian intelligence agencies had orchestrated the aircraft hijacking as part of a broader strategy aimed at inciting conflict between Pakistan and India.' Following the burning of the aircraft on Pakistani soil, in protest, the Indian government banned Pakistani aircraft from flying over Indian territory. India argued that Pakistan's failure to bring the hijackers to justice would create a precedent for future criminal acts of this nature.[65] The ban on over-flight disrupted communications between the two wings of Pakistan at a time when crucial negotiations were going on between the leaders of East and West Pakistan.

After civil strife broke out in East Pakistan, the Indian government openly expressed sympathy and support for the Bengali nationalist movement. On 31 March 1971 Prime Minister Indira Gandhi presented a resolution in the Indian parliament, urging the Pakistan government to halt the 'massacre of defenceless people' in East Pakistan.[66] The resolution expressed solidarity of the Indian people with the people of East Pakistan 'in their struggle for a democratic way' of life'.[67] Four days later, a similar resolution was adopted by the All-India Congress Committee. The Bangladesh nationalists had established a government in exile with its headquarters in Calcutta, and received financial and material assistance from voluntary organizations, as well as a massive propaganda campaign in support of the insurgent groups. India's most significant support included granting permission to the Mukti Bahini to establish their base camps in India, and the recruitment, organization and training of the Mukti Bahini by the Border Security Force (BSF) and the Army.[68] The Mukti Bahini were provided with equipment and weapons. India also launched an international, diplomatic offensive to mobilize public opinion in support of its policies on the East Pakistan crisis and the Bangladesh movement.

The massive influx of Bengali refugees into India in the wake of the civil strife bolstered India's position and provided an opportunity to internationalize the crisis. The migration put the Pakistani military authorities in an embarrassing position and highlighted the urgency of finding a solution to the crisis. Prime Minister Indira Gandhi argued that the influx of millions of refugees from East Pakistan constituted an indirect aggression on India, as it threatened to undermine India's political and economic stability. She emphasized that the refugees would go back only if East Pakistan had a government they could trust, which could come about only if the Pakistan military was withdrawn from East Pakistan and power was transferred to the Awami League leadership then based in India.

India extended all possible assistance to the Mukti Bahini in the hope that its volunteers would dislodge the Pakistan Army. The Mukti Bahini engaged in widespread guerrilla activity, but it was unable to force the Pakistan Army into submission. This compelled the Indian authorities to revise their strategy. The Indian Army directly managed the training of the Mukti Bahini personnel and planned and coordinated their operations. The BSF also played a crucial role in supporting the Mukti Bahini. At times, Indian soldiers provided fire cover to the Mukti Bahini in the border areas.

In November 1971 Indian troops began crossing the India–East Pakistan border to undertake military operations in support of the Mukti Bahini. These attacks gradually intensified and culminated in a full-fledged attack on East Pakistan by the Indian military on 21 November 1971. The Indian government's decision to intervene directly in the conflict was driven by a combination of factors, including the humanitarian crisis caused by the refugee influx, the failure of the Mukti Bahini to achieve decisive gains, and the need to demonstrate India's military capabilities in the face of a perceived threat from Pakistan.

The signing of the Treaty of Friendship and Cooperation between India and the Soviet Union on 9 August 1971 paved the way for this change.[69] This treaty was not a strict defence pact, but it did have defence implications. According to one article of the treaty, 'in the event that any of the parties is attacked or threatened with attack, the High Contracting Parties will immediately commence mutual consultations with a view to eliminating the threat and taking appropriate measures to ensure peace and security for the countries'.[70] This was followed by the arrival of the Soviet military mission, headed by Soviet Air Chief Marshal Pavel Stepanovich Kutakhov (1901–1984), to assess India's military hardware and equipment requirements. Subsequently, the Soviets promptly supplied weapons and equipment to India, providing a significant boost to India's military capabilities. This demonstrated the Soviet Union's support and endorsement of India's policies.[71]

The Yahya regime was hopeful that the Sino-Soviet split and the United States opening to China, which was made possible through Pakistan, would counteract the Indian–Soviet alliance. To strengthen their position, Yahya sent a high-powered delegation led by Air Chief Rahim Khan to China in the first week of November, which included the chief of the Air Staff and two senior officers from the Army and Navy. Bhutto was also included in the delegation at the last moment at Yahya's behest, as he thought Bhutto knew the Chinese leadership quite well and would therefore, it was believed, be of some help. Although the delegation returned with a vague assurance of Chinese support for Pakistan, Yahya Khan seemed satisfied and declared, 'If India attacks Pakistan, China will certainly intervene.'[72]

There were diplomatic efforts to resolve the Bangladesh crisis peacefully between India and Pakistan, and some conciliatory measures were taken by Yahya Khan towards East Pakistan. In early November, Yahya Khan accepted the suggestion by the United States to open negotiations with Awami League leaders and promised to return East Pakistan to civilian rule by the end of the year. The U.S. government conveyed this information to India through its ambassador in Washington, DC. However, India was no longer willing to wait as it was deeply committed to the Bangladesh movement and had completed necessary preparations for an all-out offensive. Moreover, the Soviet Union had endorsed India's new strategy, and by the third week of November, the passes on the Sino-Indian borders were snowbound, reducing the chances of Chinese intervention. The longer the climax was delayed, the greater the chances of international pressure on India and Pakistan for a peaceful resolution.

India's incursion into Pakistani territory on 21 November 1971 prompted Yahya Khan to inform the United Nations secretary general of the attack and accuse India of seeking to dismember Pakistan. The situation was further complicated by the risk of a wider conflict if India did not halt its operations. The United Nations Security Council addressed the issue, but it quickly became apparent that a resolution was unlikely. With too much time elapsed and too many casualties on both sides, neither India nor Pakistan was willing to reconsider their options.[73] Pakistan's actions (those of its top military leadership in particular) are generally accepted by historians to have enabled India to engage in war. The influx of refugees crossing over to India and military action directed against the East Pakistanis had closed all the avenues for a political settlement. Obviously having an unstable neighbour was a cause for consternation for India. Having said that, the Indian Army's invasion created such a situation whereby the birth of Bangladesh became a possibility.

In response to India's aggression, the Pakistani Army initially put up strong resistance. However, Pakistan's position quickly began to deteriorate as its army lacked public support in East Pakistan, and maintaining its supply lines became a serious problem. Guerrilla warfare intensified in the interior, particularly around Dhaka, and India established an air and sea blockade, completely isolating Pakistani troops. To release pressure on East Pakistan, Pakistan launched a counteroffensive on the West Pakistan–India border on 3 December, but this strategy proved ineffective. By 15 December, Indian troops were on the doorstep of Dhaka, and the following day, Pakistani troops in East Pakistan formally surrendered to India.[74] Earlier, on 6 December, India recognized the government-in-exile

Indian Army General Jagjit Singh Aurora and Pakistani Army General Amir Abdullah Khan Niazi in Dhaka, signing the surrender document that would end the war between the two countries and lead to the creation of Bangladesh, 16 December 1971.

of Bangladesh, which led to Pakistan severing diplomatic relations with India in response. Pakistan interpreted India's recognition of Bangladesh as the culmination of an actively pursued policy driven by India's deep hatred of Pakistan. Ten days after India's recognition, Bangladesh officially came into existence.

It is uncertain if the proposed talks between Yahya Khan and the Awami League leadership could have resolved the political conflict. However, the chance was ultimately thwarted by India's invasion of East Pakistan. Any dialogue between the Awami League and the Pakistan government would have been opposed to India's objective of creating a Bangladesh dependent on India. Despite this, the actions of the Pakistan government had inadvertently presented an opportunity for India to achieve its goals.

The East Pakistan debacle is a grim reminder of countless lives lost in a bid to perpetuate the coercive control of the eastern wing of the country by the Pakistani Army. Its role in a 'genocide' in East Pakistan evokes controversy to this day.[75] Disputes exist not only over the events surrounding the 1971 Bangladesh Liberation War but over the number of casualties, as was the case with the 1947 partition. Both Pakistan's relationship with Bangladesh and the latter's internal political development have been hindered by competing narratives of the events that followed Operation Searchlight. While the brutal operation was a grave mistake, there were also instances of atrocities committed by the Awami League in places such as Chittagong, albeit on a smaller scale. As with the 1947 partition, all sides suffered casualties and aggression, and assigning blame in binary terms oversimplifies the complex and violent reality on the ground. It is worth noting that before the war's horrific conclusion, there was a ghastly massacre of thousands of non-Bengali workers in a jute mill in the Khulna District on 28 March 1971, perpetrated by some Bengalis.[76]

The victims of the Khulna District massacre were mainly Urdu-speaking Muslim migrants from Bihar who had migrated to East Pakistan on the eve of partition. On 28 March 1971, their Bengali co-workers carried out a gruesome massacre, using brutal methods of slaughter in makeshift slaughterhouses inside the jute mill. The exact number of those who lost their lives will never be known, but it is estimated to be several thousand men, women and children. The bloated corpses of the victims clogged the rivers for days, as reported by Bose, who collected testimonies about the incident. However, it is important to note that the atrocities committed were not limited to one side, and the events that followed were complex and messy, with victims and aggressors on all sides, as in the case of the 1947 partition.[77] After Bangladesh's independence was established on 16 December, Khulna's Bengali mill workers repeated their violence against non-Bengalis, accusing them of being traitors and spies for the Pakistan Army.

In an article for *The Guardian* published on 11 May 2011, the British columnist Ian Jack revealed an important source responsible for exaggerating the events in East Pakistan. The Yahya government was eager to portray the Army as the saviour, bringing order to a country descending into civil war. Reports of cruelty and chaos leaked out, including a long report in the *Sunday Times* on 18 June 1971, which changed the world's perception of the conflict in Bangladesh. Neville Anthony Mascarenhas, an assistant editor of the *Morning News* in Karachi, was flown to Dhaka by the Pakistan military to report on the Army's positive work. However, Mascarenhas returned with a story that demonized Pakistan and the Army's atrocities against Bengalis. Unable to publish the story in Pakistan, Mascarenhas took it to London to meet with the *Sunday Times*'s editor Harold Evans, who noted in his autobiography that the Pakistan Army's 'outrages against Bengalis far outweighed those of Bengalis against non-Bengalis'.[78]

Hindus were the specific target of the Army. Senior Army officers had told Mascarenhas that 'they were seeking a final solution' and were determined 'to cleanse East Pakistan once and for all of the threat of secession, even if it mean[t] killing 2 million people and ruling the province as a colony for 30 years'.[79] Now this, without any doubt, was a statement supported by circumstantial evidence, which could at best be treated as an opinion rather than a news item based on verified facts. The *Sunday Times* ran the story across two pages under the headline 'GENOCIDE'.[80]

In 1971 Mascarenhas relocated his family to Britain before publishing his report. He later settled there permanently and made a career out of criticizing Pakistan. For over a decade, he worked with the *Sunday Times*. According to the BBC, Mascarenhas's reporting was influential in ending the war, since it helped to shift world opinion against Pakistan and encouraged India to take a decisive stance. The Indian prime minister, Indira Gandhi, later shared with Evans that Mascarenhas's report had prompted her to embark on a personal diplomatic campaign, which paved the way for armed intervention.[81]

Sarmila Bose's book *Dead Reckoning* challenges some of the prevailing narratives about the 1971 Bangladesh Liberation War. For example, she questions the accuracy of a widely reported massacre that was said to have killed 8,000 Hindus, suggesting that the actual number may have been much lower, perhaps as few as sixteen. Additionally, Bose argues that the total number of deaths during the war was likely much lower than the commonly cited figure of 3 million. Her book has been met with controversy and banned in Bangladesh. However, it also represents an important contribution to the ongoing efforts to understand the complex history of the Bangladesh Liberation War. In a critical article entitled 'Flying Blind: Waiting for a Real Reckoning on 1971', Naeem Mohaiemen engages with Bose's arguments and raises important questions about the ongoing process of reckoning with the legacy of the war.[82] Similarly, David Ludden, Mokerrom Hossain and Bina D'Costa have produced research that does not correspond with Bose's assertions.[83]

Scholars and historians have largely overlooked the Bangladesh War, but Bose's research provides a significant contribution to our understanding of the conflict. She conducted extensive research, including interviews with elderly peasants in Bangladesh and retired Army officers in Pakistan, and estimates that between 50,000 and 100,000 people, both combatants and non-combatants, died during the conflict. While it is difficult to determine the exact number of casualties, one must be cautious of unsubstantiated claims that go beyond 100,000. It is important to note that while the Pakistan Army committed atrocities during the conflict, the paramilitaries, mainly comprised of Biharis, were also responsible for the horrific persecution of Hindu Bengali men, whom they believed to be disloyal. It is important to acknowledge the suffering of all groups involved.

Additionally, it is important to investigate the actions of Bengali Muslim civilians who attacked non-Bengalis and Bengali Hindus based on their ethnic or religious identity or for material gain. This aspect of the conflict has not been thoroughly examined, but Bose's unique perspective sheds light on the complexity of the situation.

The Finale of a Tragic Episode

On 16 December 1971 General A.A.K. Niazi received the following telegram from President Yahya Khan:

> You have fought a heroic battle against overwhelming odds. The nation is proud of you. You have now reached a stage where further resistance is no longer humanly possible, nor will it serve any useful purpose. You should now take all necessary measures to stop the fighting and preserve the lives of armed forces personnel, all those from West Pakistan and all loyal elements.[84]

The dream of Pakistan's founder was shattered in just three lines, well before the nation could celebrate its 25 years of independence from British colonial rule. On 16 December 1971 the Pakistani armed forces surrendered to the joint forces of the Mukti Bahini and the Indian Army, led by Lieutenant General Jagjit Singh Arora, the general officer commanding--in-chief of the Eastern Command of the Indian Army. At 4:31 p.m., Niazi, the last corps commander of Eastern Command, signed the instrument of surrender, resulting in over 93,000 personnel, including Niazi himself and Rear Admiral Shariff, being taken as prisoners of war. The Eastern Command, civilian institutions and paramilitary forces were all disbanded. This dark day marked another partition in world history, and reality set in as East Pakistan became the newly independent state of Bangladesh. The former West Pakistan remained as the only remnant of Jinnah's vision of Pakistan.[85]

Between 1958 and 1971, two military rulers attempted to consolidate state authority and implement externally driven development strategies. They sought to avoid the unstable ministerial coalitions that had characterized Pakistan's first decade after independence. Both relied on the support of a predominantly Punjabi Army and civil bureaucracy, and extended patronage to select social and economic groups that lacked independent political bases. The collapse of these regimes underscores the limitations of state consolidation under military and bureaucratic auspices, as well as the resilience of political opposition in societies that have been systematically depoliticized.

The events of 1971 dealt a significant blow to the prestige of the Pakistan Army. However, the Army regained its footing with the Zia ul Haq coup and has since been uncompromising in its commitment to organizational and professional autonomy. Services chiefs resisted any attempts by civilian officials to interfere with promotions, transfers and postings. Yahya Khan, meanwhile, had no choice but to resign in the aftermath of the debacle. He was placed under house arrest by his successor, Zulfiqar Ali Bhutto, and died on 10 August 1980, while still in custody in Rawalpindi.

8
The Era of Populism: Zulfiqar Ali Bhutto, 1971–7

From Napoleon I imbibe the politics of power; from the pamphlet [Karl Marx's *Communist Manifesto*] I absorbed the politics of poverty.

Zulfiqar Ali Bhutto, *If I Am Assassinated*[1]

Zulfiqar Ali Bhutto's biographer, Stanley Wolpert, makes an assertion that can hardly be contested:

No individual in the history of Pakistan achieved greater popular power or suffered so ignominious a death as Zulfiqar Ali Bhutto (1928–79). Zulfi Bhutto's political rise and fall were, indeed, so meteoric as to make his name a legend in the land over which he presided for little more than half a decade prior to his hanging.[2]

It is undeniable that he sparked polarizing emotions and left contrasting impressions on his followers and opponents, making it nearly impossible to reconcile them into a cohesive representation of his character.[3] Undoubtedly, Bhutto was an exceptionally intelligent and courageous man who possessed an unwavering belief in his ability to solve any problem, overcome any obstacle and outmanoeuvre any opponent. Many consider him to be a product of his time, a period when leftist nationalism was prevalent in postcolonial politics. When he established the PPP, leaders such as Nasser in Egypt, Sukarno in Indonesia, Nkrumah in Ghana and Castro in Cuba, as well as Mao, were regarded as heroes by the left-leaning intelligentsia in the developing world. In India, Indira Gandhi was similarly seeking to break the stranglehold of the Congress's old guard through her populist campaign, which shared many similarities with Bhutto's approach.[4] Bhutto's aim was to initiate a top-down socio-economic transformation in Pakistan by nationalizing industries and directing state-led development, with the goal of achieving rapid economic growth. Unlike military rulers, Bhutto's vision was that of a 'sultanistic' dictator, focused on personal and dynastic power rather than institutional power.[5]

As Ayub Khan's most trusted aide, Bhutto played a pivotal role in shaping the former's foreign policy with his dynamic approach. However, their association came to a bitter end after the 1965 war, when Bhutto spearheaded a popular uprising against Ayub Khan that ultimately led to his resignation. Despite his political acumen, Bhutto was notorious for his distrust of his peers, to the extent that he did not even trust himself.[6] A concise portrayal of Bhutto's political journey and its eventual conclusion is captured in an analysis by Altaf Gauhar, who later became a close friend of Bhutto. He recollects that despite their bond, Bhutto seldom confided in him. In fact, when Gauhar, as chief editor of *Dawn*, wrote against the military intervention in East Pakistan, Bhutto perceived it as an attempt to undermine his government and imprisoned him without trial. Even after the High Court of Sindh and Baluchistan ruled Gauhar's detention as unlawful and ordered his release, Bhutto unapologetically stated, 'You must understand that courts do not figure in my book.'[7] Little did Bhutto know at the time that he would be sentenced to death in a highly controversial murder case, and that a ruthless military dictator would execute him in cold blood. The news of his execution was shocking, and in addition to the profound personal loss it caused, it was clear that Bhutto's death would have a long-lasting impact on the country. The event was sure to captivate the nation for years to come.[8]

Zulfiqar Ali Bhutto was born on 5 January 1928, in Larkana, Sindh, to Sir Shah Nawaz Bhutto and Khursheed Begum, née Lakhi Bai. Shah Nawaz, who was married twice, had three sons and one daughter. Zulfiqar was his father's third son but nevertheless the eldest, as his two older brothers passed away at young ages. The political heir to his father, who was the *dewan* of the princely state of Junagadh, Zulfiqar was born into a life of unparalleled privilege as a member of one of the wealthiest families in the region. His family's vast landholdings (250,000 acres of land) were so extensive that they reportedly even managed to evade the census officials of the British Raj. Sir Shah Nawaz Bhutto enjoyed a close relationship with the Raj's officials, further adding to the family's influence in the region.

Zulfiqar Ali Bhutto's family were devout followers of the Sufi saint Shahbaz Qalandar at Sehwan Sharif. As a child, Zulfiqar fell critically ill, and his mother prayed ceaselessly for his recovery. She attributed her son's eventual recovery to the miracle of Shahbaz Qalandar, cementing the family's faith in the saint's teachings and practices.[9] More than forty years later, as prime minister of Pakistan, Zulfiqar prayed at the same shrine, and ordered a pair of solid gold doors to be installed there.[10] In 1934, when Zulfiqar was just six years old, he was sent to a convent kindergarten in Karachi. However, his education was disrupted by his father's political responsibilities, which required the family to move frequently. They relocated to Bombay, and then returned to Karachi after Sindh's separation. Following Sir Shahnawaz's election defeat in 1937, the family moved back to Bombay, and Zulfiqar was enrolled at the prestigious Cathedral and John Connon School in Worli Seaface. Later he would attend St Xavier's College

Zulfiqar Ali Bhutto, 1971.

in Mumbai, where, his childhood friend and Indian politician Piloo Mody reminisced, Zulfi's subsequent passions for fine food and wine, expensive clothes and buxom women blossomed. He had been indifferent about his studies, therefore failing the first Senior Cambridge examination, which he took in 1945.[11]

Zulfiqar's access to the rich and powerful in Bombay helped him in another area of life that increasingly interested him: politics.[12] In his teenage years, Zulfiqar was eager to meet prominent figures of Indian public life. Among them was Muhammad Ali Jinnah, whose ideas he fully embraced and would continue to uphold for the rest of his life. According to Zulfiqar, Jinnah's decision to abandon his advocacy for Hindu–Muslim unity was a valuable lesson that became more relevant with the passing of time.[13]

In 1943, at the age of just thirteen, Zulfiqar's marriage was arranged to Shireen Amir Begum, the daughter of Ahmad Khan of Naudero. Ahmad Khan was the largest landowner in the Bhutto tribe, and Zulfiqar's marriage to his daughter solidified an important alliance. Ahmad Khan was the only son of Rasul Bakhsh Bhutto; he had three older sisters but no male heir of his own at the time. Shireen was ten years older than Zulfiqar, and their marriage was arranged to ensure the continuation of the Bhutto family line.[14] The marriage was arranged by Zulfiqar's father, Sir Shahnawaz. However, Zulfiqar was initially opposed to the idea and only relented when his father promised him a cricket kit from England. He later recalled being furious and not understanding what it meant to have a wife. Despite the age difference, the marriage served as a strategic move for the Bhutto family. Begum Khursheed, Zulfiqar's mother, saw the marriage as a way to secure her own future, stating that if her husband were to die, she would be thrown out; the marriage to Shireen provided an anchor for the family.[15]

Bhutto's time at the University of California, Berkeley, where he graduated from in 1950, with a political science degree, played a significant role in shaping his political views. He became interested in socialist theories and delivered a series of lectures on their feasibility in Islamic countries. He also studied the works of Marx and Engels and was influenced by the Fabian socialist Jawaharlal Nehru.

Bhutto was a strong advocate of pan-Islamism, which seeks to promote solidarity among Muslims worldwide, and he supported the cause of Palestinian Arabs for nationhood. He also supported the freedom movements of Morocco, Tunisia and Algeria from French rule. These views reflected his commitment to anti-colonialism and the empowerment of marginalized communities. Bhutto's political career was marked by both successes and controversies, and his legacy remains a subject of debate in Pakistan and beyond.

In June 1950 Bhutto embarked on a law degree at Christ Church, Oxford. During his time there, he demonstrated a strong drive and determination to complete his studies quickly. He received a BA in jurisprudence, an LLM degree in law and a postgraduate (honours) degree in political science. While at Oxford, Bhutto expressed his desire to finish his master's degree in jurisprudence in two years instead of the usual three. However, his college advisor, the historian Hugh Trevor-Roper, initially rebuked him for not wearing a gown and then explained that two years was unrealistic since Bhutto lacked Latin, which was essential to succeed in the programme. Trevor-Roper further noted that even the brightest students would struggle to complete the degree in two years.

Despite these challenges, Bhutto remained focused on his studies and went on to achieve exceptional academic success at Oxford. His tenacity and commitment to his goals were a testament to his intellect and work ethic, as well as his ambition and resilience.[16] Trevor-Roper may have made the remark in passing, but it sparked a fierce determination in Bhutto. He was determined to show that he was not just equal to but better than the brightest minds in Britain. Over the next two years, Bhutto poured his heart and soul into mastering Latin, to the point where his young wife found herself constantly administering vocabulary tests.

Bhutto's pursuit of excellence would become a hallmark of his life and career and would earn him a place among the most celebrated leaders of his time.[17] In 1952 he secured his Oxford degree with distinction and began his career as a lecturer in international law at the University of Southampton that same year. In 1953 he was called to the Bar at Lincoln's Inn, where Jinnah had been before him. Despite being a landlord and a Sindhi, Bhutto did not let his background limit his world view. His education in elite Western institutions exposed him to a range of progressive ideologies, including socialism, democracy, equality and the rights of the oppressed.

In the early 1950s, as Khrushchev's Russia rapidly caught up with the capitalist United States, several European and North American states began embracing the 'welfare state system'. At the same time, the civil rights movement in the United States was gaining momentum and national freedom movements were achieving success worldwide. These events and trends strongly influenced Bhutto's political leanings, leading him to embrace socialism and advocate for worker control over the means of production while opposing oppression.

During this period, leading economists and social scientists portrayed the state as a benign entity, while landlords and capitalists were often depicted as driven purely by self-interest or outright evil. As a result, many believed that only the state could be trusted with the responsibility of production and distribution of rewards.

In 1957 Bhutto became the youngest member of Pakistan's delegation to the United Nations, and he addressed the UN Sixth Committee on Aggression that October. He also led Pakistan's delegation to the first UN Conference on the Law of the Sea in 1958. However, Bhutto's selection for these roles was not arbitrary; it was based on his exceptional academic achievements and his growing reputation as a progressive and forward-thinking leader.

Interestingly, in Pakistan, the sports of golf and shooting have played an unexpected role in forging political connections. Many notable figures, including Ayub Khan, Zia and Musharraf, were all avid golfers. Similarly, Bhutto's passion for hunting and shooting helped him climb the ladder of political prominence.[18] It is worth noting here Horace Hildreth, who served as the U.S. ambassador in Pakistan from 1953 to 1957 and who owed his political appointment to President Eisenhower's brother, Milton, who was the president of Penn State College and a former governor of the New England state of Maine.[19] Hildreth's correspondence with his family members reveals the exceptionally close relationships he forged with key figures in Pakistani politics and business, based on personal connections rather than just transactions.[20] These relations were strengthened by the marriage of Horace's daughter Dodie to Humayun Mirza, the son of Iskander Mirza, in Karachi. The Hildreth family's shared love of hunting was another reason for the close ties they cultivated with the Pakistani elite. Horace often took advantage of his leisure time to go hunting in the outskirts of Karachi, frequently accompanied by Pir Pagaro. During one visit to Bhutto's Larkana estate, Horace was impressed by his young shooting partner, Zulfiqar Ali Bhutto, whom he considered 'one of the able and promising young men in

Pakistan ... who is friendly to the U.S.' As a result of their close relationship, Horace Hildreth recommended Bhutto to his American attorney for legal assistance in an investigation regarding Dodie's tax liabilities in Pakistan following her marriage. Bhutto, who was asked to provide legal advice, promptly responded to Hildreth's queries with detailed answers within a month. To Hildreth's surprise, Bhutto refused to accept any fee for his services. This act of kindness by Bhutto left a lasting impression on Hildreth, who felt obliged to 'make up for the kindness' in the future.[21]

Bhutto's access to Iskander Mirza was made possible through various channels. One of these was through Bhutto's wife, Nusrat (Isfahani) Bhutto, who had friendly ties with Iskander Mirza's second wife, Naheed Amirteymour, since they shared an Iranian connection. This connection proved to be another way for Bhutto to come into proximity with Iskander Mirza.[22] Humayun Mirza claims that Iskander Mirza considered Zulfiqar Bhutto his protégé and even wished to appoint him to the cabinet. However, Bhutto declined this offer and instead chose to serve under Ayub Khan. This decision was influenced by Bhutto's perception that Iskander Mirza's political prospects were dwindling. As a result, it was upon Ayub Khan's insistence that Bhutto was appointed to Pakistan's federal cabinet on 27 October 1958, becoming the youngest member in the country's history at the age of thirty.[23] In the years following his appointment to the federal cabinet, Bhutto held several key portfolios, including minister of commerce, minister of information, minister of national reconstruction and minister of fuel, power and natural resources. In 1960 Bhutto led a delegation to Moscow to negotiate a joint venture between Russia and Pakistan for oil exploration in Baluchistan. This proved to be a significant achievement, as the Soviet government provided a long-term loan of U.S.$30 million for the joint venture.[24] In 1960 Bhutto was elevated to minister of water and power, communications and industry. Despite his youth and relative inexperience, he quickly became a trusted advisor and ally of Ayub Khan, rising in power and influence. Bhutto played a vital role in the negotiations of the Indus Water Treaty with India in 1960, and the following year he negotiated an oil exploration agreement with the Soviet Union. This agreement allowed for economic and technical aid to be provided to Pakistan, which strengthened the bilateral relationship between the USSR and Pakistan.

In January 1963 Bhutto was appointed as the minister of foreign affairs, a position of greater importance that had a much-coveted portfolio. Throughout his tenure across his government roles, Bhutto's actions and initiatives reflected his clear stance. Notably, his successful negotiations of an oil exploration agreement with the USSR in 1961 and development of ties with socialist China signalled the direction he wanted Pakistan to take. Bhutto aimed to steer Pakistan away from the West and towards a more independent foreign policy. In fact, Rafique Afzal refers to him as 'one of the architects of the famous Beijing–Jakarta–Islamabad axis', and notes that he was instrumental in organizing the second Afro-Asian Conference.²⁵ Such initiatives helped Bhutto build closer ties with socialist groups in Pakistan, which later proved instrumental in the development of a PPP constituency among the country's working class, particularly the unskilled and semi-skilled sections of the proletariat.

He was a multifaceted individual who played various roles in Ayub Khan's cabinet. Apart from serving as a minister, he also demonstrated excellent organizational abilities that led to his appointment as the secretary general of the Convention Muslim League after the 1965 presidential elections. However, Bhutto's popularity and fame increased significantly during the 1965 war, particularly when he passionately advocated for Pakistan's cause before the Security Council. Although Bhutto did not publicly take credit for initiating the 1965 war with India, subsequent disclosures revealed that he was the principal advocate of a forward policy aimed at pressuring India over the Kashmir issue.

While Ayub Khan preferred limited and brief military action, he had no intention of starting a full-scale war, which the United States and the Soviet Union would not support due to their own differences. A war would only have pleased China. Consequently, the seventeen-day war ended abruptly in September. However, the Tashkent Declaration in 1966 sowed the seeds of discord between Ayub and Bhutto. Immediately after that, Bhutto resigned from his position as secretary general of the Convention Muslim League in March 1966, and their paths diverged.²⁶ A year after resigning from his post as foreign minister, Bhutto wrote a book titled *The Myth of Independence*. In the book, he argued that the Kashmir dispute was not a mere territorial conflict. He believed that if Pakistan agreed to peace without ensuring the right of self-determination for the people of Kashmir, it would pave the way for Indian dominance in South Asia, reducing smaller states to the status of Indian satellites.

In November 1967 he founded the PPP at a convention of political workers in Lahore.²⁷ The party leadership adopted a tricolour with green, black and red patches as its standard. Three catchy slogans epitomized the party's 72-page manifesto: 'Islam is our faith; democracy is our polity; socialism is our economy.'²⁸ With its famous slogan, 'Bread, clothing, shelter', the PPP pledged to work towards the establishment of an egalitarian society through the nationalization of all major industries, which also included banks and insurance companies. Bhutto's vision for Pakistan extended beyond mere military security. He believed that Pakistan needed to be free from neo-colonialist powers and their military presence on Pakistani soil, as well as from foreign military overflights. However, he was also wary of portraying socialism as a Western idea, and therefore spoke of 'Islamic socialism' to cater to Pakistani sensibilities. In a speech after the founding of the PPP, he pledged to 'establish Islamic socialism according to the wishes of Quaid-e-Azam', making it clear that he was committed to strengthening the country.

Despite this, the PPP's first manifesto was somewhat critical of the country's religious establishment, stating that dogmatic fanaticism had led to the decline of Muslim civilizations. Bhutto rejected the religious parties' powerful slogan 'Islam is in danger' by stating that it was false, and that the landlords and their puppets were the ones in danger. He also respected the ulema, but condemned those who gave fatwas after receiving money, arguing that they served the interests of the non-believers.

Sherbaz Khan Mazari, Bhutto's political contemporary and initially his detractor, noted the novelty of his style. According to Mazari, Bhutto employed a four-pronged approach in his speeches to win public support. First, he attacked the personality of Ayub Khan and the corruption scandals surrounding his family and government. Second, he criticized the Tashkent Declaration and the so-called 'great betrayal' that stemmed from it, which resonated with many Pakistanis. Third, he used fierce anti-India rhetoric to gain favour in Lahore and the populous central Punjab. And fourth, Bhutto was anti-United States in nature, taking advantage of public hostility that had resulted from the U.S. arms embargo during and after the 1965 war. By combining these tactics, Bhutto was able to establish himself as a powerful political force and gain the support of the masses.[29] Rafique Afzal succinctly captured the party's mission statement as one that emphasized the need to restructure the current colonial and capitalistic system through a socialist programme to improve the lives of the poor. The party called for the creation of a new constitution by a new assembly; nationalization of basic industries, banks and insurance companies; and reforms to better the conditions of both urban labour and rural peasantry. Additionally, it advocated for a non-aligned foreign policy; withdrawal from defence pacts such as SEATO and CENTO immediately and from the Commonwealth at a 'proper time'; solidarity with Afro-Asian and Latin American countries, particularly the Muslim ones; dissociation from the Tashkent Declaration; and the settlement of Kashmir and other disputes with India.[30]

The PPP's inaugural meeting was a momentous occasion in Pakistan's political history, since it marked the first time that socialist ideas were openly discussed. Despite the fact that only half of the expected number of delegates showed up, the meeting was still exciting. The most significant moment occurred at the end of the proceedings when the question of who should be the party's chairman was raised. Bhutto was proclaimed the leader by acclamation, and no other office bearers were elected. Although leftists such as J. A. Rahim and Mubashir Hassan may have believed that they were using him to advance their ideals, it was evident that Bhutto was using them. The party was unequivocally Bhutto's vehicle from the beginning, with all party posts under his control. He once famously remarked, 'I am the PPP.'[31]Although there have been instances of non-Bhutto office holders, internal party elections were never held until they became a legal requirement, and even then, the Bhutto family maintained control over the process – PPP officials were expected to simply carry out the agenda of the Bhutto family member in charge. Despite this, some important developments occurred during Bhutto's tenure. In 1974 he organized the Second Islamic Summit in Lahore. He also signed the Simla Agreement with India, which resulted in Pakistan regaining 13,000 square kilometres (5,000 sq. mi.) of territory occupied during the 1971 war and the release of 93,000 Pakistani prisoners of war. Bhutto established several institutions, including the National Book Foundation in September 1972, the NDFC in February 1973, Quaid-e-Azam University in February 1973 and the Port Qasim Authority in June 1973. In addition, he introduced identity cards for citizens in July 1973 and laid the foundation stone for the Pakistan Steel Mill in December 1973. Bhutto also inaugurated the Allama Iqbal Open University in May 1974 and Pakistan's First Seerat Conference in March 1976, and proposed a Third World Summit in September 1976. Bhutto banned alcohol, gambling and other un-Islamic activities and declared Friday as the weekly holiday instead of Sunday. He withdrew Pakistan from Britain's Commonwealth of Nations and the U.S.-dominated SEATO. Despite some of these achievements, Bhutto's authoritarian tendencies and mishandling of the economy eventually led to his downfall.

Zulfi Bhutto's ability to captivate large crowds through his eloquent speeches was truly remarkable. However, Bhutto's talents were not limited to just oratory. He was also a gifted writer and authored several books, including *The Myth of Independence* and *The Great Tragedy*. Bhutto's writings were known for their insightful analysis and persuasive arguments, but in addition to his political writings, he also wrote poetry in both English and Urdu.

The PPP in Power

In the first general elections, held on 9 December 1970, the PPP led by Bhutto swept to power in West Pakistan. This victory came after 23 years of independence, during which the eastern wing of the country had become increasingly marginalized and alienated. Despite this, Bhutto was unable to reach a political agreement with the Awami League, which represented Bengali nationalism and had won all but a handful of seats in the eastern wing.[32] Bhutto's intentions were increasingly perceived to be the establishment of his supremacy in West Pakistan while allowing Mujib to have complete control over East Pakistan. This perception was further strengthened when he reportedly made the statement 'udhar tum, idhar hum' at a rally, which translates to 'you there, we here'. Such statements hardly helped to dispel the perception that Bhutto was seeking to divide the country along regional lines and consolidate his own power in the west.[33] While Bhutto and his supporters maintain that the statement was simply meant to acknowledge the separate majorities of the two regions, one eyewitness insists that the comment was made in earnest. Regardless, as political divisions deepened, Bhutto saw his path to power once again through military intervention. If Mujib remained committed to the six points, the military would have only one acceptable democratic leader: Bhutto himself. With this strategy in mind, Bhutto felt confident relying on the military to propel him to power. However, Yahya's decision to postpone the National Assembly session, unwilling to move forward without the PPP's presence, proved controversial and ultimately sparked a violent backlash in East Pakistan, as many of Yahya's advisors had warned.

The growing divide between the PPP and the Awami League set the stage for Operation Searchlight, a military campaign against the Bengali insurgency, launched on 25 March 1971. The military action in East Pakistan ended in disaster, with widespread violence, displacement of people and eventual Indian military intervention. In December 1971, Bangladesh came into being, marking a catastrophic loss for Pakistan. While the military humiliation at Dhaka allowed for civilian dominance to be established, it came at the cost of the country's dismemberment. Zulfiqar Ali Bhutto emerged as a powerful leader during this tumultuous time. He drew strength from the disgrace and demoralization of the nation and, after his swearing-in ceremony as president of Pakistan, he became the CMLA, the first civilian to hold such a position among the new nations. The consolidation of power in his person and the animated popular support for his presidency proved to be the most exhilarating experience of Bhutto's life.[34] When Bhutto took over the reins of the government in December 1971, the Pakistan Army was thoroughly discredited, and the morale of the masses was at its lowest ebb. Mohammad Waseem's analysis sheds light on the significant changes that took place under Bhutto's leadership. Bhutto's assumption of power in West Pakistan represented a break not only with East Pakistan but with the first generation of leadership in the post-independence period. A whole new stratum of political leaders emerged to take up responsibilities under PPP rule from 1971 to 1977, and this transition was not limited to age alone.

A more significant change was the shift from the status quo orientation of the previous rulers of Pakistan to a commitment to economic and administrative reform, which helped re-create some of the dynamism of the independence movement in terms of mass mobilization. Waseem's analysis is apt and insightful, since it highlights the transformative impact of Bhutto's leadership on Pakistan's political landscape, especially in the aftermath of the country's dismemberment.[35]

In his first national broadcast to the nation, Bhutto acknowledged the gravity of the situation facing Pakistan and offered a message of hope and unity, declaring:

> We are in the midst of the greatest crisis our nation has ever faced, a crisis that threatens our very existence. But we must begin to

rebuild, to pick up the pieces, no matter how small, and create a new Pakistan – a Pakistan that is prosperous, progressive, and free of exploitation. This is the Pakistan envisioned by Quaid-e-Azam, and it is our duty to make it a reality. I have faith that we can do this, but I cannot do it alone. I need your cooperation, your support, and your dedication. Together, we can overcome any challenge. With your support, I am confident that we can achieve anything. I am not a magician, but I promise to do everything in my power to lead us to a brighter future.[36]

The speech was a clear reflection of the challenges facing the beleaguered Pakistani people and state. To institutionalize the supremacy of the democratic forces was indeed a daunting task because the interests of the military–bureaucratic oligarchy were so entrenched that reining them in seemed difficult, but such action was imperative for democracy to flourish.

Resistance from the Army

Despite the loss of East Pakistan, the military remained hesitant to give up control to a democratically elected government. In fact, the PPP administration had to deal with a coup attempt by around forty officers. Tensions with the military also surfaced in 1972 when a general refused to deploy troops to quell a police strike over pay in the Punjab, leading to a stand-off between the government and the military. However, it should be noted that Bhutto's efforts to reform the military and bureaucracy were also aimed at centralizing power in the prime minister's office and weakening the military–bureaucratic elite, as well as the parliament and cabinet. This approach was not surprising given Bhutto's political background, having served as a member of Ayub Khan's government early in his career.[37]

The early days of Bhutto's government were marked by a sweeping purge of the military's top brass. In the first four months of his rule, 43 senior officers who were associated with the Yahya regime were removed from their posts. The removal of Lieutenant General Gul Hassan Khan, who had served as the chief of Army staff, and Air Marshal Rahim Khan, who had been the chief of Air staff, was particularly significant as it represented a clear assertion of civilian supremacy over the military. This purge was part of Bhutto's broader efforts to consolidate power within the civilian government and reduce the influence of the military–bureaucratic elite.

To prevent the possibility of future military takeovers, the 1973 Constitution established a framework for federal, democratic structure. It included a number of clauses that were specifically designed to discourage military intervention. The Constitution ensured civilian supremacy over the military, providing a constitutional safeguard for the future.[38] Its Article 271 aimed to prevent any future military intervention by prescribing the death penalty for the Constitution's subversion. The article serves as a deterrent to anyone who might contemplate an attempt to overthrow the constitutional order through illegal means. In other words, the inclusion of this article represented the determination of the framers of the Constitution to safeguard democracy and prevent military coups from occurring in the future. Any attempt to subvert the Constitution is considered high treason, a charge that carries severe consequences.[39] In addition to implementing the measures mentioned earlier, Bhutto also sought to limit the military's long-term influence by restructuring its high command. One key change was to reduce the chief of the Army staff's tenure to three years. This move was aimed at preventing the accumulation of too much power by any one individual in the military, thus making it more difficult for the armed forces to engage in a coup or subvert civilian rule.[40]

Bhutto was concerned about the potential for political unrest and opposition to his regime and believed that the Army should not be involved in civilian affairs. He feared that if the Army intervened, they would act according to their own rules and potentially threaten the civilian government. He believed that the police and other law enforcement agencies were not sufficient to control serious agitation and that a specialized force was necessary to maintain stability and prevent the need for Army intervention. To address these concerns, Bhutto proposed the creation of a first-class security force separate from the Army.

Bhutto's views and actions can be seen as authoritarian in nature as he sought to limit dissent and maintain control over the country. However, his concerns about the Army's involvement in civilian affairs were not unfounded, since Pakistan had a history of military coups and interventions in politics. The effectiveness and impartiality of the security force that Bhutto proposed, however, remains a subject of debate.[41]

The Federal Security Force (FSF) was established in October 1972, with headquarters located in Lahore. To provide the FSF with a legal framework, an Act of parliament was passed in June 1973. However, the Army's top leadership did not welcome the creation of a new force that could operate independently of the military and showed its disapproval by refusing to provide the newly founded unit with necessary training and equipment.

The Army's reluctance to support the FSF was evident in its refusal to allow the acquisition of essential equipment, which hindered the force's ability to operate effectively. This lack of cooperation also raised questions as to the willingness of the military to accept civilian control and highlighted the challenges of balancing civilian and military power in a democratic system. Despite these challenges, the FSF continued to operate and played a role in maintaining law and order in Pakistan during a period of political and social unrest.[42]

However, to the Army's chagrin, the FSF started functioning as 'an additional coercive force'.[43] Instead of acting as a neutral force to maintain law and order, the FSF was often used as a tool to suppress opposition and silence dissenting voices. This was evident in May 1973, when the FSF disrupted rallies organized by opposition parties that were critical of the ruling People's Party. In 1975 the FSF's actions became even more alarming when a group of National Assembly members were forcibly ejected from the premises by FSF personnel. The prime minister himself acknowledged that these FSF members were acting like a group of degenerate thugs, raising concerns about the legitimacy and impartiality of the force.

These incidents highlight the dangers of creating security forces that are not accountable to civilian authorities and can be used to suppress opposition and violate the rights of citizens. The FSF's actions represent a troubling aspect of Pakistan's history and demonstrate the challenges of balancing security and civil liberties in a democratic society.[44]

Despite his efforts to limit the Army's involvement in civilian affairs, Bhutto sought to appease the military by increasing defence spending and granting military officers exemptions from land reforms. This approach led to a significant increase in Pakistan's defence expenditure, which rose by over 200 per cent during the Bhutto era.

According to Ian Talbot, during this period, the Pakistani government was spending U.S.$8 per capita on the armed forces. This disproportionate allocation of resources to the military had a significant impact on Pakistan's economy and social development, since resources that could have been used for education, healthcare and infrastructure were instead diverted towards defence spending.

Bhutto's strategy of appeasing the military while also attempting to limit its power highlights the complex relationship between civilian governments and the military in Pakistan. While it was important for civilian authorities to assert their control over the military, they also had to balance this with the need to maintain strong national defence: 'Achieving this balance is essential for building a stable and prosperous democratic society.'[45] As a result of these policies, the size and influence of the armed forces continued to grow. However, even more significant than the financial concessions granted to the military elite was the ban on public discussion of the military's failure in East Pakistan.

This embargo on public discussion prevented critical analysis of the military's actions in East Pakistan, which contributed to the loss of the territory in 1971. By suppressing open dialogue and debate about the military's role in this conflict, the government undermined accountability and transparency, which are critical components of a functioning democratic system.

The absence of accountability and transparency not only impeded the progress of a robust and efficient military but undermined the government's capacity to address impending security threats. It is imperative for democratic societies to foster open discussions and deliberations regarding military affairs, to guarantee that the armed forces answer to civilian authorities and operate in the nation's best interests.⁴⁶ The Hamood-ur-Rehman Commission was established to investigate the causes of East Pakistan's separation from the rest of the country. However, despite the commission's findings being submitted in 1972, the report was not made public until much later.

Bhutto's militaristic mode of thinking was further highlighted by his frequent anti-Indian rhetoric and his determination to build Pakistan's nuclear capabilities. His infamous statement about being willing to eat grass to acquire nuclear weapons underscored his single-minded focus on military strength.

In 1973 Bhutto inaugurated Pakistan's first nuclear plant, a move that had significant implications for the country's security and foreign policy. He also travelled extensively to Muslim countries, seeking support for his policies and committing Pakistani soldiers to fight against Israel.

Bhutto's focus on military strength and anti-Indian rhetoric helped to rehabilitate the military's reputation after the loss of East Pakistan. However, this militaristic approach came at the expense of social and economic development and contributed to Pakistan's long-standing security challenges. In the end, a more balanced and holistic approach that prioritized human development, democracy and national security was crucial to constructing a robust, stable and prosperous Pakistan.⁴⁷

Bhutto also tried hard to clip the wings of the bureaucracy, whom many critics called the 'Sultans of Pakistan' and 'the best-organized political party in Pakistan'.⁴⁸ Bhutto's announcement of Civil Service reforms was accompanied by a strong condemnation of the state of bureaucracy in the country. He emphasized that no institution had done more to harm the quality of national life than the bureaucracy, which he derogatorily referred to as *naukarshahi* (rule by servants).

This critique reflected Bhutto's broader commitment to restructuring the state and promoting a more egalitarian and inclusive society. By targeting the bureaucracy, he aimed to challenge the entrenched power structures that had long favoured the elites at the expense of ordinary citizens. Nevertheless, it is worth noting that while Bhutto's rhetoric was bold and inspiring, his reforms did not always align with his words. Despite his efforts, the bureaucracy remained a potent and frequently corrupt force in Pakistani society, and the country's governance challenges persisted.⁴⁹

Upon assuming power, Bhutto swiftly dismissed several high-ranking bureaucrats. In December 1971, just hours prior to his address to the nation, he fired Roadad Khan and imprisoned Altaf Gauhar, a close associate of former president Ayub Khan. This action was taken despite Bhutto's prior assurances that no retribution would be inflicted upon bureaucrats who had wronged him in the past.⁵⁰

Bhutto was determined to overhaul the elitist structure of the Civil Service. According to Omar Noman, the recruitment procedures and selection criteria for the service resembled those used by the British colonial government, which ensured that the top positions were controlled by a few entrenched families. Despite a vast administrative machinery of over 500,000 members, approximately five hundred bureaucrats from the Civil Service of Pakistan (CSP) cadre held the reins of power. Moreover, the annual intake of the elite corps was limited to a mere twenty individuals. To break this stranglehold, Bhutto replaced the CSP system with the linear All Pakistan Unified Grades structure, which consisted of a hierarchical but mobile framework of 22 pay scales. This restructuring also eliminated the separate entry provision into the elite corps.[51]

The initial phase of these reforms saw 'the dismissal of 1,300 Civil Servants in 1972, under a Martial Law Ordinance'.[52] To deal this decisive blow to the entrenched bureaucratic interest, Bhutto compartmentalized the bureaucratic structure into central and provincial services, and on 20 August 1973, he abolished the elite CSP cadre.[53] Despite Bhutto's efforts to reform the Civil Service, the District Management Group (DMG) still held many key positions in the central secretariat. Though the CSP cadre had been abolished, the DMG maintained its power and influence, prompting Bhutto to introduce a scheme of lateral entry for technocrats and specialists to improve efficiency. However, this move was criticized by some as it led to the appointment of sycophantic individuals, including relatives and acquaintances of federal ministers, which prompted accusations that Bhutto had created an 'army of stooges'.[54] Despite his earlier efforts to curtail the bureaucracy's power, Bhutto eventually had to rely on bureaucrats to provide administrative oversight for the numerous institutions created through his policy of nationalization. In fact, the nationalization of industries ended up strengthening the role of the bureaucracy, rather than weakening it. As Saeed Shafqat notes, investment in the public sector increased dramatically from PKR 332 million to PKR 5.4 billion between 1973–4 and 1977–8. However, investment in the private sector remained relatively low, rising only from PKR 697 million to PKR 1.1 billion during the same period. As a result, the public sector was unable to generate sufficient capital or production, becoming a burden on taxpayers. Although Bhutto had initially sought to reform the bureaucracy, his policies ultimately reinforced its power and influence.[55]

Nationalization: Two Phases

Bhutto's ideology was marked by socialism, and he promised redistributive reforms to improve the condition of marginalized segments of society. However, after coming to power, he chose to use state authority to punish resistant members of dominant social groups and reward those who supported the PPP. This approach favoured consolidation of power rather than the promotion of genuine social justice.[56] Similarly, Khalid bin Sayeed notes that 'Bhutto was primarily motivated by *animus dominandi* ... the aggrandizement of his own power,' through which 'he wanted to control every major class or interest by weakening its power base and by making it subservient to his will and policies.'[57]

Bhutto's rule was marked by a continuation of the traditional practice among Pakistani rulers of concentrating power in their own hands. Despite calls for provincial autonomy, little changed in this regard. Bhutto did not depart from this legacy, as the state structure continued to revolve around him. The policy of nationalization, which began in January 1972 with the takeover of 31 industrial units, was also aimed at consolidating his power. Although the first phase of nationalization was driven by leftist ideology, it ultimately resulted in the emergence of a form of 'state capitalism', according to Sayeed. The restructuring of credit policies affected the top 22 families that had dominated Pakistan's economy in the 1960s. Despite Bhutto's promise to redistribute wealth and empower the marginalized, his policies ultimately served to further centralize power and benefit those loyal to his regime.[58]

Land Reforms

In March 1972 Bhutto announced his land reforms, which aimed to break up the concentration of landed wealth, reduce income disparities, increase production, reduce unemployment, streamline the administration of land revenue and agricultural taxation and establish a mutually beneficial relationship between landowners and tenants. Bhutto saw these reforms as a crucial step towards social justice and the empowerment of the rural population. However, the implementation of these reforms faced numerous challenges, and many critics argued that they did not go far enough in addressing the deep-rooted problems of land ownership and distribution in Pakistan. The manifesto of the PPP stressed the importance of breaking up large estates and eliminating feudal landowners as a national necessity, and this would be accomplished through practical measures.[59]

The land reforms introduced in Pakistan under the Bhutto government had several salient features. The first phase of the reforms included ceilings on land holdings, which were set at 60 hectares (150 ac) for irrigated land, 120 hectares (300 ac) for unirrigated land, or the equivalent of 12,000 produced index units (PIUS) plus an additional 2,000 PIUS for tractor and tube-well owners. Land was redistributed without charge to landless tenants who were cultivating the resumed land, and untenanted resumed land was redistributed without charge to small owners or tenants with holdings below subsistence. The share system remained unchanged, and the landlords were responsible for paying land revenue, water rates and seed costs, while the cost of fertilizers and pesticides was shared equally between the landlords and tenants. Tenants could be evicted if they failed to pay rent or cultivate land, if they sublet their tenancy or if they rendered the land unfit for cultivation. In the second phase of the land reform, introduced in 1977, land holdings were further reduced to 40 hectares (100 ac) for irrigated land, 80 hectares (200 ac) for unirrigated land, or 8,000 PIUS equivalent. Compensation was paid to landowners at a rate of PKR 30 per PIU for the resumed land, while the redistribution of land followed the same principles as the 1972 land reform.[60]

The land reforms introduced in Pakistan failed to achieve their intended objectives. Despite the People's Party coming to power with socialist slogans and promises to redistribute resources, the landlords remained the most influential political actors in the country. The development economist S. Akbar Zaidi argues that despite the propaganda about the success of the 1972 land reforms, only a small number of people benefited from the redistribution of land. Between 1972 and 1978, only 50,548 persons benefited from the redistribution of 124,800 hectares (308,390 ac) of land. The number of landless tenants and small owners who benefited from the reforms was only 1 per cent, and even after 38 years, 6 per cent of the resumed land in 1959 remained undistributed. Additionally, 39 per cent of the land resumed under the 1972 reforms is still held by the government despite the presence of a large number of landless cultivators.[61] On 1 March 1973, the ceiling was further reduced from 200 hectares (500 ac) to 60 hectares (150 ac) of irrigated land and from 400 hectares (1,000 ac) to 120 hectares (300 ac) for semi-irrigated land. All lands in excess of 40 hectares (100 ac) were allocated to the government.

During the Bhutto regime, economic policies reflected a strong inclination towards centralized control by Islamabad, which led to mixed results. This approach was unexpected from a democratically elected leader who was supposed to be representative of the popular voice. However, the overall impact of this policy was particularly negative, not only for Pakistan's economy but for its polity. Bhutto's socialist economic model created apprehensions among the capitalist–industrial class, discouraging further investment in the country.

One such policy was the nationalization of banks and the centralization of credit disbursement, which created new social classes and strengthened the ruling elite. However, the middle-class farmers and peasants were given incentives. The penetration of banks into the agrarian structure disrupted the traditional tenant–landlord relationship and caused unrest. Additionally, agriculture suffered due to the export of labour to the Middle East, with approximately 33,000 Pakistani workers sent to Saudi Arabia, 12,000 to Libya and Dubai and 5,000 to Abu Dhabi, Jordan, Bahrain and Iran between 1972 and 1977. This labour export also led to an increase in remittances from PKR 508.8 million in 1971–2 to PKR 5.5 billion in 1976–7.

The economic changes implemented during the Bhutto regime had significant impacts on the rural structure of Pakistan, including the disruption of traditional patron–client relationships and the intensification of social tension. These changes were particularly resented by the landed aristocracy, leading to a potentially explosive situation. As a result, the economic policies affected the social and political fabric of the country, with far-reaching consequences.

Ahmadi Exclusion

A development of lasting impact during Bhutto's reign was the exclusion of followers of the Ahmadiyya denomination from the pale of Islam. Anti-Ahmadiyya sentiment had almost seventy years of history, ebbing and flowing through the years, breaking to the surface periodically – as in the 1953 disturbances. In 1974 anti-Ahmadiyya factions returned in full force, and Bhutto was left with no option but to buckle under extreme pressure. The incident that became an immediate cause for religious parties to band together, eventually turning into an agitational movement and leading to the exclusion of the Ahmadiyya people from Islam, was a scuffle between students and Ahmadi activists.[62]

In 1974 students from Nishtar Medical College in the Punjab city of Multan were on a trip when their train stopped at the small Punjabi town of Rabwah (now Chenab Nagar), home to an Ahmadiyya headquarters. The students, many of whom belonged to the student wing of the Islamic political party Jamaat-i-Islam, began chanting anti-Ahmadi slogans, leading to a physical confrontation between them and the Ahmadis. In a few days, a nationwide movement had started. Initially Bhutto hesitated, but only briefly, as the instantaneously revived Majlis-i-Tahafuz-i-Khatam-i-Nabuwwat threatened the PPP's government with direct action. To avoid confrontation with the religious right – who had great 'street power', having mastered the politics of agitation during the days of the British Raj – Bhutto decided to go with the flow.[63] The matter was referred to parliament. Such tactics have determined the subsequent course of Pakistani politics. The Ahmadis were declared a minority through constitutional amendment.

In strict compliance with constitutional requirements, the amendments were voted through secret divisions during the third reading of the bill, and 130 members of the National Assembly voted for the bill with no negative vote. During the clause-by-clause consideration of the bill, all the members from all sections of the house signified their approval by standing on their seats. The final adoption of the bill was greeted by the prolonged thumping of tables by the members. The Senate met soon after the assembly session, unanimously approved the bill without any debate and was adjourned *sine die*.[64] Every single one of the 31 senators in attendance within the house cast their vote in favour of the bill, which was spearheaded by the law minister, Abdul Hafiz Pirzada. This momentous decision, as noted by Bhutto, was described as one of the most challenging choices in Pakistan's history. Bhutto went on to emphasize that it had been made after extensive deliberations and consultations with individuals and political parties representing a wide spectrum of opinions. He said it could not have been taken without the existence of the democratic institutions of the country. Bhutto used the opportunity to reaffirm the government's determination to ensure full protection to all communities and guarantee them all the fundamental rights enshrined in the Constitution of the country. 'After today's decision it is all the more necessary to protect all the citizens of the country,' he said. 'No vandalism or humiliation of any citizen in any way will be tolerated.'[65] *Dawn* hailed a momentous occasion in Pakistan's history where, for the first time, elected representatives discussed a complex issue with democratic spirit. The National Assembly, as the country's supreme sovereign body, spearheaded the discussions.[66]

Culturally, vernacular speech and local dress rose in standing and prestige. *Sindhi kurta* (long shirts) and *shalwar* (baggy trousers) could be found in places where previously a suit and tie were the prescribed dress. Bhutto himself swapped his Savoy suits and Italian shoes for the Sindhi farmer's attire when he had to address public meetings. Folk music and culture were promoted and patronized, and it was no longer uncouth to speak in regional languages in halls of power and culture.[67] Bhutto himself spoke Urdu in an accent identifiable with the poor and dispossessed, and his spoken Sindhi also had a rural touch. His personal and ideological contradictions betrayed a promising social change. An enduring legacy of this period is the incorporation of people's rights and social justice in the national agenda. After Bhutto, no party or leader could expect to gain public support without paying at least lip service to the rights of the poor.[68] Bhutto's appeasement of the militant Sunni religious leaders by excluding the Ahmadis, however, gave in to their disruptive message that political issues should not be resolved through negotiation. Instead, threats and blackmail would be substituted for negotiation and compromise.

Generally speaking, the Bhutto era was replete with difficulties and challenges, particularly in terms of the economy. Economic trends at the international level were hardly conducive to any developing economy's growth and prosperity. Akbar Zaidi's contention also proves the same point. He says that several events that took place outside the control of the government were largely responsible for the poor performance of the economy after 1974. First, the Pakistani rupee was devalued in May 1972, which led to a positive outcome, with exports growing by over 100 per cent. However, this positive trend was short-lived as Pakistan faced massive floods in August 1973, which led to the import of food grains in considerable quantities. This was followed by a fourfold increase in international petroleum prices in October 1973, which made imports much more expensive. As a result, the prices of fertilizers, essential inputs and oil soared tremendously, leading to excessive inflation domestically. Moreover, the world recession of 1974–7, followed by OPEC price hikes, severely depressed demand for

Pakistani exports, which further affected industrial output. In 1974–5, a huge failure of the cotton crop by as much as 25 per cent occurred at a time when international cotton prices had risen, also affecting industrial output. Last, in 1976–7, the worst floods in Pakistan's history destroyed agricultural crops, forcing the government to further import food items, resulting in excessive expenditure on public good measures. All these events affected Pakistan's industrial output negatively.[69]

Foreign Policy

Bhutto's foreign policy aimed to diversify Pakistan's relations beyond the United States, since he believed that Pakistan's reliance on the States had not served its interests well. To achieve this, Bhutto withdrew Pakistan from CENTO and SEATO and established closer ties with Arab states. In addition, he worked to strengthen Sino-Pakistan relations, which had deteriorated after the 1965 war. This effort led to the historic visit of the Chinese premier Zhou Enlai to Pakistan in 1971 and laid the groundwork for the later strategic partnership between the two countries, at a time when China was isolated internationally. Bhutto's efforts to expand Pakistan's diplomatic reach were based on a desire for greater independence and self-reliance in foreign affairs and marked a departure from Pakistan's previously pro-Western stance.[70] Bhutto was a staunch supporter of an independent foreign policy for Pakistan, which he believed was heavily influenced by the United States. During his tenure as both foreign minister and prime minister, he worked towards strengthening Pakistan's ties with other countries and he notably developed a special relationship with Iran, which had previously provided military assistance to Pakistan. Overall, Bhutto's efforts were aimed at reducing Pakistan's dependence on any one country and promoting its position as an independent player in the international arena.[71] In 1974 Bhutto hosted the second Organisation of the Islamic Conference (OIC) in Lahore, inviting leaders from the Muslim world to participate and help shape a common agenda for cooperation and progress.[72] Bhutto's foreign-policy initiatives extended beyond his efforts to diversify Pakistan's relations. He also championed the cause of Afro-Asian solidarity, building strong ties with nations across Africa and Asia. By 1976 he had emerged as a leading figure in the developing world, a vocal advocate for the rights and interests of developing countries. Through these efforts, Bhutto helped to elevate Pakistan's standing on the global stage, while also advancing a vision of a more equitable and just international order.[73]

Bhutto's efforts to establish peace with India were marked by his diplomacy and negotiation skills. His primary goal was to secure the return of 93,000 prisoners of war and the territory of 13,000 square kilometres (5,000 sq. mi.) held by India without compromising on the Kashmir stance or recognizing Bangladesh, both of which were key Indian demands.

Despite India's role in the separation of Bangladesh from Pakistan, Bhutto saw the POW problem as a humanitarian issue that could be addressed at any time, whereas the territorial problem could lead to further integration of Indian-held territories over time. Indira Gandhi initially refused Bhutto's demand, but he skilfully negotiated with her, convincing her to return the territory and the POWs to Pakistan in the first stage of the Simla Agreement. Bhutto's successful negotiation with a state that had caused severe damage to Pakistan is still regarded as a remarkable diplomatic achievement.[74]

Bhutto was a visionary who possessed a vast knowledge and keen awareness of post-Second World War politics and the political history of the world. He crafted a foreign policy that brought unmatched dividends to Pakistan's foreign relations. His policy was continued by successive governments and enabled Pakistan to play a vital role in world politics. One of Bhutto's major achievements was bringing a UN resolution in 1974, which recommended and called for the establishment of a nuclear-weapon-free zone in South Asia. Along with his foreign minister, Aziz Ahmed, he aggressively attacked the Indian nuclear programme and put India in a defensive position. While Abdul Qadeer Khan was tasked with bringing the gas centrifuge technology through atomic proliferation, Bhutto promoted Pakistan as a non-proliferationist. This achievement proved Bhutto's intelligence and strategic thinking, which led to the success of Pakistan's foreign policy.[75]

Bhutto, from the 1960s, rejected SEATO and favoured a non-aligned policy, which he solidified after assuming power. He embarked on an

Zulfiqar Ali Bhutto and Colonel Gaddafi (middle), while Mujibur Rahman looks on, during the closing ceremony of the 2nd Islamic Summit Conference, Lahore, 25 February 1974. Yasser Arafat waves to the crowd.

extensive foreign trip to Southeast Asia, where he sought to establish closer ties with Vietnam, Thailand, Laos, Burma and North Korea. Bhutto also worked towards fostering positive relationships with China and the Soviet Union while building an Islamic bloc and advocating for the creation of new economic alliances, with the aim of benefiting developing nations. While Bhutto held an admiration for Japan, it did not hold a prominent position within his foreign-policy agenda. His perspective was rooted in the belief that Pakistan's interests would be better served by forging a closer relationship with China. Another significant factor contributing to Bhutto's hesitation in cultivating amicable relations with Japan was its close alliance with the United States. Nevertheless, Japan attempted to establish closer ties with Pakistan in the 1970s, sending military officials, scientists and parliamentary delegations. In 1974, when India conducted a nuclear test, code-named 'Smiling Buddha', Japan criticized India and supported Pakistan's non-nuclear-weapon policy. Japan also pledged to build several new 'peaceful' nuclear power plants.[76]

Bhutto believed that Japan had been influenced by the United States, and he saw the expansion of Japan's role in Asia as serving American interests in the region. In the 1970s Bhutto sought to establish Pakistan's independent foreign policy, with a focus on promoting economic relations rather than military alliances. As a result, Japan's influence in Pakistan diminished, despite its efforts to improve ties. Bhutto's vision for Pakistan's foreign policy was short-lived, however, as General Zia ul Haq's regime reversed many of the policy initiatives. It was only after Bhutto's execution that Pakistan–Japan ties were finally restored.[77] Bhutto worked tirelessly to improve Pakistan's relations with the Arab world and was a strong advocate for the Arab cause in the Arab–Israeli conflict. His efforts were greatly appreciated by Colonel Gaddafi of Libya, who admired Bhutto's intellectualism and considered him an inspiration. The Yom Kippur War in 1973 marked a turning point in Pakistan's relations with the Arab world.[78] Under Bhutto's leadership, Pakistan demonstrated unwavering support and a swift, unconditional offer of assistance to the Arab states. Bhutto's support for the Arab cause was not merely symbolic: he provided financial aid and political support, and even dispatched Pakistan's top fighter pilots to aid the Syrian and Egyptian air forces in their combat missions against Israel. However, Pakistan's relations with some Muslim nations, particularly Bangladesh, remained strained after the 1971 war. Eventually, under pressure from other Muslim nations and in a bid to improve regional stability, Pakistan recognized Bangladesh as an independent state in 1974. This move paved the way for the commencement of full diplomatic relations between Pakistan and Bangladesh in 1976, which has since fostered greater cooperation and understanding between the two countries.

In 1974 India conducted a nuclear test near Pakistan's eastern border, which caused concern and outrage in Pakistan. Bhutto made unsuccessful efforts to persuade the United States to impose economic sanctions on India in response. He even requested a meeting between Pakistan's ambassador to the United States and Secretary of State Henry Kissinger. However, Kissinger dismissed the idea of sanctions and suggested that Pakistan should learn to live with India's nuclear capabilities, which further strained the ties between Pakistan and the United States.

In 1976 tensions escalated further when Bhutto continued to pursue Pakistan's nuclear programme, despite U.S. objections. During a meeting, Kissinger threatened that the United States would make an example of Pakistan if Bhutto did not cancel, modify or postpone the Reprocessing Plant Agreement with France. However, Bhutto stood firm and refused to give in to U.S. pressure. He replied to Kissinger, 'For the sake of my country and its people, I do not succumb to blackmailing and threats.' Despite the strain in the relationship with the United States, Pakistan continued to pursue its nuclear programme, which eventually led to the development of its nuclear weapons capability.[79]

After the meeting with Kissinger, Bhutto shifted Pakistan's foreign-policy focus towards the non-aligned movement and worked on strengthening relations with both the Soviet Union and the United States. Here it seems appropriate to give a brief introduction of the non-aligned movement to put the whole discourse of Pakistan's foreign policy in proper perspective. The non-aligned movement (NAM) was established in 1961 to promote the interests of developing nations against the backdrop of the Cold War. During its initial three decades, this movement played a pivotal role in key global developments, including decolonization, the emergence of new independent states and the promotion of democratic principles in international relations. NAM came into existence during the Cold War era, largely driven by the efforts of influential leaders such as Josip Broz Tito of Yugoslavia, Gamal Abdel Nasser, Jawaharlal Nehru and Ahmad Sukarno. It served as a coalition of states that intentionally refrained from formal alignment with either the United States or the Soviet Union, instead opting for independence and neutrality. Bhutto was acutely aware of Britain's policy of 'divide and rule' as well as the United States' policy of 'unite and rule'.[80] He saw the non-aligned movement as a way to counterbalance the influence of the major powers and give smaller nations a voice on the world stage. The second Islamic summit in 1974 at Lahore was an elucidation of that stance.

Despite Bhutto's efforts to maintain balanced relations, his perceived closeness with the Soviet Union and his nuclear ambitions led to increased tension with the United States, which cut off military aid to Pakistan in 1979. The relationship between the two countries remained strained until the end of the Cold War.[81] In 1974 Bhutto made a historic visit to Moscow, where he sought to improve relations with the Soviet Union and the Communist bloc. This effort to alleviate tensions and promote cooperation between the two nations was the result of earlier successful collaborations such as the establishment of Pakistan Steel Mills in 1972, which was a joint venture between the Soviet Union and Pakistan. Bhutto was so invested in the project that he personally laid the foundation stone on 30 December 1973. Conceived in the 1970s as a cornerstone in the development of Pakistan's economy and industrial advancement, the Pakistan Steel Mills, also known as Pak Steel, is a massive steel-manufacturing complex located in Karachi. Established with help from the Soviet Union, it aimed to boost Pakistan's industrialization and meet the nation's growing steel needs. Situated strategically near the Arabian Sea, it could easily import raw materials and export finished steel goods. Covering around 7,700 hectares (19,000 ac), it ranks among Pakistan's largest industrial facilities and, at its peak, produced a wide range of steel products for construction, manufacturing and infrastructure. It played a crucial role in Pakistan's economic development, providing jobs and contributing to the national economy. However, over the years, it faced issues ranging from mismanagement to financial troubles and outdated technology, leading to production declines and the closure of some units. As of September 2021, Pakistan Steel Mill was grappling with severe financial and operational challenges, with government efforts under way to revive and restructure it, though its future remains uncertain.[82]

In the 1970s the erection of the integrated steel mill posed a challenge: Pakistan was inexperienced in operating such an industrial behemoth. Bhutto requested that the Soviet Union send its experts to Pakistan. Dozens of advisors, led by the Russian scientist Mikhail Koltokof, arrived in the country to supervise the construction of the mega-project, with a number of industrial and consortium companies providing financial backing.[83]

The deteriorating relationship between Pakistan and the United States was primarily due to the latter's opposition to Pakistan's nuclear deterrence programme. Despite this, President Nixon had better relations with Bhutto than did Jimmy Carter, who tightened the embargo on Pakistan and pressured the country through the U.S. ambassador, Brigadier General Henry Byroad. Carter was alarmed by Bhutto's proposed left-wing theories, which further strained relations between the two countries. In his inaugural speech, Carter expressed his commitment to seeking a ban on nuclear weapons, which further isolated Bhutto from the U.S. administration. However, under the technical guidance and diplomatic expertise of Aziz Ahmed, Bhutto managed to purchase sensitive equipment, common metal materials and electronic components, which were marked as 'common items' on their journey to Pakistan to hide their true nature from hostile officials. Pakistan's atomic bomb project was greatly enhanced despite Carter's embargo.

Meanwhile, Bhutto had initially attempted to build friendly ties with Afghanistan in 1972, but these attempts were rebuffed. Two years later, Afghanistan began covert involvement in Pakistan's Northwest Frontier Province, which led to civil disturbances, gruesome violence and a worsening of relations between the two countries. This was due to Afghan president

Zulfiqar Ali Bhutto and U.S. president Richard Nixon, Washington, DC, 1973.

Daud Khan's controversial Pashtunization policies, which Bhutto's government found deeply concerning.[84] Tensions between Pakistan and Afghanistan escalated after the ISI informed Bhutto's government that Daud was providing safe havens and training camps to anti-Pakistan militants. In response, Bhutto launched a covert counteroperation in 1974, led by Major General Naseerullah Babar, who was then director general for western fronts within Military Intelligence. The operation aimed to arm Islamic fundamentalists and instigate attacks in various parts of Afghanistan. With the help of the Pakistan Air Force, the ISI and members of the Afghan intelligence agency, a covert operation was carried out in Kabul that successfully extradited Burhanuddin Rabbani, Jan Mohammad Khan, Gulbadin Hekmatyar and Ahmad Shah Massoud to Peshawar. By the end of 1974, Bhutto had given final authorization for a covert operation to train Afghan mujaheddin to take on Daud Khan's government. This operation was ultimately successful and contributed to the downfall of Khan's regime.

By 1976 Daud had become concerned about his country's overdependence on the Soviet Union and rising insurgency.[85] On 7 June Bhutto paid a three-day state visit to Afghanistan, followed by a five-day visit of Daud to Pakistan in August 1976.[86] On 2 March 1977 an agreement was reached to resume air communications between Afghanistan and Pakistan, which signalled a further improvement in relations between the two countries. As part of the efforts to strengthen ties, Bhutto and Daud made official visits and discussed the Durand Line issue, with Pakistan pushing for its recognition as the permanent border. Many experts considered Bhutto's approach to the border issue as astute, since it increased pressure on Afghanistan and likely played a role in encouraging the Afghan government to move towards accommodation. This was an important development, given that Afghanistan had previously been heavily involved in covert activities inside Pakistan. However, these positive developments were abruptly interrupted as Bhutto was removed from power and Daud Khan was also overthrown in a military coup shortly thereafter.[87]

Bhutto's greatest achievement was the framing of Pakistan's constitution. In 1973, after much negotiation, all political leaders, including those who strongly supported regional autonomy, came to a consensus on the new constitution. This was a rare occasion in the history of Pakistan when all political parties agreed, demonstrating Bhutto's statesmanship. Although the 1973 Constitution was a consensus document that embraced a federal system, it did not prevent Bhutto from disregarding provincial rights in the name of national interest. In fact, he went so far as to dismiss the provincial governments in the NWFP and Baluchistan, which were headed by a coalition of National Awami Party (NAP) and Jamiat Ulema-e-Islam (JUI). This arbitrary action provoked regional forces, who felt that their rights were being ignored, particularly in Baluchistan, where they took up arms to fight against the national army. As a result, the issue of provincial autonomy, which had supposedly been resolved with the consensus constitution, once again became a contentious issue. Khalid Mahmud, shedding light on the impact of Bhutto's high-handedness, notes that regional forces that could have been integrated into mainstream politics were driven to desperation.[88]

Bhutto's provincial origins in Sindh, a smaller province with a history of fissiparous tendencies since the One Unit scheme in the 1950s, did not prevent him from promoting a centralized approach that stifled socio-political plurality in Pakistan. His leadership style showed little regard for building institutions that could limit his own discretion and instead focused on the personalized exercise of power. This authoritarian streak, symptomatic of his feudal upbringing, made him intolerant of dissent and prevented the growth of a more open and inclusive political culture in Pakistan.[89]

In the early hours of 4 April 1979 Zulfiqar Ali Bhutto was executed in Rawalpindi jail after a controversial trial by the military regime of General Zia ul Haq. News of his death was kept from the public until after he was buried in his ancestral village of Garhi Khuda Bakhsh. The sudden end of

Bhutto's life was a tragic outcome of his own flaws as a leader. Despite his intellectual brilliance and oratorical skills, he was consumed by his own ambition and arrogance, which led him to disregard the democratic ideals and popular support that brought him to power. As the Pakistani journalist Raza Rumi observed, 'Bhutto's downfall was not only the result of a military coup, but also of his own hubris and amnesia.'[90]

Lawrence Ziring highlights that the symptoms of decline had set in right at the very outset. After the 1970 elections, cracks appeared in the PPP ranks. Ahmed Raza Kasuri opposed Bhutto's decision to ignore Yahya's 3 March call for the formation of the National Assembly, exposing himself to Bhutto's wrath. As a result, he eventually quit the party to join the opposition. Mukhtar Rana, another independently minded political figure, known for socialist militancy, criticized what he called the 'fascist character' of the PPP. The CMLA quickly had him arrested and sentenced to five years' imprisonment. Meraj Mohammad Khan, a political activist and labour leader who was also a PPP stalwart, publicly accused Bhutto of turning the PPP into a fascist organization and the country into a dictatorship.[91]

The cascade of events that eventually led to Bhutto's downfall began with the political crisis triggered by the March 1977 general election. While the PPP secured a decisive victory, the opposition Pakistan National Alliance (PNA), a coalition of nine parties with diverse political ideologies, raised allegations of election rigging, casting doubt on the legitimacy of the PPP's triumph. In response to the escalating violence and unrest across the nation, Bhutto and his associates initially downplayed these accusations. However, as weeks passed, they came to recognize the necessity of engaging in negotiations with the opposition to address the crisis, marking the inevitability of Bhutto's downfall.

On 4 July 1977 a deal was reached between the Bhutto government and the PNA for fresh elections, but before it could be implemented, General Zia ul Haq, who had been biding his time, made his move. In the early hours of 5 July, the Army took Bhutto and the PNA leaders into custody. In a moment of cruel irony, Zia met Bhutto at the rest house where he was being held and promised him that new elections would be organized. Bhutto believed that Zia was loyal to him and would clear the way for his return to power. However, Zia had other plans.

Bhutto was charged with murder and eventually hanged on 4 April 1979, at the age of 51. As Syed Badrul Islam notes, 'Bhutto's tragedy remains unique: it was the army that raised him to prominence – and it was the army that destroyed him. Along the way, he showed promise but then declined into things Machiavellian.'[92]

The Bhutto era was characterized by populism that raised expectations that could not be fulfilled. However, the failures in delivering on those promises ultimately led to the alienation of supporters who might have otherwise stood by Bhutto. These failures were rooted in Bhutto's personality defects, which prevented him from addressing the need for building strong political institutions, decentralizing power and encouraging pluralism. By failing to do so, Bhutto became increasingly authoritarian and intolerant of dissent, which ultimately led to his downfall.

9

Piety and Praetorianism: General Zia ul Haq's Reign, 1977–88

From the ashes rose a great hypocrite, General Zia ul Haq. He promised to hold elections and reneged on that promise. He set out to establish what he called an Islamic system of government and for eleven long years the country remained enmeshed in the bushes of obscurantism and sectarianism. General Zia surpassed all other politicians in corrupting the democratic process. He exploited the politicians, including some leading ulema, with great skill, humility and piety. His grin concealed his arrogance and his cold-blooded nature. He too met a tragic end but by then he had distorted and mangled every institution, the opportunity of guiding the political process along Islamic lines was betrayed.

Altaf Gauhar[1]

Despite his harsh critics, General Zia has maintained favourable opinion among numerous bureaucrats, including veteran civil servant Roedad Khan. In his book *Dreams Gone Sour*, Khan offers a positive portrayal of Zia. According to Khan, Zia 'had an attentive ear' and would always make his interlocutors feel valued and heard. Zia would often request a brief written note on the topic and people would spend weeks writing such notes, although Zia never actually read them. Additionally, 'Zia was open to hearing opposing views and would never hold a grudge if someone spoke their mind. Overall, meeting with Zia left individuals feeling like they had made a significant contribution to the conversation.'[2]

The seasoned diplomat and former cricket commentator Jamsheed Marker describes General Zia's profile in an interesting way. The heavy, dark moustache and hooded eyelids made a somewhat sinister initial impression, but behind the thick eyeglasses sparkled a pair of bright eyes filled with intelligence and affecting a quiet attractive warmth. Although clad in uniform, his body was totally devoid of swagger, and seemed to suggest an innate modesty.[3]

Roedad Khan observes that Zia was not a garrulous person. Instead, he had a unique approach of bringing together people with divergent views and holding marathon sessions in the cabinet room to discuss complex

Piety and Praetorianism: General Zia ul Haq's Reign, 1977–88

Zia ul Haq (1924–1988).

and contentious issues. Zia enjoyed the 'clash of views, conflicting opinions and discordant notes', and relished the opportunity to hear different perspectives on a matter. By doing so, he was able to foster an environment of constructive debate and dialogue, which ultimately led to more informed and nuanced decision making.[4] Everyone was afforded the opportunity to express their opinion and be heard during cabinet meetings under Zia's leadership. If Zia ever grew tired or felt that he had heard enough, he would simply doze off without disrupting the ongoing discussion. Despite his apparent lack of engagement, he would later demonstrate his attentiveness by recalling details and insights from the meeting. This unique approach allowed for a free exchange of ideas and perspectives.

In the midst of cabinet meetings, a member of the attending staff would often arrive at the appointed time to remind Zia of the midday prayer. Zia would then proceed to the presidency mosque, sometimes accompanied by one or two individuals. Meanwhile, those who did not regularly pray would walk up and down the lawn in plain sight of Zia. Notably, Zia never pressured anyone to join him for prayers, nor did he hold it against those who chose not to participate. This demonstrated his respect for individual beliefs and practices and fostered an environment of mutual respect within the government.[5]

Zia had an uncanny similarity to Stalin and Hitler in his preference for being a night owl, and, like the German dictator, rarely appeared before noon. Zia's sleep schedule was such that he would stay up until the early hours of the morning and wake up for the early morning prayers before going back to sleep again. It was not uncommon for the green telephone (hotline) at the Army house to ring around midnight, with the operator informing the recipient that the president wanted to speak with them. Zia would come on the line, apologize for the late hour and enquire about some minor matter, expressing hope that he had not disturbed their sleep. This demonstrated his dedication to his duties and his willingness to work around the clock to ensure the smooth functioning of the government.[6]

Zia was also known to have a helpful and compassionate nature in personal matters. If an individual approached Zia with a personal problem, he would not hesitate to break or bend the rules if necessary to assist them. Despite his high-ranking position, Zia was able to command respect without inspiring fear or intimidation, and he had a unique ability to win over people's loyalty through his actions and behaviour. This speaks of Zia's character and his commitment to serving the people he led, not just in his official capacity but in his personal interactions.

Contextualizing Zia's Rise

Zia ul Haq was born into a modest Arain household in Jullundur on 12 August 1924, the second child of Muhammad Akbar, a GHQ employee (clerk) in Delhi and Simla. The Arains, known for their hard work, frugality and discipline, were a people favoured by the British and brought in to cultivate new lands in the Punjab around the cities established in the irrigated 'colonies'. As small peasant-proprietors, Zia's family likely benefited from this opportunity to work the land and establish themselves in the region.[7] As urbanization increased and the value of their land rose, many Arain families thrived and put their new-found wealth to good use. However, unlike the traditional feudal landlords of the Punjab – such as the Noons and Tiwanas of Rajput origin, who were associated with activities like afternoon tea parties, partridge shoots and polo – the Arain lacked elegance and polish. They did not indulge in activities such as patronizing dancing girls, listening to poetry during drunken evenings or having multiple marriages, which were common pastimes of the landed gentry that ultimately led to the loss of their lands. As the Pakistani academic Akbar S. Ahmad notes, the Arain instead focused their energies on their hard work and discipline, using their resources to improve their quality of life and secure their place in society.[8] Arain families invested their wealth in education, which quickly paid off. As a result, they became prominent in the legal profession among urban Muslims in the Punjab and many of them leveraged their legal expertise to enter politics.[9]

Despite the modest background of his family, Zia showed remarkable academic abilities during his schooling years. His excellent academic record allowed him to secure admission to the prestigious St Stephen's College in Delhi. In 1943 he obtained a commission in the British Indian Army's 13th Lancers. Although the British had not traditionally considered the Arain community as one of India's 'martial races', the Second World War opened recruitment for all Indian communities, 'martial' or otherwise, and Zia seized the opportunity and entered the officer corps in the Indian army. Despite feeling conservative and out of place among the Anglophile officers, Zia maintained his religious moorings and was punctual and punctilious in his prayers and other Islamic rituals. The only habit he maintained that was unbecoming of a religious person was his smoking.[10]

During the Second World War, Zia served in Burma, Malaya and Java. However, the partition of British India caused his family to uproot and leave their meagre assets behind in their native Jullundur, settling in Peshawar in the Northwest Frontier Province bordering Afghanistan. Zia's personal connection to Islam and Pakistan was revealed in his words at an International Conference on Islam in Islamabad in 1983: 'It is a vision of my mother struggling on, tired, with all her worldly possessions in her hands when she crossed the border into Pakistan. This is what Islam and Pakistan mean to me.'[11] Zia ul Haq held on to his modest beginnings and the values instilled in him by his hardworking community. His family was deeply religious and believed in a type of Islam that stressed the importance of seeking communion with God through the Quran and the teachings of the Prophet Muhammad.

After Pakistan gained independence, Zia was stationed at the Armoured Corps Centre in Nowshera, where he married Shafiqa Jahan in August 1950 and had five children. He underwent training at the U.S. Army Command and General Staff College in Fort Leavenworth, Kansas, from 1962 to 1964. During the Indo-Pakistani War of 1965, he served as a tank commander, but no significant records of his gallantry as a soldier have been reported.

Throughout his career, however, Zia took on several important assignments. After being promoted to brigadier in 1969, he was sent to Jordan from 1967 to 1970 to help train Jordanian soldiers in dealing with Palestinian dissent and lead the training mission during the 'Black September' operations. His resolute and unyielding strategic leadership proved vital to King Hussein's survival in power.[12] Zia's actions in the Black September operations appeared to defy his prescribed duties as an officer seconded from the Pakistan Army to Jordan. King Hussein's advocacy for Zia served as a reciprocal gesture, signifying to Prime Minister Bhutto that Zia possessed the requisite attributes required for crucial tasks.

Pakistani historians now contend that the appointment of General Zia to the coveted rank of Army chief was not merely an isolated event, but rather a strategic choice influenced by several key actors, including the United States and ISI. Curiously, among these stakeholders, it was the Chinese embassy that voiced reservations. The American support for General Zia can be traced back to his tenure in Jordan, where he served as a brigadier for a substantial period. During this time, Zia demonstrated his commitment and effectiveness, particularly in dealing with Palestinian opposition to King Hussein. This experience made him a favoured candidate in the eyes of U.S. decision makers. Conversely, Zia's previous association with the CIA also played a pivotal role in swaying the ISI to endorse his appointment.

Had Zia been considered for his military honours based purely on merit, it is said he would be deserving of nothing beyond the rank of brigadier.[13] However, in the aftermath of the Attock conspiracy, orchestrated by a handful of military officers in 1973, General Zia drew nearer to Bhutto. This conspiracy stemmed from the discontent of younger officers within the Army and Air Force, who held Bhutto and the senior generals responsible for the loss of East Pakistan and the defeat suffered at the hands of India. The ISI had received timely intelligence regarding this covert operation and meticulously conducted undercover surveillance on the group for several months, patiently awaiting the opportune moment to intervene. Zia, as major general, presided over the ensuing court-martial, seizing this occasion as an avenue to apprise Bhutto of the unfolding proceedings and extend his loyal services to the leader.

Ultimately, the conspirators were handed life sentences. It is worth noting that Bhutto, alongside certain senior generals, advocated for the imposition of the death penalty; however, they failed to garner a majority vote within the court in favour of such a severe sentence.[14]

On 1 April 1976 Bhutto appointed Zia ul Haq as the chief of Army staff, passing over seven other officers for the position.[15] Interestingly, the very traits that had convinced Bhutto of Zia's eligibility for the position – his piety, patriotism and professionalism – transformed him, in the circumstances of the 1977 PNA Nizam-e-Mustafa agitation, from an apolitical soldier into a successful coup maker.[16]

Popular Unrest and the Coup of 1977

Prime Minister Bhutto began facing considerable criticism and increasing unpopularity as his term progressed. Initially he targeted a leader of the opposition, Abdul Wali Khan (1917–2006), and his party, NAP.[17] Despite the ideological similarities between Bhutto's party and NAP, tensions both inside and outside the National Assembly escalated, especially after the federal government moved to remove the NAP provincial government in Baluchistan on the grounds of alleged secessionist activities. Eventually, this clash culminated in the banning of the party and the arrest of much of its leadership, following the death of a close ally of Bhutto's,

Hayat Muhammad Khan Sherpao, in a bomb blast in Peshawar. The PPP faced turmoil and inner dissensions during this period. The murder of Ahmed Raza Kasuri's father sparked public outrage and intra-party hostility as Bhutto was accused of orchestrating the crime. Powerful PPP leaders, including Malik Ghulam Mustafa Khar (from the Southern Punjab), openly condemned Bhutto and called for protests. Meanwhile, the political crisis in NWFP and Baluchistan escalated as civil liberties remained suspended and an estimated 100,000 troops deployed there were accused of human rights violations and killing numerous civilians. In response, nine opposition political parties formed the PNA on 8 January 1977.[18] Fresh elections were called by Bhutto, set to take place on 7 March 1977. Despite internal divisions, the PNA participated in the elections with enthusiasm. However, the PNA was soundly defeated, securing only 36 seats compared to the PPP's 155. After voicing allegations of election rigging, the PNA refused to accept the results, leading to a period of political turmoil.[19] Initially, the PNA claimed that the election was rigged in fourteen seats. However, later, they increased the number to forty seats in the National Assembly where they suspected election rigging. As a result, they decided to boycott the provincial elections. Despite this, there was a high voter turnout in the national elections. But the provincial elections were held amid low voter turnout and an opposition boycott. Consequently, the PNA declared the newly elected Bhutto government as illegitimate.[20] The political situation in Pakistan deteriorated rapidly as PNA leaders demanded that the Army overthrow the Bhutto regime. This led to widespread unrest and chaos. On 5 July 1977 General Zia ul Haq staged a coup known as a result of Operation Fair Play (which Bhutto labelled Operation Foul Play). Bhutto and his cabinet members were arrested, and praetorianism resurfaced, lasting for over a decade. However, towards the end of this period, steps were taken to partially civilianize the government. The 1985 party-less elections and the selection of Muhammad Khan Junejo as the prime minister were the steps in that direction.

Despite the dismissal of the Bhutto government, President Fazal Ilahi Chaudhry was persuaded to continue in office as a figurehead.[21] After completing his term, Chaudhry declined General Zia's insistence on his accepting an extension as president. As a result, General Zia assumed the office of president of Pakistan on 16 September 1978, cementing his position as the undisputed ruler of the country. Over the next six years, Zia issued several decrees amending the Constitution of 1973 and enhancing his power. The most significant was the Revival of Constitution of 1973 Order, which granted Zia the power to dissolve the National Assembly almost at will. As a result, he became the most powerful military dictator in the country's history. Despite ruling Pakistan for slightly more than eleven years, General Zia's regime came to a mysterious end when he died in a plane crash on 17 August 1988.

General Zia had ambitious plans to strengthen Pakistan's military with sophisticated American weaponry, including advanced F-16 fighter planes, AWACS reconnaissance aircraft and field equipment to outmatch India's largely Soviet-supplied arsenal. On 17 August 1988, General Zia and five of his top generals went to a desert test site to witness a demonstration of the Abrams M-1/A–1 battle tank, which the United States was pushing Pakistan to buy. Although his armoured battle experts were not keen on the tank, Zia was said to be more interested in the AWACS and wanted to observe the trials. The official party left their C-130 Hercules aircraft on the Bahawalpur airstrip and flew to the test site by helicopter. Following the morning tests, they returned to Bahawalpur for lunch before departing for Islamabad. Tragically, within minutes of take-off, the plane suddenly crashed into a dusty wasteland, killing all 34 people on board, including General Zia.[22]

There are many theories surrounding the mysterious crash that killed General Zia and his top generals, but no conclusive evidence has ever been presented to confirm any one of them. One commonly held belief within Pakistan is that the crash was a political assassination orchestrated by either the CIA or the KGB, though there is no concrete proof to support this claim. Despite Congress holding a few hearings, the FBI was kept away from the case for a year, and no official report has ever been made public. Even today, more than thirty years later, a file in the National Archives containing approximately 250 pages of documents related to the crash remains classified as secret.[23]

One conspiratorial belief is that Zulfiqar Ali Bhutto's son Murtaza Bhutto was involved in the crash. Murtaza and his younger brother Shahnawaz Bhutto founded an organization, Al Zulfiqar, to oppose Zia's military regime, advocate for the release of their father, preserve his political legacy, raise awareness about human rights abuses and advocate for democratic reforms in Pakistan. Ijaz ul Haq, Zia's son, alleged that Murtaza killed the general as part of his plot to instigate all of this: 'Ijaz ul Haq, son of Zia ul Haq, accused Mir Murtaza Bhutto of being involved in the plane crash, stating that he was "101 per cent sure" of his involvement, a year after the incident.'[24] But still, many political and higher military figures openly say that this crash was actually an assassination carried out by the CIA to kill Zia and their own ambassador, Arnold Raphael, so that the American government could conceal truths about their strategic involvements in the Soviet–Afghan war.

The Postponement of Elections and a Call for Accountability

General Zia ul Haq assumed power in Pakistan through a military coup in July 1977. Upon taking power, he promised to hold National Assembly and provincial assembly elections within ninety days and to transfer power to elected representatives of the people. He declared that his sole aim was to organize free and fair elections and that he would not deviate from the schedule. However, the promised elections did not take place within ninety days. Instead, General Zia announced a new election schedule that delayed the polls until 1979. Those polls were not at national but merely at the local level. During this period, he consolidated his power and implemented his own agenda. He promulgated several controversial laws, including the Hudood Ordinance and the Blasphemy Law, which were criticized for being regressive and discriminatory. When elections were eventually held in 1979, they were widely considered to be rigged in favour of Zia's hand-picked candidates. The elections were marred by irregularities, including allegations of ballot stuffing and intimidation of voters.

Zia's military regime was marked by authoritarianism, human rights abuses and a heavy-handed approach to political dissent. Despite his promise to hold free and fair elections and transfer power to elected representatives of the people, Zia's regime was characterized by a lack of democratic accountability and transparency.[25] In the face of such criticism, he claimed that the Constitution of Pakistan had not been abrogated but suspended under his regime.

However, in October 1977, Zia postponed the electoral plan and launched an accountability drive that mainly targeted members of the PPP. This led to accusations of political bias and a lack of impartiality in the accountability process. General Zia's reputation for constantly going back on his words earned him the nickname CMLA, 'Cancel My Last Announcement'. He later claimed that his aim was not simply to hold elections but to enforce Islam in the country, and that the date of the elections was not sacrosanct according to the Quran.

He also believed that the armed forces, not the politicians, were better suited as the people to keep Pakistan united, further undermining the prospects of a democratic transition under his regime.[26] After assuming power in a military coup, he claimed that he had rescinded his promise to hold elections within ninety days due to strong public demand for the scrutiny of political leaders who had engaged in malpractice in the past. This led to the adoption of a 'retribution first, elections later' policy that disadvantaged politicians once again.

To enforce this policy, a disqualification tribunal was formed, consisting of a High Court judge and a military officer not below the rank of brigadier. This tribunal charged 180 former members of parliament with malpractice and disqualified them from participating in politics for seven years. A White Paper was also issued, accusing the deposed Bhutto government of several wrongdoings. In response, Nusrat Bhutto, the wife of the deposed prime minister, filed a lawsuit challenging the validity of the July 1977 military coup. However, the Supreme Court of Pakistan ruled in favour of General Zia's regime, invoking the Doctrine of Necessity. The court justified the coup on the grounds of the unstable political situation at the time. This ruling not only validated the overthrow of the Bhutto regime but strengthened General Zia's hold on the government.

On 4 April 1979 General Zia ordered the execution of former prime minister Zulfiqar Ali Bhutto, who had been convicted on charges of conspiracy to murder of the dissident PPP politician Muhammad Ahmed Khan Kasuri (1903–1974). Bhutto was 'emaciated but unbowed' in his final moments, and his execution was widely condemned by the international community. This event marked a turning point in General Zia's regime and further highlighted the authoritarian nature of his rule.[27] Bhutto was hanged in Rawalpindi jail after the Supreme Court upheld the death sentence as passed by the Lahore High Court.[28] Despite numerous appeals from foreign leaders for clemency, General Zia refused to commute Bhutto's death sentence, dismissing the appeals as 'trade union activity' and upholding the verdict.

The execution of an elected prime minister by a military ruler was viewed by many as a trial and execution that had been politically motivated, with the judiciary and the military collaborating to eliminate a political rival. The hanging of Bhutto further tarnished General Zia's already controversial regime, with many criticizing his authoritarian methods and disregard for democratic principles. The legacy of Bhutto's execution and the events leading up to it continued to shape Pakistan's political landscape for decades to come.[29]

General Zia ul Haq's Military Rule and Its Dominance

General Zia consolidated his hold on power by establishing a Military Council, which he chaired, with the Joint Chiefs of Staff Committee and the services chiefs as its members. The council made the military the highest decision-making body in the country, and its decisions were implemented by a civilian bureaucracy that was closely aligned with the military. In addition to the military leadership, General Zia appointed several senior Army officers to key positions, enabling them to have significant input in policy making. The first cabinet, sworn in in 1978, was dominated by the military–bureaucratic nexus, which continued to shape decision making throughout Zia's tenure. Under Zia's rule, the military wielded enormous power and influence, and civilian institutions were subordinated to the military's interests. This had a lasting impact on Pakistan's political and social development, with the military remaining a significant force in the country's politics even after the restoration of democracy.

The entire country was divided into five zones, each zone being headed by a martial-law administrator.[30] To enforce its rule, the regime issued strict martial-law regulations, and to deal with perceived threats to its power, the regime established martial-law courts and summary military courts.

The decisions of these courts could not be appealed in any civilian court, giving the military unchecked power over the judicial system. General Zia also sought to increase the military's role in Pakistani politics, arguing that the armed forces were responsible for safeguarding not only the country's territorial integrity but its ideological foundations.[31] General Zia elaborated on his earlier statement, stating that the ideology and Islamic character of Pakistan were just as important as its geographical frontiers and territorial identity, and therefore needed to be preserved by the armed forces. Other military officers, such as General Rahim-ud Din Khan and General Khalid Mahmood Arif, expressed similar views, which implied that the military could intervene in domestic politics under the pretext of protecting Islam and Pakistan's ideology. This approach effectively granted the military commander the power to intervene in political affairs whenever he deemed it necessary to uphold these values.[32] After consolidating his power, General Zia sought to give a constitutional justification for military involvement in decision making on matters of national interest. He proposed a provision that would allow military commanders to step in during national emergencies, but these proposals were met with strong opposition from the political class. To legitimize the military's role in governance, Zia established the National Security Council (NSC). The council was empowered to make recommendations on issues such as 'the declaration of emergency under Article 232 of the Constitution, the security of Pakistan, and other matters of national importance referred to it by the President in consultation with the Prime Minister.'[33] The NSC consisted of eleven members, including the president, prime minister, chairman of the Senate, chairman of the Joint Chiefs of Staff Committee, chiefs of staff of the Army, Navy and Air Force, and the chief ministers of the four provinces. Its primary aim was to give the military commanders an unbridled role in the political and constitutional set-up, as well as to reinforce the powers of the president. However, the NSC faced strong opposition from political and civilian circles and eventually could not sustain itself.

Many retired Army officers have secured prestigious civilian positions in the federal or provincial governments or autonomous corporations. Some have even become chairmen of coveted organizations such as the Water and Power Development Authority (WAPDA), including General Fazle Raziq and General Safdar Butt. Additionally, many have been nominated to serve in the central superior services, including positions in district management, the Foreign Service of Pakistan or the police service. After retiring from their active service, numerous senior Army officers have even been appointed as ambassadors. Between 1980 and 1985, 96 officers were inducted into the selected cadres of central superior services on a permanent basis, and another 115 were re-employed on a contractual basis.[34] Under General Zia's regime, the military emerged as the most influential social institution in Pakistan's society and state. Its budget became the primary expenditure item in the national budget. Active and retired military officers were frequently appointed to high-level positions within the civil administration, and retired military personnel were also given preference in roughly 33 per cent of lower-ranked jobs within public agencies. Furthermore, the military was given access to prime urban lands, which were distributed among its officers.[35]

The Zia regime was designated as the first authentic military regime in Pakistan, since it relied entirely on the military and bestowed numerous favours upon its personnel to compensate for the lack of any genuine support base within the broader society.[36] Prior to 23 March 1985, when Muhammad Khan Junejo was sworn in as prime minister, all provincial governors were Army generals. Additionally, a significant number of Army and Air Force officers, as well as subaltern staff, were posted overseas, primarily in countries such as Saudi Arabia, Jordan, Libya, Oman and the UAE. Organizations such as the Fauji Foundation, the Shaheen Foundation and the Bahria Foundation, which represent retired military personnel, experienced substantial growth both as employers and as an agency to safeguard the interests of ex-servicemen.[37]

The bureaucracy, for the most part, welcomed the *coup d'état* in 1977. However, instead of relying solely on the bureaucracy, Zia chose to induct military personnel into the Civil Service. In February 1978 he established a civil services commission under the leadership of Justice Anwarul Haq to suggest recommendations for improving the service structure of bureaucrats. Later on, the policies formulated based on the commission's recommendations aimed at preserving the status quo, which favoured the District Management Group the most. The number of state functionaries grew significantly due to a relatively lenient approach to recruitment for new jobs during the martial-law regime, turning ministries and departments into virtual employment agencies. The number of civil servants almost doubled between 1977 and 1987, which had significant consequences for expenditure and production patterns.[38] Based on Waseem's observations, we can conclude that the administrative and economic policies of the Zia regime were focused on maintaining the status quo, which was reflective of an uninterrupted rule of the bureaucratic core of the state. Furthermore, a larger proportion of higher positions went to the military during Zia's regime than under Ayub or Yahya.[39]

Movement for the Restoration of Democracy

Zia and his supporters pursued an agenda of self-perpetuation, which involved eliminating the biggest perceived threat, Bhutto. The process of accountability was terminated on 4 April 1979, once Bhutto was out of the way. Zia then began openly aligning himself with right-wing parties, with Jamaat-e-Islami being the primary beneficiary of his so-called policy of Islamization. The state propaganda apparatus developed systematic approaches to 'depoliticize' Pakistani society. In February 1981 political parties with left-of-centre leanings, as well as certain groups of lawyers and students, launched a movement against Zia's military regime. Eleven parties came together to form the Movement for the Restoration of Democracy (MRD).[40] The first joint statement released by MRD leaders made it clear that they were demanding the withdrawal of martial law and the holding of free, fair and impartial elections to the National Assembly and the provincial assemblies under the 1973 Constitution, with the goal of transferring power to elected representatives.[41]

The MRD began to gain momentum as a serious threat to Zia and his regime in early 1981. However, their progress was hindered when, in March of the same year, a Pakistan International Airlines plane was hijacked by a dubious group known as Al-Zulfiqar. Despite the PPP's efforts to distance itself from the hijacking incident, the fact that Mir Murtaza Bhutto, the eldest son of Z. A. Bhutto, was supposedly involved in the operation had a negative impact on the movement.[42] Although the MRD regained momentum in August 1983, its impact was limited to Sindh; the Punjab, Baluchistan and the NWFD largely remained indifferent to the movement's call.[43] Smouldering discontent and intense alienation permeated the interior of Sindh, giving rise to an unabated spate of violence that 'manifested strong ethnic and regional sentiments'.[44]

Although the military regime refrained from a strategy of total suppression of dissent, it was nonetheless intolerant of harsh criticism beyond certain limits, as strict censorship was imposed to prevent the publication of views of dissenting politicians.[45] The imposition of heavy financial and legal penalties prevented private printers from publishing dissenting views in the form of booklets or pamphlets.[46] Politicians were not allowed to travel to other cities and particularly to other provinces. Hence, they could not maintain contact with the general masses.

In Baluchistan, Zia inherited a challenging situation of armed secessionist uprisings, tribal unrest and feudal clashes. However, he managed to restore some order by granting a general amnesty to those who laid down their arms and withdrew troops from the province, which ended much of the civil disobedience. After the failed military operation by Bhutto, Baluchistan had been in a state of turmoil, but Zia's decision to pursue a policy of appeasement brought normalcy to the province.[47]

Political activists were often prevented from holding meetings and many leaders and activists were put under house arrest, severely limiting the movement's effectiveness. Two additional factors contributed to the lack of support for the MRD. First, the economic situation in Pakistan improved due to development in the 1980s and remittances from expatriate Pakistanis working in the Gulf states. This prosperity dissuaded people from supporting the struggle for democracy led by politicians.

The Soviet invasion of Afghanistan and the subsequent influx of Afghan refugees provided the military regime with another pretext to maintain its grip on power. The government discouraged any attempt to launch political agitation, citing concerns that it could undermine the nation's ability to deal effectively with the political and strategic fallout of the Soviet presence in Afghanistan.[48] The Zia regime effectively mobilized Deobandi ulema, whose members are known for their strict adherence to traditional Islamic jurisprudence and emphasis on religious education in Deobandi seminaries (madrasas). Zia also lent support to religious parties of Deobandi orientation as a counterbalance to the leftist groups and parties striving for a change in government.

Fighting a War by Proxy in Afghanistan and Its Economic Implications

On 25 December 1979 the Soviet Union invaded Afghanistan. General Zia was asked by several cabinet members to refrain from interfering in the war, due to the vastly superior military power of the USSR. Zia, however, was ideologically opposed to the idea of communism taking over a neighbouring country and made no secret of his intentions of monetarily and militarily aiding the Afghan resistance (the Mujahideen). Pakistan's ISI and Special Service Group now became actively involved in the conflict, and in cooperation with the CIA and U.S. Army Special Forces supported the armed struggle against the Soviets.

President Zia's international standing greatly rose after his declaration to fight the Soviet invaders in Afghanistan, as he went from being portrayed by Western media as just another military dictator to a champion of the free world. Indeed, Pakistan–USA relations took a much more positive turn. U.S. president Jimmy Carter and his secretary of state, Cyrus Vance, had cut off U.S. aid to Pakistan on the grounds that Pakistan had not made sufficient progress on the nuclear issue. Then, on 25 December 1979, with the Soviets invading Afghanistan, Carter offered Pakistan $325 million in aid over three years. Zia rejected this as 'peanuts' while speaking to the journalists on 18 January 1980, 'without realizing the import of that snub on a U.S. President who had once been a peanut farmer in Georgia'.[49] In 1980 Carter also signed the funding that allowed less than $50 million a year to go to the Mujahideen.[50]

President Reagan came into office with a strong anti-communist stance and saw the Soviet Union as a major threat to U.S. interests. In order to counter Soviet influence in Afghanistan, Reagan and his administration decided to increase funding to the Afghan resistance and to Pakistan. Congressman Charles Wilson and CIA Afghan desk chief Gust Avrakotos played a key role in this effort by clandestinely increasing funding to the Mujahideen. The United States provided a significant amount of aid to the Afghan resistance, eventually reaching $1 billion.

The Soviet Union, faced with a growing insurgency in Afghanistan, decided to send in troops to prop up the communist government in Kabul. This move drew the United States further into the conflict, as they now saw an opportunity to fight a war by proxy against the Soviet Union. Pakistan played a key role in this conflict, serving as a conduit for U.S. aid to the Afghan resistance. Zia saw an opportunity to increase his country's influence in the region and cooperated with the United States in the effort to arm and train the Mujahideen.

The Soviet–Afghan War lasted from 1979 to 1989 and had a profound impact on the region and on international politics. It was a costly conflict for both the Soviet Union and the United States and, moreover, led to the rise of militant groups like the Taliban and al-Qaeda.[51]

President Ronald Reagan was completely opposed to the Soviet Union and its communist satellites, dubbing it 'the Evil Empire' during a speech at the British House of Commons in 1982.[52] He repeated this on 8 March 1983 while addressing the National Association of Evangelicals in Florida for the second time in his presidency. Reagan's use of the phrase was controversial, with some critics arguing that it was needlessly confrontational and could damage U.S.–Soviet relations. However, Reagan's remarks were applauded by many conservatives and helped to galvanize opposition to the Soviet Union. The phrase became emblematic of Reagan's foreign policy, which sought to counter Soviet influence around the world.

Along with increasing financial aid to Pakistan, the Reagan Administration also, in 1981, sent the first of forty F-16 jet fighters to Zia's military, which were used to help the Pakistani Air Force carry out bombing raids on Afghan targets. However, the Soviet Union maintained control of the skies over Afghanistan, making it difficult for the Mujahideen to mount effective attacks.

In 1986 a significant shift occurred in the dynamics of the conflict when the United States supplied the Mujahideen with advanced weaponry in the form of Stinger missiles. These sophisticated weapons possessed the capability to successfully intercept and destroy Soviet aircraft, marking a pivotal turning point in the war. This infusion of advanced anti-aircraft weaponry finally granted the Mujahideen control of the skies, thereby enabling them to execute more potent and strategically effective offensives against Soviet forces on the ground.

As a result, the Soviet Union declared a policy of national reconciliation to find a way out of the conflict. In January 1987, the Soviets announced that a withdrawal was no longer contingent on the make-up of the Afghan government remaining behind. During this time, Pakistan played a crucial role in supporting the Mujahideen, with the covert backing of the largest operation ever mounted by the CIA and financial support from Saudi Arabia. This aid helped to sustain the Afghan resistance and contributed to the eventual withdrawal of Soviet troops from Afghanistan in 1988. It also had significant geopolitical implications, as the Soviet defeat in Afghanistan was seen as a major blow to Soviet prestige and contributed to the eventual collapse of the Soviet Union.

The Soviet invasion of Afghanistan had a profound impact on the region, leading to an extensive stream of refugees pouring into Pakistan, totalling more than 3 million. The majority of these refugees settled in northwestern parts of Pakistan, creating tension with the local population over resources such as agricultural land, pastures and water.

As wealthy Afghan immigrants, mostly Pashtuns, arrived in Pakistan, they were able to establish businesses with the help of their Pakistani counterparts, monopolizing the sector of road transportation and acquiring assets such as cattle, houses and plots of land. In the frontier areas, where the bulk of refugee camps were built, the influx of refugees caused prices of food and other essential items to rise, leading to unemployment among the local population. The refugee crisis in Pakistan serves as a reminder of the devastating impact of war on civilian populations, and the rise of extremist groups underscores the importance of addressing the root causes of conflict and instability.

Overall, the Soviet invasion of Afghanistan had far-reaching consequences for the region, and the effects of the conflict are still felt today, one of the most significant being the emergence of drug problems in Pakistan. As the main route for the smuggling of Afghan heroin to destinations such as India, Europe, Africa and the United States, Pakistan became a hub for drug trafficking. Although opium production in Afghanistan supplemented the funds of Afghan insurgents, it also contributed to drug abuse and addiction in Pakistan. The Pashtun tribal zone became a centre for heroin production, with dozens of laboratories controlled by local tribal chiefs and government officials. The lucrative illegal business generated billions of dollars in illicit money but it also caused social frictions and political instability.

According to Ayesha Jalal, in the 1980s heroin became Pakistan's largest export. Allegations that the Army's national logistics cell (NLC) was involved in transporting narcotics from the tribal areas to Karachi added to the problem. By 1983 conservative estimates projected that there were 150,000 heroin addicts in Pakistan, a number that skyrocketed to 650,000 out of 1.9 million drug users by 1987, according to the Narcotics Control Board. Unofficial figures were appreciably higher. Estimates in 1988 put the number of heroin addicts at 1.5 million, and this in a country where a decade earlier there had been none. The drug problem in Pakistan had devastating consequences for public health, social harmony and political stability.[53]

Zia's rule brought about an alarming increase in drug addiction, which was one of the unfortunate legacies of his regime. Zia's values were revealed when he once asked if it was feasible to produce heroin solely for export.[54]

Drug money was laundered through the Bank of Commerce and Credit International (BCCI), which helped to prop up the national economy.[55]

Seeking Legitimacy: PCO and Majlis-i-Shoora

'Provisional constitutional order' (PCO) is a term commonly associated with military dictators, and is especially pertinent to Pakistan during the late 1970s and the 1980s. PCOs are essentially legal instruments used by military rulers to legitimize their control over the government, suspend or amend existing constitutions and consolidate their authority. Once in power, to provide a semblance of legality to his rule, General Zia issued a PCO in March 1981 (a tactic not unique to him, as previous military rulers in Pakistan had also used similar instruments). The PCO granted Zia sweeping powers, allowing him to make laws, amend the Constitution – in Zia's case in alignment with his ideology, introducing changes that Islamized the legal system and governance – and control all aspects of the government. Zia also manipulated the judiciary by appointing compliant judges to minimize legal challenges to his regime. Under the guise of the PCO and martial law, he suppressed political opposition, censored the media and restricted civil liberties, often harshly punishing dissent. The PCO remained in place throughout Zia's tenure; it was only after the general's demise that Pakistan began the process of returning to civilian rule and reinstating the Constitution.[56]

The PCO drafted in March 1981 set up a Federal Advisory Council, or Majlis-i-Shoora, 'to perform functions that were to be assigned to it by the President'.[57] In an effort to create a political support system for himself and his allies, Zia introduced a strategy to groom potential candidates for future elections. In addition to local officials who were already loyal to Zia, the provincial governors were tasked with recommending individuals for the council. These recommendations were based on reports from deputy commissioners and intelligence agencies, with a focus on the candidates' family backgrounds. As a result, many members of prominent feudal families were given representation in the council. The nominees to the council were expected to serve as the political arm of the Zia government, and the president could nominate up to 350 members to the Majlis. The PCO was originally intended to serve as an interim arrangement while consultations were completed regarding the affairs of the state and the restoration of democracy and representative institutions. However, it became a permanent fixture of Zia's rule, and provided a platform for Zia and his cronies to consolidate their political power – many of its members would go on to hold positions of authority in subsequent governments.

In 1982 the Majlis met for the first time, with Khawaja Muhammad Safdar from Sialkot, a veteran Muslim League worker, serving as its chairman. The council lacked the political credibility that only comes through democratic elections. As an advisory body, it had no power to make binding decisions or enforce its recommendations. Its creation was merely a gimmick by the regime, serving no real purpose or utility. It held mock discussions and was an insult to the intelligence of the Pakistani people, reminding them of their helplessness in the face of an unashamed dictator who sought to usurp the power of the state. The Majlis-i-Shoora was window dressing, backed by brute force and designed to fool the people and the world. When general elections were eventually held in February 1985, the sham council finally met its end, and everyone breathed a sigh of relief.[58]

The Referendum of 1984, the Elections of 1985 and the Eighth Amendment

In July 1983 Zia established a commission consisting of sixteen members, with Zafar Ahmad Ansari as its head, to conduct a comprehensive examination of the government systems suitable for the country, considering the conditions of the nation and the interests of the Muslim *millat* (an expression used to depict the entire Muslim world as a unified entity based on the shared religion of Islam). On 4 August 1983 the Ansari commission submitted its report, which contained certain recommendations. First was the adoption of a presidential system of government, where the head of state, called Amir-e-Mumlikat, would also be the head of government and would be elected by the central and provincial Majlis-i-Shoora. Second, elections to the Majlis-i-Shoora would be held on a non-party basis, and the candidates would be sponsored by at least 2,000 voters of a constituency. All political parties would be dissolved. Third, additional qualifications were proposed for women candidates, including that they should not be less than fifty years of age and they should produce written permission from their living husband to take part in the elections, in addition to specific qualifications like good character and knowledge of Islam.

Zia was determined to establish an Islamic system in Pakistan, as recommended by the Ansari commission. However, his cabinet colleagues, including Finance Minister Ghulam Ishaq Khan and Interior Minister Mahmoud Haroon, and external advisors advised against changing the parliamentary character of the 1973 Constitution, warning of the consequences that would ensue. Reports of agitation in Sindh under the banner of the 'Sindhu-desh movement' further convinced Zia to moderate his ambitions. In August 1983 he addressed the Majlis-i-Shoora and announced that elections to the National Assembly and provincial assemblies would be held in March 1985. He planned to announce this on 14 August but advanced his speech by two days to pre-empt an agitational campaign by the MRD. The 1973 Constitution would be restored with some amendments to correct the balance of powers between the president and the prime minister. The discussions leading up to this decision were intense, with Zia consulting his team of advisors to reach a final resolution.

After announcing the date of the general elections, Zia remained vague about the role of political parties and the process for electing the president. However, two days later, in his national address on 14 August, he clarified that the president would be elected by the two Houses of Parliament, as outlined in the 1973 Constitution. He also stated that there would be no need for a referendum on the constitutional amendments, as the Supreme Court had authorized him to make amendments as needed.

Referendum and General Elections: February 1985

In the autumn of 1984, Zia announced his intention to continue as president even after the national elections. To provide himself with the appearance of a popular mandate and legitimacy before the elections, a referendum was hastily arranged in December. The referendum proposition made it difficult for voters to oppose Zia without appearing to vote against Islam. The 'Yes' column was printed in green, the colour associated with Islam, while the 'No' column was printed in white. The referendum asked voters to endorse the process initiated by General Zia, the president of Pakistan, to bring the laws of Pakistan into conformity with the injunctions of Islam as laid down in the Holy Quran and the Sunnah of the Holy Prophet (peace be upon Him) for the preservation of the ideology of Pakistan, and for the continuation and consolidation of that process for the smooth and orderly transfer of power to the elected representatives of the people.[59]

Zia took steps to stifle the MRD's call for a boycott by making such appeals a criminal offence. As a result, the polling stations on 19 December were deserted, suggesting a much lower turnout than the official figure of 62.15 per cent, with an overwhelming 97.71 per cent of voters casting their ballots in favour of Zia ul haq to continue as the president.[60] While many right-wing enthusiasts criticize the alleged rigging and indiscretions of the Bhutto regime in the 1977 elections, they conveniently overlook the egregious exercise carried out in the name of a referendum by Zia in 1984. This referendum was widely regarded as the fraud of the century, with the state machinery being used in complete disregard of rules and regulations. Omar Noman strongly criticizes this referendum, which was marred by allegations of widespread irregularities and technical violations of the laws and ethical standards required for holding elections or referendums in any democratic society.[61]

Justice S. A. Nusrat (1924–2001), chief election commissioner from 1 March 1982 to 30 April 1989, had the longest tenure in the entire history of Pakistan. He was the person in charge of conducting the referendum that not only put Zia into an unassailable position of power but legitimized his position as ruler. Justice Nusrat, like most of his predecessors, became accomplice to the malpractices of the Zia administration. Not a single note of discord by the chief election commissioner was ever recorded. Thus the legacy continued uninterrupted. There was no dissenting voice from any member of the judiciary, just resignation to it, enabling the rot to spread, trivializing the whole exercise of elections. When the elections were held in 1985, Justice S. Usman Ali Shah, Justice Muhammad Rafiq Tarar, Justice Abdul Qadeer Chaudhry and Justice Syed Ally Madad Shah were appointed as members of the election commission.[62] These people ensured the persistence of the status quo that continues to be the hallmark of the Election Commission of Pakistan (ECP) to this day.

Following his controversial referendum, Zia called for elections to the National Assembly on 25 February 1985, as well as elections to the provincial assemblies on 28 February of that year. However, the opposition parties, or MRD, boycotted the elections due to their demands for party-based elections and the complete restoration of the 1973 Constitution not being met. These elections were known as the 'deaf and dumb elections' by the opposition, since public meetings and processions were prohibited. To further silence the opposition, Zia detained most of their leaders during the election period and insisted that political parties should not take part in the elections.

Additionally, Zia amended the 1973 Constitution through an ordinance to increase the total number of seats in the National Assembly from 218 to 237. This resulted in an increase of general seats for Muslim candidates from 200 to 207, as well as an increase of reserved seats for Baluchistan and Sindh by four and three, respectively. The number of reserved seats for women was also doubled, from ten to twenty. This move was met with criticism from opposition parties and some experts who viewed it as a ploy to manipulate election results in favour of Zia's government.

Distribution of seats in the National Assembly[63]

Province/Area	Muslim	Women	Christian	Hindu	Buddhist
Islamabad	1	-	-	-	-
FATA	8	-	4	-	-
Punjab	115	12	-	4	-
Sindh	46	4	-	-	-
NWFP	26	2	-	-	-
Baluchistan	11	2	-	-	-
Total	207	20	4	4	-

Provincial assemblies

Province	Muslim	Women	Minorities	Total
Baluchistan	40	2	3	45
NWFP	80	4	3	87
Punjab	240	12	8	260
Sindh	100	5	9	114
Total	460	23	23	506

Members of various political parties taking part in the 1985 elections

Parties	NWFP	Punjab	Sindh	Baluchistan	Total
PPP	10	31	32	6	70
PML	13	55	22	66	156
JI	7	34	18	2	61
TI	1	12	0	1	14
JUP	1	8	4	0	13
JUI	4	2	2	0	8
Progressive PP	0	4	1	0	5
MKP	1	0	0	0	1
NAP	0	2	0	0	2
PDP	0	1	0	0	1
NDP	1	0	0	1	1
Inqilabi Mahaz	0	1	0	0	1
PML (ZS)	0	1	2	0	3
Himayat-e-Zia	0	2	0	0	2
TKN	0	1	2	0	3
Masawat Party	0	1	0	2	3
Pakhtoon Itehad	0	0	1	2	3
Sawad-e-Azam	0	0	3	0	3
NAP (PK)	0	0	0	1	1
ICP	0	0	3	0	3

Voters in each province

Province	Population	N.A. seats	Voters
Punjab	47,292,441	115	21,125,289
Sindh	19,028,666	46	7,652,825
NWFP	11,061,328	26	4,173,930
Baluchistan	4,332,376	11	1,409,143
Islamabad	340,286	1	149,176
FATA	2,198,547	8	30,583

Separate Electorate for Minorities

The concept of separate electorates in Pakistan refers to a system of electoral representation that was introduced in the country during its early years following independence in 1947. This system was designed to address the political concerns of various religious and ethnic minorities, particularly non-Muslim communities, by allowing them to vote for their own representatives in separate constituencies rather than competing directly with the Muslim majority. Separate electorates were implemented as part of the Government of India Act 1935, which Pakistan inherited upon its formation. This electoral arrangement, despite its purpose, faced criticism for potentially perpetuating divisions among different communities. Over time, Pakistan has undergone significant changes in its electoral systems, with reforms aimed at striking a balance between representation of minorities and fostering a more inclusive, unified political landscape.

In 1979 an amendment to the Representation of Peoples Act 1976 introduced separate electorates, as mentioned in Articles 51 and 106, amended by RC.O.117. This was an unfortunate move, especially since there was no demand on the part of the minorities in Pakistan for separate electorates. It is a well-established constitutional practice that separate electorates for minorities are only provided on their demand and are never imposed by the majority on the minorities. In fact, the minorities in Pakistan have consistently opposed separate electorates and have demanded a joint electorate with the Muslim majority, with special seats reserved for them under the Constitution. This demand by the minorities is completely justified, as having separate electorates is an instrument for exclusion on the basis of religion.

Minorities under the Eighth Amendment

The minorities in Pakistan, though a small percentage of the population, are significant in number and were treated unfairly during the martial-law years of General Zia. The Constitution guarantees minorities the freedom to practice, profess and propagate their religions, as well as the right to establish, maintain and manage their religious institutions. The Objectives Resolution of 1949 also aimed to provide adequate provisions for the minorities to develop their cultures and safeguard their legitimate interests.

Among the minorities in Pakistan, Christians are perhaps the largest in number. They were severely affected by the nationalization of private schools and colleges in 1972, which had been established by various Christian missions throughout the country. Christian education institutions and employment in such schools and colleges were the main sources of livelihood for the native Christian population in Pakistan. However, the government took over these institutions under Martial Law Regulation No. 118 and, from 1979 onwards, it began expropriating properties under these institutions, purportedly in accordance with the regulation's provisions. This move affected the Christian occupants of these properties, who were served with eviction notices. However, the Supreme Court eventually ruled that MLR 118 did not intend to make the government the owner of these properties. Despite this ruling, and the promises made by Muhammad Khan Junejo, the prime minister at the time, these nationalized educational institutions in the Punjab were not returned to the Christians. 'The religious parties have been obstructing the government's efforts to honour the prime minister's commitment publicly.'[64]

Under the Constitution (Second Amendment) Act 1974, Ahmadis were recognized as a constitutional minority. However, they faced significant difficulties due to the enforcement of Ordinance XX of 1984, which made it a punishable offence for Ahmadis to use titles or descriptions reserved for holy personages or places of the Muslims. This created serious challenges for Ahmadis in their daily lives.

In a bail case, the Supreme Court ruled that the use of certain expressions commonly used by Muslims did not create any offence or provocation. As a result, bail was granted to those accused of using such expressions. However, in another case, the Supreme Court upheld the validity of Ordinance XX of 1984 by a majority opinion, citing that it did not violate the fundamental rights of citizens to profess, practise and propagate their religion.

It is important to note that these legal and constitutional issues have had a significant impact on the lives and rights of Ahmadis in Pakistan. The Ahmadis continue to face discrimination and persecution in many aspects of their lives, including education, employment and religious practices, and it has been argued that the 'government and civil society must take concrete steps to address these issues and ensure that the rights of all citizens, regardless of their religion or beliefs, are protected and upheld'.[65]

In light of the historical events, it is understandable that minorities in Pakistan feel insecure and vulnerable. The introduction of Article 2A through a presidential order and the Eighth Amendment only added to their anxiety and apprehension. Article 2A incorporates the principles and provisions set out in the Objectives Resolution as a substantive part of the Constitution. However, the Objectives Resolution of 1949 was subtly altered to the detriment of minorities. Specifically, its sixth paragraph was changed to read as follows: 'Wherein adequate provision shall be made for the minorities freely to profess and practice their religions and develop their cultures.'[66] The statement highlighted the concerns of minorities who felt apprehensive about the continuously deteriorating standard of judicial appointments and the expanding role of religious parties in statutory developments, as well as the introduction of separate electorates against their wishes, all of which may have led minorities to feel they were being relegated to the status of second-class citizens.

Background of National Assembly members, 1985[67]

Landlords and tribal leaders	157
Businessmen	54
Urban professionals	18
Religious leaders	6
Other	3

The MRD had appealed for the boycott of the polls, but the following table shows that their appeal did not keep the voters away from polling stations.

Voters' turnout

National Assembly	52.93
Punjab	61.80
Sindh	49.82
NWFP	47.61
Baluchistan	46.62

The exclusion of political parties and restrictions on political mobilization allowed the feudal and tribal elite to dominate the polls, resulting in the well-known landed families of the Punjab, Sindh and the NWFP, and tribal chiefs of Baluchistan, tightening their grip on the elected bodies. Additionally, the commercial elite and affluent candidates performed well in the elections. Despite most opposing political parties choosing to boycott the elections, many of the victors belonged to one party or another. General Zia, pleased with the outcome of his referendum, proceeded to tighten his grip on the opposition. Unfortunately, the main opposition leader at the time, Benazir Bhutto, made a tactical error by boycotting the non-party elections. A new generation of political leaders, including Nawaz Sharif, emerged in response to the boycott. Zia responded by imprisoning the entire opposition during the polls, leaving the field open for his henchmen to manipulate the vote in favour of parliamentarians who aligned with his regime.[68]

Ayesha Jalal's view is unassailable. She points out that after eight years of political silence, people turned out in large numbers to vote in both National Assembly and provincial assembly elections. Even some of Zia's close associates lost the election, and the only party allowed to participate, Jamaat-i-Islami, was defeated in all but a few urban constituencies in Lahore. The National Assembly election had a turnout of 52.93 per cent nationwide, while 57.7 per cent of the electorate voted in the provincial assembly elections. This overwhelming response to the electoral exercise left the MRD leadership with no political leverage during Zia's remaining three years in power. Benazir Bhutto, living in exile, was unaware of how effectively the regime had used the funds at their disposal to transform the face of Pakistani politics.[69] According to Jalal, as Zia, 'the Islamic ideologue[,] presided over the commercialization of social values and the crass monetization of politics', ideology 'took a back seat'.[70] PPP members, more focused on 'development issues' in their immediate constituencies than on 'distant national objectives ... flouted the party decision' and took part in the elections.

> In their opportunistic rush to join the ranks of those enjoying the benefits of state patronage and privilege, politics were bent out of shape. Those who entered the political fray did so more as a business [opportunity], fully aware that the more they spent on electioneering, the greater the future rewards.[71]

Despite benefiting the commercial art industry and 'ancillary businesses, the monetization of elections in Pakistan did precious little to educate the electorate about the main issues'. Voters' choices were dominated by personalities rather than problems, 'proving Zia's dictum that a thwack of the whip was all that was needed to get politicians to fall in line'.[72]

It is important to note that 1985 marked the beginning of a political culture in Pakistan characterized by the three Cs: corruption, criminalization and connivance. These vices became indispensable in Pakistani politics going forward. Politicians such as Mian Nawaz Sharif availed themselves of these vices to seize the premiership, with Benazir Bhutto countering his manoeuvres by emulating his own ways of connivance and patronage politics. Both secured power, but neither could complete a full tenure, losing the respect and trust of the people. Unfortunately, Pakistan's political landscape saw the likes of Asif Ali Zardari and others of his ilk enter the corridors of power. With no scruples worth mentioning, Zardari elevated the art of the three Cs to new heights. For him, as for the Sharifs, everything had a price, with values, ethics, honesty and integrity reduced to mere clichés. Such abstractions had no relevance when it came to the realm of politics driven by pragmatism. Idealism did not matter either, legitimizing corrupt means that took root deep enough to stymie almost every state institution. The audacity of resorting to horse-trading in this day and age highlights the need for a dispassionate analysis of what is lacking in Pakistan's political leadership.[73]

'The Mouse That Roared': Mohammad Khan Junejo

After being sworn in as prime minister on 23 March 1985, Muhammad Khan Junejo wasted no time insisting that martial law be lifted and political parties be allowed to function. Many believed that Junejo was nominated as prime minister because Zia wanted a puppet in the post. However, Junejo proved to be far from a simpleton. He was known for his impeccable honesty, strict discipline and conservative Muslim beliefs – he kept his wife at their village home and never allowed her to join him in public. Despite his unassuming demeanour, Junejo was a resolute leader who stood up to Zia and worked tirelessly to advance democracy in Pakistan.[74]

After eight long years, martial law was finally lifted on 30 December 1985, and Zia begrudgingly allowed political parties to participate in the assembly. However, Zia's willingness to share power with Junejo and his cabinet was not without conditions. To secure his position, Zia ensured that the new legislature retroactively accepted all of his actions from the past eight years, including his 1977 coup. He also manoeuvred to get several amendments passed, most notably the controversial Eighth Amendment, which gave the president sweeping powers to dissolve the National Assembly and dismiss the prime minister. These moves demonstrated that while Zia may have lifted martial law, he remained firmly in control and determined to maintain his grip on power.[75] In addition, the president was given the power to appoint key positions such as provincial governors, chiefs of the armed forces and chief justices of the Supreme and High Courts. These amendments consolidated power in the hands of one man, the president, further undermining the already fragile democratic system in Pakistan.[76] However, this amendment did reduce Zia's power – at least to a point – in one key aspect. It stated that Zia could dissolve the assembly under only two circumstances: if the cabinet had been ousted by a vote of no confidence, and it was evident that no one could form a government; or if the government could not operate in a constitutional manner.

After assuming the office, Muhammad Khan Junejo encountered his greatest political hurdle when Benazir Bhutto, leader of the opposition PPP, returned from exile in London in 1986 and addressed mammoth rallies, vowing to overthrow the government. Junejo tackled this challenge deftly, refusing to clamp down on the PPP, as Zia had expected him to.

As the days went by, the legislature yearned for greater autonomy and authority. By the start of 1988, speculations about the growing rift between Prime Minister Junejo and President Zia were rampant.[77] The divergence between the pair, and consequently the Army, became apparent as the Soviet Union announced its decision to withdraw its troops from Afghanistan. In an effort to support the UN's attempts to mediate the withdrawal, Junejo organized a round-table conference of all political parties, much to the opposition of Zia, who preferred to use the Pakistan Army to secure a Mujahideen victory. Despite Zia's disapproval, Junejo's government signed the UN-sponsored Geneva Accord on Afghanistan in April 1988. Junejo's insistence that senior generals be held accountable for the massive explosions at an ammunition dump near Islamabad (Ojri Camp) caused friction with the Army, who then pressured Zia to dismiss him. On 29 May 1988, upon Junejo's return from a visit to China, Zia declared the government dissolved and the National Assembly and provincial assemblies disbanded under the amended Constitution's section 58(2) b. Junejo was briefly placed under house arrest during this time.[78]

After ruling for eleven years, General Zia made a promise to the nation that he would hold elections within the next ninety days. However, non-party elections had led to the monetization of politics and a lack of ideological clarity among new political leaders. In 1986 Benazir Bhutto returned from exile and announced her intention to participate in the elections. As Benazir's popularity grew and international aid decreased following the Soviet withdrawal from Afghanistan, Zia found himself in a politically precarious situation.

Economic Policy

In his book *Issues in Pakistan's Political Economy* S. Akbar Zaidi notes that there were many similarities between the economic policies of the 1960s and '80s in Pakistan. Zia benefited from the initiatives of his predecessors, as well as favourable circumstances that contributed to a robust economy with high growth rates.[79] During Zia's regime, there was a gradual reversal of Zulfiqar Ali Bhutto's nationalization policy, and the process of privatization was initiated. To restore the confidence of the private sector and obtain expert industrial input into policy making, Zia appointed General Habibullah of Gandhara Industries and Mustapha Gokal, a shipping magnate, both of whom had been victimized during the previous regime. However, they were unable to influence policy making and their bid for speedy privatization was stalled by civil servants such as Ghulam Ishaq Khan, A.G.N. Kazi and Waseem Jaffrey, who preferred a gradual course of action.[80] The civil servants in power during Zia's regime had reservations about the hasty implementation of privatization, fearing potential disruptions to incomplete projects and other economic factors. However, during his eleven-year rule, the re-privatization of nationalized industries and banks allowed for the emergence of a new class of entrepreneurs, who received economic and financial incentives, becoming stakeholders in the new social order. Influence and privilege were no longer based only on personal wealth but on military rank and connections.[81]

Despite bureaucratic obstacles, the Zia government made significant strides in promoting private sector investment in various industries, including cement, fertilizer, tractors and automobiles. Additionally, the agri-processing industry, which had been nationalized in 1976, was returned to its rightful owners. To enhance output in the public sector, an Efficiency Improvement Programme incorporating balancing, modernization and replacement (BMR) was introduced. One Window Operations was also established to streamline the process of setting up industrial units and reduce bureaucratic hurdles. In order to instill greater confidence among private investors, the Zia regime initiated measures such as fiscal incentives, export promotion and import liberalization. These policy endeavours were directed at revitalizing economic growth and nurturing the emergence of a fresh wave of entrepreneurs, among whom notable figures like Nawaz Sharif, the Chaudhuris from Gujarat and General Akhtar's family ascended swiftly to prominence, establishing themselves as influential economic powerhouses and part of the new super-rich elite in Pakistan. However, despite these positive developments, there were concerns about the potential risks of a hasty privatization of large-scale, capital-intensive projects initiated under Bhutto, which had yet to be completed.[82]

Despite various incentives and inducements offered, the investors remained sceptical and cautious even at the end of the fifth five-year plan. As a result, a significant amount of investment went into real estate, leading to an unprecedented rise in landed property in urban areas. To boost investment, the Zia regime introduced additional schemes such as selective divestment of public sector industries through stock markets. Foreign-exchange bearer certificates and whitener bonds were also introduced to legalize black money and encourage investment in productive sectors rather than property, hoardings and foreign accounts. While the bond schemes showed some success, the desired results remained out of reach largely due to the credibility deficit that plagued the government's efforts.[83]

Despite the government's work to improve industry and economic standards, agriculture remained underdeveloped during the fifth and sixth five-year plans. The set targets and goals could not be achieved, with the growth rate falling short of the expected 6 per cent, hitting only 4.4 per cent. The increase in oilseed, cotton and sugar cane production remained unattainable, and the ambition to diversify agriculture by promoting major crops also failed. The high price of energy sources led to skyrocketing fertilizer prices, further contributing to the shortfall in agricultural production. World recession had a dampening effect on the growth of export crops, particularly cotton and rice. Moreover, the inordinate delay in the implementation of plans to ensure the availability of high-yield seeds also contributed to the shortfall.

In the context of the Islamization of the economy, the National Investment Trust and the Investment Corporation of Pakistan were required to operate on an equity basis instead of an interest one. To further this, interest-free counters were opened at all 7,000 branches of the nationalized commercial banks on 1 January 1980. However, interest-bearing National Savings Schemes were allowed to operate in parallel.[84]

The Zakat and Ushr Ordinance

The government introduced an Islamic wealth tax (*zakat*) and farm levy (*ushr*) with the Zakat and Ushr Ordinance on 20 June 1980, which allowed them to deduct 2.5 per cent *zakat* annually from primarily interest-bearing savings and shares held in institutions such as the National Investment Trust, the Investment Corporation of Pakistan and other companies, most of which were owned by Muslims. However, the Foreign Exchange Bearer Certificate scheme, which offered a fixed interest rate, was exempted from the compulsory *zakat* deduction. The ordinance faced strong criticism from the Shia sect, which was later exempted from the mandatory *zakat* deduction, and even the Sunni community.[85]

Reversal of Land Reforms

The Federal Shariat Court's (FSC) declaration on 13 December 1980 that the land reforms of 1972 and 1977 were in line with Islamic laws came as a surprise to General Zia. However, the traditional supporters of the landlord class, the ulema, were then brought in. Three ulema were inducted into the FSC and two into the Shariat Appellate Bench of the Supreme Court. The FSC's judgement was later reversed in 1990. During the period of martial law, many landlords reportedly asked their tenants to seek the protection of their benefactor, Bhutto. Thousands of tenants were forcefully evicted from their lands in various districts. The martial-law regime made it clear that it was not committed to redistributive agrarian policies, and it dismissed the land reforms as mere politics meant to reward supporters and punish enemies.

Empty Assurances

Despite the government's emphasis on economic growth and modernization, labour issues were neglected, and the authorities were quick to suppress any labour protests or trade union activities. Workers' demands for better wages, working conditions and social security were disregarded, and employers were given assurances of government support in suppressing any unrest. Punishments for offenders were severe, including imprisonment and whipping.

Tragically, the government's attitude towards labour disputes led to violent confrontations, such as the incident at the Colony Textile Mill in Multan where nineteen workers were killed by the police. Such incidents were symptomatic of the wider inequality and social fragmentation that characterized Zia's rule.

Although the government claimed to prioritize industrialization and economic development, there were few concrete measures taken to support these goals. The economy remained heavily reliant on foreign aid and remittances, and growth was not accompanied by significant improvements in living standards for the majority of the population.

During the eleven-year period of military rule under Zia, Pakistan experienced widespread discontent due to economic hardship and social inequality. Despite foreign military assistance, the country faced mounting challenges, including deficit financing, rising foreign indebtedness, inflation, price hikes for basic goods and a widening trade deficit. In 1982 Pakistan's foreign debt alone had reached a staggering U.S.$12 billion. Non-productive expenses also continued to rise, which contributed to an increase in Pakistan's own military expenses. The deepening of capitalist market relations, combined with corruption in the state-controlled income distribution system, further exacerbated the growing gap between the rich and the poor. This increasing inequality between different social classes led to what is known as 'relative deprivation' – that is, when improving living conditions raise expectations, but the reality of inequality fails to meet those expectations. Overall, the economic and social conditions in Pakistan under Zia's rule left many citizens feeling frustrated.[86] Eventually, the hopes were belied, resulting in an upsurge of discontent.

During Zia's regime, the influx of financial resources from abroad, coupled with huge deliveries of armaments, medicines and other goods for Afghan refugees, led to a significant increase in corruption, theft and profiteering. By the mid- to late 1980s, Pakistan's 'black' or 'shadow' economy had reached an estimated 30–40 per cent of the legal economy, exacerbating social and economic inequalities in the country.

The Zia era witnessed the emergence of a consumerist culture, with a stark divide between those enjoying opulence and material advancement, and the vast majority still struggling with poverty. The government's rhetorical emphasis on Islamic values and vernacular traditions stood in contrast to the reality of everyday life in Pakistan. This duality has persisted as a defining feature of Pakistani society.[87]

Nuclear Programme

During his rule, President Zia was determined to ensure that Pakistan would attain nuclear capability. However, this decision came with its own set of challenges. Pakistan was subjected to international pressure to sign the Nuclear Non-proliferation Treaty (NPT), but it refused to do so. This led to Pakistan being criticized on various international platforms. Zia skilfully managed to neutralize the pressure by highlighting India's nuclear ambitions and the potential security threats they posed to Pakistan.

In response to international pressure, President Zia proposed a five-point practical rejoinder. The key points of this proposal included the renouncing of nuclear weapons usage. However, the irony was that during this same period, Zia openly funded the development of a uranium enrichment plant in Kahuta under the direct supervision of the military establishment. This development caused controversy and invited international scrutiny, with Pakistan accused of pursuing a nuclear arsenal.

Despite the challenges, Zia remained committed to attaining nuclear capability, and he played a key role in establishing the foundation for Pakistan's nuclear programme. The programme was later expanded by his successors, and, eventually, Pakistan became a nuclear-armed state. Zia's determination and vision for Pakistan's nuclear programme had far-reaching consequences for the country's national security, foreign policy and relations with other countries in the region and beyond.[88]

Islamization

On 2 December 1978 General Zia addressed the nation to announce his plan of implementing an Islamic system in Pakistan and accused politicians of exploiting Islam's name for their own benefit. His Islamic system was based on a dual approach, which combined the punitive provisions of orthodox Islamic jurisprudence with market-orientated economic and social policies. The goal of establishing an Islamic order was used as a justification for suppressing dissent and discouraging demands for democracy.

To enforce this system, General Zia introduced the Hudood Ordinance in 1979, which included severe punishments such as stoning, flogging and amputations for crimes such as theft, adultery and drinking. Although these punishments were not always carried out in practice, their inclusion in the

Public flogging during Zia ul Haq's dictatorial regime, Karachi, 1980.

law helped Zia win the support of conservative Islamists and silence dissent. A parallel legal code and judicial system, based on Sharia law, were introduced.

Additionally, General Zia also implemented the *zakat* and *ushr* laws. The law of evidence was also amended, reducing a woman's evidence in financial transactions to half the weight of a man's. These measures aimed to create a more Islamic system in Pakistan, and they also reinforced gender inequality.[89]

During Zia's regime, many Muslim theologians experienced an improvement in their social status and financial well-being. Scholars of Islamic law were sought after for high-paying consultations and were able to secure lucrative administrative and judicial positions. Clerics gained control over the collection and distribution of Islamic charity taxes and aid for the impoverished, which further elevated their social status and prestige.

Zia's policy of manoeuvring was centred on the Islamization of practically every sphere of Pakistani society. He capitalized on the 'Islamic boom' in the world to make Islam the cornerstone of the Pakistani state and society, claiming it to be a novel road to development. However, there was no unity among the winners of this Islamization policy. The two main competing groups were the moderate Islam-pasand ('Islam-loving') groups and the radicals with extreme political outlooks. Since 1947 there had been a significant increase in the number of small property owners in Pakistan's cities, towns and villages, along with a rise in the underprivileged population. Both sections of society felt insecure and favoured the revival of 'true Islam' for its egalitarian provisions and ability to cleanse society of corrupt morals.

The composition of Army officers underwent significant changes during this period, with officers from an elitist background, educated during the British colonial period and trained by Americans, being replaced by their juniors from middle- or lower-middle-class backgrounds. This generation was educated and trained in Pakistan and tended to have Islamic viewpoints.

A considerable number of students, who were an important part of the democratic opposition forces, began to shift their views during this period. They put forward their own demands based on their social status and specific situation, which included uncertainty about the future and growing unemployment among certified specialists. The leftist democratic movement was unable to solve these problems, leading to disillusionment and an increasing attraction towards the Islamic alternative, which was fully supported by the authorities. The growing strength and influence of the Islamic youth student organization Islami Jamaat-i Tulaba (the youth wing of Jamaat-i-Islami) can be regarded as a confirmation of the trends mentioned.

In the spring of 1978, leftist democratic forces won the student union elections, but their influence waned as Islamic organizations gained power in the years that followed. To promote egalitarian Islamic principles, the government enacted economic measures such as the abolition of banking interest and introduction of interest-free banking, as well as mandatory Islamic taxes and inheritance laws with strong egalitarian features. The authorities also imposed strict bans on alcohol, gambling and pornography in order to restore moral values and cleanse society.

The authorities made a concerted effort to promote the influence of Islam in all aspects of Pakistan's spiritual and cultural life, including in its education system. The curriculum of schools and universities was revised to ensure compliance with Islamic principles through the study of Arabic and Islamic history and traditions and in 1980 an International Islamic University (IIU) was established in Islamabad. The number of madrasas also nearly doubled during Zia's regime. The education system was reorientated to reflect the 'Pakistani ideology', with a focus on implementing Islamic principles and protecting the country's Islamic identity.[90] There was also a deliberate effort to promote a new national narrative, in which Pakistan's history was portrayed as a string of events culminating in the creation of an Islamic state. This narrative was disseminated through various channels, including textbooks, media and speeches by government officials. As part of this effort, studying Arabic and Islamic history and traditions was given impetus, with the objective of inculcating a deeper understanding of the Islamic faith and culture among the populace.

However, this emphasis on Islamic education came at the expense of secular education, for which the government reduced funding, resulting in only two new universities being established during Zia's regime. This had a profound impact on the country's educational system, which was unable to keep pace with the growing demand for higher education, and contributed to the decline of Pakistan's intellectual and scientific capabilities. Overall, Zia's regime sought to promote a conservative, Islamic world view in all aspects of Pakistani society, including education. While this approach had some positive effects, such as the promotion of greater religious literacy, it also had negative consequences, such as the marginalization of secular education and the stunting of intellectual and scientific development.[91]

As well as the education system, the military was also restyled to suit Zia's push for Islamization and Islamic indoctrination. The armed forces were given the official duty of protecting not only national borders but ideological boundaries, which gave them greater political influence. The Federal Shariat Court, established in 1980, ensured that existing and newly adopted laws complied with Islamic injunctions, settling cases involving traditional punishments. This court introduced the system of Islamic tribunals, which were set up in localities throughout the country. Sharia (or shariat) – a buzz word during Zia's regime – or Islamic law is a comprehensive and intricate legal and ethical framework derived from the religious texts and teachings of Islam, primarily the Quran and the Hadith (sayings and actions of the Prophet Muhammad). It serves as a guide for all aspects of life, including personal conduct, family matters, business ethics and governance, encompassing both moral and legal principles. Sharia encompasses a wide range of rules and regulations, often covering areas such as worship, dietary laws, criminal justice, marriage, divorce, inheritance and more. It aims to provide a moral and legal framework for Muslims to lead their lives in accordance with Islamic values and principles, and it varies in its interpretation and application across different Muslim-majority countries and communities.[92]

After the lifting of martial law, Zia issued an order declaring Sharia supreme in Pakistan, continuing the process of Islamization and aiming to make Pakistan a 'truly Islamic' nation. However, the order required parliamentary approval, and Zia's sudden death in August 1988 prevented the bill from becoming law. While the Senate approved the bill, the National Assembly did not, and Pakistan remained on the cusp of abandoning constitutional democratic development and secularism, according to O. V. Pleshov.[93] The Islamization of Pakistani society was accompanied by an ideological Islamic indoctrination in the armed forces. General Zia emphasized that a professional soldier in the Muslim Army must fulfil the tasks set for him by the Muslim nation under the banner of Allah. According to Zia's vision, the armed forces played a crucial role in defending and promoting

Islam in the country. This indoctrination aimed to foster a sense of religious duty and devotion among military personnel, further strengthening the military's right to indulge in the political life of the country. The integration of Islamic ideology in the military created a complex dynamic between the Army and the civilian government and reinforced the military's role as a powerful force in shaping the direction of the state.[94] The military under General Zia's regime underwent a significant transformation with the Islamization of its education and training. Not only were the Sharia-based restrictions and prohibitions applied to the general population, but they were enforced in the military. Mullahs who served in the Army were promoted to religious instructor positions, and Islam was made a major subject in the contingent training programmes. Military policies were developed based on Islamic ideology, and the concept of jihad was linked to military strategy. The observance of religious rules and customs was also considered in matters of conscription and military career.[95]

The Islamization of the armed forces was influenced by several factors, including the ongoing conflict with India, Pakistan's alliance with the Afghan Mujahideen and its support for Muslim freedom fighters in Kashmir. As a result, many military personnel began to identify themselves as soldiers of Islam, particularly those whose work was closely tied to the activities of radical Islamic groups.

The directorate of the ISI, Pakistan's most powerful secret service, played a pivotal role in the country's Afghan policy from the late 1970s onwards, providing significant assistance to the Mujahideen in their fight against the Soviet occupation of Afghanistan and supporting the security forces of the Soviet-backed Afghan regime. As a result, many ISI officials who had worked closely with Islamist groups came to embrace their ideas.

Zia's push for *nizam-e-Islam* (the Islamic system) marked a drastic departure from Pakistan's predominantly Anglo-Saxon legal system. To establish an Islamic society, Zia announced the establishment of Sharia benches. However, he failed to mention that the Sharia benches' jurisdiction was limited by an overriding clause, which excluded Muslim personal law, court or tribunal procedures; fiscal law, tax and fee collection; and insurance practices and procedures from the purview of Islamic law.[96] Moreover, Zia faced resistance from the federal Sharia bench, which declared *rajm*, or stoning, to be un-Islamic. Zia reconstituted the court, hoping for a different outcome, and he got it.

The Hudood Ordinance

The term *hudood* is commonly used in Islamic social and legal literature to refer to the boundaries of acceptable behaviour and transgressions. The Hudood Ordinance of 1979 was introduced to enforce punishments for certain offences against property, including theft and robbery, under

Islamic law.[97] This law introduced severe punishments for crimes classified under *hudood*, such as theft, robbery and adultery. Instead of imprisonment or fines, amputation of the right hand from the joint of the wrist by a surgeon was prescribed for theft, while robbery carried the punishment of amputation of the right hand from the wrist and the left foot from the ankle.

Sunni denominations have minor differences in views regarding the sentencing and specifications for these laws. While some argue that since Sharia is God's law and prescribes specific punishments for each crime, they are immutable, others express concerns about the validity of Hadith, a major component of how Islamic law is created, raising questions about administering certain punishments.

In many countries, the way Islamic law is practised under *hudood* has been criticized for its incompatibility with human rights, leading to calls for an international moratorium on *hudood* punishments until greater scholarly consensus can be reached.

The Prohibition Order

Prior to 1977, the act of drinking wine or any other alcoholic drink was not a crime under Pakistan's penal code. However, in 1977 the Pakistani government made the drinking and selling of wine by Muslims illegal. This law carried a punishment of six months' imprisonment, a fine of PKR 5,000, or both. Later, this provision was replaced by the Prohibition Order, which stated that the punishment for drinking and selling alcohol by Muslims would be 80 stripes. This punishment was justified by citing an *ijma*, or consensus, of the companions of the Prophet Muhammad (peace be upon him) that had been established since the time of the second caliph, Umar.

It is important to note that the prohibition on alcohol consumption and sales only applies to Muslims in Pakistan. Non-Muslims, on the other hand, are allowed to possess licences to drink and/or manufacture alcoholic beverages, which are issued by the government. The best-known of these non-Muslim licensed manufacturers is the Murree Brewery.

The prohibition of alcohol in Pakistan is based on Islamic teachings, which consider it a sin to consume or sell alcoholic drinks. The prohibition is also meant to promote a healthy and productive society. However, the implementation of the law has been a contentious issue, with some arguing that it is not effective in curbing alcohol consumption and may lead to corruption and black-market activity. Additionally, some have criticized the law for being discriminatory against Muslims, who are not afforded the same freedoms as non-Muslims in this regard.

The Adultery (Zina) Ordinance

The Zina Ordinance replaced previous provisions relating to adultery, stipulating that both the man and the woman found guilty would be subject to severe punishment. If unmarried, they would be flogged with one hundred stripes each, whereas if married they would face the punishment of stoning to death.[98] It was argued that Section 497 of the Pakistan Penal Code dealing with the offence of adultery provided certain safeguards to the offender in as much as if the adultery was with the consent or connivance of the husband, no offence of adultery was deemed to have been committed in the eye of law. The wife, under the prevailing law, was also not to be punished as abettor. Islamic law knows no such exception.[99]

The burden of Zia's Islamization fell heavily on women, who were disproportionately affected by its inconsistencies. The Zina Ordinance, in particular, drew intense international criticism for its perceived injustices and the suffering it caused to women. Women's rights groups produced a powerful film titled *Who Will Cast the First Stone?* to highlight the oppression and injustices faced by women under the Hudood Ordinances. The first conviction and sentence under the Zina Ordinance, which called for stoning to death for Fehmida and Allah Bakhsh, was set aside in September 1981 due to national and international pressure.

Under the Zina Ordinance, many women who made allegations of rape were convicted for adultery while their rapists were acquitted, sparking widespread outrage and demands from jurists and women's activists for the law's repeal. A particularly shocking case was that of Safia Bibi, a thirteen-year-old blind girl who alleged that her employer had raped her, resulting in the birth of a son. Rather than her assailant being tried and punished, she was convicted of adultery while the rapist was acquitted. This case attracted immense publicity and condemnation from the public and the press, prompting the Federal Shariat Court to call for the case records and order Safia's release from prison on her own bond. The trial court's finding was eventually reversed on appeal, and Safia's conviction was set aside.[100] In early 1988 the stoning to death of Shahida Parveen and Muhammad Sarwar led to widespread public criticism, ultimately resulting in their retrial and acquittal by the Federal Shariat Court. The court in this case determined that notice of divorce by Shahida's former husband, Khushi Muhammad, should have been given to the chairman of the local council as stipulated under Section 7(3) of the Muslim Family Laws Ordinance 1961. This section requires any man who divorces his wife to register it with the Union Council, failing which the divorce is considered invalid and the couple can be convicted under the Zina Ordinance.

In December 1986 the International Commission of Jurists conducted a mission to Pakistan and called for the repeal of certain sections of the Hudood Ordinances related to crimes and punishments that were discriminatory towards women and non-Muslims. The commission highlighted the fact that a Muslim woman can be convicted based on the evidence of a man, and a non-Muslim can be convicted based on the evidence of a Muslim, but not vice versa. These discriminatory provisions were seen as inconsistent with the principles of justice and equality. The commission's call for reform was echoed by women's rights groups and activists who were concerned about the impact of the Hudood Ordinances on women's rights and well-being.

Blasphemy Laws

In Pakistan, the Pakistan Penal Code (PPC) and the Criminal Procedure Code were amended through ordinances in 1980, 1982 and 1986 to include a provision that criminalizes anything that implies disrespect towards Prophet Muhammad (peace be upon him), Ahl-e-Bait (the family of the prophet), Sahaba (the companions of the prophet) and Sha'ar-e-Islam (Islamic symbols). This amendment was made to protect the religious sentiments of Muslims in the country. Under this law, if anyone is found guilty of committing such an offence, they can be punished with imprisonment or a fine, or with both. This law is aimed at promoting religious harmony and tolerance in Pakistan, and to prevent any acts that could potentially incite religious hatred and violence. However, some critics argue that this law could be misused and exploited to silence dissent and stifle free speech in the country.[101]

The blasphemy laws in Pakistan have long been a subject of controversy and criticism by human rights organizations worldwide, as well as by liberals and moderates within the country. The U.S. assistant secretary of state Robin Raphel testified before a Senate foreign relations sub-committee on 7 March 1996, acknowledging that religious parties in Pakistan wield 'street power' rather than 'ballot power', which presents a major obstacle for the government to repeal the blasphemy laws. According to Raphel, more than 150 blasphemy cases had been filed in Pakistan since 1986, most of them against members of the Ahmadi community, although none had resulted in convictions. During the same period, nine cases were brought against Christians and nine against Muslims, some of which led to convictions, but no one had been executed under the law's mandatory death penalty. Some convictions had been overturned, and several individuals were still appealing their convictions. These facts highlight the controversial nature of the blasphemy laws and their selective and discriminatory application against religious minorities.

The Pakistan Penal Code (PPC) includes a set of provisions related to religious offences and their corresponding penalties. These provisions address various aspects of religious sensitivities and blasphemy laws. Section 298A pertains to the use of derogatory remarks or expressions concerning holy personages. Violation of this provision can result in a penalty of three years' imprisonment, a fine, or both. Section 298B deals with the misuse of epithets, descriptions, titles or terms reserved for specific holy personages or places by Ahmadis. Infringement of this law can lead to three years' imprisonment along with a fine. Section 298C addresses Ahmadis who call themselves Muslims, engage in preaching or propagating their faith, outrage the religious feelings of Muslims or present themselves as Muslims. Violation of this provision can result in a three-year prison term and a fine. Section 295 deals with acts that involve injuring or defiling places of worship with the intent of insulting the religion of any community. The penalty for such an offence can include imprisonment for up to two years, a fine, or both.

Section 295A covers deliberate and malicious acts intended to outrage the religious feelings of any community by insulting its religion or religious beliefs. The punishment for this offence may include imprisonment for up to ten years, a fine, or both. Section 295B pertains to the defiling of the Quran, with a penalty of imprisonment for life. Lastly, Section 295C addresses the use of derogatory remarks or expressions concerning Prophet Muhammad (peace be upon him). Violation of this provision can result in a fine and the death penalty. These provisions reflect Pakistan's legal framework concerning religious offences and the corresponding penalties aimed at maintaining social and religious harmony while safeguarding religious sensitivities.

Prayer Times

In an effort to promote religious observance and piety among the general population, instructions were issued to ensure that regular prayers were observed. As part of this initiative, arrangements were made for the performance of noon prayer (*salat al zuhur*) in various government and quasi-government offices, as well as in educational institutions. Additionally, during official functions and at airports, railway stations and bus stops, arrangements were also made for the performance of this prayer.

However, despite the implementation of these measures, the reality is that people were often allowed to skip their duties in government institutions. The strict observance of these measures was often overlooked, especially in cases where individuals were too busy with their work or when the timing of the prayer conflicts with their schedules. As a result, the intended objective of promoting religious observance and piety was not always achieved. Furthermore, some individuals simply chose not to observe the prayer, regardless of whether or not arrangements had been made for its performance.

The Reverence for Fasting Ordinance

In order to observe the Islamic month of Ramadan with complete sanctity, the government issued an *Ehtram-e-Ramazan* (reverence for the month of fasting) Ordinance. As part of this, cinemas were required to close three hours after the Maghrib (post-sunset) prayers. The intention behind the ordinance was to encourage Muslims to focus on the religious observances of Ramadan and refrain from activities that may distract them from their spiritual duties during this holy month. While the ordinance was intended to promote religious harmony and respect, it was also criticized by some for limiting personal freedom and choice.[102]

During Zia's regime, Islamization was often employed as a tool for political purposes. Unfortunately, Zia's interpretation of Islam greatly contributed to the growth of fundamentalism, obscurantism and regressive attitudes in Pakistani society. Since Zia's death in 1988, Pakistani laws have become inconsistent and unstable. This instability has led to frequent changes in the law or threats of change due to differences of opinion among ruling factions. This inconsistency and instability in the legal system has resulted in confusion and uncertainty among the general population, and it has hampered Pakistan's progress towards a more democratic and egalitarian society. Three major inconsistencies can be identified in Zia's Islamic law. The first inconsistency is between the legal norms and socially observed norms; the second is between statutory legal norms and the norms that are applied in practice in the courts (for example, *hadd*, which is a punishment for certain offences, is difficult to implement because of the strict standards of proof, confession and retraction of confession); and the third is between different formal legal norms. For instance, the courts compromise on non-compliance with the Muslim Family Laws Ordinance, but it is strictly punished under the Zina Ordinance. In addition to these inconsistencies, the Constitution guarantees equal status to women, but in practice women face discrimination in criminal law.

During Zia's martial-law regime in Pakistan, the courts were Islamized, leading to the establishment of Sharia benches and the narrowing of civilian lawyers' scope of activity. This frustrated many influential lawyers who were ready to be exploited by the opposition due to the restrictive court regulations. Women's organizations also played a crucial role in the anti-government movement as the authorities, supported by Islamists, aimed to restrict women's participation in getting jobs and professional training. This policy was viewed as a hindrance to gender equality and progress.

The Politics of Ethno-Religious Exclusion

Pakistan is a country with diverse cultural, ethnic and sectarian groups, which has resulted in inter-provincial and intra-provincial conflicts. The country has four provinces, the Punjab, Sindh, Baluchistan and Khyber Pakhtunkhwa (formerly known as the Northwest Frontier Province) and also the former Federally Administered Tribal Areas. In recent years, Pakistan has been facing the challenge of rising sectarian violence. From 1990 to 1997, over 581 deaths and 1,600 injuries were reported due to various forms of violence ranging from assassinations to bomb blasts at congregational places of worship. Moreover, individuals who were previously affiliated with sectarian militant organizations have moved to jihadist outfits, adding to the instability. As a result of sectarian terrorist attacks, the Pakistani government imposed a ban on the Sipah-e-Sahaba Pakistan (SSP) (later renamed Millet-e-Islami) and its rival Shia organization Tehrik-e-Nifaz-e-Fiqh-e-Jafaria (TNFJ) on 3 February 2002. In 2001, Lashker-e-Jhangvi, the first anti-Shia militant organization, was also banned.[103] Women's organizations and human rights activists have also raised their voices against such violence, since these attacks have adversely affected women's participation in getting jobs and professional training.[104]

The sectarian make-up of Pakistan is complex and multifaceted. With a population that is 96 per cent Muslim, the country is predominantly Sunni, with an estimated 80 per cent of Muslims adhering to this sect. However, there is a significant Shia minority, estimated to be between 15 to 20 per cent according to some sources, while the historian Qasim Zaman argues that the Shia population is closer to 14 to 15 per cent.[105] Beyond these broad categories, the Sunni population is further subdivided into four groups: Deobandis, Barelvis, Ahl-e-Hadith and followers of Jamaat-e-Islami. The last of these, founded by Maulana Abul Aala Maududi in 1942, is one of the prominent Islamist organizations in Pakistan. The Deobandi and Barelvi sects, on the other hand, trace their origins back to the religious education movements that emerged in the nineteenth century as a response to the modern educational and social institutions established by the colonial state. While the Barelvi movement has a traditional attachment to the (Muslim) Sufi shrines and the Sufis, this has led to conflicts with the Deobandi movement, which espouses a more puritanical version of Islam and views Sufi practices with scepticism. The Ahl-e-Hadith, another sect, also emerged during this period, and although it had a smaller following, its ultra-orthodox and puritanical ideas, inspired by the Wahabi movement in the eighteenth century, are significant. The Ahl-e-Hadith categorically rejects all four schools of jurisprudence.[106]

Although the Shia community in Pakistan is relatively small compared to the Sunni community, it is still diverse and is further subdivided into various subsects. The majority of Shias in Pakistan belong to the Athna

Ashari subsect, also known as the Twelvers, since they believe in the concept of twelve Imams. The Twelvers hold an overwhelming majority compared to other Shia subsects such as the Ismailis, who follow the spiritual leadership of Agha Khan, the Daudi Bohras, who follow the spiritual leadership of Syed Burhanuddin, and the Sulemani Bohras, who follow the spiritual leadership of Masood Salehbahi.

Each of these Shia subsects has its own distinct set of beliefs and practices, which can sometimes lead to tensions and conflicts within the larger Shia community. Despite these differences, the Shia community in Pakistan is united in its commitment to the faith and is actively involved in promoting the rights of the Shia minority in the country.[107] The Shia community in Pakistan shares some similarities with the Barelvis in terms of their religious practices. For instance, both communities hold saints and shrines in high esteem, as well as other aspects of Sufi Islam. Shias are primarily concentrated in Karachi, the southern Punjab and the northern areas. Prior to the Iranian Revolution in 1979, the Shias in Pakistan were politically passive. However, Zia's Sunni brand of Islamization and the Iranian Revolution led to an upsurge in Shia political activity. In fact, it was in 1979 that the first Shia political party was formed in the country, in the city of Bhakkar: TNFJ. The party aimed to promote the interests of the Shia community and advance its political agenda. Since then, various Shia political parties have emerged in Pakistan, including the Majlis Wahdat-e-Muslimeen and Shia Ulema Council. These parties have actively sought to represent the Shia community's interests and address their concerns, particularly in the face of increasing sectarian violence.[108] Its militant wing, named Sipah-e-Muhammad, was formed in 1994 in response to the activities of the SSP and Lashkar-e-Jhangvi.[109]

The Deobandi sect, in contrast to others, has gained prominence in Pakistan due to its articulate and politically dominant representation of orthodox Sunnism. The community has established its influence among the urban middle classes through its sophisticated organizational structure, extensive network of *madaris* (seminaries imparting Islamic education) and publishing activities. Despite the Deobandis' puritanical and exclusionary interpretation of Islam, their influence has managed to span across provincial and kinship divides. The JUI serves as their political voice.

The Deobandi leadership has also received support from military dictators, which has assisted the rise of this version of Islamic orthodoxy. Even General Ayub Khan, who claimed to be secular, sought the views of JUI when drafting his proposed constitution of 1962. JUI, in turn, demanded restrictions on Shia mourning processions and looked to confine their activities to Shia mosques. During Ayub's regime, more than one hundred Shias were massacred in the village of Tehri in the Khairpur district of Sindh.

The Deobandi Ulema's institutional link to the Pakistan Army was established during the rule of General Yahya Khan, who used them to counter his political opponents. During the final phase of the East Bengal struggle, the Yahya regime encouraged acts of terror conducted by the vigilante groups of Jamaat-e-Islami, Al-badr and Al-Shams. The Deobandis flourished during Zia's regime, particularly during the Afghan jihad against the Soviet occupation (1980–88). The Deobandi ulema played a significant role in the recruitment of the fighting force, and Zia's Islamization policy afforded them greater space within the corridors of power. The influx of weapons during this period contributed to mounting acts of violence by ethnic militants, sectarian organizations and drug mafias in Karachi.

Haq Nawaz Jhangvi was a Sunni cleric who founded the militant organization SSP in 1985, which later changed its name to Ahle Sunnat Wal Jamaat (ASWJ). He was a former member of the JUI, one of the largest religious parties in Pakistan, but split from the party due to his extremist views and his belief that the Shia community in Pakistan posed a threat to Sunni Islam. Jhangvi's assassination in December 1989 is widely believed to have been carried out by members of the Shia community in retaliation for his role in inciting sectarian violence. His death, however, triggered a wave of sectarian violence in Pakistan, particularly in the province of the Punjab, where the SSP had a strong presence. The SSP and other extremist groups targeted Shia Muslims and their religious gatherings, resulting in numerous attacks, bombings and shootings. The situation escalated to the point where the government declared a state of emergency in several areas of the country, and the military was called in to restore order.

The SSP and its offshoots have been responsible for some of the deadliest sectarian attacks in Pakistan's history, including that on the Hazara community in Quetta in 2013, which resulted in the death of more than one hundred people. The group has been banned by the Pakistani government but continues to operate under different names and remains a potent force in the country's religious and political landscape.[110] Confrontations between militant factions of JUI and TNFJ continue to occur regularly in Pakistan. Though there was a brief period of reduced sectarian violence following the military coup in October 1999, it did not last long. Even after its banning as part of Musharraf's crackdown on terrorism after 9/11, Lashkar-i-Jhangvi (LJ) had been implicated in several serious acts of violence. In April 2006, LJ was involved in the Nishtar Park massacre in Karachi, which claimed the lives of at least fifty individuals, including the senior leaders of Sunni Tehreek, a Barelvi organization.[111]

Even though groups like LJ and SSP are no longer operational, there remains a deep-seated support for radical interpretations of Islam among certain segments of the population. In the Khyber Pakhtunkhwa, anti-Western sentiment continues to increase, and while this form of Islamic radicalism can rally support for jihadist causes, it is also highly sectarian in nature, leading to a potentially explosive situation with regard to episodes of sectarian violence. Adding to the problem is the fact that a large number of weapons remain in circulation, despite government efforts to reduce their availability. The relatively recent phenomenon of suicide bombing is a direct result of the religious extremism that has taken hold in the region, which has proven difficult for state agencies to counter. This trend of terrorism is not limited to Pakistan, as is well known; it has become an international issue, with deep roots in the legacy of Zia's rule.

The Political Identity of Muhajirs

During Zia's regime, Pakistan saw a surge in ethnic tensions with the rise of Muhajir political identity. Muhajirs are Urdu-speaking Muslims who migrated from India during the partition in 1947.[112] According to Mohammad Waseem's analysis, the PPP had a tense relationship with Muhajirs during the Bhutto years, with riots around language issues in 1972 further fuelling their bitterness. Consequently, Zia's martial law was welcomed by Muhajirs, who felt 'delivered' from what they perceived as Sindhi rule. Muhajirs' fears of the PPP's electoral victory in Sindh drove them to support Zia, especially after the MRD began agitating in 1983. As a result, when the Muttahida Qaumi Movement (MQM) emerged in 1984, many speculated about Zia's role in its creation.

While discussing the politicization of ethnicity in Pakistan, it is important to bear in mind that the country's existing provincial boundaries do not correspond to ethnic boundaries. The ethnic groups are widely distributed across provincial boundaries, which creates a mosaic of ethnicities and the potential for both conflict and integration. While most ethnic groups have well-defined territorial domains, the Muhajir group has been concentrated in Karachi and other urban areas of Sindh, which has given them the characteristics of a local majority.

It can be argued that the politicization of ethnicity in Pakistan is largely due to historical and social factors. The ethnic and linguistic groups in Pakistan have distinct histories and cultures, and the process of migration and settlement has contributed to the intermixing of ethnicities. The Muhajir group's alienation from the PPP during the Bhutto years, riots around language issues and the MRD agitation in 1983 tied them to Zia's regime, which led to the emergence of the MQM in 1984.[113]

The root of ethnic alienation in Pakistan can be traced to the unequal distribution of resources and opportunities, resulting in the marginalization of certain groups and the mainstreaming of others. It is important to recognize that not all national groups have had equal opportunities to embark on a shared national journey. The divergent paths taken by different groups can be attributed to disparities in access to resources such as education, skills, development and representation in positions of power within the new state. These unequal distributions have perpetuated a sense of marginalization and exclusion among certain ethnic groups, creating a rift in the national fabric of Pakistan.[114]

The MQM traces its origins back to the University of Karachi, where, on 11 June 1978, Altaf Hussain founded the All-Pakistan Muhajir Student Organization (APMSO) with a small group of like-minded students. The university had several other student groups that were orientated around ethnic identities, such as the Punjabi Student Organizations, the Pakhtun Students Federation, the Baluch Students Organization and the Sindh Students Federation, but none of them provided a space for Muhajirs. Oskar Verkaaik offers a perspective on the rise of Hussain as the leader of the Muhajir students in Karachi. In 1974 a group of students in the pharmacy department of the University of Karachi formed an Intermediate Student Action Committee to demand midterm admission after the semester system was enforced at the university. Among the 27 students who failed to enrol on time was Hussain, then just 21 years old. Under his leadership, the committee successfully secured admission for the students and even forced the vice chancellor to resign. This episode established Hussain's reputation as a charismatic leader and paved the way for the formation of the APMSO, which later evolved into the MQM.[115] (After that initial success, Hussain disappeared. According to the British journalist Owen Bennett-Jones, he went to Chicago and worked as taxi driver for some time.[116])

Hussain was determined to establish a strong power base, and thus founded the MQM, leaving little room for opposition in terms of leadership. The political landscape of urban Sindh was marked by growing tension between ethnicities, and the high unemployment rate further exacerbated the situation. This provided fertile ground for 'the recruitment of young Muhajirs who were disillusioned with the mainstream political parties and eager to join an organization that would advance their interests'.[117] In 1985, a tragic traffic accident in Karachi resulted in the death of Bushra Zaidi, a student of Muhajir descent, and exposed the underlying tension that had been simmering in the city. The driver of the vehicle responsible for the accident was a Pukhtoon (Pashtun), and the transport industry in Karachi was largely controlled by Pukhtoons. This incident triggered a violent outburst, with Muhajirs attacking Pukhtoon transport workers and setting several vehicles on fire. Pukhtoons retaliated, with support from Pashto-speaking Afghan refugees who had sought asylum in Pakistan during the U.S.–Saudi-funded Islamic Mujahideen insurgency against Soviet and Afghan militaries in Soviet-occupied Afghanistan. This volatile situation demonstrated the deep-rooted ethnic tensions that had been brewing in Karachi for years.[118] By the end of the month, ethnic animosity had resulted in more than 53 people dead.[119]

The incident highlighted the ethnic differences that had become the principal determinant of Karachi's politics. On 8 August 1986 Altaf Hussain demonstrated the Muhajir community's political power at Nishtar Park, calling for the recognition of a Muhajir nationality. The size of the crowd, along with the heavily armed bodyguards surrounding Hussain, gave the Muhajirs new-found self-belief and recognition as a political force to be reckoned with. With the popularity of the MQM surging, Jamaat-i-Islami, Jamiat-e-Ulema-i-Pakistan (JUP) and the PPP lost their support base.[120]

The policies and actions undertaken during eleven years of Zia's rule had far-reaching negative consequences for Pakistan's political development, society and culture. One of the most significant changes was the military's increased involvement in the country's system of governance, leading to an overreliance on the Army establishment to hold administrative power. This trend towards military rule was accompanied by Zia's personal campaign of Islamization, which intensified contradictions between various sects and denominations, resulting in the formation of extremist groups such as SSP and TNFJ.

Another regrettable consequence of Zia's rule was the impact of the elevation of the Punjab, as he was the first 'Punjabi' among the autocratic rulers of Pakistan. This significance accorded to the Punjab province created a sense of resentment in smaller provinces. The Eighth Amendment to the Constitution of 1973, which vested the president with discretionary powers to dissolve legislative assemblies, also weakened the democratic process and political institutions.

The authoritarian regime established under Zia's rule promoted harsh reprisals, impunity and wilfulness, which created a culture of conformity, indifference and fanaticism among the population. The prevalence of drugs and 'Kalashnikov culture' – that is, the proliferation among the populace of firearms taken from Soviet caches in occupied Afghanistan, leading to increased violence and crime, and a concomitant reduction in the perception of public safety – in society was another by-product of this longlasting autocratic rule. The regime's public commitment to religious piety was also accompanied by growing materialism among the urban population, but perhaps the most significant ill effects of Zia's policies were violence and the destabilization of Pakistan's political and social order.

10

The Rule of the Troika and the Onset of 'Establishmentarian Democracy', 1988–99

The term 'establishmentarian democracy' was coined by Mohammad Waseem in his book *The Political Conflict in Pakistan*, specifically to describe the unique context of Pakistan. In this context, the term 'establishment' refers to the enduring military–bureaucratic nexus, which consistently influences how political parties define their objectives and methods. In the period covered in this chapter, Pakistan witnessed such an establishment exert control over the country's political destiny, with tacit approval from the United States.

As we delve further into the decade from 1988 to 1999, it becomes evident that, among the three key components of the ruling troika during these years, comprising the president, the commander in chief of the army and the prime minister, the last, who was the people's representative, held the weakest position. Despite carrying a substantial burden of responsibilities, the prime minister possessed limited authority, and thereby characterized the 'establishmentarian democracy' in a nutshell. The establishment maintained a stronghold on the political landscape, skilfully manipulating political parties, engineering election outcomes, shaping media narratives and controlling all facets of the free democratic system.

It is worth noting that the prevailing wisdom regarding countries like Pakistan often revolves around the concept of an illiberal hybrid regime. In this model, the influence and dominance of the establishment in shaping the political arena play a pivotal role, and this chapter will shed further light on this intricate relationship.[1] The death of Zia ul Haq on 17 August 1988 had a lasting impact on Pakistan, leading to the rise of right-wing political groups who united against the liberal left. During his eleven-year rule, Zia transformed Pakistan's political and social landscape, with a gradual shift towards religious discourse that severely limited the manoeuvrability of secular-orientated parties like the PPP in a society increasingly charged with religious fervour. This sacralization of politics had a profound and lasting effect on the country's political climate.[2]

During Zia's rule, the remaining liberal left forces were brutally silenced in favour of a puritanical and exclusionary brand of Islam promoted by its fiery advocates. This resulted in the rejection of centuries-old traditions of religious tolerance and social accommodation as heresy, or *bidah*, with religious faith becoming the sole identity marker. As a result, a sectarian divide was driven deep into Pakistani society, and Sunni–Shia clashes became common. This divisive trend had a tangible impact on Pakistan's electoral politics, with Zia's policies encouraging fundamentalist forces like the SSP, Lashkar-i-Jhangvi and Jaish-i-Muhammad with several other extremist bodies like them to take root, leading to the flouting of the state's writ in Pakistani territory.

In short, Zia's legacy posed an existential threat to the state of Pakistan. His disdain for party politics strengthened the role of ethnicity, kinship and *biraderi* (clan-based politics) to the detriment of cross-regional harmony. Ideology-based politics was replaced with money and opportunism, leading to the monetization of Pakistan's political system. Right-wing parties and groups found a lease of life, with intelligence agencies and the establishment visibly working to undermine the popular base of the PPP.

On 29 May 1988 President Zia dissolved the National Assembly and removed the prime minister under Article 58(2)(b) of the amended constitution. Prime Minister Junejo's decision to sign the Geneva Accord against Zia's wishes, along with his public statements about holding military personnel accountable for the ammunition dump explosion in Rawalpindi earlier that year, were key factors in his removal. Zia, once again, used his discretionary powers to delay elections, ignoring the constitutional requirement to hold them within ninety days of the assembly's dissolution.

However, Zia's ability to manoeuvre was increasingly restricted as Benazir Bhutto's popularity soared following her return from exile in 1986. Zia's death in August 1988 opened the way for the restoration of democracy in Pakistan. The vacuum left by his demise led to a power struggle among various factions, but, ultimately, it paved the way for the end of the military dictatorship and a return to civilian rule.

Benazir Bhutto, one of the figures who represented a return to civilian rule, was a populist leader who was forced to cover her head with a white muslin scarf (*dupatta*) and carry a rosary during her public appearances due to immense social and public pressure. The emergence of a newly affluent middle class, particularly in the Punjab, had led to a deepening of religious fervour over the previous decade, which made it difficult for Bhutto to placate her critics, despite her public demonstrations of being a devout Muslim and Pakistani woman. Bhutto's attempts to project herself as a symbol of secular liberal values were met with scepticism and criticism, as she confronted the cultural legacy of Zia's time in office.

The Members of the Troika

Although democracy was restored to Pakistan, the military retained its political influence, and the civilian governments were often manipulated

Benazir Bhutto, 1989.

by the Army. The power-sharing system that emerged, the troika, consisted of an unelected president, a chief of Army staff (COAS) and an elected prime minister. However, the president and the COAS held more power than the prime minister. The president, with the support of the Army chief, used constitutional provision 58/2B to dismiss both Benazir Bhutto and Nawaz Sharif's elected governments. Sharif, who had emerged as a protégé of Zia, sought to roll back military power, but his efforts ultimately cost him his government.

Ghulam Ishaq Khan, a main player in the troika who had begun his Civil Service career during the British Raj, rose to prominence under Zia as an economic manager and chairman of the Senate from 1985 onwards. He twice used his discretionary power to dismiss elected prime ministers. The only person in the troika with greater influence than Khan was COAS General Mirza Aslam Beg. Power emanated from General Headquarters in Rawalpindi, particularly during Zia's reign, and the pattern continues to this day. The troika initially consisted of Khan, Beg and Prime Minister Benazir Bhutto, but, as we shall see, the dynamics of the group changed over time.

Ghulam Ishaq Khan, a Pashtun belonging to the Bangash tribe, was born on 20 January 1915, in the village of Ismael Khel in Bannu District. After completing his education at Islamia College Peshawar, which was affiliated with the University of the Punjab, he joined the Provincial Civil Service in 1940 as a gazetted officer. He passed a competitive examination held by the Punjab and NWFP Joint Public Service Commission for the Executive Branch.[3]

Ghulam Ishaq Khan at the funeral for Zia ul Haq, 1988.

Initially, he held the esteemed position of assistant commissioner in Nowshera, which was considered a prestigious post during the British Raj era. Following India's partition, he joined the newly formed Civil Service of Pakistan, where his exceptional abilities quickly propelled him to success. Roedad Khan, a colleague of Ishaq Khan, recalls how he impressed senior ICS officers at inter-provincial meetings, catching the attention of the higher-ups. From that point on, his ascent to the top was meteoric, with successive governments, both civil and military, recognizing his remarkable talent.[4] After the partition, he was appointed as the home secretary of the Northwest Frontier Province. In 1956, when the One Unit Scheme was implemented, he moved to Lahore, where he served as the secretary for development and irrigation, a highly valued position in the West Pakistan government. In 1961 he was appointed as the chairman of the newly established WAPDA. Later, he served as the secretary of finance, and in 1970–71, he became the cabinet secretary.

When General Zia seized power in 1977, Ghulam Ishaq Khan was serving as the secretary general of defence. Following his retirement that year,

Zia appointed him as a federal minister, entrusting him with the responsibility of managing the economy during the military regime. In 1985 he was appointed as the chairman of the Senate, possibly at the insistence of his mentor, Zia, in the wake of the non-party elections. After Zia's sudden death, Khan was appointed as the president of Pakistan, a coveted position that gave him a leading role among the troika. He held this position until 17 July 1993, when he resigned due to a stand-off with Nawaz Sharif, the prime minister at the time. He spent his retired life in Peshawar in relative seclusion and passed away on 27 October 2006.[5]

General Mirza Muhammad Aslam Beg, who was promoted to COAS after Zia's death, was born in 1931 in the village of Muslimpatti in Azamgarh in India.[6] His family moved to Pakistan after partition in 1949. Despite having arrhythmia, a heart condition in which the heartbeat skips once after every eight beats, he was commissioned into the Pakistan Army in 1952.[7] Initially, he served in a Baluch infantry regiment, before joining the Special Service Group (SSG) in 1961. He actively participated in the wars with India in 1965 and 1971. After completing his tenure at the National Defence College, he was promoted to the rank of major general in 1978. His career trajectory took a significant turn during the Zia era when he was appointed as the chief of the general staff, a position he held from 1980 to 1985. He was later assigned the crucial role of corps commander in Peshawar, where he oversaw a significant portion of the Afghan–Pakistan border. In 1987, he was elevated to the position of vice chief of Army staff.

As commander-in-chief of the armed forces, a position he held until his retirement on 15 August 1991, Beg played a vital role in facilitating a smooth transition to democracy in 1988. In his book *Faith, Unity, Discipline* the author H. G. Kiessling notes that some officers encouraged General Beg to take over the reins of the government after Zia's sudden death. However, Beg believed that the era of dictatorships was over and that it was time to return to democracy.[8] Kiessling also notes how, by 1987, President Zia's trust in General Beg had waned, leading to his preference for Lieutenant General Zahid Ali Akbar as the vice chief.

While General Beg held a commendable reputation as a proficient military leader, he did not occupy a position within General Zia's inner circle. Instead, his elevation to the role of vice COAS owed much to the influence of former prime minister Mohammad Khan Junejo. This particular appointment represented one of the few independent decisions made by Junejo during his tenure, inadvertently exacerbating the growing schism between him and President Zia.[9]

It is worth noting that critics and adversaries of General Beg later contended that had he sought to seize power in 1988, he would have encountered reluctance from the corps commanders to rally behind him. Nevertheless, after more than a decade under the rule of a military dictator, the generals were unlikely to undergo an abrupt transformation and would have readily embraced another soldier as their commander. Lingering in the wake of the tragic demise of Zia, a sense of apprehension towards a new leader was inevitable, regardless of the prevailing circumstances. But, hypothetically speaking, had Beg attempted to assume power in August 1988, it is plausible that the disciplined Pakistan Army, moulded in the British tradition, would have acquiesced to his leadership with steadfast obedience.

General Beg was undoubtedly the most influential member of the troika. It was widely believed that Ghulam Ishaq Khan could not have dismissed the Bhutto government without General Beg's tacit support. In 1991 he had a disagreement with then prime minister Sharif regarding the first Gulf War. This caused a rift between the prime minister and his former Army backer, and it also triggered intense conflict between the ISI and Civilian Intelligence Bureau, which worked under the prime minister.[10]

Of the ruling troika's three partners, the popularly elected prime minister held the least amount of power and a bagful of responsibilities. Moreover, Benazir Bhutto's acceptance as prime minister was met with scepticism by the other stakeholders in the state apparatus. Hamza Alavi argued that four centres of power emerged on Pakistan's political scene after 1988: the prime minister, the president, the military and the USA. It was the last that came to be the most powerful among them.[11] While it is clear that U.S. ambassador Robert Oakley wielded significant influence within the corridors of power and the United States held primacy during this time, we must keep our focus on the troika as the critical subject of our enquiry here.

Benazir Bhutto's ascent to become the first female prime minister of a Muslim country was an incredible achievement, accomplished against all odds at the young age of 35. She was named 'Benazir', which means 'without a peer', after an aunt who passed away at a young age. Bhutto was proud of her election; she famously declared, 'My election was the tipping point in the debate raging in the Muslim world on the role of women in Islam,' a statement that reflected her commitment to empowering women in her country and beyond.[12] The insightful observations made by the Russian scholar Anna Suvorova in her book *Widows and Daughters* highlight a prevalent misconception regarding the powerlessness of women in Muslim society. In fact, history demonstrates that women have held high-ranking positions in traditional Islamic countries. However, the legitimacy of female leadership has been continuously challenged based on religious and traditional societal norms.[13] Benazir's competitors in politics, such as Fazal ur Rahman and Sami ul Haq, vehemently objected to her right to hold the position of prime minister due to her gender.

Benazir was the eldest child of Zulfiqar Ali Bhutto. She was born on 21 June 1953 in Karachi. She received her education at some of the most prestigious universities in the world, including Radcliffe College at Harvard University and Lady Margaret Hall/St Catherine's College at the University of Oxford. At Oxford, Bhutto studied philosophy, politics and economics as an undergraduate student. She was also elected as the president of the Oxford Union, a highly coveted position at the debating society. Her time at Oxford helped shape her into a strong, articulate and determined individual. She was born into a wealthy family, but Bhutto was committed to improving the lives of the people of Pakistan. She became a prominent figure in Pakistani politics and went on to serve as the prime minister of Pakistan twice, first from 1988 to 1990 and then from 1993 to 1996. Bhutto faced significant challenges throughout her political career, including stints in jail and accusations of corruption. However, she remained committed to her goals and continued to fight for democracy and social justice until her tragic assassination on 27 December 2007.[14]

Initially, Zulfiqar Ali Bhutto had envisioned a path for his daughter within the Foreign Service. He took deliberate steps to expose Benazir to the world of diplomacy by including her in his official journeys, as exemplified during their participation in significant events like the Simla Agreement of 1972 in India. This pivotal agreement was a crucial diplomatic effort between India and Pakistan, aiming to resolve the conflicts between the two arising from the Bangladesh Liberation War. Zulfiqar Ali Bhutto played a prominent role as Pakistan's chief negotiator during this historic event, and his daughter Benazir's presence during this time provided her with first-hand exposure to high-stakes diplomacy. It is noteworthy that Benazir, too, had expressed her own enthusiasm for a career in the Foreign Service, underscoring her alignment with her father's aspirations for her professional future. This exposure to international diplomacy and her father's influence played a pivotal role in shaping her early aspirations and career trajectory.

According to the British author Victoria Schofield in her book *Benazir Bhutto: A Political Biography*, joining the Foreign Service was an ambition that Benazir held dear; however, her eventual path in politics was largely shaped by her father's political career and his untimely death. Benazir Bhutto's initial plans to pursue a career in the Foreign Service were drastically altered by the political upheaval that her family faced. Despite this, Benazir remained a strong advocate for diplomacy and international relations throughout her life.[15]

In numerous public declarations, Benazir openly shared that it was her father's unjust execution that fuelled her entry into the realm of politics. Her determination was unwavering, driven by the profound desire to carry forward the torch of her father's legacy, one dedicated to championing the cause of democracy and social justice. The perilous and demanding landscape of Pakistani politics did not deter her; instead, it steeled her resolve to enact positive change for her nation and its people. Benazir and her mother's tireless efforts to help her father bore testament to their commitment to justice and their unyielding devotion to family. Tragically, despite their relentless endeavours, the military regime ultimately carried out her father's execution, deepening the painful scars of injustice that had spurred her into the world of politics.[16]

Benazir's life took a dramatic turn as she emerged as an ever more prominent figure in the complex realm of Pakistani politics. However, her ascent to political prominence came at a steep price, as she found herself unjustly imprisoned from 1977 to 1984. This prolonged period of incarceration exacted a heavy toll on her physical and mental well-being, testing her endurance and resolve in unimaginable ways. In her critically acclaimed autobiography *Daughter of the East*, Bhutto offers readers an intimate and unflinching glimpse into the harrowing experiences she endured during her long years of detention. In vivid and poignant detail, she recounts the isolation, the uncertainty and the relentless pressure that were her daily companions behind bars. Despite the seemingly insurmountable challenges that confronted her, Benazir remained a resilient force. She refused to be silenced, continuing her tireless fight for the restoration of parliamentary democracy. Her determination and unyielding dedication to democratic ideals serve as a testament to her enduring legacy as both a prominent figure in Pakistan's political landscape and an inspiration, one who can teach others how to face adversity and stand up for what we believe in, no matter the odds.[17]

After spending two years in exile in England, Benazir returned to Pakistan in April 1986 and was welcomed back with great enthusiasm. In July 1987 she married Asif Ali Zardari, who hails from the Nawab Shah district in Sindh and is a scion of the influential Zardari family. Together, Benazir and Asif had three children: Bilawal, Bakhtawar and Asifa. After her second term as prime minister (1993–7), she spent most of her remaining years in exile, primarily residing in Dubai. However, in 2007, she made a dramatic return to Pakistan after reaching a controversial agreement with General Pervez Musharraf, brokered by the United States through former Secretary of State Condoleezza Rice and General Ashfaq Pervaiz Kiani. This return was not without risk, and she narrowly escaped an assassination attempt upon her arrival in Karachi that October. However, Benazir's life was tragically cut short on 27 December that year, when she was killed in a second, this time successful assassination attempt in a bombing during a political rally in Liaquat Bagh, Rawalpindi. Her death left a significant leadership vacuum in Pakistani politics and she was mourned by people both in Pakistan and around the world.

To preserve the political and ideological legacy of Zia ul Haq and thwart the PPP from winning the 1988 elections, various pro-Zia groups came together to form an electoral alliance known as the Islami Jamhuri Ittehad (Islamic Democratic Alliance). This alliance included several prominent parties and groups, such as the PML, Jamaat-i-Islami, the National People's Party (NPP), Jamiat ul Ulema-e-Islam (Darkhawsti group), Jamiat-e-Mashaikh,

Jamiat-e-Ahl-e-Hadith, Nizam-e-Mustafa party, Hizb-e-Jehad and an independent group led by Syed Fakhr Imam. Additionally, the Junejo faction of the PML merged into the main body of the Muslim League, with Fida Muhammad Khan as its president and Mian Muhammad Nawaz Sharif as its secretary general.

In the post-Zia era, the military declared its intent to reduce its overt involvement in politics and supported the idea of holding national elections. However, despite this declaration, the military continued to wield significant influence in shaping the trajectory of electoral contests.[18] The ISI played a pivotal role in orchestrating an electoral alliance aimed at countering the PPP. General Hamid Gul, in particular, took a lead role in its formation, with unwavering support from General Beg. According to Kiessling, the strategy to balance the political landscape revolved around the creation of an electoral alliance comprising conservative and religious parties, aptly named the Islami Jamhoori Ittehad (IJI). Gul, the architect behind this idea, had presciently warned Beg about the potential consequences of a decisive PPP electoral victory, emphasizing the adverse implications it could have on the military's interests.[19] In a 2001 interview with *The Herald*, General Beg stated that he supported Gul's plan because the military would not have permitted Benazir to come to power otherwise. While the PPP won the 1988 election, they did not achieve a sweeping victory, and Benazir assumed the role of prime minister.[20]

Despite some rough patches, the alliance managed to stay together for some time due to the fear of the PPP. However, the pro-Zia elements successfully ousted Muhammad Khan Junejo from a position of political significance. Throughout these events, Zia's legacy remained alive and active, thanks to the establishment's stage-managing of political events.

Zia had previously dissolved the National Assembly and the provincial assemblies on 29 May and declared that the elections would be held on a non-party basis on 16 October 1988. After Zia's death, a schism of ideological perspectives swiftly manifested itself within the conservative faction, as the PML contemplated the restoration of parliamentary governance and Junejo's previously ousted administration under the auspices of General Zia. A looming apprehension prevailed within their ranks regarding the potential ascent of Benazir Bhutto to power through an electoral triumph, compelling them to employ administrative and bureaucratic stratagems to stymie such a political outcome. The newly appointed president, Ghulam Ishaq Khan, found common cause with this disposition, aligning himself with the predominant bureaucratic cohort that had tacitly acquiesced to the condemnation and execution of Zulfiqar Ali Bhutto, steadfastly supported General Zia's regime over an extended period and lucratively benefited from their association.

Benazir Bhutto remained astutely cognizant of this prevailing milieu and, in her pursuit of democratic legitimacy, resorted to legal recourse by petitioning the judiciary for the facilitation of impending elections. On 27 September 1988, the Lahore High Court, in the interest of bolstering democratic principles and political accountability, issued a ruling mandating the conduct of new elections scheduled for the forthcoming November. The full bench of the Lahore High Court declared the prevention of elections as unconstitutional. The court used its discretionary jurisdiction under Article 199 of the Constitution to stall the restoration of the assemblies and facilitate the process of party-based elections. This decision was considered by Mohammad Waseem to be a watershed moment in the political development of Pakistan.[21] Despite this judicial verdict, President Ghulam Ishaq Khan and the influential PML faction surrounding Junejo obstinately refused to concede defeat. Subsequently, they pursued legal recourse by approaching the Supreme Court of Pakistan, well aware of the close affiliations of most of the judges with the establishment.

A discernible trajectory emerged, indicating the inclination of the Supreme Court to potentially overturn the Lahore High Court's decision in favour of the petitioners. In urban centres, the appointment books of esteemed men's tailors were brimming with reservations, indicative of the anticipation among the entrenched political elites as they prepared to reassume positions of authority. Within this constellation of discontented spectators, Beg stood out, cognizant of the establishment's underlying agenda, yet harbouring ambitions of his own on the political stage. Benazir Bhutto later recounted a negotiated agreement between herself and Beg, wherein he pledged to ensure the conduct of equitable elections in November, contingent upon her endorsement of his appointment as the COAS.[22]

On 6 October 1988, Beg strategically leveraged his authority and high-ranking position by summoning the minister for justice, Wasim Sajjad, to an early morning gathering at GHQ (General Headquarters). This convocation was specifically convened for the pivotal announcement of a court ruling. Utilizing Sajjad as his intermediary, Beg expeditiously transmitted a resolute message to the judiciary, vehemently expressing his firm disapproval of any prospective reversal of the Lahore High Court's judgment. He unequivocally conveyed that such an outcome would be deemed intolerable, and it would compel him to disclose private information of great significance. Concurrently, Beg initiated consultations on this matter with the heads of the Air Force and the Navy, culminating in a joint audience with the president.

President Ghulam Ishaq Khan promptly grasped the gravity of the situation, a sentiment shared by the twelve presiding justices of the Supreme Court. Ultimately, the consensus among these stakeholders gravitated towards the decision to conduct elections in November on a partisan basis. However, it is worth noting the conspicuous influence wielded by Benazir Bhutto's political adversaries, as underscored by the timing of the court's ruling. Originally scheduled for 2 p.m., the pronouncement was not delivered until 5 p.m., indicative of the intricate dynamics at play.[23]

The 1988 Elections and Benazir as Prime Minister

The PPP entered the electoral campaign with high expectations for Benazir Bhutto, who was perceived as a confrontational leader of a resistance movement and a crusader for the restoration of democracy. The party anticipated that she would be able to galvanize the support base and secure an electoral victory.[24] Despite these high expectations, Bhutto faced numerous obstacles that made her task daunting. The political theorist Saeed Shafqat accurately observed in 1996 that

> while Benazir has proven herself to be highly skilled at mass mobilization, regime confrontation and political manipulation, she has yet to demonstrate effective managerial abilities or a commitment to progressive ideals during her tenure as prime minister. While she was successful in sustaining the Pakistan Democratic Alliance (PDA) coalition, she needs to establish herself as a consensus-building leader and a capable head of government.[25]

It is also worth noting an interview given by the former foreign secretary Shamshad Ahmad Khan to Canadian-Pakistani Internet personality Haider Mehdi, in which Khan revealed that American officials David L. Armitage (assistant secretary for international security at the Pentagon) and Richard Murphy (assistant secretary of state of the Near East and South Asia) visited Pakistan prior to the elections of 1988 and remained there for more than ten days. During the visit they urged Beg to ensure Bhutto would become prime minister. The decision to appoint her as prime minister had, clearly, already been made prior to the 1988 elections.[26]

> They met Beg, who assured them that he would pose no obstacles to Bhutto forming a government, but his concern was that she might interfere in Army promotions. Murphy and Armitage then met Bhutto and conveyed the results of their meetings to her, including Beg's concern. 'I got it,' said Bhutto, according to Armitage.[27]

In the 1988 elections, the PPP won only 92 out of a total of 207 seats, despite emerging as the largest party in the National Assembly with 38.52 per cent of the total votes cast in its favour.[28] The IJI came in second with 54 seats, the MQM with thirteen seats and the JUI with seven seats. There were also 27 independents who won seats. However, while the PPP emerged as the largest party, it fell short of securing enough seats to independently form a government. This exposed a significant vulnerability: the Pakistani establishment had played a substantial role in influencing the political landscape – to the detriment of the PPP.

As regards the provincial elections, the IJI failed to secure a single seat in Sindh, and both regional and religious parties were unable to win a significant number.[29] In general, the voter turnout for the 1988 elections was quite low, at around 40 per cent, as compared to 63 per cent in 1970, 55 per cent in 1977 and 52 per cent in 1985.[30] The demand for voters to present their identity cards during polling had a notable impact, too, on the election outcome, as approximately 12.8 percent of potential voters were unable to cast their votes. This situation posed a particular challenge for the PPP, as a significant portion of its electoral support came from the underprivileged and poorer members of Pakistan society, the majority of whom didn't have the required documents.

The electoral alliance of the IJI was largely held together by a shared hostility towards the PPP, but, despite this, the alliance had a significant impact on the outcome of the 1988 elections, particularly in the crucial electoral battleground of the Punjab.[31] The province of the Punjab emerged as a key centre of power for the IJI following its success in the provincial polls that accompanied the National Assembly elections. The IJI captured 108 out of 240 seats, with the PPP winning 94 seats and 32 seats secured by independents. The independents, coaxed by the intelligence agencies and establishment patronage, threw their support behind the IJI, giving the alliance a crucial edge in securing a majority in the provincial assembly. The IJI's strength in the Punjab was further reinforced by its by-election successes and the opportunism of the Punjabi landholding elite.[32]

In the Sindh Assembly, the PPP had a comfortable majority – 67 out of 100 seats – with the MQM coming in second place. The IJI could only secure one seat in Sindh. However, the PPP's influence in Bhutto's traditional power base had a lesser impact on the relationship between the federal government and the provinces when compared to the IJI's emergence in the Punjab. In the NWFP Assembly, which had a total of eighty seats, the IJI won 28 seats, while the PPP formed the government in collaboration with the Awani National Party (ANP), securing 32 seats. In Baluchistan, which had a total of forty seats, the PPP only managed to win three seats, while the IJI won eight, Jamiat ul Ulema-e-Islam (Fazl-ur-Rehman) won eight, the Pakistan National Party won two, the Baluchistan National Alliance won six, the Watan Party won one and independents won six.[33]

In his analysis of the PPP's poor performance in the Punjab during the 1988 elections, Waseem identifies the role of the patronage system established during Zia ul Haq's regime. According to Waseem, this system created a large network of individuals who benefited from the Zia's drive for Islamization. This network, in turn, opposed the PPP and portrayed it as an un-Islamic party. Waseem also notes that the support for this opposition came from refugees from East Punjab, especially those from the business community who feared the possibility of labour militancy if the PPP were to win. This opposition contributed significantly to the PPP's loss in the Punjab, which had previously been a stronghold of the party.[34] Consequently, the formation of the IJI, comprising various factions of Muslim Leagues and eight other parties, became possible, with a decisive contribution from Mian Sharif. He had an uncanny knack for striking deals with prospective political partners and a willingness to exert maximum governmental pressure to achieve his political and factional objectives.[35] Zahid Hussain highlights a crucial factor that contributed to the PPP's setback in the provincial assembly elections in the Punjab; according to Hussain and to some observers, apart from other factors, the complacent attitude of the provincial PPP had a hand in the party's defeat. After winning the National Assembly polls, the PPP seemed to take it easy while the IJI, on the other hand, took advantage of the situation and started promoting Punjabi nationalism.[36] The pamphlet *Jag Punjabi Jag, Teri Pag Ko Lag Gia Dagh* (Awaken, O Punjabi, Your Honour Is at Stake) played a significant role in the larger political landscape between 16 and 19 November. It was a strategic move orchestrated by intelligence agencies with the aim of discrediting the PPP. This manoeuvre was rooted in the belief that the PPP posed a threat to the interests of the military, and consequently, the interests of the nation, given the historically intertwined nature of these two entities.

The pamphlet's message was a clear reference to the Sharif-led IJI coalition's poor performance in Sindh during the elections. Notably, all IJI candidates in Sindh had lost, with the MQM and PPP securing all the seats in the province. This departure from centrist forces' previous stance was aimed at fuelling regional and parochial sentiments within the Punjab as part of their broader strategy to undermine the PPP. The campaign proved to be effective, as the IJI managed to regain some of the ground it had lost in the national elections. With the support of a friendly president, as well as the backing of the Army and intelligence chiefs, the IJI successfully seized power in the pivotal province of the Punjab, using it as a launchpad for various anti-PPP activities. This innovative approach was a testament to the ingenuity of the intelligence agencies, highlighting their ability to adapt to complex political scenarios and capitalize on emerging opportunities.[37] The president and the caretaker chief ministers of the four provinces made the PPP's task of contesting the elections even more daunting. Besides, President Ishaq Khan, reluctant to accept Benazir's leading parliamentary position, delayed the process of transition. As a result, both the PPP and the IJI began their efforts to woo smaller parties and independents. However, international and domestic pressure eventually mounted on the president to nominate Benazir as prime minister. According to Abbas Nasir in *The Herald*, 'from the outset, the Army had reluctantly allowed Ms Bhutto to take office and closely monitored every move she made during her 20-month rule.' He also suggests that 'the defence establishment would never have allowed Benazir to come to power if it had not been for pressure exerted by the United States, which controlled the Army's purse strings.'38 The role of the United States in facilitating Benazir Bhutto's ascent to the prime minister's office was significant. Robert Oakley played a pivotal role in mediating the deal between various state actors and brokering an arrangement between the president, the military and Bhutto. According to the *Daily Jang*, the u.s. ambassador helped 'smoot[h] the way' for Bhutto by mediating with the military. This intervention by the United States was part of a larger strategy to ensure stability in the region and maintain its own influence in South Asia.[39]

Benazir Bhutto faced numerous challenges when she took office as prime minister. The authoritarian regime that had ruled for over a decade had left a deep impact on all aspects of national life. In addition to dealing with the aftermath of such prolonged authoritarian rule, her government also had to grapple with a bankrupt economy, an ethnically divided and violence-prone society, pervasive corruption and a tense geopolitical environment.[40] The economy was burdened by crippling debt and military spending, exacerbating the already precarious financial situation. The lack of resources made it difficult to pursue much-needed industrialization, and providing basic welfare for the common people was a daunting task, despite it having been a key campaign slogan for the PPP. Moreover, Benazir was constrained by the amended Constitution, which was designed to perpetuate quasi-military rule. Despite her party's parliamentary majority, she struggled to maintain control over the situation. The IJI had formed the government in the largest province, the Punjab, which drew her into a never-ending confrontation that eventually led to her ousting in 1990. Although Beg claimed that the military had withdrawn from politics, the shadow of the generals remained omnipresent.[41] The military's continued influence on the government was evident from the outset, with Beg assuming the role of a powerful backseat driver. According to the *Financial Times*, 'General Beg's public statements [were] seen as key policy statements in Pakistan.'[42] It was no secret that the military had imposed certain conditions before allowing Benazir to become prime minister. These included retaining Sahibzada Yaqub Ali Khan as foreign minister, continuing the Zia regime's Afghan policy and ensuring that the defence budget remained untouched.

The newly installed government faced numerous problems, compounded by the fact that the Senate was dominated by the IJI, making the legislative process extremely challenging for the PPP. (The Eighth Amendment of the Constitution had given almost equal powers to the Senate as to the National Assembly.) In addition to these challenges, Benazir had also agreed to support Ghulam Ishaq Khan as president and to abide by the agreements signed by the interim government with the IMF.

The Worsening of Relations between Benazir and the Army

Both Benazir Bhutto and Sharif faced opposition from the military, which aimed to safeguard its professional and institutional interests. According to Saeed Shafqat, Benazir's relations with the military deteriorated for four reasons. First, she curtailed the involvement of the ISI in politics, which angered the military. In May 1989 she removed General Hamid Gul, who was instrumental in forming the IJI and shaping the Afghan policy during the Zia era, and posted him as corps commander for Multan. With the change in U.S. policy towards Afghanistan, Gul had become a liability, so Benazir replaced him with a retired lieutenant general, Shams-ur-Rehman Kallu, director general of the ISI. The military saw this as an undue interference in their professional affairs and a violation of Benazir's commitment.

Second, there was a disagreement over the appointment of the Joint Chiefs of Staff Committee (JCSC). The Eighth Amendment vested the power to appoint the JCSC in the president, but Benazir contested this position. The appointment of Admiral Iftikhar Sarohi became highly controversial, since Benazir believed that, while drawing on the executive order and the Army Act, she was authorized to retire the chairman of the JCSC. However, she eventually had to retreat, since these powers were held by the president. This led to suspicion and antagonism from both the president and the military, who believed that Benazir was deviating from her commitment not to interfere in military affairs.

These two points were only part of the bigger issue of the growing rivalry between Benazir and the military.[43] The relationship between the two grew even more strained following the Pakka Qila incident on 27 May 1990. In Pakka Qila, a Muhajir settlement located in Hyderabad, the PPP government had suspected that terrorists were seeking refuge in the area and initiated an armed operation in an attempt to flush them out. Unfortunately, this operation led to the tragic loss of at least thirty lives.

The operation itself was conducted by the police, who, unfortunately, faced resource shortages that hindered their ability to swiftly conclude the mission. Importantly, it is worth noting that there was no concrete evidence supporting the initial suspicion of terrorists held by the police or the provincial government. Following the incident, sources within the police claimed that the individuals responsible for harbouring the suspects had received protection from the ISI.

This gory incident was later seen as an ethnic conflict in which the Sindhi police massacred Muhajirs, and marked the end of the relationship between Beg, who himself was a Muhajir, and the prime minister, both personally and institutionally. It is also no secret that the proceedings, decisions and recommendations of the board were scrupulously guarded by the Pakistan armed forces.[44] In June 1990 Benazir Bhutto attempted to influence the Army's selection board by advocating for an extension of Lieutenant General Alam Jan Mehsud's term as corps commander in Lahore. However, the board did not accede to her request and instead replaced Mehsud with Lieutenant General Ashraf Janjua. This perceived interference from the prime minister proved to be a tipping point for the already strained relationship between the military high command and Bhutto's government.

Operation Midnight Jackal provides a clear example of military interference in the democratic process.[45] In 1990 the Internal Wing of the ISI reportedly hatched a plan to support a vote of no confidence against Benazir Bhutto in parliament, in order to trigger new nationwide elections. Brigadier Imtiaz Ahmad, then the additional director general of the Internal Wing, was allegedly in charge of this covert military intelligence operation, with Major Amir of the FIA serving as his counterintelligence agent.

Tensions between Bhutto and the military high command, especially General Beg, had been simmering since 1989. One major bone of contention was Bhutto's policy on Afghanistan and her decision to remove General Gul from his post.[46] Both President Ghulam Ishaq Khan and General Beg sought to make administrative changes in the civilian government to strengthen their own influence. Despite the programme's covert nature and secrecy, the Intelligence Bureau (IB), under the direction of Masood Khan, was able to track the activities of the Internal Wing and its attempts to force new nationwide elections in 1990. The Internal Wing tapped their telephones and procured videotapes of the conversations between Brigadier Imtiaz Ahmad and Major Amir. These conversations revealed that the two were attempting to financially influence and convince two senior parliamentarians belonging to the PPP.[47]

When the scandal was exposed by the IB through the news media, serious allegations were raised against Beg and President Khan. Despite efforts to authorize a court martial of General Beg, COAS denied his involvement and there was insufficient evidence to proceed. However, the Pakistan Army's JAG Corps did establish court martial hearings for Brigadier Imtiaz, who was ultimately dismissed from his one-star general rank in the Army. During his court hearings, Khan was held responsible for the scandal and testified that the primary objective of the whole exercise was to support Sharif, since the establishment was said to have preferred him as the country's prime minister. The scandal caused significant damage to the reputation of the military and raised concerns about the extent of their involvement in civilian politics.[48] Shuja Nawaz speculates that Operation Midnight Jackal was sponsored by Osama bin Laden, who, as an Islamist puritan, wanted Benazir Bhutto removed from the premiership, primarily because she was a woman.[49]

Centre–Punjab Confrontation

Right after Benazir assumed power, clashes between the federal government and the Punjab government, led by Sharif, undermined the process of democratic consolidation in Pakistan. The military's involvement in this situation can be traced back to the management of the 1988 polls and even earlier, during the Zia era.

Shahid Javed Burki maintains that, during his regime, Zia pursued a policy of restricting the support base of the PPP in the Punjab. He did this by patronizing various religious groups, traders, merchants and business groups, thus consolidating a coalition of interests who were anti-PPP. Burki's argument, however, reflects only one particular perspective on the history and politics of Pakistan and is not universally accepted.[50] Saeed Shafqat's analysis identifies General Zia's three-pronged strategy to control domestic politics, which included providing patronage to political leaders and parties willing to accept military hegemony, institutionalizing and legitimizing the role of Islam as the state religion through political and social processes, and undermining the PPP's support base in the Punjab through coercion and patronage, and by propping up new and alternative leadership.

To gain a deeper understanding of the consequences of General Zia's three-pronged strategy on Pakistani politics, let us delve into specific contexts and details. For instance, we can explore how his patronage system and the establishment of Islam as the state religion contributed to the ascendance of religious parties, amplifying their political influence in Pakistan. Additionally, we can offer concrete instances that illustrate how these policies undermined the PPP in the Punjab, including the utilization of state resources to intimidate and harass PPP supporters and leaders. By examining the multifaceted repercussions of General Zia's policies, we can paint a more comprehensive picture of their impact on Pakistani politics.[51]

Zia's retention of Sharif as chief minister of the Punjab when he dissolved the National Assembly and provincial assemblies in May 1988 proves this point. According to Shafqat, Sharif was seen as a symbol of the new realignment of socio-economic groups that Zia had carefully nurtured and encouraged in the province.[52] Sharif's leadership exemplified a continuation of Zia's policies and contributed to the preservation of the coalition of interests that supported the military's dominance in Pakistani politics.[53] During the 1988 elections, Sharif managed to ward off the PPP from the Punjab province with covert support from the military–bureaucratic nexus. His party secured 108 seats out of 240 in the provincial assembly, while the PPP won 94 seats. Thirty-two independent candidates also made their way into the Punjab Legislative Assembly. As a result, the IJI, with the support of the independents, formed a government in the Punjab. This left Benazir Bhutto to contend with not only a sceptical military but an adversarial party and leadership that, unlike her, was well entrenched in the power structure, despite being new.⁵⁴

Mian Muhammad Nawaz Sharif was born two years after his Kashmiri family migrated from Amritsar to Lahore on the eve of partition. His father, Mian Muhammad Sharif, was a shrewd businessman who sought to pass on his acumen to his sons. Nawaz Sharif attended Government College Lahore, where he was admitted on the basis of his prowess in Kushti, a form of wrestling. After graduating, he joined his family's business. However, his critics, such as Syed Haider Mehdi, contend that Nawaz was a 'failure' in the family. They believe that he was good for nothing except chauffeuring his father's friends, business associates and senior bureaucrats around in their family's Mercedes. At one point, Nawaz even expressed a desire to become an actor, and received lessons from Rangeela, a famous actor and comedian, who later had to admit his inability to train him. Nawaz had a penchant for uniforms and was made an honorary warden in full dress.⁵⁵

However, Sharif is widely regarded as the first industrialist-turned-politician to rise to prominence in Pakistan. It was during the Zia era, with the establishment's backing, that he was able to build a powerful political base for himself in the Punjab, serving as finance minister from 1981 to 1985 before assuming the role of chief minister in 1985. Sharif held this position until he became prime minister in 1990. During the 1980s and '90s, the Sharif family amassed a lot of wealth, with many of their assets acquired through bank loans.

A significant factor in Sharif's rise to power was General Ghulam Gilani Khan, the governor of the Punjab, who took the young politician under his wing and assigned various individuals to groom him for his future career. The Urdu newspapers the *Jang* and *Nawa-i-Waqt* played a key role in bringing Sharif to the forefront of politics, with the journalist Zia Shahid contributing to the cultivation of his image as an alternative leader to Benazir Bhutto.⁵⁶ Under the watchful gaze of the establishment and a group of astute civil servants – including Anwar Zahid, Akram Zaki, Haji Muhammad Akram, Pervez Masud and Saeed Mehdi – Sharif restructured the Muslim League, transforming it into a party that aligned with the interests of the establishment and the Punjabi middle classes. He formed a personalized connection with each of them, considering personal loyalty as paramount.⁵⁷

Sharif served as prime minister on three separate occasions, yet, like Benazir Bhutto, he was unable to complete a full five-year term. In fact, General Asad Durrani, the former head of Pakistan's spy agency, ISI, was critical of Sharif's leadership abilities, as he notes in his book *Pakistan Adrift*. He points out that while Sharif's appointment as prime minister was uncontested, his credentials were questionable. As chief minister of the Punjab, Sharif had generously doled out political patronage, and there were concerns that he would continue this practice in his new role. Moreover, Sharif's commitment to democracy was suspect, given his professed loyalty to General

Zia's mission and his active lobbying to postpone the 1988 elections. Finally, Durrani notes that Sharif had an extremely limited attention span – no more than three minutes, unless the topic was of personal interest – a shortcoming that would have hampered his ability to attend to the affairs of state.[58]

Upon taking office as chief minister of the Punjab in 1988, Sharif's confrontational approach and attitude towards the PPP government at the centre were evident. However, subsequent events revealed that his belligerence was propped up by the establishment's unwavering support. Benazir Bhutto, on the other hand, has been criticized for failing to improve the climate of suspicion and hostility between their parties. Had she taken conciliatory steps, Sharif may still have undermined her as a mere tool of the establishment.

As the Punjab's chief minister, Sharif vocally advocated for provincial autonomy, setting up the Bank of Punjab to further this goal. This move, however, created an environment detrimental to Pakistan's nascent democracy. As centre–Punjab confrontation escalated, Bhutto's image was tarnished, weakening her government's ability to cultivate harmonious relations with the provincial governments. A similar situation unfolded in Sindh with the MQM. The Pakka Qila incident in Hyderabad in May 1990 drove a wedge between the two parties, causing irreparable harm to both Sindh and the PPP.

Amid an atmosphere of mutual hostility among political actors, it was all too easy for the president and the Army to assert that Bhutto's government was incapable of effectively managing Pakistan's affairs. This narrative was propagated through the media, ultimately serving as the justification for the dismissal of her government.

Assessing Asif Ali Zardari's Political Legacy

Despite facing numerous obstacles, Benazir Bhutto also had to contend with the added burden of her husband, Asif Zardari, who chose not to remain anonymous and apolitical like Dennis Thatcher.[59] Zardari's statements in an interview revealed that he had been targeted as a political punching bag; as he claimed, 'I am the soft spot.' However, this was not the whole truth.[60] Zardari's presence on foreign tours and at official briefings was viewed as unnecessary and even superfluous by the military–bureaucratic establishment. Moreover, the public at large looked askance at his conduct, which rapidly earned him a reputation as a swindler who used the office of the prime minister to make shady deals, sell permits and licences and give patronage to his friends. On numerous occasions, and much to her chagrin, Benazir was told that her husband's presence was not welcome, particularly at official briefings, which only served to embarrass her further.[61] The negative public perception of Zardari, who was infamously referred to as 'Mr Ten Percent' because he was often accused of extracting kickbacks from anyone wishing to do business with his wife's government, significantly contributed to the tarnishing of Benazir's image.[62] Zardari's conduct and public reputation not only hastened Benazir's downfall but dealt a severe blow to the PPP's political standing.

In order to better understand the political challenges faced by Benazir, it is worth providing some background information on Asif Ali Zardari. The Zardari tribe trace their origin to Iranian Baluchistan, and they settled in the Nawab Shah district of Sindh several centuries ago. However, they were not considered high-ranking in feudal terms. In fact, a leaked State Department cable quoted by WikiLeaks rather harshly stated that 'post contacts suggest the Zardari tribe has little social standing with the Sindhi elite; there is a story that Sindhi children were told that "Zardari stole if something went missing".'[63] Asif Zardari's father, Hakim Ali Zardari, attempted to integrate into urban life like many others of his generation. He purchased a large house in Karachi and managed the Bambino cinema there. Asif, however, could not attend the prestigious Karachi Grammar School and instead went to Cadet College Petaro in Jamshoro, Sindh. It is rumoured that he sold tickets for his father's cinema and ran a basement disco that frequently stayed open until 4 a.m.[64] Asif Zardari was an extremely ambitious individual, constantly striving to make a splash in any way he could. A telling anecdote from his schooldays perfectly encapsulates this drive: Zardari expressed to his peers his desire to borrow PKR 5,000 to donate to a charity named the Lion's Club, his reasoning being that he would be made the chief guest and garlanded onstage in front of the social elite of Karachi, thus elevating his status. Zardari's thirst for prestige was insatiable. As one of his former schoolmates recalled, 'He was never your friend; he was your boss. You had to address him as such.'[65]

Zardari's teenage years coincided with the transformation of Karachi into a vibrant city in the 1960s. The advent of nightclubs and bars provided an escape from conservative and traditional family life for many young men and women. The easy availability of alcohol and weapons created an intense and risky environment, and Asif Zardari was one of the young men who thrived on it. He was often spotted on his 125-cc motorbike with his trousers hitched up, revealing a dagger strapped to his ankle, and was known to be fiercely protective of his reputation, never tolerating an insult to his honour.[66] Just before meeting Benazir, Zardari had ventured into the construction industry. He appeared to be an ill-suited match for Benazir – a caricature of the archetypal scoundrel who ensnares his lover with a blend of cruelty and charm. However, the Bhutto family's political struggles had shaken their innate sense of social superiority. Nusrat Bhutto, fighting multiple battles on multiple fronts, saw finding a suitable husband for her strong-willed daughter as just one of many challenges. The initial discussions between the families were derailed, but the Zardari family persisted, and in 1987 Nusrat urged Benazir to seriously consider Asif. Seeking advice,

Benazir turned to some of her friends and relatives, including her brother, Murtaza. Benazir's younger sister Sanam shared with Owen Bennett-Jones her brother's dismayed response: 'What the hell is she doing? Stop her! How can she marry Hakim Zardari's son?'[67]

When Benazir's cousin Tariq Islam stepped in as her father figure, he took it upon himself to interview Asif Zardari and posed questions Benazir had instructed him to ask. Three points were particularly important: could he provide for her financially? Would he refrain from meddling in her political affairs? And, most crucially, could he overcome any jealousy towards her interactions with male politicians? Asif, ever the charmer, gave all the right answers.[68] Some of Benazir's friends advised against the match, but she felt she had no other choice. As she explained to the *Los Angeles Times*, 'It wasn't a choice between a love marriage or an arranged marriage, but rather a choice between accepting this proposal or not getting married at all.'[69]

In July 1987 the engagement between Benazir and Asif was held in London, and Benazir marked the occasion by releasing a statement to the press. 'While I remain mindful of my religious obligations and family responsibilities,' she declared,

> I am pleased to accept the marriage proposal that has been approved by my mother, Nusrat Bhutto. Let it be known that my political commitment to Pakistan, its people, and the vision set forth by Shaheed Zulfikar Ali Bhutto for a free, democratic and equal Pakistan remains steadfast and unyielding, and will not be compromised by my impending marriage.[70]

Even as she looked ahead to married life, she was thinking of her father. It didn't sound like love, and many saw it as a union born of pragmatism.

As is often the case with wedding preparations, tensions flared during the planning process. According to reports, Asif's mother had suggested inviting General Zia to the wedding, which was completely unacceptable to the Bhuttos. It threatened to become a dealbreaker, but the Zardaris eventually relented. In *Daughter of the East*, Benazir diplomatically referred to the incident as a case of a 'false interview' that had been reported in the press.[71] The issue of Benazir's name came next, and it proved to be a contentious one for Zardari. He saw it as an opportunity to further the glory of the Zardari family, but Benazir refused to change her name. Despite his initial reluctance, Zardari eventually accepted her decision, though he would revisit the topic in later years.

In Pakistan's upper echelons, weddings are extravagant affairs, typically held at one of the country's many five-star hotels. But Benazir, always the astute politician, envisioned something grander. She hosted the celebration at her residence, 70 Clifton in Karachi, surrounded by friends from around the world. Later, she took the festivities to Lyari, a PPP stronghold in Karachi's slum district, where an estimated 75,000 supporters and well-wishers joined in the revelry. The event was replete with music, fireworks and complimentary food, much to the delight of the jubilant crowd.[72] 'It was amazing,' one party supporter later wrote:

> It was like one huge festive rally. Zia was alive but you could do anything, we drank, we smoked dope, we danced. Nobody could stop us. There was a world between Benazir's foreign guests and her adoring impoverished supporters, but both groups could agree they had never seen anything like it.[73]

(Mis)Management of the Economy

The government led by Benazir Bhutto was unable to formulate a comprehensive policy to tackle the pressing economic challenges. Despite moving away from socialist principles, the PPP appeared uncertain about its direction and lacked clarity in its vision for pursuing privatization. To address this, a high-powered committee headed by Sardar Farooq Ahmad Khan Leghari was established to streamline the privatization process. The committee assigned the Pakistan Industrial Development Corporation (PIDC) the responsibility of rejuvenating industrialization, promoting decentralization and facilitating privatization.[74] The PIDC was allocated a budget of approximately PKR 12 billion over five years to carry out these tasks. As part of its privatization efforts, the government identified five unprofitable public sector units, namely Pak-Iran Textile Mills in Baluchistan, Dir Forest Industries Complex, Shahdadkot Textile Mills in Sindh, Larkana Sugar Mills in Sindh and Harnai Mills in Baluchistan. The cumulative losses incurred by these units amounted to PKR 1.9 billion, while the PIDC's total losses were around PKR 2.5 billion. The government aimed to privatize these units to minimize losses and improve efficiency in the public sector.[75] The PPP government appeared to be committed to creating a favourable environment for the private sector to acquire the sick units. Unfortunately, the absence of a well-defined privatization policy compounded the issues, including unemployment, inflation and stagnation in the industrial sector, which demanded the government's immediate attention. Regrettably, Benazir Bhutto's energies were expended on confrontational politics instead of addressing these challenges.

Despite these difficulties, the PPP government was successful in attracting foreign investment, as noted by Saeed Shafqat.[76] Beginning in 1989, a host of multinational corporations invested in various industries, including oil exploration, textiles and fruit preservation. For instance, Cargill invested U.S.$6.4 million to establish a frozen concentrate juice plant near Sargodha, which was scheduled to commence operations in autumn 1990. Pioneer Seed began the construction of a hybrid seed plant near Lahore, investing $15 million, and the Dawood/Hercules joint venture in fertilizers also invested $325 million in the existing urea fertilizer plant. In oil exploration and drilling, Occidental, Union Texas, AMOCO and Caltex also either made fresh investments or expanded their existing operations.

Despite some minor progress, the Bhutto government failed to meet the expectations of the people during its twenty-month tenure, but this was partly due to the unrealistic expectations that had been placed upon it, given the economic and institutional limitations that impeded the restoration of democracy.[77] On 6 August 1990 the relationship between the PPP government and the establishment came to an end. President Ishaq Khan delivered the final blow at the Aiwan-e-Sadr (the presidential palace, in Islamabad) at 5 p.m., signalling the end of the political honeymoon. It was evident that the establishment had finally decided to retaliate against the PPP.[78] Shortly thereafter, Ghulam Mustafa Jatoi, the leader of the opposition, was sworn in as the designated caretaker prime minister, thus fulfilling his long-standing ambition. Alongside him, four ministers – Ghulam Mustafa Khar, Rafi Raza, Sartaj Aziz and Illahi Bux Soomro – were simultaneously sworn in. In Sindh, Governor Fakhruddin G. Ebrahim refused to dissolve the provincial assembly and was consequently replaced by Mahmoud A. Haroon, who proceeded to sign the dissolution order. Jam Sadiq Ali, who was referred to as 'the grubbiest man alive',[79] was appointed as the chief minister of the province; Amir Gulistan Janjua ousted Aftab Ahmad Khan Sherpao's government and legislature of NWFP; and Mir Afzal Khan, an industrial tycoon and former Z. A. Bhutto government minister, was appointed as the caretaker chief minister of the province. In Baluchistan, Mir Humayun Khan Marri, the son-in-law of Nawab Akbar Khan Bugti – an important Baluchistan politician who served terms as the region's chief minister and governor – became the new chief minister after the latter advised the retired governor general, Musa Khan, to dissolve the Baluchistan Assembly. In the Punjab, 'a more dignified and perhaps cosmetic exit' was arranged.[80] Rather than being dismissed, Sharif was granted time to advise Governor Mian Muhammad Azhar on the dissolution of the Punjab Assembly. Ghulam Haider Wyne, a close associate of Sharif, was appointed chief minister of the Punjab. This arrangement demonstrated the establishment's determination to prevent the PPP from returning to power. All members of the caretaker government were from the anti-PPP faction. The interim government's policies were antagonistic towards Benazir and the PPP, which significantly undermined its non-partisan ideals.[81]

The 1990 Elections

The Pakistani political landscape was tense leading up to the October 1990 elections, and expectations for the PPP to win between 75 and 110 National Assembly seats were high. However, the results were shocking, even exceeding the IJI's own optimistic projections. Historically, the PPP had performed well in economically advanced and medium- to high-prosperity districts of the Punjab, as well as in districts with large cities, except for Rawalpindi and Sialkot. Nevertheless, the 1990 elections saw a complete upheaval of the party's previous strongholds, and the PPP was essentially wiped out.

This charged political atmosphere was partly due to President Ghulam Ishaq Khan's 6 August order, which dissolved the National Assembly and dismissed Benazir Bhutto's government – the second such dismissal in less than three years. The ensuing caretaker government, made up of leaders from the IJI opposition, set new elections for 24 October, within the three-month period mandated by the Constitution. However, the legality of the president's actions and his motivations were heavily debated, leading to doubts over the transparency of the upcoming elections.

The appointment of Jatoi, the leader of the Combined Opposition Parties (COP), as caretaker prime minister only added to the controversy. There were concerns that Jatoi was too aligned with the military–bureaucratic oligarchy, and that his selection was heavily influenced by a desire to prevent Benazir's comeback. General Asad Durrani's comment that Jatoi's appointment only came after assurances of his commitment to preventing Benazir's return seems to lend credence to these fears.[82]

Jatoi was a prominent politician hailing from an established political family in the Nawab Shah district of Sindh. He was the eldest of four brothers, and his grandfather, Khan Bahadur Imam Bux Khan Jatoi, had been a member of the Bombay Legislative Assembly in the 1920s and '30s – a time when only a handful of members represented the entire province of Sindh. Jatoi was educated at Karachi Grammar School and passed his Senior Cambridge exam. In 1952 he went to England to study law but had to return home within a year due to his father's terminal illness.

Jatoi started his political career as the youngest-ever chairman of the district board of Nawab Shah in 1952. He was elected to the first provincial assembly of West Pakistan in 1958 and again in 1965. He joined the PPP in 1969 and was elected to the National Assembly in 1970. He served as a federal minister in Z. A. Bhutto's government, holding several portfolios such as Political Affairs, Ports and Shipping, Communications, Natural Resources, Railways and Telecommunications. In 1973 he was elected chief minister of Sindh and held the office until 1977, becoming the longest-serving chief minister there since Pakistan's creation.

After the imposition of martial law, Jatoi remained associated with the MRD and was arrested twice, first in 1983 and then again in 1985. He later founded his political organization, the NPP, and contested the 1988 elections but lost. Jatoi subsequently became a member of parliament for Muzaffargarh, courtesy of Ghulam Mustafa Khar, and was elected the leader of the COP in the National Assembly in 1989.

When Jatoi became the prime minister of Pakistan, he was unable to establish himself as a formidable replacement for Benazir Bhutto. His party also failed to make significant inroads into the PPP's voter bank, specifically in Sindh, in the way that the establishment had hoped. After the elections, Jatoi was removed from office, and Sharif became the prime minister. The NPP contested the 1993 elections and later joined the Benazir Bhutto government as a coalition partner, until the government's dismissal in 1996 by the PPP's own president, Farooq Leghari. In the 2002 general elections, Jatoi's party was the dominant partner in a new group called the National Alliance, which he chaired.

The elections of 1990 were marred by the caretaker government's sullied image, thanks to their attitudes towards the PPP and the manifestly selective accountability process, with investigations into corruption in the Bhutto administration. The campaign's heat ensured that the issues of ethnicity and centre–province relations were not treated constructively. Syeda Abida Hussain, the federal minister for information and broadcasting and future Washington ambassador, picked up on the theme of 'Punjabiat' and played on anti-Sindhi sentiments in a series of speeches. Addressing a large public rally at Haq Bahu Colony in Jhang on 18 October, for example, she declared that the Punjab had been deprived of its share in the Indus River by Z. A. Bhutto, and that his daughter had made Punjabi settlers in Sindh 'flee their hearths and homes'. She expressed that 'those who seek votes from the Punjab but work against its interests lose their eligibility for election in the region.' Even though the election campaign was focused on improving Pakistan's political authority and global image, no fresh ideas or strategies materialized to strengthen the country's democracy or make it less susceptible to narrow, self-serving interests.[83]

In the October 1990 general elections, the IJI emerged victorious with 105 seats in the National Assembly. In contrast, the PDA (People's Democratic Alliance), which also included the PPP as its dominant partner, secured only 45 seats. The MQM (Haq Prast) and the ANP – led by Wali Khan, who lost his own seat in the election – won fifteen and six seats, respectively. The remaining seats were divided among several parties, with three going to JUP (Noorani), two each to the Jamhoori Watan Party and Pakistan National Party and one to the Pakhtunkhwa Milli Party.

The election results were a setback for several prominent party leaders, including Wali Khan, former speaker Malik Meraj Khalid, veteran leader Nawabzada Nasrullah Khan, Maulana Fazalur Reman, minister for information and broadcasting Syeda Abida Hussain, former NWFP chief minister Aftab Ahmad Khan Sherpao, Mumtaz Bhutto and Abdul Hafeez Pirzada, who all lost their respective elections.[84]

Elections serve as a crucial indicator of the state of democratization in a country. The elections discussed here sparked a controversy that raised important questions about the relationship between elections, democratization and the resilience of democratic processes in Pakistan. The role of election observers in reporting on the process was also scrutinized. However, elections are just one aspect of the democratization process, and other factors, such as the weakness or corruption of civilian institutions, as well as socio-political and institutional characteristics, such as the nature of the military's political involvement, also significantly impacted the integrity of the democratic process and the nation's adherence to democratic values.

The fairness of the 1990 elections was strongly contested by many analysts, and allegations of rigging resonated in pro-PPP circles. The election results clearly demonstrated that the Punjab was no longer a stronghold of the PPP. The PDA, of which the PPP was the mainstay, could only secure a meagre 44 seats in the National Assembly, while the IJI, with 106 seats out of a total of 207 seats, emerged as the dominant force in the elections.[85]

The doubts surrounding the fairness of the 1990 election were indeed found to be justified. Almost six years afterwards, on 11 June 1996, during Benazir's second term in office, the retired major general Nasirullah Khan Babar, who was then serving as the minister for interior, made a speech on the floor of the National Assembly that contained contents that were highly disconcerting. In it, he presented an affidavit that had been sworn by the former director general of the ISI, retired lieutenant general Asad Durrani, on 24 July 1994. The affidavit – written while Durrani was serving as the ambassador of Pakistan in Germany – asserted that various sums of money had been disbursed to politicians and political parties forming part of the IJI to enable them to win the election. Durrani stated that, in September 1990, while he was serving as director general of the ISI, he had received instructions from General Beg, who was then the COAS, 'to provide logistical support for the disbursement of donations made by some businessmen of Karachi to the election campaign of IJI'. He was also informed that the operation had the blessings of the government, specifically President Ghulam Ishaq Khan, and proceeded to act in accordance with the instructions he had received.

Durrani delegated a group of officers to perform various tasks, which included opening cover accounts in Karachi, Quetta and Rawalpindi. Yunus Habib, the chief of Mehran Bank Limited, deposited a sum of PKR 140 million into several accounts in Karachi, and then the necessary amounts were transferred to the accounts in Quetta and Rawalpindi. The COAS or the election cell in the presidency directed the distribution of a total of PKR 6 million, while the remaining money was transferred to a special fund.[86] The table opposite shows the details and names of the recipients of money given by Durrani in his affidavit.[87]

Despite the gravity of the revelations, the case remained unresolved for nearly two decades until the Supreme Court delivered a groundbreaking judgement in 2012. This verdict had the potential to reshape the political and institutional terrain in favour of democratic ideals.[88] Yet nothing has been done to impeach those who administered the slush fund, or its recipients. The matter has been quite conveniently shoved under the carpet.

Province	Candidates and supporters	Funding (millions)
NWFP	Mir Afzal	10.0
PUNJAB	Sharif	3.5
	Lt Gen. (R) Rafaqat (for media)	5.6
	J.I.	5.0
	Abida Hussain	1.0
	Altaf Hussain Qureshi and Mustafa Sadiq	0.5
	Misc. and smaller groups	3.339
SINDH	Jatoi	5.0
	Jam Sadiq	5.0
	Junejo	2.5
	Pir Pagara	2.0
	Maulana Salah Ud-Din	0.3
	Misc. and smaller groups	5.4
BALUCHISTAN	Humayun Mari (Akbar Bugti's son-in-law)	1.5
	Jamali	4.0
	Kakar	1.0
	K Baluch	0.5
	Jam Yousaf	0.75
	Ghous Bux Bizenjo	0.50
	Nadeem Mengal	1.00
	Through Golf course	0.5
	Misc. (Bank charges, expenses, etc.)	1.1117

Sharif in Power, 1990–93

Despite the establishment's initial goodwill towards him, Sharif faced a range of grave issues upon assuming office as prime minister. The perpetuation of confrontational politics was just one aspect of the situation. Additionally, a crisis was unfolding in Sindh, where his allies managed to secure a razor-thin majority, leading to Muzaffar Ali Shah's appointment as the chief minister. He faced an ongoing battle to maintain his hold on power, and Karachi emerged as a focal point of escalating violence. The struggling economy and rampant corruption were draining the national exchequer, putting a strain on the state apparatus. Economic planning and policy formulation were dictated by the IMF and the World Bank, particularly after the drying up of U.S. aid and a sharp decline in Gulf remittances. Adding to the fiscal challenges was the suspension of $564 million of American aid after President Bush refused to certify that Pakistan did not have nuclear weapons, which resulted in the invocation of the Pressler Amendment by the U.S. Congress on 1 October 1990.[89] Consequently, the suspension of American aid in 1990–91 led to the termination of all civilian and military projects. The impact was significant, as military supplies were also affected, resulting in the cancellation of the delivery of F-16s that Pakistan had already begun paying for. Moreover, the break in relations between the two militaries lasted for over a decade, exacerbating the already strained ties between the United States and Pakistan.[90]

Sharif embarked on a policy of economic liberalization with greater zeal than the PPP had shown. In February 1991 he abolished control over foreign currency entering Pakistan and implemented various measures to promote foreign investment in the country.[91] By October, 89 state enterprises had been put up for sale.[92] The government was also faced with the necessary prospect of raising oil prices by more than 40 per cent almost immediately after Sharif assumed power.[93] The Gulf crisis of the early 1990s, sparked by Saddam Hussein's invasion of Kuwait, had profound and far-reaching consequences for Pakistan, a nation heavily reliant on the Gulf states for its economic stability. The political and economic ramifications of this crisis not only put pressure on the Pakistan government but triggered a chain of events that would profoundly impact its economy.

In addition to these issues, the coalition partners of the PML, ANP, JI, MQM and JUP were too disparate to maintain a cohesive relationship for long. Despite this, Ian Talbot considers Sharif to have been more successful than his predecessor in pushing forward legislation and forging good relationships with various groups and factions representing different units within the federation. During his tenure, the Council for Common Interest was convened, and financial assets were divided among the provinces. Furthermore, significant progress was made in March 1991 in resolving the dispute over the Indus waters. Despite these accomplishments, the Sharif government faced significant challenges.[94] The relationships of the centre and the provinces were quite harmonious, which acted as a stabilizing factor at the crucial time of the Gulf War.

Sharif's government gained considerable popularity through measures such as fixing a monthly minimum wage of PKR 1,500 for unskilled workers in July 1992. In addition, in February 1991, Sharif announced the distribution of 1.5 million hectares (3.75 million ac) of land in the Sukkur and Ghulam Muhammad Barrage areas of Sindh to landless *haris*, with each receiving 6 hectares (15 ac). These policies aimed to address the long-standing issues of poverty and landlessness faced by many in the country. They were well received by the public and helped to strengthen Sharif's political standing.[95] The 'Yellow Cab' scheme, which was announced in April 1992, was one of the most controversial measures implemented by the government. Under this scheme, the unemployed were promised a loan of up to PKR 300,000 to purchase a yellow cab. According to Waseem, around 40,000 households benefited from the loans, which were sanctioned for the purchase of 95,000 taxis, buses and coaches. Despite its controversial nature, the scheme did provide some relief for the unemployed and contributed to the government's popularity among certain segments of the population.[96]

During the first term of Sharif's administration, the private sector experienced significant growth. The government established a private airline, and a privatization commission led by General Saeed Qadir was set up to sell unprofitable units in the public sector to private entrepreneurs. Consequently, the Muslim Commercial Bank was sold to the Chinioti-Punjabi Mansha-Saphire group.[97] There was a lot of criticism surrounding the transparency of the economic measures taken by Sharif's government. The collapse of the cooperative societies, in which depositors lost PKR 20 billion, also caused a similar uproar. The majority of these societies were owned by provincial assembly members of the ruling IJI and had incurred significant bad debts, including the National Industrial Credit and Finance Corporation (NICFC) and the Services Co-operative Credit Corporation. These scams significantly damaged the credibility of the Nawaz government and provided an opportunity for the opposition to undermine their position. Benazir even sent a telegram to President Ghulam Ishaq Khan, urging him to dismiss Sharif from his post.[98] In November 1992 Benazir Bhutto orchestrated a long march on Islamabad and followed it up with a train march, aiming to unravel the Sharif-led IJI government.

This turn of events was indeed strange, given that Benazir was cosying up to the same president who represented the establishment that had earlier dismissed her own government. This incident highlights a peculiar mentality that characterizes Pakistani political culture, one that is inimical to democratic consolidation. Political rivalries often overshadow other considerations, and politicians are known to court the establishment to gain an advantage over their rivals. This widespread streak of political intolerance towards the opposition poses a significant challenge to the consolidation of democracy in Pakistan.[99] The minister of religious affairs labelled Benazir Bhutto *kafir*, while Jam Sadiq Ali went as far as calling her a terrorist.[100] During the period of civilian rule, governments would not hesitate to harass and target their opponents, just as any military ruler before them. This 'politics of malice' reached a disturbing climax on 27 November 1991, when 'five masked men broke into the Karachi residence of Veena Hayat, a close friend of Benazir Bhutto and daughter of the veteran Muslim League leader Sardar Shaukat Hayat'. Hayat accused Irfan Ullah Marwat, the son-in-law of President Ghulam Ishaq Khan and advisor on Home Affairs to the

Sindh chief minister Jam Sadiq Ali, of sending the men to attack and rape her. The severity of this crime reflects the deeply disturbing trend of political intolerance and victimization that has plagued Pakistan's democracy.[101] The case of Veena Hayat became a rallying point for various political parties and groups to come together, but the representatives of the establishment, including the president, didn't change their tactics.

Jam Sadiq Ali's reign of terror against PPP workers, carried out with the tacit approval of Ghulam Ishaq Khan, resulted in the unjust incrimination of numerous PPP members and activists. This strategy, although partially effective in suppressing political opposition, failed to quell the prevailing lawlessness that continued to plague the rural areas of Sindh. In this atmosphere, dacoit gangs operated with impunity, further exacerbating the state of lawlessness and insecurity.

This dire situation posed a significant threat not only to Pakistani citizens but to foreigners within the region. This became starkly evident when Japanese students and Chinese engineers fell victim to kidnappings in the early months of 1991. These incidents underscored the dangerous environment prevailing in the region and the urgent need for concerted efforts to restore law and order in Sindh.

The division within the MQM in Karachi led to an unprecedented wave of violence, with the party splitting into two factions – the MQM Haqiqi (Genuine) led by Aamir Khan, Afaq Ahmed and Bader Iqbal and the main faction of the MQM led by Altaf Hussain. These were trying times for the MQM. The situation took a turn for the worse following the passing of Jam Sadiq Ali on 4 March 1992, and the subsequent appointment of Asif Nawaz Janjua as the COAS, replacing Beg. It was during this period that the military initiated a significant crackdown known as Operation Clean-Up (also known as Operation Blue Fox), which commenced in May 1992, launched by the Sindh Police and Pakistan Rangers, with additional support from Pakistan Army and intelligence agencies, under a directive by Prime Minister Sharif. However, it is important to delve deeper into the events that led to this operation, particularly the Tando Bahawal incident, which took place on 5 June 1992, when a contingent of the Pakistan Army, led by Major Arshad Jamil, raided Tando Bahawal, a village on the outskirts of Hyderabad, and kidnapped nine villagers, who were taken to the bank of the Indus River near Jamshoro and gunned down.

Major Arshad Jamil had been deputed in Sindh as a part of Operation Clean-Up. The major and his *jawans* alleged that the villagers were terrorists who had links to the Indian Army and its intelligence agency – the Research and Analysis Wing (RAW). They also claimed that they had recovered a large quantity of sophisticated weapons from them.[102] The operation was started ostensibly to target terrorism, but it subsequently evolved into a witch hunt against the MQM. Leader Altaf Hussain went into exile, forcing the party, a Karachi political force since 1984, underground. In 1994 the

MQM's militant wing resisted violently. In May 1995 they launched a bloody campaign, ambushing police and attacking government offices with rocket launchers. Karachi descended into chaos as MQM and paramilitary forces clashed in the streets.

The intensity of the 1995 conflict set it apart from previous ethnic violence, drawing comparisons to Kashmir. The death toll surged to over six hundred in June and July, with months of bloodshed still ahead. Sensationalistic tabloids emerged, featuring gruesome scenes. The state adopted collective punishment, arresting over 75,000 men, often innocent friends or relatives of MQM members, who were detained, tortured and held for ransom.[103] Extra-judicial killings became commonplace. The city endured terror and economic losses, exacerbated by MQM-organized strikes, costing PKR 1 billion daily.[104]

Operation Clean-Up had a corrosive effect on Sharif's regime. He was uneasy about the operation, which strained his relations with the president and the COAS. He was also under pressure from the Gulf War and the controversial Shariat Bill, which aimed to comprehensively implement Islamic Sharia law across the country. The bill had sparked intense debates; supporters saw it as an Islamization step for justice, while opponents, including political parties and rights activists, feared it could lead to discrimination, and to the erosion of minority rights and personal freedoms. The bill was ultimately withdrawn due to widespread controversy. Sharif's problems were compounded by the economic crisis and the unravelling of the IJI coalition, which deepened the rift among the troika members. Sharif's efforts to extend the powers of the prime minister marked dissensions between him and the president and his differences grew with the Army as well.

Independent policies on Kashmir and Afghanistan further strained Sharif's relationship with the Army, since foreign policy had traditionally been the sole preserve of the latter, which didn't encourage any tangible input from the civilian leadership. However, Sharif wanted to resolve these issues by cultivating cordial relations with Pakistan's neighbours.

The selection of General Waheed Kakar as the new COAS after Asif Janjua's untimely demise in early February 1993 brought further acrimony to the relationship. Janjua had died of a heart attack while exercising on his treadmill one morning.[105] The tension between Sharif and the president had been escalating, but it reached a breaking point owing to a couple of reasons. First, Sharif voiced his intention to review the Eighth Amendment, which was seen as a direct challenge to the president's powers. Second, Sharif remained silent on the issue of Ghulam Ishaq Khan's re-election, which had been a point of contention for some time.

Sharif's exit from power was hastened by his bold televised address to the nation on 17 August 1993, in which he accused the president of conspiring against him. This speech featured his famous statement 'I will not take any dictation,' which quickly gained acclaim and helped to solidify respect for him among the populace.¹⁰⁶ Sharif evolved from a timid businessman to a courageous politician. But the wily Ghulam Ishaq Khan seized the opportunity to dismiss his government. In its place, Balkh Sher Khan Mazari was appointed as caretaker prime minister, with a sprawling cabinet mostly comprising PPP stalwarts, such as Asif Zardari, Aitzaz Ehsan and Jahangir Badar, who found their way into the corridors of power through its back doors. The sheer size of the cabinet was so massive that it was compared to the bustling Qissa Khawani Bazar at its peak. The ministers were remembered as wheeler-dealers, drug and arms smugglers and an assortment of sycophants, agents and 'saints and sinners'. To top it off, an acting prime minister was appointed, who was 'every inch an elegant hairdresser', according to Mohammad Waseem.¹⁰⁷

The Rescue of Sharif by the Judiciary

On 19 April, following the dismissal of his government and the dissolution of the legislatures, Sharif filed a petition against the actions taken by the establishment. Remarkably, 21 days later, the Supreme Court, led by Chief Justice Nasim Hassan Shah, ruled against the establishment in a landmark decision. The Supreme Court's 10–1 verdict declared that the dissolution of the government was 'not within the ambit of powers conferred' on the president by the Constitution, thus historically reversing the trend of courts siding with executive authority.¹⁰⁸

The Supreme Court's verdict in favour of Sharif's petition against the dissolution of his government had a stunning effect on both physical and ideological custodians of Pakistan's frontiers. However, despite the favourable decision, Sharif's ordeal was far from over. His former political allies, such as Mian Manzoor Ahmed Watoo and Chaudhary Altaf Hussain, had now become his inveterate foes who were granted the patronage of the president. In cahoots, they prevented Sharif from capitalizing on the court's verdict and solidifying his position in the Punjab, his political stronghold. This political crisis gave way to a constitutional crisis, which eventually required intervention from the most powerful member of the troika, the COAS. General Waheed Kakar brokered a deal that led to the resignation of both Ghulam Ishaq Khan and Sharif, paving the way for World Bank-/IMF-sponsored 'financial wizard' Moin Qureshi to take over as interim prime minister. Importantly, Qureshi's appointment came through a compromise formula brokered by General Waheed Kakar, in which the head of the caretaker set-up was to be selected through mutual agreement between the president, the prime minister and the leader of the opposition: after failing to agree on some proposed names, Sartaj Aziz, from Sharif's camp, proposed Qureshi, who was eventually approved by the president and Benazir Bhutto. Therefore, Qureshi came to power with the volition of the country's political leaders.¹⁰⁹ Waseem Sajjad, an ideologue of extreme opportunistic right-wing politics and favoured by the establishment, was appointed as president.

Qureshi was a prominent figure in the field of international finance and economics. Born in 1930, he held permanent residency in the United States and had founded his own company, the Emerging Markets Corporation. Prior to becoming prime minister of Pakistan, he had a distinguished career at several international organizations, including the World Bank, the International Finance Corporation and the IMF. At the World Bank, he held various positions, including senior vice president for finance and chief financial officer, and later senior vice president for operations. He then joined the International Finance Corporation as vice president and second in command, and later served as executive vice president and chief operating officer.

Considering his background, it was hardly unexpected that Qureshi, during his caretaker tenure, emphasized economic reform over electioneering. The primary objective of the interim administration was to execute the economic policies outlined in the structural-adjustment programme, a customary solution recommended by the World Bank and the IMF for floundering Third World economies. The economic reforms devised for Pakistan were ostensibly aimed at 'restoring Pakistan's credibility with Western lending agencies' in order to obtain additional financial flows from the IMF and the World Bank.[110] The economic programme included granting operational autonomy to the State Bank of Pakistan, introducing an agricultural income tax, devaluing the rupee by 6 per cent and withdrawing subsidies on items such as flour, ghee and fertilizers to control the budgetary deficit. However, these policies resulted in a rise in prices of essential items, which was highly unpopular.

The caretaker government shed light on the rampant corruption within Pakistan's elite, a fact that was not surprising but nonetheless shocking. It released a list of over 5,000 bank loan defaulters and beneficiaries of loan write-offs, including well-established industrial and political figures. The total amount of loan defaults and write-offs reached PKR 62 billion, causing a significant loss to economic development and acting as a major disincentive to creating a business-friendly environment that could attract foreign investment.

The 1993 National Elections

On 26 July 1993 the Ministry of Justice and Parliamentary Affairs (Parliamentary Affairs Division) issued Notification No.F.12(10)/93-P.A, appointing Justice Sheikh Riaz Ahmed, a judge of the Lahore High Court, and Justice Muhammad Bashir Ahmed Khan Jahengiri, a judge of the Peshawar High Court, as members of the Election Commission for the upcoming general elections.[111]

The 1993 elections were unique due to an amendment made in the Representation of the People Act 1976, which had been the basic law for conducting elections since 1977 and provided the statutory basis for the 1993 elections as well. Previously, the nomination form issued to candidates contained a declaration stating that they were not subject to any disqualification under Section 12 of the Act. However, on 19 August 1992 a new subsection was inserted in the Representation of the People (Amendment) Ordinance 1993 (Ordinance no. XVI of 1993), which required candidates to make additional declarations regarding loans obtained by themselves, their spouses or dependents from banks, financial institutions, cooperative societies or corporate bodies. Candidates were also required to disclose information regarding any defaults on loans of PKR 1 million or more. This was a new concept, introduced for the first time in Pakistan's electoral history.[112]

The PPP emerged as the single largest party with 86 seats, while the Pakistan Muslim League (Nawaz) (PML-N) secured 73 seats. Despite regional voting variations in the Punjab, Sharif's increasing influence was once again confirmed. In the central districts of the Punjab province, the PPP faced a dire situation as it failed to win even a single seat in major cities such as Lahore, Faisalabad, Rawalpindi, Multan, Gujranwala, Sialkot and Sargodha.[113] One possible explanation for this poor showing is the PPP's lack of organization in these localities. Additionally, as Mohammad Waseem argues, the PML-N's Yellow Cab scheme and the highly publicized Lahore–Islamabad motorway project greatly increased their vote bank.[114] In the National Assembly elections, the Pakistan Muslim League (J) managed to win six seats to the detriment of the Nawaz league. The PPP successfully kept Sharif out of power in the Punjab by forming a coalition with the PML-J and appointing Manzoor Wattoo as the chief minister.

However, the turnout of voters in the elections remained disappointingly low, with only 40.54 per cent of voters participating. This turnout demonstrated apathy among citizens, who had grown weary of corrupt, inefficient and indifferent governments. Two factors played a crucial role in tipping the balance in favour of the PPP. The first factor was the PIF (Pakistan Islamic Front), which secured only three seats in the National Assembly but was instrumental in defeating the PML-N in at least fourteen constituencies where the contest between the PPP and the PML-N was close. The PIF took away enough votes from the PML-N to ensure the PPP's victory with very narrow margins in these constituencies.

The second factor was MQM's boycott of the elections. In Karachi, thirteen seats were divided between the PML-N and the PPP, with each party securing six seats and one going to the PIF. However, had the MQM participated in the elections, all thirteen seats would have gone to it. The MQM paid a heavy price for this political lapse. Some speculate that the MQM was forced by the armed forces not to participate in the elections to the National Assembly, but this explanation is purely speculative.

Benazir Yet Again

After the elections, Benazir Bhutto returned to power at the centre. Unlike the situation in her first administration, she did not have to face a strong opposition party based on control in the Punjab. However, Sharif still retained popularity in the central urban areas of the province. In Baluchistan, the Jamhoori Watan Party of Akbar Bugti, who had formed the JWP in August 1990 following the dissolution of the Baluchistan Assembly, and the Pakistan Muslim League (Nawaz) were successful, but only in the Baluch and Pakhtoon belts, respectively. Aftab Sherpao, with unequivocal support from the centre, successfully upstaged the Sabir Shah-led Muslim League Ministry in NWFP, using all the nefarious tactics in the lexicon of politics, including bringing in a no-confidence motion with the help of independent candidates. Despite the PPP's majority in the Sindh Assembly, with Abdullah Shah as the chief minister, Karachi remained an anathema for the PPP with the MQM in the opposition camp, and it kept burning during the three years of Benazir Bhutto's reign.

Many political analysts believed that Benazir Bhutto would complete her five-year tenure after her close companion, Farooq Leghari, triumphed in the 13 November presidential election. Leghari defeated acting president Waseem Sajjad by 274 to 269 votes.[115] Leghari hailed from the Baluch Leghari tribe of Dera Ghazi Khan and was a highly educated individual with an Oxford degree. He began his career in the Pakistani Civil Services, having joined it in 1964, before eventually transitioning to politics. Initially a loyalist of the PPP, he rose to prominence as the leader of the party's parliamentary group in the Punjab following the 1988 elections. However, he later took over as minister for water and power at the centre.

After Benazir Bhutto's dismissal, Leghari briefly served as deputy opposition leader before being appointed as a minister in October 1993. Following the presidential election, Leghari appeared to be playing second fiddle to Bhutto, as evidenced by his role in the toppling of Sabir Shah's government in NWFP and the formation of Manzoor Ahmed Wattoo's government in the Punjab. Despite being a party loyalist and head of state, Leghari's image was tarnished by allegations of his involvement in the Mehran Bank scandal.[116]

In the summer of 1996, the relationship between Leghari and Bhutto began to deteriorate as the country faced institutional collapse and a worsening economic situation. Their personal relationship grew increasingly tense after Bhutto's subtle criticism of Leghari following the tragic death of her brother, Mir Murtaza Bhutto, on 20 September 1996. However, the allegations accusing Leghari of orchestrating Murtaza's murder appeared to be politically motivated manoeuvres rather than genuine accusations.[117] Despite the prime minister's disbelief, Leghari took the stunning decision to dismiss her government on 5 November 1996, using his constitutional powers as president. He reassured the public that elections would be held within the statutory ninety-day period, and appointed Malik Meraj Khalid, a founding member of the PPP, as caretaker prime minister. Though some anxiety surrounded the transition, the general elections were successfully held in February 1997.[118]

Benazir's second term in office had got off to a promising start, which made her abrupt dismissal all the more surprising. She showed remarkable political finesse by accommodating her coalition partners, such as the PML-J in the Punjab. The PPP also appointed Nawabzada Nasrullah Khan as chairman of the Kashmir Committee, Fazal-ur-Rehman as chairman of the Foreign Affairs Committee and Malik Qasim as chairman of the Anti-corruption Committee in the National Assembly. Moreover, at the PPP's behest, Malik Qasim became the leader of the House in the Senate. In addition, the son of Mustafa Jatoi was made a minister in the Sindh cabinet, while Balkh Sher Mazari's son was given a ministerial position in the Punjab cabinet. The sons of Mustafa Khar and Nasrullah Khan were also appointed as ministers in the Punjab.[119]

Despite her conciliatory policies, Benazir's attempts to improve relations with Sharif ultimately proved fruitless. Consequently, she resorted to familiar tactics, implicating her rival and his supporters in various cases of misconduct, corruption and misdemeanour. According to Saeed Shafqat, by December 1995, approximately 140 cases had been filed against Sharif and his relatives. However, the Bhutto regime was cautious not to engage in a widespread arrest of PML-N leaders and workers.[120] During this period, Benazir demonstrated a more measured approach in her dealings with the military, avoiding any potential conflicts with the top brass. As Shafqat notes, the retirement of JCSC chairman General Shamim Ahmed was managed smoothly and efficiently, in stark contrast to the contentious Sarohi affair. The selection of chiefs of air staff and naval staff was also made without causing any significant disruptions. In January 1996, General Jehangir Karamat took over as head of the Pakistan Army, marking the first time that the senior-most general had assumed the role of COAS. His appointment was widely praised by political parties and opinion leaders across the country. When the military decided to end Operation Clean-Up in Sindh in November 1994, Benazir promptly gave her approval, paving the way for the military's withdrawal from Karachi. With this development, Benazir was able to take a more assertive stance against the MQM, citing her willingness to accede to their demands.[121]

Moreover, Benazir Bhutto made every effort to safeguard the interests of the Pakistani Army, while simultaneously launching a vigorous campaign to acquire arms and munitions from various sources, including the United States. One notable achievement of her government was the Brown Amendment, which resolved a five-year-old dispute over arms that Pakistan had already paid for but had not yet received. To overcome the impasse, the House–Senate Conference Committee approved the Brown Amendment on 24 October 1995, by an 11–3 majority vote. The amendment sought a one-time waiver to the Pressler Amendment (Section 620E of the Foreign Assistance Act of 1961), which required that the U.S. president certify that any country buying U.S. military hardware was not developing nuclear weapons. When President George Bush refused to make such a certification for Pakistan in 1990, all U.S. arms deliveries to the country were suspended. Pakistan had already paid more than U.S.$600 million for the planes and an additional U.S.$368 million for other arms, which were left undelivered as a result of the freeze.[122] As alluded in the lines above, she resisted the pressures from the IMF and the World Bank to impose cuts on defence spending, and therefore in 1993–4 and 1994–5 defence expenditure exceeded one-quarter of the total budget.[123]

Despite Benazir Bhutto's efforts to maintain good relations with Army generals, her strained relationship with Leghari signalled trouble ahead. As reported by Zaffar Abbas in *The Herald*, the PPP government's third year in power highlighted the challenges faced by the administration in retaining power for the remaining two years. The government now stood on precarious ground, with a worsening economic situation, mounting tensions with the judiciary, an aggressive anti-government campaign by the opposition and growing unease among high-ranking Army officials. The recent death of her only surviving brother, Murtaza, under controversial circumstances had further undermined both the political and emotional well-being of a beleaguered Bhutto. To make matters worse, Leghari's sabre-rattling had completely altered the political landscape.[124]

Benazir's downfall can be attributed to several factors, including the worsening situation in Karachi, a struggling economy and a lack of clear strategy to address these challenges. As foreign investment began to dry up, a publication by Transparency International (a global movement working in more than one hundred countries to end the injustice of corruption) ranked Pakistan as the world's second most corrupt country, further undermining the nation's reputation. Even the IMF showed hesitation when asked to provide necessary funds, making an already difficult situation worse. The privatization process was also negatively affected, with the sale of 26 per cent of Pakistan Telecommunications being postponed indefinitely.[125] The PPP government faced severe economic challenges as foreign-exchange reserves reached critical levels. To cope with this, the government resorted to short-term loans at high interest rates, raised taxes and devalued the rupee in an October mini-budget. In the budget presented on 13 June 1996, the defence allocation was increased by 14 per cent from the previous year, reaching a staggering figure of PKR 131.4 billion.

In addition to the economic crisis, the PPP faced political challenges. The Punjab became a thorn in the party's side once again. Chief Minister Mian Manzoor Ahmed Wattoo grew increasingly uneasy with the presence of Faisal Saleh Hayat as his principal advisor. The conflict between them came to a head when Wattoo attempted to break free from the PPP's appointee in the Punjab, eventually leading to a no-confidence motion against him in the Punjab Assembly. He was replaced by Sardar Arif Nakai, causing dissension between President Leghari and Prime Minister Bhutto. Leghari had wanted Makhdom Altaf to fill the position and was reportedly upset over the developments in the key Punjab province.

Benazir Bhutto's government controversially enforced the early retirement of several Supreme Court and Provincial High Court judges, replacing them with loyal PPP members. This arbitrary move had severe repercussions for the judiciary and was widely criticized. However, Bhutto appeared to have a clear agenda and was unmindful of the negative effects of her decisions.[126]

The president, aware of the importance of upholding the Supreme Court's ruling on the judge's case, took decisive action. With the authority granted by Article 193 of the Constitution and in compliance with the court's injunction, President Leghari appointed Justice Khalilur Rehman, Mamoon Qazi and Justice Nasir Aslam Zahid as permanent chief justices of the Lahore High Court, Sindh High Court and Federal Shariat Court, respectively. This was followed by appointments to the Supreme Court and other provincial high courts. This move not only put an end to the lawyers' movement, which had demanded respect for the legal profession, but marked the beginning of a reconstruction process aimed at restoring the independence and prestige of the judiciary. President Leghari's efforts were commendable and crucial for the country's judicial system.[127] These appointments left Benazir Bhutto bewildered, since some of the judges appointed by Leghari were believed to have hostile attitudes towards the PPP. This further strained the already acrimonious relationship between the two leaders. Despite these differences, Leghari refrained from openly confronting the prime minister and exercised restraint. However, this uneasy truce did not last long, particularly when Leghari encountered the government's proposed Pakistan Petroleum Ltd deal, which would have made the businessman and hotelier Sadruddin Hashwani a major beneficiary. Besides, he returned a draft ordinance that aimed to establish a multi-billion-dollar lottery to raise funds for Pakistan's fiftieth Independence Day celebrations, objecting that the deal lacked transparency and needed to be approved by parliament.[128]

Bhutto was uncomfortable with the new-found independence of President Leghari, and she retaliated by appointing Nawaz Khokhar, a political turncoat and alleged figure in the Mehran Bank scandal, as a cabinet minister. Meanwhile, the economic situation in Pakistan was worsening, and many current and former World Bank officials of Pakistani origin were rumoured to be holding covert meetings with influential figures in Islamabad. There was talk of a new interim set-up comprising technocrats, with politicians being portrayed as corrupt and self-serving. However, the idea was opposed by both Sharif and Benazir Bhutto, and it eventually fizzled out. Sacking corrupt officials and ministers was also a contentious issue that further strained relations between the president and the prime minister.

Once again, the prime minister proved to be a weaker link in the ruling troika. One must not, however, lose sight of Benazir Bhutto's inadequacies. As Aamer Ahmed Khan perceptively commented,

> From her ill-planned Doves of Democracy Movement to the uncertain majority which she rode to her first stint as the Prime Minister, Ms. Bhutto did everything that General Zia had wanted his handpicked politicians to do. Every step she took disgraced the political process, from bribing elected representatives to secure their support in the National Assembly to letting her husband run amok in the PM's secretariat.[129]

Malik Meraj Khalid, a veteran politician from Lahore, was appointed to head the caretaker government on 5 November 1996. Born in 1916 on the outskirts of Lahore, Khalid began his political career as a member of Majlis-e-Ahrar and later joined the Convention Muslim League during the Ayub era. He was also among the founding members of the PPP and served as federal minister for agriculture after his election to the National Assembly in 1970. He also briefly served as chief minister of the Punjab. When democracy was restored in 1988, Khalid was elected speaker of the National Assembly, but subsequently struggled to win elections and eventually accepted a rectorship at the Islamic University Islamabad, effectively ending his political career. However, he returned to the limelight in 1996 following the dismissal of Benazir Bhutto on 5 November. With limited discretionary powers, Khalid's effectiveness as prime minister was questioned.

The caretaker cabinet was composed of notable figures, including President Leghari's brother-in-law, Zubair Khan, who was appointed as the commerce minister. The accomplished Mumtaz Ali Bhutto, Zulfiqar Ali Bhutto's talented cousin, was appointed as the chief minister of Sindh. Shahid Javed Burki, a distinguished economist, was entrusted with the critical portfolio of finance and played a crucial role in implementing significant economic and financial reforms. He undertook various measures to stabilize foreign exchange and reduce the fiscal deficit to 4 per cent of GDP, as per the IMF's demands. Additionally, Burki spearheaded efforts to broaden the tax base by including agricultural incomes, to restructure the management of state-owned banks and to establish a Resolution Trust Corporation to manage non-performing loans.[130]

There were two institutional reforms during this period that deserve recognition: the introduction of adult franchise in Pakistan's federally administered tribal areas (FATA) and the formation of a Council of Defence and National Security (CDNS). The introduction of adult franchise in the tribal areas was a positive step towards greater democratic inclusion. However, the establishment of the CDNS aimed to assign a permanent role to the military brass in the decision-making processes of the country, potentially legitimizing the role of the president and COAS in its governance.

Landslide Victory: Elections Bring the PML-N to Power

The process of the 1997 elections in Pakistan was marked by uncertainty and a lack of enthusiasm. There were concerns about the fate of the elections, as well as restrictions on political displays such as posters, party flags and loudspeakers. The influenza epidemic in the Punjab and the fact that the election date fell during the month of Ramadan further contributed to a sense of listlessness. Despite these challenges, the PML-N was able to secure an absolute majority, a rare feat in the country's history, by winning 135 seats in the National Assembly. The PML-N's power base remained in the Punjab, but it was also able to make inroads in Sindh, where it won fifteen seats. Meanwhile, the PPP only managed to win nineteen National Assembly seats, a relatively low number compared to the PML-N.[131] The PPP suffered significant losses in the 1997 elections, not only conceding National Assembly and provincial assembly seats in districts such as Nawab Shah, Khairpur and Jacobabad, but securing only three seats out of a total of 240 in the Punjab Provincial Assembly. Aamer Ahmed Khan's report in *The Herald* highlights that the party's vote bank, after being misused and abused for over ten years by Benazir Bhutto, failed to show up on election day. Previously able to secure at least forty seats in the National Assembly due to its consistent ability to poll over 35 per cent of the country's active electorate, the party was reduced to just eighteen seats, compared to the PML's 136. Bhutto protested, but unlike in 1990, her cries fell on deaf ears. The 3 February polls marked not only a numerical defeat for the PPP, but more starkly the death of a culture that had been in a state of constant erosion since Bhutto's return from exile a decade prior in 1986.[132]

In addition to the rise of the PML-N two other long-term trends in the 1997 elections were visible. First, there was the electoral malaise of the Islamic parties. Jamaat-e-Islami and Jamiat Ulema-e-Pakistan boycotted the elections, while Fazl-ur-Rehman's Jamiat Ulema-e-Islam only managed to win two National Assembly seats. Second, ethnic and regional identities remained strong. Despite state repression, the MQM maintained its position in urban Sindh and secured twelve National Assembly and 28 Sindh Provincial Assembly seats. Similarly, the ANP won 31 provincial assembly seats in NWFP, while the Jamhoori Watan Party and Baluchistan Nationalist Parties accounted for eighteen provincial assembly seats in Baluchistan province. These trends highlighted the complex and diverse nature of

Pakistani politics, which cannot be understood simply through the prism of party politics or national-level elections.[133]

Although the PML-N emerged victorious in the 1997 elections, the presence of ethno-nationalist identities in the country was significant, and these groups called for the recognition of pluralism through the devolution of power and resources. Therefore, despite the PML-N's 'heavy mandate' during that time, Sharif faced several daunting challenges. Apart from his complicated relationship with Leghari, who had previously been his political adversary, Sharif was also confronted with an impending economic crisis.

The instalment of the IMF loan, which had to be repaid by June 1997, was to the tune of U.S.$1.2 billion. An increasing trade imbalance and soaring prices had boxed the prime minister in. It did not seem likely that 'Pakistan would meet the IMF target of current account deficit of 4.4 per cent of GDP for 1996/7'.[134] In response to these challenges, Sharif adopted a series of populist initiatives, among which was the *Qarz Utaro, Mulk Sanvaro* (Clear Debt, Rebuild the Nation) programme. This initiative involved reaching out to Pakistani expatriates and the global diaspora community, urging them to contribute to Pakistan's economic stability by depositing a minimum of U.S.$1,000 as an interest-free loan in Pakistani banks for a period ranging from two to five years.[135] That appeal yielded positive results, but obviously it could not address Pakistan's deep-seated economic problems.

On 28 March Finance Minister Sartaj Aziz announced an economic reform package whereby the austerity measures demanded by the IMF Standby Arrangement were jettisoned in favour of supply-side economics. Through that policy, tax cuts and higher support prices had been put in place to enhance agricultural and textile production. Such an initiative was taken mainly as a result of the suspension of the IMF agreement a few days earlier. In July the Pakistan government 'was allowed to enter into a medium-term Enhanced Structural Adjustment Facility (ESAF)'.[136] It certainly helped to reduce the balance-of-payment vulnerability, but far-reaching economic reforms were required, such as widening the tax base, or measures that could result in greater direct investment and also enhance exports as well as agricultural production.

As early as 1991, the Pakistani press was printing detailed stories alleging that senior politicians were pressurizing banks into giving them multimillion-dollar bank loans. In 1998 Sharif openly admitted to having a substantial amount of outstanding loans. To solidify his immense popularity, which had surged after his pivotal decision to conduct Pakistan's nuclear tests on 28 May 1998 in Chaghi, Baluchistan, in response to India's nuclear tests conducted just a fortnight earlier, he made a resolute pledge to settle all his debts. In a televised address to the nation in June 1998, he said that the Ittefaq group of companies would offer its assets to the banks so that all the loans could be recovered.[137]

On 1 April Sharif had introduced the Thirteenth Amendment, which stripped the president of the power under Article 58-2(b) to dismiss the prime minister and dissolve the National Assembly. The tensions between the president and the prime minister came to the fore over the appointment of the Sindh governor. The PML-N wanted the MQM nominee to be appointed, whereas the president insisted on Lieutenant General Moeenuddin Haider. The conflict intensified when Sharif was compelled to award a Senate ticket to President Leghari's relative, Maqsood Leghari. The government's introduction of supply-side economics further exacerbated the rift between the two troika members. Now that Sharif was the most powerful prime minister since Zulfiqar Ali Bhutto, he could pick a fight with the president – and he did just that. Leghari had to tender his resignation on 2 December 1997. When Rafiq Tarar, a friend of Sharif's father, Mian Sharif, took over as the president just over three weeks later, Sharif's position seemed unassailable.

Rafiq Tarar, born on 2 November 1929 in Pirkot, was a relatively obscure figure prior to his appointment as the president of Pakistan. Even members of the cabinet were taken aback by his nomination, with rumours circulating that his selection was due to the backing of 'Abbaji' Mian Mohammad Sharif, the patriarch of the Sharif family.

Tarar, who came from humble beginnings, received his education at a college in Gujranwala before attending Punjab University Law College in Lahore, where he obtained his LLB in 1951. He established his legal practice in Gujranwala and gradually rose to become the chairman of the Punjab Labour Court in 1970. Four years later, he was admitted to the High Court and went on to become the chief justice of the Lahore High Court in 1989. Two years after that, he reached the pinnacle of his legal career when he joined the Supreme Court. Despite his extensive legal experience, Tarar avoided the limelight by primarily dealing with criminal cases rather than the politically contentious constitutional cases that have been a recurring theme in the annals of Pakistan's history. He was not a particularly prominent member of the Senate, which he joined in March 1997 on the PML-N ticket following his retirement from the judiciary. Some commentators characterized Tarar as a conservative and markedly hostile towards minorities, and whose appointment exemplified Pakistan's 'creeping fundamentalism'.[138]

After Farooq Leghari was ousted, Sharif locked horns with the judiciary. Ian Talbot provides insight into the confrontation between the Pakistani government and Chief Justice Sajjad Ali Shah. According to Talbot, the conflict between the judiciary and the executive was driven by the March 1996 verdict in the *Judges* case, which was a landmark legal proceeding that revolved around the appointment and removal of judges. The verdict in this case affirmed the principle that the judiciary should have a significant say in these matters, promoting judicial independence and encouraging judicial activism in the country. This decision laid the foundation for the judiciary to play a more active role in governance and decision-making processes, thus encouraging judicial activism.

Chief Justice Shah, during his tenure, started to scrutinize cases related to the government's handling of a wheat-shipping contract from the United States and allegations of the illegal distribution of residential plots by the prime minister. These actions raised tensions between the judiciary and the executive branch, as the judiciary was taking on a more assertive role in overseeing government actions.[139]

In August 1997 the conflict between the Supreme Court and the parallel justice system of summary trial courts reached its peak when the former disapproved of the latter under the Anti-terrorist Law. Justice Shah was forced to depart and was replaced by Justice Saeed uz Zaman Siddiqi as chief justice of Pakistan Supreme Court. Accusations surfaced, suggesting that Rafiq Tarar was involved in inciting a rebellion against Justice Shah by allegedly offering bribes to several judges. Reportedly, this arrangement took place in Quetta, where Justice Tarar is said to have transported briefcases filled with currency notes. With Justice Shah out of the way, Sharif had reached the pinnacle of his power and authority, having done away with both the president and the chief justice.

However, Sharif's confrontational approach with the Army led to an unexpected outcome. Notably, on 28 May 1998, Pakistan achieved the status of the world's seventh nuclear power by conducting nuclear tests. This momentous decision followed extensive contemplation, with Sharif appearing to be in favour but compelled only by mounting public pressure to give the green light. However, the nuclear explosion at Chaghi had severe economic repercussions, and American sanctions only worsened the economic situation. Sharif's government failed to come up with a viable plan to address the crisis, and the freezing of foreign currency accounts led to a wave of trenchant criticism. Sharif was unable to use the nuclear explosion to his political advantage, so he tried to turn the narrative around. In a speech, he announced that his family would restrict themselves to just one daily meal as part of their commitment to the austerity drive prompted by economic sanctions following nuclear tests. However, this declaration raised scepticism among many Pakistanis, given their prime minister's strong affection for rich Punjabi dishes – the notion of him skipping a meal appeared highly improbable.

General Jehangir Karamat's resignation, which came at the request of a civilian prime minister, marked a departure from Pakistan's historical pattern whereby the military held the upper hand. The main point of contention was the National Security Council, which Karamat strongly advocated for in his speech at the Naval Staff College. This ultimately led to a falling out between him and the prime minister. As a result, the unexpected occurred, and the COAS resigned on 6 October 1998.[140] Encouraged by this unlikely event, Sharif went on to dismiss his own handpicked COAS, General Pervez Musharraf, to replace him with General Ziauddin Butt while he was on a visit to Sri Lanka. Kiessling suggests that Sharif's father, Mian Muhammad Sharif, President Rafiq Tarar and former DG ISIS Javed Nasir, who were all members of the ultraorthodox Islamic movement Tablighi Jamaat, may have contributed to Sharif's insatiable thirst for control. Ultimately, Musharraf emerged victorious, orchestrating Pakistan's third military coup and leading to Sharif's dismissal. Perhaps these three individuals overlooked Musharraf's military record, which portrayed him as an impulsive figure.[141]

The tension between the military top brass and the prime minister had been brewing for quite some time. Sharif's initiative to bring about rapprochement between Pakistan and India sowed the seed of discord that had increased substantially in the aftermath of the Kargil operation. With this sad denouement for the nascent democracy, the military assumed the reins of power yet again.

Envoi: Similarities and Differences between Benazir and Sharif

Before concluding this chapter, it is instructive to draw a comparison between the two main contenders for power in the late twentieth century, Benazir Bhutto and Nawaz Sharif. Although they had important differences and dissimilarities, reflected in their family backgrounds, education, world views and political ideologies, both governed Pakistan in a similar fashion. They both encouraged state-owned radio and television to broadcast blatant pro-government propaganda, although Benazir Bhutto was generally more tolerant of press criticism than Sharif. She had greater sensitivity for human rights and never attacked non-governmental organizations (NGOs) in the way that Sharif did. On religious matters, Bhutto clearly had a more modernist outlook than Sharif, but she was always willing to pander to the religious lobby for short-term political advantage.

Neither of the two pushed through any significant reforms, and their most important shared characteristic in national policy terms was their ability to run up huge levels of foreign debt. By 1999, when General Musharraf took over, Pakistan owed foreign creditors over U.S.$25 billion, and debt servicing had become the largest component of the annual budget. Most of this debt had been accumulated in the 1990s.

Despite all the rhetoric about improving the lot of the poor, both lived in considerable luxury. Sharif's opulent estate of Jati Umera at Raiwind near Lahore and Benazir Bhutto's ancestral home in Larkana both boasted private zoos. Both also purchased valuable foreign properties. The extent of the Sharif family's foreign holdings has never been clear, but during his second term in office he was embarrassed by the revelation that, among many other foreign properties, he owned four luxury flats on London's

Park Lane. Likewise, according to the National Accountability Bureau, Asif Zardari owned several properties in the UK, Belgium and France, as well as a stud farm in Texas.

Although the Sharif family surrendered more than 33 industrial units to the state, subsequent investigations revealed that most of them were either inoperative or sick. According to Pakistani press reports, the total value of the units surrendered by the Sharifs was not enough to cover the amount owed to the banks. The exact amount of debt remained contested, but in November 2001 General Musharraf's military regime published a list of major loan defaulters, revealing that politicians and businessmen collectively owed PKR 211 billion (more than U.S.$3 billion or approximately £2 billion), with the Sharif family's debt alone amounting to more than PKR 3 billion (U.S.$50 million or approximately £34.5 million). However, the Pakistani press generally quotes figures two or three times higher.

Despite his immense wealth, Sharif showed little interest in paying taxes. His 1996 nomination form for National Assembly elections revealed that he had paid less than U.S.$10 in income tax between 1994 and 1996. Sharif's supporters argued that this was entirely legal and pointed out that during the same period, he paid nearly U.S.$60,000 in wealth tax. However, even if Sharif had the most skilled accountants money could buy, the amounts paid were notably low for a man whose family controlled assets worth hundreds of millions, if not billions, of dollars. Between 1988 and 1999, Pakistan borrowed and failed to repay U.S.$13 billion, with major spending projects including the Lahore-Islamabad motorway and the opulent prime ministerial Secretariat in Islamabad. A considerable amount was also spent on Sharif's Yellow Cab scheme, in which tens of thousands of taxis were distributed to towns and villages throughout the country, with the expectation that the beneficiaries would pay back the cost of the taxis, but few had ever done so. Together, these projects cost around U.S.$3 billion, leaving U.S.$10 billion unaccounted for.

Benazir Bhutto and her husband, Asif Zardari, were accused of leveraging their political power for personal gain, with the most serious charges levelled against them relating to kickbacks. The first case to reach a conclusion was the SGS *Cotecna* case. The Swiss-based company had been hired by Bhutto's government in 1994 to improve the system for collecting customs duties on imports. Sharif, determined to discredit his most popular political opponent, ordered his second government to investigate the case. The enquiry concluded that Bhutto and her husband had been paid millions of dollars in bribes as kickbacks for awarding the contract.

Geneva magistrate Daniel Devaud provided some of the most damning evidence against the Bhuttos. He found Swiss bank accounts in the name of offshore Virgin Islands companies that were, in fact, controlled by Asif Zardari. Furthermore, he revealed that Benazir Bhutto had used money from one of the accounts to buy a diamond necklace worth U.S.$175,000. The couple was convicted by Devaud, although they appealed and secured a retrial, which the Swiss abandoned when Asif Zardari became president.

11

Pervez Musharraf: An Autocrat Re-Engineering Politics, 1999–2008

Pervez Musharraf was a throwback to a bygone era in the twenty-first century, a military ruler who stood out in a world that had embraced democracy, with all its boisterousness and commotion. He firmly believed that once he relinquished his military title and left office, the country would lapse into a state of political chaos, necessitating a fresh start towards democratic ideals. Meanwhile, amid the turmoil on the national and international stages, he stood at the epicentre, commanding attention.

Musharraf's roots can be traced back to an erudite Syed family (a title denoting descent from the Prophet Muhammad) hailing from Delhi. His father, Syed Musharraf-ud-Din, was a diplomat in the Foreign Service. In his memoir *In the Line of Fire*, Musharraf fondly recollects his ancestral home, Nehar Wali Haveli, which translates to 'House Next to the Canal', situated in the old Mughal quarter of Delhi. The Haveli, characterized by its Asian-style architecture, was built around a central courtyard, a common feature of traditional homes. Musharraf's older brother, Javed, was born a year before him and proved to be a prodigious talent. Their family was complete with the arrival of their younger brother, Naved.[1]

Originally from Allahabad in Uttar Pradesh, Musharraf's family moved to Delhi, but at the time of partition in 1947, they had to migrate to Pakistan and settled in Karachi. Upon their arrival, Musharraf's father was allotted two rooms in Jacob Lines, a locality comprising long barracks with two-room units. The children were enrolled in St Patrick's High School, a missionary school in Karachi. Soon after their relocation, Musharraf's father joined the newly established Foreign Office, located in the grand Mohatta Palace building.[2] After settling in Karachi, Musharraf's father was appointed as the superintendent of the accounts department at Pakistan's embassy in Ankara, Turkey, and the family relocated there two years later. They spent seven years in Turkey, which proved to be a transformative period for Musharraf and his two brothers. He looked back at his time in Turkey with fondness. Upon returning to Pakistan, he completed his matriculation from St Patrick's High School before moving to Forman Christian College in Lahore to pursue a Freshman in Arts degree. In 1961, Musharraf joined the Pakistan Military Academy and was commissioned in an elite artillery regiment three years later. As a young officer, he saw action in the Khem Kiran, Lahore and Sialkot sectors during the 1965 war, where he served with a self-propelled artillery regiment and was awarded the Imtiaz-e-Sanad (certificate of distinction) for his gallantry.[3]

General Musharraf had a distinguished military career, with a wealth of experience in commanding troops, managing artillery and serving in key staff and instructional positions. In particular, Musharraf's time with the Special Service Group (SSG), a special operations force within the Pakistan Army that is known for its rigorous training and demanding missions, is noteworthy, as it likely gave him the valuable skills and experiences that he would draw upon throughout his career. Musharraf's service during the 1971 war was also significant. The one-month conflict saw Pakistan pitted against India in a struggle for control of what is now Bangladesh. Musharraf's role as a company commander in a commando battalion would have placed him in the thick of the fighting. Finally, Musharraf's command of two self-propelled artillery regiments had given him experience in managing the firepower of the Pakistan Army. This experience had proven particularly valuable in later years when he rose to the rank of general and ultimately became the COAS.[4]

As a brigadier, he held the prestigious command of an infantry brigade as well as the armoured-division artillery. Later, on being promoted to major general on 15 January 1991, he assumed command of an infantry division, followed by a prestigious strike corps as lieutenant general on 21 October 1995. In addition to his command roles, Musharraf also held important staff and instructional appointments. He served as deputy military secretary at the Military Secretary's Branch, and as a member of directing staff at both the Command and Staff College in Quetta and the National Defence College, and also distinguished himself at the Royal College of Defence Studies in the United Kingdom. Overall, Musharraf's military career was marked by a range of challenging and prestigious positions, demonstrating his leadership skills, strategic thinking and commitment to serving his country.[5]

On 9 April 1999 Musharraf was given the additional responsibility of serving as chairman of the JCSC. His impressive record had already caught the attention of Prime Minister Sharif, but it was unfortunately Musharraf's status as a Muhajir (Urdu-speaking migrants from Delhi who constitute an ethnic minority and reside in Karachi and Hyderabad) that Sharif believed would make him pliable and easily influenced. Despite this, there was little in Musharraf's record to suggest he was weak or subservient – his professional conduct had led him to the highest rank in the Army. It was expected that he would continue serving as COAS until November 2001, when he would retire from military life and transition to civilian life.[6]

However, two years before this expected retirement, a crucial event took place. The Kargil conflict in 1999 was a military confrontation between

India and Pakistan in the Kargil district of Jammu and Kashmir. The conflict began in May 1999 and lasted until July, when the Pakistani military, led by General Musharraf, withdrew its forces from the region. The conflict was a major embarrassment for the Pakistani government and military, as they had been caught off guard by India's response and had to withdraw their forces in defeat.

In the aftermath of the Kargil conflict, Pakistani prime minister Sharif came under intense criticism for his handling of the situation. He was accused of not being fully informed about the military operation in Kargil and of not taking adequate steps to prevent the conflict from escalating. There were also allegations that Sharif had tried to bypass the military leadership in his efforts to resolve the conflict. The situation came to a head in October 1999, when Sharif attempted to remove Musharraf from his position as COAS. In fact, on 12 October 1999, Sharif issued a decree to dismiss Musharraf from his coveted position and replace him with Lieutenant General Ziauddin Butt, a family loyalist and ISI director general.

So far as the Army top brass was concerned, after General Karamat's less-than-distinguished exit as COAS in October 1998, those in charge had resolved not to tolerate any more humiliation from the government. Both Sharif and Butt ought to have been aware of this fact. Furthermore, Musharraf had appointed generals close to him to key positions like the CGS and commander of the X Corps in Rawalpindi. However, two corps commanders, who had reputations for siding with the prime minister, seemed to overlook these warning signs. They believed that they had a golden opportunity to present a proposal to the generals while Musharraf was on his four-hour return flight from Sri Lanka to Pakistan. Their prior success in handling conflicts with the media, the judiciary and Karamat had given them an inflated sense of confidence. They also underestimated Musharraf's strength, despite the aftermath of the Kargil episode. Most generals were still firmly behind the COAS, as they believed Sharif had capitulated to Washington's demands and was personally responsible for the hasty withdrawal from Kargil. This move to remove Musharraf was seen as a grab for absolute power by Sharif, and it was met with resistance from the military establishment. Musharraf responded by leading a military coup and taking control of the government. He declared himself the chief executive of Pakistan and suspended the country's Constitution.

Much like Sharif, DG ISI Ziauddin also engaged in a high-stakes gamble. He positioned himself alongside the prime minister and surrounded himself with loyal ISI personnel. Some of the troops previously involved in hunting Osama bin Laden were redeployed, albeit for a different mission. Their objectives this time included ensuring the personal protection of Sharif and Ziauddin, as well as taking control of Pakistan's radio and television stations. On the afternoon of 12 October 1999, Sharif signed a document appointing Ziauddin as COAS. At 5 p.m., Pakistan Television made the announcement of the appointment and Musharraf's dismissal. This breaking news was reiterated repeatedly over the next hour. However, from 6 p.m., there was a conspicuous absence of information, and shortly thereafter, all radio and TV stations went off the air. GHQ had responded. Pakistan TV was now under the control of members of 111 Brigade. And their coup of the airwaves encountered only sporadic resistance from Ziauddin's supporters. A similar situation unfolded at the prime minister's official residence, which had been taken over by the same force at 6.30 p.m.[7]

The consequences of this ill-fated attempt at replacing key posts were grave for both Sharif and Ziauddin. Sharif found himself in custody and facing a court trial, with charges based on the Anti-terrorism Act, the outcome of which carried the possibility of severe penalties. Sharif remained in detention for fourteen months in Attock Fort until President Rafiq Tarar eventually granted him a pardon on 9 December 2000. However, the pardon came with the condition of his exile to Saudi Arabia. Under pressure from Riyadh and Washington, Musharraf opted to allow Sharif to leave the country, with his extended family in tow. A stipulation of the agreement was Sharif's decade-long absence from Pakistan, the precise terms of which remain undisclosed to this day. After an initial five years, the Sharif family gained more flexibility in their movements, including travel to Dubai, London and the United States. It was in 2006 that they were finally able to leave Saudi Arabia permanently, and they opted to make London their home. But their return to Pakistan remained prohibited.

Musharraf assumed charge of the government as its chief executive and on 20 June 2001 he took over as president just days prior to his planned visit for the Agra Talks with India.[8] His actions were initially met with resistance from the international community, which condemned the military takeover and called for a return to civilian rule. However, Musharraf was able to consolidate his power and remain in control of Pakistan for several years. He implemented several reforms and initiatives during his time in power, including efforts to modernize the economy and combat extremism.

The U.S. government was particularly concerned about Sharif's ousting from power. Prior to his removal, the United States had received assurances from his government that Pakistan would sign the Comprehensive Nuclear Test Ban Treaty (CTBT), a multilateral treaty that prohibits nuclear weapons testing. Additionally, American officials had been urging Sharif to take decisive action against Osama bin Laden, the founder of al-Qaeda, who was believed to be hiding in Pakistan at the time. With Sharif's dismissal, the United States was left uncertain about the future of these critical issues, and there was significant apprehension about the new military government's stance on these matters.[9]

Despite Indian demands to add Pakistan to the State Department's list of terrorist nations, Sharif had pledged to cooperate with the international community in identifying and dismantling terrorist organizations.

Additionally, Pakistan had been actively involved in combating drug trafficking. However, with the military takeover, there were concerns about the future of these initiatives, and there were significant efforts made to convince Musharraf to restore Sharif to his position as prime minister. The potential loss of progress on these crucial fronts led to heightened anxiety, as many feared that the new military government would not prioritize these issues in the same way. As a result, numerous efforts were made to persuade Musharraf to reconsider his decision and allow Sharif to return to power.[10]

Despite considerable international pressure, Musharraf refused to back down from his decision to take over the government. Even the suspension of Pakistan's membership in the Commonwealth and the European Union's condemnation of the military's intervention in Pakistan's politics were not enough to sway him. Musharraf attributed the country's instability to the misgovernance of Sharif's government, placing the blame for the turmoil and uncertainty that Pakistan had endured firmly on his administration. He argued that all the country's institutions had been systematically destroyed under Sharif's rule, and that the economy was in a state of collapse as a result.

Despite his critics, Musharraf maintained that his intervention was necessary to stabilize the country and rebuild its institutions. He was determined to bring about lasting change, even if it meant facing opposition from the international community.[11] In addition, he emphasized that the armed forces had faced relentless demands from the public, across the political spectrum, to address the rapidly deteriorating situation in the country. Despite these concerns being conveyed to the prime minister in good faith and with the country's interests in mind, there was no adequate response from the government.

Musharraf made it clear that his primary concern had always been the well-being of the country. As such, he felt compelled to act in the interest of the nation and ensure its stability, even if it meant taking decisive action that was unpopular with some. Despite criticism from certain quarters, he believed that the military's intervention was necessary to address the pressing issues facing Pakistan at the time.[12] Musharraf then turned his attention to the crux of the issue: Sharif's attempt to undermine the Pakistani Army. He expressed his frustration, saying, 'Despite all my efforts and advice, the government continued to interfere with the armed forces, which was the only remaining institution capable of maintaining stability in the country.'[13] He emphasized that he had communicated the Army's concerns to the government clearly and unequivocally. However, Sharif's administration had ignored these warnings and attempted to politicize and destabilize the Army. The former prime minister had even tried to create division among the ranks of the armed forces. Musharraf believed that the Army had been left with no other option but to step in and take control of the situation to ensure the country's stability and prevent it from descending into chaos.[14]

Musharraf, in his capacity as the Army chief and chief executive, sought to reassure the people of Pakistan that their future was secure under the leadership of the armed forces. He addressed the nation, saying, 'My dear brothers and sisters, I want to assure you that the armed forces have always been and will always be there for you. We will do everything in our power to restore order and create a better future for Pakistan.' He urged the people of Pakistan to remain calm and support the armed forces in their efforts to re-establish stability and prosperity in the country. He invoked Allah's guidance and the values of truth and honour as the guiding principles for the future of the nation.[15]

Over the next few days, the Army made moves to tighten its grip on the country. On 13 October all four provincial governments were dismissed. The following day, troops were deployed to take control of the parliament building and prevent a scheduled session of the National Assembly on 15 October, which had been called for by opposition members. As anticipated, Musharraf declared a state of emergency in Pakistan on 15 October, outlining his priorities to include economic revival, national integration and good governance. He declared himself the 'chief executive', suspended the Constitution and parliament, and mandated that the president act solely under his orders.[16]

The Army effectively imposed martial law in the country, but did not use the term 'martial law' in the proclamation or accompanying PCO in order to appease the concerns of the international community.[17] This order effectively suspended the power of the judiciary to issue orders against the chief executive and any person exercising his powers. Moreover, it

Parliament House, Islamabad.

prevented the Army court tribunal from issuing any judgement against the Army chief or any authority designated by him. However, fundamental rights, which were not in contravention of the proclamation or any further orders, would continue to be in force.[18] Musharraf issued the proclamation 'in pursuance of the deliberations and decisions of the chiefs of staff of the armed forces and Corps Commanders of the Pakistan Army'. Along with the proclamation, an order was issued stating that despite the suspension of the Constitution, Pakistan would still be governed in accordance with the Constitution true to an original text, and subject to the orders of the chief executive.[19] The duration of military rule was left unspecified, signifying the establishment of a complete military dictatorship once again, bringing the situation back to square one.

Responses to Sharif's Exit

Benazir Bhutto, the opposition leader in exile, accused Sharif of inciting the military coup against his own government by attempting to politicize the Army. According to Bhutto, Sharif had dismantled democracy since taking over and was violating the rule of law. She expressed her belief that there was no one to stop him and that the Army had to protect itself as an institution. Bhutto made these statements during an interview with Sky TV from her location in London.[20]

It is believed that Bhutto defended the Army in the hope that they would ensure her safety if she returned to Pakistan. At the time, she was under a warrant of arrest due to the corruption charges filed against her by the previous government. In April 1999 the Lahore High Court sentenced her to five years in prison. However, when she requested safe passage to return to Pakistan, the military regime denied her, since granting her a pardon could damage the Army's image of neutrality.[21]

In Karachi, people took to the streets to celebrate the removal of Sharif from power, with many blaming him for the persecution of supporters of the city's influential ethnic party, the MQM. 'The cruel and fascist ruler is gone,' exclaimed Javed Akhtar, a vocal MQM supporter. 'We have faced pressure from successive governments, but Sharif's rule was particularly ruthless,' Akhtar added. Another MQM supporter, Khalid Mehmood, said, 'At least now our boys will be safe, and there is hope for bringing peace to the city.' Farooq Sattar, an important leader of the MQM, held Sharif's government responsible for the situation, stating that the deposed prime minister had gone 'too far in his authoritarian rule'.[22] Residents in several neighbourhoods celebrated by distributing sweets, and playing pro-MQM songs.

The Grand Democratic Alliance (GDA), a multi-party alliance of political and religious parties that included Benazir Bhutto's PPP, Imran Khan's PTI and the Karachi-based Muttahida Quami Movement (MQM), played a significant role in the aftermath of Sharif's dismissal. The GDA welcomed the end of Sharif's regime and supported Musharraf's seven-point agenda on 21 October. It made this decision after a meeting in Lahore chaired by veteran politician Nawabzada Nasrullah Khan. In a statement, the GDA accused Sharif's government of conspiring to paralyse every institution of the state and expressed hope that the Musharraf regime would launch a 'ruthless' accountability drive to root out corrupt politicians.[23]

Although most political parties welcomed the military coup, the Jamaat-e-Islami was an exception. In a statement released on 15 October, the Jamaat urged the armed forces to hold 'corrupt rulers' accountable but criticized Musharraf's decision to declare a state of emergency. The statement also expressed the Jamaat's opposition to martial law and the suspension of fundamental rights, while emphasizing the party's agenda for implementing a real Islamic system in the country.[24] The statement issued by Jamaat's secretary general, Syed Munawar Hassan, further said that the Jamaat would continue its struggle for an Islamic revolution in Pakistan.

The PML led by Sharif did not react as harshly to the military takeover as expected. On 21 October, the party issued a statement demanding the immediate release of Sharif and the restoration of democracy. However, during a press briefing after a meeting of senior party leaders, former religious affairs minister Raja Zafarul Haq stated that the party wanted to avoid confrontation with the Army and requested immediate access to the detained former prime minister. Despite repeated questions from reporters, he refrained from condemning the Army's actions and simply described them as 'regrettable'.[25]

A week later, the PML-N was in disarray as its leaders were unable to determine the next course of action, and reports of widespread defections from the party were rampant. Several closed-door meetings in Islamabad among party leaders produced little in terms of a strategy. On 28 October, the former interior minister Chaudhry Shujaat Hussain told media persons in Islamabad that the Army takeover 'may be a good thing', and there was a consensus in the party to avoid a head-on confrontation with the Army over the coup.[26] One of the senior leaders of the PML-N, the retired general Abdul Majid Malik, criticized Hussain Nawaz's (Sharif's son) appeal to the Indian prime minister Atal Behari Vajpayee to intervene and save his father. Malik found it insulting that Nawaz would seek help from India instead of the United States or Britain.[27]

Initially, the dismissal of Sharif's authoritarian rule was welcomed by the people and the political class. Pakistan's history has shown that the nation as a whole has become accustomed to the false choice between democracy and dictatorship. Even the most popularly elected democratic leaders have often acted like tyrants, due to the deeply feudal mindset that prevails within the Pakistani political class. Nonetheless, it almost goes without saying that despite these shortcomings, democracy remains the only mechanism to cure political ills and to ensure good governance in Pakistan.

On 26 October, just two weeks after the military coup, Sharif was brought before an investigative team consisting of both civil and military experts. The investigation centred around Sharif's alleged refusal to allow a PIA plane carrying Musharraf and two hundred passengers to land at Karachi airport on 12 October. These investigations were seen as a precursor to charges being brought against Sharif and other political opponents of Musharraf. It was widely speculated that Sharif would face additional charges related to his alleged attempts to sow discord within the Pakistan Army and to politicize its command structure.

Finally, on 10 November, Sharif and four others were formally charged with attempted murder, hijacking and criminal conspiracy.[28] The defendants in the case, registered at the Karachi airport police station at midnight on 10 November, included Sharif, his advisor on Sindh affairs Ghous Ali Shah, former inspector general of police Sindh Rana Maqbool Ahmad, former PIA chairman and later (2017–18) prime minister of Pakistan Shahid Khaqan Abbasi and former director general of civil aviation Aminullah Chaudhry.[29]

The military regime wasted no time in taking necessary measures to ensure Sharif's swift conviction. Their first strategic move was to persuade Aminullah Chaudhry to become involved in the prosecution's case. On 24 November, news broke that Chaudhry had agreed to testify against his co-accused, Sharif, in the treason and hijacking scandal. Seeking clemency under the code of criminal procedure, Chaudhry's testimony was seen as a breakthrough for the prosecution.[30]

The military government took several significant steps to ensure the swift conviction of Sharif. First, on 2 December, the Anti-terrorism Act of 1997 was amended to allow the anti-terrorism court to hear cases involving additional sections of the Pakistan Penal Code (PPC), including offences such as hijacking and criminal conspiracy. This also authorized the court to sentence those found guilty to death, even for abetment. Thus, the stage was set for the former prime minister to be ensnared.

On 8 December a charge sheet was filed against Sharif and six others in Karachi. It accused him of waging war against the state, attempted murder, hijacking, kidnapping and criminal conspiracy. Justice Shabbir Ahmed of the Sindh High Court, who was appointed to a special anti-terrorism court to hear the case, received the charge sheet. On 18 January 2000 the court formally began proceedings against Sharif on charges of kidnapping, attempted murder, hijacking and terrorism. The charges carried the death penalty or life imprisonment. The prosecution initially did not file treason charges against Sharif. By 19 February the prosecution had concluded its case, with only 26 out of the 54 witnesses listed giving evidence; the rest were dropped.

On the opposing side of the conflict, the PML-N took legal action by filing a petition with the Supreme Court on 22 November 1999. The petition, supported by twelve individuals, including former National Assembly speaker Ilahi Bux Soomro, former Senate chairman Wasim Sajjad and Raja Zafarul Haq, demanded the reinstatement of the elected government and challenged the military takeover. In a 67-page document, the petition argued that the events of 12 October represented a 'constitutional deviation' that was 'wholly contrary to the constitution, the laws of Pakistan, and the principles of democracy'.[31]

During his testimony before the anti-terrorism court on 8 March 2000, Sharif claimed that the military coup on 12 October 1999 was motivated by his attempt to withdraw Pakistani troops from the disputed region of Kargil, which had been seized by Indian forces. According to Sharif, the coup was a 'preconceived conspiracy' against his government. He hinted that he had more information about the Kargil issue but could not disclose it publicly. He said that his policy on Kargil was aimed at 'saving the nation and its dignity' but it cost him his job. He lamented: 'I saved the nation but unfortunately, I could not save myself.'[32]

On 6 April 2000, the anti-terrorism court delivered its verdict. Sharif was found guilty of attempted hijacking and terrorism and sentenced to two terms of 25 years, each to be served concurrently. Judge Rehmat Hussain Jaffery, presiding over the court, ordered the seizure of all of Sharif's assets and property, and imposed a fine of PKR 1 million for the aforementioned charges, as well as compensation of PKR 2 million to the passengers of PIA plane PK 805.

However, the judge acquitted all six co-accused due to lack of evidence that they were involved in the hijacking conspiracy. Additionally, Sharif was acquitted of the charges of attempted murder and kidnapping.[33] The military regime was dissatisfied with the 'lenient' sentence given to Sharif and decided to take action. On 18 April they filed an appeal in the Sindh High Court seeking to overturn the ruling and instead impose the death penalty for Sharif on charges of hijacking and terrorism. At the same time, Sharif had also filed an appeal in the same court pleading for his acquittal. The Sindh High Court admitted the prosecution's appeal seeking the conversion of Sharif's life imprisonment sentence to a death penalty.[34]

The power struggle in Pakistan was unfolding as per the traditional script written by the Army, the country's dominant power centre. Musharraf was likely pleased with the verdict of the anti-terrorism court, although he continued to push for the conversion of Sharif's sentence to capital punishment. On 12 May 2000 the Supreme Court ruled that the military takeover in October 1999 was justified under the 'doctrine of necessity', which further strengthened his position.[35] The ruling was a familiar scenario in the history of Pakistan's struggle for power, since it echoed the previous decision made during the military rule of General Zia. The court justified the military takeover and gave the Army a three-year deadline to reinstate democracy. The verdict also stated that the state presented 'sufficient evidence of corruption of the former government'.[36]

It is worth noting that the ruling justifying the military coup was delivered by judges of the Supreme Court who had pledged allegiance to the military government in January. This had led to the removal of the then chief justice Saeed-uz Zaman Siddiqi and several other judges who had refused to recognize the legitimacy of the military government. In January 2000, six out of thirteen judges of the Supreme Court had declined to take oath under the PCO. The judges who took an oath under the PCO included Justice Iftikhar Muhammad Chaudhry, who later was hailed as an icon of the independence of the judiciary. In a separate judgement pronounced on 22 July, the accountability court sentenced Sharif to fourteen years in prison and banned him from holding public office for 21 years in a corruption case.

Seven-Point Agenda and Political Support

Upon taking office as chief executive, Musharraf made a pledge to implement a comprehensive seven-point agenda aimed at rebuilding national confidence and morale, strengthening the federation, reviving the economy, ensuring law and order and dispensing speedy justice, depoliticizing state institutions, devolving power to the grass-roots level and ensuring swift and across-the-board accountability. In order to prioritize and achieve tangible results, a four-point strategy was later developed, with a focus on reviving the economy, alleviating poverty, restructuring politics and devolving power to the grass-roots level. These goals were supposedly designed to improve the lives of citizens and bring about real change in Pakistan.[37]

In contrast to Zia, Musharraf did not make any promises about the future course of action when he seized power. When Musharraf met with a fact-finding team of visiting Commonwealth foreign ministers on 29 October, he told them that he could not guarantee when democracy would return to the country. He faced significant international pressure to restore democracy following his coup and was strongly criticized by both the Commonwealth and SAARC (South Asian Association for Regional Cooperation) for overthrowing a democratically elected government. In response to this pressure, he announced on 23 March 2000, just two days before the visit of President Clinton, that he would hold local-body elections later in the year, as a first step towards returning to 'real democracy'.

At a press conference, Musharraf outlined his plan for the elections, stating that the first round of local elections would be held between December 2000 and May 2001, followed by a second round of district-level elections in July 2001. By returning municipal governments to power, Musharraf argued that he was laying the foundation for a return to democracy, with a view to gradually moving towards provincial and federal elections in due course.[38]

Many saw Musharraf's promise of restoring 'real democracy' through local elections as a gimmick aimed at consolidating his personal power, similar to how Ayub Khan established basic democracies in 1962. Musharraf passionately explained his plan to hold elections at the local level as a means of devolving power to the people at the grass-roots level. Despite facing criticism both domestically and abroad, he reiterated his commitment to holding general elections after conducting local elections in July 2001, as he did during his visit to Thailand on 3 April 2000, as part of his Southeast Asian tour aimed at strengthening ties and attracting foreign investment.[39]

The extent of Musharraf's commitment to democracy can be questioned. Despite his promises to restore democracy, he issued a decree on 15 July 2000, reinstating the Islamic provisions of Pakistan's Constitution, which had been suspended since the coup. This was the second time in two months that Musharraf had bowed to demands from fundamentalist groups. In May, he withdrew a proposed amendment to the blasphemy law that was frequently used to target non-Muslim religious minorities. The decree aimed to reassert the continuity and enforceability of Pakistan's Islamic provisions, which had previously branded the Ahmadiyya sect as non-Muslims and prohibited any law that violated Islamic principles.[40]

A Critical Analysis of the 2002 Referendum

In an effort to legitimize his rule, Musharraf held a referendum on 30 April 2002. Despite independent Gallup surveys indicating a decline in his popularity leading up to the referendum, and reports from national and international media organizations and independent observers of a lacklustre turnout, the ECP reported a high turnout of 71 per cent, which was the highest in Pakistan's history. Official figures from the ECP claimed that 97.5 per cent of voters supported Musharraf, with only 2.5 per cent rejecting his candidacy. These results were met with scepticism and criticism from many both within Pakistan and abroad who questioned the transparency and fairness of the referendum.[41]

For the referendum, the voting age was lowered to eighteen years, and the traditional requirement to verify voters' eligibility through national identity cards and electoral lists was waived. In the referendum, the entire country was considered a single constituency, now with any citizens over eighteen allowed to cast a vote. According to the 1998 census, the number of people in the country aged eighteen years and above was 61.2 million. This number was estimated to have increased to 61.9 million by the date of the referendum. To ensure smooth conduct of the referendum, 87,074 polling stations and 163,641 additional polling booths were set up across the country. A team of 414,356 public sector employees was appointed to carry out various electoral duties on polling day.[42] The chief election commissioner, retired justice Irshad Hasan Khan, announced that a total of 43,907,950 votes were cast, with 42,804,030 votes in favour and 833,676 against.[43]

Despite Musharraf's victory being expected, the referendum was conducted to secure a significant turnout and confer legitimacy on his office. In pursuit of this goal, the government utilized various tactics, including associating with corrupt and criminal political figures, organizing public meetings at state expense and providing access to the entire state machinery to a select a few individuals to ensure a resounding majority. These efforts were aimed at bolstering Musharraf's position and lending credibility to his rule.[44] Taken together with the lowering of the voting age and the dismissal of identification requirements, these actions raised concerns about the fairness and transparency of the referendum, leaving many to question the legitimacy of the outcome.[45] Finally, it is worth noting that the government put significant pressure on *nazims* and councillors to support the referendum within their constituencies. Threats of withdrawal of government support were issued to thousands of local leaders who failed to muster sufficient backing for the referendum. This coercive approach was yet another attempt to manipulate the outcome of the referendum and consolidate Musharraf's power.[46]

Musharraf's campaign for the referendum started with rhetoric reminiscent of U.S. Secretary of State Colin Powell's 'you are either with us or against us' logic during the War on Terror. The general drew clear battle lines between himself and his opponents, stating that it was essential to identify those who supported his reforms and those who were against his policies. This uncompromising stance signalled his determination to crush any opposition to his rule and cement his position as the undisputed leader of Pakistan.[47] He announced it at his first public meeting in Lahore to which, according to credible reports, thousands of public sector employees had been forcibly bussed.

Typically, candidates in elections are responsible for their own electioneering expenses. However, since the government itself was conducting the referendum, it was argued that it should bear the costs associated with the process. According to reports, the government spent over PKR 100 million on a dozen or more public rallies held by Musharraf throughout the country. Officials in the federal finance ministry revealed that they had allocated a special grant of PKR 25 million to each province to cover the costs of printing and displaying posters, banners, placards, hoardings, flags and other such paraphernalia at these rallies. These expenditures raised questions about the fairness and impartiality of the referendum and fuelled concerns about the misuse of public funds for political gain.[48] In addition to the expenses associated with the public rallies, the federal government spent heavily on promotional advertisements in the national and local press and on digital election campaign activities.

With the absence of precise voter eligibility figures after the extension of franchise rights to all citizens aged eighteen and above, the ECP's assertion of a robust 71 per cent turnout was challenged by impartial observers. Their assessment considered polling irregularities, leading them to estimate the true turnout to hover between a mere 10 to 15 per cent. Such disparities cast a shadow of doubt over the referendum's legitimacy, intensifying apprehensions regarding the fairness of the electoral procedures.[49] In contrast, opposition parties claimed that the actual turnout was only 6 per cent and demanded that Musharraf consider this a vote of no confidence and step down from his post. Analysts, on the other hand, attributed the low turnout in the referendum to various factors, including the boycott by major political parties. Even the MQM withdrew its support for the referendum at the eleventh hour, further contributing to the public's apathy towards the exercise. Another possible explanation for the low turnout was the general public's disinterest in the day-to-day affairs of the government.[50]

The 2002 National Elections: Tailoring of the Electoral Rules

In early 2002 the military government proposed revisions to the electoral system to both the parliament and the provincial assemblies. On 21 August 2002 Musharraf announced the changes to the electoral system through the introduction of the Legal Framework Order 2002. It was also announced that elections to the National Assembly and provincial assemblies would be held on 10 October 2002, while Senate elections were rescheduled for 12 November.

The revised electoral system included several significant changes aimed at enhancing the democratic process. These changes included an increase in the number of seats in the National Assembly, Senate and provincial assemblies. Additionally, the number of seats reserved for women in both Houses of Parliament and provincial assemblies were also increased. The introduction of a joint electorate resulted in the abolition of the separate electorate for minority seats. Furthermore, as mentioned, the voting age was reduced from 21 years to eighteen, which allowed more citizens to participate in the democratic process.[51]

The Presidential Ordinance of July 2002 brought about a significant change in Pakistani politics by limiting the number of the prime minister's terms to two, effectively ruling out Sharif and Benazir Bhutto from holding office again. Pakistani politics, much like its South Asian counterparts, is dominated by powerful personalities rather than political parties with clear agendas and manifestos. This trend is not limited to the Sharifs or Bhuttos but can be observed across the political spectrum, including Imran Khan's Tehrik-e-Insaf, former president Farooq Laghari's Millat Party and Altaf Hussain's MQM, all of which are centred around their respective leaders. This cult of personality has been a persistent challenge for Pakistan's democratic stability and the development of a strong political system with institutionalized norms and procedures.[52] In the 2002 elections, political orientation remained unchanged, with party programmes, issues and manifestos playing little to no role. The 2002 elections were conducted on a joint electoral basis with a total of 272 seats for the National Assembly and 577 seats for the provincial assemblies across four provinces, including ten reserved for minorities and sixty reserved for women. The allocation of seats for women was determined by the proportional strength of the political parties in the general elections.[53] An encouraging number of women participated in the 2002 elections by contesting direct seats. It was a landmark moment in the history of Pakistan's elections, as 126 women contested for National Assembly and provincial assembly seats from the Punjab. This showed a positive trend of increasing women's participation in electoral politics. The surprisingly liberal nature of the Musharraf regime, coupled with awareness campaigns launched by NGOs, played a pivotal role in changing the conventional thinking of the masses and leaders, resulting in this positive development.

The 2002 elections saw an important development in the form of the slogans raised by political parties. However, even more interesting was the use of slogans by voters themselves to draw attention to their issues. One such popular demand was 'Roti Do, Vote Lo' (Give us Bread, We'll Give You Our Vote), which was heard in nearly all slum areas, constituting thousands of voters. Other similar slogans that gained popularity included 'Pani Do, Vote Lo' (Give Us Water, We'll Give You Our Vote) and 'Dispensary Do, Vote Lo' (Give Us a Dispensary, We'll Give You Our Vote).[54]

In the late 1970s, the majority of religio-political parties formed an alliance against the Bhutto government with the sole aim of ousting him from power. Similarly, in the 2002 elections, the religio-political parties formed an alliance known as the Muttahida-Majlis-e-Amal (MMA), comprising six religious parties. MMA had been hand in glove with Musharraf as it was given rule over NWFP. In addition to this, there were other electoral alliances, such as the National Alliance headed by Laghari, which included the Sindh Democratic Party and the PML-Q, also vying for power.[55]

The October 2002 elections resulted in a hung parliament, as the lower house of parliament's party profile shifted from a two-party-led system to a distinctive triangular representation. Despite this change, the PPP, one of the two previous major parties, managed to survive.[56] Two newcomers with familiar faces, namely the Pakistan Muslim League (Q) and the MMA, joined forces with the PPP in the lower house of parliament. In addition, ethnic parties such as the MQM and JWP made notable strides in their participation. Despite grappling with formidable challenges, the PML-N threw its hat into the electoral ring but emerged with a modest presence.

Meanwhile, other parties like the PPP (Sherpao) and PTI, led by Imran Khan, struggled to leave a substantial mark. In the National Assembly, the PML-Q won 77 seats, PPP-P 62, MMA 45, independents thirty, PML-N fifteen, MQM thirteen and NA thirteen, with several other parties winning only one to four seats each.

Musharraf not only restricted the mainstream parties PPP and PML-N but cultivated the religious parties and aided their coalition. Additionally, official support was given to the PML-Q, which became known as the 'King's Party'. The overall voter turnout was 40.69 per cent, with Islamabad having the highest turnout of 51.16 per cent, followed by the Punjab at 45.55 per cent, Sindh at 37.72 per cent, NWFP and tribal areas at 31.42 per cent and Baluchistan at 28.66 per cent. Despite all efforts, including pre-poll and polling-day rigging by the military government, the pro-government political parties, particularly the PML-Q and National Alliance, fell short of the necessary majority to elect a prime minister.[57] The election laws were frequently changed within one month of the 2002 elections to favour pro-government parties, and according to these laws, reserved seats were allocated based on the percentage of seats held by a political party in the National Assembly and provincial assemblies.

After the elections, Musharraf transferred some powers to the newly elected parliament in November 2002. The National Assembly then elected Mir Zafarullah Khan Jamali as the prime minister of Pakistan, and he subsequently formed his own cabinet. Jamali, a Baluch politician, was born on 1 January 1944 in the small village of Roojhan Jamali, located in Baluchistan's Nasirabad division. He hailed from a political family, with his father, Mir Shahnawaz Khan Jamali, being a *jirga* member and local landlord. Mir Zafarullah's grandfather, Mir Jaffar Khan Jamali, was a close friend of Muhammad Ali Jinnah.[58] He made history by becoming Pakistan's first Baluch prime minister. After completing his primary education in Baluchistan, he moved on to Lawrence College, Ghora Galli, for his secondary education. Later, he earned a master's degree in history from Government College, Lahore. While studying there, he was also known for his passion for hockey.

In the 1970s Jamali was a member of the provincial cabinet in the government of the PPP. Later in the 1980s, he served as a minister of various departments in the government of General Zia. Despite being considered for the position of prime minister in the 1980s, he was never appointed to the role. However, he had the opportunity to serve as the chief minister of Baluchistan on multiple occasions. During the 1990s, he was an important member of the PML-N. After the removal of Sharif, Jamali joined the newly formed faction of the Muslim League, the PML-Q, which was established to support General Musharraf.

Jamali was elected as Pakistan's prime minister on 21 November 2002, after weeks of political negotiations. With no party able to secure a majority in parliament, Jamali managed to secure the position with the help of a few defectors from the PPP to the PML-Q. He was seen as a close ally of Musharraf and supported his political and economic policies. Jamali promised to work towards restoring democracy in Pakistan and oversaw a broad political coalition during his tenure. However, his position was short-lived as he resigned on 26 June 2004, due to deteriorating relations with Chaudhry Shujaat Hussain,[59] a main force behind the PML-Q and a seasoned politician from Gujrat, who replaced him as interim prime minister. Some analysts speculate that it was the result of many aspiring politicians seeking to unseat him.

On 1 January 2004 Musharraf won a confidence vote in the Electoral College of Pakistan, which includes both Houses of Parliament and the four provincial assemblies. He secured 658 out of 1,170 votes, representing a 56 per cent majority, though members of the opposition and particularly those from religious parties walked out in protest. According to Article 41(8) of the Constitution of Pakistan, this vote meant that Musharraf was 'deemed to be elected' to the office of president, extending his term up to 2007. Unlike his 2002 referendum, which was widely criticized, Musharraf's election through the Electoral College received greater acceptance both inside and outside Pakistan.[60]

Chaudhry Shujaat Hussain served as interim prime minister before the National Assembly elected Shaukat Aziz, a former vice president of Citibank and head of Citibank Private Banking, as the new prime minister. After taking the oath of office, Aziz pledged to seek guidance from the president to ensure good governance.[61] The new government was widely perceived as being heavily influenced by Musharraf, who continued to hold the positions of president, head of state and COAS, and remained a central figure in the new dispensation, leading some to characterize it as a puppet government.[62]

The Seventeenth Amendment

After more than a year of political debates between supporters and opponents of Musharraf, the Constitution (Seventeenth Amendment) Act of 2003 was passed in December of that year, resulting in several changes to Pakistan's Constitutionincluding the integration of the Legal Framework Order. The amendment reversed the Thirteenth Amendment, reinstating the president's control over the prime minister and National Assembly. However, the role of the MMA in the passage of this amendment was dubious.

Musharraf's LFO was incorporated into the Constitution with a few modifications, one of which was the addition of Article 63(1)(d), effective 31 December 2004. The aim of this change was to prevent an individual from holding both a political office, such as the president, and an 'office of profit', usually held by a career government official, such as the COAS. However, the amendment had a loophole that allowed parliament to pass a law later that year allowing the president to hold both positions. He also regained the authority to dissolve the National Assembly, subject to approval or veto by the Supreme Court of Pakistan, and a governor's power to dissolve a provincial assembly was now subject to the Supreme Court's approval or veto. Article 152-A, which dealt with the National Security Council, was annulled, and its legal basis became an ordinary law, the National Security Council Act of 2004. The LFO had added ten laws to the Sixth Schedule, which was a list of 'laws that are not to be altered, repealed, or amended without the previous sanction of the President'. After this amendment, five of those laws would lose their Sixth Schedule protection after six years. The four laws that established the system of democratic local governments would be unprotected, which had raised concerns among opponents of the change that authoritarian provincial governments might disempower or even dismantle the system of local democracies.[63]

The Devolution Plan (Education and Health)

In late 1999 the idea of devolving power to the grass-roots level was introduced. The National Reconstruction Bureau (NRB), headed by Lieutenant General Tanvir Naqvi, spearheaded a discourse and consultation process with various stakeholders, including politicians, media and civil society. This led to the eventual promulgation of the Local Government Ordinance and the holding of multi-stage elections for local bodies.[64] Although the structure of political decentralization had been partially established, its capacity to deliver remained uncertain. After nearly two years of implementation, it became clear that the system could not meet the expectations set for it.[65] Numerous factors contributed to the inefficient public-service delivery during the devolution process. Chief among these was the lack of clarity in the rules of business, which left citizens unsure of their rights and responsibilities. This led to tensions between district *nazims* and district coordination officers (DCOs), as well as between *nazims* and district police officers (DPOs). While some districts were fortunate enough to see positive results from the devolution system, with *nazims* and other district officers able to establish a working rapport, most areas experienced a standstill. With no established institutional arrangements, things were being run on an ad hoc basis.[66]

Critics of the system also pointed fingers at Civil Service inertia, which they believed played a role in the system's failure. While it is true that the devolution process deprived the bureaucracy of the absolute powers they had previously enjoyed, tensions between *nazims* and district officers responsible for various departments at the Civil Secretariat were primarily caused by the fact that provincial governments were the ones responsible for recruiting these officers, with districts having no say in their hiring and firing. Additionally, some officials who had no relationship with the district *nazims* were still required to serve under them, further complicating matters.[67]

The relationship between provincial and local governments was marked by tension and conflict. One notable example was the strained relationship between the MMA government in NWFP and the district governments in the province. The situation became so dire that Musharraf had to intervene in order to prevent the system from collapsing altogether.[68] While the devolution plan initially stipulated that local governments would work within the provincial framework, it ultimately led to provinces feeling that their already limited autonomy had been further diminished.

One of the key features of the devolution plan was the establishment of community citizen boards (CCBs) to mobilize resources at the local level and address governance issues and citizen accountability. As per the plan, CCBs were expected to contribute one-fifth of the cost for improving public facilities or managing new development initiatives, with the remaining four-fifths to be provided by the local government.[69] The dual role of CCBs presented an inherent conflict, since they were expected to act as both development partners and watchdogs of the process. The 20:80 partnership model had the potential to bring about significant changes in traditional power dynamics. But there were concerns that this model might open the door for local elites to exert influence over decision-making processes that were previously the sole purview of the bureaucratic system. Furthermore, in numerous regions, these CCBs were not set up at all, resulting in local governments being unable to allocate funds.

The same fate befell public safety commissions (PSCs), as high-handedness on the part of the police continued unabated and even increased noticeably. *Nazims* found themselves helpless in resolving police-related issues affecting their constituents.[70]

The devolution plan placed the responsibility of developmental work in the hands of local governments. However, in well-functioning democracies, parliamentarians are typically engaged in both legislation and the development process, making them genuine stakeholders in the latter. Some parliamentarians believed that without their involvement in the development programme under the devolution plan, they would be unable to retain their seats in parliament.[71]

Fiscal decentralization proved to be another thorny issue in terms of the relationship between provincial and district governments. The implementation of fiscal decentralization varied across provinces. For instance, in the Punjab, district allocations were categorized as one-line items in the provincial budget, and the lower tiers, such as district councils or municipal committees, were involved in fiscal transfers.[72] In contrast, in Sindh, the accountant general's office was responsible for disbursing payments allocated by the provincial government, and the allocations were subject to specified heads of accounts. This made it challenging for districts to effectively utilize the funds. In neither case, however, were the districts raising resources locally.[73]

The district governments that were newly formed became heavily reliant on federal transfers, which led to a contentious situation as there were complaints about delays in payments due to procedural bottlenecks. These delays had a significant impact on the implementation of development projects.

The policy organization the International Crisis Group argued in March 2004 that the rationale for Musharraf's devolution plan was a ruse to bring legitimacy to his rule.[74] The Musharraf government's devolution plan was distorted even further through rigged polls in order to ensure regime survival as it entered its sixth year. However, this political engineering only led to increased divisions at the local and provincial levels and ultimately engendered greater political violence. The consequences of this manipulation were dire, resulting in the loss of at least sixty lives and leaving more than five hundred people injured during the local elections.[75]

The military government presented the devolution plan as a solution to improve public services and attract donor support. However, instead of being a technocratic solution or an effort to empower people, the devolution process was merely a political gimmick to prolong military power.[76] In the absence of representative governance, persistent ethno-regional and political disaffection posed serious risks to the country's political development and economic viability.[77]

The electoral process had worsened already strained relations between the central government and the four provinces, leading to a low-level insurgency over political issues and resource allocation in Baluchistan.[78] The local elections in Pakistan had severe consequences. The country was already divided along ethnic lines, and the elections further exacerbated local clan and ethnic rivalries. The participation of women in politics decreased, and the elections weakened and divided political parties. As a result, there was constant erosion of the political space for secular democratic parties, which provided a big boost to extremist and religious groups and factions. The situation in Karachi was particularly volatile, with the smouldering embers of violence threatening to conflagrate. This divisive atmosphere posed serious risks to Pakistan's political development and economic viability.[79]

Dawn reported on 8 August 2004 that representatives from civil society and NGOs had rejected the devolution plan, referring to it as a 'destruction plan'.[80] They argued that it disrupted the chain of command at provincial and local government levels, and that it was conceptually flawed, eroded political accountability and created societal chaos. The plan, introduced by the NRB, was widely criticized for being misleading and lacking in transparency.[81] Experts widely criticized the devolution plan for lacking political legitimacy and for being an attempt to erode the political system at the grass-roots level. They argued that the plan had created unrest in the entire hierarchy of the local government system, leaving people uncertain about whom to report to.[82]

The group of experts, who worked closely with local government representatives, expressed their view that the system introduced by the devolution plan was a combination of decentralization and delegation of power, rather than a true devolution of power at the grass-roots level. They pointed out that this lack of true devolution was the reason why positive impacts were not being seen and why a tug of war had started among legislators, union councils, *nazims* and bureaucrats.[83]

> The lack of political will and capacity at the district level has resulted in millions of rupees lying unutilized with the district governments. The responsibility for allocating these funds, planning developmental projects, and ensuring accountability remains unclear. This has led to confusion and inaction, with no one taking ownership of the process.[84]

Structural Reforms in the Police

The legal framework of the police underwent a significant change due to the implementation of the Devolution of Power Plan. The plan aimed to transfer the authority of the provincial government to the districts and introduce public accountability of the police. To achieve this goal, the office of the district magistrate was abolished in 2001 and a system of PSCs was introduced.[85] These changes were incorporated into a new police law, which was promulgated in 2002. The Police Order 2002 not only provided for the PSCs but established a professional Police Complaints Authority, enhanced powers for the inspector general of police, and the separation of the watch and ward and investigation functions of the police.[86]

A report from Lahore, which was published in *Dawn* on 3 January 2005, indicated that the implementation of the Police Order 2002, even after the amendments, would require a substantial amount of time.[87] The process of selecting six independent members for the National Public Safety Commission was still ongoing when the National Assembly speaker nominated elected members. The provincial public safety and complaint commissions were yet to be established, while the district public safety commissions had been partially set up in all provinces. The Punjab had 31 out of 34 districts covered, Sindh had twelve out of sixteen, Baluchistan had twenty out of 26 and NWFP had 22 out of 23.

According to Articles 97 and 98 of the law, the government was to appoint six members of the Federal Police Complaints Authority based on the recommendations of the Federal Public Service Commission. However, the process of selecting these members was still ongoing. The implementation of the law required serious commitment from all stakeholders, which was starkly missing.[88]

The National Accountability Bureau

The National Accountability Bureau (NAB) was established under the National Accountability Ordinance 1999 as the successor to the Ehtesab Bureau. Initially, the NAB carried out its operations across the country from Islamabad until March 2000, when regional offices were established. As the organization evolved over the years, its policies, structures and processes underwent several transitions. In 2002, the National Anti-corruption Strategy (NACS) was approved, and the NAB was entrusted with two additional functions, namely awareness and prevention, in addition to its primary function of enforcement.[89] Subsequently, the NAB also acquired the Anti-corruption Operations (ACO) and Economic Crime Wing (ECW) of the Federal Investigation Agency (FIA), along with their manpower, budget and workload. As a result of these changes and the evolving nature of the organization, there were several attempts to restructure it.[90]

Following the change of leadership in November 2005, a comprehensive evaluation of the NAB's existing policies, structures and processes was deemed necessary. The organization adopted a new operational methodology and organizational structure, which reorganized its main tasks into four functional divisions: Operations, Prosecution, Awareness and Prevention and Human Resource and Finance.

It should be noted that the NAB has been widely viewed as a powerful tool for the president and the establishment to suppress independent-minded politicians who deviated from the norms established by state functionaries. Moreover, the NAB had played a significant role in forging the ruling coalition led by the PML-Q by pressuring politicians with questionable credentials to support Musharraf's allies in power. As a result, these politicians not only evaded accountability but received yet another opportunity to enrich themselves.

The Charter of Democracy

The Charter of Democracy was approved and signed by former prime ministers Benazir Bhutto and Sharif in May 2006, after several hours of clause-by-clause discussions by the enlarged negotiating teams of the PPP and the PML-N in London. The purpose of the charter was to unite the two parties against dictatorship and commit to restoring the Constitution to its original form. They agreed that free and fair elections were not possible under the supervision of Musharraf, and promised to return to the country together before the election. They also pledged not to approach the Army for support or sign any military agreement in their pursuit of power. The

Pervez Musharraf, 2005.

signing of the charter, known as *Misaq-e-Jamhouriyat*, became a significant event in the political history of Pakistan against martial law.

The Charter of Democracy outlined various key decisions, such as bringing the 1973 Constitution back to its original form, passing the budget for defence in parliament, establishing a commission for the appointment of judges of the Supreme Court, making the tribal areas of FATA part of the Frontier Province, and investing more power in the 'Legislative Council' established in the northern regions for the benefit of the people. The abolition of the National Security Council, forming the Defence Committee of the Cabinet, establishing the 'Truth and Reconciliation Commission' to investigate incidents like Kargil, and the NAB's own accountability were also emphasized.

The charter also stressed the importance of cordial relations with India and Afghanistan and resolving the Kashmir issue according to UN conventions. Similarly, it was decided to appoint an election commissioner with the advice of the government and opposition for free elections. The intelligence agencies would be accountable to the government, and their political cells would also be abolished.

A Second Stint of Presidency and the National Reconciliation Ordinance

On 28 November 2007, Musharraf retired as COAS. He took oath for the second term as civilian president of Pakistan on 29 November 2007. For that, Musharraf reached a compromise through the infamous NRO, which was issued on 5 October 2007. Representatives of Benazir and Musharraf held at least five meetings between 2005 and 2006. These discussions also included Tariq Aziz; General Ashfaq Parvez Kayani, the DG of the ISI; and later General Hamid Javed, Musharraf's chief of staff. These meetings were initially arranged and facilitated by the British Foreign Office. However, when an agreement was imminent, London allowed the USA to take over. The military proposed that they only deal with Benazir and not Zardari, which Benazir successfully rejected. After a tumultuous process of building trust with the Army and overcoming internal opposition within the PPP, Benazir and Musharraf finally met face to face on 24 January 2007.[91]

Musharraf spoke about the need for positive changes that could create a better political environment in the country by eliminating the politics of vengeance and persecution. He explained that after consulting with his colleagues in the government and various political leaders, they decided to provide a general amnesty to politicians as a step towards achieving this goal. 'Our decision to offer this amnesty was aimed at promoting a more conducive political climate in the country,' Musharraf stated.[92] According to him, the period between 1988 and 1999 was characterized by political confrontations, retribution, victimization and reciprocal legal action against one another by the political parties. He stated that the government aimed to put an end to this culture, and as such, they made the decision to close the numerous cases that had been lingering for up to fifteen years, with some never even having been initiated. The general amnesty would help to put an end to the cycle of legal battles and promote a more peaceful and stable political environment.[93] Musharraf emphasized that the NRO was not aimed at benefiting any particular political party. Rather, it was a means to create an environment of reconciliation and positive politics in the country. To ensure transparency, a committee was established to review the pending cases and distinguish between genuine and false allegations. The committee would dismiss cases that lacked merit while pursuing those with credible evidence. Additionally, Musharraf explained that the NAB would continue to investigate corruption cases with proper evidence. The NAB had played a significant role in recovering substantial sums of money from politicians, bureaucrats, businessmen, bankers and armed forces personnel. The fear of God had been instilled in the minds of powerful and influential individuals, thanks to the NAB's work.[94] However, the fact remains that, despite its implications for the country's governance, the agreement brokered by the Americans and the British resulted in more than 8,000 bureaucrats, government officials, bankers and politicians charged with corruption offences between 1986 and 1990 receiving amnesty, including Benazir and Zardari. According to documents provided by the NAB to the Supreme Court, these individuals were suspected of embezzling PKR 1,060 billion from Pakistan, with Benazir and Zardari together accounting for 140 billion of that total.[95] In addition, it is important to note that PKR 2 billion of Pakistani taxpayers' money was previously spent on pursuing corruption cases against Benazir and Zardari in Swiss courts, which makes the NRO even more significant. The NRO also resulted in the annulment of thousands of cases of murder and assassination believed to have been committed by the MQM, further demonstrating the far-reaching effects of this ordinance.[96]

Musharraf disclosed that the proposed Parliamentary Ethics Committee, which was mentioned in the NRO, would keep a strong check on political victimization, if any, and ensure transparency in the election process.[97] The NRO facilitated the return of former prime minister Benazir Bhutto from self-exile in London to lead her PPP in the upcoming parliamentary elections as its chairperson. Prime Minister Shaukat Aziz further stated that the national reconciliation agreement, which had been approved by the cabinet, was a positive step towards resolving Pakistan's long-standing political turmoil and promoting harmony in the country.

A Beleaguered State of the Economy

Following the nuclear tests in Baluchistan in May 1998, the United States and the North Atlantic Treaty Organization (NATO) imposed economic sanctions on Pakistan. When Musharraf seized power in a *coup d'état* in 1999, Pakistan was expelled from the Commonwealth, exacerbating the country's economic problems. Many experts deemed Pakistan a failed state: it was on the verge of bankruptcy, and investor confidence had hit rock bottom. In fact, when Musharraf assumed power, Pakistan was technically bankrupt, with both remittances and export income in decline. The IMF and the World Bank had also suspended their programmes with Pakistan.[98] Pakistan was at risk of defaulting, but both Islamabad and its creditors had a mutual interest in avoiding this scenario in order to prevent further economic damage. Throughout Musharraf's tenure, the economic situation improved significantly. One of his most noteworthy achievements was increasing Pakistan's foreign-exchange reserves, in U.S. dollars, from $1.6 billion when he assumed power to $14.3 billion when he left office.[99]

Annual growth of 4.2 per cent had increased to 7 per cent by the time he resigned. Foreign direct investment reached a record level of over $5 billion in 2006–7.[100] The IMF's 2007 assessment highlighted that the Musharraf administration's prudent macroeconomic management and extensive structural reforms had significantly contributed to the high GDP growth, a decrease in the debt burden and an improved business environment in Pakistan.[101]

Musharraf also succeeded in garnering substantial foreign aid during his tenure. Specifically, between the 9/11 attacks and 2007, Pakistan received a substantial $12.3 billion in overt U.S. aid. This figure encompassed four main funding streams: coalition support funds, budget support, security assistance and development aid. What's more, it was likely to have been matched or even surpassed by classified funds allocated for intelligence operations and covert military endeavours.¹⁰² Hence, the real total of U.S. aid to Pakistan post-9/11 might be nearer to $20 billion. The international community extended support to Pakistan's anti-terrorism efforts by restructuring its debts, resulting in savings of hundreds of millions of dollars and facilitating access to new loans. Consequently, the foreign-exchange reserves increased to over $16 billion in 2006, but at the same time the foreign debt hit an all-time high of $40 billion. The government claimed that the economy had grown in several sectors and that per capita income in Pakistan had more than doubled in the previous seven years as a result. Nevertheless, the Musharraf regime failed to address the structural socio-economic weaknesses that continued to hinder sustainable growth, such as a lack of export diversification, low taxation rates, poor infrastructure and inadequate investment in human capital. The last contributed to lower productivity and demand. The gains made in reducing indebtedness and increasing foreign reserves post-9/11 were a one-time windfall.¹⁰³

Musharraf's Compromise on Corruption

The results of a poll conducted by Dawn News, Indian Express and CNN-IBN showed that the majority of respondents believed that corruption increased during the Musharraf era. Additionally, an Asian Development Bank report on the state of the country during Pakistan's sixtieth Independence anniversary described the country as having 'poor governance, endemic corruption, and social indicators that are among the worst in Asia'.¹⁰⁴ The allegations that corrupt servicemen were not being prosecuted and their practices were condoned due to the junta's clout had been in circulation. The Pakistani media alleged that the previous governments' individual corruption was substituted by the Pakistan Army's institutionalized corruption, awarding land deeds and a life of luxury to its officers. In her book *Military Inc.*, Ayesha Siddiqa Agha reveals the commercial character of the Pakistan Army, which has evolved into the largest corporate body in the country.¹⁰⁵

Despite promising to prioritize the elimination of corruption after the 1999 coup, it quickly became apparent that Musharraf was willing to compromise on this commitment if it served his political interests. In exchange for validating his coup, the judiciary secured a guarantee that judges would not be investigated for corruption, and the military announced that journalists would not be investigated either in an effort to maintain positive press coverage.

However, by 2002, the regime's commitment to fighting corruption had all but disappeared. Moreover, there were allegations that corrupt service personnel were not being held accountable due to the military's influence, with some suggesting that institutionalized corruption had replaced individual corruption under previous governments.¹⁰⁶

Admiral Mansur ul-Haq (1937–2018) served as chief of naval staff from 1994 to 1997. However, rumours about his alleged involvement in taking kickbacks on defence contracts began circulating shortly after he assumed the role. These rumours were linked to payments made during the technology transfer of submarines from France.[107] The civilian government under Benazir Bhutto yielded to pressure from other service chiefs who believed that formally charging ul-Haq with taking kickbacks on defence contracts would undermine the prestige of the armed forces. After Musharraf's coup, the new authorities claimed to be committed to pursuing the case, and in May 2001, they managed to gather enough evidence to extradite Mansur ul-Haq from the United States to face charges in Pakistani courts. However, by the end of that year, the military's commitment to the anti-corruption drive had waned. In a deal struck with the National Accountability Bureau, ul-Haq paid back $7.5 million to the state, but he did not face imprisonment, despite admitting to misappropriating the money. This case followed a pattern: by early 2002, several politicians found that their corruption cases had been dropped. It is worth noting that the amount ul-Haq promised to repay was equivalent to 1,270 years of an admiral's salary, or twice the annual salary bill for the Navy's entire personnel, as pointed out by a Pakistani journalist.[108]

The military's excuse for the softened approach towards white-collar crime was that finding solid evidence had been difficult and time-consuming. However, the real reason was that the Army viewed legal cases as useful tools to control politicians. They could revive corruption cases against any politician who crossed the line of acceptable criticism of the military, while dropping cases against those who acquiesced to the military regime.

Musharraf's failure to confront corruption reached its climax in 2007, when he faced increasing pressure from the United States to allow Benazir Bhutto, who was in self-imposed exile, to return to Pakistan. In 2003, a Geneva magistrate had found Bhutto and her husband guilty of money laundering.[109] The Pakistani government alleged that Benazir Bhutto and Asif Zardari had bought Rockwood Palace, a country home in the UK, using money obtained through kickbacks. In 2006 Lord Justice Collins, an English judge, stated that there was a 'reasonable prospect' of the Pakistani government proving this claim. However, Bhutto and Zardari employed various tactics to delay the case and avoid a verdict. One of their strategies, which ultimately proved to be somewhat embarrassing, was to have Zardari declared mentally ill. His lawyers submitted documents from doctors claiming that he suffered from severe psychiatric problems, including dementia, major depressive disorder and post-traumatic stress disorder.[110] When he became president, his aides were quick to say that even if dementia was not an irreversible illness, he had fully recovered.

Benazir Bhutto was also embroiled in allegations related to the UN oil-for-food scandal. The Independent Inquiry Commission led by former U.S.

Federal Reserve head Paul Volcker investigated the scandal in 2005 and found that over 2,000 companies had made illegal payments to Saddam Hussein's government in Iraq, breaching UN sanctions. One of these companies was Petroline FZC, based in the United Arab Emirates. The inquiry found that the company had traded U.S.$144 million of Iraqi oil and made illegal payments of U.S.$2 million to Saddam's regime. According to documents from Pakistan's National Accountability Bureau, Benazir Bhutto was the company's chairwoman.[111]

The exposure of international cases of corruption was not limited to foreign jurisdictions alone, since many of these cases were also brought up within Pakistan. In addition, numerous cases involving kickbacks came to light in the country, including corrupt deals related to gold import licences, Polish tractors and French fighter jets.[112] Musharraf was convinced of Bhutto's corruption and initially pledged to convict her. He stated unequivocally in 2001 that legal action would be taken against her. However, it proved to be a more complicated task than anticipated. Bhutto's lawyers, both at home and abroad, managed to impede any progress in the courts. As time passed, and Musharraf's popularity dwindled, he found himself increasingly reliant on support from political parties. Meanwhile, allegations of corruption against other politicians continued to surface, putting pressure on Musharraf to address the issue.

Benazir Bhutto proposed a deal to her members of the National Assembly (MNAs) in which she requested that they not block Musharraf's election as president in October 2007 in exchange for amnesty. The Americans supported this plan with enthusiasm, since they believed that Bhutto's comeback to Pakistani politics would create a favourable scenario for them, with a democratic and legitimate leader committed to fighting Islamic radicalism working alongside Musharraf, who had the support of the Army and the ability to get things done.[113]

The idea that Benazir Bhutto and Musharraf could work together was overly optimistic. The two leaders lacked trust in each other, and it was inevitable that their relationship would deteriorate. Despite this, the 2007 NRO was negotiated after several clandestine meetings in Dubai between Musharraf and Bhutto. The terms of the agreement meant that both Bhutto and Zardari's corruption cases were dismissed, while Sharif remained vulnerable to prosecution if necessary. This outcome disgusted most Pakistanis. Musharraf, who had initially promised swift justice when he came to power in 1999, had abandoned the rule of law by making a secret deal with one of the politicians he had once criticized.

Musharraf and the Judiciary

On 9 March 2007 Musharraf suspended the chief justice of Pakistan, Justice Iftikhar Muhammad Chaudhry.[114] The circumstances surrounding the detention of Justice Chaudhry are somewhat disputed. In an interview with Geo TV, Musharraf claimed that Justice Chaudhry himself requested a meeting with him, during which Musharraf presented evidence related to abuse-of-office charges made against Chaudhry. However, other sources assert that Chaudhry was summoned by Musharraf to his Army residence in Rawalpindi and asked to explain his position on a list of charges brought against him by various parties. Chaudhry refused to resign and was subsequently detained. The accuracy of Musharraf's version is contested, since the affidavit Chaudhry presented in the Supreme Court contradicts it, stating that he had requested an appointment with the president and was not asked to resign. Following Chaudhry's detention, Justice Javaid Iqbal was appointed as the acting chief justice of the Supreme Court.[115]

Musharraf's decision to suspend Justice Chaudhry caused an uproar among Pakistani lawyers and civil society. On 12 March 2007 lawyers across Pakistan began boycotting all court procedures to protest against the suspension, which they saw as unconstitutional. Thousands of lawyers, dressed in their professional attire, took to the streets in all major cities, condemning the move. The support for the ousted chief justice continued to grow, and, by May, protesters and opposition parties organized huge rallies against Musharraf's regime. In response, Musharraf's tenure as Army chief was challenged in the courts. Unfortunately, rallies held by political parties, including the MQM, turned violent, resulting in more than forty deaths in the streets of Karachi on 12 May. The offices of AAJ TV were also damaged in the crossfire, and opposition parties alleged that the government and rangers had failed to stop the violence.

On 20 July 2007 the Supreme Court of Pakistan reinstated Chaudhry as chief justice and dismissed the misconduct charges filed against him by Musharraf. However, the situation changed on 3 November when Musharraf declared a state of emergency, leading to the dismissal of Chaudhry and several other members of the judiciary, including Justice Rana Bhagwan Das. This move sparked widespread outrage among the general public and members of civil society, leading to an unprecedented clamour for justice.

The Lal Masjid Siege

The Lal Masjid (Red Mosque) issue proved to be a significant embarrassment for the Musharraf regime. However, it is important to note that the blame for the unfortunate incident cannot be entirely attributed to Musharraf. The issue had a complex history that dated back to the Zia era. Maulana Muhammad Abdullah, a Deobandi cleric and founder imam of the mosque, was a close friend of Zia ul Haq and an avid supporter of the extremist group SSP.[116] Unfortunately, he was killed in 1998 allegedly by Shia militants. The mosque has been in a central area of Islamabad since 1965, and its clerics have been actively supporting the Taliban in Afghanistan while promoting the Deobandi puritanical brand of Islam. In 2006 Abdul Aziz, the eldest son of Maulana Abdullah, issued a fatwa stating that Army personnel fighting the Taliban would be denied a Muslim burial, and the Lal Masjid administration published fifty preliminary guidelines for the enforcement of Sharia in Pakistan. As a result, it became a significant centre for recruiting fighters for the Afghan jihad.[117] In 2007 the Lal Masjid clerics made headlines by challenging the authority of the state for the first time. Abdul Aziz even went so far as to threaten the government with a brigade of suicide bombers if they tried to prevent the implementation of Sharia law and attacked the Lal Masjid and its affiliated seminaries.[118] Gradually, the situation deteriorated, leading to an open confrontation between Maulana Abdul Aziz, his younger brother Abdul Rashid Ghazi and state agencies.[119]

The confrontation with the Army began when Ume-Hassan, the principal of Jamia Hafsa and wife of Maulana Abdul Aziz, encouraged female students to take over a nearby children's library and abduct Chinese women whom they accused of running a brothel. This incident escalated the protests that had started in January 2007 when the government demolished illegally constructed mosques in Islamabad. For years, the Capital Development Authority (CDA) had turned a blind eye to the expansion of the Lal Masjid and Jamia Hafsa. The vigilante actions of the Jamia Hafsa students, who sought to impose Sharia law, led to clashes with male students from the Lal Masjid. The latter group also resorted to unlawful acts such as destroying CDs and cassettes put up for sale in local shops.[120]

The defining moment of the Lal Masjid stand-off came on the morning of 8 July 2007, when the government delegation, led by Shujaat Hussain, announced that negotiations with the militants who assumed control of the mosque had made some progress, but no agreement could be reached due to the clerics' refusal to accede to the demands of state agencies. The stand-off persisted for several days, during which Abdul Rashid Ghazi, the deputy cleric of the mosque, held the fort with several hundred students and militants, including young girls. When negotiations failed to yield results, the troops were given the go-ahead to storm the complex, code-named Operation Sunrise, with the objective of capturing or killing the militants if they resisted and rescuing the students held as hostages.[121] The operation resulted in a substantial loss of life, including that of a military colonel. The incident triggered an unending spate of suicide bombings in Pakistan, which led to *The Economist* characterizing Pakistan as 'the world's most dangerous place' on its title page and in its lead story. *Newsweek* later echoed the same sentiment.[122]

The military operation at the Lal Masjid was deemed successful, but it ultimately resulted in an escalation of insurgencies in Waziristan through the newly formed Tehrik-e-Taliban Pakistan (TTP). Following a brief incarceration, Maulana Abdul Aziz was released and publicly denounced suicide attacks and bombings, although he thanked Allah for empowering individuals like Fazlullah and Sufi Muhammad to enforce Sharia. Punjab-based sectarian militants from groups such as SSP and Lashkar-i-Jhangvi joined the TTP, and for the first time, the state of Pakistan became a target, particularly in the Pashtun areas and eventually in the Punjab itself. As time passed, these attacks became more daring, targeting the Army and the ISI, who had formerly helped nurture and protect these militant organizations. In July following the Lal Masjid operation, there was an average of one suicide attack per day. These attacks targeted security forces, government buildings and Western symbols in Pakistan, such as the Marriott Hotel in Islamabad, which was hit in September 2008. Although Musharraf survived more than one assassination attempt, Benazir Bhutto fell victim to the mounting violence, which, in 2008 alone, saw more than 2,000 terrorist attacks resulting in the death or injury of around 7,000 people.[123]

The Pakistan Institute for Peace Studies released a report in which it revealed alarming statistics regarding the country's security situation in 2007. According to the report, there were 1,503 violent incidents in that year alone, which included terrorist attacks and political and sectarian clashes, resulting in 3,448 deaths and 5,353 injuries. These figures represented a significant increase of 128 per cent and 491.7 per cent over the 2006 and 2005 numbers, respectively. Out of these, there were sixty suicide attacks, which claimed 770 lives and injured 1,574 people. Additionally, there were twelve political clashes, which caused 64 fatalities and an equal number of injuries. Security personnel were particularly vulnerable, and terrorists targeted them in several attacks, killing 232 soldiers, 163 paramilitary personnel and 71 policemen. The Lal Masjid operation, conducted in July, coincided with a wave of violence that saw fifteen suicide attacks in NWFP, Islamabad and the Punjab, resulting in the loss of 191 lives and injuries to 366 others.[124]

Foreign Policy

In the aftermath of the devastating 11 September 2001 attacks, Musharraf aligned himself with the United States in its war against the Taliban government in Afghanistan following an ultimatum by then U.S. president George W. Bush. To assist in the effort, Musharraf agreed to provide the United States with the use of three airbases for Operation Enduring Freedom. These events presented overwhelming challenges for Musharraf as the magnitude of the attacks on New York and Washington, DC, reverberated around the world. The world's only superpower had been attacked on its own soil, and its own aircrafts had been used as a weapon. This tragedy dealt a severe blow to the pride of the United States, and it was clear that the country would respond with a fierce determination, akin to that of a 'wounded bear'.[125] The validity of these concerns was soon confirmed as the

U.S. government identified al-Qaeda, based in neighbouring Afghanistan under the protection of the Taliban, international pariahs, as the perpetrator. Ironically, Pakistan was the only country that maintained diplomatic relations with the Taliban regime and its leader, Mullah Omar. The morning after the attacks, Musharraf was presiding over a meeting in the Governor House, Karachi, when he received a call from U.S. Secretary of State Colin Powell. Powell's message was unambiguous: 'You are either with us or against us.' It was a blatant ultimatum that left no room for ambiguity. At the time, Pakistan's director general of the ISI was in Washington, where he met with the U.S. deputy secretary of state, Richard Armitage. In what is widely regarded as the most undiplomatic statement ever made, Armitage told the director general that Pakistan had to choose whether it was with America or the terrorists. If Pakistan chose the latter, he warned, it should be prepared to be bombed back to the Stone Age. It was a shockingly barefaced threat, but it was clear that the United States had decided to retaliate with full force.[126]

After considering all available options, particularly given that India had already offered its bases to the United States, Musharraf felt he had no choice but to comply with their demands. Pakistan's military and economic vulnerabilities, along with a lack of unity that was necessary to mobilize the country for confrontational action, left Musharraf with little choice but to align with the Americans.

Colin Powell and other officials met with Musharraf to establish the framework for cooperation in the prosecution of the 'War on Terror'. On 19 September 2001 Musharraf addressed the people of Pakistan and stated that, while he opposed military tactics against the Taliban, Pakistan risked being attacked by both India and the United States if it did not cooperate. In 2006 Musharraf reiterated that he had been pressured into taking this stance by threats from the United States. In his memoirs, he revealed that he had even 'war-gamed' the possibility of the United States becoming an adversary and concluded that it would ultimately result in defeat for Pakistan.[127]

A parallel development was taking place alongside this. Anti-American sentiment had deeply permeated the country, and even senior Army officers were not immune to it. *The Guardian* reported on 22 July 2004 that Omar Sheikh, a British-born Islamist, had wired U.S.$100,000 to Mohammed Atta, the lead hijacker of the 9/11 attacks, on the instructions of General Mahmoud Ahmad, the former head of Pakistan's ISI.[128] After the *Wall Street Journal* exposed Ahmed for sending money to the hijackers, Musharraf forced him to retire. However, the 9/11 commission did not investigate this funding due to a lack of credibility. Then, in September 2007, following the Lal Masjid incident, Ayman Zawahiri, al-Qaeda's leader and deputy of Osama bin Laden, urged his followers to wage a holy war against Musharraf and the Pakistani Army.[129]

Musharraf was serving as the COAS during the Mujahideen incursion into India from Pakistan-administered Kashmir in the summer of 1999. While Pakistan maintained that these were Kashmiri freedom fighters from Indian-controlled Kashmir, subsequent events revealed that they were Pakistani paramilitary soldiers supporting separatists on the mountaintops. Following intense fighting and significant loss of life, Pakistani soldiers were eventually withdrawn due to pressure from the international community, primarily the United States.[130] In the book *Battle Ready*, co-authored by former CENTCOM commander-in-chief Anthony Zinni and novelist Tom Clancy, a different version of events is presented. According to Zinni and Clancy, it was Musharraf who pushed Sharif to withdraw Pakistani troops from Kargil after realizing that the situation was unwinnable. Additionally, an ex-official of the Musharraf government, Hassan Abbas, has claimed that Musharraf had planned the entire operation and convinced Sharif to implement it.[131] Benazir Bhutto provided insight into Musharraf's intentions to attempt the Kargil infiltrations much earlier, in an interview with a leading daily newspaper. According to Bhutto, Musharraf had boasted that he would 'hoist the flag of Pakistan atop the Srinagar Assembly' if his plan was executed. This statement suggests that Musharraf had long harboured plans for the Kargil conflict and had an ambitious objective in mind.[132] According to the PML-N, Musharraf had orchestrated the Kargil intrusions but became flustered when the conflict with India broke out, prompting him to inform Sharif. The timing of the Kargil incident, which followed the Lahore Peace Summit earlier that year, only intensified the already-present suspicion towards Musharraf in India.

Starting in the middle of 2004, Musharraf initiated a series of talks with India aimed at resolving the long-standing Kashmir dispute. The talks covered a range of issues, including the Wullar Barrage and Kishanganga power project, the Baglihar Dam on the Chenab River in Jammu and Kashmir, the disputed Sir Creek estuary at the mouth of the Rann of Kutch, the Siachen glacier, the status of Gurdaspur and Ferozepur, Hindu–Muslim relations, autonomy for Sikhs in the Indian Punjab and minority rights. Additionally, India raised concerns about Pakistan's alleged sponsorship of 'cross-border' terrorism.[133] Following a meeting with Indian prime minister Manmohan Singh in 2007, Musharraf declared that the efforts to normalize relations between India and Pakistan were 'irreversible'.[134]

One of the most notable controversies during Musharraf's administration was the revelation of nuclear proliferation by Abdul Qadeer Khan, the metallurgist considered to be the father of Pakistan's nuclear bomb. Musharraf has denied any knowledge or involvement by Pakistan's government or Army in this proliferation, and has faced criticism for publicly condemning Khan, who was once considered a national hero. Khan was later pardoned following confession in exchange for cooperation in the investigation, but remained under house arrest for a significant period of

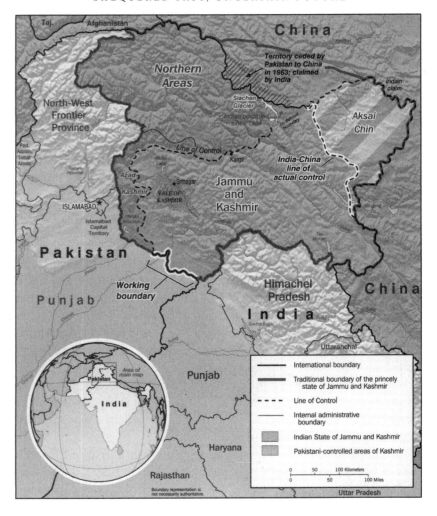

The disputed area of Kashmir, 2002.

time.[135] Later, however, Khan claimed that his confession was not given freely. Musharraf's popularity was declining, as evidenced by a survey conducted by *Dawn* that showed that 54.5 per cent of urban Pakistanis believed that the military should have no role in politics, and 65.2 per cent wanted Musharraf to step down. *The Economist* also voiced criticism against Musharraf, accusing him of destabilizing Pakistan through the imposition of emergency measures. The magazine suggested that it was high time for him to step down and let the democratic process proceed unhindered.[136]

As we come to the end of this chapter, it is crucial to delve into the profound impact that 9/11 had on not only the Pakistani state but Pakistani society. Pakistan's identity revolves around Islam, which unfortunately faces suspicion and disapproval from individuals worldwide. The Pakistani diaspora has had to confront xenophobia and blatant hostility, prompting a realignment of the Pakistani people with the global community. It is worth exploring the crucial role played by Pakistani artists and laureates in this realignment.

Cultural Representations of Pakistani Identity after 9/11

With their intricate interplay, of the diverse identities that shape Pakistani society, art and literature serve as crucial tools in challenging the narrow definitions of Pakistan, particularly those imposed by the West. The terrorist attacks on 11 September 2001, which ushered in a binary view of the world as 'with us or against us', marked a pivotal moment for Pakistani literature and its global recognition, particularly in the West.[137] Since 2001, the West's increasingly Islamophobic perspective has compelled Pakistani literature to distance itself from violence by actively condemning it. Unfortunately, violence had become deeply ingrained in Pakistani society during the 1990s, fuelled by the lingering gun culture from the Soviet–Afghan War, Zia-era policies and the state's backing of groups such as the Taliban in Afghanistan and the Hizb-ul-Mujahideen in Kashmir.

Omar Shahid Hamid's novels are particularly notable for their portrayal of the ethnic violence perpetrated by the MQM in Karachi. In works such as *The Prisoner* and *Party Worker*, Hamid deftly caricatures the city's political figures, while vividly depicting the violence and militancy that had tragically become a part of everyday life.[138] Likewise, Fahmida Riaz's novel *Hum Log* (We, the People) skilfully captures the ethnic violence that plagued Karachi, tracing its roots back to the broader sweep of history and drawing a poignant connection with the politics surrounding Bengali separation in 1971.[139]

In Karachi, both political and cultural representation – through literature and media – has seen a shift in demographics. The migrant presence, once considered foreign at partition, has now surpassed the native Sindhi presence. The new literature emerging from Karachi reflects this reality; it writes back to the native, autochthonous tradition while also challenging Islamophobic representations of Pakistan in global media. The city's dominance of English-language writers, many now based in the United States or the UK, highlights its urban focus and well-developed educational infrastructure. Karachi also hosted Pakistan's inaugural international literary festival in 2010, which has since been replicated in Lahore and Islamabad, with the Lahore festival even travelling to London and New York. Post-9/11, international pressure forced Pakistan to revise its alliances and address its violent past. As a result, Pakistani literature in English has been striving to portray the country as a non-violent society. A prime example is Mohsin Hamid's *The Reluctant Fundamentalist*, which follows the radicalization of a young Westernized Pakistani man, Changez, who returns to Lahore after the upheaval of global events in the United States.[140] The novel's enigmatic conclusion leaves unresolved the question whether Pakistani society is inherently violent. As the story draws to a close, it remains uncertain whether Changez harbours violent intentions towards the American to whom he has recounted his life story, or whether the American himself is plotting violence against Changez. Meanwhile, Mohammed Hanif's *Our Lady of Alice Bhatti* offers a distinct portrayal of violence that takes on a different form altogether.[141]

Kanza Javed's *Ashes, Wine and Dust* skilfully shifts the narrative lens away from war and religious violence, instead illuminating the devastating effects of violence against women and minorities. Similarly, the novel highlights how Pakistan has often been the victim of violence, rather than its sole perpetrator, as underscored by a heart-wrenching suicide blast.[142] Pakistani literature that defies Islamophobic stereotypes represents the country's pluralistic and tolerant identity and highlights the internal resistance against extremism and terrorism. These novels portray the multidimensional aspects of Pakistani society, countering one-dimensional portrayals that fuel negative stereotypes.

Despite state policies that reinforce an 'anti-India' identity, Pakistani literature has been influenced by Indian writers and publishers, with several Pakistani writers gaining global popularity through Indian publishing houses. Notably, Asif Farrukhi's Shahrazad has republished Shamsur Rahman Faruqi's *Kayi Chaand Thay Sar-e-Asmaan* (Multiple Moons in the Sky), widely considered the greatest Urdu novel of the last two decades.[143]

To comprehend the inclinations in Pakistani literary history, it is vital to consider the interactions among bickering neighbours. Pakistani writing in English, both fiction and non-fiction, witnessed a surge after 9/11, and its global recognition is well documented. Recent studies on the history of Pakistani anglophone literature, such as the reissue of Tariq Rahman's *History of Pakistani Literature in English*, have contributed to this field.[144] Muneeza Shamsie's *Hybrid Tapestries*, and *The Routledge Companion to Pakistani Anglophone Writing* edited by Aroosa Kanwal and Saiyma Aslam, provide evidence of the critical mass generated by the humanities in Pakistan.[145] Works by Uzma Aslam Khan (*The Geometry of God* and *Trespassing*), Mohsin Hamid (*Moth Smoke, The Reluctant Fundamentalist, How to Get Filthy Rich in Rising Asia* and *Exit West*), Kamila Shamsie (*Kartography, Salt and Saffron, Burnt Shadows* and *Home Fire*), Nadeem Aslam (*Maps for Lost Lovers, The Wasted Vigil* and *The Blind Man's Garden*), Mohammed Hanif (*A Case of Exploding Mangoes, Our Lady of Alice Bhatti* and *Red Birds*), Bilal Tanweer (*The Scatter Here Is Too Great*), Aamer Hussain (*Another Gulmohar Tree*) and Daniyal Mueenuddin (*In Other Rooms, Other Wonders*) have found an audience, both local and global, wider than any of the earlier Pakistani writers.

Critically acclaimed and translated into various languages, the works of Pakistani writers have aided in the decolonization and indigenization of the English language and literature, fostering a more dialectical dialogue between cultures and promoting a global sense for the humanities. The youth of today, in contrast to previous generations, are more in tune with the international culture of humanities-led social reform and social justice, a result of their identification with global practices and vocabulary through social media. The ever-expanding reach of the Internet has played a significant role in this development. While assumptions about English writing in Pakistan suggest that it is the domain of a circumspect liberal elite, writers such as Bapsi Sidhwa, Mohammed Hanif, Kamila Shamsie, Uzma Aslam Khan and Ali Sethi challenge these notions by advocating for Pakistan's idea, nation and state as well as its creation.[146] This significant observation suggests that the elite education and English access previously seen as promoting anti-Pakistan agendas are now recognized as vital tools in defending Pakistan. While these writers of fiction aim to align the policies of the state with Pakistani society, they do not necessarily challenge the notion of the nation state's failure, instead focusing on the successes achieved by Pakistan and Pakistani society.

Tariq Ali's *Islam Quintet* explores the mythology and traditions of Muslim Spain, as earlier traced by Intizar Hussain.[147] Claire Chambers notes that this novel series is about Muslim societies in decline.[148] A repressive Catholic society replaces the tolerant, pluralistic society of Moorish al-Andalus.[149] Tariq Ali's novel's brief recapture of Jerusalem represents the revival of the tolerant Islamicate empire, connecting historical dots from Moorish Spain to Mughal India for Intizar Hussain. In 1989, Sara Suleri Goodyear gained literary prominence with *Meatless Days*, a memoir of pre-radicalized Pakistan.[150] Suleri was born in Pakistan as one of six children to Mair Jones, a British professor who moved to Pakistan with her husband, Ziauddin Ahmad Suleri, a Pakistani journalist. Sara spent her early years in Pakistan and London, but mainly grew up in Lahore.[151] The book's most captivating aspect is how geography intertwines with Sara's recollections of specific individuals, blurring the lines between them. She notes how London, with its ability to evoke a sense of home, now recalls Shahid, Sara's brother. Meanwhile, Lahore remains inseparable from memories of Ifat, her late sister, who had a special connection to the city.[152] Throughout the novel, Suleri evokes a sense of loss, from the loss of relationships and words to the loss of culture, history, audience and geography. She poignantly recounts a brief congregation in Lahore before returning to a more geographical reality. Shahid's words on the phone from England, 'We're lost, Sara,' are a sobering reminder of their shared feeling of being adrift. 'Yes, Shahid, we're lost,' Sara responds, encapsulating the novel's pervasive sense of displacement.[153]

Despite the role of English-language fiction in countering Western Islamophobia and reshaping Pakistani literature and identity, Urdu continues to hold a significant place. This is exemplified by Mohammed

Hanif's *A Case of Exploding Mangoes*, which highlights Urdu's continuing relevance.[154] The novel satirizes Zia ul Haq's dictatorship and was initially praised in English but caused controversy when translated into Urdu in 2019. The state's resistance to the Urdu version suggests it assumes Urdu readers favour theocratic militarization, while the English-reading audience is deemed insignificant. Umera Ahmed's *Pir-i-Kamil* (The Perfect Mentor) is a polemical Urdu novel that presents a certain Islamic identity as the true identity of a Pakistani citizen and justifies the denial of Ahmadiyya rights, making it the most impactful Urdu novel since 9/11.[155] Ahmed's novel launched her into national prominence, and she capitalized on the boom of private television by becoming a successful TV serial writer.

While the production of high-quality Urdu literature has declined in the past decade, the rise of Urdu television channels and radio stations indicates a growing demand for humanities content. However, the representation of social hierarchies, gender issues and state narratives in privately owned media demonstrates the unrealized ideal of independent media. In the 2010s, controversial TV dramas such as *Meray Paas Tum Ho* (I Have You) and the military-sponsored production *Ehd-e-Wafa* (Pledge of Allegiance), and movies like *Waar* (The Strike), *Yalghaar* (Assault) and *Parwaaz Hai Junoon* (Soaring is Passion), demonstrate how the state police are viewed. Nonetheless, social media remains a democratizing space for Pakistani society, as evident in the vigorous critique of state-sponsored media on these platforms. This counternarrative on social media is a necessary corollary to the acceptance and popularity of the humanities.

In addition to Intizar Hussain, Mustansar Hussain Tarar (who has been Pakistan's most widely read and prolific Urdu writer over the past three decades), in his novel *Bahao* (The Flow), ventures on a daring quest to unearth an indigenous connection between the cultural heritage of the Punjab and Sindh, exploring the possibility that some of the roots of Punjabi customs may have originated from the culture of the Sindh Valley.[156] Similarly, *Raakh* (Ashes) takes as its canvas the entire history of the country up until its publication in 2003.[157] Abdullah Hussain, who was already a widely revered author with his 1964 novel *Udaas Naslain* (The Weary Generations), wrote *Nadaar Log* (Deprived Peoples) in 1996.[158] The novel asserts that with proper leadership and an honest commitment to state building, the new state could have protected its destitute. It is a stark, postcolonial work that scathingly criticizes the failure of the postcolonial state to become a unified nation.

Among Urdu-reading audiences, a young writer who has gained significant relevance in the past decade is Ali Akbar Natiq, whose 2014 novel *Nau Lakhi Kothi* (The Bungalow Worth Nine Lakhs) tells a story that connects the Raj era with post-partition Pakistan.[159] However, Natiq does not explore autochthonous links or allude to local anti-colonial heroes of his region, such as Ahmad Khan Kharal (1785–1857), who are so significant to the decolonizing trend of recent scholarship.[160] The concept of decolonization has been present in Pakistani literature through oral tradition, but university academics, trained and influenced by Western discourses, have chosen not to engage with these literary strains.

Pakistani literature and art serve as powerful tools for challenging narrow definitions of the country, particularly those imposed by the West. The events of 9/11 marked a pivotal moment in Pakistani literature, and since then, Pakistani literature in English has striven to portray the country as a non-violent society. Novels such as *The Reluctant Fundamentalist* by Mohsin Hamid and *Our Lady of Alice Bhatti* by Mohammed Hanif portray the multidimensional aspects of Pakistani society, countering one-dimensional portrayals that fuel negative stereotypes. Pakistani literature that defies Islamophobic stereotypes represents the country's pluralistic and tolerant identity and highlights the internal resistance against extremism and terrorism.

The Musharraf era was dominated by the military establishment, which has long held sway over Pakistani politics. Since 1954, when the military first gained a foothold in the state apparatus, both the military and the bureaucracy have ignored the general will expressed through the ballot box. Musharraf, however, sought to break from this tradition by keeping politicians at arm's length and relying instead on experienced consultants from international banks and monetary institutions. Interestingly, Pakistani military high command has an obsession with the technocratic set-up they have installed, despite its repeated failures. The same strategy adopted by Musharraf led to a radical restructuring of the Civil Service, with power shifting away from traditional centres. Politicians were treated with disdain and subjected to media trials, while institutions such as the NAB and RAB were designed to keep them marginalized.

Musharraf was the undisputed kingpin of this system, with all power emanating from him. The legislative bodies were nothing more than pliable instruments in his hands, while the unwavering support of the Army and the trust of the United States bolstered his position even further. He favoured military action over negotiated settlements, as demonstrated by his handling of the Akbar Bugti-led insurgency in Baluchistan and the Lal Masjid issue in Islamabad. Musharraf's authoritarian tendencies were severe, but compared to his predecessors, he was less of an autocrat. Minorities fared better under his regime than under Zia ul Haq, and he initially liberalized the press, allowing private television channels to flourish. However, this new-found media freedom ultimately worked against him, leading to the imposition of emergency rule.

Musharraf faced prosecution after being ousted from power, and fearing incarceration, he fled to Dubai, where he lived until his death on

5 February 2023. Despite his shortcomings, Musharraf's legacy is complex, and his tenure marked a departure from the traditional nexus between the military and bureaucracy in Pakistani politics.

12
A Decade of Uncertainty, 2008–18

In this chapter, a decade's worth of events will be scrutinized, spanning from political instability to economic constraints, natural disasters and, most notably, widespread violence, including devastating suicide bombings that caused immense destruction and loss of life. Throughout this tumultuous period, Pakistan was plagued by extreme chaos and uncertainty, as its political leadership failed to demonstrate the necessary vision and resolve to steer the nation out of crisis. This was largely due to flawed policies that were unilaterally formulated and half-heartedly executed. The decade in question began with an election, which ushered in a new era of governance.

The 2008 Elections in Pakistan

General elections were to be held on 18 February 2008, but the lead-up to the vote was tense. There was widespread apprehension, fear of violence and uncertainty. There was concern about the possible rigging of the electoral process, which gave rise to a great atmosphere of mistrust. Moreover, the unabated spate of violence fuelled fear of more bloodshed and uncertainty, particularly after the bomb blast at Sazgar.[1] In October 2007 in Karachi, a large procession of PPP supporters had gathered to welcome Benazir Bhutto upon her arrival at the airport. They were making their way towards Quaid-e-Azam's mausoleum, with their leader in tow, when tragedy struck. Just after midnight, suicide bombers triggered their explosive devices manually, resulting in a devastating attack. The first bomber approached Benazir's security guards, who had formed a human chain around her truck to keep potential bombers away, and detonated himself, which created a path for the second bomber to carry out their deadly mission. The second bomber brazenly walked over the dead and dying guards, filling the air with bright white flashes before the explosion rocked the vehicle, killing three people on board.[2] A total of 146 people were either killed or severely injured, and the area was littered with body parts. Miraculously, Benazir survived the attack, as she had retreated into the body of the bus just ten minutes prior to the incident. She was tired after hours of waving and her ankles were swelling, making her decision to retreat into the bus all the more fortuitous.³ Only two months later, the successful assassination of Benazir Bhutto on 27 December in Rawalpindi significantly increased the volatility of the political environment. Aspirations and hopes to vote out a military-sponsored government after a five-year term also accompanied the process, calling for political change.⁴

The backdrop to Pakistan's parliamentary elections of 2008 was the tragic assassination of Benazir Bhutto. As a result of this horrific event, the election schedule that was originally set for 8 January had to be postponed, ostensibly due to security concerns. However, it later emerged that the Musharraf-led establishment, comprising the senior ranks of the military, Civil Service and other elites who shared power only when required, feared a significant groundswell of public support for the PPP.⁵ In the wake of Benazir's assassination, campaigning was significantly subdued, with public rallies being seriously curtailed. But even before her untimely death, there were doubts about whether the elections would take place at all. Despite a power-sharing agreement between President Musharraf and Benazir Bhutto, prompted by the United States, a state of emergency was imposed on 3 November 2007.⁶ The initiative taken was a pre-emptive strike intended to stall the Supreme Court's impending verdict against Musharraf's re-election as president by the outgoing parliament in October. There was widespread belief that his election as president was unconstitutional. Even though the state of emergency cast doubt on the election, the date was eventually announced on 20 November, leaving the contestants just seven weeks to prepare.⁷ The state of emergency remained in effect until 15 December, and media restrictions were maintained throughout the election campaign. These limitations were eventually lifted after the election; however, the judges who had been dismissed during the state of emergency were not reinstated. As a result, some political parties, such as the Jamaat-i-Islami, one of the main parties in the MMA, and Tehrik-e-Insaf, along with Baluchi nationalist parties within the All-Parties Democratic Movement (APDM), opted to boycott the elections in protest. The PML-N, led by Nawaz Sharif, also considered joining the boycott but ultimately decided against it when the PPP announced its intention to proceed with the election. This move helped to limit the impact of the boycott.⁸ The ninth general elections were held on 18 February amid an atmosphere of uncertainty and fear, and the electoral results completely reshaped the national political landscape. The voters rejected the political opportunism of the PML-Q, which comprised most of the PML(N)'s deserters, and the religious extremism that flourished under the dictatorial regimes of Zia and Musharraf, opting instead for those who opposed the dictators. In the Punjab, the PML-N emerged as the majority party, while in Sindh, the PPP took the lead; the ANP was ahead in Khyber Pakhtunkhwa, and independents and the PML-Q in Baluchistan due to the boycott of the APDM. At the centre, the PPP emerged as the largest party, followed by the PML-N in second place and PML-Q in third. The only clear conclusion to draw from the 18 February election was that the people of Pakistan had lost faith in the policies of the Musharraf regime.[9] The return from exile of leaders such as Benazir Bhutto and Nawaz Sharif generated much enthusiasm in the election campaign, although the latter was not allowed to run for office. However, due to security concerns, the personal campaign remained lacklustre, particularly after the tragic incident of Benazir's assassination. Even before that, the local authorities, controlled by pro-incumbent politicians, had been granted the power to ban public gatherings and rallies, citing the possibility of terrorism.

During the campaign for the National Assembly elections, two main issues dominated the discourse. The first was the status of President Musharraf. The PML-N demanded his removal, citing his unconstitutional re-election by the outgoing parliament, and the reinstatement of the Supreme Court judges, including Justice Iftikhar Muhammad Chaudhry. The PPP, on the other hand, was more cautious and open to a future power-sharing deal with Musharraf. After Benazir's assassination, the PPP demanded a UN investigation, but remained conciliatory towards the president.[10]

During the election campaign, the economy emerged as the second major issue, with a focus on soaring inflation, high fuel prices, the energy crisis and wheat shortages. The ruling PML-Q was heavily criticized for mismanaging the economy, despite some local developmental successes and a respectable growth rate. The energy and food crisis had a severe impact on the common people, leading to a loss of popularity for the ruling party, but state authorities continued to support the PML-Q. Despite pre-election negotiations with the PPP, Musharraf urged voters to support the PML-Q. However, after Benazir's assassination, the PML-Q distanced itself from Musharraf, criticizing his hand-picked prime minister, Shaukat Aziz, for the food shortage and government policies in Baluchistan. Before the election, concerns were raised about the exclusion of millions of voters from the electoral roll. Those without a national identity card, even if they were on the electoral roll, were not allowed to vote.[11]

The fact that the majority of the caretaker administration had previous affiliation with the PML-Q remained a contentious issue. The Election Commission's partisan nature was also a cause for concern, since it failed to effectively enforce legal bans on the misuse of state resources and official positions.[12] There was also a growing concern about the biased media coverage given to the ruling party in the state-run media. According to a report by Reporters Without Borders in 2008, almost 85 per cent of the airtime was dedicated to Musharraf and the PML-Q. Furthermore, restrictions were imposed on privately owned media, which were required to comply with a voluntary code of conduct. Those who refused to comply, such as GEO TV, were ultimately blocked.[13] The polling results were as expected, and once again, a hung parliament was produced. None of the mainstream political parties, namely the PML-Q, PML-N or PPP, were able to secure a clear majority to form the government. In contrast, the religio-political alliance of MMA suffered a significant decline in strength in the parliament. This outcome suggested that their previous victory was either aided by the intelligence services or a result of certain geopolitical realities.[14] To the surprise and shock of many, Major General Ehtesham Zamir, former head of the powerful political cell of the ISI, delivered a devastating blow to Musharraf. General Zamir quite categorically blamed the president for ordering manipulation before and after the 2002 elections. In an interview with *The News* on 24 February, Zamir admitted that he had manipulated 'the last elections at the behest of President Musharraf'.[15] The timing of General Zamir's revelation held particular significance, as it undermined General Musharraf's credibility at a crucial juncture when his political fate hung in the balance. This revelation was pivotal, casting doubt on General Musharraf precisely when he needed steadfast support the most. Importantly, General Zamir's assessment extended beyond mere timing, as he went on to characterize the 2008 elections as fairer compared to those in 2002 when expressing his views on the electoral process. The voter turnout during the election was low, at 44 per cent, with significant variation across provinces. Turnout was notably lower in Khyber Pakhtunkhwa and Baluchistan due to the APDM boycott, leading to voter apathy. In FATA, concerns over high levels of violence kept many from casting their votes.

After the election, three political players emerged: Musharraf, the former ruling party PML-Q, and all other opposition parties. Initially, the PML-N and the PPP pledged to cooperate in the new parliament and not undermine each other. However, this agreement was short-lived as Asif Zardari reneged on a promise he had made earlier with the PML-N leadership.[16]

Despite securing 121 seats in the National Assembly, the PPP was unable to acquire the simple majority required to form the government on its own. Thus, it formed a coalition government with the second-largest party, the PML-N (with 91 seats in the National Assembly), along with the ANP and the MMA. The 2008 election results showed the decline of the religious-political alliance MMA due to its failure in ensuring good governance. The impact of provincialism on Pakistani politics was evident in the 2008 elections, with the PPP winning in Sindh, the PML-N in the Punjab and the ANP in Khyber Pakhtunkhwa. Most political parties had a presence only in one or two provinces, with only the PPP and the PML-Q securing representation in all four provinces. The failure of the ECP to address allegations of irregularities undermined the impartiality of the electoral machinery for national elections. According to Human Rights Watch, 'the commission's structure, which has wide powers to investigate complaints and take action, also suggests that it will not rule fairly in the election.'[17] As expected, the MQM joined the PPP as a coalition partner at the centre, which became crucial after the latter decided to break ties with the PML-N. The PPP nominated Syed Yousaf Raza Gilani, its second vice chairman, for the premiership after much wrangling among contenders such as Shah Mehmood Qureshi, Makhdum Amin Fahim and Ahmed Mukhtar for the coveted post within the party. Gilani took oath as Pakistan's eighteenth prime minister of Pakistan on 25 March 2008.[18]

The Zardari–Gilani Duo

The 2008 elections in Pakistan were widely considered to be the fairest since 1971, marking a positive step towards greater transparency and democracy in the country. As a result of these elections, Asif Ali Zardari, the widower of the late Benazir Bhutto, unexpectedly rose to a position of political leadership in Pakistan.[19] Similar to Benazir Bhutto's victory in 1988, the hopes that the 2008 elections would bring about a new era of stability were not realized. Once again, a prolonged period of military-backed rule gave way only to a precarious democracy. Allegations of corruption, reminiscent of the 1990s, resurfaced, though this time it appeared that judicial intervention rather than executive action might lead to the downfall of a democratically elected government. The post-2008 era shared with the 1990s a looming economic crisis and a deteriorating governance situation, both of which were worsened by the costly War on Terror; government estimates suggested that Pakistan had spent U.S.$31.4 billion on the conflict by 2008–9.[20] The Zardari era cannot be dismissed as a mere repetition of the failed democratization of the late twentieth century. Valuable political lessons were learned, as evidenced by the avoidance of the zero-sum game between the PPP and PML-N that plagued the 1990s. Although tensions ran high and outright confrontation was not uncommon, the official opposition remained critical of the military instead of conspiring with it to remove the government. President Zardari's professed commitment to a politics of reconciliation was more than just empty words. He made genuine efforts to curtail presidential power and address long-standing grievances stemming from centre–provincial relations.[21]

When Musharraf resigned, the PPP nominated Zardari as its presidential candidate, while the PML-N put forward the former chief justice of the Supreme Court, Saeed-ud-Zaman Siddiqui. Zardari won a comfortable majority on 6 September and was sworn in as president three days later. It was an ironic twist of fate that one of the most maligned figures in the country had assumed the presidential office. Had Benazir been alive, this miracle would never have occurred. With Zardari's tarnished reputation, any hope of positive change during his tenure was too much to expect. After nine years of military-backed political rule, the country's political institutions were in a state of disrepair.[22] In this context, it would have required a leader with unwavering commitment to the democratic cause and exceptional political acumen to steer Pakistan towards a sustainable democratic system. Unfortunately, the country's political leadership lacked the necessary determination, vision and devotion to the cause of genuine democracy. As a result, during Zardari's five-year tenure as president, democracy in Pakistan remained fragile and barely managed to survive. However, Ayesha Jalal highlights that Zardari demonstrated remarkable political finesse in navigating the challenging transition after Benazir's untimely demise, proving himself to be a skilled political operator with a keen sense of when and how to make necessary compromises.[23]

Despite having won the presidential election, Zardari faced significant obstacles in turning his victory into power. Some of Benazir's supporters, without any concrete evidence, harboured suspicions that he was involved in his wife's assassination. To counter these perceptions, Zardari made his first official visit as president to the Bhutto mausoleum, paying respects to his wife and asserting his position as her political heir. He also followed the tradition of the Bhutto family by visiting the shrine of Lal Shahbaz Qalandar and referencing 'the Bhutto doctrine' in his early speeches. However, none of these efforts were enough to win over the Bhutto family. Fatima Bhutto, in particular, was vocal about her disapproval of Zardari, despite his acquittal of involvement in her father's murder, stating that her 'blood froze' on the day Zardari assumed the presidency.[24] Mumtaz Bhutto, who was Zulfiqar's cousin and a long-time ally, was deeply disturbed by the situation. He said, 'It is unjust to hold an old and illustrious family responsible for the misdeeds of the Zardaris, who have tarnished the family's name.' According to Tariq Ali, even when Benazir was alive, many of her closest supporters in the PPP were growing increasingly dissatisfied with Zardari. They blamed his avarice and his tendency to act like a mafia boss for her previous two stints in power ending in failure.[25]

There were also anxieties about Zardari's physical and mental health. In addition to rumours about his suffering from heart issues and bouts of depression, there was the awkward fact that, when he was facing his legal cases in the UK and Switzerland, a doctor had diagnosed him with dementia.[26] While there was no evidence that he had that ailment, foreign interlocutors were dismissive of his abilities. WikiLeaks later revealed that the UK's most senior Foreign Office official considered Zardari to be 'clearly a numbskull'. A NATO official would later describe him as 'unable to engage PermReps [that is, national governments' permanent representatives or ambassadors to NATO] in a strategic level discussion of the situation in South Asia'.[27] On the other side of the Atlantic, Zalmay Khalilzad, a high-ranking U.S. diplomat with a focus on South Asia and Afghanistan, described Zardari's beliefs as 'madness'. Zardari apparently expressed that the United States was behind the Taliban's suicide bombing campaign in Pakistan, and Khalilzad considered this to be a serious statement.

Meanwhile, Zardari's meetings with Barack Obama did not go smoothly. The U.S. president became irritated by Zardari's tendency to speak for up to forty minutes without interruption, repeatedly referring to U.S. aid to Pakistan as 'my money'. Zardari also claimed that, although Obama was surrounded by highly educated individuals, he had the advantage of having a 'PhD in life'. This behaviour led to Obama reportedly trying to avoid one-on-one meetings with him.[28] Pakistan's closest ally, Saudi Arabia, expressed its doubts about Zardari, with King Abdullah referring to him as a 'rotten head' and 'the greatest obstacle to Pakistan's progress'. China also had reservations about him and his wife, viewing them as too pro-American. Beijing was displeased with Zardari's failure to prioritize China as his first foreign visit, and his excuse that his trips to London and Dubai were made in a private capacity did not appease them. His commitment to honouring Z. A. Bhutto's legacy regarding the Pakistan–China relationship also fell short of their expectations. Furthermore, his primary focus in his first encounter with the Chinese leadership was to avoid the constraints of an IMF reform

Asif Ali Zardari, 2010.

programme by relying on significant amounts of Chinese funding, which China denied.²⁹

The security crisis in Pakistan was accompanied by a broader crisis in governance, which was partly due to the federal government's lack of competence and coherence. President Zardari was known for his deal-making skills, but not for his ability to articulate a strategic vision. The lack of coordination was thrust into the limelight by the 24/7 news coverage of politics, which was made possible by the proliferation of cable networks during the first decade of the twenty-first century. No other popularly elected government in Pakistan's history had faced such intense scrutiny. The media frenzy reached its peak when Zardari was absent from the country during the catastrophic July–August 2010 floods. The rise of judicial activism, which was a legacy of the Musharraf era, further contributed to the challenges posed to a beleaguered government.³⁰

The PPP-led government took over an economy in decline in 2008. The country's economic situation had been worsened by factors such as high debt, but a temporary respite was provided by relief and debt rescheduling, along with a significant influx of foreign investment and remittances from overseas Pakistani workers. Unfortunately, this created an unsustainable consumption-led boom in the post-9/11 period. As a result, the

Asif Ali Zardari and U.S. president Barack Obama, 2012.

country's GDP grew at an average annual rate of 6.1 per cent in the five years leading up to 2005–6.[31] President Musharraf and his technocratic prime minister Shaukat Aziz were hailed for Pakistan's fast-paced economic growth. However, their reliance on external capital flows failed to address long-standing issues such as low taxation rates and overdependence on the textile industry. Human development levels also remained alarming. The Musharraf regime chose to ignore warning signs of increasing budgetary debt and pressure on foreign-exchange reserves, leading to mounting political opposition and a deteriorating security situation from 2006–7 onwards. The rising commodity prices had a significant external impact, and fuel and food subsidies further increased indebtedness. According to the February 2008 polls, the economic growth of the earlier Musharraf era was a thing of the past.[32] The security and economic crises in Pakistan were becoming more interconnected, with direct foreign investment declining as suicide bombings damaged infrastructure and employment opportunities. The extension of militant control in northwestern Pakistan also disrupted the education of many young people. Even prior to the major setback of the 2010 floods, the security situation had a negative impact on the economy, causing it to lag behind the recovery of other Asian economies from the global recession. This slow growth, coupled with persistent inflation, widened the gap between the rich and poor, similar to the situation during the last democratic interlude of the 1990s.[33] Likewise, the newly elected government faced a severely deteriorating security situation. Since 2007, militant groups had increasingly targeted Pakistan's 'apostate' rulers with their firepower. Talbot's assertion that the state had created conditions conducive to jihadist organizations gaining financial autonomy and infiltrating local communities is accurate. Furthermore, the revelation of Osama bin Laden's long-term presence in Pakistan exposed the existence of small cells within the security apparatus with the ability to pursue their own agendas independently of their superiors. The state's use of Islamic proxies as part of a long-term strategy had consequences that it ultimately paid dearly for.[34] Following the 2008 elections, there was a brief respite from the wave of suicide attacks, and the elections themselves were conducted without major incidents. The revival of the Pakhtun ANP raised hopes for a potential path towards a peaceful resolution to the conflict in the tribal areas through dialogue. However, these hopes were soon dashed as the state became increasingly involved in the conflict, leading to a surge in militant attacks, including suicide bombings in Pakistani cities.[35] The decision to launch a large-scale military offensive was driven by the deteriorating situation in the Malakand division. It had become clear to both politicians and the public that the state's authority was being undermined, and that militancy was not just an external problem arising from U.S. intervention in Afghanistan but a threat to Pakistan's existence. However, one should not exaggerate the new national unity of purpose in security matters that the

PPP government had claimed. Later surveys have revealed that while there was widespread hostility towards the Pakistani Taliban (TTP), sectarian groups and militants who had long been associated with the Kashmir jihad still enjoyed support.[36] This was the context in which Yousaf Raza Gilani assumed the position of Pakistan's prime minister.

Yousaf Raza Gilani came from an influential and spiritual family in Multan. His father was a descendant of Syed Musa Pak, a prominent spiritual figure from the Iranian province of Gilan. One of Gilani's maternal aunts married Pir Pagara (Ali Mardan Shah from Sangar in Sindh). Gilani began his political career in 1978 with the PML during the General Zia's martial-law regime. He was appointed to the Muslim League Central Working Committee and served as minister of housing and works from April 1985 to January 1986, and then as minister for railways from January 1986 to December 1986 in Prime Minister Muhammad Khan Junejo's cabinet. After a short stint with the Muslim League, Gilani joined the PPP in 1988 and has remained a loyal and steadfast supporter ever since. During the first term of Benazir Bhutto's government (1988–90), Gilani served as minister of tourism from March 1989 to January 1990 and then as minister of housing and works from January 1990 to August 1990.[37] During the second tenure of Benazir Bhutto, Gilani was elected as the speaker of the National Assembly and remained in that position until February 1997. He served as a member of the National Assembly from Multan on numerous occasions, and in the 2008 general elections, he emerged victorious over PML-Q candidate Sikandar Hayat Bosan.[38] In 2001 Gilani was sent to prison by General Musharraf and served a five-year sentence following a conviction over illegal government appointments. As a result, he was unable to contest the 2002 elections. While in prison, Gilani wrote a book called *Chah-e-Yousaf se Sada* (Echoes from Yousaf's Well).

Following the restoration of democratic rule, corruption resurfaced as a major issue within the PPP government, reminiscent of the 1990s. Gilani was accused of misappropriating a gift donated by Emine Erdoğan for flood victims, which remained unaccounted for. As a result, the Supreme Court dismissed Gilani as premier and issued arrest warrants for their first nominee, Makhdoom Shahabuddin. Raja Pervez Ashraf emerged as the coalition's preferred candidate for prime minister, receiving 211 votes, while PML-N candidate Sardar Mehtab Abbasi received 89 votes. However, Ashraf's reputation was steeped in controversy. When he was nominated as the PPP's candidate, a corruption case against him from his tenure as water and power minister was still in court. He had also been blamed for the government's inability to resolve the energy crisis, earning him the nickname 'Raja Rental' due to allegations of corruption in power plants.[39]

In the post-Benazir era, corruption had been accepted as a norm by the PPP's top leadership. But, Talbot contends, 'this time it seemed that judicial activism, rather than executive action, could signal the end of a democratically elected government'.⁴⁰ The inability of the Zardari–Gilani government to bring back Iftikhar Chaudhry as chief justice is a perplexing issue. Chaudhry had gained tremendous support from the public during the lawyers' movement. Reinstating the ousted chief justice would have been a powerful demonstration of the government's commitment to the rule of law and justice. The fact that they failed to do so is a testament to their political incompetence, which dealt a significant blow to their popularity. As public pressure mounted, Sharif led a long march to Islamabad, compelling General Ashfaq Parvez Kayani to take action. The reinstatement of Justice Chaudhry largely because of the tacit support of General Kiyani created a new challenge for the Zardari–Gilani government during the remainder of their tenure.

President Zardari's public commitment to a politics of reconciliation was not merely rhetoric. He attempted to roll back presidential power and tried to address long-standing grievances arising from centre–provincial relations. The constitutional achievements were overshadowed by the ongoing security crisis.⁴¹ The period following 2008 was characterized by the looming threat of economic crisis and a deteriorating state of governance. The War on Terror and the consequent surge in suicide bombings had a devastating impact on economic activity, bringing it to a near standstill. Government data revealed that the relentless wave of militancy had caused a loss of U.S.$31.4 billion to Pakistan by 2008–9.⁴²

The state's authority in North and South Waziristan, as well as in Swat Valley, had virtually ceased to exist. State authorities had to revise their earlier position with regard to the Taliban and jihadists who had once acted as their proxies. By 2008–9, the United States' War on Terror in northwestern Pakistan had become Pakistan's own conflict. Consequently, the decades-long strategy of using Islamic proxies in the struggle with India had come back to haunt Pakistan with a vengeance.⁴³ Securing its own facilities proved to be a daunting task for the military. Well-coordinated attacks on the general headquarters in Rawalpindi in October 2009 and on the Mehran naval base near Shahrah-e-Faisal in Karachi on 22 May 2011 exemplified this difficulty. The Mehran naval base attack was particularly lethal, since the attackers held commandos at bay for seventeen hours and resulted in the destruction of two P-3C Orion maritime surveillance aircraft.⁴⁴ The attack on an ammunition factory near Islamabad, the massive explosion at the Marriott Hotel in September and the subsequent attack on the bus transporting the Sri Lankan cricket team from their hotel to the stadium in Lahore in March transformed Pakistan into one of the most dangerous places on the planet. The Sri Lankan cricketers escaped unharmed, primarily because of the driver, who heroically steered the bus to safety, but six policemen died in that extremely well-coordinated attack. These incidents shattered any hope of international teams returning to the cricket-crazy country and raised serious questions about the government's policy on extremism.⁴⁵ Concomitantly, the mounting human toll in drone strikes orchestrated by the United States and a reaction against the latter's unilateral action that resulted in the killing of Osama bin Laden provoked another shift in public opinion, as support for military action against militancy waned in June 2011.[46]

Economic Challenges

In 2008 the PPP-led government inherited an economy in decline. Despite debt rescheduling, relief and a surge in foreign investment and remittances from overseas Pakistani workers, the post-9/11 period had seen an unsustainable consumption-led boom. The challenges that Pakistan faced from 2006 to 2007 were exacerbated by mounting political opposition and a deteriorating security situation. During this time, the Musharraf regime seemed to overlook the warning signals indicating a growing budgetary debt and mounting pressure on foreign-exchange reserves. The situation was further complicated by the surge in commodity prices and the need for subsidies on fuel and food, which only added to the country's indebtedness.

As the calendar turned to February 2008 and Pakistan prepared for polls, it became increasingly evident that the era of economic growth under Musharraf's leadership was drawing to a close. The country's security and economic crises had become inextricably linked. The wave of suicide bombings not only claimed human lives but wreaked havoc on infrastructure and shut down economic prospects, diminishing employment opportunities. The deteriorating security scenario in northwestern Pakistan disrupted the education of the youth, casting a long shadow on their futures.

Despite these mounting challenges, the new government led by the PPP found itself entangled in post-election political struggles, notably with the PML-N and grappling with defining the president's role. Consequently, the growing economic crisis did not receive the attention it urgently required.

By the autumn of 2008, inflation had surged to alarming levels, surpassing 25 per cent due to the relentless rise in oil prices. Foreign investment dwindled as the global banking crisis took its toll, and the rupee faced depreciation. Concurrently, exports collapsed at a time when the costs of importing essential food and energy resources were soaring. This precarious situation raised the ominous prospect of Pakistan defaulting on its external debt.

Foreign-exchange reserves had dwindled to a mere U.S.$3.4 billion by November 2008, equivalent to just a month's worth of imports. It was at this juncture, following President Zardari's visit to Beijing in October, that it became abundantly clear that China would not be coming to Pakistan's financial rescue. In a stark reversal of his earlier stance, Zardari had no choice but to seek support from the IMF, a pivotal moment in Pakistan's quest to navigate the treacherous waters of economic instability.

Stabilization occurred with the current-account deficit narrowing from 8.5 per cent of GDP in the fiscal year 2007–8 to a projected 2–3 per cent for

2009–10. The budget deficit also narrowed, and inflation dropped from its peak of 25 per cent in November 2008 to 13 per cent. The improved economy saw an upturn in portfolio investment, but the government's attention remained divided due to ongoing political struggles.[47] Nonetheless, even before the major setback of the 2010 flood disaster, the security situation had a constricting impact on the economy. The slowing pace of growth, along with persistent inflation, resulted in increasing poverty and inequality. This situation resembled that of the last democratic interlude of the 1990s. The IMF mission in mid-July 2010 expressed concern over uncontrolled expenditure, rising inflation, slow revenue reforms and poor performance in the power sector.[48]

The devastating floods that hit Pakistan in July and August 2010 left an indelible mark on the country. The floods affected more than 20 million people, destroying approximately 875,000 homes and causing around U.S.$1 billion worth of damage to crops. The floods were triggered by an unprecedented 72-hour rainfall in Khyber Pakhtunkhwa and Azad Kashmir at the end of July, which saw the former receive four times its average monsoon rainfall in just ten days, with a staggering 346 centimetres (136 in.) of rain falling from 28 July. This led to flash floods from the rivers Kabul and Swat, as well as the inundation of the Swat Valley, which left a trail of destruction and devastation in its wake.[49] The overwhelming of the Taunsa Barrage, along with breaches in the Muzaffargarh and TP Link canals, wreaked havoc in the Muzaffargarh district, the most severely affected district in the Punjab. Over 2.5 million people were displaced, and hundreds of villages were destroyed. The devastation sparked a debate about engineering flaws, the need for more dams and barrages, the Irrigation Department's culpability for failing to maintain embankments and the reality that some flood protection schemes thought to have been in place only existed on paper.[50] Amid discussions centred on the devastating floods, the predominant focus was a blame-shifting narrative. Yet, it remained an undeniable fact that the primary catalyst for this calamity was the silting of canals and riverbeds, an unfortunate elevation that exacerbated the disaster's impact. Allegations reverberated through the air like an echo. It was alleged that certain officials, with a purported intention to shield urban areas from the deluge, deliberately breached canals and embankments, consequently redirecting the water's devastating flow towards the rural expanses of Upper Sindh and away from the urban hubs.

As the torrents of flooding continued their relentless course into the heart of Sindh, the finger of blame pointed towards influential landowners, their alleged actions now under scrutiny. Accusations were rife that some of these powerful individuals had ingeniously diverted the inundating floodwaters away from their own estates, in turn inundating the fields and homes of less privileged communities.

The repercussions of this disaster extended beyond the immediate realms of environmental catastrophe. In the wake of the inundation of Dera Allah Yar and the surrounding Jaffarabad district, a turbulent undercurrent of inter-provincial tensions began to brew between Baluchistan and Sindh. In this complex narrative, Baluch authorities vehemently asserted that their counterparts in Sindh had deliberately breached canals and embankments, engineering the flow of water in their direction.[51]

The floods not only necessitated a huge rescue and relief operation but threatened to undermine Pakistan's halting recovery from the 2009 recession. Some estimates were that up to 2 percentage points could be taken off the projected growth rate in GDP of 4.5 per cent.[52] In addition to the damage to an already weak infrastructure and the worsening of the power supply situation, standing crops of rice and cotton were destroyed in the Punjab and Sindh. In the Punjab alone more than 647,500 hectares (1.6 million ac) of crops were inundated.[53] The cotton crop in the major cotton-growing district of Rahim Yar Khan was 20 per cent lower in 2010–11 than in the previous year. This decline had an unfavourable impact on Pakistan's textile industry, which is central to the country's exports. Furthermore, the slowing down of GDP growth came at a time when the youth bulge in the population was generating additional labour demands, with the working-age population increasing annually at around 2.4 per cent.[54]

The Emergence of Tehrik-e-Taliban Pakistan

Understanding the origins of the Pakistan Taliban requires examining the context of two pivotal conflicts: the Afghan jihad of the 1980s and the U.S. invasion of Afghanistan after 9/11. Pakistani militants who participated in the Afghan jihad returned home to find their tribal areas lawless, their government neglectful and no rehabilitation programmes available. As a result, some of these fighters redirected their focus and violence towards Pakistan. Among them was Sufi Muhammad, a former Jamaat-e-Islami leader who left the group in 1981 due to 'irreparable ideological differences' regarding the use of force. Jamaat-e-Islami adhered to non-violence but supported the Afghan jihad.[55] Upon returning from Afghan jihad to Pakistan in 1989, Sufi Muhammad founded the Tehrik-e-Nifaz-Shariat-Mohammadi (TNSM) with the aim of imposing Sharia in Dir, Khyber Pakhtunkhwa. The TNSM later became a precursor to the Tehrik-e-Taliban Pakistan, with Sufi Muhammad's son-in-law, Fazlullah, succeeding him as the group's leader.

In the aftermath of the U.S. declaration of war in Afghanistan in 2001, various militant groups, including the TNSM, seized upon a compelling narrative of resistance. This narrative was framed around opposing the perceived 'occupation' in Afghanistan by American forces and, concurrently, critiquing the Pakistani government's alignment with the United States, particularly in the rugged and lawless tribal regions.

Context here is crucial. The U.S. military's intervention in Afghanistan following the attacks of 11 September 2001 not only shook the geopolitical landscape but stirred regional tensions. In this milieu, groups like the TNSM found fertile ground to rally support against American forces in Afghanistan and the Pakistani government's collaboration with Washington. These narratives of resistance were not merely ideological but also had significant geopolitical ramifications, shaping the dynamics of the region for years to come.

Groups like the TNSM established their own courts, which offered swift justice, and launched terrorist attacks against the Pakistani state. Mullah Fazlullah, also known as 'Mulla Radio', became a prominent figure in the movement, using daily FM radio broadcasts throughout 2006 and 2007 to advocate for jihad against the U.S. 'invaders' in Afghanistan. He also issued fatwas against girls' schools, labelling them as 'centres of all evil'.[56] Despite the growing threat posed by precursors to the TTP, the Pakistani state initially failed to recognize them as an existential threat. The state's complicity in the Afghan jihad, combined with the belief that the militants were 'our brothers' and could be contained, led to a lack of action. Between 2005 and 2007, General Musharraf's government attempted three successive peace deals with the precursors to the TTP. These agreements ultimately failed, but they served to legitimize the militants and their cause in the eyes of the public.

Moreover, these deals provided logistical support to the militants, allowing them to regroup and expand. Following a 2005 deal with the militant Baitullah Mehsud, General Safdar Hussain of the Pakistani Army declared that Mehsud was 'not a rebel but a patriotic citizen and soldier' of Pakistan. Such statements helped to perpetuate a false narrative that the militants were simply misguided patriots and further emboldened their extremist activities.[57] Haji Omar and Baitullah refused to back down from their insurgency and publicly declared their intention to continue their jihad against the U.S.-led coalition in Afghanistan. However, events in the summer of 2007, particularly those that unfolded at Islamabad's Lal Masjid, marked a turning point for these groups.

The militant brothers at the Lal Masjid, Abdul Aziz and Abdul Rashid Ghazi, were openly inspired by Osama bin Laden and known for their incendiary rhetoric from the pulpit. The mosque also served as a training ground for students who would later join various militant groups operating in the northwest region of Pakistan, as they had done during the Afghan jihad of the 1980s. Additionally, Abdul Aziz's wife ran the women's wing of the Lal Masjid, known as Jamia Hafsa.

In 2007 students from Jamia Hafsa formed vigilante groups and began patrolling the streets of Islamabad with sticks, attempting to enforce Sharia law. They raided massage parlours, video shops and hotels, further stoking tensions in the region.[58] Musharraf launched an operation against the

Swat Valley.

madrasa; the Army raided the mosque and scores of seminary students were killed, along with Abdul Rashid Ghazi.[59]

The action proved to be too much for the public's appetite, and too late to be effective. Abdul Aziz threatened Musharraf with retaliatory attacks, and 'publicly thanked Allah for giving Fazlullah and Sufi Muhammad the power to enforce Sharia'.[60] The state lost the war of public opinion and of narrative, especially in the newly free media environment that Musharraf himself had set up. Soon after this, the TTP was officially born, and the spike in terrorist attacks was unmistakable.[61]

The state continued to shuffle its feet on the militants. Baitullah and Fazlullah were declared 'patriotic' in a confidential media briefing in 2008.[62] In early 2009 the TTP managed to seize control of the Swat Valley in Khyber Pakhtunkhwa, prompting the federal government under Zardari and the provincial government headed by the secular ANP to sign a peace deal with the TTP. As a result, Sharia law was imposed in Swat in an effort to quell the violence. Government officials at the time viewed this as a positive development, since it was seen as bringing swift and fair justice to an area that had long been lacking it.

Even the chief minister of Khyber Pakhtunkhwa remarked that 'there was a vacuum in the legal system' and that 'the people demanded this, and they deserved it.' However, the peace deal ultimately proved to be short-lived, as the TTP went back on their promises and resumed their attacks on the Pakistani state shortly thereafter.[63] The state's inability to recognize the existential threat posed by the Pakistan Taliban and its continued violence can be traced back to its complicity in the Afghan jihad. Having used jihadists to further its strategic interests in Afghanistan and Kashmir, the state continued to view them as 'brothers' even when they turned against

Pakistan. As a result, the state believed that it could contain these groups. This narrative was driven by the state's actions, which included successive peace deals and talks with the TTP. The attack on Malala Yousafzai in 2012 was a stark reminder that these groups could not be contained, and the state's image of the Pakistan Taliban needed to change.[64]

The Mumbai Attack

During the operation against militants in South Waziristan and Swat, relations between India and Pakistan soured. The reason for this was an alleged attack carried out by militants linked to the Lashkar-i-Tayyiba in Mumbai, India, on 26 November 2008. This deadly attack on India's financial capital brought the two nuclear-armed countries to the brink of war. Faced with this precarious situation, the Pakistani Army high command had to redeploy its units from the northwestern tribal areas to the eastern border. This move provided a reprieve for the militants in South Waziristan and Swat, as pressure on them eased.[65] The Mumbai attacks of 2008, which resulted in the deaths of 166 people and left around three hundred injured, were rooted in the conflicts raging in Afghanistan, FATA and Kashmir. Pakistan's foreign minister, Shah Mahmood Qureshi, was present in New Delhi when the attacks were carried out, but the Indian government strongly criticized Pakistan for not taking responsibility for the attacks. The Army chief denied Pakistan's involvement, and this fuelled the anger of the Indian people, who felt that Pakistan should hand over or prosecute Hafiz Muhammad Saeed, the leader of Lashkari-Tayyiba, who was believed to have planned the attack.

The Indian government was outraged by the refusal of the Pakistani authorities to take action against Saeed. Despite the conviction and sentencing of the sole surviving assassin, Ajmal Kasab, to death four years later, India felt that justice was not fully served. The refusal of Pakistan to take responsibility for the Mumbai attacks and hand over Saeed added fuel to the already tense relations between the two neighbouring countries.[66]

Salman Taseer's Murder

Salman Taseer, the charismatic and prominent governor of the Punjab, was assassinated by one of his own security guards, who would later become a household name. The guard, Malik Mumtaz Hussain Qadri of the Punjab Elite Force, shouted 'Allah-o-Akbar' before firing two magazines of a sub-machine gun at the governor in Kohsar Market in Islamabad, and then surrendered to law enforcement officials.[67] Qadri later admitted to killing Taseer because of his vocal opposition to Pakistan's controversial blasphemy law.[68] On that fateful day, Governor Salman Taseer arrived in Islamabad and, after conducting official meetings, he headed to the popular cafés in Kohsar Market, accompanied by over a dozen guards, including nine personnel of the Elite Force. Taseer had just finished his meal when the perpetrator, Qadri, shot him. According to police officers, Qadri emptied his gun and then loaded it with another magazine, firing a second round of thirty bullets at the governor. Taseer fell to the ground and, by most accounts, died instantly.

As news of the governor's assassination spread, leaders of the PPP, who were present in the capital, visited the hospital where his body was being held. Distraught and grief-stricken, they spoke of the immense loss his death would bring to the party. Leaders of other parties, including the PML-N, also paid their respects at the hospital. The first official to confirm the identity of the killer was Interior Minister Rehman Malik. The killer had been stationed in Rawalpindi and had been on the governor's guard duty at least three times before the attack.

After the autopsy, which concluded that the governor had been hit by forty bullets, 26 of which were lodged in his body and fourteen of which exited, the body was taken to Lahore for burial from Chakala Air Base in a C-130 aircraft.

Asiya Factor

To provide context for Taseer's assassination, it is necessary to recount the story of Asiya Bibi, a Christian woman who in June 2008 offered water from a well to a group of Muslim women working in the fields. The women refused to drink from her, claiming she was a non-Muslim, and Bibi allegedly made an insulting remark about the Prophet Muhammad. The Muslim women informed the village cleric, who alerted the police. Bibi was charged with blasphemy, a crime punishable by death in Pakistan. This seemingly innocuous incident quickly became a national display of bigotry, intolerance and fanaticism. Taseer emerged as one of Bibi's most prominent supporters, visiting her in prison and holding a press conference with her, and promising to obtain a presidential pardon for her. Although the pardon was prevented by court order, Taseer continued to publicly criticize the blasphemy law.

However, the religiously oriented population in Pakistan, inflamed by influential clerics, did not interpret Taseer, the Governor of Punjab, as rendering assistance to a woman from a religious minority. Regardless of her alleged transgressions, these individuals staunchly believed that Taseer should not have intervened in a case that pertained to the honour of the Prophet. Instead, he was seen as a traitor and renegade. In Urdu media outlets, mosque sermons and mass rallies, Bibi's case became a national symbol of defiance and of asserting Muslim supremacy over 'the other'. Christianity symbolized the West, and Taseer was part of the English-speaking elite who were seen as being in cahoots with 'the enemy'. Taseer's public support for a woman who allegedly insulted the Prophet Muhammad (peace be upon him) was seen as ample evidence, in their minds, of a global conspiracy against Islam and Muslims.

Following Taseer's assassination, the PPP leadership expressed their shock and horror at the heinous crime. However, few showed the courage to attend his funeral. President Zardari praised Taseer's courage and resilience but did not attend the funeral. The PPP spokesman called the assassination 'ghastly' and demanded that the perpetrators be punished, while Zardari delegated attendance at the funeral to the Sindh chief minister Qaim Ali Shah and his sister Faryal Talpur. The absence of the PPP leadership at Taseer's funeral highlighted the dangerous and divisive nature of religious extremism in Pakistan.

Certain Pakistani religious leaders went to the extent of praising the assailant who took the life of the governor and advocated for a boycott of the ceremonies associated with Taseer's final rites in Lahore. One religious party in particular, the Jamaat-e-Ahl-e-Sunnat Pakistan, issued a warning that those who expressed grief over the assassination could suffer the same fate. The party stated, 'No Muslim should attend the funeral or express any kind of regret or sympathy over the incident for Salman Taseer.'[69] They claimed that anyone who expressed sympathy for the death of a blasphemer was committing blasphemy themselves. The TTP also threatened that anyone offering prayers for Taseer would be guilty of blasphemy.

Despite the backlash, the funeral prayers were eventually led by Allama Afzal Chisti of the ulema wing of the PPP. The chief cleric of the Badshahi mosque, who had initially agreed to lead the funeral prayers, backed out at the last moment, saying he was going out of town. Taseer was finally buried at a military cantonment graveyard in Lahore.

Qadri was held in custody on five-day remand following his arrest. During his appearance in court on 9 January 2011, he confessed to killing Taseer. Despite this confession, more than three hundred lawyers offered to represent him pro bono. Qadri was sent to Adiala Jail in Rawalpindi on fourteen-day judicial remand on 10 January 2011. Owing to security issues, his trial for murder was held in the prison four days later.

On 10 October 2011 Qadri was found guilty of murder and condemned to death. He filed an appeal in Islamabad High Court against his death sentence, and the appeal was admitted on 11 October 2011. However, his appeal was rejected in December 2015, and he was eventually hanged on 29 February 2016, at around 4:30 a.m., at Adiala Jail. His funeral was held on 1 March 2016 at Liaqat Bagh in Rawalpindi and was attended by over 100,000 people, including Hamid Saeed Kazmi, the federal minister for religious affairs at the time of Taseer's assassination. It was also noted that Barelvis attended the funeral in large numbers. Qadri was buried in the Bara Kahu district of Islamabad.[70] Importantly, Qadri's hanging gave rise to the religio-political party Tehreek-i-Laibaik-Ya-Rasool Allah.[71]

The Raymond Davis Incident

The Raymond Davis case stands out as a pivotal 'diplomatic tempest' that truly strained the diplomatic ties between Pakistan and the United States. Davis, an American national, took the lives of two Pakistanis by shooting them on a bustling road in Lahore on 27 January 2011. Tragically, a third Pakistani citizen lost his life when a vehicle attempted to rescue him from the scene of the incident.[72] Davis, after killing those individuals, tried to escape the scene but passers-by held him. Different questions were raised after the incident, igniting heated debate. Who was Raymond Davis? What was the job for such a person whose status is not exactly diplomatic? What is immunity according to international law? A weapon was also recovered from his custody, which made his role and status in Pakistan considerably suspect in the eyes of people as well as the government.[73] This incident and the way it was handled alluded to a prevailing perception regarding the United States' involvement in Pakistan's internal affairs. Over a period of time, this perception had solidified in the public consciousness, suggesting that the United States had been actively engaged in undermining the stability of Pakistan. This belief stemmed from the widely held notion that the CIA had established and operated a clandestine spy network within Pakistan. This network was seen as a tool used by the United States to exert influence and potentially manipulate the country's political landscape, fuelling suspicions and concerns about the extent of foreign interference in Pakistan's internal affairs. The case had strained the bilateral relations between the two countries with anti-U.S. groups stressing that the Pakistani government must resist the American call to free Davis.

There was initial confusion about Davis's status after he was arrested in Lahore. Reports referred to him as a diplomat, then as a consular employee and later as a plain civilian on a business visa. The U.S. embassy later confirmed that he worked as a technical advisor, but an *ABC News* report raised suspicions of a possible CIA connection, since Davis was associated with a security firm in Florida. U.S. state officials clarified that he was not an employee of the Lahore consulate, but of the embassy in Islamabad. The crucial question was whether Davis had diplomatic immunity or not, which was governed by the Vienna Convention on Diplomatic Relations. Pakistan had passed legislation incorporating the convention into domestic law in 1972. Article 29 of the convention states that a diplomatic agent's person is inviolable, and they are not subject to arrest or detention.[74]

The U.S. government maintained a straightforward position from the beginning: Raymond Davis was an employee of the U.S. consulate in Lahore, and he had shot two men in self-defence. Because of these two factors, the Americans argued that he was entitled to diplomatic immunity, and that the government of Pakistan was obligated to release him under the Vienna Convention. President Obama supported this position, and Senator John

Kerry even visited Pakistan in an attempt to resolve the complex issue.[75] Threats from various U.S. lawmakers of halting aid to Pakistan were also made. One senior U.S. administration official said, 'The longer this goes on, the higher the potential cost in the relationship.' 'Sooner or later, if they can't resolve it, Congress is going to start sending some signals.'[76]

Complying with the wishes of the United States was not as simple as U.S. officials had thought. It involved a political cost, which President Zardari and his colleagues were acutely aware of. They needed American funding, but at the same time, exposing themselves to anti-American sentiments, which had surged exponentially across Pakistan, could potentially cut short their political careers. The public was incensed over Davis's actions, adding fuel to the fire of the already widespread perception that Americans were a source of discontent and terror in Pakistan. Conspiracy theories had taken root in the minds of many Pakistanis, with Davis being portrayed as a CIA agent or an employee of Blackwater, an American private military contractor firm that was established on 26 December 1996 by Erik Prince, a former Navy SEAL officer, whose activities are shrouded in complete mystery. Its connection to the incident further outraged Pakistanis, who had embraced various conspiracy theories about Blackwater/Xe Services and their ilk running around Pakistan.[77]

The Raymond Davis incident also exposed a rift within the ruling party regarding the Davis case. During a cabinet reshuffle, Foreign Minister Shah Mehmood Qureshi was reportedly removed due to his differing opinion on the Raymond Davis issue. Qureshi stated that he had been pressured by Washington to release Davis, but he refused to comply because Davis did not have diplomatic status.[78] Religious and political parties in Pakistan exerted immense pressure on the PPP-led government not to give in to U.S. demands, since it was a matter of sovereignty and national dignity. They demanded that Davis be tried in Pakistani courts and receive due punishment. Despite the public outrage, a Pakistani court acquitted Davis of murder charges and released him, allegedly after a deal was struck involving 'blood money' paid to the victims' families. Washington officials tried to spin the situation positively, claiming that his release meant a return to normalcy in relations between the two countries. However, this case became a severe test of ties between the United States and Pakistan, with anti-U.S. groups demanding the Pakistani government resist U.S. calls to release him. Nonetheless, the Pakistani leadership, deemed spineless by some, ultimately succumbed to American pressure.

The Killing of Osama bin Laden

In May 2011 U.S. intelligence discovered that Osama bin Laden, the mastermind behind the 9/11 terrorist attacks, was living in a secure compound in Abbottabad, a city near Islamabad in Pakistan. In a daring operation on a clear night, U.S. Navy SEALS raided the compound and killed bin Laden without facing significant resistance. After visually identifying his body at the site of the raid, U.S. forces took his remains out of Pakistan for further examination and DNA identification. Bin Laden's body was then given a sea burial. The successful operation was a major victory for the United States in its fight against terrorism, but it also raised questions about Pakistan's role in harbouring the world's most wanted terrorist.[79] Hours after its confirmation, bin Laden's death was announced by President Obama in a televised address. 'I expected my most difficult call to be with Pakistan's beleaguered president, Asif Ali Zardari, who would surely face a backlash at home over our violation of Pakistani sovereignty,' Obama wrote. 'When I reached him, however, he expressed congratulations and support. "Whatever the fallout," he said, "it's very good news".'[80]

Apart from President Zardari, U.S. officials also contacted the then Army chief of Pakistan, General Ashfaq Parvez Kayani, who asked the United States to be transparent about the raid so that the Pakistani public's reaction could be managed. According to Obama, he did not involve the Pakistani government in the raid because he suspected that certain elements within the country maintained links with the Taliban and al-Qaeda. A secret Pakistani investigation of the operation, which was leaked to *Al Jazeera*, concluded that the operation was a 'great humiliation' for Pakistan, the worst since the 1971 war with India. The United States had carried out a 'hostile military mission deep inside Pakistan' without informing Islamabad, and the Pakistani security establishment had no idea bin Laden was hiding in Abbottabad, or in fact anywhere in Pakistan. If this claim is to be given any credence, then it suggests that the Pakistani establishment and its intelligence apparatus were in a state of utter disarray.

The Salala Incident

On 26 November 2011 NATO helicopters launched an attack on a Pakistani checkpoint in Salala, resulting in the death of at least 24 Pakistani security personnel and injuring twelve soldiers. The checkpoint was located in the Tehsil Bayzai area of Mohmand Agency on the Pakistan–Afghan border, in close proximity to Afghanistan's Kunar province.[81] The attack occurred when forty soldiers were stationed at the checkpoint, and the continued shelling resulted in the loss of lives of security personnel and civilians in nearby areas. The incident was vehemently condemned by Syed Masood Kausar, the governor of Khyber Pakhtunkhwa, who stated that it was an attack on Pakistan's territorial sovereignty and such cross-border attacks could not be tolerated any more. The incident came a day after a meeting between the chief of Army staff General Ashfaq Parvez Kayani and the commander of coalition forces in Afghanistan General Allen Jones to discuss measures of enhancing border control on both sides. The attack caused a marked deterioration in the already strained relations between the United States and Pakistan, which had had a tumultuous year, marked by incidents such as the bin Laden raid, the jailing of a CIA contractor and U.S. accusations that Pakistan backed a militant attack on the U.S. embassy in Kabul. The increase in U.S. drone strikes on militants in recent years had also caused unease in Islamabad, which claimed that the campaign killed more Pakistani civilians in the border area than militants.[82]

After the attack on Pakistani security personnel by NATO helicopters, Prime Minister Yousuf Raza Gilani described it as 'outrageous' and immediately took action by convening an emergency cabinet meeting. Despite being in his hometown at the time, he cut short his visit to return to Islamabad to address the situation. The Pakistani government also issued a statement from the Foreign Ministry, stating that the prime minister would be taking up the matter with NATO and the United States 'in the strongest terms'. This swift response from the Pakistani government reflected the severity of the attack and their determination to address it through diplomatic channels.[83] The cabinet was informed that NATO's force in Afghanistan was investigating and had expressed condolences to the families affected. The assault occurred at the Salala checkpoint, located about 2.5 kilometres (1.5 mi.) from the Afghan border, around 2 a.m. local time (9 p.m. GMT). Pakistani troops retaliated as best they could, according to the Pakistan Army's source. General Kayani had denounced the 'blatant and unacceptable act' and urged for 'strong and immediate action to be taken against those responsible for this aggression'.[84] General John R. Allen, the commander of the International Security Assistance Force (ISAF), issued a statement expressing his commitment to thoroughly investigate the incident and determine the facts. 'This incident has my highest personal attention,' he said, 'and I offer my most sincere and heartfelt condolences to the families and loved ones of any members of Pakistan Security Forces who may have been killed or injured.'[85] Shortly after the attack, Pakistan closed the border crossing for supplies bound for NATO forces in Afghanistan – a move that had been used in the past as a form of protest. According to the BBC's correspondent Syed Shoaib Hasan in Karachi, Pakistani officials were furious and denied any militant activity in the area at the time of the NATO attack. This incident appeared to be yet another setback for U.S.–Pakistan relations, which had only just begun their slow recovery following the unilateral U.S. raid that killed Osama bin Laden in Pakistan in May.

The Memogate Scandal and Civil–Military Relations

A scandal erupted in Pakistan when a secret memo was published in October 2011, which requested assistance from Washington to control the Pakistani military. The memo caused tension between the country's government, led by President Zardari, and the influential military. Pakistan's ambassador to the United States, Husain Haqqani, was implicated in the scandal, as the memo was delivered to the U.S. military chief. Haqqani denied any involvement in the memo and its request for help with the military due to the domestic unrest that arose following the death of Osama bin Laden. The scandal, known as 'memogate', further increased the pressure on Zardari's already unpopular government.

Despite the presence of a civilian president in Pakistan, the military maintained an immense degree of political and economic power. Since 1951, when General Ayub Khan took charge as the Army chief, the military had effectively governed the country, either directly or indirectly. Despite repeated attempts by civilian leaders to limit its influence, the military establishment had stubbornly resisted such efforts.

Ambassador Haqqani was accused of writing the memo to Admiral Mike Mullen, a former top U.S. military officer, requesting his help in establishing a 'new security team' in Islamabad that would be favourable to Washington. The memo was published in a Pakistani English-language newspaper and on *Foreign Policy*'s website. While Haqqani initially denied any knowledge of the document, Mullen's spokesperson confirmed that he had received it but had dismissed it as lacking credibility. Haqqani continued to deny any involvement with the memo. If it was authentic, it could reinforce the politically explosive allegation that the Pakistani government colluded with the United States to undermine the interests of the country and its Army.[86]

Although the United States had injected substantial amounts of aid into Pakistan, the Western nation remained deeply unpopular in the country. Detractors of the government and individuals linked to the military incited the scandal. As a result of the affair, Haqqani offered to resign, and Zardari could have been targeted if allegations that he authorized the memo had proven to be true. Some had speculated that Zardari was forced to dismiss Haqqani, his close confidant.

In addition, Pakistani newspaper *The News* published transcripts of conversations between Haqqani and Mansoor Ijaz, a U.S. citizen of Pakistani descent who claimed to have conveyed the memo to Mullen through an intermediary, as instructed by Haqqani. The transcripts indicated that Haqqani purportedly collaborated with Ijaz to draft the memo and urged him to proceed with the plan.[87]

After delivering the memo, Ijaz reportedly warned Haqqani, 'The ball is in play now. Make sure you have protected your flanks.' The memo accused General Kayani of orchestrating a plot to overthrow the government following the assassination of bin Laden. This claim sparked a remarkable wave of domestic criticism against the Army. The memo implored Mullen to intervene directly with Kayani to halt the supposed conspiracy.

Some analysts believe that the memo was a machination of the military intended to humiliate the government or remove Haqqani from his position. 'Could Haqqani/Zardari be that staggeringly out of touch with reality?' asked political commentator Cyril Almeida in *Dawn*. 'Or is the more likely scenario (though far from certain) that the boys, meaning the Army establishment, are up to their tricks again?'[88] Mansoor Ijaz initially disclosed the scandal himself in a *Financial Times* column on 10 October, adding to the confusion surrounding the affair. In an interview with *Dawn*, he explained that he wrote the column to defend Admiral Mullen's criticism of Pakistan's alleged support for militants and mentioned the memo to strengthen his argument. (It is worth noting that Ijaz has a history of making claims about being well connected to u.s. politicians.)

According to Ijaz's *Financial Times* piece, on 9 May – a week after the u.s. special-forces operation that resulted in Osama bin Laden's death – a senior Pakistani diplomat, namely Haqqani, urgently requested that he relay a message from President Zardari to White House national-security officials. The message was to bypass Pakistan's military and intelligence channels, given that the discovery of bin Laden on Pakistani soil had humiliated Zardari's civilian government, which he feared would lead to a military takeover. To avoid such a situation, Zardari needed an American show of support to end any possibility of a coup, and he needed it fast.

Following the humiliating breach of Pakistani sovereignty by u.s. special forces during the raid on Osama bin Laden's hideout, both the military establishment and the ISI were criticized for their alleged involvement in harbouring bin Laden for six years. President Zardari's government was also looking for a scapegoat. In an effort to prevent a possible military takeover, a senior Pakistani diplomat contacted Ijaz to deliver a message from President Zardari to u.s. Navy admiral Michael Mullen, who had a strong relationship with Pakistan. Despite the admiral's warnings, it seems that Pakistani military and intelligence chiefs did not take heed, leading to attacks against u.s. and NATO troops in September, which Admiral Mullen claimed were done 'with ISI support'.[89] The crux of the matter was that Ijaz was accusing Pakistan's intelligence services of waging a covert war against the United States, perhaps as retaliation for the raid on bin Laden's compound or in pursuit of national interests that sought to restore Taliban rule in Afghanistan. According to Ijaz, the ISI embodied the radicalism that underpins Pakistan's foreign policy, and the time had come for America to take decisive action to shut down the political and financial support that sustained this organ of the Pakistani state, which had consistently undermined global anti-terrorism efforts. Ijaz believed that measures like the bill then moving through Congress to stop aid to Pakistan were inadequate, and more precise policies were needed to excise the cancer that the ISI and its rogue elements had become in the Pakistani state.[90] Ijaz did not view the Pakistani people as enemies of the United States, nor did he hold the civilian government responsible for the country's troubles. Rather, he saw the real threat as coming from a state apparatus that fuelled extremism among Pakistan's Islamist population and directed their jihadist ambitions towards regional adversaries and global targets. To effectively combat terrorism, it was imperative to address the root cause by curbing the influence of this dangerous entity within Pakistan's political and security establishments. This would require a concerted effort by the international community to dismantle the terror infrastructure and disrupt its sources of funding and support.[91]

In June 2012 the Supreme Court formed a commission to investigate the matter and announced its verdict, confirming that Hussain Haqqani had indeed passed on messages, as claimed. Throughout this period, the government had consistently denied issuing any such instructions. General Kayani, on the other hand, did not take any action and allowed the crisis to continue, hoping that it would weaken the civilian administration further. Eventually, the military settled for Haqqani's resignation as ambassador and his de facto exile to the United States, rather than pursuing treason charges against him.[92]

The Election of 2013

The PML-N was widely expected to win the 2013 elections and become the largest party in the National Assembly, with the Pakistan Tehreek-i-Insaf as the runner-up. Despite using every available trick to win the elections, the Nawaz League only managed to secure 47.4 per cent of the total seats, amounting to 129 out of 272 seats, or 32 per cent of the total registered votes. However, an intriguing aspect of the election was the increased voter turnout, from 44 per cent to 55 per cent, which suggested PTI's success in mobilizing new voters.[93] The Muslim League (Nawaz) was anticipated to dominate the 2013 National Assembly elections with PTI as the runner-up.

The Punjab remained the Muslim League's stronghold, and it won 120 out of 148 National Assembly seats from there. It secured six seats from Khyber Pakhtunkhwa, two from FATA, and one each from Sindh and Baluchistan, demonstrating its lopsided representation and Punjab-centric politics. Despite this, nineteen independents joined its ranks, and with the help of 41 reserved seats for women and minorities, the tally reached 189 in the National Assembly, which had a total strength of 342 seats. Thus, the Muslim League (Nawaz) had a simple majority in the lower house.

PTI could not win more than 28 seats, despite a spirited election campaign, which was a paltry 10.2 per cent of the total seats in the National Assembly. PTI was the third-largest party, while the PPP had won 36 seats and emerged as the second-largest party, with almost 15 per cent of the total votes cast in its favour.[94]

Surprisingly, the ANP was completely wiped out in Khyber Pakhtunkhwa, and Fazal ur Rahman's Jamiat Ulema-i-Islam didn't fare much better than the ANP. The PPP's claim that the results were manipulated was dismissed because its defeat had been anticipated. Many of its supporters either did not come out to vote or opted to vote for other parties. Much of its support base was eroded by PTI's aggressive politicking.

Although the May 2013 elections marked the first democratic transition from one civilian government to another, the PML-N did not enjoy its victory for long. PTI accused the PML-N of rigging the elections and embarked upon a relentless campaign to discredit the PML-N victory. This campaign led to marches and sit-ins in Islamabad from August to November 2014, in which PTI and Tahir ul Qadri's Pakistan Awami Tehreek (PAT) joined forces. Interim chief minister Najam Sethi was alleged to have helped the PML-N win around 35 seats more than it had actually secured.

In Pakistan's 2013 general election, which was held on 11 May 2013, the results were met with allegations of rigging and manipulation. Imran Khan, the leader of the PTI party, and his supporters were among the most vocal critics of the election's integrity, claiming that the results were engineered in favour of the PML-N party.[95]

Allegations of Rigging

The allegations of rigging and manipulation stemmed from the ECP handling of the election process. Khan and his party believed that the ECP failed to ensure a fair and transparent election. PTI claimed that there were irregularities in the voting process, including polling stations that were shut down before the official closing time, widespread use of fake ballot papers and the improper use of voter identification cards. Moreover, the party accused the ECP of being biased towards the PML-N, claiming that it allowed the party to violate the election code of conduct.[96]

Besides these allegations, Imran Khan called for an independent investigation into the election results. He even refused to accept the results of the election, which his party lost, and called for re-election in the constituencies where rigging was alleged. Khan's allegations and his refusal to accept the results of the election led to political instability in Pakistan, with his party's supporters holding several protests and sit-ins across the country. In August 2014 PTI held a massive sit-in protest in Islamabad to put pressure on the government to conduct an independent enquiry into the alleged rigging.[97] The protests created a tense political climate and hampered the government's efforts to address critical national issues.

The PML-N government responded to the allegations by inviting PTI to participate in a judicial commission to investigate the rigging allegations. The commission was formed in June 2014 and was headed by the retired justice Nasir-ul-Mulk. The commission's report, which was released in July 2015, concluded that while there were some irregularities, there was not enough evidence to support the claims of widespread rigging. Despite the commission's findings, Khan refused to accept the report, claiming that it was biased and that the commission was unable to carry out a comprehensive investigation due to the government's interference.

The purpose of Imran Khan's 2014 sit-in protest in the capital city of Pakistan was to demand a vote recount in four constituencies, but the government refused to meet his demands. The sit-in, which lasted for more than one hundred days, attracted thousands of supporters and caused major disruption to daily life in the city. The protest also sparked controversy and debates about democracy, political ethics and the role of opposition parties in Pakistan.[98] Despite the government's refusal to accept Khan's demands, the protest helped to raise awareness about electoral transparency and accountability in the country. The sit-in was called off only after the Army Public School incident, which will be discussed later.

Imran Khan's allegations and his refusal to accept the results of the election led to political instability and protests across the country. The formation of the judicial commission and its subsequent report failed to satisfy Khan and his supporters, who continued to insist that the election was rigged. The allegations of rigging in the 2013 election continued to be a contentious issue in Pakistani politics, and the government's efforts to address these issues remained unsuccessful.

The Pashtun Tahafuz Movement

The Pashtun Tahafuz Movement (PTM) sprang from humble beginnings in May 2014, when a group of eight students from Dera Ismael Khan, a major city in Khyber Pakhtunkhwa, founded the Mahsud Tahafuz Movement. However, on 1 February 2018, the group changed its name to the more inclusive 'Pashtun Tahafuz Movement'. Despite its relatively low profile, the PTM gained national prominence in January 2018 when it launched a justice movement for Naqeebullah Mehsud, a young man killed in a fake police encounter orchestrated by Rao Anwar, a police officer based in Karachi. Rao Anwar claimed that Naqeebullah had links with the TTP, Lashkar-e-Jhangvi (LeJ) and the Islamic State of Iraq and the Levant (Daesh). His claims were termed false and baseless. The PTM's protest against extrajudicial killings and human rights abuses by state security forces quickly spread throughout Pakistan and attracted international attention.[99] Regrettably, limitations on media freedom have hindered open, candid and informed discussion on the nature and drivers of the PTM. The discourse surrounding the PTM is mostly propagated by Western scholars, journalists and writers from mainland Pakistan, who base their arguments on a combination of colonial stereotypes about Pashtuns and a statist view of politics in the Pashtun region. The state has accused the PTM of being financed and supported by foreign powers, and it has relied on repressive tactics to suppress the movement. However, these measures have proven to be unsuccessful. The most significant lesson from the past events was that oppressive and coercive tactics had not weakened the movement or decreased its support. On the contrary, these measures seemed to have further radicalized the movement's followers and bolstered its claims regarding ethnic discrimination by state institutions. A different, more political approach is necessary to address the PTM. Therefore, it is imperative to have a thorough understanding of the movement for those who seek to find a mutually agreeable resolution.[100]

The PTM emerged as an organic political force, rooted in the collective and individual experiences of Pashtuns in the unique socio-political milieu of the post-9/11 world. Spearheaded by educated Pashtun youth, this movement has been simmering in the Pashtun region for several decades. Manzoor Pashteen, a human rights activist from South Waziristan, leads the movement, which also includes prominent activists such as Ali Wazir, Mohsin Dawar, Mir Kalam, Alamzaib Mahsud, Abdullah Nangyal, Fazal Khan, Gulalai Ismail, Sanna Ejaz, Wranga Loni and the late Arman Loni, Arif Wazir, Usman Kakar and Noor Islam Dawar.

The PTM is a non-violent and peaceful resistance movement that operates within the lawful boundaries of the Constitution of Pakistan. However, constraints on media freedom have hindered an open and informed discussion about the movement's nature and drivers. Stereotypical views propagated by mainstream Pakistan about the Pashtun region do not reflect the reality of the Pashtun people. The PTM's members have experienced a range of traumatic events, including killings, displacements, enforced disappearances, ethnic profiling, humiliation and destruction of livelihoods and ways of life.

Pashtun labourers, students and salaried classes have borne the brunt of the crises caused by terrorism and the accompanying politics of fear and discrimination. The repressive tactics used against the PTM have only strengthened the movement's claims of ethnic discrimination by state institutions.

The most remarkable feature of the movement is the leading role of educated youth from middle and lower middle classes. These young people had to leave their homes and spend their formative years in major urban centres of the country post-9/11 for livelihood and studies. However, Pakistan's policy of militant sponsorship began to backfire, and militants started wreaking havoc in mainland Pakistan, causing Pashtuns living in urban centres to bear the brunt of backlash by the state and society.

Confronted with an existential crisis of identity, many university students turned to books and study circles and became politically active in both physical and digital spaces well before the founding of the PTM. With the proliferation of digital technology and social media, they connected with Pashtun youth from other parts of Pakistan with shared experiences. Through this shared experience of navigating the crisis, a political consciousness emerged that sought recognition, fair treatment and lasting peace for Pashtuns within the constitutional framework of Pakistan.[101]

This political consciousness embodies both continuity and change in the traditional Pashtun nationalism. The movement is rooted in a secular–progressive ideology and is critical of the military's alleged support for Islamic militants. It serves as a vehicle for Pashtun ethnicity to articulate its grievances, demanding a continuation of classical Pashtun nationalism. The PTM's narrative has been heavily influenced by Pashtun nationalist parties that have long been critical of Pakistan's Afghan policy, dating back to the days of Zulfiqar Ali Bhutto. They have consistently accused the military establishment of using Islamic militants as a tool of domestic and regional policy. The PTM believes that the growth of religious militancy in the Pashtun region is primarily a consequence of decades of investment in jihad and extremism. The PTM is a unique departure from classical Pashtun nationalism, as it is spearheaded by Pashtun individuals who belong to the lower middle class and hail from ex-FATA (mainly Waziristan). This region remained at the margins of Pashtun politics for decades, and thus, the PTM represents the interests and aspirations of Pashtun 'have-nots' both economically and politically. The movement's appeal transcends tribal and geographical boundaries, but its strongest support base lies in areas that have been historically neglected by Pakistan's economic and political spheres, such as ex-FATA, southern parts of Khyber Pakhtunkhwa and northern Baluchistan. Due to this modest socio-economic and regional background, the PTM's relationship with Pashtun nationalist elites is rocky and ambiguous.

What sets the PTM apart from other nationalist movements is that it draws its primary inspiration from actual social and political experiences of Pashtuns in the post-9/11 world, rather than abstract references to historical Pashtun territory or imagined futures. The PTM foregrounds the misery, destruction and disruption caused by war in a region that was often ignored by the media and independent researchers. The movement rejects the false binary of 'pro-military operation versus anti-military operation' and calls for a fairer and more critical engagement with the Pakistani state. Although PTM leadership may not have strong feelings about the Durand Line, they clearly want to revisit the current relationship with the Pakistani state and demand a more just and equitable engagement that challenges the hegemonic narratives of the state and its policies that have fomented terrorism.

The young members of the PTM are notable for their rejection of orientalist myths that portray Pashtuns as savage, naive, revengeful and emotional beings. Instead, they challenge these stereotypes through their words and actions, drawing attention to the diverse and complex nature of Pashtun society. In doing so, the PTM is reviving a youth-led, progressive and democratic politics that is sorely needed in a country where right-wing tendencies have gained a foothold in the body politic. By engaging with the PTM in a meaningful way, it may be possible to address the grievances of those who have suffered in war-torn areas and help build a more inclusive, federal and democratic Pakistan.

Challenges Posed to the PML-N Government

When the Muslim League (Nawaz) assumed power in Pakistan in 2013, they faced a multitude of challenges right from the start. The country was grappling with a surge in terrorism, while frequent power outages and rising inflation had stirred public discontent. Political polarization had rendered consensus on critical issues nearly unattainable. Amid these challenges, the tragic Model Town incident occurred, featuring a violent clash between authorities and Tahir ul Qadri's supporters, resulting in casualties and prompting concerns about the government's use of force. This event also ignited calls for accountability and justice, further highlighting the intricate political and security dynamics the party had to navigate during its tenure.

The Model Town Incident

On 17 June 2014 a violent clash occurred in Model Town, Lahore, resulting in the tragic deaths of fourteen individuals, while dozens more were left injured. Tahir ul Qadri's supporters had gathered outside his offices, and tensions escalated when police attempted to remove barriers from the area. Despite the police's claims of restraint, the situation intensified as more officers arrived on the scene. Tragically, two women lost their lives in the riots, and Qadri's supporters retaliated by throwing stones. PAT has been identified as the group behind the protests.[102] Sadly, such issues should have been resolved through negotiation instead of resorting to strong-arm tactics.

The chief minister of the Punjab, Shahbaz Sharif, took swift action following the tragic incident by ordering a judicial inquiry. In a public statement, he expressed deep remorse over the loss of life, stating, 'The killings that occurred in Model Town are a tragedy that pains me deeply. My heart goes out to the families of those who lost their loved ones.' He also emphasized his commitment to non-violent conflict resolution, saying, 'I believe in peaceful protest and cannot even imagine using force against anyone. If I am found responsible for this incident, I will immediately resign from my position.'[103] However, the incident was largely brushed under the rug. Officials at Jinnah Hospital in Lahore confirmed that the deceased had sustained bullet wounds, while Abdul Rauf stated that the hospital had treated eighty people for injuries, with forty of them having bullet wounds. Critics have lambasted the authorities for their heavy-handed response to Qadri's supporters, noting that the barricades had been installed there for more than four years and erected with the consent of local residents to enhance security. Meanwhile, Qadri, speaking via video link from Canada, condemned the police raid on his Lahore headquarters during a news conference. While he urged his followers to continue protesting, he implored them to do so peacefully and to refrain from damaging any property.[104] Later, during an interview conducted by this author, a police officer who wished to remain anonymous claimed that the killing had been orchestrated by intelligence agencies to discredit the political government. These allegations were later brought to the attention of Prime Minister Nawaz Sharif, who then confronted Army chief General Raheel Sharif about the matter. The matter was then hushed up, to the benefit of both the parties. The toll of lives lost lingered unacknowledged, with Justice Ali Baqar Najfi's report, which squarely implicated Rana Sana Ullah and Dr Tauqir, the Chief Minister's secretary, as culprits in the tragedy, relegated to the archives of neglect.

The Army Public School Massacre in Peshawar

On 16 December 2014 a horrific attack took place at Army Public School in Peshawar, in which 141 people, 132 of whom were innocent children, were brutally killed by militants from the TTP. The attackers were later reported to have been killed by military officials. Reports indicated that all seven of the attackers wore suicide bomb vests. The militants scaled the school walls and started their assault with a bomb blast. The attack left scores of people injured, and parents were frantically searching for their missing children as survivors were admitted to hospitals. In a heart-wrenching account, Shahrukh Khan, a seventeen-year-old student, told the BBC how he hid under a desk as the attacker entered his classroom and opened fire, killing his friends. The militants continued their rampage, going from one classroom to another, shooting indiscriminately. A group of ten friends tried to run away and hide, but only one survived. Witnesses described seeing pupils lying dead in the corridors, and one girl managed to escape by pretending to be dead, covered in blood from those around her. It is important to note that many of the victims were children of military personnel, and most of them were sixteen or younger.

A Taliban spokesman told BBC Urdu that the attack was in retaliation for military operations. Despite international condemnation, Pakistan's policy makers struggled to come to grips with various shades of militants, citing a 'lack of consensus' and 'large pockets of sympathy' for religious militants as major stumbling blocks. When Army chief General Raheel Sharif launched an indiscriminate operation against militant groups, including the Pakistani Taliban, Punjabi Taliban, al-Qaeda and the Haqqani network, the country's political leadership chose to remain largely silent, highlighting the ongoing challenges in addressing extremism in the region.[105]

Dawn Leaks

The *Dawn* Leaks controversy in 2016 involved the alleged leaking of sensitive government information to the newspaper *Dawn*. Journalist Cyril

Almeida was the main character of the whole saga. It revolved around a news report published by *Dawn* on 6 October 2016, which claimed that there had been a high-level civil–military meeting in Pakistan discussing the issue of tackling militant groups, particularly those accused of carrying out acts of terrorism in India.

According to the report, the civilian government had informed the military leadership of Pakistan's increasing isolation in the international community and requested their agreement on several key actions by the state. *Dawn* claimed that the government had asked intelligence agencies to abstain from interfering if law enforcement agencies took action against militant groups. The meeting concluded by reaffirming that the Army and intelligence agencies would continue to play a leading role in the country's fight against terrorism.[106]

The stand-off between the Pakistan Army and the political leadership, led by Sharif, came to a head with the *Dawn* Leaks, which reflected the Army's constant efforts to undermine the country's elected government.[107] After receiving the report, Sharif issued a series of instructions, which included dismissing his special assistant on foreign affairs, Tariq Fatemi, and taking action against the principal information officer, Rao Tehsin. The federal minister for information and broadcasting, Pervaiz Rasheed, was removed from his position on 29 October, making him the biggest casualty of the investigation into the national-security breach. Interior minister Chaudhry Nisar Ali Khan later acknowledged that Rasheed had failed to prevent the controversial news from being released.[108]

The government's release of instructions regarding the *Dawn* Leaks report prompted a swift and public rejection by the Army, which was apparently angered by the government's actions. The report, which concerned differences between the military and the civilian government in their approaches to fighting terrorist groups, was the subject of an inquiry committee that included representatives from the ISI agency and Military Intelligence. The committee recommended strong action against the journalist Cyril Almeida for writing the report, but the government did not act on this recommendation. The Army believed that the prime minister's principal secretary, Fawad Hasan Fawad, was a key part of the problem, since he was the one issuing instructions on behalf of the prime minister. This caused tensions between the military and the government, with analysts such as Abid Hussain suggesting that the Army was seeking to keep the government in a state of flux and portray politicians as corrupt and ineffective. Some also believed that the Army saw its role being reduced in the future and was therefore trying to maintain its power and influence over national affairs.[109] The *Dawn* Leaks highlighted the complex and sensitive nature of civil–military relations in Pakistan and raised questions about the role of the military in national-security decision-making.

Power Failure and IPPS

In 1985 the government of Pakistan teamed up with the World Bank to devise a long-term strategy for the development of Pakistan's power sector. The primary objective was to provide reliable and steady power to fuel economic growth. However, with demand for energy growing at 12 per cent while supply was only increasing at 7 per cent annually, power outages were rampant and adversely affecting industry and agriculture, resulting in considerable output losses. If this gap continued, it was estimated that the country would lose approximately U.S.$1 billion annually in GDP due to a shortage of 2,000 megawatts of electricity. With only 40 per cent of the population having access to electricity and per capita consumption at a mere 4 per cent of the United States' consumption and 24 per cent of Malaysia's, Pakistan was lagging behind and had to catch up quickly. Unfortunately, the Government of Pakistan was facing a significant financial crunch and lacked the resources necessary for infrastructure development. As a result, the private sector was invited to develop new generating capacity, as it was expected to supplement public sector generation and attract additional equity and debt resources while improving efficiency in the energy sector.

The implementation of the new energy policy coincided with a period of high political volatility in the early 1990s. After the first Benazir Bhutto government was dismissed by President Ghulam Ishaq Khan in 1990, Sharif initiated several free-market reforms and signed Pakistan's first independent power producer (IPP) contract for the largest power sector project with the Hub Power Company in 1992. During Benazir Bhutto's second tenure, the government signed several IPP contracts under the 1994 Power Policy, and in June 1996, Pakistan's first private sector power plant, the Hub Power Company (Hubco), began operating.

In February 1997 the Muslim League government of Nawaz Sharif won the elections, and in 1998 the government started investigating IPP contracts signed under the previous government. Unfortunately, the IPP crisis continued unabated, resulting in serious repercussions for international investor confidence. Nonetheless, almost U.S.$4.8 billion of private investment in the power sector has occurred to date, with IPPs accounting for nearly 17 per cent of the country's total electricity generation.[110]

Since May 1998 an important issue facing Pakistan policy makers had been whether IPPS produced expensive electricity. It was contended that IPPs' expensive power had rendered the state utility, the Water and Power Development Authority (WAPDA), bankrupt. It was also alleged that IPPs had indulged in corruption and colluded with WAPDA officials to get their signatures on contracts that allowed procurement of expensive power by WAPDA, which it could ill afford.

Established in 2010, the Independent Power Producers Association (IPPA) was an organization that worked in an advisory capacity to IPPs in

Pakistan. It also acted as a bridge between IPPs and the government for resolution of their common issues. The main functions of IPPA were to liaise with relevant ministries of the federal as well as provincial governments; represent IPPs with NTDC, NEPRA and other relevant authorities; collect, prepare and circulate relevant statistics and information of the power sector of Pakistan to its members and to the public; prepare research reports and publications relevant to the power sector and represent IPPs in policy making and to the media.

Independent power producers were entities set up to develop, own and operate power plants to produce electricity for sale under long-term contracts to power purchasers such as Central Power Purchase Agency-Guarantee (CPPA-G) and K-Electric. They played a pivotal role in solving electricity shortages and supplementing the government's endeavours to create a competitive energy market, but other industry players, such as NEPRA, had also appreciated the higher performance and efficiency of IPPs as compared to public sector generators.

Member IPPs had generation facilities ranging between 84 megawatts and 1,292 megawatts gross. They mainly used natural gas, with high-speed diesel (HSD) as a backup fuel or residual fuel oil (RFO). Some companies, including member IPPs, had also initiated the establishment of a diverse range of power generation facilities. These encompassed wind power plants harnessing the energy of the wind, solar power plants utilizing sunlight to generate electricity, coal-fired power plants relying on the combustion of coal for energy production, and hydropower plants tapping into the potential energy of flowing water to generate electrical power. Pakistan had finally overcome its chronic power shortage and simultaneously broken its decades-long addiction to imported furnace oil as the main fuel for power generation. But the feat had come at a steep price.

In the recent past, the country has found itself entangled in a fervent debate concerning the fate of its power sector. It has grappled with soaring electricity bills and enduring blackouts, issues that have plagued the nation for some time. The incapacity to fully operate all its power plants, along with the associated financial burdens, played a substantial role in exacerbating these challenges. Consequently, the circular debt within the power sector experienced a staggering escalation, surging from PKR 315 billion (U.S.$2 billion) in 2015 to an astonishing PKR 2.2 trillion (U.S$12.7 billion) by 2022.[111]

Soaring Electricity Prices

Pakistan's power sector has been facing a critical juncture as the country grapples with high electricity payments and persistent blackouts. According to some estimates, the country has been paying around PKR 850 billion (U.S.$5.41 billion) annually in capacity charges over the past few years, with projections indicating that this figure could soar beyond PKR 45 trillion

(U.S.$9.2 billion) by 2023. This would make it larger than the country's current peacetime defence budget.

While capacity charges are not technically a budgetary item and are instead paid through power bills sent to consumers, the escalating cost of surplus power generation has resulted in a continuous rise in consumer power tariffs. This has led to inflation, eroded industrial competitiveness and required increased government-funded subsidies on power tariffs to shield export-orientated industries from the full impact of tariff hikes.

Since the government is the sole buyer of power in Pakistan, any costs associated with capacity charges have to be borne by consumers or subsidized by the government. During 2022, the government disbursed over PKR 470 billion (equivalent to U.S.$3 billion) in power subsidies. This expenditure stood as one of the most significant items within the current expenditures category, and it necessitated substantial reductions as part of the IMF programme that Pakistan was endeavouring to reinitiate in 2023. Only two years prior, this figure stood at approximately PKR 90 billion (equivalent to U.S.$573 million). Looking ahead, as capacity payments are anticipated to surge due to an excess of power supply, the subsidy expenditure is expected to escalate even more steeply in the upcoming years. This development poses a significant fiscal challenge for the government, rendering the subsidies unsustainable and compelling it to consider further increase in power tariffs, thus placing it in the onerous position of having to raise rates substantially. This will burden consumers even more, exacerbating inflation and pricing Pakistani exports out of global markets.

In addressing Pakistan's power sector crisis, the PTI government had encouraged the textile export industry to transition away from gas-fuelled captive power plants, which had been installed in response to power shortages following 2008. The PTI government held the belief that significant power consumers, such as the export industry, should rely on the national grid to fulfil their energy needs. Nevertheless, the industry resisted this proposition, contending that grid power was prohibitively expensive.

In January 2021, the government announced an average 15 per cent tariff increase, citing 'compulsory payments' associated with the recent expansion of power generation capacity. This increase, however, amounted to less than a quarter of what was necessary to counteract the escalating costs resulting from the influx of new power plants coming online.[112]

A Crisis Foretold

In November 2014, the governments of Pakistan and China signed an agreement to develop related energy projects based on market-based principles of openness, equality and mutual benefit.[113] The agreement listed fourteen projects as 'prioritized' and seven others as 'actively promoted'. In 2016 these projects were initiated, and Pakistan's power generation capacity was just below 20,000 megawatts with almost two-thirds of the power generated by hydroelectric and furnace oil-based plants. The system added two plants fired by LNG (liquified natural gas), which contributed 1,673 megawatts of generation. However, the government's projections showed that by 2018, 13,207 megawatts would be added to the system as the Chinese power plants reached commercial operations. Plants running on imported coal and LNG accounted for slightly over half or 6,900 MW of this capacity.[114]

The next round of capacity expansion began in 2019 and ran until 2022, adding 20,380 megawatts to the system, with hydroelectric being the largest share at 9,010 megawatts, followed by nuclear at 4,400, and then local coal at 3,300. The completion of all projects in the pipeline by 2023 was expected to double the country's total power generation capacity, reaching up to 53,504 megawatts.[115] According to the government's projections at the time, Pakistan's demand for power was projected to be 25,961 megawatts by June 2018, assuming a GDP growth rate of around 6 per cent (in fact, growth crashed to near zero in 2018). At that point, the country's total generation capacity would be 30,938 megawatts, of which 25,590 megawatts would be available at any given time. The projections showed a surplus emerging in 2018, even with a growth rate of 6 per cent.[116]

Renewable sources such as solar photovoltaic, wind and hydro were expected to account for nearly 43 per cent of total generation capacity, up from 37 per cent in 2016, while coal-based generation was projected to reach 17 per cent of the total, up from 0.3 per cent in 2016. With these new additions, Pakistan was on course to bridge its chronic shortfall in power generation capacity and reach a long-sought goal of diversifying its fuel mix away from expensive furnace oil. Under the old power policies of the 1990s, almost 70 per cent of all power generation used thermal sources such as furnace oil and gas. As the period of gas shortages began after 2005, reliance on furnace oil only increased, straining foreign-exchange reserves and driving up the price of power. Under the new capacity expansion plan agreed with the Chinese, the share of generation based on furnace oil was expected to decline to 11 per cent of the total by 2022, by which time all the projects were supposed to have commenced commercial operation.

However, concerns began to mount within the government about the impact these capacity additions would have on the fiscal account, as well as the foreign-exchange requirement under increased imports of LNG and coal. The same projections made in 2016 by the power division showed capacity payments going up twofold by 2018. Internal documents within the power division showed that capacity payments, which stood at PKR 272 billion in 2015, or approximately 30 per cent of total generation cost, would rise sharply to PKR 630.8 billion by 2018, or almost 50 per cent of the total generation cost. That figure was hit in the year 2019 instead, and according to the power minister, was projected to rise to PKR 1.455 trillion by 2023. The power sector regulator, NEPRA, had provided a more complex picture for the spiralling costs that had weighed on power generation. In its annual report, NEPRA stated that the cost of generation had been increasing due to multiple factors. These had included mismanagement by the distribution companies, non-availability of LNG for the more efficient newer plants, excessive levies and surcharges on grid power to aid the government's revenue effort and transmission constraints in some newer plants, among others.[117]

Although the Chinese capacity expansion had helped to overcome power generation shortfalls in Pakistan, more chronic problems of a creaking transmission network and a poor bill recovery track record, as well as keeping emissions under check, had remained in place. Members of the previous government (PML-N) who had commissioned those power plants had argued that their projections had been based on continuing 6 per cent to 7 per cent growth rates in the economy.[118] With the coming of the PTI government in 2018, the growth rate had plunged to below 2 per cent and went negative in 2020 as COVID-19 lockdowns swept the country. 'You don't factor in recessions when making power sector capacity expansion plans,' said a bureaucrat who had worked under the previous government's power team.[119]

Today, Pakistan is embroiled in a fierce debate over whether it was poor planning or bad management of the power sector and the wider economy that had burdened the country with excess power generation capacity. What is harder to debate, however, is the mounting bill.

The China–Pakistan Economic Corridor

The China–Pakistan Economic Corridor (CPEC) is a bilateral project aimed at enhancing and improving infrastructure within Pakistan to facilitate better trade with China and further integrate the countries of the region. It was launched on 20 April 2015, when Chinese president Xi Jinping and Pakistani prime minister Nawaz Sharif signed 51 agreements and memorandums of understanding valued at U.S.$46 billion. In 2016 the announcement of joint space and satellite initiatives between Pakistan and China, spurred by the CPEC, followed suit.

The CPEC was conceived as a part of the larger Belt and Road Initiative, which seeks to improve connectivity, trade, communication and cooperation between the countries of Eurasia, announced by China in 2013. Due to its potential impact on the region, the CPEC has been compared to the Marshall Plan for the rebuilding of post-Second World War Europe. As a result, numerous countries have expressed interest in participating in the initiative.[120]

Specifically with reference to Pakistan, the CPEC is rooted in the long-standing bilateral relations between Beijing and Islamabad that date back to the 1950s. It represents a significant evolution in the China–Pakistan partnership, introducing an economic dimension to a relationship that had primarily been diplomatic and strategic. The proposed CPEC rail and road networks are strategically designed to build upon Pakistan's existing infrastructure, making use of operational or in-progress rail lines and roads, with necessary upgrades where needed. Among the noteworthy existing infrastructure assets that the CPEC aims to utilize are the Karakoram Highway, linking China's Xinjiang region to Pakistan's Gilgit Baltistan region, and the Gwadar port along the Arabian Sea.

The primary objectives of the CPEC are twofold: first, to modernize Pakistan's transportation systems, encompassing road, rail, air and energy infrastructure; and second, to establish connectivity between Pakistan's deep-sea ports, Gwadar and Karachi, and China's Xinjiang province and beyond via overland routes. This strategic initiative seeks to reduce both the time and cost associated with transporting goods and energy resources, including natural gas, to China. By doing so, it offers an alternative route that circumvents the Straits of Malacca and the South China Sea.[121]

The CPEC represented a comprehensive framework for regional connectivity with far-reaching ambitions that extended beyond China and Pakistan. Its objective was to create mutual benefits not only for these two countries but for Iran, Afghanistan, the Central Asian republics and the broader region. The initiative aimed to bolster geographical linkages by improving road, rail and air transportation systems; fostering seamless exchanges of goods and people; nurturing cross-cultural understanding through academic and cultural initiatives; and significantly boosting trade and commercial activities. The ultimate goal was to optimize energy production and distribution, facilitating cooperation on a win–win basis and ultimately culminating in a well-connected, integrated region characterized by shared destiny, harmony and development.

In essence, the CPEC represented a pivotal step towards economic regionalization within the context of an increasingly globalized world. It was founded on the principles of promoting peace, fostering development and establishing a conducive framework for all stakeholders involved. The project held the promise of a brighter future for the entire region, underpinned by peace, robust economic development and sustainable growth.[122]

However, the Pakistan Democratic Movement (PDM), an alliance of opposition political parties in Pakistan that was formed in September 2020, has been critical of the CPEC and had raised concerns about the terms of the agreements between China and Pakistan. Since coming to power, the PDM government expressed reservations about some of the projects under the CPEC, citing worries about their financial viability and transparency. The government had also sought to renegotiate the terms of some of the projects. In December 2020 Pakistan's minister for planning, development and special initiatives, Asad Umar, stated that the government would undertake a review of all CPEC projects to ensure that they were aligned with the country's development priorities. The PTI government had been quite keen to renegotiate the terms of some of the projects, including the Main Line–1 railway project, which had been mired in controversy over its financing and awarding of contracts.

Despite these concerns, the Chinese government and companies involved in the CPEC expressed their commitment to the projects and had stated that they were moving forward. In March 2021 Pakistan's minister for economic affairs, Khusro Bakhtiar, stated that the government was fully committed to the CPEC and that the projects under the initiative were progressing well. As of the time of writing, the overall status of CPEC projects under the PDM government remains unclear. While the government (of PDM) has expressed its commitment to the initiative, it has also sought to renegotiate the terms of some projects, which has led to some delays. The future of the CPEC under the PDM government remains uncertain.

The Panama Scandal

In 2016 a massive leak of documents known as the Panama Papers scandalously revealed famous individuals using offshore entities to avoid taxes and engage in other forms of financial fraud. These documents consisted of 11.5 million leaked financial and attorney–client details of more than 214,488 offshore entities created by the Panamanian law firm Mossack Fonseca. These entities were allegedly used to evade taxes and commit various forms of financial wrongdoing.[123] On 3 April 2016 the German newspaper *Süddeutsche Zeitung* released data it had obtained by an anonymous source under the title the 'Panama Papers'. The papers had around five hundred Indian names, which included several Bollywood personalities, such as Amitabh Bachchan, his daughter-in-law Aishwarya Rai and the actor Ajay Devgan, businessman Vijay Mallya, the former solicitor general of India Harish Salve, and the most wanted underworld figure in the continent, Iqbal Mirchi, who was allegedly Dawood Ibrahim's right-hand man. The Panama Papers exposed alleged illegal properties worth around PKR 207,780 million (approx. £578 million) of these five hundred Indians who were named in the documents.

To date, the whistle-blower who leaked the information to the German journalists remains anonymous, and even the reporters who worked on the investigation do not know their identity. The whistle-blower cited income inequality as the reason for leaking the documents and told the journalist that his 'life was in danger'. The International Consortium of Investigative Journalists (ICIJ) later posted the full document on its website.

Following the publication of the papers, several countries launched separate investigations into the matter and identified many high-profile individuals across the world involved in illegal activities. In India, the government formed a multi-agency group (MAG) comprising central investigative agencies to monitor a probe into the Panama Papers and similar leaked global tax cases. The MAG included officials from the Enforcement

Directorate (ED), the Reserve Bank of India (RBI) and the Financial Intelligence Unit (FIU). The MAG stated that as of 1 October 2021, a total of PKR 203,530 million undisclosed credits had been detected with respect to 930 India-linked entities in the Panama and Paradise Paper leaks.[124]

Sharif's Sentencing

Pakistan's political leader, Nawaz Sharif, along with his daughter and son-in-law, received a historic corruption verdict on 6 July 2018, which included prison sentences. The National Accountability Bureau (NAB), Pakistan's anti-graft court, sentenced Sharif to ten years in prison and fined him U.S.$10.6 million on corruption charges related to the 2016 Panama Papers revelations about his family's overseas properties. The court also convicted Sharif's daughter, Maryam Safdar, to seven years in prison and his son-in-law, Muhammad Safdar, to one year in prison. Despite the verdict, Sharif and his daughter denied any wrongdoing and labelled the sentence 'politically motivated', according to the BBC. Shahbaz Sharif reportedly referred to the court's decision as 'undemocratic'.[125] In April 2016 the ICIJ conducted a probe based on files leaked from Mossack Fonseca. The investigation revealed that Sharif's children were connected to offshore companies that owned four flats in a luxury apartment block in London.[126]

Following the allegations, Sharif was first disqualified from office in July 2017, and then later received a lifetime ban from politics in April 2018. He had ten days to appeal the verdict at the Islamabad High Court. This landmark ruling marked the first time a former Pakistani prime minister had been convicted of corruption, leading many political commentators to consider it a historic event. According to journalist and analyst Zahid Hussain, speaking to CNN, this decision may well spell the end of the Sharif political dynasty. It's worth noting that this sentence came just a few weeks before Pakistan's scheduled general elections on 25 July.[127]

The 2018 Elections

The 2018 elections proved to be a major setback for the PPP as it faced its worst defeat since 1997. The party secured only 43 out of 272 general seats, accounting for a mere 15.8 per cent of the total votes. This sharp decline in popularity can be attributed to a series of allegations of corruption and incompetence that were levelled against the party.

The 2018 elections marked a fierce competition between the PML-N and PTI, led by the charismatic former cricket champion Imran Khan. The PML-N suffered greatly due to the Panama Papers scandal, which implicated its top leadership in several instances of corruption. Despite numerous attempts by Nawaz Sharif to justify his family's properties, his explanations failed to convince the public. As a result, the PML-N emerged as the runners-up in the elections, having won 64 seats, whereas PTI won a majority with

116 seats. Notably, Imran Khan achieved a historic milestone by winning all five seats he contested. At the provincial level, PTI secured enough seats to form governments in both the Punjab and Khyber Pakhtunkhwa.

Overall, the 2018 elections marked a significant shift in Pakistani politics as dynastic politics and corruption lost their appeal among voters. It was a clear indication that the Pakistani people were seeking a change in leadership and governance and had placed their trust in PTI and Imran Khan to deliver on their promises of a new Pakistan.[128]

The PPP hardly posed a challenge at the national level, with negligible representation in Khyber Pakhtunkhwa, Baluchistan and Islamabad. The party's only success in the FATA was securing a single seat in the Parachinar constituency of the Kurram tribal agency. In the Punjab, the PPP's meagre success amounted to a mere six seats, including Rawalpindi II, won by party heavyweight Raja Pervaiz Ashraf, and three seats in Muzaffargarh district, secured by members of the influential Khar clan – one of the PPP founding social groups. The party's success in Rahim Yar Khan was limited to two seats, one of which went to the Jamaldinwali family, an old Darbari political family that traces its roots back to the pre-independence days of Bahawalpur as a princely state.

However, the PPP's stronghold lay in its home province of Sindh, where it won 36 of 61 National Assembly seats and 76 of 126 seats in the Sindh Provincial Assembly, forming the government. The party's dominance extended across both sides of the Indus River plain in urban and rural Sindh. Both PPP leaders won their home constituencies, with Bilawal Bhutto Zardari emerging victorious in Larkana I and Asif Ali Zardari in old Nawabshah I, renamed Shaheed Benazirabad I. The party suffered setbacks, however, losing Jacobabad and Ghotki II to members of the Maher tribe and the Mirpurkhas I seat to an independent candidate. The PPP's biggest loss came in Karachi, where it managed to win just one of twenty seats, with the rest going to PTI. The party even lost its historic stronghold of Lyari, where Bilawal Bhutto Zardari was defeated by the PTI candidate.

The PPP's strength in Sindh lies in a moderate form of soft Sindhi nationalism, which contrasts with the plethora of small, militant Sindhi nationalist and separatist movements in the province. Both Zulfiqar and Benazir Bhutto are revered as martyrs who championed the essentially secular, nationalist and populist politics of the independence-era Muslim League. However, the current PPP leader, Bilawal Bhutto-Zardari, the son of Benazir and Asif, has yet to demonstrate the political acumen and intellectual prowess of his forebears, particularly his grandfather Zulfiqar. Moreover, the party continued to suffer from the tainted reputation and dubious business dealings of Bilawal's father, who had been somewhat of a liability for the PPP. The co-leaders have made no efforts to strengthen the party organization they inherited, which had been a recurring weakness of the PPP.

Bhutto-Zardari's campaign efforts failed to inspire voters, and his proposal for a new province of South Punjab or Seraikistan failed to resonate with voters in Multan, the trans-Indus districts or the old state of Bahawalpur, except among the Jamaldinwali Makhdooms. In any case, the 2018 elections proved unfavourable for the PPP, dealing a major blow to dynastic politics, which had hitherto dominated Pakistani politics.

IN SUMMARY, THE DECADE from 2008 to 2018 in Pakistan was marked by turmoil and instability. Corruption scandals, judicial activism, political polarization and a widening gulf between politicians and military top brass had made Pakistani politics murky and its economy barely sustainable. The killing of Osama bin Laden in Pakistan by American SEALs further tarnished Pakistan's global image and raised questions about the capacity of its intelligence agencies and defence personnel. Memogate, *Dawn* Leaks and the Panama Papers scandal highlighted the lack of trust between Pakistan's Army and civilian leadership, as well as the involvement of Pakistani politicians in money laundering and kickbacks. Since the post-Zia ul Haq era, the Pakistani establishment has worked to undermine governments led by political leaders, indicating a desire to perpetuate political instability in order to remain relevant in the corridors of power. Memogate and *Dawn* Leaks can be seen as attempts by the civilian power elite to contain the overriding power held by the Army top brass. In conclusion, it is safe to say that no group, party or faction in Pakistan's political spectrum now aspires to collude with the Army establishment for any length of time. Any political party or faction that colludes with the military or establishment is prone to tarnishing its political credibility, as has recently been evident in the case of those who were part of the PDM government. Overall, this was not a decade worth celebrating.

13

Imran Khan Takes Charge

> Mistakes, or missteps, that might have felled another career in Islamic Pakistan gilded his international reputation. He was the errant achiever who irritated the mullahs when he rubbed the red cricket ball on his white trousers near the groin but raised a cheer from the young and an indulgent blush from aunties. Great looks, good diction, and a friends' list that included Princess Diana: What more could a generation ask for? Even the British tabloids could not wear him down. Pakistan had never had a superstar like Imran Khan, loved by Lahore and London.
>
> M. J. Akbar[1]

Imran Ahmed Khan Niazi, a sporting icon, philanthropist and politician, served as the 22nd prime minister of Pakistan from 2018 to 2022.[2] He rose to popularity as the finest all-round cricketer Pakistan has ever produced, and is credited for leading Pakistan to its first ever Cricket World Cup title in 1992, which made him the most successful cricket captain of Pakistan's sporting history. He also established the first cancer hospital in Pakistan, in Lahore, after losing his mother to the deadly disease, and has been involved in raising funds for various health and educational projects. His transformation from the biggest heartthrob of cricket to an influential politician has been fraught and has spanned more than two decades.

He retired from cricket in 1992 and entered politics by forming his own party – Pakistan Tehreek-e-Insaf (Movement for Justice). He came into politics with a vision to make Pakistan a welfare state. His party, PTI, promised a new Pakistan with a corruption-free system, merit-based governance and justice for all. In the 2018 general election, PTI emerged as the single largest party and it formed a coalition government with the support of independents, the PML-Q, the Baluchistan Awami Party and the MQM. After a long struggle, Khan became the prime minister of Pakistan in August 2018. Since then, he has faced numerous challenges, as a political leader and as the head of the government, and most recently, as a man behind bars.[3]

One of the most significant challenges faced by Imran Khan as prime minister was the economic crisis in Pakistan. The country was facing a

Imran Khan, 2019.

severe balance-of-payments crisis by the latter years of the 2010s, with a huge current-account deficit and declining foreign reserves. To tackle this issue, Khan's government initiated a series of measures, from imposing taxes on luxury goods to reducing non-development expenditures and seeking loans from friendly countries such as China, Saudi Arabia and the United Arab Emirates. However, these measures did not produce the desired results and Pakistan's economy continued to struggle.[4]

Another major challenge for Imran Khan's government was corruption. During his election campaign, Khan promised to root out corruption from the country's political and administrative system. However, some of his party members were accused of corruption themselves, which tarnished PTI's image. Khan's anti-corruption campaign was criticized for being selective and targeting only the opposition parties, particularly the PML-N and the PPP.[5]

Furthermore, Khan's government was accused of suppressing freedom of expression and violating human rights. Journalists, activists and opposition leaders were arrested, and their voices were silenced.[6] The government was also accused of using excessive force against peaceful protesters, particularly those who were demanding justice for the PTM.

Despite these challenges, Imran Khan's government took some positive steps. It launched the Ehsaas programme, which aimed to reduce poverty and improved social protection, and the Kamyab Jawan programme, which aimed to provide employment and entrepreneurship opportunities for youth. Moreover, the government was actively pursuing the CPEC project, which aimed to boost economic development in Pakistan.[7]

An Icon Who Needs No Introduction

Imran Ahmed Khan Niazi, born on 5 October 1952, hails from a prosperous Pashtun–Niazi family of Lahore, Pakistan. He completed his early education at Aitchison College, Lahore, and later attended the Royal Grammar School Worcester, England, before pursuing higher education at Keble College, at the University of Oxford.[8] In 1975 he graduated with a degree in philosophy, politics and economics, laying a strong foundation for his future endeavours in politics and public service.[9] A legendary cricketer, he made his debut for Pakistan in 1971, on a tour of England, marking the beginning of a long and illustrious career. In 1974 he captained the Oxford University side, displaying his leadership skills at a young age. He played county cricket for Worcestershire from 1975 to 1977, before joining Sussex in 1978, where he spent the majority of his professional career until 1988.[10] He received the Cricket Society Wetherall Award for being the leading all-rounder in English first-class cricket in 1976 and 1980, and was honoured with the Sussex Cricket Society Player of the Year award in 1985.

As a cricketer, Khan's career reached its peak during his captaincy of the Pakistan national side between 1982 and 1992. He led the team in 48 test matches, winning fourteen, losing eight and drawing 26. In the one-day international (ODI) format, he played 139 matches, winning 77, losing 57 and tying one. The 1992 Cricket World Cup was the pinnacle, as he led his team, famously known as 'Imran's Cornered Tigers', to a historic victory. The team's remarkable performance, winning against almost every opponent on their home ground, cemented Khan's status as a legend. Aside from his on-field achievements, Khan also made a significant contribution to the game by advocating for neutral umpires, which changed the nature of cricket to this day. On his retirement from cricket, he left behind an impressive record of 3,807 runs and 362 wickets in tests, and 3,709 runs and 182 wickets in ODIs, not to mention numerous records.[11] His legacy as a cricketer and a leader in the sport remains unmatched.[12]

He was awarded the second-highest civilian award, Hilal-e-Imtiaz, from the government of Pakistan. In 2004 he received the Lifetime Achievement Award at the Asian Jewels Awards, London, for his support for various charity programmes. He was given the Humanitarian Award at the 2007 Asian Sports Awards in Kuala Lumpur for setting up the first cancer hospital in Pakistan. He received the special silver jubilee award, along with other cricket legends, at the inaugural Asian Cricket Council (ACC) Awards in Karachi in 2009. The same year, he was also inducted into the International Cricket Council (ICC) Hall of Fame as part of its centennial year celebration. The Royal College of Physicians of Edinburgh awarded him an honorary fellowship towards his efforts for cancer treatment in Pakistan in 2012. He was declared 'Person of the Year 2012' by the Asia Society and listed at number three in the 'top nine world leaders' by GlobalPost.[13]

The end of his cricketing journey was only the beginning of his now world-renowned philanthropy work. Deeply affected by his mother's battle against cancer, Imran Khan vowed to build and run a cancer hospital that would treat the poor for free. It was a monumental endeavour and there were many detractors, but Khan was undeterred. While watching his mother suffer, he had realized that early diagnosis and proper treatment were both unavailable and ill-affordable for the poorest in his country. Having resolved to do the impossible, he set his considerable energy and commitment to the task, and within a short span of two years he launched the biggest crowd-funded campaign in Pakistan to make his mission a reality. Shaukat Khanum Cancer Hospital, a world-class facility, opened its wards for the treatment of the poorest citizens of Pakistan on 29 December 1994. Today, the hospital treats 70 per cent of its patients for free and has its current biggest facility in Peshawar. Pakistan's largest tertiary-care cancer centre at Karachi was completed in late November 2022, with the installation of equipment carried out throughout 2023.[14] Over PKR 50 billion has been spent on the treatment of the poor since the hospital's opening.[15]

Imran Khan's philanthropic endeavours and his interactions with the common people of Pakistan paved the way for his foray into politics. His movement for upholding the law; promoting equality, meritocracy and the development of human capital; and, most importantly, eradicating corruption took hold as he connected with the marginalized masses of the country. Khan's journey to discover his roots took him across the nation, and he found his purpose in serving the underprivileged.[16]

The once-shy cricketer, who always challenged the norm, found his true calling on 25 April 1996, when he officially formed his political party, PTI. In the first election PTI contested in 1997, it failed to win a single seat. However, in the October 2002 elections, Imran Khan was elected as a Member of Parliament of the National Assembly from Mianwali, and his party managed to secure a solitary seat. Grateful to the people of the region, Imran Khan began work on a top-class university called Namal College in 2008. The college, an associate of the University of Bradford, also established the Imran Khan Foundation. In recognition of his contributions, Imran Khan has been honoured as a chancellor at the University of Bradford. Situated in a remote area against a picturesque mountain backdrop, 90 per cent of the students at Namal College hail from humble backgrounds and study on scholarships.

Imran Khan's personal life has been marked by a series of high-profile marriages. In May 1995 he married Jemima Goldsmith, the daughter of a wealthy British businessman, in a traditional Islamic ceremony held in Paris. The couple later remarried in a civil ceremony in Richmond, London. Together they have two sons, Sulaiman Isa and Kasim. Their marriage ended in divorce in June 2004, due to challenges adapting to life in Pakistan, according to Jemima.[17] Khan's decision to enter politics had a negative impact on his marriage, as he faced criticism from opponents who questioned his connection to Zionists because of his marriage to a woman of Jewish heritage. In January 2015 he tied the knot a second time with Reham Khan, a British Pakistani journalist and television personality, in a private ceremony at his Islamabad residence, despite objections from his family. Unfortunately, their marriage was short-lived, and they divorced a few months later, in October 2015.

Finally, in February 2018, Imran Khan married Bushra Manika, a Pakistani spiritual guide who had been counselling him for several years. Their union was a more low-key affair, but it has been reported that Bushra's influence on Khan has been significant, particularly in matters of faith and spirituality.

Pakistan Tehreek-i-Insaf

Imran Khan's rise to become the 22nd prime minister of Pakistan was a remarkable achievement, and marked the culmination of his 22-year-struggle in the political arena. Until 2011 he was a vocal critic of the politics of 'electables', whom he saw as opportunistic figures who perpetuate a culture of patronage and corruption within political parties and governments. In the early days of his political career, Khan surrounded himself with principled and honourable politicians such as Mairaj Muhammad Khan, but despite their efforts, PTI remained a peripheral player in Pakistani politics.[18]

However, Khan's fortunes changed when he held a rally in Lahore on 30 October 2011. The *Daily Telegraph* hailed the rally as the return of a political powerhouse that stunned both the media and the politicians. Some believed that Khan had the backing of the country's powerful military establishment after it was unable to fully bring the PML-N into its fold to overthrow the then PPP government, following an acute split between the PPP government and the military over the 'Memogate' scandal. Regardless, Khan emerged as a serious contender in Pakistani politics.

Over the next eighteen months, Khan was joined by several respectable personalities such as retired justice Wajeehuddin, Shah Mehmood Qureshi and Makhdoom Javed Hashmi, who had left the PPP and the PML-N, respectively. By the time the 2013 general elections were announced, Khan had a sizable number of former PML-Q leaders in his party, many of them deserters from PML-N. PTI's increasing popularity among the youth and the media raised genuine concerns among the PPP's and PML-N's leaders with respect to their political clout. However, despite a strong campaign, PTI failed to win the expected number of seats at the centre and sat on the opposition benches with 32 seats. Nonetheless, the party formed a government in Khyber Pakhtunkhwa after striking an alliance with Jamaat-i-Islami. The PML-N won the largest number of seats in the National Assembly, and Nawaz Sharif became prime minister for the third time. However, Khan refused to accept the election results, and within months he had taken to the streets, staging sit-ins and rallies against what he termed 'organized rigging'.

Throughout the PML-N's 2013–18 tenure, Khan continued with his unrelenting rigging narrative, agitating against the alleged injustice. Even a 2015 report on rigging by a judicial commission, which was set up following Khan's 126-day sit-in outside parliament, failed to satisfy Khan. Then, the Panama Papers were leaked to the media completely out of the blue. Since it mentioned Sharif and his family, the report provided Khan with just the right pretext to escalate his agitational mode of politics. Henceforth, Khan fanned a vicious narrative of corruption to discredit the PML-N. However, just discrediting the government was not enough; Khan made utopian promises to the people and the media to bring them to his side. Although PTI's provincial government in Khyber Pakhtunkhwa was hardly exemplary, it still announced a '100-day agenda', which it planned to implement if elected to power. The agenda was rife with religious references from the model state of Medina and virtually promised to create an egalitarian society, presenting crucial challenges in simple and populist terms.[19]

In the elections of 2018, PTI fielded candidates from 248 National Assembly seats, with 136 seats from the Punjab, 46 from Sindh, 38 from Khyber Pakhtunkhwa, fourteen from Baluchistan, eleven from FATA and three from Islamabad.

Political Objectives

PTI had been a vocal opponent of Musharraf's decision to join the U.S.-led War on Terror following 9/11. The party had consistently advocated for dialogue with the Taliban as opposed to launching military campaigns against them. In addition, PTI vehemently protested against U.S. drone strikes in Pakistan's tribal areas, which it considers to have fuelled the growth of militancy in the region.[20]

In 2014 PTI staged a 126-day-long sit-in at Islamabad's Red Zone, alleging that the ruling PML-N party had won the 2013 election through rigging. PTI demanded an investigation into the matter and the resignation of then prime minister Nawaz Sharif. The sit-in was called off by Khan in December 2014 following the Army Public School massacre in Peshawar. The party also demanded Nawaz's resignation in 2016 after the Panama Papers leaks revealed that his children owned offshore companies.[21]

PTI launched the Billion Tree Tsunami initiative in the Khyber Pakhtunkhwa province to combat deforestation and promote environmental conservation, successfully planting an incredible 1 billion trees in the province – an undoubtedly impressive feat. In 2017, following an investigation into Nawaz's assets, he was disqualified by the Supreme Court for failing to declare a receivable salary as an asset in his 2013 nomination papers. PTI's consistent stance on accountability and transparency in politics has resonated with many Pakistanis.

Vision for Pakistan: State of Medina

Imran Khan's admiration for Medina as a model for Pakistan in the twenty-first century requires careful consideration. The pre-modern world's socio-political realities were simpler than today's globalized world, where greater mutual practices have become the norm. It would be impossible to revive its principles after fourteen centuries in today's new socio-political context, but nevertheless Khan drew parallels between the principles established in Medina's historical context – along with contemporary governance systems in Scandinavia and China – to serve as a tangible and relevant exemplar from which Pakistan could draw valuable lessons. Khan's adept utilization of historical references from various epochs to craft a political discourse that fosters positive outcomes indeed merits commendation.

First, Khan's linkage of Medina's principles with the governance systems of Scandinavian countries underscores the importance of a sociocultural synthesis of freedom and regulation. Scandinavian nations, renowned for their progressive societies and high standards of living, exemplify how effective governance can harmoniously blend individual freedoms with regulatory frameworks that ensure social equity and cohesion. This sociocultural synthesis has resulted in a model society and state where citizens enjoy both personal liberties and a robust social safety net – and offers a demonstration for Pakistan to achieve similar outcomes through a well-crafted governance strategy.

Second, Khan's reference to China's governance system highlights the pragmatic approach taken by the Chinese government in eradicating poverty. China's remarkable progress in lifting millions of its citizens out of poverty in a relatively short period serves as a pertinent case study for Pakistan. By recognizing China's success in addressing poverty as the shortest route to economic development, Khan underscored the need for Pakistan to adapt and implement effective poverty alleviation measures to catalyse its own socio-economic progress.

Pakistan's limited sociocultural adaptability, which hinders its ability to synthesize diverse systems, presented a challenge for Khan's vision. In Pakistan, there exists a prevailing belief in the necessity of a comprehensive code of life that is perceived as timeless and universal, thus making the process of forging a synthesis challenging.

Khan as a Bête Noire of Dynastic Politics

Despite no longer holding a position of power, Khan has continued to impress with his eloquence and charisma as a politician. His ability to deliver impactful speeches remains undiminished, reflecting his dedication to the political arena and his capacity to inspire and engage his audience, both within Pakistan and the wider world.[22]

Khan became a symbol of opposition to the insidiousness of dynastic politics, long considered a scourge on Pakistani society and governance. He has repeatedly decried the sense of entitlement and lack of accountability that pervades this system, tracing its roots back to the feudal era. In his view, true social justice and the rule of law can only be achieved by breaking free from the grip of political dynasties, which he regards as the main obstacle to the smooth functioning of democracy in Pakistan. Thus he has emerged as a powerful voice advocating for the end of dynastic rule and the ushering in of a new era of meritocracy and accountability. Dynastic politics is a common occurrence in South Asia due to the prevalence of strong family structures and feudalism. However, this practice is being challenged across the continent. Despite corruption scandals, public fallouts and tragedies, two political dynasties have managed to maintain their hold on power for extended periods: the Gandhis in India and the Bhutto-Zardari family in Pakistan.

Bilawal Bhutto-Zardari: Heir to a Political Dynasty

At barely nineteen years old, Bilawal Bhutto-Zardari, as the son of former Pakistani president Asif Ali Zardari and murdered ex-prime minister Benazir Bhutto, inherited a role in a dynasty steeped in power and bloodshed. Three days after his mother's assassination in December 2007, Bilawal took over her position as chairman of the PPP. Despite being suddenly catapulted to the top of the political echelon, he initially kept a low profile and focused on finishing his history degree at the University of Oxford. However, he returned to Pakistan in 2010 and took on an increasingly active role as PPP chairman. At the age of 29, he ran for parliament for the first time, campaigning to implement his mother's vision of a 'peaceful, progressive, prosperous, democratic Pakistan'.

According to the polls, the PPP was projected to secure a third-place finish in the elections, with PTI and the outgoing PML-N expected to take the top two spots. In the 2013 elections, the PPP had suffered a significant defeat, narrowly holding onto its second-place position. Therefore, some argued that this time around, even though the party came in third, it represented an improvement over the dire predictions.

The weight of his family legacy cast a long shadow over Bilawal, making it challenging for him to escape constant comparisons with his iconic mother and grandfather, Zulfiqar Ali Bhutto. As the heir to one of South Asia's most renowned political dynasties, he faced the daunting task of not just following in their footsteps but also carving out his own path and identity in the political arena.

His appointment as party chairman was considered a strategic move to consolidate the party using the Bhutto legacy: the PPP was founded, and has always been led, by a Bhutto family member. As Bhutto-Zardari made his first public appearance before the world in the wake of his mother Benazir's assassination, his father announced that his son would be linked with his mother's famous last name. Bilawal Zardari became Bilawal Bhutto-Zardari.

Bilawal, meaning 'one without equal', was born in September 1988, a month before his mother was first elected prime minister. While friends of Benazir Bhutto have said that she always envisaged her son becoming her political heir, they agreed that she would not have wanted him to have to bear that burden so young. Bilawal spent most of his life outside Pakistan, travelling with his mother – who went into self-imposed exile in 1999 – between London and Dubai, and then studying in Oxford. He did speak Urdu, but like Benazir, his first language was English, and his Urdu accent was just as Anglicized as that of his mother. However, language never stopped her from reaching a mass audience, and it remained to be seen if it would present a long-term barrier to her son. In joining Oxford's Christ Church college, he followed in the footsteps of both his mother and his grandfather. Bilawal quoted his mother at his first press conference in 2007, saying: 'My mother always said democracy is the best revenge.' He did not look entirely at ease as party supporters broke into chants of: 'Bilawal, step forward! We are with you!'[23]

After the fall of Khan's government on 10 May 2022, Bilawal was appointed as Pakistan's foreign minister at the age of 33, making him one of the world's youngest foreign ministers. He was faced with a heap of diplomatic issues, many of which had existed well before his birth, including relations with India. His first foreign mission was to accompany Prime Minister Shahbaz Sharif to Saudi Arabia, a key trade partner and regular source of relief for Pakistan's struggling economy.

On assuming the role of foreign minister, Bilawal embarked on numerous extensive travels – though without a clear objective. Notably, he has failed to articulate any discernible foreign-policy agenda or issue any relevant policy statements. Consequently, many view him as the most widely travelled yet least effective foreign minister in Pakistan's history. It is widely speculated that his constant globetrotting is merely a publicity stunt, aimed at furthering his political career and fulfilling his father's aspiration to see his son as prime minister. However, this approach comes at a significant cost to the public. It is noteworthy how the Pakistani elite views the importance of the people's mandate. There is a widespread belief that fostering strong relationships with influential figures in American power corridors will ultimately lead to gaining political power in Pakistan. However, this approach raises questions about the true priorities and values of the elite, and whether they are truly committed to serving the needs and interests of the Pakistani people.

While Bilawal consistently paints the party as progressive and dedicated to serving the people, his leadership journey reveals some nuances.

Despite his persuasive rhetoric, Bilawal has struggled to emerge as an autonomous leader and build a team that reflects his unique vision. Instead, he often appears overshadowed by the formidable presence of his father, who some believe may still wield significant influence over the party's decisions. This dynamic could potentially limit Bilawal's capacity to play a substantial role in Pakistan's political arena in the immediate future. One of the factors contributing to this perception is Bilawal's relatively limited personal experience and his constrained ability to shape the selection of party candidates. Moreover, he has faced criticism for being more of a symbolic figurehead for the PPP, with little concrete evidence to support his claims of leadership and effectiveness.

In terms of his key stances, Bilawal has positioned himself as a staunch advocate for democracy, while also expressing reservations about judicial activism. He has consistently advocated for peaceful relations between Pakistan and India and has been vocal about safeguarding the rights of Pakistan's religious minorities. As the 2024 election loomed, Bilawal underscored the PPP's commitment to its original slogan, which centres on providing fundamental necessities such as food, clothing and shelter to the people.

Bilawal's leadership journey within the PPP presents both challenges and opportunities. While he champions important causes and ideals, his ability to assert his independence and influence the party's direction remains under scrutiny. Bilawal is considered progressive, and he has frequently spoken out on the rights of women and minorities. With more than half of Pakistan's population aged 22 or below, his being social-media-savvy is also a hit with the younger voters. His success in shaping the PPP's future will likely depend on his capacity to navigate these complexities and establish a distinct leadership identity.[24]

Bilawal is often derided for his limited command of Urdu, the national language. However, in certain circles, lacking fluency in Urdu is considered a hallmark of elite and sophisticated individuals. This attitude raises questions about the perception and value assigned to language skills in Pakistani society, and whether it is truly a reflection of the country's diverse linguistic landscape. Moreover, Bilawal seems to be out of touch with the sociopolitical realities of Pakistan. Political commentators have mixed opinions on his abilities and are divided on how long he can maintain good relations with Sharif from the rival PML-N party. Analyst Hasan Askari Rizvi believes that Bilawal is an untested missile, while fellow analyst Farzana Bari thinks that he is intelligent enough to hold the fort. He has a long way to go, and despite all the privileges and entitlement, his destiny as political leader is shrouded in uncertainty.[25]

The Political Dynasty of the Sharifs

The Sharif family originally comes from Jati Umra in Amritsar but moved to Pakistan in 1947 and settled in Lahore. Mian Muhammad Sharif, who came from an artisanal background, had an extraordinary business acumen and social skills, and aspired to exponential expansion in his business. He initiated into politics his son, Muhammad Nawaz Sharif, who was elected chief minister of the Punjab in 1985. Despite having a limited attention span and oratory skills, Nawaz was ambitious and his patience for dissent wore off over time. In his formative years in politics, his father was his greatest asset and stage-managed most of his political manoeuvres.[26]

The Sharifs relied on the establishment's support not only for the acquisition of power but for its sustenance; the family was invested in approaching people with power and cultivating connections with them. The establishment adopted Nawaz Sharif as its protégé against the charismatic and politically astute Benazir Bhutto. For years, the establishment hounded Benazir because she was Zulfiqar Ali Bhutto's daughter, and elections were managed to the benefit of Sharif.

Shahbaz Sharif, a proponent of grandiose projects rather than substantive reform, ventured into practical politics in 1990. His political approach leaned towards favouring individuals professing unwavering loyalty to the Sharif family, reflecting the intertwining dynamics of dynastic politics and the politics of patronage. In such a milieu, the significance of merit often diminishes, and the rule of law finds itself compromised. When politics becomes synonymous with an unquenchable thirst for power, the very mechanisms designed to curb corrupt practices begin to crumble. Notably, during the Sharif era, Pakistan witnessed a significant deceleration in its trajectory of social development. Furthermore, the entry of the Sharif family's second generation into politics, exemplified by Hamza Shahbaz, the son of Shahbaz Sharif, and Maryam Nawaz, the daughter of former prime minister Nawaz Sharif, underscores the need for training and acclimatization within the realm of political leadership. Their transition into the intricate fabric of Pakistani politics warrants careful consideration and nurturing.

Maryam Nawaz's Political Stance

Maryam Nawaz had been at the forefront of a movement aimed at countering perceived military intervention in Pakistan's political landscape. A notable illustration of this unfolded during a public gathering held in Gujranwala on 16 October 2020, where she vehemently criticized high-ranking military officials. She and her father maintained that the military conspired against their government by framing them in corruption cases and rigging the 2018 election that brought Imran Khan to power. Despite sedition charges filed against her, Maryam remained critical of the military and Khan's government for restricting the media, abducting journalists and harassing political activists. She has drawn comparisons to Benazir Bhutto, whom many think she tries to emulate.[27] However, in contrast to Benazir Bhutto, Maryam Nawaz has displayed a sharp and sometimes even indecorous tone, especially in her remarks about her political adversaries, whom she has labelled as 'incompetent', and particularly Imran Khan, whom she has characterized as a *fitna* – someone who foments discord. In her trenchant critique of the PTI government, she has specifically targeted Imran Khan and those who willingly dissolved their own governments in the Punjab and Khyber Pakhtunkhwa but who are now staging street protests.

Maryam Nawaz consistently assures the public in her speeches that the PML-N possesses the strategies and determination required to rectify the nation's economy and put it on a path towards development. However, given the failure of Ishaq Dar as finance minister in the PDM government to rescue Pakistan from its economic crisis, questions arise regarding what cards Maryam and her party have left to play in addressing Pakistan's economic woes. Pakistan has been grappling with a historic economic crisis characterized by a continuous depreciation of the rupee, a rapid surge in inflation rates and dwindling foreign reserves, all of which have generated significant uncertainty among the populace.

As the chief organizer and later the senior vice president of the PML-N, she seems determined to fortify the party's foundations and infuse a new lease of life among its ranks. However, amid the rhetorical flourishes and fervour of her speeches, her vision for Pakistan's future seems clouded by confusion. Instead of offering concrete policy guidelines to address the economic crisis, she frequently resorts to personalized attacks on Imran Khan. The bitterness and animosity evident in her rhetoric have, unfortunately, had a detrimental impact on both her party and her own political prospects. Moreover, her alleged possession of and threats to release compromising videos involving significant figures in Pakistan's political landscape have alienated serious-minded individuals from her and her party. Such tactics, rather than garnering support, have tarnished her image.

Based on her recent performances, Maryam Nawaz appears to be facing an uphill battle in Pakistani politics. Her divisive rhetoric and controversial actions have led some to perceive her as a non-starter, detracting from her ability to present a compelling and constructive vision for Pakistan's future. In the face of the nation's pressing economic challenges, a more substantive and inclusive approach may be required to win the confidence of the electorate and achieve meaningful change.

Dynasties in Pakistan's Politics

Political parties that rely on dynastic rules often operate like mafia organizations, with the leader – a godfather-like figure – holding unchecked power and no accountability to the people. Justice Asif Saeed Khosa, in his verdict on Panamagate, was spot on when he branded the dynastic ruling elites as a type of Sicilian mafia.[28] 'Behind every great fortune there is a crime,' wrote Justice Khosa, quoting Mario Puzo's novel, which itself was inspired by a line by Honoré de Balzac: 'The secret of a great success for which you are at a loss to account is a crime that has never been found out, because it was properly executed.'[29]

In the case of Pakistan's parties, decisions are made unilaterally, with no democratic or consultative process, and the PML-N is run more like a business than a political entity. Disputing Justice Khosa's assertion proves challenging, due to the evident priorities and performance of these politicians and their parties, which have effectively functioned as their personal fiefdoms. On top of that, these parties lacked any meaningful agenda to improve the lives of the poor and have frequently flouted the law and the country's constitution to suit their own interests. Shahbaz Sharif's government, in power from 10 May 2022 to 12 August 2023, was a clear testament to such a self-serving agenda, as the party transformed the nation into a fascist state without precedent in its history. The callous manner in which they handled the 2022 floods serves as a prime example of their indifference to the suffering of ordinary citizens.

In the face of such arbitrary and unbridled power, Imran Khan remains the only real challenge to this reign. However, it is crucial for Khan to comprehend, as articulated by Tasneem Noorani, that his 26-year endeavour will be in vain unless there is a lasting transformation in Pakistan's political culture. To witness the tangible outcomes of his struggle and establish a legacy that endures beyond his time, the only viable course of action is to institute a rule-based framework within PTI, underpinned by grass-roots democracy within the party.[30]

Challenges on the Economic Front

The Imran Khan government faced numerous economic challenges after taking office in 2018, ranging from structural issues to political instability and external shocks. One of the most significant had been the country's balance-of-payments crisis. Pakistan had been running a current-account deficit for several years, which led to a depletion of foreign-exchange reserves. This left the country vulnerable to external shocks, such as fluctuations in oil prices, and made it difficult to attract foreign investment.[31]

Another major challenge was the fiscal deficit. Pakistan had struggled to maintain fiscal discipline, with the government frequently overspending and relying on borrowing to finance its expenditure.[32] This led to a significant increase in public debt, which put pressure on the country's finances and limited its ability to invest in critical areas such as education and healthcare.

In addition to these structural issues, Khan's government also faced political instability, which compounded its economic challenges. The government had been unable to build a broad-based consensus around its economic policies, which made it difficult to implement the necessary reforms.[33] This was exacerbated by frequent changes in the cabinet, which had resulted in a lack of continuity and of consistency in policy.

External shocks also significantly impacted the government. The COVID-19 pandemic, for example, had a severe impact on the Pakistani economy. The closure of international borders and disruptions to global supply chains from 2020 led to a significant drop in remittances and exports, which Pakistan is heavily reliant on and which therefore further strained the country's finances.[34]

To address these economic challenges, the government implemented a range of policies, including measures to reduce the fiscal deficit, such as cutting subsidies and increasing taxes. The government had also sought to attract foreign investment, with a particular focus on investment from China through the CPEC.[35] However, these policies had provided mixed results. While there were some improvements in the balance of payments and public finances, progress was markedly slow, and the country remains vulnerable to external shocks.[36] In addition, there were concerns about the government's ability to implement reforms effectively, given the ongoing political instability and lack of consensus around its policies. But the Khan government managed to mobilize support from the Middle East to address the balance-of-payments deficit, including seeking financial support from friendly countries.[37] The Saudis, the UAE and Qatar provided substantial assistance, while China redefined the CPEC investment programme and made a deposit. Malaysia and Turkey also expressed interest in investing in areas where they had a comparative advantage.[38]

The Pandemic and Its Management

In December 2019 the COVID-19 outbreak began in Wuhan, China. The World Health Organization (WHO) declared the resulting pandemic as the sixth public health emergency of international concern on 30 January 2020. Given Pakistan's population of over 200 million and its struggling healthcare and economic systems, the country was considered a potential hotspot for the virus. However, Pakistan was able to address the challenge and suffered relatively mild consequences.[39]

On 26 February 2020 the first COVID-19 cases were reported in Islamabad and Karachi. Given the country's high population and status as one of the most densely populated nations in Asia, coupled with Karachi being Pakistan's largest metropolitan city, Pakistan was highly vulnerable to the outbreak. Prior to this, the Centers for Disease Control and Prevention had already issued a level 3 warning for international travellers to Pakistan, taking into account the country's weak infrastructure and history of previous outbreaks. It was vital for the government to respond timely and appropriately to prevent the spread of the disease, which was initially difficult to contain due to non-compliance with rules and delayed reporting of symptoms by the general population.

As of 10 April 2020 Pakistan had reported 4,601 confirmed COVID-19 cases with a death toll approaching 66, but there was a mixed response from the community. Some people in Pakistan – as well as people in other countries – considered the virus to be a hoax or propaganda, which undermined the efforts of the government and agencies in their attempts to control the spread of the pandemic. Despite these challenges, the Pakistani government received praise from international organizations for its efforts to curb the spread of the virus and ensure the safety of its citizens. One of the government's first steps was to establish functional emergency operation centres and identify the origin of the virus. Detailed history-taking of patients was crucial in understanding the outbreak and identifying their contact with others in the community. This helped to isolate infected areas, and individuals with a recent history of international travel were monitored closely as neighbouring countries reported a high number of cases. Border control was also implemented, despite strong public response, and quarantine houses were designated near borders and airports to isolate individuals entering Pakistan. These measures helped to contain the spread of the virus and gain the confidence of affected individuals and their families.[40]

As the WHO reported an alarming increase in new cases of COVID-19 across the globe, it became apparent that the disease's spread was no longer limited to those with recent travel history in highly affected regions. More drastic measures became necessary, not only at the local level but on a national and international scale, to combat the pandemic. To ensure the safety of its citizens, the Pakistani government imposed travel restrictions to limit virus transmission from other countries. However, this left many individuals stranded at the borders, necessitating the development of quarantine facilities to isolate them from the rest of the community. After being quarantined for at least two weeks, those who did not show symptoms could return to their home towns and notify authorities of any symptoms. Developing these shelters was a massive undertaking, with more than 3,000 pilgrims arriving from Iran in the first week of March 2020 alone, requiring quarantine shelters in Taftan and Chaman. Later, the government decided to relocate the pilgrims to quarantine centres set up in their respective provinces. Despite this, there were many problems, including cramped living conditions, unhygienic facilities and shortages of food, water, medication and physicians, which drew widespread criticism from national news outlets and social-media users.

One of the first steps taken was to enforce well-planned lockdowns in major cities. These lockdowns were imposed during different hours in various regions, and public spaces such as parks, wedding halls, schools and offices were closed until further notice. Despite pressure from provincial governments and the opposition, this was a necessary measure to curtail the spread of the disease. Eateries, grocery stores, pharmacies and fruit and vegetable shops were allowed to remain open. The closure of prayers at mosques, including Friday prayers, was another step taken by the government that faced significant opposition. When reports of virus transmission began to emerge, particularly in the federal capital, Islamabad, the government took the initiative to seal off areas that reported infections. Samples were tested by the National Institute of Health, Islamabad, and analysed by epidemiologists of the COVID-19 Nerve Centre, following which a notification was issued. This strategy not only helped to curb the spread of the infection but facilitated contact tracing and further testing of the public.[41]

During the early months of the pandemic, the country's testing capacity was limited. High-income countries were conducting large-scale randomized tests to estimate the actual number of confirmed cases, but Pakistan was forced to carry out priority-based testing and rely on the enforcement of strict quarantine and isolation strategies. Nevertheless, contact tracing was an effective strategy that not only helped to limit the spread of the virus but predicted its route through different regions of the country and across different age groups. The government gradually increased the testing capacity of laboratories and the availability of testing kits, and by June 2020 up to 30,000 tests were conducted daily to ascertain the pace of spread and formulate future strategies accordingly. Both of these strategies provided valuable insights into the differences in the clinical manifestation of COVID-19 in people with different demographic and health backgrounds.

The Field Epidemiology Laboratory Training Programme

The Training Programmes in Epidemiology and Public Health Interventions Network is a vast network consisting of 75 field epidemiology training programmes operating in more than one hundred countries, including Pakistan. Following the WHO's declaration of COVID-19 as a public health emergency of international concern, alumni from the Field Epidemiology Training Programme in Pakistan took swift action and implemented standard operating procedures (SOPs) for COVID-19 screening at international airports. Additionally, they designed and implemented a real-time data entry system to screen travellers arriving from high-risk countries.

To ensure public safety, SOPs were developed for public areas and were strictly enforced. These guidelines included maintaining social distancing of at least 1 metre (3 ft), wearing masks, frequently sanitizing touched surfaces, practising good hand hygiene and following general hygiene rules such as avoiding touching the face, nose or eyes and coughing or sneezing into an elbow or a paper napkin instead of hands. Authorities in various parts of the country took disciplinary action against those who violated the SOPs, in line with the recommendations of the National Command and Control Centre of Pakistan. The centre focused on implementing strict administrative actions; enforcing the track, trace and quarantine strategy; and ensuring compliance with SOPs.

The local and federal governments in Pakistan initiated campaigns to spread awareness about COVID-19 risks, signs and symptoms. The WHO mobilized Pakistan's polio vaccination programme, consisting of over 265,000 community health workers and vaccinators, to provide infrastructure for tracking and tracing cases early and spreading awareness in remote rural areas. Text messages were sent to mobile networks, daily reminders were given about SOPs and fines were imposed for non-compliance. Caller tunes warned about the risks, spread and complications and about the awareness of SOPs, and recorded messages were changed according to the situation. The emergence of COVID-19 posed problems in Pakistan due to limitations in the healthcare system, poor infrastructure, uneven access to healthcare, resistance from various social, political, cultural and religious groups, political instability, economic fragilities and mistrust among the public. The government launched relief schemes to tackle the economic crisis, allowed construction and daily-wage workers to resume work and requested home quarantine for mild or asymptomatic cases to ease burdens on health workers and medical practitioners.

The shortage of ventilators was a major issue for Pakistan's health departments, but the National Radio and Telecommunications Corporation produced their own locally. COVID-19 caused unexpected rates of mortality and morbidity worldwide, with new mutant strains causing a third wave. Pakistan tackled the pandemic through various measures, including preparing special wards and using resources like polio and dengue teams, creating awareness messages and alleviating the economic burden of the people by giving subsidies on various items of necessity. With government efforts and public support, active cases in Pakistan steadily declined from their peak in June 2020. As of 1 October 2020, there were 312,263 confirmed cases and 6,479 deaths.[42]

The Ehsaas Programme

In March 2019, an ambitious social safety and poverty alleviation programme for the welfare of the public was launched by Prime Minister Imran Khan. The programme, called Ehsaas (Compassion), aimed to bring significant changes in poverty alleviation underpinned by the strategic deployment of data and technology. According to the prime minister, the first change that would be brought under the poverty alleviation plan would be amending Article 38(D) of the Constitution. The clause included provisions for providing people with food, shelter, clothing, education and healthcare. However, the provision in its current form was only a policy recommendation. Khan stated that the government needed to bring an amendment to the Constitution to make it a 'fundamental right' so that the state could guarantee these five necessities to the people.[43] On 7 April 2019, Khan unveiled a comprehensive policy statement, spanning fifteen pages, that delineated the contours of the Ehsaas programme. The policy framework underscored several key objectives, including the creation of precision-targeted safety nets, the advancement of financial inclusion, the promotion of women's economic empowerment, and the mitigation of challenges affecting social welfare.

By leveraging data-driven insights and technology-enabled targeting mechanisms, the Ehsaas programme aimed to identify and assist those segments of the population that were considered as the most vulnerable and in need of social support. Precision safety nets were designed to ensure that assistance reached the intended beneficiaries with greater accuracy and efficiency, minimizing the risk of resources being misallocated or diverted.

Financial inclusion was another central pillar of the Ehsaas programme. Recognizing that access to financial services was a critical driver of economic empowerment and poverty reduction, the initiative sought to expand financial inclusion across the country. By facilitating access to formal financial services, such as banking and savings accounts, the programme aimed at empowering individuals and families to better manage their finances, save for the future and participate more actively in the economy. In all, it is intended as a means of enhancing the financial resilience of vulnerable populations.

Women's economic empowerment constituted a vital component of the Ehsaas programme. Pakistan, like many other countries, grapples with gender disparities in economic participation and access to economic opportunities. To address this challenge, the initiative aimed to facilitate women's access to income-generating activities, entrepreneurial opportunities and financial resources. By fostering economic empowerment among women, the programme aimed to enhance their socio-economic status, reduce gender-based disparities and contribute to broader societal development.

'Elite capture', a phenomenon where the affluent or influential segments of society exploit social welfare programmes for their own benefit, was another critical issue that the Ehsaas programme sought to confront. This challenge has plagued many social welfare efforts in Pakistan, leading to the diversion of resources away from those in genuine need. To counter the problem and to promote greater equity and justice in resource allocation, the programme implemented a range of measures and safeguards, including transparent and accountable disbursement mechanisms, robust monitoring and evaluation systems, and increased scrutiny of programme beneficiaries.

The programme represents a substantial and forward-looking approach to social welfare in Pakistan, and aims to usher in a new era of social policy that is more equitable, efficient and responsive to the needs of the most vulnerable segments of society. Prime Minister Imran Khan, in his official capacity, heralded the Ehsaas initiative as the most extensive and ambitious poverty alleviation programme ever embarked on within the borders of Pakistan. He unequivocally articulated the government's unwavering commitment to collaborating with diverse stakeholders in a collective endeavour to uplift millions from the grips of poverty, with the ultimate objective of fortifying the foundations of the nation.[44] The Poverty Alleviation Coordination Council, an institution presided over by Sania Nishter, who has the rank of a federal minister and is entrusted with the oversight of the Ehsaas programme, meticulously crafted an extensive initiative that revolved around three central pillars: the enhancement of human-capital formation, the reinforcement of institutional capacities, and the mitigation of financial impediments that hindered access to essential healthcare and education services. This programme specifically targeted a spectrum of marginalized demographics, encompassing the extremely impoverished, persons with disabilities, the unemployed, economically disadvantaged farmers, labourers facing financial hardships, individuals suffering from undernourishment, students hailing from low-income backgrounds, underprivileged women and senior citizens grappling with financial constraints. It promoted a government-wide multi-sectoral collaboration, federal–provincial joint leadership and the role of the private sector. Additionally, the programme aimed to create jobs and livelihood opportunities.[45]

The job of running the council was bestowed upon Nishtar in recognition of her extensive and distinguished background spanning civil society, governmental affairs, international development, policy formulation, advocacy and humanitarian efforts. She has garnered substantial acclaim as a distinguished health expert and a committed activist, possessing first-hand expertise in the establishment of institutions, fundraising endeavours and the cultivation of partnerships. Notably, during her tenure as a minister in the 2013 interim government, Nishtar played a pivotal role in the re-establishment of Pakistan's Health Ministry. Moreover, she founded Heartfile, a non-profit think tank, in 1998, which is dedicated to the critical analysis of healthcare systems and the formulation of solutions aimed at enhancing them to attain universal health coverage, not only within Pakistan but in various other developing nations. She was accorded the honour of being appointed as the co-chair of the WHO's high-level commission, specifically addressing non-communicable diseases.[46]

Health Card

On 19 August 2020 Khan launched the Sehat Insaf Card initiative in the province of Khyber Pakhtunkhwa, Pakistan. This initiative marked a significant step towards advancing the principles of universal health coverage (UHC) in the country. Notably, the concept of a universal health card had its origins in the WHO's recommendations, emphasizing equitable access to essential health services for all individuals and communities.

The journey towards UHC in Pakistan had commenced earlier in the province of Khyber Pakhtunkhwa with the introduction of the Sehat Sahulat Programme (SSP, or Health Facility Programme) in 2015. The SSP represented an initial effort to provide comprehensive health coverage to vulnerable populations in the province, aligning with the principles of UHC and striving to make quality healthcare services accessible to all, regardless of their socio-economic status.

Khan's emphasis on extending health insurance coverage to the entire population through the Sehat Insaf Card initiative reflected a commitment to helping the millions of people of Pakistan as well as being a pivotal step towards the realization of an Islamic welfare state. Under this initiative, approximately 6 million families in the province were provided with an annual health insurance cover of PKR 1 million. This significant coverage extension aimed to benefit the entire population of 40 million residents in Khyber Pakhtunkhwa by facilitating their access to essential medical treatments and services.

The Sehat Insaf Card initiative operated by enabling beneficiaries to access free medical treatment not only at public healthcare facilities but at a network of over 250 private hospitals across the country. This comprehensive approach to healthcare delivery sought to address the healthcare needs of individuals and families while fostering collaboration between the public and private healthcare sectors. This initiative exemplified the government's dedication to ensuring that quality healthcare services were not merely a privilege for a few but a fundamental right accessible to all segments of society.[47] After Khyber Pakhtunkhwa, Khan launched a health insurance programme for all residents of the Punjab.[48]

One of the distinctive features of the Sehat Insaf Card scheme was its strategic focus on incentivizing private sector investment in healthcare, particularly in areas that were remote and underserved. In many impoverished regions across Pakistan, access to healthcare services was severely limited, with shortages of medical facilities and healthcare professionals, including doctors. This scarcity of healthcare infrastructure and personnel posed significant challenges to addressing the healthcare needs of vulnerable populations.

To mitigate these challenges, the Sehat Insaf Card initiative sought to leverage private sector involvement in the construction and operation of hospitals in these underserved areas. By encouraging such investment, the programme aimed to bridge the healthcare gap and provide residents of remote and impoverished regions with access to essential medical services. This approach recognized the potential of private sector entities to contribute to expanding healthcare infrastructure, thereby enhancing the availability of healthcare facilities and healthcare providers in areas where they were most needed.

The Ehsaas Saylani Langar Scheme

The Ehsaas Saylani Langar Scheme inaugurated by Imran Khan in Islamabad on 6 October 2019, marked a significant step in the government's pursuit of establishing a welfare state in Pakistan. Through the establishment of 112 free meal stations across the country, the scheme aimed to address the fundamental issues of hunger and malnutrition by providing free meals to those in need three times a day.

During the inauguration of the first Ehsaas Saylani Langar in the federal capital, Khan articulated his vision for a new Pakistan characterized by equitable wealth distribution, where taxes levied on the affluent would be directed towards the betterment of the impoverished segments of society. He acknowledged the prevailing economic disparities that had perpetuated the enrichment of the wealthy while deepening the impoverishment of the underprivileged. However, Khan also acknowledged the complexity of addressing these deeply rooted grievances and recognized the necessity of time and concerted effort.

Khan underscored the virtue of serving the poor and vulnerable, emphasizing the importance of benevolent actions as a means of seeking divine blessings. He identified the government's Ehsaas programme as the most extensive poverty eradication initiative in the nation's history, reflecting the administration's determination to ensure that hunger would no longer afflict any citizen. In parallel, Khan emphasized the government's commitment to fostering economic growth through the promotion of trade and industry while simultaneously addressing the plights of the less fortunate. He reiterated the principle of progressive taxation, where the wealthy would contribute more to support the impoverished, in line with the overarching vision of transforming Pakistan into a welfare state. The prime minister also highlighted the numerous welfare programmes initiated by the PTI-led government, all aimed at meeting the essential needs of the people.

The collaboration between the Ehsaas programme and Saylani Welfare International Trust in launching the Langar project underscored the government's commitment to partnership and shared responsibility in the pursuit of social welfare. Sania Nishtar, the chairperson of Ehsaas, received commendation for her effective implementation of the programme and the alignment of her efforts with the prime minister's vision.

Bashir Farooqi, the founder of Saylani Trust, lauded Khan for his unwavering dedication to realizing the concept of a welfare state in Pakistan. In a notable gesture, Khan actively participated in the Langar project by sharing a meal with those present on its inauguration. He demonstrated his commitment to the cause by queuing alongside labourers, waiting for his turn to receive food. This act underscored the significance of dignity and equality for all in the pursuit of a more just and compassionate society.[49]

Khan's Initiatives for the Homeless Population

After coming to power, Khan fulfilled his campaign promise of creating four shelters for the homeless in Peshawar, pledging that 'poor people will no longer sleep on footpaths or spend nights in the open'. The new shelters were capable of housing more than four hundred people. Khyber Pakhtunkhwa chief minister Mahmood Khan had previously announced that basic facilities would be available to homeless people, including women, children and disabled persons. In Lahore, the provincial capital of the Punjab, the first phase of the project was launched. Khan had previously instructed the provincial government to provide 'all household facilities' to those living in the shelters. There had been plans to build four more shelters in other parts of the province.[50]

Khan transferred the control of five *panahgahs* (shelters for the homeless) in the federal capital to Pakistan Baitul Maal (PBM) and instructed them to be remodelled within three months. During a visit to the *panahgah* at Tarlai, the prime minister conducted an extensive inspection of the facilities and shared a meal with the residents, signalling his personal commitment to the welfare of the homeless population – an empathetic act that humanized his leadership. However, it was evident that the local administration faced considerable challenges in operating the *panahgahs*, given the absence of financial support from the government. In response to this pressing issue, Khan articulated a vision wherein more than one hundred *panahgahs* across the nation would meet uniform standards and offer comparable facilities.

To realize this vision, Pakistan Poverty Alleviation (PPA) and PBM were entrusted with the task of elevating the *panahgahs* to a higher standard. In a significant administrative move, control over the *panahgah* in Islamabad was transferred from the Islamabad Capital Territory (ICT) administration to PBM. This transfer aimed to enhance the sustainability of these shelters and streamline their operations.

While the establishment of shelter homes under the prime minister's leadership garnered widespread acclaim, it was notable that these facilities operated on a 'help yourself' basis, placing an additional financial and administrative burden on already financially constrained local authorities. It is worth noting that the government had not allocated specific funds for the operation of these *panahgahs*, raising concerns about their long-term viability in the absence of adequate financial support.[51] But the act of drawing attention to the plights of the homeless and the need to improve welfare standards served as an inspiration for voluntary initiatives, fostering a collective response to social challenges.[52]

Pakistan's Environmental Initiatives under PTI Leadership: Global Recognition

PTI's environmental initiatives started receiving global acclaim. On Twitter (now X), the prime minister shared a video from the World Economic Forum (WEF) in May 2021, providing an overview of Pakistan's eco-friendly policies. He remarked, 'Internationally, PTI's environmental policies are gaining recognition, particularly our green recovery program in response to the Covid-19 pandemic and our comprehensive Climate Action Plan.'[53]

The WEF video spotlighted three key strategies that Pakistan had undertaken to pave the way for a more environmentally sustainable future: the goal of sourcing 60 per cent of its energy from renewable sources by 2030, the cancellation of coal projects in favour of hydroelectric power, and the creation of more than 85,000 green jobs across the nation. Under Khan's leadership, Pakistan embarked on a journey to cultivate green spaces, securing a substantial U.S.$180 million in funding for the establishment of fifteen new national parks. Simultaneously, the nation initiated a groundbreaking U.S.$500 million 'green Eurobond' and assigned a tangible monetary value to its green spaces, streamlining efforts to safeguard them.

It is very important to note that Pakistan stands as one of the world's most susceptible countries in the face of climate change. Over the past decade, from 2013 to 2023, the nation has already weathered a series of extreme climatic events, including devastating floods, torrential monsoon rains and scorching heatwaves. Astonishingly, despite contributing a significantly smaller share of greenhouse gas emissions, Pakistan was ranked fifth on the Global Climate Risk Index 2020, compiled by the Germanwatch think tank. This index identifies Pakistan as one of the countries most severely impacted by global warming since the year 2000.

The PTI government placed a strong emphasis on tree planting as a critical component of its countermeasures against climate change. In 2018 Imran Khan initiated the ambitious 10-Billion Tree Tsunami project, which aimed to address the increasing issues of rising temperatures, flooding, droughts and other extreme weather events in Pakistan that were closely linked to climate change. Pakistan had recorded over 150 extreme weather events between 1999 and 2018, resulting in a total economic cost of U.S.$3.8 billion, as reported by Germanwatch.

Despite these challenges, Pakistan faces a significant deficiency in forest cover, with less than 6 per cent of its total area being forested. The country is categorized as 'forest-poor', and each year thousands of hectares of forest land are lost due to unsustainable logging practices and the clearance of land for small-scale farming. Reforestation is a way to prevent flooding, stabilize rainfall, provide cool spaces, absorb heat-trapping carbon dioxide emissions and protect biodiversity. The 10-Billion Tree project aimed to scale up the success of the earlier Billion Tree Tsunami in Pakistan's Khyber Pakhtunkhwa province, where the government had been planting trees since 2014. With PKR 7.5 billion (U.S.$46 million) in funding, the project was expected to help Pakistan combat climate change and mitigate its effects.[54]

The Green Initiative Summit

At the Green Initiative Summit in 2021, Imran Khan urged the world to take climate change more seriously. He outlined the steps taken by Pakistan on this front and warned of the consequences if immediate measures were not taken to address the problem. The prime minister pointed out that just 10 per cent of the world's countries were responsible for emissions causing environmental damage. He shared that Pakistan had been among the ten countries most vulnerable to climate change and had faced 152 extreme weather events over the past ten years. Pakistan's future climate adaptation costs – to safeguard the land and its citizens from further disaster – have been estimated at between U.S.$6 billion and U.S.$14 billion. Khan said that before the world took any action, Pakistan had decided that, for its own survival, it must do whatever was possible.

The country would shift 60 per cent of all its energy production to clean sources by 2030. Moreover, the government planned to shift 30 per cent of all transport to electric vehicles by 2030 and committed to not initiating any new coal projects. He shared that the government had already shelved 2,400 megawatts of coal projects and replaced them with 3,700 megawatts of hydroelectricity. Pakistan had already planted 2.5 billion trees of the 10-billion target, and Khan further stated that the government planned to plant 1 million more mangroves by 2023. It had expanded green parks in the country by 50 per cent during the pandemic. The premier added that his government had also provided 'green' jobs; that is, jobs related to improving the environment. He said that 85,000 jobs had already been created in this area, and the number was expected to rise to 200,000 by 2022. His government had also been working towards the restoration of wetlands: in 2021 the World Bank ranked Pakistan as the top country for using development finance for climate-friendly initiatives and had given examples of green bonds, blue bonds, nature bonds and a mechanism devised by the government for the transition to clean energy.[55]

The prime minister also highlighted that glaciers were melting at a rapid pace due to climate change and, as a result, Pakistan and several other countries were at risk of facing water scarcity. He termed climate change 'one of the biggest crises' facing the world today, and that the problem had been visible twenty years ago but, unfortunately, the world had failed to recognize the threat. On 24 October 2021 he met with special presidential envoy for climate John Kerry to discuss the importance of reinforcing national and global efforts against the existential threat of climate change. During the meeting, Khan shared Pakistan's perspective on the challenges faced by the country and other developing nations due to climate change, highlighting the country's experience with launching nature-based solutions such as the Plant for Pakistan campaign. The ongoing collaboration between Pakistan and the USA on climate change and the environment was also reviewed. Khan expressed satisfaction with the inaugural meeting of the U.S.–Pakistan Climate and Environment Working Group, which explored potential areas of cooperation on climate action. Kerry acknowledged Pakistan's initiatives to fight climate change and briefed Khan on measures taken by the Biden administration for developing a broad global consensus on climate action ahead of the UNFCCC Conference of Parties (COP26). The two sides agreed to work closely to determine the next steps in building an effective framework of cooperation. The ongoing situation in Afghanistan was also discussed, with Khan stressing the importance of a peaceful and stable Afghanistan for Pakistan and the rest of the region, and the need for positive engagement and the release of economic resources and financial assets for the welfare of the Afghan people.[56]

The Miyawaki Forest

Imran Khan inaugurated Islamabad's first ever Miyawaki forest, which also marked the beginning of the Spring Tree Plantation Campaign 2021. The campaign was launched in the capital as part of the federal government's commitment to fighting climate change. The prime minister spoke about the Miyawaki method, stating, 'I have launched urban forestry on the lines of [the] Miyawaki technique in Japan where the trees grew ten times faster and thirty times denser.' According to Khan, Miyawaki 'is the best way to fight pollution'. The unique technique, pioneered by the Japanese botanist Akira Miyawaki, involves planting dozens of native species in the same area, close to each other, ensuring that the plants receive sunlight only from the top so that they grow upwards rather than sideways.[57]

Khan's Ambitious Vision: Construction of Ten Dams for Water and Energy Security

On 12 August 2021, Imran Khan pledged to construct ten dams in a decade to address the challenge of water scarcity in the country. He emphasized the need for storage to cope with the needs of people and farmers in the future. The groundbreaking ceremony of the Tarbela-5 (T5) expansion project was held, which aimed to generate 1,530 megawatts of electricity, provide 1.34 billion units of power to the national grid and create 3,000 jobs. The project's objective was to achieve clean energy and allow Pakistan to contribute to the fight against global warming. Khan criticized previous governments for not constructing water reservoirs due to lack of long-term planning and signing exorbitant contracts that put a burden on consumers. Due to the expensive electricity, the industry couldn't compete with the global market until the government provided subsidies. The prime minister mentioned that China's success was due to long-term planning and emphasized that the construction of reservoirs was essential to store and supply water throughout the year, since 80 per cent of Pakistan's rivers received water inflow within three to four months. Khan hoped that construction of the Mohmand dam would be completed by 2025 and the Diamer-Bhasha dam by 2028, which would protect future generations. He also noted that he appreciated the performance of the Water and Power Development Authority chairman, retired lieutenant general Muzammil Hussain, for continuing the construction of dams despite COVID-related restrictions. Moreover, Federal Minister for Energy Muhammad Hammad Azhar called on the prime minister to brief him on the country's overall energy situation, and Finance Minister Shaukat Tarin updated him on the progress of the Kamyab Pakistan Programme. Khan expressed satisfaction over the programme, stating that it would provide employment opportunities, affordable housing and agricultural machinery to the people, making it the first project of its kind in the country's history.[58]

The construction of ten dams, including the Bhasha and Dasu dams, was expected to play a pivotal role in ensuring food security in the country. Khan emphasized that these dams, which are being built under the vision of a clean and green Pakistan, hold great significance in addressing the nation's water and energy needs. The Diamer–Bhasha dam, currently in its initial construction stages, is a concrete-filled gravity dam situated on the Indus River. It is located between the Kohistan district in Khyber Pakhtunkhwa and the Diamer district in Gilgit Baltistan. This dam site is near a place called Bhasha, which is approximately 40 kilometres (25 mi.) downstream from Chilas town and 315 kilometres (195 mi.) from the Tarbela dam. Upon completion, this colossal dam will create a 3.2-million-hectare (8 million ac) reservoir, standing at a towering height of 272 metres (892 ft), making it the tallest roller compact concrete (RCC) dam in the world. The Dasu Hydropower Project is a runoff river project on the Indus River located 7 kilometres (4 mi.) upstream of Dasu town, Kohistan district, Khyber Pakhtunkhwa. The site is 74 kilometres (46 mi.) downstream of the proposed Diamer-Bhasha dam site and 350 kilometres (217 mi.) from Islamabad. Along with generating cheaper electricity, these projects aim to make the country's 3 million hectares (8 million ac) of land cultivable and ensure food security.[59]

Voting Rights for Expatriates

In November 2021, the government achieved a major victory when two amendments to the Elections Act 2017 were passed in a joint sitting of parliament. These amendments, which related to electronic voting machines and the right of overseas Pakistanis to vote, were significant reforms that aimed to give the Pakistani diaspora a voice in the country's democratic process. The Indian and Chinese diaspora have played a crucial role in improving the state of investment in their respective countries. These diasporas, which comprise millions of people spread across the globe, have a deep connection with their home countries and are highly invested in their growth and development. As a result, they have been instrumental in attracting foreign investment and promoting economic growth in India and China.

In recent years, both India and China have taken steps to leverage the potential of their diaspora communities. For example, India has implemented various policies aimed at engaging with its diaspora and encouraging them to invest in the country.[60] These policies include the establishment of the Overseas Indian Facilitation Centre and the introduction of the Pravasi Bharatiya Divas, an annual event that brings together members of the Indian diaspora from around the world.[61] Similarly, China has also recognized the importance of its diaspora in promoting economic growth and has implemented policies to encourage investment from overseas Chinese. These policies include the establishment of the China Overseas Exchange Association and the introduction of the Overseas Chinese Investment Fund.[62]

The Indian and Chinese diasporas have made notable contributions to the political processes in their respective countries. By granting a voice to these diasporas in decision making, these nations have successfully tapped into their communities' knowledge and expertise, using their networks to attract investments. Regrettably, the same cannot be said for Pakistan, despite its sizable diaspora. Pakistan has not fully harnessed the potential of its diaspora to foster economic growth. If Pakistan had engaged its overseas community more actively in the electoral process, it might have attracted economic investments similar to India and China. Therefore, it is crucial for Pakistan to connect with its diaspora and formulate policies that encourage investment and stimulate economic development.

On 25 May 2022, the National Assembly approved a bill that deprived overseas Pakistanis of their right to vote from abroad. Under the new law, these citizens could only cast their votes while residing in Pakistan. This decision had been met with criticism from some quarters, with calls for reserved seats for the Pakistani diaspora. The matter had been sent to a standing committee for further consideration, but at that time, overseas Pakistanis were excluded from the country's electoral process. This move marked a setback for efforts to increase democratic participation in Pakistan, particularly among those living outside the country. The right to vote is a fundamental aspect of any democratic system and denying it to certain citizens undermines the legitimacy of the entire process. The decision to reverse this reform also came after years of legal battles and court orders to grant overseas Pakistanis the right to vote. The fact that the electoral body failed to do so effectively, even in the face of a Supreme Court order, is deeply troubling and calls into question the competence and commitment of those responsible for ensuring free and fair elections in Pakistan.

Overall, while there may be arguments for and against the inclusion of overseas Pakistanis in the electoral process, this decision represents a step backwards for democracy in the country. As Pakistan continues to navigate the complex challenges of political stability and economic development, ensuring that all citizens have a voice in their government will be crucial.

'The End of an Era': The Formation of the PDM

In 2020 the PDM was launched as a multi-party opposition movement against the PTI government. The broad-based political alliance initially denounced military intervention in politics, yet eventually collaborated with the Army establishment to remove Imran Khan from power. There are widespread allegations suggesting that Shahbaz Sharif maintained consistent communication with the General Headquarters, and even reports claiming that he resorted to being clandestinely transported in the boot of a car.[63] The PDM planned countrywide rallies and a 'long march' in January 2021, with the action plan culminating in March before the 2021 Senate elections. The opposition announced that it would use all available tools, including no-confidence motions. However, the PML-N and PPP had their own manifestos and political interests, and each sought to remain relevant in the political process. In 2019 both parties vowed to launch an agitation against the government, but ultimately they were unable to remove the Senate chairman.[64]

In October 2019 the PPP and PML-N, in collaboration with the Jamiat Ulema-i-Islam (Fazal ur Rahman Group) (JUI-F), announced their intentions to agitate against the PTI government. While the PPP and PML-N initially supported the JUI-F-led Azadi march, they did not endorse the final sit-in, which left Fazlur Rehman and his followers alone. This was partly due to Rehman's insistence on keeping his plans confidential and not sharing them with his alliance partners. Furthermore, both the PPP and PML-N were unwilling to participate in an indefinite sit-in. Despite the opposition's decision to abandon the JUI-F's sit-in, Fazlur Rehman managed to re-establish himself as a significant player in Pakistani politics. Rehman has a long history of moving from one opposition alliance to another since the 1970s, and he has formed alliances with many unexpected partners. However, his madrasa-based support remains his one constant and allows him to sustain his brand.

Nevertheless, his constant swinging could undermine the opposition's efforts to establish a robust front against the government.

Additionally, PML-N leaders were wary of Zardari, given his past decision to undermine his commitment to the PML-N by removing the Senate chairman and forging an agreement with the civilian government to gain political mileage. Conflicting viewpoints were also evident among senior leaders of the party. Senior PPP leader Chaudhry Aitzaz Ahsan expressed reservations about the alliance, cautioning his party to be careful in their dealings with the PML-N.[65]

The PPP maintained a more neutral position towards the current regime, in contrast to the PML-N, which adopted a more confrontational approach. In March 2018 the PPP, PTI and a group of independent senators from Baluchistan backed Sadiq Sanjrani in an attempt to counterbalance the PML-N's hold on the Senate. However, this alliance was short-lived. The first cracks appeared in December 2018 when the PTI-led federal government placed several PPP leaders, including Zardari, his sister Faryal Talpur and son Bilawal on the Exit Control List following the compilation of a report by the Supreme Court-mandated joint investigation team. Moreover, many PPP leaders were facing serious corruption allegations and were rumoured to be seeking a deal with the establishment regarding their cases with the National Accountability Bureau (NAB). The opposition's alliance was tested once again when PML-N stalwart Khawaja Asif expressed his mistrust of Zardari following the PDM's launch. This statement prompted PML-N leader Mian Nawaz Sharif to issue a statement expressing his 'great deal of respect' for Zardari. This development once again highlighted the fragile nature of the opposition's alliance.[66]

As per expert analysis, the repeated efforts by the opposition to unseat Khan from his position proved unsuccessful. One key factor contributing to this failure was the absence of a unified agenda and purpose within the PDM. This lack of coherence stemmed from fundamental disparities in the ideologies and objectives of the constituent parties. Instead of presenting a cohesive front, it often appeared that individual party interests were prioritized over the collective movement's broader objectives.

Had the opposition been willing to set aside their personal agendas and pool their efforts towards shared goals, the PDM would have had the potential to emerge as a potent political force. It is worth noting that this might explain the reluctance to hold elections in the country, as the fractured nature of the opposition hindered the formation of a unified and effective political alternative.[67]

However, the PDM reached an understanding with the establishment, which paved the way for Khan's exit from power. The PTI government detained and arrested around five hundred opposition figures and activists, mainly from the PML-N, prior to the first PDM rally on 16 October. On 19 October Muhammad Safdar, Maryam Nawaz's husband and a prominent

PML-N figure, was arrested, a day after the second PDM rally in Karachi. The aforementioned events significantly contributed to the already prevalent political instability in the country.

Subsequent revelations, as exemplified by statements made by Khuram Dastgir, a prominent figure within the PML-N, bear testament to an intriguing narrative. Dastgir, during a televised appearance, articulated that General Qamar Javed Bajwa initiated contact with the opposition, effectively orchestrating a convergence of their disparate political forces in a concerted effort to remove Imran Khan from office. Dastgir further contended that failure to undertake such a collaborative endeavour would likely have resulted in an extended tenure for Khan at the helm of Pakistan's political landscape. These revelations shed light on the intricate behind-the-scenes manouvring within Pakistan's political arena and raise pertinent questions regarding the role of key actors in shaping the nation's political trajectory.[68] Such statements were sufficiently evident to suggest that General Bajwa was the mastermind behind these manoeuvres. He held meetings with various opposition leaders, urging them to join forces and overthrow Khan's government. The alternative presented was dire: if they did not comply, General Faiz Hameed would be appointed as the Army chief, and opposition leaders would continue to languish in jail while Khan remained in power for another decade.[69]

The disclosure of a secret meeting between a senior PML-N leader and the Army chief further compromised the party's position and was seen as an attempt to derail the PDM's efforts. The PML-N's interactions with the military, while simultaneously criticizing its interference in politics, undermined its credibility with politically conscious citizens. Moreover, to tighten the noose around the PPP, the NAB issued an arrest warrant for PPP chairperson Zardari. While denouncing the government, PPP spokesperson Senator Mustafa Nawaz Khokhar labelled the PTI government as an authoritarian regime and lambasted it for fabricating cases against opposition parties and leaders. In the past, the opposition movement might have succeeded given the growing public discontent with the PTI government and its struggle to manage multiple economic issues, including inflation and unemployment, exacerbated by the global pandemic.[70] Although the PDM played a role in destabilizing Khan's government, the decisive factor in his ousting was the role of the establishment. General Bajwa effectively utilized his position and power to unite the disparate political parties and ensure Khan's removal with minimal disruption.

On 9 April 2022 Khan was removed from power. The establishment of the PDM was the first step in this process, which, despite facing internal frictions, eventually settled on a conciliatory tone at the behest of the military establishment. Khan's foreign-policy initiatives were another reason for his disagreement with the establishment, since for decades it had been regarded as the sole domain of the Army.

Foreign Policy

After his election victory, Imran Khan's conciliatory statements and the presence of Indian former cricketer Navjot Singh Sidhu during his oath-taking ceremony on 18 August 2018 gave the impression that he would articulate his foreign-policy guidelines regarding Afghanistan, India and the United States. However, in his seventy-minute televised address, he conveyed a different message and seemed to articulate his foreign-policy preferences exactly like his predecessors, which disappointed many. There was a widespread perception that Pakistan's foreign policy remained subservient to its powerful military establishment – one of the major reasons for Nawaz Sharif's fall from grace was his crossing the red line on Afghanistan, India and the United States. Imran Khan assumed charge of the government at a time when Pakistan confronted a few major challenges on the foreign-policy front. The country's relationship with the United States was at its lowest ebb, while its eastern neighbour, India, had doubled efforts to further isolate Pakistan on the international level. The Financial Action Task Force (FATF), the global financial watchdog, had placed Pakistan on the grey list at a time when the country needed an immediate bailout package of U.S.$12 billion, and the United States had frozen aid to Pakistan for its alleged failure to take serious steps in fighting terrorism. Pakistan's foreign-policy challenges were mounting: its relationship with the United States was at a low point, and India was working to isolate it. Compounding these issues, President Ashraf Ghani of Afghanistan had accused Pakistan of backing the Taliban, while the United States sought to end its long campaign in the country. Against this backdrop, Imran Khan's independence and willpower could have been crucial in resetting Pakistan's relationships with its neighbours. If Pakistan's powerful security establishment had agreed, Khan could have helped to bring the Taliban to the negotiating table, potentially resolving the ongoing conflict in Afghanistan. Furthermore, Khan's social work and experience as a successful sportsman gave him a strong foundation to help unite his country and strengthen its position on the global stage.[71]

Imran Khan's past successes, driven by his independence, determination and straightforwardness, suggested he could find solutions for regional peace and stability. However, his inability to make decisions independently might have been a limitation. Analysts at the time believed that if Khan could have persuaded the military to improve relations with the United States, Afghanistan and India, it would have been a remarkable accomplishment. While Khan did not discuss foreign policy in his inaugural speech, Foreign Minister Shah Mahmood Qureshi's news conference provided some hope. Qureshi passed on a message of peace to Afghanistan and India and dispelled the notion that the security establishment was driving Pakistan's foreign policy.[72] The opening of the Kartarpur Corridor was a significant gesture that held promise for improving Pakistan's relationship with India.

The Kartarpur Corridor

The prospect of amicable relations between India and Pakistan has faced challenges ever since the latter's creation, especially the issue of Kashmir. In 2019 India was reportedly planning to carry out a military operation in Kashmir and had offloaded ammunition in Balakot. In response, Pakistan retaliated by shooting down a couple of Indian Air Force aircraft and capturing their fighter pilot, Abhinandan Varthaman. This episode created a considerable amount of acrimony between the two nations. On 6 August 2019 the Indian government made a significant move by revoking the special status, or autonomy, granted to the state of Jammu and Kashmir under Article 370 of the Indian Constitution.[73] This region, which comprises the larger part of the disputed territory of Kashmir, has been a subject of contention among India, Pakistan and China since 1947. The revocation was accompanied by several actions taken by the Indian government, including the sudden severing of communication lines in the Kashmir Valley.[74] To quell any potential uprising, thousands of additional security forces were deployed to the area. Additionally, numerous prominent Kashmiri politicians, including the former chief minister, were apprehended by authorities. Government officials have asserted that these actions were taken with the aim of preventing potential violence. The decision to revoke certain provisions was justified by the Indian government to facilitate the state's residents in accessing various government programmes, such as reservation, the right to education and the right to information.[75] Any possibility of a thaw in the relationship between India and Pakistan was effectively vanquished by this aggressive act. The decision to annex Kashmir was seen by Pakistan as an act of hostility, and it intensified the differences between the two nations. India and Pakistan were on the brink of war, and the tension between the two countries led to a suspension of the Kartarpur Corridor, following concerns raised about the potential for it to be used as a political tool.[76]

The Kartarpur Corridor, which connects the Sikh holy shrine of Kartarpur Sahib in Pakistan to the Indian border town of Dera Baba Nanak, has immense historical and cultural significance. It was opened in 2019 as a gesture of goodwill between India and Pakistan, allowing Indian Sikh pilgrims to visit the Kartarpur Sahib Gurdwara, where the founder of Sikhism, Guru Nanak, spent his last eighteen years. This holy site is considered the second most important in Sikhism. But the significance of the Kartarpur Corridor lies not just in its religious importance but in its potential to improve India–Pakistan relations. The two countries have a long and troubled history that comprises multiple conflicts and wars, but the Kartarpur Corridor represents a rare instance of cooperation and dialogue between the two neighbours.[77] The corridor has the potential to boost the economies of both countries. The project of opening it up has already created

Kartarpur Sahib Gurdwara.

jobs and opportunities for local communities in the area, and it could pave the way for increased trade and tourism between India and Pakistan. As the former Indian Minister for External Affairs, Sushma Swaraj, noted in a tweet, 'It is a corridor of infinite possibilities.' Prior to the construction of the corridor, pilgrims had to undertake a gruelling 125-kilometre (78 mi.) journey under strict visa regulations. The corridor itself leads directly from the border to the Gurdwara, with fenced-off sides that restrict travel to the shrine alone. To make the journey, pilgrims must register in advance with the Indian Ministry of Home Affairs, which compiles a list of travellers to send to Pakistan for approval. While a visa is not required, pilgrims must carry their passport and the electronic travel authorization issued by the ministry. As a goodwill gesture, Khan waived two requirements for Sikh pilgrims: they no longer needed to carry their passports (only valid identification) and they were not required to register ten days in advance. He also announced that pilgrims would not be charged the usual U.S.$20 entry fee on the day of the corridor's inauguration on 12 November 2019, the anniversary of Guru Nanak's birth.[78]

The Kartarpur Corridor serves as a powerful symbol of improving relations between India and Pakistan, highlighting the unifying force of religion. For decades, the Sikh community had yearned for visa-free access to the Kartarpur shrine following the partition of the subcontinent in 1947. After the shrine fell within Pakistan's borders, it became nearly inaccessible to Sikhs residing in India. In 1999, during his historic bus journey from Delhi to Lahore, former Indian prime minister Atal Bihari Vajpayee proposed the concept of a visa-free corridor as a means to enhance relations with Pakistan. Subsequently, following renovation by the Pakistani government, the Kartarpur shrine was reopened to Indian visitors in 2000. However, at that time, only those with valid visas were permitted to visit, and the numbers were limited. Despite the Indian government's repeated efforts to address the issue, little progress was made towards fully opening the corridor until November 2019. It was the assumption of power by the Imran Khan government that catalysed the construction process on the Pakistani side. Shortly after, India announced its decision to build its portion of the corridor (although Indian officials claimed it was not intended as a response to the Pakistani proposal).

The Kartarpur Corridor stands as a significant symbol of religious harmony, peace and cooperation between India and Pakistan. Its importance transcends religious boundaries, as it holds the potential to enhance economic ties between the two nations. However, it is imperative that both India and Pakistan diligently preserve the Kartarpur Corridor as a beacon of hope and cooperation, ensuring that political tensions do not compromise its future.

Sino-centric Foreign Policy

Imran Khan repeatedly emphasized the importance of the Pakistan–China relationship, calling it the 'cornerstone of its Pakistan's foreign policy', and both sides reiterated their support on issues concerning each other's core interests. During a meeting with Chinese president Xi Jinping, Pakistan expressed its commitment to the One-China Policy and support for China on various issues. In a joint statement released after the meeting, the leaders of the two countries discussed the entire spectrum of bilateral relations, the regional situation and the international political landscape. Khan appreciated Xi's Belt and Road Initiative (BRI), highlighting the contribution of the CPEC to Pakistan's economic and social development. The two sides reviewed bilateral cooperation and mutual support after the COVID-19 outbreak and decided to enhance cooperation in developing emergency response systems, public health infrastructure and joint ventures for the development of the pharmaceutical industry in Pakistan. They also agreed to fully utilize the second phase of the Pakistan–China Free Trade Agreement and to strengthen cooperation in e-commerce and logistics. Both sides were satisfied with the successful holding of the 15th Session of the Pakistan–China Joint Committee on Economic, Trade, Scientific and Technical Cooperation in December 2021. Pakistan and China agreed to celebrate the Pakistan–China Year of Tourism Exchanges in 2023 and establish strong links between the tourism promotion agencies and private enterprises of the two countries, building on the Memorandum of

Understanding (MOU) on Tourism Exchanges and Cooperation signed in November 2022. They also agreed to continue defence cooperation at various levels, stressing its importance for regional peace and stability. The leaders emphasized the need to resolve all outstanding disputes and underscored that a stable Afghanistan was essential for regional prosperity. The Chinese leadership was briefed on the Kashmir conflict and reiterated that it should be resolved based on the UN Charter, relevant Security Council resolutions and bilateral agreements. Khan welcomed and reiterated support for the Global Development Initiative proposed by President Xi Jinping and invited him to pay a state visit to Pakistan.[79]

During their meeting at the prestigious Great Hall of the People in Beijing, Khan engaged President Xi Jinping on various significant aspects of the Pakistan–China relationship. In a resolute commitment, Khan affirmed his determination to carry forward the ambitious and somewhat contentious U.S.$50-billion CPEC project and expressed his deep appreciation for the increased Chinese investments in the CPEC's Phase II, with a primary focus on industrialization and enhancing the well-being of the people. The discussions between the two leaders extended to encompass bilateral cooperation between Pakistan and China, in addition to their exchange of perspectives on both regional and global matters. Looking to the past, Khan underscored the paramount significance of Pakistan's enduring and unwavering friendship with China, which has consistently stood as a cornerstone of Pakistan's foreign policy.

In a gesture of felicitation, Khan commended China for the impeccable organization of the 24th Olympic Winter Games in Beijing. He underscored the unwavering support that Pakistan receives from its trusted partner and 'iron brother'. Khan provided President Xi with insights into Pakistan's geo-economic vision and the government's comprehensive policies aimed at fostering growth, development and regional connectivity. Furthermore, he shared his concerns regarding the escalating polarization in the global arena, a phenomenon fraught with significant risks for developing nations.

Highlighting the importance of ongoing agreements, both leaders celebrated the accords reached in domains such as industrial cooperation, space exploration and vaccine collaboration, especially pertinent in the midst of a global pandemic. They underscored the pivotal role of Gwadar in the CPEC, recognizing it as a central pillar and a critical nexus in regional connectivity.

Khan extended a warm invitation to President Xi to visit Pakistan and Pakistan expressed its unwavering support for China on issues surrounding Taiwan, the South China Sea, Hong Kong, Xinjiang and Tibet. Both leaders acknowledged that a peaceful and stable Afghanistan would substantially contribute to economic development and enhanced connectivity within the region. They jointly called upon the international community to provide assistance to the Afghan people.

Furthermore, Khan raised pertinent concerns about the atrocities being perpetrated in the illegally occupied Indian cities of Jammu and Kashmir, as well as the persecution of minorities in India. He emphasized that these actions posed a tangible threat to regional peace and stability, underscoring the importance of addressing these issues on the global stage.[80]

In a notable diplomatic development during March 2022, Chinese Foreign Minister Wang Yi embarked on a three-day visit to Pakistan, where he engaged with Khan. During this visit, the leaders reaffirmed their shared vision of bolstering the strategic partnership between their nations. Their discussions encompassed a comprehensive commitment to not only see the CPEC project through to its completion but to nurture and advance bilateral relations. President Arif Alvi of Pakistan reiterated that the friendship with China represented a core aspect of Pakistan's national policy, a sentiment heartily concurred with by Wang Yi. The Chinese foreign minister, in his visit, made it abundantly clear that the steadfastness of China–Pakistan relations and their enduring friendship remained unwavering.

Amid these diplomatic engagements, the discussions extended to the regional geopolitical landscape and broader global issues. Wang Yi's visit, notably, occurred against a backdrop of certain reports suggesting Beijing's concerns regarding how the new government in both Gilgit Baltistan and Azad Kashmir, led by PTI, would navigate Chinese investments within the ambit of the CPEC. (Worth mentioning is India's vocal protestation against the CPEC, contending that it traversed Pakistan-occupied Kashmir.)

China's investments in Pakistan have far exceeded the U.S.$50 billion mark, spanning a range of development initiatives as part of President Xi's ambitious Belt and Road Initiative. The CPEC itself is a meticulously planned network of transportation infrastructure, encompassing roads, railways and energy projects, designed to connect China's resource-rich Xinjiang Uyghur Autonomous Region with Pakistan's strategically vital Gwadar Port, situated on the Arabian Sea.[81]

Complex Dynamics Surrounding Imran Khan's Foreign Policy and Political Challenges

Russia backed Imran's claim of a 'foreign plot' that he made when he was ousted from power on 9 April 2022. Russia accused the United States of 'shameless interference' in Pakistan's internal affairs, stating that ongoing political developments 'left no doubt' that the United States intended to punish the 'disobedient' PTI chief. A statement from the Russian Foreign Office criticized the United States for allegedly conspiring to overthrow the Pakistani prime minister, claiming that the opposition was colluding with the Western superpower. The National Assembly's deputy speaker rejected the no-trust vote, endorsing the government's claim that the opposition was conspiring with a 'foreign power' against the prime minister. The ruling triggered a political and constitutional crisis, and the matter was put before the Supreme Court to decide its legality. Russian Foreign Ministry spokesperson Maria Zakharova accused the United States of exerting 'rude pressure' on Khan and demanding ultimatums and cited PTI's claim that the U.S. deputy secretary of state for South Asia called upon Pakistani diplomats to condemn the balanced reaction of the Pakistani leadership to events in Ukraine as evidence of U.S. involvement. The Russian Foreign Office accused foreign funds of being used to bribe dissenting party members and stated that partnerships with the United States were only possible if Imran was removed from power. The premier had claimed that a conspiracy against him was inspired and financed from abroad, and the Russian Foreign Office hoped that Pakistani voters would be informed of these circumstances in the upcoming elections. The motion of no confidence against Khan was dismissed under Article 5 and the National Assembly was dissolved by the president on the advice of the prime minister. Former foreign minister Shah Mahmood Qureshi claimed that external interference in the country's internal affairs was the primary cause of anxiety in Pakistani society, and that the National Security Committee had reported foreign interference and deemed it inappropriate. Intelligence had found no credible evidence to endorse the prime minister's complaint of a foreign conspiracy, according to an official with knowledge of the development.[82]

Imran Khan's meeting in February 2022 with Russian president Vladimir Putin, the first by a Pakistani leader in 23 years, came amid escalating tensions between Russia and the West over Ukraine. The visit, which focused on mutual concerns over Taliban-controlled Afghanistan and regional security cooperation, could be seen as an implicit endorsement of Putin's actions. Discussions also included plans for a U.S.$2.5-billion natural-gas pipeline between Karachi and Kasur. This meeting demonstrated the increasing strategic importance of Pakistan and Russia to each other, signalling a shift in the geopolitics of the region.[83]

Did Putin intentionally time his well-planned invasion of Ukraine to coincide with the arrival of Pakistani prime minister Imran Khan and his delegation in Moscow? Or was there an unspoken policy alliance between the two leaders, who were seeking to demonstrate their power and influence as crucial regional players? It's unclear whether Khan was caught off guard by Putin's announcement, or whether the ministries had been covertly informed. Regardless, Khan's foreign-policy strategy had been to strengthen regional ties, and this required alliances with neighbouring countries. As the world becomes more multipolar, poise and pragmatism are essential for building strong regional alliances. Pakistan's foreign policy had been geared towards strengthening regional ties due to the emergence of two potential regional alliances: the China–Russia alliance and the Japan–India–U.S. alliance. Although Russia had traditionally been allied with India, the U.S. invasion of Afghanistan had led to Russian-hosted peace talks between the Taliban and the Afghan government, which had softened Russia's stance towards Pakistan. This had opened the possibility of a China–Russia–Pakistan alliance, leaving India isolated. The prime minister's choice not to voice the Uyghur issue or condemn Russia's attack on Ukraine had not been difficult in the context of global politics and had been seen as a message to the West to stop intimidating Pakistan.

The United States has a history of interfering in regime changes around the world, and Pakistan and Sri Lanka's abstention from voting against Russian aggression in Ukraine may have led to Biden's assistant secretary of state Donald Lu's mission to topple both regimes. Immediately afterwards, Lu had a meeting with Pakistani envoy Asad Majeed, where he warned that failure of the vote of no confidence would lead to consequences. The minutes of this meeting were received on 7 March and the no-confidence motion was filed on 8 March. On 16 March protests against the Rajapaksa regime were launched in Sri Lanka. Sri Lanka has grappled with economic difficulties since the global crisis of 2008. However, recent events, including the timing of protests and the prominent role of Internet activism, have raised questions about whether these developments could be indicative of a 'colour revolution' – that is, one that typically involves a sequence of peaceful, often large-scale, protests and movements that seek political change through non-violent means.

A democratically elected government should prioritize economic prosperity, but not at the cost of compromised sovereignty and a slave mentality. We can instead focus on green energies and less consumerism to maintain our independence in foreign and internal policies. It is the right and responsibility of the people to ensure that democracy remains in their hands and that their elected leaders act in their best interests.[84]

One may argue that Khan's decision to form a new alliance with China, Russia and Turkey marked a departure from the traditional pro-Western American-centric foreign policy. This shift appeared to be a major point of contention for General Bajwa. Ironically, Khan sought advice from foreign-policy experts and consulted with Bajwa before proceeding to align with Russia. After forging a consensus, Khan travelled to Moscow to negotiate a deal to purchase oil and wheat at reduced rates. While in Russia, the Ukraine invasion occurred, and Khan received criticism from Western states for undertaking that visit. He was also criticized for remaining neutral rather than siding with the West. Contrary to the Pakistani government's publicly declared stance of maintaining a neutral position and refraining from taking sides, General Bajwa took a rather audacious step in an unprecedented move for a Pakistani COAS. On 1 April 2022, during the Islamabad Security Dialogue, the general openly criticized Russia's actions in Ukraine. This action, it seems, may have been an attempt to signal to the Western nations that Khan's administration held views that are not entirely in alignment with Western (particularly American) interests. Bajwa's decision can be interpreted as an attempt to appease Western nations, potentially at Khan's expense.[85]

Differences between Khan and Qamar Bajwa

Of paramount significance, transcending the PDM's endeavours to remove Imran Khan from office and the contours of his foreign-policy initiative, lies the pivotal episode wherein Khan declined to heed the counsel of his COAS to effectuate a change in the leadership of Khyber Pakhtunkhwa and Punjab provinces. This refusal engendered a discernible strain in the relationship between the two leaders.

General Bajwa expressed a preference for Aleem Khan as the chief minister of the Punjab, a preference purportedly rooted in the business affiliations that Aleem Khan shared with the father-in-law of Bajwa's son. Notably, both individuals are prominent figures in the real-estate sector, thereby sharing a connection founded on mutual business interests. Intriguingly, a similar sentiment was expressed by General Ijaz Amjad, the father-in-law of Qamar Javed Bajwa, who also harboured a favourable disposition towards Aleem Khan.

Matters escalated when Bajwa announced a change in DG ISI. Replacing a serving DG ISI constitutionally is the sole prerogative of the prime minister, not the Army chief. Khan called out Bajwa and made him follow the constitutional procedure, which further soured their relationship. The no-confidence motion moved by the PDM was a legitimate constitutional move for the removal of a sitting prime minister, and it was suspected to have had the active support of Bajwa. Many analysts tended to overlook the fact that prior to the no-confidence motion, some of Khan's party members were enticed to defect and offered bribes. As a result, twenty members of parliament were kept in Sindh House, a guest house owned by the Sindh government in the capital. These turncoats played a crucial role in Khan's removal from power. It is worth noting that Khan did not attempt to entice opposition members to switch sides in exchange for financial gain, which is both ethically and morally commendable.

The dynamics surrounding Chief Justice Omer Atta Bandial's extraordinary late-night *suo motu* intervention and his active engagement in parliamentary affairs necessitate closer examination. This particular episode marked a unique moment in the history of the Supreme Court. The court was convened during the late hours, purportedly with the intention of pre-empting any potential countermove by Imran Khan, which could have disrupted a meticulously devised strategy to remove him from power. Central to this turn of events was Chief Justice Bandial's pronouncement wherein he declared the dissolution of the National Assembly by Deputy Speaker Qasim Suri null and void. This declaration effectively facilitated the transition of government, underscoring the pivotal role played by the judiciary in the unfolding political landscape.

Shahbaz Sharif, younger brother of the deposed Nawaz Sharif and three-time chief minister of the Punjab, replaced Khan as the prime minister. Shahbaz had a reputation as a competent administrator, but he also carried the stigma of corruption as well as money laundering.[86] In fact, he was on bail when he was sworn in as the prime minister, undergoing charges of money laundering in the Pakistani courts. About 60 per cent of his cabinet members, including the prime minister himself, were on bail facing corruption charges in the trial courts.

The public's reaction to Imran Khan's dismissal was different from previous removals of sitting prime ministers. Khan took over in 2018 with the reputation of being Mr Clean, and his financial integrity survived despite attempts by his adversaries to besmirch it. While some PTI ministers and advisors were accused of and charged with corruption, the vast majority of Pakistanis view Khan as honest. High inflation during his term eroded much of the public support, but compared to the PDM's performance, PTI's inflation figures are now being accepted as a job well handled under particularly trying circumstances. This factor has led to a surge of support for the PTI and its leader. Khan's stand on resisting American attempts to make Pakistan subservient to U.S. global interests resonated with a large section of the public, particularly among the intelligentsia. Shahbaz Sharif and his cabinet's reluctance to approach Russia for the purchase of considerably cheaper oil and gas, despite these already being imported by neighbouring India, because of fears of upsetting the USA was intriguing. The decision had led to an increase in fuel costs – the principal factor in the uncontrolled rise in inflation – and appeared to substantiate and strengthen Khan's assertion that the United States conspired with the Sharifs and Zardaris to affect a regime change.

In retrospect, the remarkable surge in public support for Khan's rallies throughout the nation was a noteworthy development. Nevertheless, his return to power in the foreseeable future appears highly implausible. The outcome of the election for twenty seats during the by-polls in the Punjab on 17 July 2022 underscored the electoral prowess of PTI. Nonetheless, the durability of his political popularity has always remained uncertain, especially since the establishment's support has shifted away from him.

Khan's rise and ousting from the government is typical of Pakistan's political history. The political engineering that brought him to power in 2018 and led to his downfall in 2022 and the subsequent decimation of PTI is very similar to earlier military interventions (for example, in 1988–99). Some historical parallels can also be drawn between Zulfiqar Ali Bhutto and Imran Khan. Both were populists who promised to transform Pakistan, but ultimately they failed not only because of the establishment's vested interests but because of their own character flaws. They were temperamentally unsuited to the politics of collaboration. Yet cross-party cooperation is required to begin the process of resetting the civilian–military balance and bringing about the structural economic reform necessary to end dependency. While Bhutto and Khan set out to establish a new politics, they ended up relying on the same patron–client pattern (by getting 'electables' on board), and so the insidious corrupting influence that has prevailed in Pakistan since 1947 continued. Interestingly, both men linked their ousting with Western opposition to their policy, thereby playing into an anti-American sentiment within Pakistani popular culture that can be dated to the 1960s.

Contemporary Pakistan is, of course, very different to the country of the Bhutto years in the 1970s, so parallels should not be played up too much. For a start, it is more conservative in religious and political outlook. But society has changed in other ways as well. Indeed, Imran Khan's boldness in attacking the military reflects the confidence brought first by PTI's appeal (through adroit social-media use) to the 'youth bulge', whose urban element is better educated and informed than ever before, and second to a politically active diaspora. Indeed, it could be argued that Khan has effectively copied from Narendra Modi's populist playbook in acquiring financial, lobbying and media support through courting Pakistanis living in the USA and the UK.

Initially, Imran Khan's ability to reach out to Pakistani youth and the hope of his addressing mounting structural problems attracted the establishment's attention, the so-called 'Project Imran'. It was possible on his ousting that there was still a way back for him, despite the feathers he had ruffled following the vote of no confidence. However, following the events of 9 May 2023, and the latest upheavals in the 2024 elections, this seems a distant dream.

PAKISTAN'S CURRENT CRISIS is more serious than any previously experienced, particularly with a backdrop of climate change, which could provide an existential threat not just to Pakistan but to much of South Asia. There is now an environmental imperative for greater regional cooperation in addition to hopes of a peace dividend if Indo-Pakistan relations can be normalized. Indeed, the question must be raised: can there ever be a fully consolidated Pakistani democracy with a reset in civilian–military relations without some degree of normalization between the 'distant' neighbours? The replacement of a strategy-centric approach to national security with a human-centric one surely requires a normalization of relations with New Delhi. A Modi victory in the Indian elections of mid-2024 is not as certain as was once thought; and PML-N's Sharif has been appointed prime minister once more following a hugely controversial election period.[87] In future, might Rahul Gandhi and Bilawal Bhutto-Zardari deliver on the hopes raised in 1988 by Rajiv Gandhi and Benazir Bhutto and secure a peace dividend for the subcontinent?

14

Regime Change and a Year of Uncertainty,

2022–3

Throughout Pakistan's history, no prime minister has managed to complete a full five-year term without encountering assassination, hanging or removal through martial law or by the president under the Eighth Constitutional Amendment. Pakistan's history was marked by frequent regime changes, often carried out through unconstitutional means. However, in the case of Imran Khan, there was a shift in the status quo: it was a vote of no confidence that led to regime change.[1] This time, despite Imran Khan's allegations of a foreign conspiracy leading to the premature end of his tenure, the change in leadership was carried out in a constitutional manner.

However, Khan's allegations were met with scepticism by the opposition, who rejected his claims of foreign interference. The director general of Inter-services Public Relations stated that there was no evidence of a foreign conspiracy, though there had been interference leading to the deposition of Khan. Thus a debate ensued regarding how it was possible for such interference to occur without a conspiracy. However, it was later revealed that Bajwa had enlisted the services of a lobbying firm to depict Khan as anti-American and to secure clearance for another term for Bajwa as COAS in Pakistan. Hussain Haqqani acted as a conduit for Bajwa, despite the Pakistan Army labelling him a traitor due to his involvement in the Memogate scandal. A coalition of around a dozen political parties managed to remove Khan from power, triggering a political and economic crisis in Pakistan. However, despite frenzied efforts and intense lobbying, spearheaded by Bajwa's father-in-law, Bajwa was not granted any further extension. On 29 November 2022 he was made to retire, but the problems he left behind were too substantial to be easily resolved by his replacement.

According to Imran Khan, the U.S. assistant secretary of state for South and Central Asian affairs had warned the Pakistani envoy that there would be consequences if the prime minister survived a no-confidence vote in the National Assembly. Subsequently, he levelled an accusation against Bajwa, holding him responsible for orchestrating a regime change to fulfil his personal interests. Khan stated that Bajwa had clear aspirations to enhance his influence in state affairs through political manipulation. Looking back, the unchecked power that Bajwa possessed and exercised without consequence has caused irreparable harm to the Pakistani state and its economy, as well as its political institutions. Instead of implementing significant reforms within the Army, he appeared to be more focused on interfering in politics and helping his colleagues and relatives accumulate wealth.[2]

General Qamar Javed Bajwa served as the COAS from 29 November 2016, when he was appointed by Prime Minister Nawaz Sharif, to 29 November 2022. The decision to give him such authority surprised few, since Sharif had a track record of appointing individuals without strong connections or qualifications to key positions. According to analysts, Bajwa's father-in-law, Major General Ijaz Amjad, lobbied on Bajwa's behalf, drawing upon his connections with the Sharif family that he had established during his tenure as general officer commanding in Lahore.

Bajwa got his early education at Sir Syed College and Gordon College in Rawalpindi and graduated from the Pakistan Military Academy in Kakul in 1980. He also received training from the Canadian Army Command and Staff College and the Naval Postgraduate School in Monterey, California. In the selection of the sixteenth Army chief of Pakistan, Sharif had a good pool of candidates to choose from. The top four candidates were all highly qualified and experienced, but none had served in senior positions in the ISI, which was a concern for the prime minister. Ultimately, Bajwa was chosen for the position.

Bajwa had served as the commander of the X Corps in Rawalpindi, which encompassed all of Kashmir and the northern areas, and had experience serving on the Line of Control in Kashmir, too. As a major general, he had transformed the School of Infantry and Tactics in Quetta to focus on irregular warfare. He was the recipient of several prestigious awards, including Nishan-e-Imtiaz, Hilal-e-Imtiaz, the Turkish Legion of Merit and the Order of the Military Merit, presented by the king of Jordan, Abdullah II.

There were rumours that Bajwa was an Ahmadi, which had been declared a non-Muslim group during the elder Bhutto's tenure. However, as Shuja Nawaz avers, Sharif chose not to disqualify him on these grounds. Bajwa's marriage to the niece of a famous Ahmadi war hero was cited as proof of this allegation, but his father-in-law declared himself to be a Sunni while in service.[3]

Bajwa's extension as the COAS in August 2019, granted by Imran Khan, was a significant and somewhat controversial development, as it followed a series of consultations and discussions within the Pakistani government and military hierarchy. The extension of Bajwa's tenure was made possible through the passage of a bill in the National Assembly of Pakistan, the lower house of parliament. This bill, known as the Army Act Amendment Bill (or simply the Bajwa Extension Bill) aimed to amend the Army Act of 1952 to allow for the extension of the COAS's tenure beyond the previously stipulated retirement age. The bill sought to address the need for flexibility in appointing and extending the term of the COAS. It also emphasized the importance of establishing clear term limits for future COAS appointments to ensure transparency and accountability within the military establishment. It argued that in certain situations, such as regional security challenges and for continuity of military leadership, it was imperative to grant extensions to the COAS. The bill underwent thorough debate and scrutiny by lawmakers, where various arguments were presented both in favour and against the extension. After extensive discussions and deliberations, the National Assembly endorsed the bill, thereby approving General Bajwa to continue his service as COAS until 29 November 2022. This endorsement was seen as an expression of confidence in his leadership and a recognition of the security challenges faced by Pakistan at that time, particularly related to counterterrorism operations and regional geopolitics.[4]

Since the bill was the legal framework through which the extension of Bajwa's tenure was granted, the process adhered to constitutional procedure, but the extension generated mixed reactions among political parties and the public. While some believed it was necessary for stability and continuity, others criticized it as an overreach of executive power.

During his time as COAS, Bajwa carried out counterterrorism operations nationwide in February 2017 and was in charge of Khyber-4 in July 2017. Khyber-4 was a significant military operation to target militant groups and their strongholds in the Khyber Agency of Pakistan's FATA. This operation aimed to eliminate terrorist threats, disrupt their infrastructure and enhance security in the region, furthering Pakistan's efforts in the fight against terrorism.

A New Government

On 10 April 2022 the PDM government came to power and claimed that the country was better off without the previous regime, which they labelled as corrupt, vindictive and inefficient. However, the aftermath of the regime change only served to exacerbate the political crisis and plunged the country into economic turmoil. The situation was far from straightforward, and Pakistan continued to grapple with the consequences of the regime change.

Shahbaz Sharif's enduring aspiration to ascend to the role of Pakistan's prime minister had materialized. Upon assuming leadership, his administration was anticipated to prioritize economic revival, a commitment he and his supporters had vocally underscored. Nevertheless, despite a full year in power following the ousting of Khan's government and the appointment of two finance ministers, the PDM had faltered in delivering a coherent and effective economic strategy. In stark contrast, Prime Minister Khan contended that his administration had successfully achieved an impressive annual growth rate of 5.97 per cent, accompanied by record-breaking remittances and historically high levels of exports. These accomplishments played a pivotal role in re-establishing a degree of stability in the economy, which had previously suffered from volatility as a consequence of regime transitions. However, it is worth noting that negotiations with the IMF, a vital institution for Pakistan's economic sustenance, encountered persistent setbacks. The IMF's stipulated conditions on Pakistan had grown increasingly stringent, thereby exacerbating the plight of the general populace, who grappled with mounting inflation and the consequent surge in consumer prices.

Moreover, the rupee's precipitous devaluation against the U.S. dollar had reached alarming proportions, yet the government appeared to exhibit a degree of insensitivity to this precarious economic predicament. Notably, the devaluation of the national currency bore significant ramifications for various sectors, including imports, exports and foreign-debt servicing, and was in need of a robust government response.

In addition to these economic challenges, the government under Shahbaz Sharif notably expanded its cabinet, comprising an expansive roster of approximately ninety members. This expansion raised pertinent questions regarding the efficiency and cost-effectiveness of governance, as well as the allocation of public resources, amid concerns over administrative bloat and its potential impact on the delivery of public services. Such an expansion warranted closer scrutiny within the broader context of governmental effectiveness and accountability.

Upon assuming political authority, the PDM government adeptly curtailed the operational scope of the NAB, thereby exerting a notable influence on its functions. A conspicuous policy shift transpired wherein instances of corruption involving sums less than PKR 500 million were tacitly legitimized, thereby imparting a discernible impression of the government's limited commitment to principles of accountability and transparency. Additionally, it became evident that cases implicating PDM members in acts of misappropriation of public funds or money laundering were systematically dismissed, thereby laying bare the government's propensity for selective dispensation of justice. This policy stance underscored the government's inclination to adopt a discerning and discretionary approach to matters of legality and accountability.

Concurrently, a persistent and aggressive smear campaign was initiated against Imran Khan, marked by concerted efforts to implicate him in what was known as the Tosha Khana case. This particular case pertains to an incident where Khan had ostensibly engaged in the purchase and subsequent sale of a wristwatch and revolved around allegations related to the acquisition and disposition of luxury watches by various political figures in Pakistan. Imran Khan's involvement in this case was framed as an attempt to tarnish his reputation and insinuate potential wrongdoing. It is imperative to note, however, that the purchase and sale of the watch were entirely legitimate and devoid of any unlawful activity.

The incessant chorus of accusations and insinuations against Khan persisted unabated until there emerged allegations of similar practices involving prominent members of PML-N and former president Asif Ali Zardari from the PPP. This revelation cast a spotlight on the government's apparent hypocrisy, highlighting a stark contrast between the treatment of Khan and other political figures regarding similar accusations. Nevertheless, Khan was incarcerated in Attock Jail, where he was detained in a cell typically reserved for individuals accused of more serious criminal offences, a measure lacking legal justification. As *Dawn* reported, 'The court sentenced Imran – who was absent from court – to three years of imprisonment and imposed a fine of PKR 100,000.'[5] Ironically, individuals who absconded with significantly larger items remain immune from legal consequences.

This episode underscores the complex dynamics of political discourse and accountability in Pakistan, where allegations and counter-allegations in high-profile cases are often subject to political manipulation and selective scrutiny. It serves as a poignant example of how the interpretation and framing of legal cases can have significant implications for public perception and the broader political landscape.

A period characterized by oppressive measures unfolded as Khan spearheaded a long march on 25 May 2022, advocating for national elections. This event underscored the government's apparent political short-sightedness. Rather than permitting peaceful assembly and expression of support by PTI adherents, the government opted for a heavy-handed approach, employing brute force that encroached upon the fundamental rights and privacy of individuals. Notably, police personnel, acting on the government's directives, forcefully entered the residences of those suspected of harbouring loyalty to PTI, without legal warrants, and subjected them to physical brutality. Additionally, this crackdown resulted in property damage and the rough treatment of protesters.

This robust and authoritarian response not only revealed the government's limited capacity for tolerating dissent but further sullied the already tarnished image of PML-N. A more conciliatory approach could have potentially afforded the government the moral high ground. However, it instead chose to double down on its authoritarian tactics, thereby exacerbating an already tense political atmosphere.

In the initial phases of the government's tenure, public sentiment had become notably characterized by widespread discontentment, primarily stemming from a confluence of economic factors. Chief among these factors was a substantial escalation in petrol and diesel prices, coupled with heightened gas and electricity tariffs. It is imperative to underscore that these economic adjustments disproportionately affected the middle- and lower-income strata of the population, rendering them particularly susceptible to the precipice of impoverishment.

Additionally, significant criticism was directed towards the imposition of taxes as delineated in the 2022–3 federal budget. Of particular concern was the apparent incongruence between the imposition of these taxes and a simultaneous lack of substantial reductions in imports. This disjunction provoked widespread debate and scrutiny, with many contending that a more comprehensive approach to fiscal management was essential to mitigate adverse economic impacts. Furthermore, a pervasive perception of elite hypocrisy had taken root within the public consciousness. This perception was fuelled by a stark contrast between ostentatious displays of extravagance and the concurrent exhortation for austerity measures directed at the broader populace. The ruling elites' conspicuous participation in lavish events and consumption practices were deemed incongruent with the austere expectations imposed upon the citizenry.

These multifaceted issues illuminate the complex interplay of economic policy, public perception and governance within the contemporary political landscape. They underscore the imperative for governments to formulate coherent and equitable economic policies that address the specific vulnerabilities of different societal strata. Additionally, it emphasizes the significance of maintaining public trust and credibility through consistent and transparent governance practices, particularly in matters relating to fiscal policy and austerity measures.[6] The 'Turnaround Pakistan' conference convened in Islamabad (on 28 June 2022) served as a pertinent illustration of a broader issue that transcended political affiliations. The substantial financial resources expended on such an event, amounting to millions of rupees, raised legitimate questions about its efficacy in delivering tangible outcomes commensurate with its cost. This fiscal outlay underscored the necessity for rigorous scrutiny and assessment of the cost–benefit ratio of such initiatives, given their implications for public finances.

Interestingly, the economic repercussions of the aforementioned measures, albeit unintended, appear to have played a role in inadvertently bolstering the political fortunes of PTI and its chairman, Imran Khan. The economic challenges that would have beset the PTI government had it remained in power were multifaceted, spanning a spectrum of critical issues. The cumulative weight of these challenges would have posed a formidable obstacle to their electoral prospects in the 2024 general elections. However, the abrupt change in regime dynamics introduced a new dimension to the political landscape. This shift, in turn, led to public contemplation regarding the legitimacy of the PML-N and its underlying motivations. This introspection spoke to the broader implications of regime change on public perception, trust and the prevailing discourse surrounding governance.

This nuanced analysis underscored the imperative for impartial examination of the multifaceted factors contributing to political transitions, financial prudence in government spending and the intricate interplay of electoral dynamics within the realm of Pakistani politics. Furthermore, it emphasized the need for an objective and comprehensive understanding of the consequences of political transitions on public sentiment and the prevailing democratic discourse.

The revelation that twenty PTI parliamentarians had their loyalties effectively acquired and were subsequently accommodated at Sindh House carries substantial implications, providing a lens through which to scrutinize the involvement of various elements, including the establishment. These actions, allegedly conducted under the influence of General Bajwa and associates within the intelligence agencies, introduce complexities into the political landscape. The disclosure of such activities had evidently eroded the moral credibility of the PDM coalition, prompting questions regarding the ethical dimensions of political conduct within the country. This development raises concerns about the transparency and integrity of the political process, necessitating a closer examination of the mechanisms through which political allegiances are formed and manipulated.

The by-elections held in the Punjab in July 2022 offer additional insights into the evolving political dynamics. They serve as an empirical measure of the PML-N's popularity, and the results appeared to indicate a decline in the party's electoral support. An impartial analysis of these results is essential to gauge the broader shifts in political sentiment and voter preferences within the region. It is noteworthy that Pakistan has grappled with recurring political, economic and social crises over time. These challenges can be traced, in part, to the historical and contemporary suppression of democratic processes. A scholarly examination of this phenomenon is essential to unravel the complex web of factors contributing to the nation's welfare and the well-being of its citizens. Such an analysis should remain objective and unbiased to foster a deeper understanding of Pakistan's political landscape and its impact on the broader socio-economic context.

Subsequent to his deposition from office, a notable shift occurred in Imran Khan's narrative. Initially, he attributed his removal to a perceived conspiracy orchestrated by the United States, accusing the country of engineering the regime change. However, approximately one year later, Khan altered his stance, asserting that the conspiracy had its origins within Pakistan itself, with the active involvement of the PDM. In this revised narrative, the United States was purportedly approached to facilitate the process by providing a cipher for his ousting. Moreover, Khan claimed that this intricate conspiracy involved the lobbying efforts of Husain Haqqani in the United States.

Of significant note is Khan's accusation directed at the army chief, alleging the granting of an NRO-2 (national reconciliation ordinance 2) – signifying a willingness to absolve those implicated in corruption and money laundering – to a purported 'cabal of crooks' in exchange for another term extension. Khan emphasized the stark contrast between his government's tenure and the one-year rule of the PDM coalition, underscoring his administration's accomplishments in transitioning the country from a state grappling with terrorism to promoting tourism. In contrast, he contended that the 'cabal of crooks' had effectively managed to close corruption cases amounting to PKR 1,100 billion during their brief time in office.

Khan levelled criticism at the PDM government, citing the instrumental use of the NAB and the Federal Investigation Agency (FIA) as tools for the targeted harassment of political opponents. Specifically, he contended that approximately two hundred cases were filed against himself and other prominent leaders of PTI. Additionally, Khan raised concerns over the inadequacy of the security measures provided to him, alleging that the government had failed to ensure his safety. In a more serious accusation, he asserted that there were attempts on his life, amounting to allegations of assassination plots. This set of allegations and claims was emblematic of the broader discourse surrounding political rivalries and the instrumentalization of state institutions for political ends.

Pakistan had previously confronted a multifaceted crisis characterized by several interlinked challenges, notably including a pronounced economic downturn, devastating floods and a critical energy shortage. This complex predicament had been further exacerbated by issues of weak governance and political instability, which had, in turn, engendered corruption and the proliferation of detrimental consequences for the nation's fiscal stability. Importantly, Pakistan's significant reliance on imports, particularly in the realm of energy resources, had rendered it highly susceptible to fluctuations in global oil and gas prices. This structural vulnerability had amplified the challenges posed by external economic shocks. In response to these formidable challenges, the international community had pledged a substantial sum of U.S.$9 billion in support for Pakistan. Key contributors to this pledge had included China and Saudi Arabia. However, the actual disbursement of these pledged funds failed to materialize, due to a prevailing trust deficit between the PDM government and the donor countries. Moreover, underlying these pledges had been implicit expectations, raising the likelihood that these countries had anticipated reciprocal actions or policy adjustments from Pakistan in exchange for their support.

While U.S.$9 billion had undoubtedly represented a substantial amount, it is important to acknowledge that it alone had been insufficient to fully extricate Pakistan from its multifaceted crisis. Nevertheless, the value of securing IMF funds had lain in its potential to serve as a critical stopgap measure. Beyond the immediate financial infusion, IMF support had played a crucial role in rebuilding confidence within the global financial community, thus facilitating the resumption of private investment flows into the country. This facet had been of paramount significance in the broader context of Pakistan's economic stabilization efforts.

In summation, Pakistan's past challenges had been underscored by a confluence of economic, environmental and governance-related issues.

The international community's past financial commitments, though substantial, had been contingent on trust-building efforts and had entailed implicit expectations. Consequently, while they had provided valuable support, the comprehensive resolution of Pakistan's past crisis had necessitated multifaceted strategies that had extended beyond immediate financial injections.

Pakistan found itself in a state of heightened vulnerability to climate-induced disasters, underscoring the imperative for bolstering domestic preparedness and resilience. Concurrently, foreign aid initiatives stood as instrumental tools in mitigating the aftermath of devastating floods. However, the restoration of foreign reserves assumed pivotal significance. Such an undertaking served as a linchpin in fostering international confidence in Pakistan's capacity to meet its debt obligations effectively.[7]

Press Freedom in Pakistan

In the third week of August 2022, Imran Khan found himself entangled in a legal and political quagmire, with authorities charging him under the nation's anti-terrorism law. This development followed a contentious political rally in Islamabad, where Khan launched an acerbic tirade against both law enforcement agencies and a judicial officer, Zeba Chaudhary.

In a parallel move, Pakistan's apex media regulatory body imposed a ban on the dissemination of Khan's speeches, citing the purported dissemination of 'hate speech' targeting 'state institutions and officers'. This ban on his speeches exacerbated the already simmering political tensions within the country.

Khan, since his removal from power in April 2022 through a parliamentary no-confidence motion, had been actively engaged in organizing massive rallies across Pakistan, endeavouring to pressurize the establishment to hold elections. During the August rally, Khan publicly pledged to pursue legal action against police officers and a female judge, alleging that a close associate, his chief of staff, Shehbaz Gill, had suffered torture while in police custody. This was reiterated during another rally held the very next day, where Khan asserted that the police had acted under duress from 'neutrals', a term frequently employed to allude to Pakistan's influential military establishment. He queried the ostensibly neutral stance of these entities, questioning the veracity of their claims to impartiality.

The legal consequences of these developments were of significant import. Imran Khan, at that time, faced the possibility of a protracted prison sentence, as he had been charged with menacing police officers and a judge. It is worth noting that, during his campaign against the government, Khan had not been detained for the less severe charges levelled against him. He had, however, been granted protective bail, granting him respite to prepare for his anticipated appearance before an anti-terrorism court in Islamabad. The treatment of Khan and the unfolding legal proceedings have been closely scrutinized, as they carry implications not only for Imran Khan but for the broader political terrain of Pakistan.

As the administration aimed to quell Imran Khan's ongoing popularity among the public, media freedom suffered as a primary casualty. Pakistan had, since 2006–7, nurtured a relatively vibrant media sector that represented a spectrum of political perspectives and opinions. Nevertheless, in the years following, successive governments and the military establishment progressively restricted media freedom, posing a threat to pluralism and journalistic independence in the nation. This was achieved by establishing new 'red lines' regarding sensitive topics. In the past, this practice of silencing the media had been limited. The PTM case is perhaps the most conspicuous example; reporters were instructed to exercise caution in their reporting to avoid contradicting the official narrative. However, the latest trends in curtailing media freedom have increasingly focused on major cities, with restrictions becoming more pronounced during the tenure of the PML-N party from 2013 to 2018 and PTI from 2018 to 2022.

As domestic politics and the media landscape in Pakistan have become more polarized, successive governments have resorted to arbitrary and politically motivated power grabs to suppress political dissent and weaken the opposition, further undermining media freedom and democracy in the country. Since 2013, efforts to constrain the press have employed various tactics, including legal mechanisms, physical coercion, violence against journalists and media blackouts. Although politicians had made promises to enhance press freedoms while out of office, the press environment continued to deteriorate throughout successive administrations.

For instance, the PML-N had pledged to enact a journalists' protection law in its 2013 election manifesto, but it remained unimplemented until 2018. Instead, in 2016 Pakistan's National Assembly passed the Prevention of Electronic Crimes Bill (2015), which granted substantial censorship powers to enforcement agencies with regard to the Internet. It received criticism for its broad discretion.[8] In the same year, Pakistan found itself ranked among the ten worst countries for Internet freedom, and it held the unenviable fourth position among the ten worst countries for journalists. During the period spanning from May 2017 to April 2018, which marked the final years of the PML-N's tenure, there were a reported 157 attacks on journalists. Additionally, notable armed assaults were perpetrated against prominent journalists, including Hamid Mir in 2014 and Cyril Almeida in 2016. The latter incident resulted in Almeida being 'restricted from leaving the country' in the aftermath of his report on a civil–military dispute, famously referred to as the '*Dawn* Leaks'.

Following a pattern established by prior administrations, the coalition government led by the PML-N initially made assurances of press reforms and expressed its intention to potentially 'disband' the Pakistan Media

Development Authority (PMDA). Prime Minister Shahbaz Sharif vociferously emphasized his commitment to freedoms of press and speech. However, despite these bold pledges, the state of press freedom appeared to have demonstrably deteriorated. This time, journalists who aligned with the PTI narrative of 'regime change' found themselves subjected to censorship and violence.[9]

Media censorship and the suppression of dissent had cast a shadow over the supporters of the ousted government. A prominent pro-PTI journalist, Imran Riaz Khan, had been detained on 5 July, facing seventeen treason charges, while Ayaz Mir, a senior journalist then affiliated with Dunya TV, had endured a physical assault by unidentified assailants a week prior for his critical stance against the military establishment. These incidents set in motion a series of government actions that took aim at pro-PTI journalists and media outlets.

On 12 August the government had revoked the operating licence of ARY News, citing the broadcast of 'seditious content' during an interview with Shahbaz Gill, Imran Khan's chief of staff. Subsequently, the government initiated an investigation into ARY CEO Salman Iqbal and other journalists in connection with the controversial remarks made during the interview. The absence of due process in the actions taken against ARY News had garnered criticism, notably from PPP senator Farhat Ullah Babar, who cautioned against the arbitrary use of state power, warning that such practices could yield adverse consequences.[10]

Legal mechanisms were frequently employed as a tool to suppress dissent, serving as a smokescreen behind which the military exerted its influence. The military establishment maintained a complex relationship with the media, often targeting journalists who criticized its involvement in politics. Daniel Bastard, the head of RSF's Asia-Pacific Desk (Reporters sans frontières), contended that the harassment of journalists recurred as the military clandestinely intervened to exert control over Pakistan's journalists.[11]

The press environment was further shaped by domestic polarization, wherein media outlets became amplifiers for the powerful elite, the incumbent government or the military establishment. In December 2020 the official Twitter handle of PTI issued a list of journalists categorized as 'good' and 'bad', with the latter mainly belonging to Jang Group's Geo TV, accused of 'constructing narratives for the corrupt'. Conversely, 'good journalists', predominantly affiliated with ARY News, were celebrated as 'brave and bold' individuals championing the cause of 'truth and justice'. This polarization within the media landscape contributed to a lack of cohesive response from media platforms.

The suppression of dissenting voices threatened to become ingrained in Pakistan's political culture. However, targeting and penalizing dissenting voices constituted a self-inflicted wound, as it did not eliminate dissent but rather underscored the heavy-handed tactics of the state, jeopardizing the democratic institutions vital for the state's long-term sustainability. Consequently, governing authorities should refrain from politically weaponizing their power by constricting space for dissent. Similarly, the media should prioritize the collective defence of journalism in Pakistan over political partisanship, thereby demonstrating and reinforcing their indispensable role in fostering democracy and disseminating information.

Media censorship stood as a formidable impediment to the transparency of the elections that had taken place, which, even at that juncture, had been anticipated to grapple with a myriad of challenges. These challenges had encompassed institutional mistrust and deep-seated apprehensions regarding electoral integrity. Instead of engaging in the politicization of the media, the incumbent government would have been better served by championing the cause of heightened media freedom. This could have been achieved through a concerted effort to repeal laws that constricted press freedom and by steadfastly safeguarding the inherent right to freedom of expression. Such a commitment not only would have aligned with democratic principles but would have underscored its indispensability as a hallmark of a vibrant democratic trajectory for Pakistan.

It was imperative to recognize that media censorship not only curtailed the fundamental right to free expression but jeopardized the core values of a democratic society. By embracing and actively promoting media freedom, the government could have signalled its dedication to fostering a democratic landscape wherein diverse voices, opinions and perspectives could thrive. Such an environment had been crucial in the context of elections, as it had enabled citizens to access a broad spectrum of information, engage in informed decision making and hold their representatives accountable. Moreover, it had served to enhance public trust in the electoral process itself.

However, the challenges that faced Pakistan's media landscape should not be underestimated. Achieving meaningful media freedom had required not only legislative reforms but a cultural shift that championed openness, pluralism and the vitality of a free press. Furthermore, the government's role had extended beyond legislative changes; it had needed to actively promote a culture of tolerance and respect for diverse viewpoints, both within its own institutions and within society at large.

As Pakistan endeavoured to navigate the complex terrain of democratic governance and electoral transparency, the imperative to protect and foster media freedom had emerged as a pivotal and enduring component of this journey. By taking tangible steps to ensure that the media can operate without fear of censorship or reprisal, Pakistan can lay the foundation for a more vibrant, accountable and democratic future.

Unveiling the Harsh Reality: The Stigma Associated with Arshad Sharif's Murder

Arshad Sharif, a prominent Pakistani journalist who had sought refuge within Kenya, died in October 2022 in Nairobi, when law enforcement personnel there, under the mistaken presumption that they were pursuing a vehicle associated with a child abduction case, shot at the car he was in. Sharif, having been a vocal critic of the government of Pakistan, had been compelled to flee his homeland in response to grave death threats. In a poignant revelation, Sharif's wife revealed that her husband was the victim of a sustained harassment campaign over the course of several months in 2022, and a former Pakistani minister has posited that Sharif's death was in fact a calculated act of murder. Consequently, the circumstances surrounding his unfortunate demise have engendered a cloud of suspicion, prompting not only profound denunciation across Pakistan, but a collective demand for answers by both impartial observers and political figures. There have also been vociferous calls from the media fraternity for a comprehensive and impartial inquiry into the incident.

Kenya has a historical record of police-related fatalities and instances of brutality, a lamentable trend that has seen a staggering total of 1,286 documented cases since 2007.[12] The Independent Policing Oversight Authority (IPOA) undertook a formal inquiry into Sharif's murder, and the Foreign Press Association of Africa (FPA) issued a call to the Kenyan government, beseeching it to investigate the incident.[13]

It is imperative to acknowledge the global context of press freedom and journalist safety in this discourse. Pakistan placed ninth on the Committee to Protect Journalists (CPJ) 2020 Global Impunity Index. This index, meticulously crafted, not only assesses and quantifies the environments wherein journalists regularly face the gravest of risks to their lives, but surveys places where perpetrators are able to evade accountability for their actions. Pakistan needs to address the gravity of this reality.[14]

Beyond the ambit of his journalistic vocation, Sharif was involved in the groundbreaking Netflix documentary *Behind Closed Doors*, which explored the world of money laundering and ill-gotten wealth, a scourge endemic within Pakistan. By virtue of its exposé, *Behind Closed Doors* found itself casting aspersions upon some of the most entrenched and potent political figures within Pakistan's corridors of power.

In essence, this cinematic foray represented an act of remarkable audacity, underscoring Sharif's sagacious investigative acumen and unwavering determination to illuminate the truth of the seediest areas of Pakistani society.[15] By unmasking the nefarious activities of those in positions of power, the documentary had the potential to upend the corrupt and entrenched status quo, bringing about a seismic shift in the country's political landscape.

Sharif's death continues to elicit outpourings of grief, and the shadow of uncertainty surrounding it continues to be confounded by discordant narratives emanating from the Kenyan law enforcement authorities. There has been no consensus on what actually happened. One rendition proffers the narrative that the law enforcement officers, in a tragic misapprehension, perceived the vehicle in which Sharif was travelling as a stolen van, resulting in the fatal encounter. In stark contrast, another narrative asserts that the tragic sequence of events was set in motion by an alleged provocation, with one of the vehicle's occupants purportedly initiating gunfire against the police.

The perplexing question arises: by what means did the Kenyan police commit the grievous error of misidentifying Sharif's Toyota Land Cruiser as a mere delivery van? This inquiry raises concerns about not only the adequacy of police training but the overall competence of law enforcement personnel in the field. Why, in the face of what they perceived as a stolen vehicle, did they not opt for the conventional procedure of immobilizing it by shooting at its tyres? This question delves into the critical realm of police tactics and decision making – particularly police protocols and the discernment exercised by officers in high-pressure situations, where lethal force is resorted to – which is too large to address here.

The intricate tapestry of Arshad Sharif's trajectory unveils a compelling narrative that transcends borders. Prior to his fateful sojourn in Kenya, Sharif had temporarily gone to the United Arab Emirates. Sharif's legal representative, Shoaib Razzaq, disclosed that the Pakistani government had formally initiated proceedings to seek his extradition from Dubai. It was within the sanctuary of Kenya that Sharif sought refuge, where he found solace in the presence of friends and contacts who rallied to his side during his time of need. At the time of his death, Sharif was accompanied by a compatriot, believed to be a resident of Kenya. While the precise link between Kenya and Sharif's investigative pursuits remains enigmatic, his demise thrust the Kenyan police force into the spotlight. Their historical record, marred by allegations of extrajudicial killings, abductions and the systemic torture of suspects, emerges as a disquieting backdrop to this narrative.[16] Despite accusations of police officers' involvement in criminal activity, no cases have yet gone to trial. Sharif had many enemies in Pakistan and faced possible sedition charges before leaving the country. Accusations regarding his death have been made by various figures, including former minister Faisal Vawda, who alleged that the plan to kill Sharif was hatched in Pakistan, and Lieutenant General Nadeem Ahmed Anjum, the head of military intelligence, who named several individuals, including senior media figures, who might have been involved in Sharif's movements and death. The military denies any involvement, but the credibility of this denial remains a big question mark.[17]

Human Rights Watch Slams Pakistan

During Imran Khan's tenure as the head of Pakistan's government, his administration garnered widespread condemnation from both domestic and international human rights organizations. Foremost among these critical voices was Human Rights Watch (HRW), a prominent international human rights advocacy group headquartered in the United States. In an annual report, HRW delivered a scathing assessment of the Pakistani government's policies and actions, particularly in the context of an expanding crackdown on various segments of the population, including citizens, journalists and political opposition figures.

The central focus of HRW's critique pertained to several key areas, namely freedom of expression and religion, women's rights, and alleged instances of abuse perpetrated by Pakistan's law enforcement agencies and security forces. HRW contended that the Pakistani authorities had instrumentalized sedition and counterterrorism laws as tools to curtail dissent and exert control over civil society organizations critical of the government. Additionally, they undertook vigorous measures to suppress members and supporters of opposition political parties, thereby further narrowing the democratic space within the nation.

It is crucial to note that Khan's PTI-led coalition attempted to rectify perceived corruption within the prior administrations. However, under his rule, there emerged conspicuous indications of enhanced governmental oversight and influence over the journalistic community and media organizations. Journalists who dared to offer critiques of the government faced a harrowing spectrum of consequences, including abductions, physical assaults, gun violence and legal charges invoking sedition and other purported offences.

NGOs operating within Pakistan reported instances of intimidation, harassment and surveillance orchestrated by state authorities, engendering a palpable climate of fear and constraint. Furthermore, the government imposed bureaucratic hurdles that hindered the registration and operational efficacy of international humanitarian and human rights organizations within the nation's borders.

HRW's comprehensive report presents a stark portrait of the state of human rights and civil liberties in Pakistan during Imran Khan's tenure. The complex interplay of political agendas, institutional actions and societal repercussions underscores the profound implications of these developments for the country's democratic and human rights landscape, as well as its standing within the global human rights discourse.[18] This context is marred by the ever-increasing deployment of stringent blasphemy laws that are wielded indiscriminately against both religious minorities and members of the predominant Muslim community.

The HRW report provides disheartening documentation of widespread human rights transgressions, wherein women and children are portrayed as particularly vulnerable. The litany of abuses includes instances of violence, sexual assault, homicide, acid attacks, domestic brutality and coerced marriages. The grim reality is mirrored in Pakistan's disconcerting ranking of 167th out of 170 countries on the Georgetown University Global Women, Peace, and Security Index, reflecting the stark disparities in gender equality and safety. In addition to this distressing situation, human rights defenders estimate that a staggering 1,000 women fall victim to so-called 'honour killings' annually, emblematic of the deeply entrenched cultural and societal challenges confronting Pakistan.

In tandem with these domestic issues, HRW levelled accusations against Pakistani security forces, implicating them in a litany of human rights violations ranging from arbitrary detentions devoid of formal charges to extrajudicial killings. Concurrently, the report elucidated the persistence of violent attacks targeting both civilians and security personnel, perpetrated by armed groups that include the Tehrik-e-Taliban Pakistan, al-Qaeda and the Baluch Liberation Army.

The analytical purport of this comprehensive report is profound, offering a sobering insight into the various human rights challenges endemic to Pakistan. These issues are not isolated but rather interconnected, reflecting the intricate interplay of legal, societal and political forces that shape the country's human rights landscape. Consequently, there is an imperative to craft an approach to address these entrenched issues, not only from the perspective of domestic policy reform but within the broader context of international human rights discourse and advocacy.'[19]

Khan's Anti-Government Rallies

In a formal declaration, Imran Khan proclaimed the PTI's intention to orchestrate a significant political demonstration at Islamabad's Parade Ground on 2 July 2022. This rally was slated to serve as the inaugural salvo in a series of nationwide protests that had been conceived as a response to mounting concerns over inflationary trends and amendments to NAB legislation. The alterations to the NAB law that Imran Khan vociferously opposed had contained provisions with far-reaching implications. Notably, changes stipulated that inquiries into assets held in the names of family members could no longer be subject to scrutiny. Moreover, the legislation's retroactive effect from the year 1999 had the potential to exonerate individuals with political affiliations who may have been implicated in cases of corruption or financial impropriety.

Central to Imran Khan's call to action was a fervent plea directed at PTI supporters, beseeching them to actively participate in rallies within their respective cities, positing their involvement as a crucial investment in the 'future of their generations'. The core impetus behind the protests lay in Khan's vehement concerns over fundamental breaches of the constitutional order. It was of paramount importance, Khan acknowledged, to uphold the citizenry's prerogative to subject their elected representatives to scrutiny and accountability, particularly in matters related to fiduciary stewardship.

PTI, he declared, intended to contest changes within the judicial sphere by bringing a case to the Supreme Court. In doing so, PTI's intended recourse through legal channels underscored the party's commitment to upholding constitutional principles and seeking redress within the established framework of the Pakistani legal system.[20]

Imran Khan warned of the deleterious consequences of the NAB changes, which he perceived as an erosion of accountability mechanisms, which would have repercussions on the integrity of the nation's democratic institutions and financial probity. He suggested that Pakistan could devolve into a 'banana republic'. In substantiating his claim, he cited an alarming figure, alleging that corrupt elements, who had ostensibly misappropriated PKR 1.1 billion in public funds, were absolved of liability through the amendments to the NAB laws. Khan emphatically emphasized the noteworthy milestones achieved during the tenure of his government, including the surge in the nation's exports, an achievement he attributed to the burgeoning demand and export orders in the textile sector, primarily centred in Faisalabad. This commendable upswing in economic activity had, however, precipitated an unforeseen challenge: a shortage of labour within the booming textile industries.

Regrettably, Imran Khan lamented a distressing turn of events wherein the once-vibrant factories in Faisalabad had begun to shutter their operations, owing to the lack of workers available to keep up with the industry's surging demand. This unwelcome development, he contended, had given rise to an alarming escalation in unemployment rates. He ascribed these economic setbacks to the implementation of flawed policies by previous administrations characterized by corruption and inefficacy.

To substantiate his claims and elucidate the PTI government's accomplishments, Imran Khan referred to the statistical data gleaned from economic survey reports. According to these reports, the PTI government had not only created a conducive environment for economic growth but had surpassed its predecessors, the PML-N and PPP, in terms of job creation. He underscored that this notable feat had been achieved notwithstanding formidable challenges, such as the global COVID-19 pandemic, which had tested the resilience of economies worldwide.

In a bid to foster a comprehensive assessment of the PTI government's performance, Khan extended an open invitation to the populace. He encouraged citizens to undertake a rigorous comparative analysis, juxtaposing the current administration's achievements with those of the previous regimes. In doing so, he sought to engender a nuanced understanding of the socio-economic landscape, thereby contributing to a more informed discourse on Pakistan's recent political and economic history.[21]

The Assassination Attempt on Imran Khan

The assault on Imran Khan on 3 November 2022, an event supporters contended was an assassination attempt, elicited widespread international condemnation. Imran Khan had been spearheading a 'long march' of protests in Wazirabad, a locality situated in the northeastern region of Pakistan, to vociferously advocate for early elections to pave the way for his political resurgence. During the march Khan was speaking to throngs of assembled supporters atop a truck, encircled by aides and party members, when he found himself suddenly engulfed by a hail of gunfire. An assailant managed to shoot him in the leg before being intercepted by a courageous bystander. There was one fatality and at least ten people were injured; some contended that there was more than one attacker that day, though reports have been disputed. Khan was tended to, ushered into his bulletproof car and rushed to Shaukat Khanum Hospital in Lahore.

The attack had reverberations: schools closed in Islamabad following a call for nationwide protests by PTI. The gravity of the situation was underscored by President Arif Alvi, a founding member of PTI, who unequivocally labelled the attack as a 'heinous assassination attempt'.[22] Swift condemnation of the incident emanated from various quarters, including from Khan's political adversaries. Prime Minister Shahbaz Sharif promptly initiated an investigation into the matter.

Pakistan, already grappling with a protracted economic crisis and the devastating aftermath of recent floods, was in the throes of once more witnessing a recurrence of political violence. Not only that, but there was a whiff of conspiracy about the incident. In the immediate aftermath of the shooting, individuals within Khan's inner circle intimated that he had harboured suspicions implicating current political leaders, including Sharif, the interior minister and even a military general, in the orchestrating of the attack. A spokesman for Khan, Raoof Hasan, had asserted on the BBC's *Newshour* that the government had been actively pursuing Khan's physical elimination.

Subsequently, the police disclosed a video confession ostensibly recorded with the assailant who had purportedly attempted to assassinate Khan. When questioned about his motivations for the assault, the assailant claimed, 'He was misguiding the people. I wanted to kill him. I tried to kill him.' However, concerns have persisted regarding the circumstances under which this interview was conducted, and Khan's allies have dismissed the video as an attempt at obfuscation.

As of the present moment, the one suspect who was in custody has also been granted bail. The ramifications of this attack resonate deeply within Pakistan's socio-political landscape, evoking questions regarding political stability, security and the rule of law. The episode stands as a stark testament to the tumultuous nature of the nation's political discourse, underscored by the persistent spectre of violence and its implications for democratic processes and governance.[23]

Imran Khan, undeterred by the assassination attempt, led thousands of supporters in a 'long march' to Islamabad, calling for immediate elections. This march aimed to garner support following his removal from office via a no-confidence vote in April, which he attributed to collusion between Pakistan's opposition parties and the United States. Khan's recovery in the hospital saw him accusing Shahbaz Sharif, Interior Minister Rana Sanaullah and Army Major General Faisal Naseer of plotting against him. However, these allegations were denied by the military and Sharif's government, prompting calls for a judicial investigation. During an interview with journalist Piers Morgan, Khan disclosed two alleged assassination plots against him, but provided limited details. From Lahore, he warned that Pakistan teetered on the brink. He implored Supreme Court Chief Justice Umar Ata Bandial to intervene, citing a lack of trust in institutions.[24]

Khan's Popularity Soars

A recent Gallup poll reveals growing frustration among Pakistanis regarding the country's economic challenges, with 62 per cent of respondents attributing soaring inflation to the current coalition government, the PDM. The nation's precarious financial situation, teetering on the edge of default, has placed economic concerns at the forefront for voters.[25]

Simultaneously, Imran Khan has experienced a surge in support, with his approval ratings climbing from 36 per cent in January 2022 to 61 percent in February 2023. This suggests that many Pakistanis view Khan – who has steadfastly demanded free and fair elections while firmly rejecting any compromise on corruption, and has dismissed the need for military support and accused the PDM government of negatively impacting the economy – as a potential remedy for the nation's economic and political woes.[26]

Khan has emphasized that his party enjoyed the people's backing, obviating the necessity for military assistance. Khan contended that the caretaker government's primary duty was to oversee elections, highlighting incidents of violence and arrests during a PTI election rally.

Khan accused the government of fearing electoral scrutiny and alleged their intent to obstruct the elections. Khan decried the government's alleged pursuit of chaos, citing police aggressiveness towards PTI activists. However, he remained resolute in not affording the government the opportunity to disrupt the electoral process. Khan also accused the PDM of attempting to disqualify or imprison him to secure electoral victory and underscored his PTI party's preference for simultaneous elections, including for the National Assembly.[27]

The aftermath of the regime change in Pakistan highlighted the shortcomings of the new government and its impact on the country's political and economic stability. Shahbaz Sharif's government was unable to address the economic crisis during its year in power from April 2022 to August 2023. Its failure to effectively negotiate with the IMF and its selective approach to justice have exacerbated the situation, resulting in increased inflation and a devaluing currency. Furthermore, the government's use of authoritarian tactics, such as cracking down on protesters, eroded its credibility.

In addition to these issues, the tragic murder of Arshad Sharif and the bold assassination attempt on Imran Khan raised doubts about the PDM government's commitment to democracy. This inadvertently boosted support for the previous government and its leader, Khan.

IN THE PURSUIT of a more promising future for the citizens of Pakistan, it has been imperative to delve into the root causes of the nation's political and economic tribulations. The ascendant popularity of Imran Khan, as discerned through his electoral victories in by-elections, was a noteworthy phenomenon. These triumphs were achieved despite a backdrop of scepticism regarding the impartiality of the electoral commission and the overt backing of the establishment.

Nonetheless, the actions of the PDM government, which stood accused of constitutional transgressions and a disregard for the tenets of the rule of law, revealed a palpable reluctance to conduct elections in the regions of the Punjab and Khyber Pakhtunkhwa, even when confronted with a constitutional deadline. Regrettably, the unequivocal directives of the Supreme Court were met with non-compliance. Many speculated that the government was intentionally postponing the electoral process, awaiting a moment when they could be assured of Imran Khan's exclusion from returning to power. Furthermore, the 'establishment' perpetually floated the notion of instituting a technocratic government for a period of two to three years, ostensibly to address the pressing economic challenges before the resumption of elections. This proposition, while captivating, was often regarded as fantastical and far-fetched.

It is incumbent upon us to recognize that substantial reforms can only come about when there exists a genuine political resolve, coupled with an unwavering commitment to the principles of the rule of law and constitutional supremacy. These are invaluable lessons, yet it appears that Pakistan's de facto leaders remain obstinately disinclined to assimilate them, thereby ushering in an era of uncertainty in the present and an unpredictable trajectory for the nation's future.

Epilogue

> The only true prison is fear, and the only real freedom is freedom from fear.
>
> Aung San Suu Kyi

In an ironic twist, the use of fear is promoted in Pakistan under the guise of protecting freedom. The word *azadi* can be translated into English as 'independence', 'freedom' or 'liberation', each with subtly different connotations. Independence typically refers to the self-governance and sovereignty of a nation, state or country. While Pakistan has celebrated its independence for 77 years, the nation's ruling elite have been more concerned with their own interests and external dependencies than with the collective will and interests of the people. As a result, Pakistan is still largely dependent on foreign resources, with America controlling the largest share. In such a scenario, it is hard to say that Pakistan is truly independent.

Freedom lies at the core of a citizen's rights, encompassing the ability to express oneself, take action, and gather and hold personal beliefs. Yet, in Pakistan's society, which is marked by social hierarchies, freedom often remains a distant goal rather than a tangible reality. To truly protect freedom, a robust justice system is essential, but unfortunately, Pakistan lacks such a system. As a result, it appears unlikely that we will see true liberty realized in the near future.

When the Muslim League leadership took charge after gaining independence, they were filled with enthusiasm at the prospect of wielding power. However, they seemed unprepared and unwilling to bear the accompanying responsibilities. This led to a prevailing sense of mistrust that permeated the national narrative. The public began to view their representatives as inept, ignorant and corrupt, creating a disconnect between authority and responsibility. It is also worth noting that our non-political elite showed a greater inclination to change masters rather than to embrace true independence, including sovereignty.

Such endeavours have been in progress since 1951, facilitated by prominent figures such as Malik Ghulam Muhammad, Chaudhary Muhammad Ali, Iskander Mirza and Ayub Khan. During the 1950s, the United States

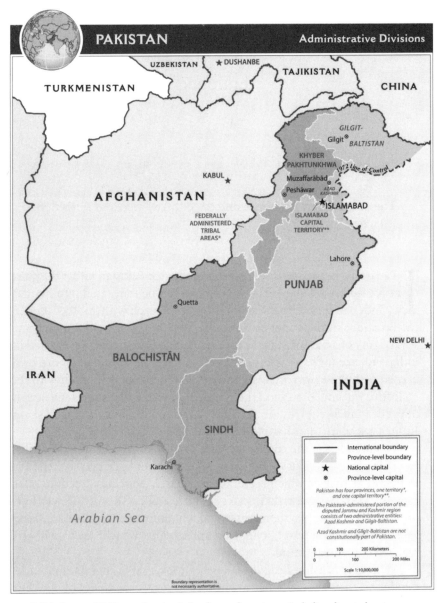

Political map of Pakistan, showing its borders and provinces, including disputed regions and their administrative entities.

regarded these individuals as sympathetic to its interests. Despite the United States exhibiting no evident inclination to offer sustained support, these non-political actors persisted in engaging in manoeuvres aimed at garnering American attention. Eventually, the United States was wooed and SEATO and CENTO were signed. Was the will of the people taken into account when signing these pacts? There seems to have been no specific benefit.

Epilogue

The second concept shrouded in ambiguity is that of sovereignty. Sovereignty has been ambivalent for Pakistani state managers from the outset. It is not clear whether the term was used before the Objectives Resolution in 1949, so it is necessary to investigate the speeches of Quaid-e-Azam to determine if he used the term, and if so, in what context. If we look at the issue differently, it can be inferred that the North Indian Muslim elite did not aspire to be a sovereign entity. Iqbal valued freedom, but he vacillated between individual freedom and its ties to the Muslim *ummah*. In general, the Muslim political elite showed little enthusiasm for achieving sovereignty, so it was neither defined nor conceptualized after independence. It was only mentioned ambiguously in the Objectives Resolution. The Muslim political elite wanted to rid themselves of Hindu domination, and they had valid reasons for choosing that path. Therefore, the argument that Pakistan did not experience a colonial moment has some validity. The top echelon of South Asian Muslims, mostly in north India, had little objection to British rule or to their presence in the subcontinent. Even today, Pakistani textbooks do not teach about colonialism and its consequences. That is why Pakistan is described as a neo-colonial state instead of a postcolonial polity, because it is yet to be independent in its decision making. Neo-colonialism is the continuation or reimposition of imperialist rule by a state (usually a former colonial power) over another nominally independent state (usually a former colony). Kwame Nkrumah, Ghana's first president, coined the term 'neo-colonialism' in 1965 to describe the influence of former imperial nations on ex-colonies in the areas of economy, language, culture and political philosophy. The term 'postcolonial state' usually refers to the new nation states that emerged from the decolonization process in the post-Second World War period. Another term sometimes used is the 'developmental state'. The postcolonial state exhibited many features of the colonial state in its political formation. In postcolonial countries, the anti-colonial/imperialist impulse is relatively strong, and the people of these countries are conscious of their sovereignty, which is tied to public sentiment and expression. In neocolonial polities, sovereignty and freedom hold only semantic value. All major decisions are made at the behest of metropolitan centres located in the imperialist world. After reviewing Pakistan's political history, the nation clearly falls into the latter category.

Pakistan emerged as a nation state on 14–15 August 1947, underpinned by an ideology of pan-Islamism. However, Khalid bin Sayeed described the creation of Pakistan as an 'aberration from the norm' due to its unique concept. Nation states usually exist in contradistinction to unilateralism drawn from a universal ideology, like pan-Islamism. The Muslim leadership in Pakistan validated its claim for a separate state by foregrounding the category of 'Muslim' as universal. Pakistan drew its *raison d'être* from religion, which made it a contradiction in terms. It is practically a nation state predicated on the ideology drawn from pan-Islamism. This paradox presented an opportunity to craft innovative solutions by amalgamating the political threads linked to both tradition and modernity. However, such an ambition was an exceedingly tall order considering the leadership vacuum that ensued after the passing of Jinnah. Nonetheless, the potential for creative synthesis remained, awaiting a visionary leader to rise to the challenge.

Pakistan's founding fathers (Allama) Muhammad Iqbal and Quaid-e-Azam Muhammad Ali Jinnah, the former an ideological/philosophical and the latter a political leader, set in motion a process of dialectics of ideas culminating in a new synthesis. Any socio-political formation like Pakistan, containing contradictory currents (cultural, ethnic, sectarian or linguistic), has the potential to evolve into a plural sociocultural space with a powerful ethos. Such a synthesis can only be brought about by an effective leadership, which Jinnah tried to do when he addressed the Constituent Assembly in Karachi on 11 August 1947.

However, Jinnah's demise derailed the whole process, and the reins of power fell into the hands of a military–bureaucratic oligarchy, which indisputably tilted towards the United States. The process of constitution-making slowed down, and the erosion of democratic institutions stymied the state's bid to acquire a representative character. Consequently, any effective arbitration between disparate cultural, religious or sectarian groups became a virtually impossible proposition. Socio-political synthesis came to a halt, and forces of exclusion were unleashed. Despite catastrophic ramifications, the military–bureaucratic clique, referred to now as the establishment, continues to wield all powers, and civilian/elected representatives are allowed extremely limited space.

Zahid Hussain, in one of his pieces for *Dawn*, describes the establishment in Pakistan as the 'deep state cooperative federation' of the Pakistan armed forces, the Pakistani intelligence community and other pro-military government officials and civilians. He laments the fact that the establishment has a long history of meddling in politics, reinventing political discourse and structure to fit its own agenda. Having ruled Pakistan for almost three decades, both directly and indirectly, it tends to pull strings from behind the scenes, ousting elected governments, conjuring up pressure groups, causing splits in parties and dividing their vote bank. Moreover, it finances opposition parties to unhinge elected set-ups to maintain its stranglehold on political power. The usual perception is that politicians want to be on the right side of the armed forces to share power with them. The Asghar Khan case, when the establishment distributed funds to parties it wanted to share power with, is a vivid testimony to this. Although some politicians have stood up to the military's hegemonic role and continued political interference, there has never been a dearth of civilian leaders willing to do the establishment's bidding for a share in power. In the absence of a representative character, mediatory options that require negotiation have not been adopted. Coercive (and exclusionary) mechanisms have been used without giving any consideration to the consequences they may yield. Resultantly, epithets like *ghadar* (traitor), *kafir*, infidel and *fasiq o fajir* are used in profusion.

From 1949, with the passage of the Objectives Resolution and the establishment of Majlis-i-Tahafuz-i-Khatam-i-Nabuwwat (MTKN), exclusion became a defining feature of the Pakistani polity. The anti-Ahmadi movement in 1953 was launched by clerics associated with MTKN calling for Ahmadis' exclusion from the fold of Islam. In 1974, MTKN bounced back with such severity that Zulfiqar Ali Bhutto's government eventually gave in, and Ahmadis were declared non-Muslims by the parliament. Bhutto could not resolve that issue through dialogue. That opened the door for yet another exclusion, that of Shias.

Exclusion was not confined to casting out religious minorities only; cultural and linguistic specificities of different groups and factions were also called into question. The military–bureaucratic oligarchy orchestrated this xenophobic trend. The language movement in East Bengal (later East Pakistan and eventually Bangladesh in 1971) in the early 1950s was a case in point. Political injustice and travesties done in the realms of culture and language paved the way for the separation of East Pakistan in December 1971. Bengalis, despite their majority, were denied their proportion of representation, and the principle of parity was introduced.

The Bengali language was given the status of a national language after prolonged agitation that resulted in significant loss of life. General Ayub Khan's centralized control, his strong-arm tactics and his visible bias against Bengalis became the foremost cause of their separation. General Yahya Khan, his successor, resorted to extreme violence to suppress dissidents in East Pakistan, which proved disastrous and resulted in the severing of the eastern wing of the country. With democratic institutions denied an opportunity to strike firm roots and attain maturity in Pakistan, the political issues were settled through physical suppression instead of negotiation. Pakistan, despite 77 years of existence, has failed to evolve to the level whereby it can resolve its issues through negotiation, which is a cause for concern. Intimidation instead of negotiation has been the ploy used by the state authority to settle contentious issues.

During General Zia's eleven years of draconian rule (1977–88), coercion and exclusion were institutionalized as policy. The Hudood Ordinance was promulgated to limit the freedom of women. The Zakat and Ushr Ordinances were enforced, which drove a wedge between Shias and Sunnis. Shias protested against this arbitrary legislation, which they thought was undue interference in their religious practice. Therefore, General Zia orchestrated the establishment of the SSP, an anti-Shia militant group. A blasphemy law was implemented, which was used as an instrument of repression against minorities. In this regard, the year 1979 was crucial because of the Soviet Union's invasion of Afghanistan, Zia's Islamization process and the Iranian revolution that mobilized the Pakistani Shia community. These developments strengthened puritanical tendencies that accorded legitimacy to religious exclusion. The Pakistani citizenry was divided not only in terms of ethnic/linguistic differentiation but in sectarian terms, Muslim and non-Muslim. Thus, exclusion became standard practice during those eleven years.

Zia died on 17 August 1988, and the rule of the troika and the establishmentarian democracy began, with American oversight. In such models of government, forged as they are as military bureaucracies, democracy mostly exists as a ruse – the real authority is exercised by the army-led establishment. Pakistan had six prime ministers during this period (Benazir Bhutto and Nawaz Sharif each had two stints as prime minister) and four chiefs of the armed forces (General Asif Nawaz died prematurely). In this period, the Army chief was the strongest member of the troika, and the elected prime minister was the weakest and most vulnerable. Therefore, no government could complete its full term. Dissolution of the Assembly was the recurrent feature. Zia's legacy reigned supreme as religious extremism and sectarian antagonism became evident social trends. Horse-trading, corruption and jobbery became prevalent as never before. Both contenders for the slot of prime minister, Benazir Bhutto and Nawaz Sharif, competed in the realm of corruption. In October 1999, this period of (mis)rule came to an end when General Pervez Musharraf deposed Nawaz Sharif, who tried to sack the former upon his return from an official visit to Sri Lanka.

The top brass of the Pakistani military reacted strongly, resulting in the unceremonious ousting of Prime Minister Nawaz Sharif during General Pervez Musharraf's reign (1999–2008), which was characterized by religious militancy and sectarian antagonism. Events such as 9/11 greatly damaged Pakistan's reputation. Musharraf acquiesced to U.S. pressure to launch a war on terror against the Taliban government in Afghanistan, which had enduring repercussions on Pakistan. This, along with other incidents, polarized Pakistani politics and strengthened religious fundamentalism. Like his predecessors, Musharraf suffered from a legitimacy deficit, and thus had to align his interests with politicians of dubious reputation.

The Red Mosque incident in 2007 proved to be a turning point that led to the emergence of militant organizations such as the Tehrik-e-Taliban Pakistan and Lashkar-i-Taiba. These groups unleashed a reign of terror from 2007 until 2018, significantly contributing to the ripping apart of Pakistan's social fabric. The gory upshot of religious militancy was the assassination of Benazir Bhutto in December 2007, and the killing of Akbar Bugti, which resulted in political instability in Baluchistan. Like dictators before him, Musharraf wore the garb of a messiah and tried to engage in political re-engineering, which paved the way for corrupt politicians such as Sharif and Bhutto to stage a comeback.

Epilogue

Nawaz Sharif (left) and prime minister of India Narendra Modi, New Delhi, 2014.

The period of civilian rule that followed Musharraf's regime was characterized by a distinct lack of continuity. From Asif Zardari's tenure (2008–13) to subsequent prime ministers, including Nawaz Sharif (2013–17), Shahid Khaqqan Abbasi (2017–18) and Imran Khan (2018–22), the landscape of leadership constantly shifted. None of them were allowed to complete their full term, resulting in an average government tenure of merely three to three and a half years.

The true locus of power remained the Army, which exercised significant influence over a wide array of matters, ranging from foreign policy and political alliances to the management of financial institutions, utility stores, the National Logistic Cell and Defense Housing Societies. Moreover, the Army's sway extended into the realm of the judiciary. Despite instances of blatantly disregarding the Constitution, Army chiefs have managed to evade prosecution.

Pakistan experienced its worst possible state of chaos under President Zardari. Incidents such as the killing of Osama bin Laden in Abbottabad by U.S. marines, Raymond Davis's killing of three people in Lahore; the Salalla incident, where several Pakistani troops were killed by the Americans; and the Memogate scandal, where Zardari sought American help against his deposition orchestrated by Pakistan's Army, added to the chaos. There was an unending spate of suicide bombings and drone attacks that caused substantial collateral damage, and corruption soared to unprecedented levels. The dismal state of the economy, coupled with bad governance, was the legacy of PPP government under Asif Ali Zardari.

Things stabilized somewhat under Nawaz Sharif's government. His brother Shahbaz Sharif kept a firm hold on the Punjab, the biggest and most resourceful province. However, in 2016, General Raheel Sharif completed his term as Army chief, and Nawaz Sharif picked General Qamar Javed Bajwa as his successor. As events unfolded, it became clear that Bajwa was more interested in politics than in the affairs of the Army. He proved to be a corrupt conspirator, as his family members accumulated billions of rupees, primarily from the business of real estate. Apart from Bajwa assuming the impregnable slot of chief of Army staff things went awry for Sharif when the Panama Papers scandal hit the house of Sharif. Nawaz Sharif's loss of power and defeat in the 2018 elections dealt a severe blow to his political career. He and his associates blamed General Bajwa for their defeat. Imran Khan, a renowned cricketing icon and philanthropist, took over as the 22nd prime minister of Pakistan at a time when the country was facing numerous challenges, including locust attacks, the COVID-19 pandemic, U.S. indifference and strained relations with India's Narendra Modi.

Khan confronted a formidable challenge, grappling with a media landscape often adversarial, a vociferous opposition and an Army chief renowned for navigating both sides of the political spectrum. In the face of these formidable obstacles, Khan embarked on a course aimed at aligning Pakistan more closely with China, a move that is widely perceived as the principal catalyst for his removal from power by the military leadership and the ISI on 9 April 2022. Since his removal from power, Khan's popularity has soared, and he has remained a thorn in the side of both the PDM government, a thirteen-party alliance, and the establishment. Khan encountered numerous challenges, from minor disputes about his character to accusations of terrorism and treason, all of which were subject to dispute.

At the moment, Pakistan's economy remains on the brink of disaster. Given these circumstances, the future of beleaguered Pakistan does not hold much promise, particularly given its 77-year history of turmoil. Throughout Pakistan's history, the establishment has steadily enhanced its influence, encompassing domestic politics, national security, governance and foreign and economic policies. Its presence is palpable in every sphere, from the media, judiciary and academic institutions to business. The establishment, which refers to the military and its associated institutions, reacts strongly whenever civilian leaders try to restrict the military to its constitutional duty of protecting Pakistan and its people from foreign threats. Instead of accepting these limits, the establishment takes actions to weaken elected governments and disrupt the democratic process. At the same time, it maintains the appearance of being impartial and supportive of democratic governments. However, this facade of neutrality and support has come to be seen in a negative light, as it is perceived as a cover for actions that undermine civilian authority and the democratic system.

To steer Pakistan towards certainty and stability, what steps must be taken? The foremost and most vital precondition is to establish the rule of law. It is the fundamental principle that must be upheld by the Pakistani people, and any violation of rules or the Constitution must result in accountability. Rule of law dictates that governments should operate under general legislation that is applicable to both governors and citizens, as opposed to irregular decrees and *ad hominem* proclamations. This provides citizens with the ability to accurately anticipate the legal implications of their actions, eliminating any 'surprises' that may arise from legislation. The laws must also adhere to certain substantive principles and rights without violating them. An independent judiciary must defend the rule of law, which plays a crucial role in protecting civil and political rights, as well as civil liberties. It also must safeguard the equality and dignity of citizens.

The rule of law acts as a safeguard against tyranny, ensuring that rulers do not become corrupt or despotic. Fair, just and impartial laws protect individuals from the government's highhandedness, organizations and other mafia networks. A welfare state is a desirable goal that is sustained by the rule of law. It is characterized by a durable system of laws, institutions, norms and community commitments that ensures accountability. Both government and private actors are held accountable under laws that are clear, publicized, stable and applied consistently.

The rule of law is closely linked to democratic ideals, where citizens elect their leaders and the government is bound by the law. Equality is fundamental to the rule of law, and no individual should face any form of distinction or discrimination. The right to equal protection of the law is a fundamental principle in a democratic society. It guarantees that all individuals, regardless of their economic status, ethnicity, religion or political affiliation, are entitled to the same protection.

This concept comprises three fundamental principles. First, authorities should not interfere with or punish individuals unless they have violated the law. Second, the law applies to everyone, and no one is above it. Third, a bill of rights is unnecessary since judicial decisions determine the general principles of the Constitution and the rights of private individuals.

To achieve stability, it is imperative to implement wide-ranging reforms aimed at civilianizing the structure of governance. One of the critical steps in this regard is to significantly rationalize the powers and role of the Army top brass. The Pakistani Army chief currently holds a position of unparalleled strength and influence, making the position one of the most powerful jobs in the world.

It is essential to ensure that the appointment of top officials within the military is not left solely at the discretion of one person. Civilian input in the selection of the corps commanders and promotions beyond the rank of brigadier must be made mandatory. The excessive perks and privileges awarded to top Army officers require drastic rationalization, as their documented assets are astonishingly greater than those of any other citizen in Pakistan. To achieve stability and certainty in Pakistan, it is crucial to re-evaluate the role of the ISI's internal wing. This department should either be abolished entirely or have its role completely redefined. The fact that the Army's military intelligence exists alongside the ISI, which operates under the Army chief's authority, is unprecedented. In order to prevent the Army's interference in politics – the root cause of many issues – the ISI should be civilianized like other intelligence agencies around the globe.

In essence, a comprehensive overhaul of the military structure is necessary, with a shift towards a more civilian-orientated system of governance. This would help to ensure that the Army is not overly dominant and operates within its designated role as a protector of the nation's borders, rather than as a wielder of political power. Such reforms would go a long way in promoting transparency, accountability and stability within the country, ultimately benefiting all its citizens.

Another crucial aspect of ensuring stability in Pakistan is the reform of its judiciary system. The selection of judges must be made through a rigorously conducted competitive examination process and they should undergo training courses at every stage of their career. Politicians must not have any say in their selection and appointment process, and a system of accountability should be in place to ensure that any judge found guilty of corruption is held responsible for their actions.

Unfortunately, since 2007, judges have started conducting themselves like politicians, which is in direct contradiction to the long-standing convention that they are meant to comply with. This must be addressed, and measures should be taken to ensure that the judiciary functions independently and upholds the rule of law. By implementing these reforms, Pakistan can establish a fair and impartial judicial system that serves its citizens and promotes the stability of the country as a whole.

To address the deeply ingrained issue of dynastic politics in Pakistan, it is imperative that elections within political parties become mandatory. Any party that fails to adhere to this requirement should not be allowed to participate in national elections. This is a crucial step towards breaking the cycle of political dynasties that have plagued Pakistani politics for far too long. By making internal party elections mandatory, aspiring politicians would have a fair chance to compete for positions of power and influence within their respective parties, regardless of their family background or connections. This would promote a more merit-based political culture and encourage talented individuals to enter politics, rather than merely candidates relying on family connections.

Furthermore, this would also help to ensure that political parties are more representative of the broader population and not just a few powerful families. By promoting a more inclusive and democratic internal party structure, Pakistan can take a significant step towards establishing a more vibrant and equitable political landscape.

After establishing the rule of law, freedom of the press is arguably the most critical aspect for progress and growth. As emphasized previously, freedom is a *sine qua non* for both material and sociocultural advancement. Freedom of speech, thought and action are key factors in driving progress and evolution, and freedom of the press plays a vital role in promoting intellectual vibrancy within a society. It creates a robust public sphere that fosters creative processes, allowing for the free exchange of ideas and opinions. This, in turn, fuels innovation, critical thinking and the development of a more engaged and informed citizenry.

Thus safeguarding freedom of the press is crucial for ensuring a healthy and thriving democracy. It enables citizens to access accurate and diverse information, to hold their leaders accountable, and to participate actively in public discourse. By prioritizing freedom of the press, Pakistan can create an environment that encourages progress, growth and a vibrant exchange of ideas.

REFERENCES

1 From Prehistory to the Early Modern Era, 3800 BCE to 1707 CE

1 For exclusion of the pre-Muslim period from Pakistan's history, see A. H. Nayyar and Ahmed Salim, *The Subtle Subversion: The State of Curricula and Textbooks in Pakistan* (Islamabad and New York), pp. 66–71.
2 For further details, see Jamil Jalibi, , vol. II (Lahore, 2015), pp. 375–718.
3 Irfan Habib, *A People's History of India*, vol. I: *Prehistory* (New Delhi, 2001), p. 1.
4 Ibid., p. 6.
5 Ibid.
6 The Siwalik Hills, also called the Siwalik Range (Siwalik, also spelled Shiwalik (from Sanskrit, meaning 'Belonging to [the God] Shiva'), is a sub-Himalayan range of the northern Indian subcontinent. It extends west-northwestward for more than 1,600 kilometres (1,000 mi.) from the Tista River in Sikkim state, northeastern India, through Nepal, across northwestern India, and into northern Pakistan. Though only 16 kilometres (10 mi.) wide in places, the range has an average elevation of 900 to 1,200 metres (3,000–4,000 ft). It rises abruptly from the plain of the Indus and Ganges (Ganga) rivers (south) and parallels the main range of the Himalayas (north), from which it is separated by valleys.
7 Habib, *A People's History of India*, vol. I, p. 7.
8 For more details see 'Ramapithecus', *Encyclopaedia Britannica*, www.britannica.com, accessed 5 February 2024.
9 Habib, *A People's History of India*, vol. I, p. 21.
10 Mortimer Wheeler, *Civilizations of the Indus Valley and Beyond* (London, 1966), p. 9.
11 A. H. Dani, *A Short History of Pakistan*, vol. I: *Pre-Muslim Period* [1967], ed. I. H. Qureshi (Karachi, 2019), p. 32.
12 Ibid.
13 Ibid.
14 Ibid., p. 26.
15 Ibid.
16 Ibid.
17 The archaeological site of Kot Diji is adjacent to Khairpur district in Sindh. The remains of Kot Diji consist of two parts: the citadel area on high ground, and the outer area. The Pakistan Department of Archaeology excavated at Kot Diji in 1955 and 1957. See Yahya Amjad, *Tarikh-i-Pakistan: Qadim Daur-Zamana-i-Qabal az Tarikh* (Lahore, 1989), p. 245.
18 Irfan Habib, *People's History of India*, vol. II: *The Indus Civilization* (New Delhi, 2015), p. 9.
19 Ibid.
20 Ibid.

21 Kalibangān is a town located on the left or southern banks of the Ghaggar in Tehsil Pilibangān, between Suratgarh and Hanumangarh in the Hanumangarh district, Rajasthan, India, 205 kilometres (127 mi.) from Bikaner. For further details, see B. B. Lal, 'The Indus Civilization', in *A Cultural History of India*, ed. A. L. Basham (New Delhi, 1975), p. 11.
22 Habib, *People's History of India*, vol. II, pp. 10–11.
23 Ibid., p. 11.
24 Ibid.
25 Ibid., p. 12.
26 Ibid., p. 36.
27 Amjad, *Tarikh-i-Pakistan*, p. 266.
28 Chris Scarre and Brian M. Fagan, *Ancient Civilizations* (New York and Oxon, 2016), p. 6.
29 Habib, *People's History of India*, vol. II, p. 14.
30 Ibid., pp. 15–16.
31 D. N. Jha, *Ancient India: In Historical Outline* (New Delhi, 2009), p. 32.
32 Amjad, *Tarikh-i-Pakistan*, pp. 281–4.
33 For architecture and town planning, see Wheeler, *Civilizations of the Indus Valley and Beyond*, pp. 14–34.
34 Habib, *People's History of India*, vol. II, p. 42.
35 Pandit Madho Sarup Vats (1896–1955) was an Indian archaeologist and Sanskrit scholar who held the position of director general at the Archaeological Survey of India from 1950 to 1954. He is most notably recognized for his pivotal role in overseeing the excavations at Mohenjo Daro starting in 1924. Sir Robert Eric Mortimer Wheeler (1890–1976) was a distinguished British archaeologist renowned for his significant archaeological findings in both Great Britain and India. He is also celebrated for his pioneering contributions to the advancement of scientific methods within the field of archaeology.
36 Habib, *People's History of India*, vol. II, p. 45.
37 Ibid., pp. 45–6.
38 Ibid.
39 A. L. Basham, *The Wonder That Was India* [1954] (Karachi, 2004), pp. 19–20.
40 For exhaustive detail on trade, see Amjad, *Tarikh-i-Pakistan*, pp. 286–93.
41 Habib, *People's History of India*, vol. II, p. 47.
42 Ibid., pp. 47–8.
43 S.M.S. Sajjadi, F. Foruzanfar, R. Shirazi and S. Baghestani, 'Excavations at Shahr-i Sokhta: First Preliminary Report on the Excavations of the Graveyard, 1997–2000', *British Journal of Persian Studies*, XLI/1 (2003), pp. 21–97.
44 Habib, *People's History of India*, vol. II, pp. 48–9.
45 Claudio Giardino, *Magan: The Land of Copper: Prehistoric Metallurgy of Oman* (Oxford, 2019), pp. 7–19.
46 Habib, *People's History of India*, vol. II, p. 49.
47 Ibid.
48 Ibid., p. 62.
49 Jha, *Ancient India*, p. 39.
50 Habib, *A People's History of India*, vol. II, p. 62.
51 Ibid., pp. 63–4.
52 Dani, *A Short History of Pakistan*, vol. I, pp. 1–2.
53 Wendy Doniger, *The Hindus: An Alternative History* (New York, 2009), pp. 90–91.
54 Romila Thapar, *A History of India*, vol. I (London, 1990), p. 23.
55 Ibid., p. 18.
56 Ibid.
57 Ibid.

58 Dani, *A Short History of Pakistan*, vol. I, p. 50.
59 Thapar, *History of India*, vol. I, pp. 1–20.
60 Dani, *A Short History of Pakistan*, vol. I, p. 51.
61 Thapar, *History of India*, vol. I, p. 25.
62 Touqir Ahmad Warraich, 'Gandhara: Appraisal of Its Meaning and History', *Journal of Research Society of Pakistan*, XLVIII/1 (2011), p. 1.
63 Muhammad bin Naveed, 'Gandhara Civilization', www.worldhistory.org.com, 7 July 2015.
64 Ibid.
65 Ibid.
66 For the Kushans, see Burton Stein, *A History of India*, 2nd edn (Hoboken, NJ, 2010), p. 86.
67 Mortimer Wheeler, *Five Thousand Years of Pakistan* (London, 1950), pp. 26–47.
68 For Taxila as the centre for learning, see Dani, *A Short History of Pakistan*, vol. I, p. 88.
69 John Keay, *India: A History: From the Earliest Civilisations to the Boom of the Twenty-First Century* (London, 2000), pp. 143–4.
70 Muhammad bin Naveed, 'Gandhara Civilization'. Also see Basham, *The Wonder That Was India*, pp. 49–59.
71 Muhammad bin Naveed, 'Gandhara Civilization'.
72 Ibid.
73 Ibid.
74 Barbara and Thomas Metcalf, *A Concise History of Modern India* (Cambridge, 2006), p. 3.
75 Ibid.
76 Ibid.
77 Richard M. Eaton, *India in the Persianate Age: 1000–1765* (London, 2019), p. 3.
78 Ibid.
79 The Slave (Mamluk) dynasty (1206–90), Khiliji dynasty (1290–1330), Tughlaq dynasty (1330–1413), Syed dynasty (1414–51) and Lodhi dynasty (1451–1526). For details, see S.A.A. Rizvi, 'The Muslim Ruling Dynasties', in *A Cultural History of India*, ed. A. L. Basham (Delhi, 1983), pp. 245–65.
80 Prithviraja III (Sanskrit: Pṛthvī-rāja; r. c. 1177–92 CE), popularly known as Prithviraj Chauhan or Rai Pithora, was a king from the Chauhan (Chahamana) dynasty who ruled the territory of Sapadalaksha, with his capital at Ajmer in present-day Rajasthan. K. S. Lal, *The Legacy of Muslim Rule in India* (New Delhi, 1992), p. 76.
81 For example, James Mill, *The History of British India* (London, 1817).
82 Peter Hardy, 'Islam in Medieval India', in *Sources of Indian Tradition*, vol. I: *From the Beginning to 1800*, ed. Ainslie T. Embree (New Delhi, 1992), p. 465.
83 Metcalf and Metcalf, *A Concise History of Modern India*, p. 5.
84 K. K. Khullar, *Amir Khusrau aur Humara Mushtarka Culture* (New Delhi, 1983).
85 Saiyid Athar Abbas Rizvi, *A History of Sufism in India: Early Sufism and Its History in India to AD 1600* (Lahore, 2004), p. 170; S. M. Ikram, *History of Muslim Civilization in India and Pakistan: A Political and Cultural History* (Lahore, 2007).
86 See Aziz Ahmad, *Studies in Islamic Culture in the Indian Environment* (Oxford, 1964), pp. 115–18; and Manan Ahmed Asif, *The Loss of Hindustan: The Invention of India* (Lahore, 2022), pp. 121–8 and 132–3.
87 For more detail on Amir Khursu, see Tabasum Kashmiri, *Urdu Adab ki Tarekh: Ibtada say 1857 Tak* (Lahore, 2020), pp. 29–35.
88 Khullar, *Amir Khusrau aur Humara Mushtarka Culture*.
89 Waheed Mirza, *The Life and Works of Amir Khusru* (Calcutta, 1936).
90 Gopi Chand Narang, *Amir Khusrau ka Hindavi Kalam* (Lahore, 2021).
91 Ibid.

92 Ibid.
93 Janet Lippman Abu-Lughod, 'The World System in the Thirteenth Century: Dead-End or Precursor?', in *Islamic and European Expansion: The Forging of a Global Order*, ed. Michael Adas (Philadelphia, PA, 1993), pp. 75–102.
94 Ivan Hrbek, 'Ibn Battuta', *Encyclopaedia Britannica*, www.britannica.com, accessed 7 August 2022.
95 S.A.A. Rizvi, *The Wonder That Was India, 1200–1700* (New Delhi, 1994), p. 182.
96 Metcalf and Metcalf, *A Concise History of Modern India*, p. 6.
97 Ibid.
98 Richard M. Eaton, *The Rise of Islam and the Bengal Frontier, 1204–1760* (Berkeley, CA, 1993), p. 30.
99 Susan Bayly, *Caste, Society and Politics in India from the Eighteenth Century to the Modern Age* (Cambridge, 1999), p. 50.
100 Metcalf and Metcalf, *A Concise History of Modern India*, pp. 5–20.
101 The Quwwat-ul-Islam Mosque is one of the oldest surviving mosques in India, and it was solely built to celebrate the victory of Mohammed Ghuri against the Rajputs. Initially, the building of the mosque was started by Qutub-ud-din Aibak as a token of respect for his master Mohammed Ghuri when the latter became the sultan. Rizvi, *The Wonder That Was India*, pp. 277–9.
102 Metcalf and Metcalf, *A Concise History of Modern India*, p. 6.
103 For greater details on Sufism, see S.A.A. Rizvi, *A History of Sufism in India* (New Delhi, 2012). Also see Annemarie Schimmel, *Mystical Dimensions of Islam* (Lahore, 2006).
104 Metcalf and Metcalf, *A Concise History of Modern India*, p. 6.
105 For details on Mughals, see Harbans Mukhia, *The Mughals of India* (Malden, MA, 2004); John F. Richards, *The Mughal Empire* (Cambridge, 2000); Ishwari Prashad, *A Short History of Muslim Rule in India: From the Advent of Islam to the Death of Aurangzeb* (New Delhi, 2018) and S. M. Ikram, *History of Muslim Civilization in India and Pakistan* (Lahore, 2007).
106 Ahmad, *Studies in Islamic Culture in the Indian Environment*; Yohanan Friedmann, *Shaikh Aḥmad Sirhindī: An Outline of His Thought and a Study of His Image in the Eyes of Posterity* (New Delhi, 2000).
107 Jha, *Ancient India*, p. 19.
108 For details, see John Richards, *The Mughal Empire* (Cambridge, 2000), pp. 196–204.
109 For details, see Marshal G. S. Hodgson, *The Venture of Islam*, vol. III: *The Gunpowder Empires and Modern Times* (Chicago, IL, 1974), pp. 16–22.
110 For that debate see Metcalf and Metcalf, *A Concise History of Modern India*, pp. 2–4.
111 Richards, *The Mughal Empire*, p. 150. Also see Daud Ali, *Courtly Culture and Political Life in Early Medieval India* (Cambridge, 2004).
112 Metcalf and Metcalf, *A Concise History of Modern India*, p. 30.
113 Muzaffar Alam, *The Crisis of Empire in Mughal North India: Awadh and Punjab* (New Delhi, 1997), pp. 20–31.
114 Metcalf and Metcalf, *A Concise History of Modern India*, p. 30.
115 Ibid., pp. 30–31.
116 Ibid.
117 Ibid., p. 31.
118 Ibid.
119 Ishrat Haque, *Glimpses of Mughal Society and Culture: A Study Based on Urdu Literature, in the 2nd Half of the 18th Century* (New Delhi, 1992), pp. 38–40.

References

2 British Rule and the Rise of Muslim Nationalism

1. Philip Lawson, *The East India Company: A History* (London, 1993), pp. 16–17.
2. Tania Sengupta, 'Indian Subcontinent: 1750–1947', in *Sir Banister Fletcher's Global History of Architecture*, vol. I (London, 2020).
3. P. J. Marshall, 'Warren Hastings', *Encyclopaedia Britannica*, www.britannica.com, accessed 16 August 2022.
4. On the Battle of Buxar, see Asim Umair, *Battle of Buxar* (Delhi, 2018), pp. 10–40; for Mir Jaffar, see Humayun Mirza, *From Plassey to Pakistan: The Family History of Iskander Mirza, the First President of Pakistan* (Lahore, 2002), pp. 1–50.
5. For the Battle of Plassey, see Stuart Reid, *The Battle of Plassey, 1757: The Victory That Won an Empire* (London, 2017), p. 10; Sudeep Chakravarti, *Plassey: The Battle That Changed the Course of Indian History* (New Delhi, 2020), pp. 15–30.
6. Marshall, 'Warren Hastings'.
7. The phrase 'military fiscalism', coined by Martin Wolfe in the context of Renaissance France, is frequently used to suggest a co-evolution of fiscal capacity and military capacity.
8. Sugata Bose and Ayesha Jalal, *Modern South Asia: History, Culture, Political Economy* (Lahore, 2011), p. 55.
9. Ramkrishna Mukherjee, *The Rise and Fall of the East India Company: A Sociological Appraisal* (Lahore, 1976), p. 409.
10. *Talukdars*, or *taluqdars*, were aristocrats who formed the ruling class during the Delhi sultanate, Bengal sultanate, Mughal Empire and British Raj. They were owners of vast tracts of lands, consistently hereditary, and were responsible for collecting taxes. Priyanka Chanana, 'Caste Ties, Allodial Rights and Colonial Administration in Oudh during Summary Settlement and after 1858: The *Taluqdar* Association and the British Policies up to 1870s', *Proceedings of the Indian History Congress*, LXXIV (2013), pp. 458–69.
11. Hafeez Malik, *Moslem Nationalism in India and Pakistan* (Washington, DC, 1963), p. 202.
12. Ibid., p. 201.
13. Kenneth W. Jones, *Socio-Religious Reform Movements in British India* (Cambridge, 1999), pp. 18–19.
14. Ibid., pp. 20–21.
15. Ibid., p. 21.
16. Peter Hardy, *The Muslims of British India* (Cambridge, 1972), p. 56.
17. Ayesha Jalal, *Partisans of Allah: Jihad in South Asia* (Lahore, 2008), p. 1.
18. Rajmohan Gandhi, *Punjab: A History from Aurangzeb to Mountbatten* (New Delhi, 2013), p. 160.
19. Khushwant Singh, *Ranjit Singh: Maharajah of the Punjab* (London, 1962), p. 163.
20. Olaf Caroe, *The Pathans: 550 BCE–AD 1957* (Karachi, 1976), pp. 297–8.
21. Jalal, *Partisans of Allah*, p. 1.
22. Bose and Jalal, *Modern South Asia*, p. 58.
23. Ibid., p. 59.
24. Ibid.
25. Aloys Sprenger, an Austrian orientalist, pursued a multidisciplinary academic path, delving into medicine, natural sciences and oriental languages during his studies at the University of Vienna. In 1836 he relocated to London, collaborating with the Earl of Munster on the latter's project titled 'History of Military Science among the Muslim Peoples'. Later, in 1843, he made another move, to Calcutta, where he assumed the role of principal at Delhi College. In this capacity, Sprenger facilitated the translation

of numerous European textbooks into Hindustani, contributing significantly to educational endeavours in the region. For exhaustive detail, see Ikram Chaghatai, 'Dr Aloys Sprenger and the Delhi College', in *The Delhi College: Traditional Elites, the Colonial State, and Education before 1857*, ed. Margrit Pernau (New Delhi, 2006), pp. 105–24.

26 Bernard S. Cohn, *Colonialism and Its Forms of Knowledge* (Princeton, NJ, 1996), p. 49.
27 Syed Waqar Azeem, *Fort William College: Tehreek aur Tarikh* (Lahore, 2001), p. 20.
28 Cohn, *Colonialism and Its Forms of Knowledge*, p. 49.
29 Ibid.
30 Ibid.
31 Sisir Kumar Das, *Sahibs and Munshis: An Account of the College of Fort William* (New Delhi, 1960), pp. 7–21.
32 Ibid.
33 'Mir Amman Dehlvi', www.rekhta.org.com, accessed 17 August 2022.
34 Das, *Sahibs and Munshis*, pp. 13–14; Annemarie Schimmel, *Classical Urdu Literature from the Beginning to Iqbāl* (Wiesbaden, 1975), p. 207.
35 Jamil Jalibi, *Tareekh e Adab e Urdu* (Lahore, 2015), p. 407; Das, *Sahibs and Munshis*, pp. 101–2.
36 Ibid.
37 'Clapham Sect', *Encyclopaedia Britannica*, www.britannica.com, 4 August 2016.
38 Ibid.
39 Edmund Burke (1729–1797) is celebrated for his advocacy of Catholic emancipation, his pivotal role in the impeachment of Warren Hastings from the East India Company, and his unwavering resistance to the French Revolution. His intellectual foundation was significantly shaped by the profound ideas of John Locke and David Hume. Stanley Ayling, *Edmund Burke: His Life and Opinions* (New York, 1988).
40 Saiprasad Bejgam, 'Education in India during the British Rule', *The Medium*, www.medium.com, accessed 25 August 2022.
41 It is debated at length in Hardy, *The Muslims of British India*, pp. 61–2.
42 Tahir Kamran, 'Punjab, Punjabi and Urdu, the Question of Displaced Identity: A Historical Appraisal', *Journal of Punjab Studies*, I/14 (2007), pp. 11–25.
43 Sati, or suttee, was a practice, now mostly historical, in which a widow sacrifices herself by sitting atop her deceased husband's funeral pyre. Tania Sengupta, 'Indian Subcontinent, 1750–1947', p. 4, available online at www.discovery.ucl.ac.uk, accessed 30 August 2022.
44 Ibid.
45 According to the doctrine, any Indian princely state under the suzerainty of the East India Company (EIC), the dominant imperial power in the Indian subsidiary system, would have its princely status abolished (and therefore be annexed into British India) if the ruler was either 'manifestly incompetent or died without a male heir'. John Keay, *India: A History* (New York, 2000), p. 433.
46 Percival Spear, *A History of India*, vol. II: *From the Sixteenth Century to the Twentieth Century* (New Delhi, 1990), p. 145.
47 Altaf Hussain Hali, *Hayat-e Javed*, trans. K. H. Qadri and David Mathews, quoted in M. J. Akbar, *Tinderbox: The Past and Future of Pakistan* (New Delhi, 2011), p. 82.
48 Christopher Bayly, *Recovering Liberties: Indian Thought in the Age of Liberalism and Empire* (Cambridge, 2012), p. 214.
49 For details on Syed Ahmed Khan, see Christian W. Troll, *Sayyid Ahmad Khan: A Reinterpretation of Muslim Theology* (New Delhi, 1978).
50 Jawaharlal Nehru, *The Discovery of India* (New Delhi, 1989), p. 390.
51 Hardy, *The Muslims of India*, pp. 94–104.

References

52 Ibid., pp. 104–15. Also see Farzana Shaikh, *Community and Consensus in Islam: Muslim Representation in Colonial India, 1860–1947* (Cambridge, 1989), pp. 83–9.
53 On Dar ul Ulum Deoband, see Barbara Metcalf, *Islamic Revival in British India: Deoband, 1860–1900* (Princeton, NJ, 1982). Also see Zia-ul-Islam Faruqi, *The Deoband School and the Demand for Pakistan* (London, 1963); and Mehbub Rizvi, *Tarikh-i-Dar ul Ulum Deoband: Bar-i-Saghir key Musalmanon ka sab sey bara Karnama* (Lahore, 2005).
54 Metcalf, *Islamic Revival in British India*, p. 4.
55 S. M. Ikram, *Modern Muslim India and Birth of Pakistan* (Lahore, 1990), pp. 123–37.
56 Mirza Asad Ullah Khan Ghalib, *Kulliyat-e-Nasr-e-Ghalib* (Naval Kishor, 1877), p. 382.
57 Saqib Saleem, *Year 1857: In the Words of Ghalib* (New Delhi, 2021), p. i.
58 Clara E. Councell, 'War and Infectious Diseases', *Public Health Reports (1896–1970)*, LVI/12 (1941), pp. 547–73.
59 For further insights, see David Arnold, 'The "Discovery" of Malnutrition and Diet in Colonial India', *Indian Economic and Social History Review*, XXXI/1 (1994), pp. 1–26.
60 Belkacem Belmekki, 'A Wind of Change: The New British Colonial Policy in Post-Revolt India', *Atlantis: Journal of the Spanish Association of Anglo-American Studies*, XXX/2 (2008), p. 122.
61 Swapna M. Banerjee, 'Blurring Boundaries, Distant Companions: Non-Kin Female Caregivers for Children in Colonial India (Nineteenth and Twentieth Centuries)', *Paedagogica Historica: International Journal of the History of Education*, XLVI/6 (2010), p. 781.
62 Ibid.
63 Nicholas Mansergh, *The Commonwealth Experience* (London, 1969), p. 256.
64 For details on Raja Ram Mohan Roy, see 'Ram Mohan Roy', *Encyclopaedia Britannica*, www.britannica.com, accessed 16 October 2022.
65 The Editors of Encyclopaedia Britannica, 'sanatana dharma', *Encyclopaedia Britannica*, 7 September 2023, www.britannica.com/topic/sanatana-dharma, accessed 13 October 2023.
66 Allan Octavian Hume (1829–1912) was a British administrator in India who entered the Indian Civil Service in Bengal in 1849. 'Hume was among the leading spirits in the founding of the Indian National Congress. On his retirement from the Civil Service in 1882, he involved himself in political activities aimed at giving Indians a more democratic, representational government and was one of the conveners of the first session of the Indian National Congress, held at Bombay (Mumbai) in 1885. He served as general secretary of the Congress for its first 22 years.' 'Allan Octavian Hume', *Encyclopaedia Britannica*, www.britannica.com, accessed 10 August 2022. For Sir Syed Ahmed Khan, see Altaf Hussain Hali, *Hayat-i-Javaid* (Delhi, 1939); and Dietrich Reetz, 'Enlightenment and Islam: Sayyid Ahmad Khan's Plea to Indian Muslims for Reason', *Indian Historical Review, Delhi*, XIV/1–2 (1988), pp. 206–18.
67 Tariq Rahman, *From Hindi to Urdu* (Karachi, 2011), p. 50.
68 Ikram, *Modern Muslim India and the Birth of Pakistan*, p. 39.
69 Ibid.
70 Ibid.
71 The Hindu Mela, inaugurated in 1867 in the vibrant city of Calcutta, bore the dual mantle of a political and cultural festival. Its fundamental aim lay in cultivating a profound sense of nationalistic fervour within the urban populace, encouraging them to embrace locally crafted goods over the imported British-made alternatives. Sailendra Nath Sen, *An Advanced History of Modern India* (New Delhi, 2010), p. 235.
72 Ikram, *Modern Muslim India and the Birth of Pakistan*, p. 495.
73 Ibid.

74 Ibid.; James Tod, *Annals and Antiquities of Rajasthan; or, The Central and Western Rajpoot States of India* (London, 1914).
75 Ikram, *Modern Muslim India and the Birth of Pakistan*, p. 39.
76 Ibid., p. 497.
77 Bengal was partitioned largely for administrative reasons. It was too large a province to be affectively administered. Therefore, it was divided in 1905, which obviously had communal implications. The newly created province of East Bengal had a Muslim majority which was resented by the Hindu Bengali elite. On the Swadeshi movement, see Sumit Sarkar, *Swadeshi Movement, 1905–1908* (New Delhi, 1973).
78 On the deplorable situation that Muslims found themselves in, see Abdul Hamid, *Muslim Separatism in India: A Brief Survey, 1858–1947* (Lahore, 1967).
79 Syed Razi Wasti, *Lord Minto and the Indian Nationalist Movement, 1905–1910* (Oxford, 1964).
80 On Muhammad Ali Jinnah, see Stanley Wolpert, *Jinnah of Pakistan* (New York, 1984); Ayesha Jalal, *The Sole Spokesman: Jinnah, the Muslim League and the Demand for Pakistan* [1985] (Cambridge, 1994); Ajeet Javed, *Secular and Nationalist Jinnah* (New Delhi, 2009); Sikandar Hayat, *The Charismatic Leader: Quaid-i-Azam Mohammad Ali Jinnah and the Creation of Pakistan* (Karachi, 2014); and Yasser Latif Hamdani, *Jinnah: A Life* (Karachi, 2022).
81 Hamdani, *Jinnah*, p. 9.
82 Hector Bolitho, *Jinnah: The Creator of Pakistan* (London, 1954), p. 3.
83 Sikandar Hayat, 'The Political Transformation of the Quaid', *Hilal*, www.hilal.gov.pk, accessed 22 August 2023. More information can be found in Hayat, *The Charismatic Leader*; and Vasant Narayan Naik, *Mr Jinnah: A Political Study* (Bombay, 1947).
84 Sheela Reddy, *Mr and Mrs Jinnah* (Gurgaon, 2017), pp. 170–200.
85 Sarojini Naidu, *Mohomed Ali Jinnah: An Ambassador of Unity: His Speeches and Writings, 1912–1917* (Warangal, 1918). Originally, Gopal Krishna Gokhale coined the term 'Ambassador of Unity' for Jinnah. Sarojini used it in her writings and speeches.
86 Liaquat Ali Khan, *Pakistan the Partition of India* (Mumbai, 2008), pp. 20–30.
87 Jaswant Singh, *Jinnah: India, Partition, Independence* (New Delhi, 2010), pp. 200–230.
88 B. R. Nanda, *Road to Pakistan: The Life and Times of Mohammad Ali Jinnah* (London, 2013), pp. 50–70.
89 Jalal, *The Sole Spokesman*, pp. 120–60.
90 Hayat, *The Charismatic Leader*, pp. 150–200.
91 Farzana Shaikh, *Making Sense of Pakistan* (New York, 2009), pp. 60–100.
92 Saleena Karim, *Secular Jinnah and Pakistan: What the Nation Doesn't Know* (Lahore, 2017), pp. 90–100.
93 Jalal, *The Sole Spokesman*, pp. 170–240.
94 K. L. Shrimali, *The Wardha Scheme: The Gandhian Plan of Education for Rural India* (New Delhi, 1949).
95 Christophe Jaffrelot, *A History of Pakistan and Its Origins* (London, 2004), pp. 60–120.
96 For details see Jamal Malik, *Islam in South Asia* (Leiden, 2020), pp. 434–80.
97 Iftikhar H. Malik, *The History of Pakistan* (London, 2008), p. 200.
98 This reference to A. G. Noorani is cited in Hayat, 'The Political Transformation of the Quaid'.
99 On Gandhi, see Ramachandra Guha, *Gandhi: The Years That Changed the World, 1914–1948* (London, 2018).
100 Khalid bin Sayeed, *Pakistan: The Formative Phase, 1857–1948* (Oxford, 1968), p. 40.
101 The Rowlatt Acts (February 1919) were legislation passed by the Imperial Legislative Council, the legislature of British India: 'The acts allowed certain political cases to be tried without juries and permitted internment of suspects without trial. Their object was to replace the repressive provisions of the wartime Defence of India Act (1915)

by a permanent law. They were based on the report of Justice S.A.T. Rowlatt's committee of 1918'. 'Rowlatt Acts', *Encyclopaedia Britannica*, www.britannica.com, accessed 10 September 2022. See also Sayeed, *Pakistan*, p. 46.
102 Ibid.
103 Barbara Metcalf, *A Concise History of Modern India* (Cambridge, 2006), p. 169.
104 Sayeed, *Pakistan*, pp. 46-7.
105 On the Khilafat movement, see M. Naeem Qureshi, 'The Indian Khilāfat Movement (1918-1924)', *Journal of Asian History*, XXII/2 (1978), pp. 152-68; and M. Naeem Qureshi, *Pan-Islam in British Indian Politics: A Study of the Khilafat Movement, 1918-1924* (Leiden, 1999).
106 Guha, *Gandhi*, pp. 344-5.
107 For details, see Shahid Amin, *Event, Metaphor, Memory: Chauri Chaura, 1922-1992* (Berkeley, CA, 1995), pp. 11-40.
108 M. K. Gandhi, *Indian Home Rule* (Natal, 1910).
109 On Ambedkar, see Christophe Jaffrelot, *Dr Ambedkar and Untouchability: Analysing and Fighting Caste* (London, 2005).
110 Malik, *Moslem Nationalism*, pp. 240-46.
111 F. K. Khan Durrani, *The Meaning of Pakistan* (Lahore, 1946), p. 156, cited ibid., p. 240.
112 Ibid.
113 Ibid.
114 Ibid., p. 241.
115 The issue of Shahid Gunj revolved around the Abdullah Khan Ki Masjid mosque, located in the Landa bazaar at some distance from Lahore Railway Station. Khan-i-Saman of Dara Shikoh (the kitchen-in-charge of the Crown prince of the Mughal emperor Shah Jehan), whose name was Abdullah Khan, built the mosque in the seventeenth century. Before the onset of the Sikh rule, the mosque was in use, but when the Sikhs rebelled against the Mughals, the governor of the Punjab Nawab Moin-ul-Mulk was entrusted with the task of quelling the resistance. In those days, adjacent to the mosque was a *kotwali* (police station) where criminals or dissidents were executed. One of those fighting against the Mughal state was Taru Singh, who was brought to this *kotwali* to be tortured and executed. The Sikhs subsequently built a *samadh* (a monument for the dead) named Shahid Gunj on the spot where Singh had breathed his last, which was subsequently converted into a Gurudwara. For further details, see Tahir Kamran, 'Majlis-i-Ahrar-i-Islam: Religion, Socialism and Agitation in Action', *South Asian History and Culture*, IV/4 (2013).
116 Sayeed, *Pakistan*, pp. 96-7.
117 Ahmad Saeed deals with this episode of history in greater detail in Ahmad Saeed and Kh. Mansur Sarwar, *Trek to Pakistan* (Lahore, 2003), pp. 233-4.
118 Jalal, *The Sole Spokesman*, pp. 4-5.

3 Bloodied Partition and the Punjab's Bifurcation: 1947

1 Kirpal Singh, ed., *Select Documents on Partition of Punjab-1947: India and Pakistan: Punjab, Haryana, and Himachal-India and Punjab-Pakistan* (Delhi, 1991).
2 The Punjab became a major recruiting area because of the crucial loyalty of its population during the 1857 revolt. The growth of the ideology of 'martial races' in the 1880s further cemented the linkage between certain areas of the Punjab and military service.
3 Ethnographic surveys, census reports and district gazetteers, too, quite significantly contributed to feelings of communal difference. In addition, separate electorates were introduced for urban constituencies from 1883. In order to repel the onslaught of the Christian missionaries several reform movements representing all major religions in

the Punjab sprang up. The most significant in its impact was the Arya Samaj. They emulated the Christian missionaries by deploying aggressive tactics.

4   For more detail, see N. Gerald Barrier, *The Punjab Alienation of Land Bill of 1900* (Durham, NC, 1966).
5   Ian Talbot, *Punjab and the Raj, 1849–1947* (New Delhi, 1988).
6   Ian Talbot, 'The Unionist Party and Punjabi Politics, 1937–1947,' in *The Political Inheritance of Pakistan*, ed. D. A. Low (London, 1991), pp. 86–105.
7   Kirpal Singh, *The Partition of the Punjab* (Patiala, 1989), pp. 10–11.
8   Ibid., pp. 11–12.
9   Gurharpal Singh and Giorgio Shani, *Sikh Nationalism: New Approaches to Asian History* (Cambridge, 2021).
10 Singh, *Select Documents on Partition of Punjab-1947: India and Pakistan: Punjab, Haryana, and Himachal-India and Punjab-Pakistan*, 8.
11 Ian Talbot, *Khizr Tiwana: The Punjab Unionist Party and the Partition of India* (Karachi, 2002).
12 Ibid., p. 151.
13 For their influence and the political role in the colonial Punjab, see David Gilmartin, *Empire and Islam: Punjab and the Making of Pakistan* (Berkeley, CA, 1988).
14 This franchise was still restricted because of property and educational qualifications. In the 1945–6 elections, men and women of 21 years or above were entitled to vote on the very low qualifications of literacy, property, income and being combatants in the First World War. A landlord paying five rupees in land revenue, an owner of property worth PKR 5,000, all income tax payers and persons able to write an application for inclusion in the voters' list had the right to vote. Iftikhar Ahmad, *Pakistan General Elections: 1970* (Lahore, 1970), p. 2. According to Keith Callard, in any location more than 15 per cent of the total population was entitled to vote. Keith Callard, *Pakistan: A Political Study* (London, 1957), p. 77.
15 T. T. Yong, '"Sir Cyril Goes to India": Partition, Boundary-Making and Disruptions in the Punjab', *International Journal of Punjab Studies*, IV/1 (1997), p. 4.
16 The Congress won 51 seats in the Punjab Assembly under the leadership of Bhim Sen Sachar. The Unionist Party only secured eighteen, whereas the Panthic Pratinidhi Board had 22 and the Coalition Ministry mustered a total of 94 members. Talbot, *Khizr Tiwana*, pp. 197–9.
17 Khizr Hayat was denounced as a traitor by the Muslim League, who regarded him as part of an anti-Pakistan movement. Satya Mehta Rai, *Legislative Politics and Freedom Struggle on the Panjab, 1897–1947* (New Delhi, 1984), p. 318.
18 Ian Talbot has deployed the term 'consociationalism' while discussing the Unionist Party's political philosophy with respect to the Punjab, which had a heterogeneous communal demography. According to Arend Lijphart, the polysyllabic synonym for consociational democracy is 'power sharing'. Arend Lijphart, 'Definitions, Evidence, and Policy: A Response to Matthijs Bogaards' Critique,' *Journal of Theoretical Politics*, XII/4 (1 October 2000), p. 427. For detailed reference see the Epilogue to Rai's *Legislative Politics*, pp. 237–45.
19 The Panthic Party was a political party in India in the 1940s that focused on the Sikhs. Sardar Swaran Singh and Baldev Singh were prominent members of this party, both of whom later joined the INC and rose to the status of cabinet ministers in the Union Government of India. Swaran Singh was the longest-serving defence minister of India whereas Baldev Singh held the same portfolio from 1947 to 1952.
20 Rai, *Legislative Politics*, p. 204.
21 Talbot, *Punjab and the Raj, 1849–1947*, p. 227.

22 Sir Evan Meredith Jenkins was born on 2 February 1896. His ingress into the Civil Service in the year 1920 marked the inception of a distinguished service tenure, predominantly within the region of the Punjab, which, during that epoch, stood as a crucible of complex socio-political dynamics. Yet Jenkins's story extends far beyond the confines of regional service. In 1937 he ascended to the distinguished position of chief commissioner of Delhi, a role of considerable significance within the administrative framework of colonial India. Transitioning seamlessly into a pivotal role, he assumed the mantle of secretary of the Department of Supply from 1940 to 1943, underscoring his multifaceted acumen in managing vital governmental functions during a period of considerable global upheaval. The zenith of his administrative career, however, manifested in his tenure as private secretary to the viceroy and personal secretary to the governor general from 1943 to 1946, emblematic of his proximity to the epicentre of British colonial rule in India. This role positioned him as a principal conduit of communication between the highest echelons of colonial authority and the myriad complexities of the Indian subcontinent. Yet it is in the crucible of transition that Jenkins's legacy takes its most poignant form. Tasked with the stewardship of the Punjab as its acting governor from 1946 to the momentous date of 15 August 1947, he presided over a region poised on the precipice of historical transformation. His governance during this pivotal period, fraught with challenges and the imminent partition of India, merits meticulous scrutiny, as it encapsulates the confluence of administrative prowess, diplomacy and statesmanship in the face of epochal change. Jenkins thus emerges as a quintessential figure in the complex tapestry of British India, his life and career emblematic of the nuanced interplay of imperial authority and the tumultuous milieu of a nation on the cusp of independence. For details, see Farah Gul Baqai, 'Sir Evan Jenkins and the 1947 Partition of the Punjab,' *Pakistan Journal of History and Culture*, XXVII/1 (2006), p. 20.

23 'The Partition of the Punjab', *Broadlands Archives*, MS62/MB/1/D/259 (March 1947), p. 652.

24 Ibid.
25 Ibid.
26 Ibid.
27 Ibid.
28 Ibid.
29 See Government of India Act 1935, section 93, pp. 61–2.
30 Ibid.
31 'The Situation in the Punjab: Unrest over Its Partition, the Organisation of the Punjab Assembly, Etc.,' *Broadlands Archives* (April 1947), MS62/MB/1/D/264.
32 'The Partition of the Punjab,' March 1947, p. 652.
33 Baldev Singh (1902–1961), a member of the Chokar sub-caste from the village of Dumana in the Ambala district, hailed from a family of substantial wealth with a background in the steel industry. His journey into Sikh politics commenced in 1937 when he secured a seat in the Punjab Assembly. He generously supported various initiatives of the Akali party, including the establishment of the Sikh National College in Lahore. In June 1942 he played a pivotal role in the Sikander–Baldev Pact, an agreement with the Unionists that saw the Akalis cease their protest against Sikander Hayat's government. Baldev Singh was a key participant in the negotiations for the transfer of power and subsequently assumed the role of the first defence minister in the Nehru administration. He continued to oversee Sikh affairs until 1957, when Sawarn Singh took his place. Khushwant Singh, *A History of the Sikhs*, vol. II: *1839–1964* (Princeton, NJ, 1966), pp. 249–50.

34 Singh to Lord Wavell, 11 March 1947.
35 'The Partition of the Punjab,' March 1947, p. 652.
36 Talbot, *Punjab and the Raj, 1849–1947*, p. 227.
37 On the morning of 4 March, Hindu students clashed with the police outside Government College and later attacked a police station. The violence claimed five lives and led to another episode of rioting, setting a precedent of arson attacks on Hindu businesses in the walled city. Shops in Sua Bazar and Rang Mahal were set ablaze. G. D. Khosla, *Stern Reckoning: A Survey of the Events Leading up to and Following the Partition of India* (Delhi, 1989), p. 101.
38 According to Waseem, 'Many ex-servicemen carried weapons with them which enhanced their power to inflict damage on the rival community because of their professional training in the use of arms and fresh experience on the war front.' For details see Muhammad Waseem, 'Partition, Migration and Assimilation in Pakistani Punjab', *International Journal of Punjab Studies*, IV/1 (1997), pp. 63–84.
39 Donald L. Horowitz, *The Deadly Ethnic Riot* (Berkeley, CA, 2001), p. 150.
40 Talbot, *Punjab and the Raj, 1849–1947*, p. 228.
41 Ravinder Kaur, 'The Last Journey Exploring Social Class in the 1947 Partition Migration', *Economic and Political Weekly*, 41 (2006), pp. 2221–8.
42 C. Dass Dutt, 'The Punjab Riots and Their Lessons, 30 April 1947, S. P. Mukherjee Papers IV File 17, Nehru Memorial Museum Library', in *The Deadly Embrace*, ed. Ian Talbot (Karachi, 2007), p. 4.
43 'The Situation in the Punjab.'
44 Governor to Viceroy, no. 64-G, Confidential 617-S, 20 March 1947. Mountbatten Collection, Southampton University Archives.
45 Jenkins to Viceroy, no. 666, 30 April 1947.
46 Mountbatten to Jenkins about Jinnah and Liaquat, 5 May 1947, MB1/D265, Mountbatten Collection, Southampton University Archives.
47 Telegram (Grade C) from Governor to Viceroy, no. 28-G, 6 March 1947, Confidential 439-S (TOR-0630), MB1/D259. Mountbatten Collection, Southampton University Archives.
48 Ibid.
49 Ibid.
50 Ibid.
51 Ibid.
52 Ibid.
53 Ibid.
54 Singh, *Select Documents on Partition of Punjab-1947: India and Pakistan: Punjab, Haryana, and Himachal-India and Punjab-Pakistan*, 120.
55 Jenkins to Viceroy, no. 662, 31 March 1947, MD1/D264. Mountbatten Collection, Southampton University Archives.
56 Ibid.
57 Resolution passed by the Congress Working Committee on 8 March 1947 in New Delhi, MB1/D267, Mountbatten Collection, Southampton University Archives.
58 Letter to Nehru by non-Muslim Punjabis, 2 April 1947, MB1/D264, Mountbatten Collection, Southampton University Archives.
59 Baldev Singh to Lord Wavell, 11 March 1947, MB1/D264, Mountbatten Collection, Southampton University Archives.
60 Copy of the Resolution No. IX adopted by the Working Committee of the Shiromani Akali Dal, Amritsar in its meeting held on 16 April 1947, MB1/D259, Mountbatten Collection, Southampton University Archives.
61 The Shiromani Akali Dal (SAD), or Supreme Akali Party, is a centre right Sikh-centric state political party in Punjab, India. Akali Dal was formed on 14 December 1920 as

a task force of the Shiromani Gurudwara Prabandhak Committee, the Sikh religious body. The Akali Dal considers itself the principal representative of Sikhs. In the provincial election of 1937, it won ten seats. The Akalis sat in opposition and made occasional forays into reaching an understanding with the Muslim League, which never reached fruition. Ashutosh Kumar, 'Electoral Politics in Punjab: Study of Akali Dal', *Economic and Political Weekly*, XXXIX/14/15 (2004), pp. 1515-20.
62 Ibid.
63 Cypher Telegram (OTP) from Viceroy to the Secretary of Punjab Repeated Governor of Punjab (Immediate), no. 992-S, 5 May 1947 (TOD-2200), Mountbatten Collection, Southampton University Archives. 'Certainly, in recent conversations which Mieville and I have had with Jinnah he did not appear seriously to contest the need for partition but seemed even grateful for 17 districts of the Punjab.'
64 Extract from the Viceroy's First Staff Meeting, 25 March 1947, MB1/D264, Mountbatten Collection, Southampton University Archives.
65 The scheme was discussed as the Viceroy's Conference Paper No. 7: Partition of the Punjab, 25 March 1947, MB1/D264, Mountbatten Collection, Southampton University Archives.
66 Sir B. N. Rau's Scheme for Regional Ministries, 25 March 1947, MB1/D259, Mountbatten Collection, Southampton University Archives.
67 Ibid. In the abstract of B. N. Rau's scheme given in MB1/D259, the 'joint territory' comprising the Lahore Division is not mentioned as such. However, in the text Viceroy's Conference Paper No. 7, the provision of the 'joint territory' is mentioned.
68 Ibid.
69 Ibid.
70 Jenkins to G.E.B. Abell, 31 March 1947, Secret. DO. NO.G.S.179, Mountbatten Collection, Southampton University Archives.
71 Ibid.
72 Ibid.
73 In a letter to Abell, Jenkins stated, 'If the plan is ever presented, I would start with the regions defined as in Sir B. N. Rau's draft rule 1. I would, if necessary, transfer the Amritsar district to the eastern region, and keep only the remaining five districts of the Lahore Division in the Central region.' Cited in Tahir Kamran, 'The Unfolding Crisis in Punjab, March-August 1947: Key Turning Points and British Responses', *JPS*, XIV/2 (2007), p. 188.
74 Three ministers for each regional subject would expect to be served by separate departments, but they would find in practice that in a subject like education regional autonomy can be applied only in a very limited sphere. The big policy questions in education are, namely, the improvement of university education, the length of primary education and compulsion to attend and complete studies, and the pay of the teachers. These questions are closely linked with finance, and for obvious reasons no one region could get out of step with the others in dealing with them. See ibid., p. 208.
75 In his opinion, partition was not workable: 'The Punjab as we know it is largely an artificial creation of Irrigation Engineers. During a period of anarchy our vast canal system would not be maintained and parts of it might be deliberately destroyed. Without it we could support perhaps two-thirds of our 1947 population, which must be roughly 30 million ... It is unlikely that one community could conquer and hold the entire Punjab; and the result of a "civil war" would in fact be a partition, the parties to which would have destroyed the administrative machine, the irrigation system, and other props of orderly Government'. 'The Partition of the Punjab', 7 March 1947, Mountbatten Collection, Southampton University Archives, no. 653.

76 Memorandum by the Punjab Sikh and Hindoo members of the Constituent Assembly, 'The Partition of the Punjab', *Broadlands Archives* (April 1947), MS62/MB/1/D/260.
77 Talbot, *Punjab and the Raj, 1849–1947*, p. 231.
78 Governor to Viceroy, 15 June 1947, no. 683, MB1/D261, Mountbatten Collection, Southampton University Archives.
79 Partition Proceeding, Government of India, vol. VI, p. 2, in Singh, *The Partition of the Punjab*, p. 47.
80 Singh, *The Partition of the Punjab*, vol. I, p. 48.
81 *Civil and Military Gazette* (Lahore), 15 June 1947.
82 Baldev Singh to Mountbatten, 27 April 1947, MB1/D260.
83 Quoted in Kamran, 'The Unfolding Crisis in Punjab'.
84 'The Partition of the Punjab,' *Broadlands Archives* (April 1947), MS62/MB/1/D/260
85 Yong, 'Sir Cyril Goes to India', p. 4.
86 Ibid.
87 Indian Independence Act, Section 9(b), in Singh, *The Partition of the Punjab*, p. 54. Mamdot, Sachar and Swaran Singh to Governor on Partition Committee, Lahore, 17 June 1947, MB1/D261.
88 Minutes, viceroy's meeting, Lahore, 22 July 1947, MB1/D262.
89 Mamdot, Sachar and Swaran Singh to Governor on Partition Committee, Lahore, 17 June 1947.
90 Sachdev was a senior ICS officer and Jenkins appointed him as the partition commissioner, whereas Syed Yakub Shah was additional secretary to the Finance Department, Government of India. Ibid.
91 Note on a meeting on partition preliminaries held at Government House, Lahore, at 10 a.m. on Monday, 16 June 1947, MB1/D261, Mountbatten Collection, Southampton University Archives.
92 Ibid.
93 'A Dispute in Partition Committee, Jenkins to Viceroy', no. 696, 13 July 1947, MB1/D267, Mountbatten Collection, Southampton University Archives.
94 'Issues Connected with the Partition Work in the Punjab, Note by the Viceroy', 20 July 1947, MB1/D267.
95 Singh, *The Partition of the Punjab*, p. 69.
96 Ibid.
97 A Joint Defence Council was established on 30 June under the then commander-in-chief. Governor generals of India and Pakistan and the defence ministers and other parliamentarians of both dominions were its members. The Ludhiana district was included in the list of disturbed areas on 24 July 1947. For details, see ibid., pp. 125–32.
98 Robin Jeffrey, 'The Punjab Boundary Force and the Problem of Order, August 1947', *Modern Asian Studies*, VIII/4 (1974), pp. 491–520.
99 Communiqué regarding the Joint Defence Council's meeting held on 29 August 1947, Lahore, MB1/D268, Mountbatten Collection, Southampton University Archives.
100 Lord Mountbatten was the chairman of the council and the meeting was attended by the governor generals of India and Pakistan, the prime ministers of India and Pakistan, the defence ministers of the two dominions, the governors of the two Punjabs, the supreme commander (Field Marshal Sir Claude Auchinleck), the commander-in-chief of the Pakistan Army (General Sir Frank Messervy), commander-in-chief of the Indian Army (General Sir Rob Lockhart) and the commander of the Punjab Boundary Force (Major General Rees). Ibid.
101 The *Nawa-i-Waqt* (Lahore), 28 June 1947.
102 Listowel to Mountbatten, 13 June 1947, in *Constitutional Relations between Britain and India: The Transfer of Power, 1942–1947*, vol. XI: *The Mountbatten Viceroyalty:*

Announcement and Reception of the 3 June Plan, ed. N. Mansergh and E.W.R. Lumby, (London, 1981), p. 336.
103 Yong, 'Sir Cyril Goes to India', p. 7.
104 Ibid., p. 6.
105 Cyril Radcliffe, Report of the Punjab Boundary Commission, paragraph 3, Delhi, 12 August 1947, MB1/D267, Mountbatten Collection, Southampton University Archives.
106 Ibid., para. 6.
107 Yong, 'Sir Cyril Goes to India', p. 15.
108 Radcliffe, 'Report of the Punjab Boundary Commission', para. 9.
109 Ibid.
110 Ibid.
111 Yong, 'Sir Cyril Goes to India', p. 12.
112 Radcliffe, 'Report of the Punjab Boundary Commission', para. 10.
113 Ibid., para. 11.
114 Yong, 'Sir Cyril Goes to India', p. 13.
115 Ibid.
116 Ibid.
117 Ibid.
118 Radcliffe, 'Report of the Punjab Boundary Commission', para. 12.
119 Ibid.

4 Multiple Challenges, Limited Options: Making Sense of the Early Problems

1 Faiz Ahmed Faiz, *Colours of My Heart*, trans. Baran Faroouqui (New Delhi, 2017).
2 Rajeswari Sunder Rajan, *Real and Imagined Women: Gender, Culture and Postcolonialism* (London, 1993), p. 97.
3 Inayat Ullah, *State and Democracy in Pakistan* (Lahore, 1997), p. 15.
4 Ibid., p. 19.
5 Ibid., p. 20.
6 Ayesha Jalal, *Democracy and Authoritarianism in South Asia: A Comparative and Historical Perspective* (Lahore, 1995), p. 10.
7 Ibid., p. 18.
8 Ibid., p. 19.
9 Ian Talbot, *Pakistan: A Modern History* (London, 2005), p. 54.
10 Asma Barlas, *Democracy, Nationalism and Communalism: The Colonial Legacy in South Asia* (New York, 1995), cited ibid.
11 For details on 'viceregalism', see Khalid bin Sayeed, *Pakistan: The Formative Phase, 1857–1948* (Karachi, 1994), pp. 279–81.
12 Ikram Ali Malik, *A Book of Readings on the History of the Punjab: 1799–1947* (Lahore, 1985), p. 179.
13 Ibid., p. 60.
14 Ian Talbot, *Punjab and the Raj, 1849–1947* (New Delhi, 1988), pp. 10–50.
15 According to the idea of 'martial races', specific ethnic, religious, caste or societal communities were perceived as having a heightened level of masculinity and unwavering loyalty, and consequently were deemed exceptionally well suited for military duties. This 'martial-race' concept, as a tool of imperial authority, was employed to justify and manage colonial governance in the Indian subcontinent. It drew upon cultural and racial ideologies while simultaneously leveraging pre-existing divisions related to 'caste', religion and social strata. For a detailed analysis, see Roy Kaushik, 'Martial Race Theory and Recruitment in the Indian Army during Two World Wars', in *Manpower and the*

Armies of the British Empire in the Two World Wars, ed. Douglas E. Delaney, Mark Frost and Andrew L. Brown (New York, 2021), pp. 86–100.
16 Ian Talbot, 'The Punjab under Colonialism: Order and Transformation in British India', *Journal of Punjab Studies*, XIV/1 (Spring 2007), p. 4.
17 Gavin Rand and Kim A. Wagner, 'Recruiting the "Martial Races": Identities and Military Service in Colonial India', *Patterns of Prejudice*, XLVI (2012), pp. 232–54.
18 Talbot, *Pakistan*, p. 56.
19 Ibid.
20 Ibid.
21 This section of Chapter Four has been taken from Tahir Kamran, *The Humanities in Pakistan (1990–2020)*, World Humanities Report, CHCI (2022).
22 For a detailed discussion of these figures, see Khawaja Zakariya, *Chand Aham Jadeed Shair* [A Few Important Past Poets] (Faisalabad, 2020); and Zahid Munir Amir, *On the Wings of Poesy: Prof. Ghulam Jilani Asghar on Modern Urdu Poetry* (Lahore, 2007).
23 Ashfaq Ahmed, *Gadariya* (Lahore, 1995).
24 Ashfaq Ahmed, *Khel Tamasha* (Lahore, 2013). The protagonist of this novel and his characterization are uncannily reminiscent of the figure of Dao ji from his short story 'Gadariya'.
25 For details, see Sajjad Zaheer, *The Light: The History of the Movement for Progressive Literature in the Indo-Pak Subcontinent* (Karachi, 2006).
26 Faiz Ahmad Faiz, 'Dast-i-Saba' [Hand of Morning Breeze], in *Nuskha Hai Wafa* [Prescriptions of Fidelity] (Lahore, 1985), pp. 20–22.
27 Khawaja Muhammad Zakariya, interview with the author, Lahore, 11 May 2020.
28 Mushtaq Bilal, *Writing Pakistan: Conversations on Identity, Nationhood and Fiction* (Noida, 2016), p. 100.
29 Muhammad Umar Memon, 'Partition Literature: A Study of Intizar Husain', *Modern Asian Studies*, XIV/3 (1980), pp. 378–9.
30 Mushtaq Ahmed Yusufi, *Aab-i-Gum* (Karachi, 1990); Matt Reeck and Aftab Ahmad, trans., *Mirages of the Mind* (Noida, 2014). See also Mehr Afshan Farooqi, 'Ab-e gum, or "Disappeared Water" as a Metaphor for Language, Location, and Loss', *Critical Quarterly*, LII/3 (2010), p. 78.
31 See *Gosha-i-Yusufi*, Mushtaq Ahmad Yusufi, Arts Council of Pakistan Archives, Karachi, www.youtube.com, accessed 28 September 2023.
32 Mukhtar Masood, *Harf-i-Shauq* (Lahore, 2017).
33 Ayesha Jalal, *The State of Martial Rule: The Origin of Pakistan's Economy of Defence* (Lahore, 1999), p. 27.
34 Ibid.
35 Ibid.
36 Yasser Latif Hamdani, *Jinnah: A Life* (Karachi, 2022), p. 286.
37 Ibid.
38 Jalal, *The State of Martial Rule*, p. 28.
39 Hamdani, *Jinnah*, p. 354.
40 Jalal, *The State of Martial Rule*, pp. 28–9.
41 Ibid., p. 29.
42 Chaudhri Muhammad Ali, *The Emergence of Pakistan* (Lahore, 1992), p. 333.
43 Ibid., p. 334.
44 Regarding details of the establishment of radio, see Z. A. Bokhari, *Sarguzasht* (Lahore, 2013), pp. 355–73.
45 'Pakistan International Airlines', www.piac.com.pk, accessed 15 August 2022.
46 'Karachi and the Crown: Life in Pakistan's Capital City during the Dominion Years: 1947 to 1956', www.karachiandthecrown.blogspot.com, accessed 12 August 2022.

References

47 An important study on this aircraft is Major General Ali Hamid, 'A 1949 Air Crash That May Have Changed Pakistan's History', *Friday Times* (Lahore), December 2019.
48 'Railway', *Banglapedia*, www.en.banglapedia.org, accessed 11 October 2023.
49 Ali, *The Emergence of Pakistan*, p. 339.
50 Saila Parveen and I. M. Faisal, 'People versus Power: The Geopolitics of Kaptai Dam in Bangladesh', *International Journal of Water Resources Development*, XVIII/1 (July 2010), pp. 197–208.
51 'Warsak Power Rehabilitation', www.wapda.gov.pk, accessed 13 August 2022.
52 Ali, *The Emergence of Pakistan*, p. 340.
53 'Within the first few months of partition over 5.5 million Muslims entered Western Punjab and about 3.8 million non-Muslims, from both urban and rural areas, fled to India.' Jalal, *The State of Martial Rule*, pp. 78–9.
54 For an in-depth analysis of post-partition Punjab, see Ilyas Chattha, 'Faction-Building in Pakistan: Sir Francis Mudie and Punjab Politics, 1947–1949', *Contemporary South Asia*, XXII/3 (2014), pp. 225–39.
55 Tariq Ali, *Pakistan: Military Rule or People's Power?* (New Delhi, 1970), p. 41.
56 Ralph Braibanti, *Research on the Bureaucracy of Pakistan* (Durham, NC, 1969), p. 97.
57 M. Rafique Afzal, *Pakistan: History and Politics, 1947–1971* (Karachi, 2001), p. 15.
58 Ibid.
59 Nafis Ahmad, *Economic Geography of East Pakistan* (London, 1958), p. 211.
60 Afzal, *Pakistan*, p. 16.
61 Ibid.
62 Ibid.
63 Ibid., p. 17.
64 Jalal, *The State of Martial Rule*, p. 38.
65 Ibid., p. 41.
66 Afzal, *Pakistan*, p. 18.
67 Stephen P. Cohen, *The Pakistan Army* (Karachi, 1984), p. 17.
68 Hein G. Kiessling, *Faith Unity Discipline: The ISI of Pakistan* (London, 2023), pp. 13–14.
69 Ibid., p. 16.
70 Fazal Muqeem, *The Story of the Pakistan Army* (Lahore, 1964), p. 40.
71 Afzal, *Pakistan*, p. 18.
72 'Thomas Wynford Rees', *Dictionary of Welsh Biography*, www.biography.wales.com, accessed 15 August 2022.
73 Afzal, *Pakistan*, p. 19.
74 After General Frank Messervy and General Gracey, Ayub Khan was appointed as the chief of the armed forces. Ibid.
75 Sikandar Hayat, *Aspects of Pakistani Movement* (Islamabad, 2016), p. 145.
76 Pyarelal, *Mahatma Gandhi: The Last Phase*, vol. II (Ahmedabad, 1956), p. 180.
77 Ali, *The Emergence of Pakistan*, p. 180.
78 Alan Campbell-Johnson, *Mission with Mountbatten* (London, 1952), p. 100.
79 Ibid., pp. 70–80.
80 Quoted in the *Daily Hindu* (Madras), 16 January 1950.
81 Lord Ismay, *Memoirs* (London, 1960), p. 420.
82 Ian Stephens, *Pakistan* (London, 1963), p. 180.
83 Ali, *The Emergence of Pakistan*, p. 189.
84 Ibid., p. 23.
85 Ibid.

86 Raj Mohan Gandhi, *Patel: A Life* (Ahmadabad, 1996), p. 438; Yaqoob Khan Bangash, *A Princely Affair: Accession and Integration of Princely States in Pakistan, 1947–55* (Karachi, 2015), p. 113.
87 Afzal, *Pakistan*, p. 23.
88 Being a landlocked state, Hyderabad was wholly dependent on India for access to the sea. The dynasty was founded in the early eighteenth century by Mir Qamar-ud-din Khan Siddiqi Bayafandi (1671–1748), also known as Chin Qilich Kamaruddin Khan, Nizam-ul-Mulk, Asaf Jah and Nizam I, the first *nizam* (ruler) of Hyderabad, a trusted nobleman and general of the Mughal emperor Aurangzeb. Mir Osman Ali Khan, Asaf Jah VII GCSI GBE (1886–1967) was the last *nizam* of the princely state of Hyderabad, the largest princely state in British India. Ali, *The Emergence of Pakistan*, pp. 278–9.
89 Afzal, *Pakistan*, p. 24.
90 Wilfred Cantwell Smith, 'Hyderabad: Muslim Tragedy', *Middle East Journal*, IV/1 (January 1950), pp. 27–51.
91 Ibid.
92 Ali, *The Emergence of Pakistan*, p. 282.
93 Kalim Siddiqui, *Conflict, Crisis and War in Pakistan* (London, 1972), p. 112.
94 Jalal, *The State of Martial Rule*, p. 56.
95 Ibid., p. 57.
96 Ibid.
97 Ibid.
98 Ibid.
99 Talbot, *Pakistan*, p. 433.
100 Jalal, *The State of Martial Rule*, p. 58.
101 Ibid.
102 Ibid.
103 Ibid., p. 59.
104 Ibid.
105 Talbot, *Pakistan*, p. 116.
106 Ibid., p. 117.
107 'Pakistan: The End of the Water Dispute', *Round Table*, CCI (September 1960), p. 72.
108 Talbot, *Pakistan*, p. 112.
109 Ibid., p. 113.

5 The Faltering Years of a Nascent State, 1947–58

1 Subrata Kumar Mitra, ed., *The Post-Colonial State in Asia: Dialects of Politics and Culture* (Lahore, 1988), p. 3.
2 Ishtiaq Hussain Qureshi, *Ulema in Politics* (Karachi, 1974), pp. 356–7.
3 Tahir Kamran, 'The Genesis, Evolution and Impact of "Deobandi" Islam on the Punjab: An Overview', in *Faith-Based Violence and Deobandi Militancy in Pakistan*, ed. Jawad Syed, Edwina Pio, Tahir Kamran and Abbas Zaidi (London, 2016), pp. 65–92.
4 Mohammad Waseem, *Politics and the State in Pakistan* (Islamabad, 2007), p. 51.
5 Tahir Kamran, 'The Pre-History of Religious Exclusionism in Contemporary Pakistan: *Khatam-e-Nubuwwat* 1889–1953', *Modern Asian Studies*, XLVI/6 (2015), pp. 1–35.
6 Tahir Kamran, 'The Making of a Minority: Ahmadi Exclusion through Constitutional Amendments, 1974', *Pakistan Journal of Historical Studies*, IV/1–2 (2019), pp. 55–84.
7 It is pertinent to mention here that the Ahmadiyya community was a movement founded in 1889 in Punjab to follow the teachings of Mirza Ghulam Ahmad (1835–1908). Its deviation from mainstream Islamic thought meant that many Muslims considered the movement to be heretical.

8 Kamran, 'The Pre-History of Religious Exclusionism'.
9 Ibid.
10 Tahir Kamran, 'Pakistan: A Failed State?', *History Today*, LXVII/9 (2017), pp. 26–7.
11 Ibid.
12 Hasan Askari Rizvi, *Military and Politics in Pakistan: 1947–1997* (Lahore, 2000), p. 61.
13 Ibid.
14 Ibid.
15 Ibid.
16 Quoted ibid., p. 63.
17 Ibid., p. 65.
18 Tariq Ali, *Pakistan: Military Rule or People's Power* (Delhi, 1970), p. 89.
19 Ibid.
20 Khalid bin Sayeed has reflected quite profoundly about this development in his book *Pakistan: The Formative Phase, 1857–1948* (London, 1968).
21 Hamza Alavi, 'The State in Post-Colonial Societies: Pakistan and Bangladesh', *New Left Review*, 74 (1972), p. 59.
22 Ibid.; for more details, see Farooq Sulehria, 'From Overdeveloped State to Praetorian Pakistan: Tracing the Media's Transformations', in *New Perspectives of Pakistan's Political Economy*, ed. Matthew McCartney and S. Akbar Zaidi (Cambridge, 2019).
23 Ian Talbot, *Pakistan: A Modern History* (London, 2006), p. 4.
24 Ibid.
25 Mohammad Waseem, *Politics and State in Pakistan* (Islamabad, 2007), pp. 51–2.
26 Tahir Kamran, 'Islam, Urdu and Hindu as the Other: Instruments of Homogeneity in Multicultural Society', in *Composite Culture in a Multicultural Society*, ed. Bipin Chandra and Sucheta Mahajan (New Delhi, 2006), pp. 93–122.
27 Before 1937, the Muslim League was not religiously orientated. I am not using the term 'secularism' because had it been secular then it would not have trodden the separatist course. Then, it represented the salariat class, as Hamza Alavi terms it.
28 Muhammad Azeem, 'The State as a Political Practice: Pakistan's Postcolonial State beyond Dictatorship and Islam', *Third World Quarterly*, XLI/10 (2020), pp. 1670–86.
29 Talbot, *Pakistan*, p. 21.
30 Stephen Cohen, *The Idea of Pakistan* (Washington, DC, 2004), p. 71.
31 Ibid., p. 23.
32 Tahir Kamran, *Democracy and Governance in Pakistan* (Lahore, 2008), p. 18.
33 Talbot, *Pakistan*, p. 30.
34 Alan Campbell Johnson, *Mission with Mountbatten* (London, 1952), p. 156.
35 'Freedom and After', *Dawn* (Delhi), 18 August 1947.
36 Khalid bin Sayeed, *Pakistan: A Formative Phase, 1857–1948* (Karachi, 2007), p. 227.
37 The comprehensive study on Jinnah's powers and discretion is Khalid bin Syeed's article, 'The Governor General of Pakistan', *Pakistan Horizon*, VIII/2 (June 1955), pp. 330–39.
38 Sayeed, *Pakistan: A Formative Phase*, p. 229.
39 Ibid., p. 235.
40 Hamza Alavi, 'Authoritarianism and Legitimation of State Power in Pakistan', in *The Post-Colonial State in Asia: Dialects of Politics and Culture*, ed. Subrata Kumar Mitra (Lahore, 1998), p. 31.
41 Ibid., p. 39.
42 Ibid., p. 40.
43 Omar Noman, *Pakistan: A Political and Economic History since 1947* (New York, 1990), p. 10.
44 Fatima Jinnah, quoted in Sayeed, *Pakistan*, p. 83.
45 Ibid., p. 9.

46 Tahir Amin, *Ethno-National Movements in Pakistan's Domestic and International Factors* (Islamabad, 1993), p. 73.
47 Zahid Chaudhry, *Pakistan key Siyasi Tarikh*, vol. IV: *Jinnah Liaqat Tazaad aur Punjabi Muhajar Tazaad* (Lahore, 1990), pp. 130–77.
48 Noman, *Pakistan*, p. 10.
49 Alavi, 'Authoritarianism and Legitimation of State Power in Pakistan', p. 42.
50 Ibid.
51 Noman, *Pakistan*, pp. 11–12.
52 Ibid., p. 12.
53 Ibid., p. 10.
54 For details, see Hamid Khan, *Constitutional and Political History of Pakistan* (Karachi, 2005).
55 Waseem, *Politics and State in Pakistan*, p. 61.
56 Ayesha Jalal, *Democracy and Authoritarianism in South Asia: A Comparative and Historical Perspective* (Lahore, 1995), pp. 224–5.
57 Talbot, *Pakistan*, p. 26.
58 'When Urdu was elevated to the status of a national language, the Bengalis who were deeply attached to their own language and continued to venerate Bengali literature organized protest movements culminating into riots. The movement in support of the Bengali language was suppressed by the state machinery on 21 February 1952. In the course of that violence many people lost their lives. Not only the event is commemorated each year by a Remembrance Day, but it also proved to be a beginning of the end.' Tahir Kamran, 'Islam, Urdu and Hindu as the Other: Instruments of Cultural Homogeneity in Pakistan', in *Composite Culture in a Multicultural Society in Pakistan*, ed. Bipan Chandra and Suchita Mahajan (New Delhi, 2007), p. 109.
59 Ramachandra Ghua, 'Language Politics in Jinnah's Pakistan Has Parallels in Modi's India', *The Wire*, https://thewire, 28 October 2018.
60 Tariq Rahman, *Language, Ideology and Power: Language-Learning among the Muslims of Pakistan and North India* (New Delhi, 2008), pp. 270–71.
61 *Quaid-e-Azam Muhammad Ali Jinnah, Speeches as Governor General of Pakistan (1947–1948)* (Karachi, n.d.), p. 9, quoted in Waseem, *Politics and State in Pakistan*, p. 101.
62 Karimuddin Ahmed, *The Social History of Pakistan* (Dhaka, 1967), pp. 111–12, quoted in Waseem, *Politics and State in Pakistan*, p. 101.
63 Y. A. Mitha, 'Linguistic Nationalism in Pakistan', unpublished M.Phil. diss., University of Sussex, 1985, quoted in Talbot, *Pakistan*, p. 26.
64 Ibid., p. 271.
65 Alyssa Ayres, *Speaking Like a State: Language and Nationalism in Pakistan* (New York, 2009), p. 42.
66 Rafiqul Islam, 'The Language Movement', in *Bangladesh: History and Culture*, ed. S. R. Chakravarty and Virendra Narain (New Delhi, 1986), p. 82, quoted ibid.
67 Aqil Shah, *The Army and Democracy: Military Politics in Pakistan* (Cambridge, 2014), pp. 31–2.
68 Ibid., p. 32, citing Diljit Singh, 'Military Education in India: Changes from the British Tradition', *United Services Institution Journal*, I (1974), p. 229.
69 Rizvi, *Military and Politics in Pakistan*, p. 70.
70 Ibid.
71 Ibid., p. 72.
72 Ibid.
73 Ibid., p. 73.
74 Ibid.

References

75 Humayun Mirza, *From Plassey to Pakistan* (Lahore, 1999), pp. 176–7.
76 Kamran, *Democracy and Governance in Pakistan*, p. 35.
77 Jalal, *Democracy and Authoritarianism in South Asia*, p. 22.
78 Jalal, *The State of Martial Rule: The Origins of Pakistan's Political Economy of Defence* (Cambridge, 1990).
79 Zahid Hussain, 'The First Five Year Plan Size, Objectives and Limitations', annual address delivered on 5 November 1956 at the conference of West Pakistan economists, p. 2.
80 Noman, *Pakistan*, p. 15.
81 S. Akbar Zaidi, *Issues in Pakistan's Economy* (Karachi, 1999), p. 500.
82 Ibid.

6 Praetorianism Unbound (Ayub Khan's Rule), 1958–69

1 Malik Feroz Khan Noon served as a member of the Punjab Legislative Council during 1921–3, 1924–6, 1927–30 (minister for local self-government) and 1930–36 (minister for education); and as a member of the Punjab Legislative Assembly during 1946–7 and 1951–5. He also functioned as governor of East Pakistan during 1950–53; as chief minister of Punjab during 1953–5; and as prime minister of Pakistan during 1957–8. For details, see Feroz Khan Noon, *From Memory* (Lahore, 1969).
2 Ian Talbot, *Pakistan: A Modern History* (London, 2005), p. 126.
3 Hamza Alavi, 'Authoritarianism and Legitimation of State Power in Pakistan', in *The Post-Colonial State in Asia: Dialects of Politics and Culture*, ed. Subrata Kumar Mitra (Lahore, 1998), p. 47.
4 *Dawn*, 7 October 1958; *Dawn*, 12 October 1958.
5 G. W. Choudhury, *The Last Days of United Pakistan* (London, 1974), p. 13.
6 Alavi, 'Authoritarianism and Legitimation of State Power in Pakistan', p. 48.
7 Khalid Mahmud, 'The Development of Federalism in Pakistan', in *Problems and Politics of Federalism in Pakistan*, ed. Pervaiz Iqbal Cheema and Rashid Ahmad Khan (Islamabad, 2006), p. 19.
8 Shuja Nawaz, *Crossed Swords: Pakistan, Its Army, and the Wars Within* (Karachi, 2017), p. 139.
9 Ibid.
10 Mohammad Waseem, *Politics and the State in Pakistan* (Islamabad, 2007), p. 141.
11 Ayesha Jalal, *The Struggle for Pakistan: A Muslim Homeland and Global Politics* (Cambridge, 2014), p. 101.
12 Kalim Siddique, *Conflict, Crisis and War in Pakistan* (London, 1972), p. 89. Also see Mohammad Ayub Khan, *Friends Not Masters* (Oxford, 1967), p. 39.
13 Hector Bolitho, *Jinnah: Creator of Pakistan* (Karachi, 1966), p. 207.
14 Ian Stephens, *Pakistan* (New York, 1964), pp. 249–50.
15 Siddique, *Conflict, Crisis and War in Pakistan*, p. 90.
16 Nawaz, *Crossed Swords*, p. 142.
17 Siddique, *Conflict, Crisis and War in Pakistan*, p. 90.
18 Humayun Mirza, *From Plassey to Pakistan: The Family History of Iskander Mirza, the First President of Pakistan* (Lahore, 2002), p. 139.
19 Khan, *Friends Not Masters*, p. 38.
20 Ibid., p. 21.
21 Abul Kalam Azad, *India Wins Freedom* (Calcutta, 1959), pp. 125–7.
22 Khan, *Friends Not Masters*, p. 40.
23 Ibid.
24 Alavi, 'Authoritarianism and Legitimation of State Power in Pakistan'.
25 Omar Noman, *Pakistan: A Political and Economic History since 1947* (London and New York, 1990), p. 35.

26 Tahir Kamran, *Democracy and Governance in Pakistan* (Lahore, 2008), p. 47.
27 Rounaq Jahan, *Pakistan: Failure in National Integration* (Lahore, 2019), pp. 55–6.
28 Khan, *Friends Not Masters*, p. 187.
29 Altaf Gauhar, *Ayub Khan* (Lahore, 2000), p. 176.
30 Ibid., p. 160.
31 Khan, *Friends Not Masters*, p. 54.
32 Ibid.
33 Nawaz, *Crossed Swords*, p. 260.
34 J. S. Bains, 'Some Thoughts on Pakistan's New Constitution', *Indian Journal of Political Science*, XXIII/1 (January–December 1962), p. 212.
35 Ibid.
36 Hasan Askari Rizvi, 'Federalism: Conceptual and Practical Issues', in *Problems and Politics of Federalism in Pakistan*, ed. Cheema and Khan, p. 13.
37 Cited by Ayaz Muhammad and Muhammad Kaleem, 'Marriage of Convenience between Military and Local Government', *European Journal of Social Sciences*, XXVII/3 (2012), p. 383.
38 Cheema and Khan, eds, *Problems and Politics of Federalism in Pakistan*, p. 19.
39 Talbot, *Pakistan: A Modern History*, p. 157.
40 Habib Jalib, 'Dastoor', *Ravi Magazine*, www.ravimagazine.com, accessed 6 May 2023.
41 Kamran, *Democracy and Governance in Pakistan*, p. 50.
42 Noman, *Pakistan*, p. 44.
43 Waseem, *Politics and the State in Pakistan*, p. 155.
44 Ibid., p. 149.
45 Zamir Niazi, 'Towards a Free Press', in *Old Road, New Highways: Fifty Years of Pakistan*, ed. Victoria Schofield (Karachi, 1997), p. 182.
46 'Woman in the News; Ayyub's Election Foe Fatima Jinnah', *New York Times*, 16 December 1964.
47 Ibid.
48 Gauhar, *Ayub Khan*, p. 276.
49 Mujibur Rahman was the son of a middle-class landowner: 'He studied law and political science at the Universities of Calcutta and Dhaka. Although jailed briefly as a teenager for agitating for Indian independence, he began his formal political career in 1949 as a co-founder of the Awami League. The league advocated political autonomy for East Pakistan in 1960s. Mujib's arrest in the late 1960s incited mob violence that eroded the Pakistani president Ayub Khan's authority in East Pakistan. In the elections of December 1970, Mujib's Awami League secured a majority of the seats in the National Assembly and demanded independence for East Pakistan. Troops from West Pakistan were sent to regain control of the eastern wing but were defeated with the help of India. East Pakistan, renamed Bangladesh, was proclaimed an independent republic in 1971, and in January 1972 Mujib became the first prime minister installed under the country's new parliamentary government. Faced with increasing problems, Mujib took tighter control and assumed the presidency in January 1975. He, along with most of his family, was killed in a coup d'état just seven months later.' 'Mujibur Rahman', *Encyclopaedia Britannica*, www.britannica.com, accessed 26 September 2022.
50 Gauhar, *Ayub Khan*, p. 277.
51 Roedad Khan, *Pakistan: A Dream Gone Sour* (Lahore, 1997), p. 44.
52 'Democratising Pakistan? II', *Daily Times*, www.dailytimes.com.pk.
53 Hasan Zaheer, *The Separation of East Pakistan: The Rise and Realization of Bengali Muslim Nationalism* (Karachi, 1994), p. 87.
54 Quoted in Irfan Waheed Usmani, 'Print Culture and Left-Wing Radicalism in Lahore, c. 1947–1071', unpublished PhD thesis, National University of Singapore, 2016, p. 292.

References

55 Saadia Toor, *The State of Islam: Culture and Cold War Politics in Pakistan* (London, 2011), pp. 86–9.
56 Irfan Waheed Usmani offers a graphically detailed analysis of this aspect of Ayub's regime; see 'Print Culture and Left-Wing Radicalism in Lahore, Pakistan, c. 1947–1971', PhD dissertation, National University of Singapore, 2016.
57 Kamran, *Democracy and Governance in Pakistan*, p. 52.
58 Lawrence Ziring, *Pakistan at the Crosscurrent of History* (New York, 2003), pp. 108–9.
59 Waseem, *Politics and the State in Pakistan*, pp. 269–70.
60 Akmal Hussain, *Pakistan, Institutional Instability and Underdevelopment: State, People and Consciousness* (Lahore, 2023), pp. 78–9.
61 Rounaq Jehan, *Pakistan: Failure in National Integration* (New York, 1972), p. 26.
62 Ibid., p. 25.
63 Noman, *Pakistan*, p. 27.
64 Ibid.
65 Sherbaz Khan Mazari, *A Journey to Disillusionment* (Karachi, 1999), pp. 989–9.
66 Ibid., p. 99.
67 Ayesha Jalal, *The State of Martial Rule: The Origin of Pakistan's Economy of Defence* [1990] (Lahore, 1999), p. 304.
68 Charles Kennedy, *Bureaucracy in Pakistan* (Karachi, 1987).
69 Jalal, *The State of Martial Rule*, p. 303.
70 For details of the operation of basic democracies, see Government of Pakistan, Bureau of National Construction, *Four Studies in Basic Democracies* (1964).
71 G. W. Choudhury, *The Last Days of United Pakistan* (Bloomington, IN, 1974), p. 13.
72 Ibid., cited in Arnold J. Toynbee, 'Communism and the West in Asian Countries', *Annals of the American Academy of Political and Social Sciences* (July 1961).
73 S. M. Naseem, 'Economists and Pakistan's Economic Development: Is There a Connection?' *Pakistan Development Review*, XXXVII/4, Part II (Winter 1998), pp. 410–14.
74 Choudhury, *The Last Days of United Pakistan*, p. 304.
75 Planning Commission 1960, Second Five-Year Plan, 1960–1965, Karachi, Government of Pakistan.
76 Kamran, *Democracy and Governance in Pakistan*, p. 57.
77 Ibid., p. 58.
78 Hussain, *Pakistan, Institutional Instability and Underdevelopment*, pp. 84–5.
79 Pakistan Economic Survey in Noman, *Pakistan*, p. 37.
80 Khan, *Pakistan: A Dream Gone Sour*, p. 42.
81 Ibid., pp. 42–3.
82 Ibid., p. 44.
83 Nawaz, *Crossed Swords*, pp. 204–5.
84 Rizvi, *Military and Politics in Pakistan*, p. 139.
85 Gauhar, *Ayub Khan*, p. 308.
86 Isha M. Kureshi, 'The Mysterious Rann of Kutch', *Dawn*, www.dawn.com.pk, 3 June 2009.
87 Gibraltar Planning Directive 17 May 1965, in Mahmud Ahmed, *History of the Indo-Pak 1965 War* (Islamabad, 2006), p. 29.
88 Gauhar, *Ayub Khan*, p. 313.
89 Rahman, *Pakistan's Wars*, p. 114.
90 Ibid., p. 117.
91 Gauhar, *Ayub Khan*, p. 325.
92 Nawaz, *Crossed Swords*, p. 211.
93 Ibid., p. 212.
94 Ibid.

95 Ibid., p. 208.
96 Rahman, *Pakistan's Wars*, p. 122.
97 For the details on the danger posed to Lahore in 1965, see Nawaz, *Crossed Swords*, pp. 220–24.
98 Nawaz, *Crossed Swords*, p. 236; Rahman, *Pakistan Wars*, p. 129.
99 Dr Hemant Kumar Pandey and Manish Raj Singh, *India's Major Military and Rescue Operations* (New Delhi, 2017), p. 101.
100 This phrase has been borrowed from Samuel Finer, *The Man on Horseback: The Role of the Military in Politics* (London, 2002).
101 Khan, *Pakistan: A Dream Gone Sour*, p. 43.
102 Sayeed, *Politics of Pakistan*, pp. 62–3.

7 Praetorianism under General Yahya Khan and East Pakistan's Separation, 1969–71

1 Lawrence Ziring, *Pakistan in the Twentieth Century: A Political History* (Karachi, 1997), p. 648.
2 Hamza Alavi, 'Authoritarianism and Legitimation of State Power in Pakistan', in *The Post-Colonial State in Asia: Dialects of Politics and Culture*, ed. Subrata Kumar Mitra (Lahore, 1988), p. 40.
3 For his short biographical note, see Ian Talbot, *Pakistan: A Modern History* (London, 2005), p. 436. On his life and career, see Brigadier A. R. Siddiqi, *General Agha Mohammad Yahya Khan: The Rise and Fall of a Soldier, 1947–1971* (Karachi, 2020).
4 Shuja Nawaz, 'Non-Fiction: The Saga of Yahya Khan', *Dawn*, www.dawn.com.pk, 24 January 2021.
5 Siddiqi, *General Agha Mohammad Yahya Khan*, p. 41.
6 'Yahya Khan', *New World Encyclopedia*, www.newworldencyclopedia.org.com, accessed 5 February 2024.
7 Lawrence Ziring, *Pakistan: At the Crosscurrent of History* (London, 2003), p. 115.
8 'Good Soldier, Yahya Khan', *Time Magazine*, www.time.com, 2 August 1971.
9 Ibid.
10 G. W. Choudhury, *The Last Days of United Pakistan* (London, 1974), p. 49.
11 Rafique Afzal, *Political Parties in Pakistan, 1969–1971*, vol. III (Islamabad, 1988), p. 4.
12 Choudhury, *The Last Days of United Pakistan*, p. 50.
13 Ibid.
14 Hassan Askari Rizvi, *Military and Politics in Pakistan: 1947–1997* (Lahore, 2000), p. 182.
15 Ibid., p. 183.
16 American Consul General Lahore to Department of State, 22 January 1963, 790D.00/1–1663, Box 2116, National Archives at College Park. Quoted in Talbot, *Pakistan: A Modern History*, p. 187.
17 Afzal, *Political Parties in Pakistan, 1969–1971*, p. 8.
18 Ibid., p. 89.
19 Mohammad Waseem, *Politics and the State in Pakistan* (Islamabad, 2007), p. 240.
20 Ibid., p. 241.
21 Ibid., p. 239.
22 The plan was launched on 1 July 1970. In that plan, PKR 49 billion was allocated to the public sector and PKR 26 billion to the private sector. For details, see Rizvi, *Military and Politics in Pakistan*, p. 185.
23 Ibid.
24 Fazal Muqueem Khan, *Pakistan's Crisis in Leadership* (Islamabad, 1973), pp. 25–9.
25 Waseem, *Politics and the State in Pakistan*, p. 242.

26 Elizabeth Kolbert, 'Adus Sattar, Ex-Leader of Bangladesh, Dies', *New York Times*, www.nytimes.com, 6 October 1985; Rizvi, *Military and Politics in Pakistan*, p. 187.
27 Afzal, *Political Parties in Pakistan, 1969–1971*, p. 21.
28 Jalal, *The State of Martial Rule*, p. 309.
29 Omar Noman, *The Political Economy of Pakistan* (Abingdon, 1988), p. 44.
30 Ziring, *Pakistan*, p. 117.
31 Waseem, *Politics and the State in Pakistan*, p. 243.
32 Jalal, *The State of Martial Rule*, p. 309.
33 Talbot, *Pakistan*, p. 195.
34 Shuja Nawaz, *Crossed Swords: Pakistan, Its Army, and the Wars Within* (Karachi, 2017), p. 260.
35 Ibid.
36 Ibid., p. 261.
37 Ibid.
38 For Operation Blitz, see Kamal Mateen Uddin, *Tragedy of Errors: East Pakistan Crisis* (Lahore, 1994), pp. 241–3.
39 Nawaz, *Crossed Swords*, p. 264.
40 Siddiqi, *General Agha Mohammad Yahya Khan*, p. 141.
41 Nawaz, *Crossed Swords*, p. 265.
42 Ibid.
43 See for details on Operation Blitz, see Siddiq Salik, *Witness to Surrender* (Karachi, 1977), pp. 39–40.
44 Nawaz, *Crossed Swords*, p. 265.
45 Mateen Uddin, *Tragedy of Errors*, pp. 241–2.
46 He was a reserved officer who was given the sobriquet 'Butcher of Baluchistan' for his vigorous prosecution of military action in 1958 against dissident tribesmen in that province fighting under the flag of Nawab Nowroz, or Nowroz Khan (also known by Baluchs as Babu Nowroz), the head of the Zarakzai tribes of Baluchistan. Tikka's mind was reportedly unclouded by strategic thinking or complicated vocabulary. He was expected to get the job done in short order. Nawaz, *Crossed Swords*, p. 30; also see Muqeem Khan, *Pakistan's Crisis in Leadership*, p. 60.
47 Sarmila Bose, *Dead Reckoning: Memories of the 1971 Bangladesh War* (Karachi, 2011), p. 21.
48 Rizvi, *Military and Politics in Pakistan*, p. 191.
49 Ibid.
50 Waseem, *Politics and the State in Pakistan*, p. 246.
51 Jalal, *The State of Martial Rule*, p. 310.
52 Noman, *Pakistan*, p. 46.
53 Ibid., p. 47.
54 Rizvi, *Military and Politics in Pakistan*, p. 199.
55 Aijaz Ahmad, 'The Rebellion on 1983: A Balance Sheet', *South Asia Bulletin*, 1/4 (1984), p. 43.
56 Sarmila Bose, 'Anatomy of Violence: Analysis of Civil War in East Pakistan in 1971', *Economic and Political Weekly*, www.epw.in.com, 8 October 2005.
57 Ahmad Salim, 'Bangladesh and Dismemberment of Pakistan', *The Herald*, https://herald.dawn.com, April 1997.
58 Khalid Hasan, *Rearview Mirror: Four Memoirs* (Islamabad, 2002), p. 103.
59 Zulfiqar Ali Bhutto, *The Great Tragedy* (1971), pp. 78–9.
60 Amir Abdullah Khan Niazi, *The Betrayal of East Pakistan* (Karachi, 1999), pp. 10–80.
61 See for reference a piece by Babar Sattar, 'Bigoted and Smug', *Dawn*, www.dawn.com.pk, 23 December 2013.

62 Niazi, *The Betrayal of East Pakistan*, p. 40. For the details on Mukti Bahini, see Sadiq Salik, *Witness to Surrender* (Karachi, 1977), pp. 99–106.
63 Muazzam Hussain Khan, 'Osmany, General Mohammad Ataul Ghani', *Banglapedia: National Encyclopedia of Bangladesh*, www.banglapedia.com, accessed 1 February 2024.
64 Rizvi, *Military and Politics in Pakistan*, p. 204.
65 For details, see L. F. Rush Brook Williams, *The East Pakistan Tragedy* (London, 1972), pp. 121–6.
66 Government of India's note to the Government of Pakistan, 3 March 1971, *Pakistan Horizon*, XXIV/2 (1971), pp. 118–19.
67 Article in *The Guardian*, 1 April 1971, cited in Rizvi, *Military and Politics in Pakistan*, p. 203.
68 For a detailed analysis of India's assistance to the Bangladesh movement, see Hasan Askari Rizvi, *Internal Strife and External Intervention: India's Role in the Civil War in East Pakistan* (Lahore, 1981), pp. 162–213.
69 Rizvi, *Military and Politics in Pakistan*, p. 204.
70 Ibid.
71 Ibid.
72 *Pakistan Times*, 9 November 1971.
73 Ziring, *Pakistan at the Crosscurrent of History*, p. 126.
74 Rizvi, *Military and Politics in Pakistan*, p. 206.
75 On genocide with reference to east Pakistan see Tariq Rahman, *Pakistan's Wars* (Lahore, 2022), pp. 242–3.
76 Bose, 'Anatomy of Violence'.
77 Ibid.
78 Tahir Kamran, 'Reading Bengal Genocide, Differently', *The News*, www.thenews.com.pk, 13 December 2020.
79 Ibid.
80 Ibid.
81 Ibid.
82 Quoted from 'Understanding Bangladesh's War of Liberation: A Discussion on Sarmila Bose's *Dead Reckoning*', *Economic and Political Weekly*, www.epw.in.com, 8 October 2005.
83 David Ludden, 'The Politics of Independence in Bangladesh', *Economic and Political Weekly*, XLV/35 (2011), pp. 79–85; Mokerrom Hossain, 'Bangladesh War of Independence: A Moral Issue', *Economic and Political Weekly*, XLIV/5 (2009), pp. 26–9; Bina D'Costa, 'War Crimes, Justice and the Politics of Memory', *Economic and Political Weekly*, XLVIII/12 (2013), pp. 39–43.
84 Siraj Khan, 'Playing the Fiddle while Dhaka Burned: How We Ended Up with a Leftover Pakistan', *Friday Times*, www.fridaytimes.com.pk, 17 December 2021.
85 Ibid.

8 The Era of Populism: Zulfiqar Ali Bhutto, 1971–7

1 Zulfiqar Ali Bhutto, *If I Am Assassinated*, p. 223, available at https://bhutto.org, accessed 17 October 2023.
2 Stanley Wolpert, *Zulfi Bhutto of Pakistan: His Life and Time* (Karachi, 1993), p. 7.
3 Ibid.
4 Anatol Lieven, *Pakistan: A Hard Country* (London, 2012), p. 71.
5 Ibid.
6 Altaf Gauhar, *Ayub Khan: Pakistan's First Military Ruler* (Lahore, 1996), p. 27.
7 Ibid.
8 Ibid.

9   Wolpert, *Zulfi Bhutto of Pakistan*, p. 19.
10 Ibid.
11 Piloo Mody, *Zulfi, My Friend* (Delhi, 1973), p. 27. Syeda Hameed, *Born to Be Hanged: Political Biography of Zulfiqar Ali Bhutto* (New Delhi, 2017), p. 4.
12 Owen Bennett-Jones, *The Bhutto Dynasty: The Struggle for Power in Pakistan* (New Haven, CT, 2020), p. 38.
13 Ibid.
14 Hameed, *Born to Be Hanged*, p. 3.
15 Ibid.
16 Wolpert, *Zulfi Bhutto of Pakistan*, p. 50.
17 Bennett-Jones, *The Bhutto Dynasty*, p. 42.
18 In fact, Ian Talbot's *History of British Diplomacy in Pakistan* (Abingdon, 2021) delves into this topic.
19 Ibid., pp. 76–7.
20 Ibid.
21 Hildreth to Bhutto, 4 May 1955, Horace Hildreth Papers Coll 1601, 33/2, Maine Historical Society, Portland, cited in Talbot, *History of British Diplomacy in Pakistan*, p. 78.
22 Ibid.
23 Humayun Mirza, *From Plassey to Pakistan: The Family History of Iskander Mirza, the First President of Pakistan* (Lahore, 2002), p. 227.
24 Hameed, *Born to Be Hanged*, p. 12.
25 Rafique Afzal, *Political Parties in Pakistan, 1958–1969* (Islamabad, 1986), p. 187.
26 Ibid.
27 Ian Talbot, *Inventing the Nation* (London, 2000), p. 208.
28 Afzal, *Political Parties in Pakistan, 1958–1969*, vol. I, p. 190.
29 Sherbaz Khan Mazari, *A Journey to Disillusionment* (Karachi, 1999), p. 140.
30 *Foundation and Policy, Pakistan People's Party* (Lahore, 1968), cited in Afzal, *Political Parties in Pakistan, 1958–1969*, p. 190.
31 Bennett-Jones, *Bhutto Dynasty*, p. 60.
32 Talbot, *Inventing the Nation*, p. 208.
33 See Shuja Nawaz, *Crossed Swords: Pakistan, Its Army, and the Wars Within* (Karachi, 2017), p. 264.
34 Lawrence Ziring, *Pakistan in the Twentieth Century: A Political History* (Karachi, 1997), p. 375.
35 Mohammad Waseem, *Politics and the State in Pakistan* (Islamabad, 2007), p. 284.
36 Wolpert, *Zulfi Bhutto of Pakistan*, p. 172.
37 Sugata Bose and Ayesha Jalal, *Modern South Asia: History: Culture, Political Economy* (Lahore, 2011), p. 182.
38 'Its third schedule contained an oath which serving members of the military were to take forswearing political activities of any kind.' Ian Talbot, *Pakistan: A Modern History* (London, 2005), p. 223.
39 Ibid.
40 Hassan Askari Rizvi, *Military and Politics in Pakistan: 1947–1997* (Lahore, 2000), p. 214.
41 Omar Noman, *Pakistan: A Political and Economic History since 1947* (New York, 1990), p. 59.
42 Ibid.
43 Ibid.
44 Ibid.
45 Talbot, *Pakistan*, p. 223.
46 Noman, *Pakistan*, p. 60.

47 Salman Taseer, *Zulfiqar Ali Bhutto: Bachpan sey Takhta-i-Dar Tak* (Lahore, 1988), p. 168.
48 For a detailed account of Pakistani bureaucracy, see Charles Kennedy, *Bureaucracy in Pakistan* (Karachi, 1987).
49 Talbot, *Pakistan*, p. 227.
50 Wolpert, *Zulfi Bhutto of Pakistan*, p. 173.
51 Noman, *Pakistan*, p. 61.
52 Ibid.
53 Ibid.
54 Talbot, *Pakistan*, p. 228.
55 Saeed Shafqat, *Political System of Pakistan and Public Policy* (Lahore, 1989), p. 10.
56 Bose and Jalal, *Modern South Asia*, pp. 182–3.
57 Khalid bin Sayeed, *Politics in Pakistan*, p. 91.
58 Ibid.
59 Ibid.
60 Ibid.
61 S. Akbar Zaidi, *Issues in Pakistan's Economy* (Karachi, 2005), p. 39.
62 Tahir Kamran, 'Pakistan: A Failed State?', *History Today*, LXVII/9 (2017), p. 30.
63 *Dawn*, 8 September 1974.
64 Ibid.
65 Tahir Kamran, 'The Making of a Minority: Ahmadi Exclusion through Constitutional Amendments, 1974', *Pakistan Journal of Historical Studies*, IV/1–2 (Summer–Winter 2019), p. 75.
66 *Dawn*, 8 September 1974.
67 Abdul A. Qadeer, *Pakistan: Social and Cultural Transformations in a Muslim Nation* (Lahore, 2011), p. 29.
68 Ibid.
69 Ibid., p. 41.
70 Iqbal Ahmad, 'Bhutto's Foreign Policy Legacy', *Dawn*, www.dawn.com.pk, 5 April 2009.
71 For details on Bhutto's vision about Pakistan's foreign policy, see Bhutto, *The Myth of Independence* (Karachi, 1969).
72 Ayesha Jalal, *The Struggle for Pakistan: A Muslim Homeland and Global Politics* (Cambridge, MA, 2014), p. 200.
73 Ibid.
74 On the Simla Agreement, see Mody, *Zulfi, My Friend*, pp. 142–50.
75 Ahmad, 'Bhutto's Foreign Policy Legacy'.
76 Rashid Ahmad Malik, 'Pakistan–Japan Relations: Continuity, Convergence and Divergence (1971–1977)', *Routledge Publications* (2009), pp. 145–90.
77 Ibid.
78 Talbot, *Pakistan*, pp. 238–9.
79 Jalal, *The Struggle for Pakistan*, p. 200.
80 Bhutto, *The Myth of Independence*, pp. 9–10.
81 Ibid., p. 30.
82 Farhan Zaheer, 'A Look Back at the History of PSM', *Express Tribune*, 10 November 2013, https://tribune.com.pk.
83 For details, see Muhammad Ahsen Chaudhry, 'Pakistan's Relations with U.S.S.R', *Asian Survey* (1966), pp. 492–500. M. Iqbal, Falak Sher, Rehmat Ullah Awan and Khalid Javed, 'Cultural Relations between Pakistan and the Soviet Union during Ayub Khan's Period', *Pakistaniaat: A Journal of Pakistan Studies*, III/3 (2011), pp. 60–72.
84 Dalip Mukerjee, 'Afghanistan under Daud: Relations with Neighboring States', *Asian Survey*, XV/4 (April 1975), pp. 301–12.

85 'Mohammad Daud Khan', *Encyclopedia Britannica*, www.britannica.com, accessed 9 November 2022.
86 Mukerjee, 'Afghanistan under Daud'.
87 Hanif ur Rahman, 'Pak–Afghan Relations during Z. A. Bhutto Era: The Dynamics of Cold War', *Pakistan Journal of History and Culture*, XXXIII/2 (2012), pp. 23–42; Anees Jillani, 'Pak–Afghan Relations, 1958–1988', *Pakistan Horizon*, XLVI/1 (January 1993), pp. 35–45.
88 Khalid Mahmud, 'The Development of Federalism in Pakistan', in *Problems and Politics of Federalism in Pakistan*, ed. Pervaiz Iqbal Cheema and Rashid Ahmad Khan (Islamabad, 2006), p. 21.
89 Ibid.
90 Cited in Syed Bader ul Islam, 'When Bhutto Forgot His People', *Daily Star*, www.thedailystar.net, accessed 14 October 2023.
91 Ziring, *Pakistan in the Twentieth Century*, p. 377.
92 'The Fall of Zulfiqar Ali Bhutto', *Daily Observer*, www.observerbd.com, 5 July 1977.

9 Piety and Praetorianism: General Zia ul Haq's Reign, 1977–88

1 Altaf Gauhar, cited in Roedad Khan, *Pakistan: A Dream Gone Sour* (Lahore, 1997), pp. 81–2. A former bureaucrat and trusted confidant of Ayub Khan who later ventured into journalism, Altaf Gauhar offers a keen and perceptive evaluation of Zia ul Haq's character and legacy, serving as an apt prelude to this chapter.
2 Ibid., p. 81.
3 Jamsheed Marker, *Cover Point: Impressions of Leadership in Pakistan* (London, 2021), p. 115.
4 Khan, *Pakistan*, p. 81.
5 Ibid.; however, the assertion that as president Zia never minded if his friends and cronies did not join him for prayer is unpersuasive when tested against Zia's intolerance for progressive forces and his orders for compulsory *namaz* in offices. See Zahid Akhtar Masood, 'Dictatorship in Pakistan: A Study of Zia Era, 1977–88', *Pakistan Journal of History and Culture*, XXXII/1 (2011), p. 4.
6 Ibid.
7 Shahid Javed Burki, 'Pakistan under Zia: 1977–1988', *Asian Survey*, XXVIII/10 (1988), pp. 1083–4.
8 Akbar S. Ahmad, *Pakistan Society: Islam Ethnicity and Leadership in South Asia* (New York, 1986), p. 159.
9 Burki, 'Pakistan under Zia', p. 1084.
10 Masood, 'Dictatorship in Pakistan', p. 4.
11 Quoted in Ahmad, *Pakistan Society*, p. 160.
12 Shaikh Aziz, 'A Leaf from History: Enter: Ziaul Haq', *Dawn*, www.dawn.com, 12 May 2013.
13 Hein G. Kiessling, *Faith Unity Discipline: The ISI of Pakistan* (London, 2023), p. 35.
14 Seyyed Vali Reza Nasr, *The Vanguard of the Islamic Revolution: The Jama'at-i Islami of Pakistan* (Berkeley, CA, 1994).
15 The generals who had been superseded were Mohammad Sharif, Mohammad Akbar Khan, Aftab Ahmad Khan, Azmat Bakhsh Awan, Agha Ibrahim Akram, Abdul Majeed Malik and Ghulam Gilani Khan. Aziz, 'A Leaf from History'.
16 Talbot, *Pakistan*, p. 255.
17 On Wali Khan, see 'Wali Khan: An Appraisal, Special Report', *The News*, www.thenews.com.pk, 24 April 2006.
18 They were Jamaat-i-Islami, Tehreek-i-Istaqlal, Jamiat ulma-i-Islam, Jamiat Ulema-i-Pakistan, Muslim League, Pakistan Democratic Party, Khaksar Tehreek, Awami National

Party. For details see Bashir Ahmad, 'PNA Movement', *Journal of the Punjab University Historical Society*, XXXI/1 (January–June 2018), pp. 37–49.
19   Tahir Kamran, *Election Commission of Pakistan: Role in Politics* (Lahore, 2009), pp. 115–23.
20   For details, see Ghafoor Ahmad, *Aur Phir Martial Law Aa Gaya* (Lahore, 2000).
21   Talbot, *Pakistan*, p. 50.
22   Barbara Crossette, 'Who Killed Zia?', *World Policy Journal*, XXII/3 (Fall 2005), pp. 94–5.
23   Ibid., p. 94.
24   Ibid., p. 95.
25   Hasan Askari Rizvi, 'The Paradox of Military Rule in Pakistan', *Asian Survey*, XXIV/5 (May 1984), p. 538.
26   Ayesha Jalal, *The Struggle for Pakistan: A Muslim Homeland and Global Politics* (Cambridge, MA, 2014), p. 219.
27   Ibid., p. 222.
28   Ibid., p. 218.
29   For details, see Colonel Rafiuddin, *Bhutto key Akhari 323 Din* (Lahore, 2007).
30   After declaring martial law in July 1977, General Zia established a military council as the supreme governing body and partitioned the country into five distinct zones: Zone A for Punjab, Zone B for NWFP, Zone C for Sindh, Zone D for Baluchistan and Zone E for the Northern Areas. Hina Altaf, 'History of Military Interventions in Political Affairs in Pakistan', MA thesis, City University of New York, 2019, p. 26.
31   *The Muslim*, 14 March 1984.
32   Hassan Askari Rizvi, *Military and Politics in Pakistan: 1947–1997* (Lahore, 2000), p. 256.
33   Ibid., p. 257.
34   Ibid.
35   Ayesha Siddiqa, *Military Inc.: Inside Pakistan's Military Economy* (Karachi, 2007).
36   Mohammad Waseem, *Politics and the State in Pakistan* (Islamabad, 2007), p. 366.
37   Talbot, *Pakistan*, p. 246.
38   Waseem, *Politics and State in Pakistan*, p. 373.
39   Ibid.
40   The parties forming the MRD were the Pakistan People's Party, the National Democratic Party (NDP); the Pakistan Democratic Party (PDP); Tehrik-e-Istiqlal; the Pakistan Muslim League (Khairuddin-Qasim Group); Qaumi Mahaz-e-Azadi; the Pakistan Mazdoor Kisan Party; Jamiat Ulema-i-Islam (JUI), which subsequently opted to split on the question of participation in the MRD; the Pakistan National Party (PNP); Awami Tehrik; and the National Awami Party (Pakhtoonkhwah). For a detailed account on MRD, see Sherbaz Khan Mazari, *A Journey to Disillusionment* (Karachi, 1999), p. 537.
41   Rizvi, *Military and Politics in Pakistan*, p. 253.
42   For details, see Mazari, *A Journey to Disillusionment*, pp. 538–9.
43   For a view to the contrary, see Malik Hammad Ahmad, 'The Struggle for Democracy in Pakistan: Non-Violent Resistance to Military Rule 1977–88', PhD thesis, Warwick University, 2015.
44   Mazari, *A Journey to Disillusionment*, pp. 554–5.
45   Zamir Niazi, *The Web of Censorship* (Oxford, 1994).
46   Tahir Kamran, *Democracy and Governance in Pakistan* (Lahore, 2008), p. 111.
47   Talbot, *Pakistan*, p. 252.
48   Mazari, *A Journey to Disillusionment*, p. 255.
49   Shuja Nawaz, *Crossed Swords: Pakistan, Its Army, and the Wars Within* (Karachi, 2017), p. 370.
50   Kamran, *Democracy and Governance in Pakistan*, p. 113.

References

51 Ibid.
52 Ibid., p. 114.
53 Jalal, *The Struggle for Pakistan*, p. 242.
54 Ibid.
55 Ibid.
56 For context to PCO, see Martin Lau, *The Role of Islam in the Legal System of Pakistan* (Leiden, 2005), pp. 131–42.
57 Sartaj Aziz, *Between Dreams and Realities: Some Milestones in Pakistan's History* (Karachi, 2020), p. 58.
58 'The Federal Council [Majlis-e-Shoora] (1981–85)', History Pak, www.historypak.com, accessed 12 October 2023.
59 Kamran, *Election Commission of Pakistan*, p. 136.
60 Ibid.
61 For details, see Omar Noman, *Pakistan: A Political and Economic History since 1947* (New York, 1990), pp. 125–38.
62 See Election Commission of Pakistan, *Report on the General Elections 1985*, vol. I, (Islamabad, 1986).
63 'Politics without Parties, a Report on the 1985 Partyless Election in Pakistan', Society for the Advancement of Education (SAHE), Lahore, 1988, pp. 11–12 and 15.
64 On Christians, see Tahir Kamran, 'Community of the Marginalized: State, Society and Punjabi Christians', *South Asian Review*, XXI/2 (2010), pp. 66–83.
65 Tahir Kamran, 'The Making of a Minority: Ahmadi Exclusion through Constitutional Amendments, 1974', *Pakistan Journal of Historical Studies*, IV/1–2 (2019), pp. 55–84.
66 Hamid Khan, *Constitutional and Political History of Pakistan* (Karachi, 2009), p. 20.
67 *Dawn*, *Jang* and *The Herald*, cited in Noman, *Pakistan*, p. 127.
68 Jalal, *The Struggle for Pakistan*, p. 243.
69 Ibid.
70 Ibid.
71 Ibid.
72 Ibid.
73 Tahir Kamran, 'Politics and a Sense of History', *The News*, www.thenews.com.pk, 27 March 2022.
74 Ahmad Rashid, 'Obituary: Muhammad Khan Junejo', *The Independent*, 19 March 1993.
75 Article 58-2b, Constitution of 1973. See Khan, *Constitutional and Political History of Pakistan*, pp. 509–18.
76 Aziz, *Between Dreams and Realities*, p. 66.
77 For details, see Noman, *Pakistan*, pp. 136–8.
78 Rashid, 'Obituary'.
79 S. Akbar Zaidi, *Issues in Pakistan's Economy* (Karachi, 1999), p. 124.
80 For the military's role in Pakistan's economy, see Ayesha Siddiqa, *Military Inc.: Inside Pakistan's Military Economy* (Karachi, 2007), pp. 139–51.
81 Abdul A. Qadeer, *Pakistan: Social and Cultural Transformations in a Muslim Nation* (Lahore, 2011), p. 31.
82 For causes of high growth, see Zaidi, *Issues in Pakistan's Political Economy*, pp. 116–17.
83 Noman, *Pakistan*, pp. 180–87. Also see *World Development Report* (World Bank, 1984) for comments on the Fourth Five-Year Plan.
84 Noman, *Pakistan*, pp. 180–87.
85 Ibid., p. 154.
86 Vyacheslav Y. Belokrenitsky and Vladimir N. Moskalenko, *A Political History of Pakistan: 1947–2007* (Karachi, 2013), p. 285.
87 Qadeer, *Pakistan*, p. 33.

88 Belokrenitsky and Moskalenko, *A Political History of Pakistan*, p. 279.
89 Qadeer, *Pakistan*, p. 31.
90 Belokrenitsky and Moskalenko, *A Political History of Pakistan*, pp. 283–4.
91 Ibid., p. 284.
92 For greater details, see Waael B. Hallaq, *Sharī'a: Theory, Practice, Transformations* (Cambridge, 2009).
93 Belokrenitsky and Moskalenko, *A Political History of Pakistan*, p. 283.
94 Cohen, *The Pakistan Army*, p. 86.
95 *Newsline*, Karachi, September 2001, pp. 36–42.
96 Federal Shariat Court, 'Chapter 3', www.federalshariatcourt.gov.pk, accessed 14 October 2023.
97 For details, see ibid., citing the Hudood Ordinance 1979.
98 Owen Bennett-Jones, *Pakistan: Eye of the Storm* (New Haven, CT, 2009), pp. 20–21.
99 Noman, *Pakistan*, p. 145.
100 Asifa Quraishi, 'Her Honour: An Islamic Critique of the Rape Provisions in Pakistan's Ordinance on *Zina*', *Islamic Studies*, XXXVIII/3 (Autumn 1999), pp. 403–31.
101 Adeel Hussain, *Revenge, Politics and Blasphemy in Pakistan* (London, 2022), pp. 126–7.
102 Khan, *Constitutional and Political History*, p. 505.
103 Qasim Zaman, *Islam in Pakistan: A History* (Princeton, NJ, 2018), p. 180.
104 Tahir Kamran, 'Contextualizing Sectarian Militancy in Pakistan: A Case Study of Jhang', *Journal of Islamic Studies*, XX/1 (2009), pp. 55–85.
105 Qasim Zaman, *Islam in Pakistan*, p. 180.
106 For details, see Tahir Kamran, 'Salafi Extremism in the Punjab and Its Transnational Impact', in *Communalism and Globalization in South Asia and its Diaspora*, ed. Deana Heath and Chandana Mathur (London, 2010).
107 Andreas Rieck, *The Shias in Pakistan: An Assertive and Beleaguered Minority* (London, 2015).
108 Kamran, 'Contextualizing Sectarian Militancy in Pakistan', p. 71.
109 Mariam Abou Zahab, *Pakistan: A Kaleidoscope of Islam* (London, 2020), pp. 91–5.
110 Ibid., pp. 56–7.
111 Declan Walsh, 'Karachi Bomb Attack Leaves at Least 45 Sunni Worshippers Dead', *The Guardian*, www.theguardian.com, 12 April 2006.
112 Mohammad Waseem, *Political Conflict in Pakistan* (London, 2021), p. 71.
113 Rasul Bakhsh Rais, *Islam, Ethnicity, and Power Politics: Constructing Pakistan's National Identity* (Karachi, 2017), pp. 120–21.
114 Ibid., p. 121.
115 Oskar Verkaaik, *Migrants and Militants: Fun and Violence in Pakistan* (Princeton, NJ, 2004), pp. 60–61.
116 Bennett-Jones, *Pakistan*, p. 56.
117 Ibid.
118 Nadeem Farooq Paracha, 'Born to Run: The Rise and Levelling of the APMSO', *Dawn*, www.dawn.com.pk, 23 August 2012.
119 Bennett-Jones, *Pakistan*, p. 56.
120 Ibid., p. 57.

10 The Rule of the Troika and the Onset of 'Establishmentarian Democracy', 1988–99

1. Mohammad Waseem, 'Conclusion: Political Parties in an "Establishmentarian Democracy"', in *The Political Conflict in Pakistan* (London, 2021), pp. 318–19; Marium Mufti, Sahar Shafqat and Niloufer Siddiqui, eds, *Pakistan's Political Parties: Surviving between Dictatorship and Democracy* (Lahore, 2020).
2. Lawrence Ziring, 'Public Policy Dilemmas and Pakistan's Nationality Problem: The Legacy of Zia ul-Haq', *Asian Survey*, XXVIIII/8 (August 1988), pp. 796–8.
3. Roedad Khan, *Pakistan: A Dream Gone Sour* (Karachi, 1997), p. 101.
4. Ibid.
5. Ian Talbot, *Pakistan: A Modern History* (London, 2005), pp. 428–9.
6. Colonel Ashfaq Hussain, *Iqtidar key Majbooriyan: General Mirza Aslam Beg key Swaneh Hayat* (Lahore, 2021), pp. 22–4.
7. Ibid., p. 41.
8. Cited in Nadeem Farooq Paracha, 'The Rise and Fall of "General Glasnost"', *Dawn*, www.dawn.com.pk, 2 October 2016.
9. Hein G. Kiessling, *Faith, Unity, Discipline: The ISI of Pakistan* (London, 2023), p. 73.
10. Talbot, *Pakistan*, p. 421.
11. Hamza Alavi, 'Authoritarianism and Legitimation of State Power in Pakistan', in *The Post-Colonial State in Asia: Dialects of Politics and Culture*, ed. Subrata Kumar Mitra (Lahore, 1998), p. 66.
12. Benazir Bhutto, *Daughter of the East: An Autobiography* (London, 2007), p. v.
13. Anna Suvorova, *Widows and Daughters: Gender, Kinship, and Power in South Asia* (Oxford, 2019), p. 147.
14. Ayesha Jalal, *The Struggle for Pakistan: A Muslim Homeland and Global Politics* (Cambridge, 2014), p. 260.
15. Victoria Schofield, *The Fragrance of Tears: My Friendship with Benazir Bhutto* (Karachi, 2020), p. 22.
16. Anita M. Weiss, 'Benazir Bhutto and the Future of Women in Pakistan', *Asian Survey*, xxx/5 (May 1990), pp. 433–45.
17. Bhutto, *Daughter of the East*, pp. 1–50.
18. Saeed Shafqat, *Civil–Military Relations in Pakistan: From Zulfiqar Ali Bhutto to Benazir Bhutto* (Boulder, CO, 1997), p. 225.
19. Paracha, 'The Rise and Fall of "General Glasnost"'.
20. Ibid.
21. Mohammad Waseem, *Politics and the State in Pakistan* (Islamabad, 2007), p. 425.
22. Muhammad Ali Shaikh, *Benazir Bhutto* (Karachi, 2000), p. 110.
23. Kiessling, *Faith, Unity, Discipline*, p. 75.
24. Shafqat, *Civil–Military Relations in Pakistan*, p. 226.
25. Saeed Shafqat, 'Pakistan under Benazir Bhutto', *Asian Survey*, XXXVI/7 (1996), p. 655.
26. 'Haider Mehdi interview with Shamshad Ahmad Khan', *Haider Mehdi's Perspectives*, www.youtube.com, 18 January 2023.
27. Shuja Nawaz, *Crossed Swords: Pakistan, Its Army, and the Wars Within* (Karachi, 2017), p. 414.
28. The PPP got exactly as many votes in 1988 as it managed to get in 1970. However, it got fewer seats because of the electoral alliance between its opponents in 1988.
29. Tahir Kamran, *Election Commission of Pakistan: Role in Politics* (Lahore, 2009), p. 70.
30. Talbot, *Pakistan*, pp. 294–5.
31. Kamran, *Election Commission of Pakistan*, p. 155.

32 Landholders such as Khuda Bakhsh Tiwana from Khushab won the election as an independent and promptly allied themselves with the IJI. For details, see Talbot, *Pakistan*, p. 295.
33 Ahmed Salim, *Tootti Banti Assemblian aur Civil Military Bureaucracy* (Lahore, 1990), p. 336.
34 Waseem, *Politics and the State in Pakistan*, pp. 434–5.
35 Ibid., p. 435.
36 *The Herald* (January 2008), p. 80.
37 Kamran, *Election Commission of Pakistan*, p. 154.
38 Ibid., p. 87.
39 *Jang*, 2 December 1988; *The Independent*, 1 December 1988.
40 *The Herald* (January 2008), p. 79.
41 Shafqat, *Civil–Military Relations in Pakistan*, p. 229.
42 Quoted in Tahir Kamran, *Democracy and Governance in Pakistan* (Lahore, 2008), p. 141.
43 Shafqat, *Civil–Military Relations in Pakistan*, pp. 229–30.
44 Ibid., pp. 230–31.
45 'Return of the "Midnight Jackal?"', *Dawn*, 8 April 2009, www.dawn.com.pk.
46 Kamran Khan, 'Major Amir Has a Murky Past', *Dunya News*, www.dunyanews.com.pk, 30 January 2014.
47 Asad Durrani, *Pakistan Adrift: Navigating Troubled Waters* (London, 2018), p. 31.
48 For details on 'Midnight Jackal', see Idrees Bakhtiar and Zafar Abbas, 'The Mysterious Case of Operation Midnight Jackal', *The Herald*, August 1994.
49 Nawaz, *Crossed Swords*, p. 432.
50 Shahid Javed Burki, 'Pakistan's Cautious Democratic Course', *Current History* (March 1992), pp. 117–22.
51 Saeed Shafqat, 'The Formation, Development, and Decay of the P–Nawaz', in *Pakistan's Political Parties: Surviving between Dictatorship and Democracy*, ed. Mariam Mufti, Sahar Shafqat and Niloufer Siddiqui (Lahore, 2020), p. 45.
52 Shafqat, *Civil–Military Relations in Pakistan*.
53 Ibid., p. 231.
54 Ibid.
55 Syed Haider Mehdi, 'Sharif: Traitor or Trader', *Insaf Blog*, www.insaf.pk.com.
56 Zia Shahid, *Mera Dost: Sharif: Wazir-i-Khazana sey Wazir-i-Ala aur Wazarat-i-Uzma sey Adiyala Jail Tak* (Lahore, 2018), pp. 23–7.
57 Author's interview with a retired bureaucrat who worked with Sharif in various capacities, 10 April 2019.
58 Durrani, *Pakistan Adrift*, p. 31.
59 For his profile, see Talbot, *Pakistan*, p. 445.
60 Schofield, *The Fragrance of Tears*, p. 159.
61 Shafqat, *Civil–Military Relations in Pakistan*, p. 233.
62 'Meet Mr. 10 Percent', *Chicago Tribune*, 13 September 2008, www.chicagotribune.com.
63 'Profile: PPP Co-Chair Asif Zardari', Wikileaks (ISLAMABAD 00001368003 OF 003), 31 March 2008, cited in Owen Bennett-Jones, *The Bhutto Dynasty: The Struggle for Power in Pakistan* (New Haven, CT, 2020), p. 152.
64 Ibid.
65 Ibid.
66 Ibid.
67 Ibid., p. 153.
68 Ibid.
69 Tyler Marshall, 'Political Maverick Bows to Muslim Custom', *Los Angeles Times*, 7 August 1987, cited ibid.

70　Bennett-Jones, *Bhutto Dynasty*, p. 153.
71　Bhutto, *Daughter of the East*, p. 358.
72　Bennett-Jones, *Bhutto Dynasty*, p. 154.
73　Ibid.
74　Shafqat, *Civil–Military Relations in Pakistan*, p. 233.
75　Ibid.
76　Ibid., p. 234.
77　Talbot, *Pakistan*, p. 310.
78　'The Empire Strikes Back', *The Herald* (1990).
79　Durrani, *Pakistan Adrift*, p. 26.
80　'The Empire Strikes Back'.
81　Shafqat, *Civil–Military Relations in Pakistan*, p. 235.
82　Durrani, *Pakistan Adrift*, p. 26.
83　Talbot, *Pakistan*, pp. 311–12.
84　National Democratic Institute for International Affairs, *The October 1990 Elections in Pakistan* (Washington, DC, 1991), p. 196.
85　Ibid., p. 236.
86　Ibid.
87　Ibid.
88　Ibid.
89　Jalal, *The Struggle for Pakistan*, pp. 272–3.
90　Ibid.
91　*Dawn*, 8 February 1991.
92　Talbot, *Pakistan*, p. 315.
93　*Dawn*, 16 November 1990.
94　Mohammad Waseem, 'Pakistan's Lingering Crisis of Diarchy', *Asian Survey*, XXXII/7 (July 1992), p. 626.
95　*Dawn*, 8 February 1991.
96　Waseem, *The 1993 Elections in Pakistan* (Karachi, 1994), p. 122.
97　Talbot, *Pakistan*, p. 320.
98　*Dawn*, 8 November 1991.
99　Talbot, *Pakistan*, p. 321.
100　Ibid. *Kafir* is a pejorative term to outcast any individual from the fold of Islam, and carries much significance in the Pakistani context.
101　Ibid.
102　Dr Mazhar Abbas, 'A Lone Fighter', *News on Sunday* (Lahore), 22 February 2022, www.thenews.com.pk.
103　Vazira Fazila-Yacoobali, 'The Battlefields of Karachi: Ethnicity, Violence and the State', *Journal of the International Institute*, IV/1 (Fall 1996).
104　Ibid.
105　Nawaz, *Crossed Swords*, p. 458.
106　An interview of the author with a retired bureaucrat who worked with Sharif in various capacities on 10 April 2019.
107　Waseem, *The 1993 Elections in Pakistan* (Lahore, 1994), p. 47.
108　S. Yasmeen, 'Democracy in Pakistan: The Third Dismissal', *Asian Survey*, XXXIV/6 (1994), p. 581.
109　Durrani, *Pakistan Adrift*, p. 46.
110　Talbot, *Pakistan*, p. 331.
111　*Report on the General Elections, 1993*, vol. I (Islamabad, n.d.), p. 13.
112　Ibid., p. 16.
113　'People's Verdict', *Newsline* (October 1993); *Dawn*, 8 October 1993.

114 Waseem, *The 1993 Elections in Pakistan*, pp. 168–9.
115 Ibid., pp. 191–204.
116 'Sharif declared in the National Assembly on May 31 (1994) that President Farooq Leghari was involved in the scandal and had used the Mehran Bank to sell off a worthless piece of land for 15 million rupees. The president confirmed that the land had indeed been sold through Younus Habib but denied the opposition leader's charge that there was any illegality involved in the deal.' See Tahir Amin, 'Pakistan in 1994: The Politics of Confrontation', *Asian Survey*, xxxv/2 (February 1995), p. 141.
117 'Murtaza was killed as he returned from that rally. Much of what happened is contested, but it is generally accepted that he was heading back to his house in a convoy of four cars when he came across a police checkpoint right outside 70 Clifton. When he got out of his car, there was shooting; he was hit and left bleeding to death on the street for at least twenty minutes.' For details, see Bennett-Jones, *Bhutto Dynasty*, p. 203.
118 On elections of 1996 and the role of the caretaker government, see Talbot, *Pakistan*, pp. 349–58.
119 Shafqat, *Civil–Military Relations in Pakistan*, pp. 240–41.
120 Ibid., p. 241.
121 Ibid., pp. 241–2.
122 M. M. Ali, 'Brown Amendment Prepares Way for Arms Delivery to Pakistan', *Washington Post*, December 1995, www.wrmea.org.
123 Kamran, *Democracy and Governance in Pakistan*, pp. 157–8; Ayesha Siddiqa-Agha, 'Political Economy of National Security', *Economic and Political Weekly*, xxxvii/44–5 (2002), pp. 4545–9.
124 Zafar Abbas, 'The Final Countdown', *The Herald* (October 1996).
125 *Far Eastern Review*, clix/26 (27 June 1996), p. 67.
126 Lawrence Ziring, *Pakistan: At the Crosscurrent of History* (London, 2003), p. 236.
127 Lawrence Ziring, *Pakistan in the Twentieth Century: A Political History* (Karachi, 1997), p. 570. For further details, see Hamid Khan, *A History of Judiciary in Pakistan* (Karachi, 2016), pp. 230–38.
128 Ibid.
129 Aamer Ahmed Khan, 'The Great Debacle', *The Herald*, March 1997.
130 Talbot, *Pakistan*, p. 350.
131 Government of Pakistan, '1997 General Election Report', vol. I (Islamabad, 1997), pp. 1–3.
132 Khan, 'The Great Debacle'.
133 For details on the electoral results of provincial assemblies, see Mohammad Waseem, 'Pakistan Elections 1997: One Step Forward', in *Pakistan 1997*, ed. Craig Baxter and Charles H. Kennedy (Karachi, 1998), pp. 10–12.
134 Talbot, *Pakistan*, p. 359.
135 Ibid., pp. 359–60.
136 Ibid., p. 60.
137 Owen Bennett-Jones, *Pakistan: Eye of the Storm* (New Haven, ct, 2009), p. 237.
138 Talbot, *Pakistan*, p. 444.
139 Ibid., p. 361.
140 Kathy Cannon, 'Army Chief Steps Down in Pakistani Quarrel', *Washington Post*, 8 October 1998.
141 Kiessling, *Faith, Unity, Discipline*, p. 141.

11 Pervez Musharraf: An Autocrat Re-Engineering Politics, 1999–2008

1. Pervez Musharraf, *In the Line of Fire: A Memoir* (London, 2008), pp. 10–100.
2. Ibid.
3. Ian Talbot, *Pakistan: A Modern History* (London, 2005), p. 445.
4. 'General Musharraf', Pakistani American Business Executives Association, www.pabe.org.
5. Ibid.
6. Lawrence Ziring, *Pakistan: At the Crosscurrent of History* (London, 2003), p. 266.
7. Hein G. Kiessling, *Faith, Unity, Discipline: The ISI of Pakistan* (London, 2023), p. 144.
8. For details, see Musharraf, *In the Line of Fire*, pp. 296–8.
9. Ziring, *Pakistan*, p. 267.
10. Ibid., p. 268.
11. 'General Musharraf's Address to the Nation, 13 October 1999', www.pakistani.org, accessed 14 October 2023.
12. Ibid.
13. Ibid.
14. Ibid.
15. Ibid.
16. Tahir Kamran, *Democracy and Governance in Pakistan* (Lahore, 2008), p. 175.
17. Ibid.
18. Ibid.
19. Ibid., p. 176.
20. Sumita Kumar, 'Sharif vs. Musharraf: The Future of Democracy in Pakistan', *Strategic Analysis*, XXIV/10 (January 2001), pp. 1861–75.
21. Ibid.
22. Ibid., p. 1865.
23. Kamran, *Democracy and Governance in Pakistan*, p. 177.
24. Ibid.
25. Kumar, 'Sharif vs. Musharraf: The Future of Democracy in Pakistan'.
26. Ibid.
27. Ibid.
28. Kamran, *Democracy and Governance in Pakistan*, p. 179.
29. Ibid.
30. Ibid.
31. D.M.A. Faiz, K. Hussain and A. Iqbal, 'Zia ul Haq Vis a Vis Musharraf: A Comparative Overview of Politics in Pakistan: Social Sciences', *International Research Journal of Management and Social Sciences*, III/1 (2021), pp. 16–24.
32. Ibid.
33. Luke Harding, 'Sharif Sentenced to Life for Musharraf Plot', *The Guardian*, www.theguardian.com, 7 April 2000.
34. Ibid.
35. Hamid Khan, *A History of the Judiciary in Pakistan* (Oxford, 2016), pp. 36–7.
36. Faiz, Hussain and Iqbal, 'Zia ul Haq Vis-a-Vis Musharraf', pp. 16–24.
37. Khan, *A History of the Judiciary in Pakistan*, p. 150.
38. Human Rights Watch background briefing, 'Pakistan: Entire Election Process "Deeply Flawed"', *Human Rights Watch*, 9 October 2002.
39. Faiz, Hussain and Iqbal, 'Zia ul Haq Vis-a-Vis Musharraf'.
40. Ibid.
41. Masoud Ansari, 'How the Referendum Was Won', *Newsline*, Karachi, May 2002.
42. Ibid.

43 Ibid.
44 Ibid.
45 Ibid.
46 Ibid.
47 Ibid.
48 Ibid.; also see Ayesha Jalal, *The Struggle for Pakistan: A Muslim Homeland and Global Politics* (Cambridge, 2014), p. 329.
49 Kamran, *Democracy and Governance in Pakistan*, p. 186.
50 Ibid.
51 Tahir Kamran, *Election Commission of Pakistan: Role in Politics* (Lahore, 2009), p. 213.
52 Ibid.
53 Ali Javed Naqvi, *Election 2002: The White Paper* (Lahore, 2002), pp. 80–104.
54 Syed Karim Haider, *Pakistan General Elections 2002* (Lahore, 2004), p. iv.
55 Ibid., p. iii.
56 Mohammad Waseem, 'The 2002 Elections: A Study of Transition from Military to Civilian Rule', in *New Perspectives on Pakistan: Vision for the Future*, ed. Saeed Shafqat (Karachi, 2007), pp. 258–9.
57 Kamran, *Election Commission of Pakistan*, p. 216.
58 His biographical sketch was given under the title 'Former PM Zafarullah Jamali Passes Away at 76', *Dawn*, www.dawn.com.pk, 2 December 2020.
59 For Ch. Shujaat Hussain's profile see his autobiography, Shujaat Hussain, *Such To Yeh Hai* (This Is a Truth) (Lahore, 2018).
60 *Dawn*, www.dawn.com.pk, 2 December 2020.
61 *Dawn*, 28 August 2004.
62 Jalal, *The Struggle for Pakistan*, p. 335.
63 For a detailed analysis, see Kamran Aziz Khan, '17th Constitutional Amendment and Its Aftermath: The Role of Muttahidda Majlis-i-Amal (MMA)', *Pakistan Vision*, IX/2 (2008), pp. 103–4.
64 Syed Tanwir Husain Naqvi, 'The Triad of Governance, Devolution, and National Prosperity', *Pakistan Development Review*, XLII/4, Part II (2003), pp. 629–40.
65 Riaz Ahmed Shaikh, 'Politics in Pakistan: Parvaiz Musharaf's Military Rule in Perspective', *International Journal of South Asian Studies*, III/1 (2010), p. 14.
66 Kamran, *Democracy and Governance in Pakistan*, p. 191.
67 Ibid.
68 For details, see Naqvi, 'The Triad of Governance, Devolution, and National Prosperity', pp. 629–40.
69 Kamran, *Democracy and Governance in Pakistan*, p. 192.
70 Ibid.
71 Ibid.
72 Ibid.
73 Ibid.
74 'Devolution in Pakistan: Reform or Regression?', *Crisis Group*, report (22 March 2004), www.crisisgroup.org, accessed 14 October 2023.
75 Ibid.
76 Ibid.
77 Ibid.
78 'Pakistan: The Worsening Conflict in Balochistan', *Refworld*, www.refworld.org, September 2006.
79 Kamran, *Democracy and Governance in Pakistan*, p. 193.
80 *Dawn*, 8 August 2004.
81 Ibid.

82 Ibid.
83 Ibid.
84 Ibid.
85 For details, see Muhammad Zakir Abbasi and Razia Mussarrat, 'Devolution of Powers to Local Governments in Pakistan during Musharraf Regime', *Pakistan Journal of Social Sciences*, XXXV/2 (2015), pp. 891–901.
86 For police reform under Musharraf, see 'Reforming Pakistan's Police', *Crisis Group*, report (14 July 2008), www.crisisgroup.org, accessed 14 October 2023.
87 *Dawn*, 3 January 2005.
88 Ibid.
89 Kamran, *Democracy and Governance in Pakistan*, p. 196.
90 National Accountability Bureau Ordinance, 16 November 1999, www.pakistani.org.
91 Owen Bennett-Jones, *The Bhutto Dynasty: The Struggle for Power in Pakistan* (New Haven, CT, 2020), p. 214.
92 Kamran, *Democracy and Governance in Pakistan*, p. 197.
93 Ibid.
94 Ibid.
95 Imran Khan, *Pakistan: A Personal History* (London, 2011), p. 292.
96 Ibid.
97 Kamran, *Democracy and Governance in Pakistan*, p. 198.
98 Owen Bennett-Jones, *Pakistan: Eye of the Storm* (New Haven, CT, 2009), p. 303.
99 Ibid.
100 International Monetary Fund, 'Pakistan IMF Country Reports No. 08/21' (January 2008), p. 3.
101 Ibid.
102 Ibid.
103 Ian Talbot, *Pakistan: A New History* (Karachi, 2012), pp. 173–4.
104 Kamran, *Democracy and Governance in Pakistan*, p. 199.
105 Ayesha Siddiqa, *Military Inc.: Inside Pakistan's Military Economy* (Karachi, 2007), p. 70.
106 Bennett-Jones, *Pakistan*, pp. 299–300.
107 *Dawn*, 17 July 2002.
108 Bennett-Jones, *Pakistan*, p. 300; and Siddiqa, *Military Inc.*, p. 247.
109 For details, see Raymond Baker, *Capitalism's Achilles Heel: Dirty Money and How to Renew the Free-Market System* (Hoboken, NJ, 2005), pp. 78–82.
110 Michael Peel and Farhan Bokhari, 'Doubts Cast on Zardari's Mental Health', *Financial Times*, 25 August 2008.
111 Sabir Shah, 'Zardari, Benazir also Faced Charges of Having Offshore Businesses', www.thenews.com.pk, 10 April 2016.
112 Baker, *Capitalism's Achilles Heel*, p. 79.
113 Bennett-Jones, *Pakistan*, p. 302.
114 For a detailed account, see Khan, *A History of the Judiciary in Pakistan*, pp. 344–70.
115 Ibid., pp. 344–57.
116 Jalal, *The Struggle for Pakistan*, p. 341.
117 Ibid.
118 Qasim Zaman, *Islam in Pakistan: A History* (Princeton, NJ, 2018), p. 259.
119 Tahir Kamran, 'Pakistan: A Failed State?', *History Today*, LXVII/9 (2017), p. 35.
120 Talbot, *A New History*, p. 193.
121 Qudssia Akhlaque, 'It's "Operation Sunrise" not "Silence"', *Dawn*, 12 July 2007.
122 *The Economist*, 5–11 January 2008.
123 Talbot, *A New History*, p. 193.

124 Mushfiq Murshid, 'The Vicious Cycle of Extremism and Politics', *Dawn*, 4 February 2008.
125 Musharraf, *In the Line of Fire*, p. 70.
126 Ibid.
127 Ibid.
128 Michael Meacher, 'The Pakistan Connection', *The Guardian*, 22 July 2004.
129 Akhlaque, 'It's "Operation Sunrise" not "Silence"'.
130 For details, see Nasim Zehra, *From Kargil to the Coup: Events That Shook Pakistan* (Lahore, 2019).
131 Moeed Yusuf, 'The Kargil Crisis', in *Brokering Peace in Nuclear Environments: U.S. Crisis Management in South Asia* (Stanford, CA, 2019), pp. 53–82.
132 M. Siddique ul Farooque, *Kargil: Adventure or Trap, Whitepaper* (Delhi, 2006), p. 22.
133 Yusuf, 'The Kargil Crisis', p. 60.
134 Ibid.
135 Kamran, *Democracy and Governance in Pakistan*, p. 204.
136 Quoted ibid.
137 Musharraf, *In the Line of Fire*, p. 201.
138 Omar Shahid Hamid, *The Prisoner* (Delhi, 2013); Hamid, *The Party Worker* (Delhi, 2017).
139 Fahmida Riaz, *Hum Log* (Karachi, 2013).
140 Mohsin Hamid, *The Reluctant Fundamentalist* (Karachi, 2007).
141 Mohammed Hanif, *Our Lady of Alice Bhatti* (London, 2011).
142 Kanza Javed, *Ashes, Wine and Dust* (New Delhi, 2015).
143 Shamsur Rahman Faruqi, *Kayi Chaand Thay Sar-e-Asmaan* (New Delhi, 1998). The work was translated into English by Faruqi himself, under the title *The Mirror of Beauty* (New Delhi, 2013).
144 Tariq Rahman, *A History of Pakistani Literature in English: 1947–1988* (Lahore, 1990).
145 Muneeza Shamsie, *Hybrid Tapestries: The Development of Pakistani Literature in English* (Karachi, 2017); Aroosa Kanwal and Saiyma Aslam, eds, *Routledge Companion to Pakistani Anglophone Writing* (London, 2019).
146 For Cara Cilano's comment, see Mushtaq Bilal, *Writing Pakistan: Conversations on Identity, Nationhood and Fiction* (Noida, 2016), p. 19.
147 Ali's work is a series of historical novels that treat the history of the long encounter between Islam and the West: *Shadows of the Pomegranate Tree*; *The Book of Saladin*; *The Stone Woman*; *A Sultan in Palermo*; *Night of the Golden Butterfly*.
148 Claire Chambers, *British Muslim Fictions: Interviews with Contemporary Writers* (Basingstoke, 2011), p. 37.
149 Ali, *Shadows of the Pomegranate Tree*.
150 Sara Suleri Goodyear, *Meatless Days* (Chicago, IL, 1991).
151 Later, as an adult, Suleri moved to the United States. After receiving her PhD from Indiana University in 1983, she taught at Yale University.
152 Lucy Scholes, 'Meatless Days: A Bewitching Memoir about Growing Up in Newly Created Pakistan', *The National*, www.thenational.ae, 12 February 2018.
153 Hira Shah, '"Meatless Days" – A Saga of Personal Loss and Political Turmoil', *Daily Times*, www.dailytimes.com.pk, 11 September 2018.
154 Mohammed Hanif, *A Case of Exploding Mangoes* (New Delhi, 2009).
155 Umera Ahmed, *Pir-i-Kamil* (Lahore, 2004).
156 Mustansar Hussain Tarar, *Bahaao* (Lahore, 1992).
157 Mustansar Hussain Tarar, *Raakh* (Lahore, 2003).
158 Abdullah Hussain, *Udaas Naslain* (Lahore, 2015); and *Nadaar Log* (Lahore, 1996).
159 Ali Akbar Natiq, *Nau Lakhi Kothi* (Lahore, 2014).

160 For Ahmad Khan Kharral, see Turab ul Hassan Sargana, *Punjab and the War of Independence, 1857–1858: From Collaboration to Resistance* (Karachi, 2020).

12 A Decade of Uncertainty, 2008–18

1 Owen Bennett-Jones, *The Bhutto Dynasty: The Struggle for Power in Pakistan* (New Haven, CT, 2020), p. 220.
2 Ibid.
3 Ibid.
4 *Dawn*, www.dawn.com.pk, 19 October 2007; *Al Jazeera*, www.aljazeera.com, 29 December 2007; Tahir Kamran, *Election Commission of Pakistan: Role in Politics* (Lahore, 2009), p. 223.
5 Ron Suskind, *The Way of the World: A Story of Truth and Hope in an Age of Extremism* (New York, 2008), p. 268; Benazir Bhutto, *Reconciliation: Islam, Democracy, and the West* (London, 2008), pp. 5–8; Ayesha Jalal, *The Struggle for Pakistan: A Muslim Homeland and Global Politics* (Cambridge, 2014), pp. 346–50.
6 'November 3 Emergency Revisited', *Dawn*, www.dawn.com.pk, 1 November 2008.
7 Bennett-Jones, *The Bhutto Dynasty*, pp. 220–30; Mary Englar, *Benazir Bhutto: Pakistani Prime Minister and Activist* (Mankato, MN, 2006), pp. 1–40; Libby Hughes, *Benazir Bhutto: From Prison to Prime Minister* (Bloomington, IN, 2000), p. 25; Heraldo Muñoz, *Getting Away with Murder: Benazir Bhutto's Assassination and the Politics of Pakistan* (New York, 2014), p. 60.
8 Kamran, *Election Commission of Pakistan*, p. 224.
9 Ahsan ur Rahim, *The Dynamics of Electoral Politics in Pakistan: A Study of General Election 2008* (independently published, 2018), pp. 10–11; Iffat Humayun Khan, *Electoral Malpractices during the 2008 Elections in Pakistan* (Karachi, 2012), pp. 10–15; Aqil Shah, *The Army and Democracy: Military Politics in Pakistan* (Cambridge, MA, 2014), pp. 30–35; Mariam Mufti, Sahar Shafqat and Niloufer Siddiqui, eds, *Pakistan's Political Parties: Surviving between Dictatorship and Democracy* (Lahore, 2020), p. 70.
10 Kamran, *Election Commission of Pakistan*, p. 225.
11 Raja Asghar, 'PPP, PML-N in Sight of Magical Number', *Dawn*, www.dawn.com.pk, 20 February 2008.
12 Kamran, *Election Commission of Pakistan*, p. 226.
13 'Bhutto's Party Seeks Coalition', *Al Jazeera*, www.aljazeera.com, 20 February 2008.
14 Kamran, *Election Commission of Pakistan*, p. 226.
15 'Political Management Done in 2002 Polls', *Dawn*, www.dawn.com.pk, 27 February 2008.
16 Irfan Ghauri, 'Political Musings: The Kingmakers and Their Prime Ministers', *Express Tribune*, www.tribune.com.pk, 11 March 2016.
17 'Pakistan: Election Commission Not Impartial', *Human Rights Watch*, www.hrw.org.com, 12 February 2008.
18 '2007 Country Reports on Human Rights Practices – Pakistan', *Refworld*, www.refworld.org, 11 March 2008.
19 Talbot goes on to say: 'Asif Zardari, who had married Benazir in December 1987, claimed that charges against him were politically motivated. While he may have favoured friends and family, his portrayal as "Mr. 10 per cent" was exaggerated. In all he spent 11 years in jail facing various corruption and criminal charges. He left Pakistan to go overseas for medical treatment after being granted bail in mid-2004.' Talbot, *Pakistan: A New History* (Karachi, 2012), p. 200.
20 Sartaj Aziz, 'The Economic Cost of Extremism', in *Pakistan's Quagmire: Security, Strategy and the Future of the Islamic-Nuclear Nation*, ed. Usama Butt and N. Elahi (New York, 2010), p. 80.

21 Talbot, *A New History*, p. 205.
22 Ibid., pp. 210–24.
23 Jalal, *The Struggle for Pakistan*, pp. 300–360.
24 Hilary Synnott: *Transforming Pakistan: Ways Out of Instability* (London, 2009), p. 181.
25 Tariq Ali, *Uprising in Pakistan: How to Bring Down a Dictatorship* (New York, 2018), pp. 10–20.
26 Asad Hashim, 'Public Support for Militancy', *Dawn*, 22 June 2010, www.dawn.com.pk.
27 Bennett-Jones, *The Bhutto Dynasty*, p. 220; Jalal, *The Struggle for Pakistan*, p. 254.
28 Bennett-Jones, *The Bhutto Dynasty*, p. 252; 'Obama Calls Pakistan's Zardari, Urges More Effort', *Reuters*, www.reuters.com, 26 October 2010.
29 Jalal, *The Struggle for Pakistan*, p. 254.
30 Talbot, *A New History*, p. 200.
31 Synnott, *Transforming Pakistan*, p. 56.
32 Pakistan's GDP growth rate reached a peak of 8.6 per cent in 2004–5.
33 William B. Milam, *Bangladesh and Pakistan: Flirting with Failure in South Asia* (London, 2009), p. 137.
34 Talbot, *A New History*, p. 220.
35 Ibid., p. 236.
36 Asad Hashim, 'Public Support for Militancy', *Dawn*, 22 June 2010, www.dawn.com.pk.
37 Yousaf Raza Gilani, *Chah-e-Yousaf se Sada* (independently published, 2016), pp. 113–15.
38 Kamran, *Election Commission of Pakistan*, pp. 228–9.
39 *Dawn*, www.dawn.com.pk, 22 June 2012.
40 Ian Talbot, *A History of Modern South Asia: Politics, States, Diasporas* (New Haven, CT, 2016), p. 280.
41 Ibid., p. 50.
42 'War on Terror Cost Pakistani Economy $40 Bn: Minister', *South Asia News*, www.southasianews.com, 27 October 2009.
43 S. Iqbal, 'Foreign Direct Investment Falls by 58 Pc in First Quarter', *Dawn*, www.dawn.com.pk, 16 October 2009.
44 Salman Masood and David E. Sanger, 'Militants Attack Pakistani Naval Base in Karachi', *New York Times*, www.nytimes.com, 22 May 2011.
45 Jalal, *The Struggle for Pakistan*, p. 77.
46 Stanley B. Sprague, *Pakistan since Independence: A History, 1947 to Today* (Jefferson, OH, 2020), p. 100.
47 *Dawn*, www.dawn.com.pk, 1 December 2010; and *Monthly Economic Update and Outlook*, December 2010, published by the Government of Pakistan Finance Division Economic Adviser's Wing.
48 'IMF Concerned over Rising Expenditure, Inflation', *Dawn*, www.dawn.com.pk, 19 July 2010.
49 Augustine Anthony and Michael Georgy, 'Pakistan Floods Destroy Crops and Could Cost Billions', *Reuters*, www.reuters.com, 12 August 2010.
50 Shakeel Anjum, 'Investigation into Taunsa Bund Breach Underway', *Express Tribune*, www.tribune.com, 9 September 2010.
51 'Overview of Economy', *Economic Survey, 2010–11*, www.finance.gov.pk.
52 'Pakistan Floods "Hit 14m People"', *BBC News*, www.bbc.co.uk, 6 August 2010.
53 Aroosa Masroor, 'These Are Not Pakistan's Worst Floods', *Express Tribune*, www.tribune.com, 23 August 2010.
54 Jehangir Karamat, 'Pakistan's Water World: The Political and Economic Impact of the Recent Floods', *Brookings*, www.brooking.com, 17 August 2010; 'Pakistan Flood Impact Assessment', *World Food Program Report* (September 2010).

55 Hassan Abbas, *The Taliban Revival: Violence and Extremism on the Pakistan–Afghanistan Frontier* (New Haven, CT, 2015), pp. 60–100.
56 Madiha Afzal, *Pakistan under Siege: Extremism, Society, and the State* (Gurgaon, 2018), p. 45.
57 Abbas, *The Taliban Revival*, p. 112.
58 William Dalrymple, 'Days of Rage', *New Yorker* (23 July 2007).
59 N. Elahi, *Terrorism in Pakistan: The Tehreek-e-Taliban Pakistan (TTP) and the Challenge to Security* (London, 2019), p. 100.
60 Talbot, *A New History*, p. 194.
61 Afzal, *Pakistan under Siege*, p. 46.
62 Abbas, *The Taliban Revival*, p. 120.
63 Pamela Constable, 'Islamic Law Instituted in Pakistan's Swat Valley', *Washington Post*, www.washingtonpost.com, 17 February 2009.
64 Afzal, *Pakistan under Siege*, p. 47.
65 BBC News, www.bbc.co.uk, 27 November 2008.
66 *Dawn*, www.dawn.com.pk, 27 November 2008.
67 *Dawn*, www.dawn.com.pk, 5 January 2010.
68 A detailed account has been published by Salman Taseer's son, Shahbaz Taseer. See Shahbaz Taseer, *Lost to the World: A Memoir of Faith, Family, and Five Years in Terrorist Captivity* (New York, 2022), pp. 32–40; Imran Khan, *Pakistan: A Personal History* (London, 2011), pp. 347–8.
69 Salman Siddiqui, 'Hardline Stance: Religious Bloc Condones Murder', *Express Tribune*, www.tribune.com.pk, 5 January 2011.
70 BBC News, 5 January 2011, www.bbc.co.uk.
71 For a detailed analysis, see Tahir Kamran, 'Unpacking the Myth of Barelvi Eclecticism: A Historical Appraisal', in *Rethinking Pakistan: A Twenty-First-Century Perspective*, ed. Bilal Zahur and Raza Rumi (Lahore, 2018), pp. 53–65.
72 For the accused's version of events, see Raymond Davis and Storms Reback, *The Contractor: How I Landed in a Pakistani Prison and Ignited a Diplomatic Crisis* (Dallas, TX, 2017), pp. 20–60.
73 Shuja Nawaz, *The Battle for Pakistan: The Bitter U.S. Friendship and a Tough Neighbourhood* (Karachi, 2019), pp. 83–91.
74 'Raymond Davis Case', *History Pak*, www.historypak.com.
75 S. R. Subramanian, 'Abuse of Diplomatic Privileges and the Balance between Immunities and the Duty to Respect the Local Laws and Regulations under the Vienna Conventions: The Recent Indian Experience', *Chinese Journal of Global Governance* (October 2017), pp. 182–233.
76 *Dawn*, www.dawn.com.pk, 28 January 2011.
77 C. Christine Fair, 'Diplomatic Duplicity', *Foreign Policy*, www.foreignpolicy.com, 18 February 2011; Madiha Afzal, 'On Pakistani Anti-Americanism', *Brookings*, www.brooking.com, 19 November 2013.
78 *Express Tribune*, www.tribune.com.pk, 15 November 2011.
79 *Dawn*, www.dawn.com.pk, 2 May 2011; Nicholas Schmidle, 'Getting Bin Laden: What Happened That Night in Abbottabad', *New Yorker*, www.newyorker.com, 1 August 2011.
80 *News International*, www.thenews.com.pk, 18 November 2020.
81 For an in-depth and detailed analysis, see Nawaz, *The Battle for Pakistan*, pp. 148–71.
82 *Dawn*, www.dawn.com.pk, 27 November 2011.
83 *News International*, www.thenews.com.pk, 27 November 2011.
84 BBC News, www.bbc.co.uk, 26 November 2011.

85 Ibid.
86 *Dawn*, www.dawn.com.pk, 18 November 2011.
87 Chris Allbritton, 'Pakistan's Envoy to U.S. Quits over Coup Memo', *Reuters*, www.reuters.com, 22 November 2011.
88 *Dawn*, www.dawn.com.pk, 18 November 2011.
89 Hussain Nadim, *Aid, Politics and the War of Narratives in the U.S.–Pakistan Relations: A Case Study of Kerry Lugar Berman Act* (London, 2022), pp. 90–130; Christophe Jaffrelot, *The Pakistan Paradox: Instability and Resilience* (New Delhi, 2016), pp. 200–220.
90 Haroon Rashid, 'Pakistan's "Memogate" Bodes Ill for Zardari', BBC *News*, www.bbc.co.uk, 16 December 2011. Also see Akmal Hussain, *Pakistan, Institutional Instability and Underdevelopment: State, People and Consciousness* (Lahore, 2023), pp. 220–22.
91 Mansoor Ijaz, 'Time to Take on Pakistan's Jihadist Spies', *Financial Times*, www.subs.ft.com, 10 October 2011.
92 Ilhan Niaz, 'History (of Pakistan, 1947–2017)', in *Europa World Regional Series* (2018), pp. 1–16.
93 Ibid.
94 A. Rasheed, 'The 2013 Elections in Pakistan: A Post-Mortem', *Journal of Democracy*, XXVI/4 (2015), pp. 84–98.
95 Shamsul Islam, '2013 Election "Rigging": Imran Khan calls for "Trial of Troika"', *Express Tribune*, https://tribune.com.pk, 25 May 2014.
96 I. Khan, 'The 2013 General Elections in Pakistan: An Analysis of Rigging Allegations', *Commonwealth and Comparative Politics*, LVI/3 (2018), pp. 303–24.
97 I. Hussain, 'The Rigging of the 2013 General Elections in Pakistan: A Forensic Analysis', *Round Table*, CVII/4 (2018), pp. 491–501.
98 'Imran Khan's Protest in Islamabad, What You Need to Know', *The Guardian*, www.theguardian.com, 18 August 2014.
99 Rafiullah Kakar, 'Politics: De-Mystifying the PTM', *Dawn*, www.dawn.com.pk, 23 February 2020.
100 Nadeem F. Paracha, 'The Pakhtun Identity Crisis', *Dawn*, www.dawn.com.pk, 15 April 2018.
101 M. Ilyas Khan, 'Manzoor Pashteen: The Young Tribesman Rattling Pakistan's Army', BBC *News*, www.bbc.co.uk, 23 April 2018.
102 *Dawn*, www.dawn.com.pk, 18 June 2014.
103 *Express Tribune*, www.tribune.com.pk, 18 June 2014.
104 BBC *News*, www.bbc.co.uk, 17 June 2014.
105 *Dawn*, www.dawn.com.pk, 17 December 2014.
106 Azhar Khan and Baseer Ahmad, 'What Are the "Dawn Leaks"? A Look into Pakistan's Headline-Making News Scandal', ARY *News*, https://arynews.tv, 2 May 2017.
107 For a dispassionate analysis, see Nawaz, *The Battle for Pakistan*, pp. 183–4.
108 Cyril Almeida, 'Exclusive: Act against Militants or Face International Isolation, Civilians Tell Military', *Dawn*, www.dawn.com.pk, 6 October 2016.
109 Khan and Ahmad, 'What Are the "Dawn Leaks?"' Also see Hussain, *Pakistan, Institutional Instability and Underdevelopment*, pp. 222–6.
110 Independent Power Producers Association, www.ippa.com.pk, accessed 10 October 2023.
111 Fahd Ali and Fatima Beg, *The History of Private Power in Pakistan* (Islamabad, 2007), pp. 13–16.
112 Khurram Husain, 'Pakistan Pays Heavy Price for Excess Power Generation Capacity', *The Third Pole*, www.thethirdpole.net, 10 March 2021.

113 'The Economic Diplomacy of the China–Pakistan Economic Corridor', The Wilson Center, 20 December 2017.
114 Ibid.
115 Vaqar Ahmed and Sakib Sherani, 'Pakistan's Electricity Crisis: Can the China–Pakistan Economic Corridor (CPEC) Offer Solutions?', *Brookings Institution*, www.brooking.com, 13 February 2019.
116 'Pakistan's Power Crisis: How Did We Get Here?' *Dawn*, www.dawn.com.pk, 2 October 2020.
117 Ibid.
118 Ibid.
119 Munir Ahmad, 'China–Pakistan Economic Corridor: Boon or Bane?', Carnegie Endowment for International Peace, 20 November 2019.
120 'China Pakistan Economic Corridor', *Encyclopaedia Britannica*, www.britannica.com, accessed on 15 October 2023.
121 Siegfried O. Wolf, *The China–Pakistan Economic Corridor of the Belt and Road Initiative: Concept, Context and Assessment* (Cham, 2019), pp. 10–40; Jeremy Garlick, *Reconfiguring the China–Pakistan Economic Corridor: Geo-Economic Pipe Dreams versus Geopolitical Realities* (London, 2022), p. 56; Sujan R. Chinoy, *China–Pakistan Economic Corridor (CPEC): The Project and Its Prospects* (New Delhi, 2021), p. 70.
122 'CPEC', www.cpec.gov.pk; 'The China Pakistan Economic Corridor: View the Ground', www.wilsoncentre.org, accessed 15 October 2023.
123 Hasham Cheema, 'Papers Probe Unfolded', *Dawn*, www.dawn.com.pk, 3 April 2016.
124 *Economic Times*, www.economictimes.indiatimes.com, 21 December 2021.
125 BBC News, www.bbc.co.uk, 6 April 2016.
126 Ibid.
127 Quoted in Scilla Alecci, 'Former Pakistan PM Sharif Sentenced to 10 Years over Panama Papers, International Consortium of Investigative Journalists, 6 July 2018.
128 Saeed Shah, 'Ex-Cricket Star Imran Khan Headed for Pakistan Election Victory', *Wall Street Journal*, www.wsj.com, 25 July 2018.

13 Imran Khan Takes Charge

1 M. J. Akbar, 'Imran Khan: The Reckoning', *Open Magazine*, 8 April 2022, www.openthemagazine.com.
2 See www.thefamouspeople.com.
3 'Pakistan's Economic Crisis: Why Imran Khan's Government Is on Shaky Ground', *The Guardian*, 22 May 2019.
4 Ibid.
5 'Imran Khan's Selective Anti-Corruption Drive', *Al Jazeera*, www.aljazeera.com, 17 May 2021.
6 Asad Hashim, '"Silenced": Pakistan's Journalists Decry New Era of Censorship', *Al Jazeera*, www.aljazeera.com, 15 August 2019.
7 Aamir Yasin, 'Imran Launches Ambitious Scheme to Reduce Poverty', *Dawn*, www.dawn.com, 28 March 2019.
8 Christopher Sandford, *The Cricketer, the Celebrity, the Politician: Imran Khan* (London, 2009), pp. 21–9.
9 Ibid., p. 52.
10 'Imran Khan: From Cricketing Glory to Political Stardom', BBC News, www.bbc.com, 18 August 2018.
11 'Imran Khan – Stats – Batting Analysis – Test Cricket', ESPN *Cricinfo*, www.espncricinfo.com.
12 Peter Oborne, *Wounded Tiger: A History of Cricket in Pakistan* (New York, 2015).

13 Ibid., pp. 20–70.
14 See, for reference, 'Project Update: Shaukat Khanum Memorial Cancer Hospital and Research Centre, Karachi', https://shaukatkhanum.org.pk/shaukat-khanum-hospital-karachi.
15 Imran Khan, *Pakistan: A Personal History* (London, 2012), pp. 15–35.
16 Ibid., pp. 88–105.
17 Ibid., pp. 76–85.
18 'Tehreek-e-Insaf, Political Party, Pakistan', *Encyclopaedia Britannica*, www.britannica.com.
19 Samina Ahmed, 'Imran Khan's Fall: Political and Security Implications for Pakistan', *Crisis Group*, www.crisisgroup.org, 13 April 2022.
20 See 'Pakistan Tahreek-i-Insaf', *Dawn*, www.dawn.com.pk, 12 July 2018.
21 Asad Hashim, 'Pakistan's Imran Khan Leads Lahore Protests', *Al Jazeera*, www.aljazeera.com, 15 December 2014.
22 Tahir Kamran, 'The State of Medina and the Pakistani Context', *News International*, www.thenews.com.pk, 1 December 2019.
23 See BBC *News*, www.bbc.co.uk, 25 July 2018.
24 See *Dawn*, www.dawn.com.pk, 12 July 2018.
25 *Le Monde*, www.lemonde.com, 27 April 2022.
26 Tahir Kamran, 'Dynastic Politics in South Asia-II', *News International*, www.thenews.com.pk, 15 May 2022.
27 See DW, www.dw.com, 25 October 2020.
28 '13 Damning Remarks Made by Justice Khosa on Panamagate', www.dawn.com, 20 April 2017.
29 See *Dawn*, www.dawn.com.pk, 21 February 2018.
30 Tasneem Noorani, 'Dynastic Politics', *Dawn*, www.dawn.com.pk, 12 June 2022.
31 'Pakistan Faces Balance of Payments Crisis', *News International*, www.thenews.com.pk, 28 August 2022.
32 See *Pakistan Today*, www.pakistantoday.com.pk, 31 March 2019.
33 See *Dawn*, www.dawn.com.pk, 15 August 2018.
34 'Pakistan Development Update', *World Bank*, July 2020, www.worldbank.com.
35 'IMF Program Aims to Fix Pakistan's Fiscal Deficit', *The Nation*, www.thenation.com.pk, 10 November 2019.
36 'Pakistan Government's Economic Reforms Remain a Work in Progress', *Arab News*, www.arabnews.com, 15 February 2021.
37 Shahid Javed Burki, *Pakistan: Statecraft and Geopolitics in Today's World* (Karachi, 2022), pp. 10–20.
38 Ibid.
39 Hashaam Akhtar et al., 'Pakistan's Response to COVID-19: Overcoming National and International Hypes to Fight the Pandemic', JMIR *Public Health Surveillance* (2021), pp. 1–9.
40 Ibid.
41 Faran Emmanuel et al., 'Pakistan's COVID-19 Prevention and Control Response Using the World Health Organization's Guidelines for Epidemic Response Interventions', *Cureus: Journal of Medical Science* (January 2023).
42 Akhtar et al., 'Pakistan's Response to COVID-19'.
43 See *Dawn*, www.dawn.com.pk, 27 March 2019.
44 See 'Ehsaas Strategy', JMIR *Publications*, www.pass.gov.pk, 17 September 2020.
45 See *Daily Times*, www.dailytimes.com.pk, 9 April 2019.
46 See *Dawn*, www.dawn.com.pk, 16 May 2019.
47 *Dawn*, www.dawn.com.pk, 20 August 2020.

References

48 See the Punjab Health Initiative Management Company, www.phimc.punjab.gov.pk, accessed 13 October 2023.
49 See *Express Tribune*, www.tribune.com.pk, 7 October 2019; *Dawn*, www.dawn.com, 7 October 2019.
50 See *Arab News*, www.thearabnews.com, 15 December 2018.
51 See *Dawn*, www.dawn.com.pk, 8 September 2020.
52 See *News International*, www.thenews.com.pk, 15 October 2020.
53 'Government's Climate Conservation Policies Being Recognised Globally: Imran', *Pakistan Today*, www.pakistantoday.com.pk, 14 March 2021.
54 See *Express Tribune*, www.tribune.com.pk, 14 March 2021.
55 See *Dawn*, www.dawn.com.pk, 25 October 2021.
56 See *Pakistan Today*. www.pakistantoday.com.pk, 26 July 2021.
57 See *Express Tribune*, www.tribune.com.pk, 17 February 2021.
58 See *Express Tribune*, www.tribune.com.pk, 13 August 2021.
59 See *Express Tribune*, www.tribune.com.pk, 19 May 2021.
60 'India's Diaspora Policy', Ministry of External Affairs, Government of India, www.mea.gov.in, accessed 3 May 2023.
61 'The Pravasi Bharatiya Divas (PBD) Convention', Ministry of External Affairs, Government of India, www.mea.gov.in, accessed 3 May 2023.
62 'The State Council Information Office of the People's Republic of China', State Council Information Office, People's Republic of China, http://english.scio.gov.cn, accessed 3 May 2023.
63 Michael Kugelman, 'Pakistan's Anti-Government Movement May Hit the Brick Wall of the Security State', *Foreign Policy*, www.foreignpolicy.com, 27 October 2020.
64 See *Dawn*, www.dawn.com.pk, 25 July 2019.
65 Asim Yasin, Mumtaz Alvi and Muhammad Anis, 'Choosing Chairman: PTI in Bed with PPP for Senate', *The News*, www.thenews.com.pk, 12 March 2018.
66 M. Ziauddin, 'PTI Joins PPP, But It's No Alliance!', *Tribune*, www.tribune.com.pk, 10 March 2018.
67 Malik Muhammad Ashraf, 'Successes and Failures of PDM', *Pakistan Today*, www.pakistantoday.com.pk, 17 August 2023.
68 See Khuram Dastgir talking to TV anchor, www.youtube.com, accessed 30 September 2023.
69 Mubasher Bukhari, 'Nawaz Sharif Accuses Pakistan's Army Chief of Toppling His Government', *Reuter*, www.reuters.com*s*, 17 October 2020.
70 Baqir Sajjad Syed, 'Opposition Leaders Told Not to Drag Military into Politics', *Dawn*, www.dawn.com.pk, 22 September 2020.
71 Ahmed Awais Khaver, Muhammad Awais Umar and Shafqat Munir Ahmad, 'Evaluating Foreign Policy of Pakistan in the Context of Strategic Coercion', Sustainable Development Policy Institute (July 2019), available at www.jstor.org.
72 Daud Khattak, 'Imran Khan's Foreign Policy Approach', *The Diplomat*, www.thediplomat.com, 21 August 2018.
73 'India Revokes Kashmir's Special Status', *Al Jazeera*, www.aljazeera.com, 4 September 2019.
74 Ibid.
75 'India Revokes Special Status of Kashmir, Putting Tense Region on Edge', *Washington Post*, www.washingtonpost.com, 5 August 2019.
76 Anna V. Bochkovskaya, 'The Kartarpur Pilgrimage Corridor: Negotiating the "Line of Mutual Hatred"', *International Journal of Religious Tourism and Pilgrimage*, IX/2 (July 2021), pp. 28–37.
77 Helen Regan, Sophia Saifi and Manveena Suri, 'India–Pakistan "Peace Corridor" Opens Sikh Temple to Tourists', *CNN*, www.cnn.com, 7 November 2019.

78 'The Long Road from Kartarpur to Peace', *Indian Express*, www.indianexpress.com, 2 December 2018.
79 *Express Tribune*, www.tribune.com.pk, 6 February 2022.
80 Ibid.
81 NDTV, www.ndtv.com, 10 September 2018.
82 *Express Tribune*, www.tribune.com.pk, 5 April 2022.
83 'Imran Khan Goes to Moscow as Pakistan Romances Russia', *Foreign Policy*, www.foreignpolicy.com, 23 February 2022.
84 'Geopolitics of Imran Khan's Russia Visit', *Express Tribune*, www.tribune.com.pk, 8 April 2022.
85 See *Dawn*, www.dawn.com.pk, 2 April 2022.
86 David Rose, 'Did the Family of Pakistani Politician Who Has Become the Poster Boy for British Overseas Aid STEAL Funds Meant for Earthquake Victims?', *Mail on Sunday*, www.dailymail.co.uk, 14 July 2019.
87 Hannah Ellis-Petersen, 'Shehbaz Sharif Elected as Prime Minister of Pakistan', www.theguardian.com, 3 March 2024.

14 Regime Change and a Year of Uncertainty, 2022–3

1 Moonis Ahmar, 'A Year after the Regime Change', *Express Tribune*, www.tribune.com, 1 April 2023.
2 Ahmad Noorani, 'Local and Foreign Assets of General Qamar Javed Bajwa and Family', www.youtube.com, 21 November 2022.
3 Shuja Nawaz, *Crossed Swords: Pakistan, Its Army, and the Wars Within* (Karachi, 2017), p. 200.
4 For a perspective on Bajwa's extension, see Madiha Afzal, 'The Curious Case of the Pakistani Army Chief's Extension', *Brookings*, www.brookings.edu, 4 December 2019.
5 Umar Burney, 'Imran Arrested after Islamabad Court Finds Him Guilty of "Corrupt Practices" in Toshakhana Case', *Dawn*, www.dawn.com, 5 August 2023.
6 'Pakistan Fuel Price Crisis as Economic and Political Crisis Deepens', *New York Times*, 27 May 2022, www.nytimes.com; 'Amid Economic Turmoil, Pakistan Hikes Up Fuel Prices', *Al Jazeera*, www.aljazeera.com, 29 January 2023.
7 'Pakistan's Economic Crisis', *Brookings Institution*, 1 February 2023, www.brooking.com.
8 Furqan Khan, 'Press Freedoms in Pakistan: As Polarization Deepens, Journalism Pays the Price', *South Asian Voices*, www.southasianvoices.org, 1 September 2022.
9 Lynne O'Donnell, 'Pakistan's New Media Crackdown Threatens Press Freedom', *Foreign Policy*, www.foreignpolicy.com, 28 Februry 2022.
10 'Who Was Arshad Sharif, the Pakistani Journalist Shot Dead in Kenya?', *Indian Express*, www.indianexpress.com, 25 October 2022.
11 'Behind Pakistan's Civilian Government, Army Tightens Its Grip on Journalists', https://rsf.org, accessed 6 January 2024.
12 'Arshad Sharif's Murder Is a Stark Reminder That Pakistani Journalists Are Not Safe', *Friday Times*, www.fridaytimes.com, 26 October 2022.
13 Furqan Khan, 'Arshad Sharif's Death and Political Polarization in Pakistan', *South Asian Voices*, www.southasianvoices.org, 25 October 2022.
14 *The Guardian*, www.guardian.com, 24 October 2022.
15 'Pakistani Journalist's Killing in Kenya "a Pre-Meditated Murder"', *The Guardian*, www.guardian.com, 9 December 2022.
16 'Pakistan Forms Committee to Investigate Arshad Sharif's Murder', *Al Jazeera* www.aljazeera.com, 26 October 2022.
17 Emmanuel Igunza, 'Arshad Sharif: Mystery over Killing of Pakistani Journalist in Kenya', BBC *News*, www.bbc.co.uk, 29 October 2022.

References

18 'HRW Slams Pakistan for "Forcibly Evicting" Farmers for Infrastructure Project', *New Arab*, www.newarab.com, 12 April 2023.
19 Asad Hashmi, 'HRW Slams Pakistan over Dissent Crackdown, Alleged Rights Abuses', *Al Jazeera*, www.aljazeera.com, 14 January 2022.
20 'Imran Announces Anti-Government Rallies in Major Cities on July 2', *Express Tribune*, www.tribune.com.pk, 25 June 2022.
21 Ibid.
22 'Shooting of Former Pakistani PM Imran Khan Sparks Outrage', www.aljazeera.com, 3 November 2022.
23 *BBC News*, www.bbc.co.uk, 4 November 2022.
24 *Al Jazeera*, www.aljazeera.com, 10 November 2022.
25 'Imran Khan's Popularity Soars Ahead of Vote, Pakistan Survey Shows', *Straits Times*, www.straitstimes.com, 7 March 2023.
26 *Bloomberg*, www.bloomberg.com, 7 March 2023.
27 *Pakistan Today*, 9 March 2023.

BIBLIOGRAPHY

Journal Articles

Abbasi, Muhammad Zakir and Mussarrat Razia, 'Devolution of Powers to Local Governments in Pakistan during Musharraf Regime', *Pakistan Journal of Social Sciences*, xxxv/2 (2015), pp. 891–901

Ahmad, Bashir, 'PNA Movement', *Journal of the Punjab University Historical Society*, xxxi/1 (January–June 2018), pp. 37–49

Alavi, Hamza, 'The State in Post-Colonial Societies: Pakistan and Bangladesh', *New Left Review*, 1/74 (July–August 1972), pp. 59–81

Amin, Tahir, 'Pakistan in 1994: The Politics of Confrontation', *Asian Survey*, xxxv/2 (February 1995), pp. 140–46

Arnold, David (1994), 'The "Discovery" of Malnutrition and Diet in Colonial India', *Indian Economic and Social History Review*, xxxi/1 (1994), pp. 1–26

Azeem, Muhammad, 'The State as a Political Practice: Pakistan's Postcolonial State beyond Dictatorship and Islam', *Third World Quarterly*, xli/10 (2020), pp. 1670–86

Bains, J. S., 'Some Thoughts on Pakistan's New Constitution', *Indian Journal of Political Science*, xxiii/1–4 (January–December 1962), p. 212

Banerjee, Swapna M., 'Blurring Boundaries, Distant Companions: Non-Kin Female Caregivers for Children in Colonial India (Nineteenth and Twentieth Centuries)', *Paedagogica Historica: International Journal of the History of Education*, xlvi/6 (2010), p. 781

Baqai, Farah Gul, 'Sir Evan Jenkins and the 1947 Partition of the Punjab', *Pakistan Journal of History and Culture*, xxvii/1 (2006), p. 20

Bose, Sarmila, 'Anatomy of Violence: Analysis of Civil War in East Pakistan in 1971', *Economic and Political Weekly*, 8 October 2005

Burki, Shahid Javed, 'Pakistan under Zia: 1977–1988', *Asian Survey*, xxviii/10 (October 1988), pp. 1083–4

——, 'Pakistan's Cautious Democratic Course', *Current History* (March 1992), pp. 117–22

Cantwell Smith, Wilfred, 'Hyderabad: Muslim Tragedy', *Middle East Journal* (January 1950), pp. 27–51

Chanana, Priyanka, 'Caste Ties, Allodial Rights and Colonial Administration in Oudh during Summary Settlement and after 1858: The Taluqdar Association and the British Policies up to 1870s', *Proceedings of the Indian History Congress*, lxxiv (2013), pp. 458–69

Chattha, Ilyas, 'Faction-Building in Pakistan: Sir Francis Mudie and Punjab Politics, 1947–1949', *Contemporary South Asia*, xxii/3 (2014), pp. 225–39

Chaudhry, Muhammad Ahsen, 'Pakistan's Relations with USSR', *Asian Survey*, vi/9 (1966), pp. 492–500

Crossette Barbara, 'Who Killed Zia?', *World Policy Journal*, xxii/3 (Fall 2005), pp. 94–102

Faiz, Muhammad Aslam, Hussain Kiran and Iqbal Abid, 'Zia ul Haq Vis-a-Vis Pervez Musharraf: A Comparative Overview of Politics in Pakistan', *International Research Journal of Management and Social Sciences*, III/1 (2022), pp. 16–24

'Government of India's Note to the Government of Pakistan, 3 March 1971', *Pakistan Horizon*, XXIV/2 (1971), pp. 118–19

Iqbal, M., Falak Sher, Rehmat Ullah Awan and Khalid Javed, 'Cultural Relations between Pakistan and the Soviet Union during Ayub Khan's Period', *Pakistaniaat: A Journal of Pakistan Studies*, III/3 (2011), pp. 60–72

Jeffrey, Robin, 'The Punjab Boundary Force and the Problem of Order, August 1947', *Modern Asian Studies*, VIII/4 (1974), pp. 491–520

Jillani, Anees, 'Pak–Afghan Relations, 1958–1988', *Pakistan Horizon*, XLVI/1 (January 1993), pp. 35–45

Kamran, Tahir, 'Contextualizing Sectarian Militancy in Pakistan: A Case Study of Jhang', *Journal of Islamic Studies*, XX/1 (2009), pp. 55–85

——, 'Community of the Marginalized: State, Society and Punjabi Christians', *South Asian Review*, XXI/2 (2010), pp. 66–83

——, 'Majlis-i-Ahrar-i-Islam: Religion, Socialism and Agitation in Action', *South Asian History and Culture*, IV/4 (2013)

——, 'The Pre-History of Religious Exclusionism in Contemporary Pakistan: Khatam-e-Nubuwwat 1889–1953', *Modern Asian Studies*, XLVI/6 (2015), pp. 1–35

——, 'Pakistan: A Failed State?', *History Today*, LXVII/9 (2017), pp. 26–32

——, 'The Making of a Minority: Ahmadi Exclusion through Constitutional Amendments, 1974', *Pakistan Journal of Historical Studies*, IV/1–2 (2019), pp. 55–84

Kaur, Ravinder, 'The Last Journey: Exploring Social Class in the 1947 Partition Migration', *Economic and Political Weekly*, XLI/22 (2006), pp. 2221–8

Khan, Kamran Aziz, '17th Constitutional Amendment and Its Aftermath: The Role of Muttahidda Majlis-i-Amal (MMA)', *Pakistan Vision*, IX/2 (2008), pp. 101–21

Kumar, Ashutosh, 'Electoral Politics in Punjab: Study of Akali Dal', *Economic and Political Weekly*, XXXIX/14–15 (2004), pp. 1515–20

Kumar, Sumita, 'Sharif vs. Musharraf: The Future of Democracy in Pakistan', *Strategic Analysis*, XXIV/10 (January 2001), pp. 1861–75

Ludden, David, 'The Politics of Independence in Bangladesh', *Economic and Political Weekly*, XLVI/35 (2011), pp. 79, 81–5

Masood, Zahid Akhtar, 'Dictatorship in Pakistan: A Study of Zia Era, 1977–88', *Pakistan Journal of History and Culture*, XXXII/1 (2011), pp. 1–27

Memon, Muhammad Umar, 'Partition Literature: A Study of Intizar Husain', *Modern Asian Studies*, XIV/3 (1980), pp. 378–9

Muhammad, Ayaz, and Kaleem Muhammad, 'Marriage of Convenience between Military and Local Government', *European Journal of Social Sciences*, XXVII/3 (2012), pp. 381–90

Mukerjee, Dalip, 'Afghanistan under Daud: Relations with Neighboring States', *Asian Survey*, XV/4 (April 1975), pp. 301–12

Naqvi, Syed Tanwir Husain, 'The Triad of Governance, Devolution, and National Prosperity', *Pakistan Development Review*, XLII/4, Part II (2003), pp. 629–40

Naseem, S. M., 'Economists and Pakistan's Economic Development: Is There a Connection?', *Pakistan Development Review*, XXXVII/4, Part II (Winter 1998), pp. 410–14

Naveed, Muhammad bin, 'Gandhara Civilization', www.worldhistory.org, 7 July 2015

Parveen, Saila, and I. M. Faisal, 'People versus Power: The Geopolitics of Kaptai Dam in Bangladesh', *International Journal of Water Resources Development*, XVIII (21 July 2010), pp. 197–208

Quraishi, Asifa, 'Her Honour: An Islamic Critique of the Rape Provisions in Pakistan's Ordinance on Zina', *Islamic Studies*, XXXVIII/3 (Autumn 1999), pp. 403–31

Qureshi, M. Naeem, 'The Indian Khilāfat Movement (1918–1924)', *Journal of Asian History*, XXII/2 (1978), pp. 152–68

Rahman, Hanif ur, 'Pak–Afghan Relations during Z. A. Bhutto Era: The Dynamics of Cold War', *Pakistan Journal of History and Culture*, XXXIII/2 (2012), pp. 23–42

Rand, Gavin, and Kim A. Wagner, 'Recruiting the "Martial Races": Identities and Military Service in Colonial India', *Patterns of Prejudice*, XLVI/3–4 (2012), pp. 232–54

Reetz, Dietrich, 'Enlightenment and Islam: Sayyid Ahmad Khan's Plea to Indian Muslims for Reason', *Indian Historical Review*, XIV/1–2 (1988), pp. 206–18

Rizvi, Hasan Askari, 'The Paradox of Military Rule in Pakistan', *Asian Survey*, XXIV/5 (May 1984), pp. 534–55

Sajjadi S.M.S., F. Foruzanfar, R. Shirazi and S. Baghestani, 'Excavations at Shahr-i Sokhta: First Preliminary Report on the Excavations of the Graveyard, 1997–2000', *British Journal of Persian Studies*, XLI (2003), pp. 21–97

Sayeed, Khalid bin, 'The Governor General of Pakistan', *Pakistan Horizon*, VIII/2 (June 1955), pp. 330–39

Siddiqa-Agha, Ayesha, 'Political Economy of National Security', *Economic and Political Weekly*, XXXVII/44–5 (November 2002)

Shafqat, Saeed, 'Pakistan under Benazir Bhutto', *Asian Survey*, XXXVI/ 7 (1996), pp. 655–72

Talbot, Ian, 'The Punjab under Colonialism: Order and Transformation in British India', *Journal of Punjab Studies*, XIV/1 (Spring 2007), pp. 3–10

Warraich, Touqir Ahmad, 'Gandhara: Appraisal of Its Meaning and History', *Journal of Research Society of Pakistan*, XLVIII/1 (2011), pp. 1–20

Waseem, Muhammad, 'Pakistan's Lingering Crisis of Diarchy', *Asian Survey*, XXXII/7 (July 1992), pp. 617–34

——, 'Partition, Migration and Assimilation in Pakistani Punjab', *International Journal of Punjab Studies*, IV/1 (January–June 1997), pp. 63–84

Weiss, Anita M., 'Benazir Bhutto and the Future of Women in Pakistan', *Asian Survey*, XXX/5 (May 1990), pp. 433–45

Yacoobali, Vazira Fazila, 'The Battlefields of Karachi: Ethnicity, Violence and the State', *Journal of the International Institute*, IV/1 (1996)

Yasmeen, S., 'Democracy in Pakistan: The Third Dismissal', *Asian Survey*, XXXIV/6 (1994), pp. 572–88

Yong, Tan Tai, '"Sir Cyril Goes to India": Partition, Boundary-Making and Disruptions in the Punjab', *International Journal of Punjab Studies*, IV/1 (1997), pp. 1–20

Ziring, Lawrence, 'Public Policy Dilemmas and Pakistan's Nationality Problem: The Legacy of Zia ul-Haq', *Asian Survey*, XXVIII/8 (August 1988), pp. 795–812

Books

Abbas, Hassan, *The Taliban Revival: Violence and Extremism on the Pakistan–Afghanistan Frontier* (New Haven, CT, 2015)

Adas, Michael, ed., *Islamic and European Expansion: The Forging of a Global Order* (Philadelphia, PA, 1993)

Afzal, Madiha, *Pakistan under Siege: Extremism, Society, and the State* (Gurgaon, 2018)

Afzal, Muhammad Rafique, *Political Parties in Pakistan*, vol. III: *1969–1971* (Islamabad, 1988)

——, *Pakistan: History and Politics, 1947–1971* (Karachi, 2007)

——, *A History of the All-India Muslim League, 1906–1947* (Karachi, 2013)

Afzal, Rafiq, *Political Parties in Pakistan, 1958–1969* (Islamabad, 1986)

Ahmad, Akbar S., *Pakistan Society: Islam Ethnicity and Leadership in South Asia* (New York, 1986)

Ahmad, Aziz, *Studies in Islamic Culture in Indian Environment* (Oxford, 1964)

Ahmad, Ghafoor, *Aur Phir martial Law Aa Gaya* (Lahore, 2000)

Ahmad, Iftikhar, *Pakistan General Elections:1970* (Lahore, 1970)
Ahmad, Nafis, *Economic Geography of East Pakistan* (London, 1958)
Ahmed, Ashfaq, *Gadariya* (Lahore, 1995)
——, *Khel Tamasha* (Lahore, 2013)
Ahmed, Mahmud, *History of the Indo-Pak 1965 War* (Islamabad, 2006)
Ahmed, Umera, *Pir-i-Kamil* (Lahore, 2004)
Akbar, M. J., *Tinderbox: The Past and Future of Pakistan* (New Delhi, 2011)
Alam, Muzaffar, *The Crisis of Empire in Mughal North India: Awadh and Punjab* (New Delhi, 1997)
Ali, Chaudhri Muhammad, *The Emergence of Pakistan* (Lahore, 1992)
Ali, Daud, *Courtly Culture and Political Life in Early Medieval India* (Cambridge, 2004)
Ali, Tariq, *Pakistan: Military Rule or People's Power?* (New Delhi, 1970)
Altaf, Hina 'History of Military Interventions in Political Affairs in Pakistan', MA thesis, City University of New York, 2019, p. 26
Amin, Shahid, *Event, Metaphor, Memory: Chauri Chaura, 1922–1992* (Berkeley, CA, 1995)
Amin, Tahir, *Ethno-National Movements in Pakistan's Domestic and International Factors* (Islamabad, 1993)
Amir, Zahid Munir, *On the Wings of Poesy: Prof. Ghulam Jilani Asghar on Modern Urdu Poetry* (Lahore, 2007)
Amjad, Yahya, *Tarikh-i-Pakistan: Qadim Daur-Zamana-i-Qabal az Tarikh* (Lahore, 1989)
Asif, Manan Ahmed, *The Loss of Hindustan: The Invention of India* (Lahore, 2022)
Ayling, Stanley, *Edmund Burke: His Life and Opinions* (New York, 1988)
Azad, Abul Kalam, *India Wins Freedom* (Calcutta, 1959)
Azeem, Syed Waqar, *Fort William College: Tehreek aur Tarikh* (Lahore, 2001)
Aziz, Khurshid Kamal, *The Making of Pakistan: A Study in Nationalism* (Lahore, 2002)
Aziz, Sartaj, *Between Dreams and Realities: Some Milestones in Pakistan's History* (Karachi, 2020)
Baker, Raymond, *Capitalism's Achilles Heel: Dirty Money and How to Renew the Free-Market System* (Hoboken, NJ, 2005)
Bangash, Yaqoob Khan, *A Princely Affair: Accession and Integration of Princely States in Pakistan, 1947–55* (Karachi, 2015)
Barrier, N. G., *The Punjab Alienation of Land Bill of 1900* (Durham, NC, 1966)
Basham, L., ed., *A Cultural History of India* (New Delhi, 1983)
——, *The Wonder That Was India* [1954] (London, 2014)
Baxter, Craig, and Charles H. Kennedy, eds, *Pakistan 1997* (Karachi, 1998)
Bayly, Christopher, *Recovering Liberties: Indian Thought in the Age of Liberalism and Empire* (Cambridge, 2012)
Bayly, Susan, *Caste, Society and Politics in India from the Eighteenth Century to the Modern Age* (Cambridge, 1999)
Belokrenitsky, Vyacheslav Y., and Vladimir N. Moskalenko, *A Political History of Pakistan: 1947–2007* (Karachi, 2013)
Bennett-Jones, Owen, *Pakistan: Eye of the Storm* (New Haven, CT, 2009)
——, *The Bhutto Dynasty: The Struggle for Power in Pakistan* (New Haven, CT, 2020)
Bhutto, Benazir, *Daughter of the East: An Autobiography* (London, 2007)
Bhutto, Zulfiqar Ali, *The Myth of Independence* (Karachi, 1969)
——, *The Great Tragedy* (Pakistan People's Party, 1971)
——, *If I Am Assassinated*, https://bhutto.org/wp-content/uploads/2020/12/If-I-am-Assassinated-Zulfikar-Ali-Bhutto.pdf
Bilal, Mushtaq, *Writing Pakistan: Conversations on Identity, Nationhood and Fiction* (Noida, 2016)
Bokhari, Z. A., *Sarguzasht* (Lahore, 2013)

Bibliography

Bolitho, Hector, *Jinnah: Creator of Pakistan* (Karachi, 1966)
Bose, Sarmila, *Dead Reckoning: Memories of the 1971 Bangladesh War* (Karachi, 2011)
Bose, Sugata, and Ayesha Jalal, *Modern South Asia: History, Culture, Political Economy* (Lahore, 2011)
Braibanti, Ralph, *Research on the Bureaucracy of Pakistan* (Durham, 1969)
Burki, Shahid Javed, *Pakistan under the Military: Eleven Years of Zia Ul-Haq* (New York, 1991)
——, *Pakistan: Statecraft and Geopolitics in Today's World* (Karachi, 2022)
Callard, Keith, *Pakistan: A Political Study* (London, 1957)
Cantwell Smith, Wilfred, *Modern Islam in India (and Pakistan): A Social Analysis* (Lahore, 1947)
Caroe, Olaf, *The Pathans: 550 BC–AD 1957* (Karachi, 1976)
Chakravarti, Sudeep, *Plassey: The Battle That Changed the Course of Indian History* (New Delhi, 2020)
Chambers, Claire, *British Muslim Fictions: Interviews with Contemporary Writers* (Basingstoke, 2011)
Choudhury, G. W., *The Last Days of United Pakistan* (Bloomington, IN, 1974)
Cohen, Stephen P., *The Pakistan Army* (Karachi, 1984)
——, *The Idea of Pakistan* (Washington, DC, 2004)
Cohn, Bernard, *Colonialism and Its Forms of Knowledge* (Princeton, NJ, 1996)
Das, Sisir Kumar, *Sahibs and Munshis: An Account of the College of Fort William* (New Delhi, 1960)
Doniger, Wendy, *The Hindus: An Alternative History* (New York, 2009)
Durrani, Asad, *Pakistan Adrift: Navigating Troubled Waters* (London, 2018)
Eaton, Richard M., *The Rise of Islam and the Bengal Frontier, 1204–1760* (Berkeley, CA, 1993)
——, *India in the Persianate Age: 1000–1765* (London, 2019)
Englar, Mary, *Benazir Bhutto: Pakistani Prime Minister and Activist* (Mankato, MN, 2006)
Faiz, Ahmad Faiz, 'Dast-i-Saba' [Hand of Morning Breeze], in *Nuskha Hai Wafa* [Prescriptions of Fidelity] (Lahore, 1985)
Farooque, Siddique ul, *Kargil: Adventure or Trap, Whitepaper* (Delhi, 2006)
Faruqi, Shamsur Rahman, *Kayi Chaand Thay Sar-e-Asmaan* (New Delhi, 1998)
Faruqi, Zia-ul-Islam, *The Deoband School and the Demand for Pakistan* (London, 1963)
Finer, Samuel, *The Man on Horseback: The Role of the Military in Politics* (London, 2002)
Friedmann, Yohannan, *Shaikh Aḥmad Sirhindī: An Outline of His Thought and a Study of His Image in the Eyes of Posterity* (New Delhi, 2000)
Jaffrelot, Christophe, *Dr Ambedkar and Untouchability: Analysing and Fighting Caste* (London, 2005)
Gandhi, Rajmohan, *Patel: A Life* (Ahmadabad, 1990)
——, *Punjab: A History from Aurangzeb to Mountbatten* (New Delhi, 2013)
Gauhar, Altaf, *Ayub Khan: Pakistan's First Military Ruler* (Lahore, 1996)
Ghalib, Mirza Asad Ullah Khan, *Kulliyat-e-Nasr-e-Ghalib* (Lucknow, 1877)
Giardino, Claudio, *Magan: The Land of Copper: Prehistoric Metallurgy of Oman* (Oxford, 2019)
Gilani, Yousaf Raza, *Chah-e-Yousaf se Sada* (Lahore, 2016)
Gilmartin, David, *Empire and Islam: Punjab and the Making of Pakistan* (Berkeley, CA, 1988)
Guha, Ramachandra, *Gandhi: The Years That Changed the World, 1914–1948* (London, 2018)
Habib, Irfan, *Peoples History of India*, vol. I: *Prehistory* (New Delhi, 2001)
——, *People's History of India*, vol. II: *The Indus Civilization* (Lahore, 2004)
Hali, Altaf Hussain, *Hayat-i-Javaid* (Delhi, 1939)
Hallaq, Waael B., *Sharī'a: Theory, Practice, Transformations* (Cambridge, 2009)
Hamdani, Yasser Latif, *Jinnah: A Life* (Karachi, 2022)
Hameed, Syeda, *Born to Be Hanged: Political Biography of Zulfiqar Ali Bhutto* (New Delhi, 2017)

Hamid, Abdul, *Muslim Separatism in India: A Brief Survey, 1858–1947* (Lahore, 1967)
Hamid, Mohsin, *The Reluctant Fundamentalist* (Karachi, 2007)
Hamid, Omar Shahid, *The Prisoner* (Delhi, 2013)
—, *The Party Worker* (Delhi, 2017)
Hanif, Mohammed, *A Case of Exploding Mangoes* (New Delhi, 2009)
Haque, Ishrat, *Glimpses of Mughal Society and Culture: A Study Based on Urdu Literature, in the 2nd Half of the 18th Century* (New Delhi, 1992)
Hardy, Peter, *The Muslims of British India* (Cambridge, 1972)
Hasan, Khalid, *Rearview Mirror: Four Memoirs* (Islamabad, 2002)
Hasan, Zaheer, *The Separation of East Pakistan: The Rise and Realization of Bengali Muslim Nationalism* (Karachi, 1994)
Hayat, Sikandar, *The Charismatic Leader: Quaid-i-Azam Mohammad Ali Jinnah and the Creation of Pakistan* (Karachi, 2014)
Hodgson, Marshal, *The Venture of Islam*, vol. III: *The Gunpowder Empires and Modern Times* (Chicago, IL, 1974)
Hughes, Libby, *Benazir Bhutto: From Prison to Prime Minister* (Bloomington, IN, 2000)
Hussain, Abdullah, *Nadaar Log* (Lahore, 1996)
—, *Udaas Naslain* (Lahore, 2015)
Hussain, Adeel, *Revenge, Politics and Blasphemy in Pakistan* (London, 2022)
Hussain, Akmal, *Pakistan, Institutional Instability and Underdevelopment State, People and Consciousness* (Lahore, 2023)
Hussain, Ashfaq, *Iqtidar key Majbooriyan: General Mirza Aslam Baig key Swaneh Hayat* (Lahore, 2021)
Hussain, Ishrat, *Pakistan: An Economy of an Elitist State* (Karachi, 2020)
Ikram, S. M., *Modern Muslim India and Birth of Pakistan* (Lahore, 1990)
—, *History of Muslim Civilization in India and Pakistan: A Political and Cultural History* (Lahore, 2007)
Jahan, Rounaq, *Pakistan: Failure in National Integration* (Lahore, 2019)
Jalal, Ayesha, *The Sole Spokesman: Jinnah, the Muslim League and the Demand for Pakistan* (Cambridge, 1985)
—, *Democracy and Authoritarianism in South Asia: A Comparative and Historical Perspective* (Lahore, 1995)
—, *The State of Martial Rule: The Origin of Pakistan's Economy of Defence* (Lahore, 1999)
—, *Partisans of Allah: Jihad in South Asia* (Lahore, 2008)
—, *The Struggle for Pakistan: A Muslim Homeland and Global Politics* (Cambridge, 2014)
Jalibi, Jamil, *Tareekh e Adab e Urdu*, vol. II (Lahore, 2015)
Javed, Ajeet, *Secular and Nationalist Jinnah* (New Delhi, 2009)
Javed, Kanza, *Ashes, Wine and Dust* (New Delhi, 2015)
Jha, D. N., *Ancient India: In Historical Outline* (New Delhi, 2009)
Johnson, Alan Campbell, *Mission with Mountbatten* (London, 1952)
Jones, Kenneth, *Socio-Religious Reform Movements in British India* (Cambridge, 1999)
Kamran, Tahir, *Democracy and Governance in Pakistan* (Lahore, 2008)
—, *Election Commission of Pakistan: Role in Politics* (Lahore, 2009)
Kanwal, Aroosa, and Saiyma Aslam, eds, *Routledge Companion to Pakistani Anglophone Writing* (London, 2019)
Kashmiri, Tabasum, *Urdu Adab ki Tarekh: Ibtada say 1857 Tak* (Lahore, 2020)
Keay, John, *India: A History from the Earliest Civilisations to the Boom of the Twenty-First Century* (London, 2000)
Kennedy, Charles, *Bureaucracy in Pakistan* (Karachi, 1987)
Kiessling, Hein G., *Faith Unity Discipline: The ISI of Pakistan* (London, 2023)
Khan, Ayub, *Friends Not Masters* (Oxford, 1967)

Bibliography

Khan, Hamid, *Constitutional and Political History of Pakistan* (Karachi, 2005)
Khan, Iffat Humayun, *Electoral Malpractices during the 2008 Elections in Pakistan* (Karachi, 2012)
Khan, Imran, *Pakistan: A Personal History* (London, 2012)
Khan, Roedad, *Pakistan: A Dream Gone Sour* (Karachi, 1997)
Khosla, G. D., *Stern Reckoning: A Survey of Events Leading up to and Following the Partition of India* (New Delhi, 1989)
Khullar, K. K., *Amir Khusrau aur Humara Mushtarka Culture* (New Delhi, 1983)
Lal, K. S., *The Legacy of Muslim Rule in India* (New Delhi, 1992)
Lawson, Philip, *The East India Company: A History* (London, 1993)
Lieven, Anatol, *Pakistan: A Hard Country* (London, 2012)
McCartney, Matthew, and Akbar Zaidi, *New Perspectives on Pakistan's Political Economy: State, Class and Social Change* (Cambridge, 2019)
Malik, Hafeez, *Moslem Nationalism in India and Pakistan* (Washington, DC, 1963)
Malik, Hammad Ahmad, 'The Struggle for Democracy in Pakistan: Non-Violent Resistance to Military Rule 1977–88', PhD thesis, Warwick University, 2015
Malik, Ikram Ali, *A Book of Readings on the History of the Punjab: 1799–1947* (Lahore, 1985)
Malik, Jamal, *Islam in South Asia* (Leiden, 2020)
Mansergh, Nicholas, *The Commonwealth Experience* (London, 1969)
——, and E.W.R. Lumby, eds, *Constitutional Relations between Britain and India: The Transfer of Power, 1942–1947*, vol. XI: *The Mountbatten Viceroyalty: Announcement and Reception of the 3 June Plan* (London, 1981)
Marker, Jamsheed, *Cover Point: Impressions of Leadership in Pakistan* (London, 2021)
Masood, Mukhtar, *Harf-i-Shauq* (Lahore, 2017)
Mateen Uddin, Kamal, *Tragedy of Errors: East Pakistan Crisis* (Lahore, 1994)
Mazari, Sherbaz Khan, *A Journey to Disillusionment* (Karachi, 1999)
Metcalf, Barbara, *Islamic Revival in British India: Deoband, 1860–1900* (Princeton, NJ, 1982)
——, and Thomas Metcalf, *A Concise History of Modern India* (Cambridge, 2006)
Milam, William B., *Bangladesh and Pakistan: Flirting with Failure in South Asia* (London, 2009)
Mill, James, *The History of British India* (London, 1817)
Mirza, Humayun, *From Plassey to Pakistan: The Family History of Iskander Mirza, the First President of Pakistan* (Lahore, 1999)
Mirza, Waheed, *The Life and Works of Amir Khusrau* (Calcutta, 1936)
Mitra, Subrata Kumar, ed, *The Post-Colonial State in Asia: Dialects of Politics and Culture* (Lahore, 1988)
Mody, Piloo, *Zulfi, My Friend* (Delhi, 1973)
Mufti, Marium, Sahar Shafqat and Niloufer Siddiqui, eds, *Pakistan's Political Parties: Surviving between Dictatorship and Democracy* (Lahore, 2020)
Muhammad Ali Shaikh, *Benazir Bhutto* (Karachi, 2000)
Mukherjee, Ramakrishna, *The Rise and Fall of the East India Company: A Sociological Appraisal* (Lahore, 1976)
Mukhia, Harbans, *The Mughals of India* (Malden, 2004)
Muñoz, Heraldo, *Getting Away with Murder: Benazir Bhutto's Assassination and the Politics of Pakistan* (New York, 2014)
Muqeem, Fazal, *The Story of Pakistan Army* (Lahore, 1964)
Musharraf, Pervez, *In the Line of Fire: A Memoir* (London, 2008)
Narang, Gopi Chand, *Amir Khusrau ka Hindavi Kalam* (Lahore, 2021)
Nasr, Seyyed Vali Reza, *The Vanguard of the Islamic Revolution: The Jama'at-i Islami of Pakistan* (Berkeley, CA, 1994)
Natiq, Ali Akbar, *Nau Lakhi Kothi* (Lahore, 2014)

Nawaz, Shuja, *Crossed Swords: Pakistan, Its Army, and the Wars Within* (Karachi, 2017)
——, *The Battle for Pakistan: The Bitter U.S. Friendship and a Tough Neighbourhood* (Karachi, 2019)
Nayyar, H., and Ahmed Salim, *The Subtle Subversion: The State of Curricula and Textbooks in Pakistan* (Islamabad, n.d.)
Nehru, Jawaharlal, *The Discovery of India* (New Delhi, 1989)
Niazi, Amir Abdullah Khan, *The Betrayal of East Pakistan* (Karachi, 1999)
Niazi, Zamir, *The Web of Censorship* (Oxford, 1994)
Noman, Omar, *The Political Economy of Pakistan* (Oxon, 1988)
——, *Pakistan: A Political and Economic History since 1947* (New York, 1990)
Noon, Firoze Khan, *From Memory* (Lahore, 1969)
Oborne, Peter, *Wounded Tiger: A History of Cricket in Pakistan* (New York, 2015)
Pandey, Hemant Kumar, and Manish Raj Singh, *India's Major Military and Rescue Operations* (New Delhi, 2017)
Pernau, Margrit, ed., *The Delhi College: Traditional Elites, the Colonial State, and Education before 1857* (New Delhi, 2006)
Prashad, Ishwari, *A Short History of Muslim Rule in India: From the Advent of Islam to the Death of Aurangzeb* (New Delhi, 2018)
Qadeer, Abdul A., *Pakistan: Social and Cultural Transformations in a Muslim Nation* (Lahore, 2011)
Qureshi, Ishtiaq Hussain, *Ulema in Politics* (Karachi, 1974)
——, *A Short History of Pakistan* (Karachi, 2019)
Qureshi, M. Naeem, *Pan-Islam in British Indian Politics: A Study of the Khilafat Movement, 1918–1924* (Leiden, 1999)
Rafiuddin, Colonel, *Bhutto key Akhari 323 Din* (Lahore, 2007)
Rahman, Tariq, *A History of Pakistani Literature in English: 1947–1988* (Lahore, 1990)
——, *Language, Ideology and Power: Language-Learning among the Muslims of Pakistan and North India* (New Delhi, 2008)
——, *From Hindi to Urdu* (Karachi, 2011)
——, *Pakistan's Wars: An Alternative History* (Lahore, 2022)
Rai, Satya M., *Legislative Politics and Freedom Struggle on the Panjab, 1897–1947* (New Delhi, 1984)
Rais, Rasul Bakhsh, *Islam, Ethnicity, and Power Politics: Constructing Pakistan's National Identity* (Karachi, 2017)
Rajan, Rajeswari Sunder, *Real and Imagined Women: Gender, Culture and Postcolonialism* (London, 1993)
Reid, Stuart, *The Battle of Plassey, 1757: The Victory That Won an Empire* (London, 2017)
Riaz, Fahmida, *Hum Log* (Karachi, 2013)
Richards, John F., *The Mughal Empire* (Cambridge, 2000)
Rieck, Andreas, *The Shias in Pakistan: An Assertive and Beleaguered Minority* (London, 2015)
Rizvi, Hasan Askari, *Internal Strife and External Intervention: India's Role in the Civil War in East Pakistan* (Lahore, 1981)
——, *Military and Politics in Pakistan: 1947–1997* (Lahore, 2000)
Rizvi, Mehbub, *Tarikh-i-Dar ul Ulum Deoband: Bar-i-Saghir key Musalmanon ka sab sey bara Karnama* (Lahore, 2005)
Rizvi, S.A.A., *The Wonder That Was India: 1200–1700* (New Delhi, 1994)
——, *A History of Sufism in India: Early Sufism and Its History in India to AD 1600* (Lahore, 2004)
Saeed, Ahmad and Sarwar, Kh. Mansur, *Trek to Pakistan* (Lahore, 2003)
Saleem, Saqib, *Year 1857: In the Words of Ghalib* (New Delhi, 2021)
Salik, Sadiq, *Witness to Surrender* (Karachi, 1977)

Bibliography

Salim, Ahmed, *Tootti Banti Assemblian aur Civil Military Bureaucracy* (Lahore, 1990)
Samad, Yunas, *A Nation in Turmoil: Nationalism and Ethnicity in Pakistan: 1937–1958* (New Delhi, 1995)
Sandford, Christopher, *The Cricketer, the Celebrity, the Politician: Imran Khan* (London, 2009)
Sargana, Turab ul Hassan, *Punjab and the War of Independence, 1857–1858: From Collaboration to Resistance* (Karachi, 2020)
Sarkar, Sumit, *Swadeshi Movement: 1905–1908* (New Delhi, 1973)
Sayeed, Khalid bin, *Pakistan: The Formative Phase, 1857–1948* (Oxford, 1968)
——, *The Political System of Pakistan* (Boston, MA, 1967)
Scarre, Chris, and Brian Fagan, *Ancient Civilizations* (New York and Oxon, 2016)
Schimmel, Annemarie, *Classical Urdu Literature from the Beginning to Iqbal* (Wiesbaden, 1975)
——, *Mystical Dimensions of Islam* (Lahore, 2006)
Schofield, Victoria, *The Fragrance of Tears: My Friendship with Benazir Bhutto* (Karachi, 2020)
Sen, Sailendra Nath, *An Advanced History of Modern India* (New Delhi, 2010)
Shafqat, Saeed, *Political System of Pakistan and Public Policy* (Lahore, 1989)
——, *Civil–Military Relations in Pakistan: From Zulfiqar Ali Bhutto to Benazir Bhutto* (Boulder, CO, 1997)
Shah, Aqil, *The Army and Democracy: Military Politics in Pakistan* (Cambridge, MA, 2014)
Shahid, Zia, *Mera Dost: Nawaz Sharif: Wazir-i-Khazana sey Wazir-i-Ala aur Wazarat-i-Uzma sey Adiyala Jail Tak* (Lahore, 2018)
Shaikh, Farzana, *Community and Consensus in Islam: Muslim Representation in Colonial India, 1860–1947* (Cambridge, 1989)
——, *Making Sense of Pakistan* (Karachi, 2018)
Shamsie, Muneeza, *Hybrid Tapestries: The Development of Pakistani Literature in English* (Karachi, 2017)
Shrimali, K. L., *The Wardha Scheme: The Gandhian Plan of Education for Rural India* (New Delhi, 1949)
Siddiqa, Ayesha, *Military Inc.: Inside Pakistan's Military Economy* (Karachi, 2007)
Siddiqi, A. R., *General Agha Mohammad Yahya Khan: The Rise and Fall of a Soldier: 1947–1971* (Karachi, 2020)
Siddiqui, Kalim, *Conflict, Crisis and War in Pakistan* (London, 1972)
Singh, Gurharpal, and Giorgio Shani, *Sikh Nationalism: From a Dominant Minority to an Ethno-Religious Diaspora* (Cambridge, 2022)
Singh, Khushwant, *Ranjit Singh: Maharajah of the Punjab* (London, 1962)
——, *A History of the Sikhs*, vol. II (Princeton, 1966)
Singh, Kirpal, *The Partition of the Punjab* (Patiala, 1989)
——, ed., *Select Documents on Partition of Punjab, 1947* (New Delhi, 1991)
Spear, Percival, *A History of India*, vol. II: *From the Sixteenth Century to the Twentieth Century* (New Delhi, 1990)
Sprague, Stanley B., *Pakistan since Independence: A History, 1947 to Today* (Jefferson, NC, 2020)
Stein, Burton, *A History of India* (Hoboken, 2010)
Stephens, Ian, *Pakistan* (New York, 1964)
Suleri Goodyear, Sara, *Meatless Days* (Chicago, IL, 1991)
Suskind, Ron, *The Way of the World: A Story of Truth and Hope in an Age of Extremism* (New York, 2008)
Suvorova, Anna, *Widows and Daughters: Gender, Kinship, and Power in South Asia* (Oxford, 2019)

Synnott, Hilary, *Transforming Pakistan: Ways out of Instability* (London, 2009)
Talbot, Ian, *Punjab and the Raj, 1849–1947* (New Delhi, 1988)
——, *India and Pakistan: Inventing the Nation* (London, 2000)
——, *Pakistan: A Modern History* (London, 2005)
——, ed., *The Deadly Embrace* (Karachi, 2007)
——, *History of British Diplomacy in Pakistan* (Abingdon, 2021)
——, *Khizr Tiwana, the Punjab Unionist Party and the Partition of India* (Karachi, 2023)
Tarar, Mustansar Hussain, *Bahaao* (Lahore, 1992)
Tariq, Shameem, *Raakh* (Lahore, 2003)
——, *Ghalib Aur Humari Tehreek-e-Azadi* (Mumbai, 2007)
Taseer, Salman, *Zulfiqar Ali Bhutto: Bachpan sey Takhta-i-Dar Tak* (Lahore, 1988)
Taseer, Shahbaz, *Lost to the World: A Memoir of Faith, Family, and Five Years in Terrorist Captivity* (New York, 2022)
Thapar, Romila, *A History of India*, vol. 1 (London, 1990)
Tod, James, *Annals and Antiquities of Rajasthan; or, The Central and Western Rajpoot States of India* (London, 1914)
Toor, Saadia, *The State of Islam* (London, 2011)
Troll, Christian W., *Sayyid Ahmad Khan: A Reinterpretation of Muslim Theology* (New Delhi, 1978)
Ullah, Inyat, *State and Democracy in Pakistan* (Lahore, 1997)
Umair, Asim, *Battle of Buxar* (Delhi, 2018)
Usmani, Irfan Waheed, 'Print Culture and Left-Wing Radicalism in Lahore, Pakistan, c. 1947–1971', PhD thesis, National University of Singapore, 2016
Verkaaik, Oskar, *Migrants and Militants: Fun and Violence in Pakistan* (Princeton, NJ, 2004)
Waseem, Mohammad, *Politics and the State in Pakistan* (Islamabad, 2007)
——, *The Political Conflict in Pakistan* (London, 2021)
Wasti, Syed Razi, *Lord Minto and the Indian Nationalist Movement, 1905–1910* (Oxford, 1964)
Wheeler, Mortimer, *Civilizations of the Indus Valley and Beyond* (London, 1966)
Williams, Rush Brook, *The East Pakistan Tragedy* (London, 1972)
Wolpert, Stanley, *Jinnah of Pakistan* (New York, 1984)
——, *Zulfi Bhutto of Pakistan: His Life and Time* (Karachi, 1993)
Yusufi, Mushtaq Ahmed, *Aab-i-Gum* (Karachi, 1990)
Zahab, Mariam Abou, *Pakistan: A Kaleidoscope of Islam* (London, 2020)
Zaheer, Sajjad, *The Light: The History of the Movement for Progressive Literature in the Indo-Pak Subcontinent* (Karachi, 2006)
Zahur, Bilal, and Raza Rumi, ed., *Rethinking Pakistan: A Twenty-First-Century Perspective* (Lahore, 2018)
Zaidi, S. Akbar, *Issues in Pakistan's Economy* (Karachi, 1999)
Zakariya, Khawaja, *Chand Aham Jadeed Shair* [A Few Important Past Poets] (Faisalabad, 2020)
Zaman, Qasim, *Islam in Pakistan: A History* (Princeton, NJ, 2018)
Zehra, Nasim, *From Kargil to the Coup: Events That Shook Pakistan* (Lahore, 2019)
Ziring, Lawrence, *Pakistan in the Twentieth Century: A Political History* (Karachi, 1997)
——, *Pakistan at the Crosscurrent of History* (London, 2003)

ACKNOWLEDGEMENTS

Throughout the course of writing this book, I found myself incurring numerous debts of gratitude, ones that I hold in the highest regard. At the forefront of my acknowledgements, I extend my heartfelt thanks to Michael Leaman, the astute director of the renowned publishing house Reaktion Books, for his unwavering faith in my abilities. It was his persuasive conviction that ignited the spark in me to embark on the formidable task of chronicling the rich history of Pakistan. To him, I am eternally indebted.

A profound debt of gratitude is also owed to the distinguished Professor Ian Talbot, who, in addition to being a friend, has been a trusted philosopher and guide throughout my academic journey. Professor Talbot's remarkable generosity in investing his time and wisdom, especially in mentoring young historians, is a testament to his enduring commitment to the field. His invaluable insights were instrumental in shaping my manuscript, as he meticulously reviewed every word and provided suggestions that enriched the study in ways beyond measure. It is not just this author, but the majority of historians from Pakistan, who find themselves indebted to Professor Talbot for his invaluable guidance and counsel.

A special mention must be reserved for Dr Kevin Greenbank, a luminary in the academic realm, whose association with the Centre of South Asian Studies and his role as vice president of Wolfson College, University of Cambridge, speaks volumes about his standing in the scholarly community. Dr Greenbank's meticulous scrutiny of the draft was nothing short of transformative. With his discerning eye and profound expertise, he assumed a central role in the refining of the text to reach its zenith, eradicating ambiguities that might have otherwise lingered and elevating the manuscript to its fullest potential.

Dr Greenbank's contributions extend far beyond mere academic aid; his sincere advice and unwavering support have been instrumental in realizing numerous milestones throughout my academic career. His generosity in providing access to invaluable archival sources and his sage counsel on how to refine my occasionally verbose writing style incur a debt of gratitude that transcends words. His influence has not only enriched the content but left an indelible mark on my approach to scholarship, for which I am profoundly indebted.

Furthermore, my heart brims with gratitude towards Professor Hussain Ahmed Khan and Dr Mehboob Ahmed, both esteemed colleagues and cherished friends, whose unwavering support and insightful guidance have been pivotal in shaping this narrative. Their scholarly contributions not only illuminated uncharted avenues but unearthed hidden sources that might have otherwise remained elusive, significantly enriching the profound depth and expansive breadth of this study.

Within the esteemed sphere of my colleagues, I owe a profound debt of gratitude to Ms Shandana Waheed, Dr Waqas Sajjad and Rabia Piracha. Their invaluable assistance transcended the conventional boundaries of collaboration, as they played a vital role in meticulously refining the manuscript. Their adeptness in the intricacies of the citation process ensured the study's adherence to rigorous academic standards, underpinning its integrity with unwavering diligence.

From the dedicated team at Reaktion Books, I extend my heartfelt appreciation to Amy Salter, the editor of the manuscript who tirelessly toiled to enhance the text. Her unrelenting commitment to identifying errors and ambiguities was indispensable, and her efforts have played a significant role in making this book a truly worthwhile read. I wish to express my profound gratitude to a number of individuals who played pivotal roles in the realization of this work. Foremost, my heartfelt appreciation extends to the talented picture editor, Alexandru Ciobanu. With unwavering dedication and painstaking effort, he meticulously curated a collection of pertinent images through his extensive resources. Alex's professionalism left an indelible mark on me, and his invaluable contributions to this project are deeply acknowledged.

I must also extend my sincere thanks to Mr Zahid Hussein, who generously permitted the use of his evocative photograph capturing the harrowing moment of a man being flogged during the Zia ul Haq era. His photographic artistry, documenting a tumultuous period in history, enriches this work.

In my pursuit of historical depth, I was fortunate to have the support of Adeel Ijaz, a promising young scholar in the field of history. His boundless potential became a guiding light whenever I found myself in need of additional sources. It is through the presence of such promising young minds that our optimism remains unwavering, even in the face of the daunting challenges that Pakistan grapples with today.

I would be remiss not to acknowledge the invaluable assistance of Shahrukh Baloch, whose expertise proved indispensable in the labyrinth of references that often appeared insurmountable. Baloch, a young scholar endowed with a rare talent for research methodology, lent his expertise to this endeavour, for which I am sincerely grateful.

Moreover, I owe a debt of gratitude to the *Journal of Punjab Studies*, which published my article 'Unfolding Crisis in Punjab, March–August 1947: Key Turning Points and British Responses' in 2007. This evolved into Chapter Three of this book, with certain refinements. I extend my profound appreciation to Dr Shinder Thandai, the steward of the journal, for his unwavering support. Furthermore, I must acknowledge my own publication, *The Humanities in Pakistan (1990–2020)*, issued by the Board of Regents of the University of Wisconsin System. Several passages from this publication have been seamlessly integrated into chapters Four and Eleven, enhancing the depth and context of this work.

Finally, I am pleased to express my deepest gratitude to my dear wife, Ayesha, who has embodied the age-old adage that behind every successful man stands an equally exceptional woman. Her unwavering support and encouragement have consistently fuelled my academic pursuits to their fullest potential. I am equally thankful for my son, Saad, whose unique form of support has been a pillar of strength. My daughter, Khadija, with her unwavering expectations of me as a historian, has significantly contributed to this endeavour. I acknowledge their indispensable roles with the utmost sincerity.

To all those mentioned and countless others who have contributed to this project in various capacities, I offer my sincerest thanks, as your support and guidance have been immeasurable in bringing this work to fruition.

PHOTO ACKNOWLEDGEMENTS

The author and publishers wish to express their thanks to the sources listed below for illustrative material and/or permission to reproduce it. Some locations of works are also given below, in the interest of brevity:

Bettmann/Getty Images: pp. 172, 214; British Library, London: p. 70; European Soil Data Centre (ESDAC): p. 176; Flickr: pp. 53 (photo Guilhem Vellut, CC BY 2.0), 421 (photo U.S. Institute of Peace, CC BY 2.0); photo Zahid Hussein, all rights reserved: p. 276; Iqbal Academy Pakistan, Lahore: p. 67; Keystone Press/Alamy Stock Photo: p. 162; Library of Congress, Geography and Map Division, Washington, DC: pp. 12, 370, 482; from *Modern Review*, 1/2 (February 1907): p. 48; Nationaal Archief, The Hague: pp. 68, 94, 220; National Archives and Records Administration: pp. 151 (Harry S. Truman Library and Museum, Independence, MO), 168 (Lyndon Baines Johnson Library and Museum, Austin, TX), 242 (Richard Nixon Library and Museum, Yorba Linda, CA), 293 (National Archives at College Park, MD), 384 (Barack Obama Library, Hoffman Estates, IL); National Library of Australia, Canberra: p. 79; Robert Nickelsberg/Getty Images: p. 294; photo Prime Minister's Office, Government of India (Government Open Data License (GODL) India): p. 487; from the *Railway Gazette* (24 October 1947): p. 118; TopFoto: p. 157; Unsplash: pp. 18 (Noman Bukhari), 452 (Azam Ch); photo U.S. Department of State: p. 383; photo U.S. Navy: p. 359; Wikimedia Commons: pp. 21 (photo Smn121, CC BY-SA 3.0), 30–31 (photo Fazeela Jamil, CC BY-SA 4.0), 32 (photo Teseum, CC BY-SA 4.0), 33 (photo Mhtoori, CC BY-SA 4.0), 40 (photo Ammarkh, CC BY-SA 4.0), 43 (photo Noman Ilahi, CC BY-SA 4.0), 138 (Mhtoori, CC BY-SA 4.0), 167 (photo Ziegler175, CC BY-SA 3.0), 342 (photo Usman Ghani, CC BY-SA 3.0), 392 (photo Muh.Ashar, CC BY-SA 3.0).

INDEX

Page numbers in *italic* refer to illustrations

10-Billion Tree Project 425, 442–3

Aali, Jamil ud Din 175
Abbasi, Shah Khaqan 345
Abdali, Ahmad Shah 45
Abdullah, Shaikh 132, 185
Adamjee 114
Adharba'ijan 35
Adilshahi sultanate 44
Afghanistan 10, 17, 24, 29, 32, 49, 107, 108, 136, 305, 321, 359, 385, 393, 399, 415, 444, 450, 454
    and Benazir Bhutto 306
    Taliban in 366, 368, 371, 392, 401, 456
    U.S. invasion of 390–91, 457, 486
    and Z. A. Bhutto 241–3
    see also war, Soviet–Afghan
Agra 13, 340
Ahmad Rana Maqbool 345
Ahmad, Aziz 36
Ahmad, Mirza Ghulam 137
Ahmadi exclusion 235–6, 267, 348
Ahmed Hassan Dani 28
Ahmed, Umera (Pir-i-Kamil) 374
Ahsan, S. M. 197, 198
Aibak, Qutbu'd-din 37
Al Qaeda 136, 259, 340
Al Zulfiqar 252, 257
Ala-ud-Din Khalji 35
Alexander (of Macedonia) 30, 33, 35
Ali, Chaudhary Muhammad 141, 150, 161, 169
Ali, Haider 47
Ali, Jam Sadiq 313, 319, 320
Ali, Sethi 373
Ali, Sher 202
Ali, Tariq 140, 373, 382
Allahabad address 77
Almeida, Cyril 401, 409, 470

Altyn Depe 25
Alvi, Arif 455, 478
Ambedkar, Bhimrao Ramji 76, 78
Amin, Nurul 206
Amri Nal 17, 18
Amri 17
Anjuman Ittehad-ul-Muslimeen 128
Ansari commission (1983) 262
Ant-Qadiani/Ahmadi movement 137, 157, 158
Arabian Peninsula 13
Arachosia 32
Archean age 14
Arif, Khalid Mehood 255
Army Public School Incident (APS) 408–9
Aryans 27, 28
Ashoka 32
Ashraf, Raja Pervez 386
Asiya, Bibi 394–5
Aslam, Nadeem 372
Aslam, Saiyma 372
Assam Bengal Railway 115
Auchinleck 97, 121, 122, 164
Awadh 42, 49
Awami League 152, 162, 173, 177, 203, 206, 207, 210, 213, 214, 226, 227
Ayurveda 39
Aziz, Abdul 366–7, 391, 392
Aziz, Sartaj 313, 323, 331
Aziz, Shaukat 353, 361, 379, 385

Bactria 27
Baghdad 35
Bahrain 25, 27
Bajaur 29
Bajwa, Qamar Javed 449, 457, 458, 461, 462, 463, 467, 488
Balakot 18, 23
Bampur 16

Bangladesh
  creation 208, 209, 211, 213–15, *214*, 217, 227, 238–9
  diplomatic relations 240
  Liberation War 214, 216, 297
  map of as East Pakistan *176*
  origins of national consciousness 155
Bannerji 20
Barelwi, Syed Ahmed 51–2
Basic Democracies 177–80
Battle of Burki 187
Battle of Buxer 48
Battle of Dograi 188
Battle of Hydaspes 30
Battle of Plassey 48
Beg, Mirza Aslam 293, 295–6, 299, 301, 304, 305, 316
Begam Khurshid 219, 221
Begum, Shireen Amir 220
Bentinck, William 57
Bhakra Dam 132
Bhakti movement 36, 39
Bharuch 23
Bhir Mound 32
Bhutto, Benazir 269–72, 292–3, *293*, 295–300, 301–17, 319, 322, 326–8, 329, 334, 335, 343, 350, 359–64, 367, 377–9, 381, 386, 410
Bhutto, Murtaza (son of Zulfiqar) 252, 257, 311, 325, 327
Bhutto, Nusrat 223, 253, 310, 311
Bhutto, Shahnawaz (son of Zulfiqar) 252, 310
Bhutto, Sir Shahnawaz 219, 220, 221
Bhutto, Zulfiqar Ali 169, 173, 185, 186, 206, 207, 208, 212, 217, 218–45, 220, 238, 242, 249–58, 263, 272, 273, 296, 297, 299, 311, 313, 315, 330, 332, 382, 383, 406
Bhutto-Zardari, Bilawal 11, 298, 418–19, 427, 428, 429, 448, 460
Bindusara 32
biraderi 145, 292
blasphemy laws 282–3
Bombay 47, 50, 57, 60, 67, 73, 112, 114, 119, 219–20, 314
  see also Mumbai Attack
Brahmaputra 14
Bronze Age 16
Bugti, Akbar Khan 313, 325, 376
Bukhara 35
Buner 29

Bush, George 327, 368
Butt, Zia ud Din 334, 339, 340

Calcutta/Kolkata 47, 48
Cambrian Period 14
Carnatic Wars 49
Carter, Jimmy 241, 258
Cawthorne, Walter Joseph 122
Chaghi (Baluchistan) 332
Chalcolithic era 18
Chambers, Clair 373
Chandragupta 32
Chanhu Daro 23, 26
Charter of Democracy 358–9
Chaudhary Iftikhar Muhammad 347, 365, 379, 387
Chaudhary, Aminullah 345
Chaudry, Fazal Illahi 251
Chauri Chaura 75
China 7, 184, 223, 224, 239, 383–4, 388, 412–13, 426, 446, 453–7, 468, 488
China–Pakistan Economic Corridor (CPEC) 414–16, 433, 453
Chitral 129
Chundrigar, Ibrahim Ismael 161
Clive, Robert 48
College, Fort William 55–6
constitutional history of Pakistan
  constitutional crisis (1993) 322
  constitutional framework for 104, 134
  delays 140–41, 152, 160
  dismissal of elected governments 293, 300, 326
  LFO of Yahya Khan 202–3
  validity 202
  see also individual constitutions; provisional constitutional order (PCO)
Constitution of 1956 8–9, 134, 152, 162, 175
  criticism of 164
  Jinnah and the formation of the Constitution 71–3, 146–7, 148, 484
  suspension of 164
Constitution of 1962 169–71, 168–70, 179, 192, 286
  abrogation of 196, 199
Constitution of 1973 9, 225, 228–9, 236, 243–4, 257, 262, 263–4, 267, 271, 353
  amendments 235–6, 251, 263, 267, 271, 290, 292, 304, 353–4
  Charter of Democracy (2006) 358–9
  constraints of 304

Ehsaas Programme (2019) amendments to 437
flouting of 432, 487
referendum by Zia (1984) 263, 269
reinstatement of Islamic practice *see* Islam and Islamization
suspension of (Musharraf) 339, 342, 343
suspension of (Zia) 253
use as justification for military actions 255
women 284
Constitution of India 76, 77, 78, 131
Cornwallis, Lord 50
Curzon, Lord 60–61, 66

Daimabad 24
Damascus 37
Damb Buthi 19
Damb Sadaat 17
Das, Rana Bhagwan 365
Dasht Valley 16
Daulah, Siraj-ud- 48
Daultana, Mumtaz Muhammad Khan 85, 88, 95, 117, 139, 203
Davis, Raymond (incident) 396–8
Dawn Leaks 408
Derawar fort 43
Dharmarajika monastery 32
Dholavira 23
Dilmun 25
Din, Muiz-ud 52–3
Dipalpur Canal 132, 133
Dogra, Gulab Singh 129
Dogra, Hari Singh 129, 130, 131
drugs and drug trafficking 260–61, 287, 290, 341
Durrani, Asad 314, 316, 317

Eaton, Richard M. 34
EBDO 171
Ebrahim, Fakhruddin G. 313
Ehsan, Aitzaz 322
Election Commission of Pakistan (ECP) 264, 324, 379
Elizabeth I 47
Enlai Zhou 237
Euphrates 16

Fahim, Makhdum Amin 381
Faiz, Faiz Ahmad 175
Faraizi movement 50–51

Farrukhi, Asif 372
Faruqi, Shams ur Rahman 372
Faylakah 25
Federal Security Force (FSF) 229, 230
Federally Administered Tribal Areas (FATA) 330, 359, 393, 406
Firoz Shah Tughluq 38

Gandhara Motors 174
Gandhara/Gandhara Civilization 29, 30, 31, 32, 33, 45
Gandhi, Indra 211, 218, 238
Gandhi, Mohandas Karamchand 70, 71–5, 94, 120, 124, 139
Ganga 13, 14, 211
Ghazna 38
Ghaznawi, Mahmud 38
Gilbert, Richard 180
Gillani, Yousaf Raza 381, 386–7, 398, 399
Godavari basin 24
Goodyear, Sara Sulehri 373, 374
Gopi Chand Narang 36
Gracey, Douglas 122, 155, 164, 167
Grama 29
Grand National Alliance (GDA) 343
Gul, Hamid 299, 305, 306
Gumla 19
Gupta Empire 31, 32, 33

Habib, Irfan 19, 26
Hakra-Gagger 13, 17, 19, 21
Hamid, Mohsin 371–2, 375
Hamid, Omar Shahid 371
Hamood ur Rahman Commission 230
Hanafi law 37
Hanif, Muhammad 372–3
Haq, Ijaz ul 252
Haq, Mansur ul 363
Haq, Raja Zafar ul 346
Haq, Zia ul 136, 217, 222, 239, 244–90, 247, 291–2, 294–5, 299, 302, 304, 305–7, 312, 346, 347, 366, 374, 375, 378
Haqqani, Hussain 400, 401, 402
Harappa 17–19, 20–27, 21
Haroon, Mahmoud 313
Harvard Advisory Group 179, 180
Haryana 17, 20
Hashim, Abul 124
Hassan, Mubashir 225
Hassan, Syed Munawar 344
Hastinapur 27

Hastings, Warren 47, 48
Hayat, Faisal Saleh 328
Helmand 17
Hephthalites 31, 33
Hijrat 110
Hildreth, Horace 222, 223
Himalayas 14
Hooghly 47
Hudood Ordinance 275, 279–83
Huns (white) 31, 32, 33
Hunza Valley 30–31
Hunter Committee 74
Hussain Aamer 372
Hussain, Abdullah 374
Hussain, Abida 315, 317
Hussain, Altaf 288–90, 321, 351
Hussain, Chaudhary Shujaat 344, 353
Hussain, Intizar 108, 109, 110, 373, 374
Hussain, Zahid 180
Hussein, king of Jordan 248, 249
Hyderabad state 127–8
Hyderabad 13, 42, 305, 338

Ibn Battuta 37
Imam, Syed Fakhar 298
India, political map of 79
Indian National Congress (INC) 46, 63–5, 69, 111, 112, 125, 144, 165
Indus Water Basin Treaty 133
Iqbal, Allama Muhammad 67, 76–7
Islam and Islamization 8, 276–84, 348, 194, 226, 281, 371
  of the economy 273
  idea of Islam as cornerstone of Pakistan 134–8, 141, 143, 144
  'Islamic socialism' 224
  Islamic welfare state 439
  Jamaat-e-Islami revolution 344
  and the military 278–9
  under Musharraf 348
  prohibition 280–81
  radicalism and radical interpretations of 287–8, 292
  Shariat Bill 278, 321
  shariat and the Shariat Court 274, 275, 278
  tool of political mobilization 149
  Titu Mir as proponent of 52
  and women 275, 281–2, 284, 296
  in Yahya Khan's LFO (1970) 201–3
  Zia as 'Islamic ideologue' 269
Zia's policies 246, 249, 253, 255, 257, 261, 262, 263, 274, 275–80, 284–6, 287, 290, 291, 302, 307, 486
  see also blasphemy laws; Hudood Ordinance; Ramadan
Islami Jamhuri Ittehad (IJI) 298, 299, 301, 302, 303
Islamophobia 371–2, 373–4
Ispahani, Mirza Ahmad 114–15
Issa, Qazi Faiz 141

Jaffar, Mir 48, 49, 53
Jallianwala Bagh Massacre 74
Jamaat-i-Islami 344, 378, 390
Jamali, Mir Zafarullah Khan 352–3
Jamia Hafsa 366, 391
Jamil Jalbi 36
Janjua, Asif Nawaz 320, 321
Jati Umera 334
Jatoi, Ghulam Mustafa 313, 314–15, 326
Javed, Kanza 372
Jenkins, Evan 86–7, 89-90, 91, 92, 93, 96–7, 100
Jha, D. N. 26
Jhangvi, Haq Nawaz 287
Jinnah, Fatima 172, *172*, 173
Jinnah, Muhammad Ali 67–72, *68*, *70*, *172*
  mausoleum of *138*
Jirga 107
Jizya 37, 38
Johnson, Lyndon B. *168*
Julludur 248, 249
Jumna 13
Junagarh 127–8
Junejo, Muhammad Khan 251, 256, 267, 270–72, 386

Kakar, Abdul Waheed 321, 322
'Kalashnikov culture' 290, 371
Kalat 16
Kalibangan 17, 19, 23, 24
Kandahar 16
Kandyan kingdom 49
Kanishka stupa 30
KANUPP 183
Kanwal, Aroosa 372
Karamat, Jehangir 326, 333, 339
Kargil operation 334, 338, 339, 346, 369
Karnafuli Multipurpose Project 116
Kartarpur Sahib Gurdwara 452

Index

Kashmir 10, 24, 100, 120, 122, 129–32, 156, 164, 167, 184–7, 190–91, 196, 224, 238, 321, 339, 359, 369, *370*, 392, 393, 451, 455
Kasim, Mir 48
Kasuri, Ahmed Raza 251, 254
Kayani, Ashfaq Pervaiz 298–9, 360, 387, 398, 401
Kechi Beg 17
Kenyapithicus 15
Khalid, Malik Meraj 315, 326, 329–30
Khalilzad, Zalmay 382
Khan Liaquat Ali 135, 148, 151, *151*, 155
khan of kalat 107
Khan, Abdul Hamid 197, 210
Khan, Abdul Qadeer 238, 369
Khan, Abdul Qayyum Khan 130, 131, 162
Khan, Abdul Wali 250, 315
Khan, Air Marshal Asghar 123
Khan, Amir Muhammad (of Kalabagh) 174
Khan, Ayub 123, 140, 141, 156, 157, 158, 161–93, *168*, 194, 196, 197, 199, 218, 219, 222, 223, 224, 228, 256, 286, 348, 400
Khan, Ghazanfar Ali 89
Khan, Ghulam Ishaq 262, 272, 293–5, *294*, 299, 300, 303, 304, 305, 313, 314, 316, 319, 320, 322, 410
Khan, Imran 7, 8, 10, 343, 350, 352, 403, 404, 417, 420–27, *421*, 429–36, 438, 440, 442, 443, 444, 447, 449, 450, 453, 455, 456, 458–61
Khan, Monem 174
Khan, Musa 186, 187
Khan, Nawabzada Nasullah 315, 326, 344
Khan, Noor 197, 198, 199
Khan, Rahim ud Din 255
Khan, Sahibzada Yaqub Ali 203–5, 304
Khan, Sir Ahmed Khan 46, *48*, 58–9, 80
Khan, Tikka 205, 206, 208
Khan, Uzma Aslam 372
Khan, Yahya 163, 192, 194–217, *195*, 227, 229, 256
Khar, Malik Ghulam Mustafa 251, 313, 315, 326
Kharal, Ahmad Khan 375
Khilafat Movement 75
Khuhro, Ayub 140
Khurasan 44
Khusrau (Amir) 35–8
Khwarizm 35
Khyber Pass 27, 166, *167*
Kidarites 33

Kissinger, Henry 240
Kohtras Buthi 19
Kokcha River 24
Kosygin, Alexei 189
Kot Diji 13, 17–22
Krishak Praja Party 148
Kujula Kadphises 29
kula 29
kulapa 29
Kulli 16, 17, 19
Kunal region 19
Kuntasi 23
Kushan 29, 32, 33

labour disputes 156, 181, 274, 302
Laden, Osama bin 136, 305, 339, 340, 385, 388, 391, 397–9, 401
Lahore Museum 53
Lahore Resolution 46, 78
Lal Masjid 365–7, 375, 391
land reforms (under Bhutto) 233–5
language controversy 154–5
Larkana 17, 19, 219, 222, 335
Lasbela 16
Lashkar-i-Jhangvi 285, 286, 287, 292, 367, 404
Lashkar-i-Tayyiba 393
Legal Framework Order 201–3, 350, 353
Leghari, Farooq 312, 315, 325–6, 327, 328, 329, 331, 332, 350
Lothal 23, 24, 25, 26, 27
Lucknow 13
Lucknow Pact 69

Mackenzie, Holt 50
Madhopur Headworks 132
Madhya Pradesh 24
Madras/Chennai 47, 50
Magadha 31, 32
Mahabharata 27
Mahalwari system 50
Majlis-i-Ahrar 137, 329
Majlis-i-Shoora 261–2
Majlis-i-Tahfuz-i-Khatam-i-Nabuwat (MTKN) 137
Makran 16, 25
Malabar coast 37
Maliki Law 38
Mamdot, Iftikhar Hussain Khan 86, 87, 90, 100, 117, 139
Mandal, Jogindar Nath 135

Mankiyala 32
Mansoor, Ijaz 400–402
Manto, Saadat Hasan 109, 205
Marathas 42, 44, 49
Marshall, John 19–20
Marshall, P. J. 48
martial castes 106
Marwar 44
Masulipatnam 47
Maududi, Abul Ala 285
Mauryan Empire 32
mausoleum of Shah Rukn-e Alam *40*
Mazari, Balakh Sher 322, 326
Mediterranean 14, 38
Mehmood Sherani 36
Mehsud Baitullah 391
Memogate Scandal 399–402
Menon, V. P. 130
Mesopotamia 25, 27
Messervy, Francis 122, 155
Mewar 44
Minto-Morley Reform 66
Miocene period 15
Mir, Safdar 175
Mir, Taqi Mir 45
Mirza, Iskander 140–41, 149, 151, 158, 161, *162*, 163–5, 168, 175, 197, 222, 223
Miyan, Dudu 51
Miyawaki forest 444
Mlecca 35
Model Town Incident 407–8
Modi, Narendra 7, 11, 460, *487*, 488
Mohenjo Daro 17–23, *18*, 26
Mortimer Wheeler 15, 23
Mountbatten, Louis 82, 83, 84, 89, 91, 93–4, *94*, 96, 100, 101, 112, 121, 125–6, 130, 165, 167
Movement for Restoration of Democracy (MRD) 256–8, 263, 264, 268
Mueenuddin, Daniyal 372
Mughal Ghundai 19
Mughal 39, 40, 41, 42, 43, 44, 45, 47, 49, 55, 59, 70, 128, 148, 163, 337, 373,
Muhammad bin Qasim 13, 37, 45
Muhammad, Malik Ghulam 141, 149, 150, 151, *157*, 161
Muhammad, Sufi 390, 392
Mukhtar, Ahmed 381
Mukti Bahini 210, 210, 211, 212, 217
Mulk, Nizamu'l 42
Mumbai Attack 393

Munro, Thomas 50
Musharraf, Pervez 222, 334, 335, 337–76, *359*, 377, 378, 385, 388, 391
Muslim Nationalism 65–73
Muttahida Majlis-i-Amal (MMA) 351, 378, 380
Muttahida Qaumi Movement (MQM) 288–90, 301, 302, 315, 318, 321, 324, 327, 331, 332, 343, 350, 351, 365, 381
Muzaffargarh 315

Nageshwar 23
Nagwada 19
Naidu, Sarojini 69
Nal-Hingol Valley 16, 19
Namazga culture 25
Naqai, Sardar Arif 328
Naqvi, Tanvir 354
Narmada River 23
National Accountability Bureau (NAB) 335, 358, 360
National Reconciliation Ordinance (NRO) 360, 361, 364, 367
National Reconstruction Bureau (NRB) 354, 357
nationalization 199, 218, 224, 225, 232–4, 267, 272–3
Natiq, Ali Akbar 374–5
Nawaz, Hussain 344
Nehru Report 71
Nehru, Jawaharlal 72, 91, 101, 125, 129, 131, 132, 221, 240
Niazi, Amir Abdullah Khan 209–10, 216–17
Nixon, Richard 241, *242*
non-nuclear-weapon policy 239
Noon, Feroze Khan 89, 149, 161, 162
Northwestern Railway 116
nuclear programme and capability 183, 231, 240, 241–2, 258, 275, 318, 327, 332, 333–4, 340, 361, 370, 413
see also non-nuclear-weapon policy
Nusrat, S. A. 263–4

Oakley, Robert 303
Obama, Barack 383, *384*, 398
Objective Resolution 135, 136, 267, 268
oligarchy 134, 139, 150, 160, 161, 176
Operation Blitz 204–5
Operation Clean-Up 320–21, 326
Operation Desert Hawk 185
Operation Enduring Freedom 367
Operation Fair Play 251

Index

Operation Gibraltar 184, 185, 186–90, 191
Operation Grand Slam 186–7, 190
Operation Midnight Jackal 305
Operation Riddle 187
Operation Searchlight 208, 210, 227
Operation Sunrise 367
Operation Windup 188
Orient Airways 114–115
Oxford (Christ Church college) 221
Oxus Valley 16, 24

Pagaro, Pir 222, 386
Pak Airways 115
Pakistan Democratic Movement (PDM) 171, 415, 416, 419, 431, 447, 448, 449, 458, 459, 463, 464, 467, 468, 479, 480, 488
Pakistan Eastern Railway 115
Pakistan Institute of Development Economics (PIDE) 180
Pakistan Muslim League Nawaz (PML-N) 324, 330–33, 346, 351, 369, 378, 379, 380, 381, 386, 402, 403, 404, 407, 410, 414, 417, 421, 424–5, 427, 431–2, 447–9, 465–7, 470
Pakistan Muslim League (Q) 351, 352, 353, 378, 379, 380, 386
Pakistan National Alliance (PNA) 244, 245, 250, 251
Pakistan People's Party (PPP) 191, 192, 224, 225, 226, 228, 230, 233, 291, 302–2, 307, 312, 313, 379, 380, 381, 403
Pakistan, political map of 482
Pakistan Steel Mill 226, 241
Pakistan Tehreek-i-Insaf (PTI) 343, 378, 402, 403, 412, 414, 417–18, 419, 420, 421, 423, 424, 425, 427, 431, 432, 440, 442, 447–56, 459, 460, 465, 466, 467, 468, 470–71, 475–9
Panama Scandal 416–18, 419, 425, 432, 488
Panjshir Valley 24
Parliament House, Islamabad 342
Pashtun Tahafuz Movement (PTM) 404–7
Periano Ghundai 19
PICIC 159
PIDC 159, 312
PINSTECH 183
Pirpur report 78
Pirzada, Ghulam Muhy-ud-Din 197, 198, 201
Pleistocene 14
Poonch 130, 186

power generation and capacity 116, 223, 311–12, 410–14, 444–5
Press and Publication Ordinance 172
Pressler Amendment 318, 327
Prithviraj Chauhan 35
Progressive Papers Limited 172
Progressive Writers Association 10, 108, 109
provisional constitutional order (PCO) 261–2, 342, 347
public flogging 275, 276
Public and Representatives Office (Disqualification) Act (PRODA) 105, 140
Punjab Alienation of Land Act 82
Punjab Boundary Commission 98–101
purohita 29

Qadir, Manzoor 169
Qadiri, Mumtaz 393, 394
Qadri, Tahir ul 403, 407, 408
Qalander, Shahbaz 219, 382
Qureshi, Moin 322–3
Qureshi, Shah Mehmood 381, 393, 397, 424, 450, 456
Quwwat-ul-Islam Mosque 38

Radcliffe, Cyril 96, 98–100, 125–6, 132
Rahim, J. A. 225
Rahman, Mujibur 173, *174*, 177, 191, 203, 205, 206, 207, 208, 226, 227, *238*
Rahman, Tariq 372
Raiwind 335
Raja, Khadim Hussain 199
Rajasthan 17, 20
Ramadan 284
Ramapithecus 15
Ramayana 27
Ranade, Mahadev Govind 44
Rann of Kutch 184–5, 369
Raphael, Arnold 252
Ras al-Junayz (Oman) 25
Rashtra 29
Rashtriya Swayam Sevak Sangh 85
Ratanpur 23
Read, Alexander 50
Reagan, Ronald 258, 259
referendum (under Musharaf) 348–50, 353
refugees 88, 114, 116, 117–18, 120, 133, 174, 302
  Afghan refugees 258, 260, 274, 289
  Bengali refugees 211
  migration of refugees *118*, 212–13

Rehman Dheri 17, 18
Rehman, Fazl ur 302, 315, 326, 331, 403, 447
Republican Party 152, 161
Riaz, Fahmida 371
Rice, Condoleezza 298
Richard, John 40
Rig Veda 28
Rohira 18
Round Table Conference 71, 83
Rowlett Committee Report 73
Roy, Raja Tridev 206
Ryotwari system 50

Saeed, Hafiz Muhammad 393
Safdar, Khawaja Muhammad 261
Sajjad, Waseem 300, 322–3, 346
Salala incident 398–9
Salt Range 14
Sassanians 33
Sauda, Mirza Muhammad Rafi 45
Saudi Arabia 260, 340
Saxena, Bhimsen 42
Scythians 32
Scytho-Parthians 33
Sehwan Sharif 219
Senani 29
Seventeenth Amendment 353–4
Shah, Ghaus Ali 345
Shah, Justice Sajjad Ali 333
Shah, Nadir 44
Shah, Nasim Hassan 322
Shahab, Qudrat Ullah 175
Shahi Tump 16
Shahr-i Sokhta 25
Shamsie, Kamila 372
Shamsie, Muneeza 372
Shapur I 33
Shariatullah, Haji 50, 51
Sharif, Arshad 473, 474, 480
Sharif, Mian Muhammad 332, 334
Sharif, Nawaz 269, 270, 272, 293, 299, 303, 307–9, 313, 317–25, 329, 331, 332, 334, 335, 339–41, 343–5, 350, 378, 408, 410, 414, *487*
Sharif, Raheel 408, 409
Sharif, Shahbaz 407, 417, 428, 430
Shastri, Lal Bahadur 189
Shehr-e-ashoob 45
Sherpao, Aftab Ahmad Khan 313, 315, 325
Shivaji 44
Shortughai 24, 25

Siachen Glacier 369–70
Siddiqi, Saeed uz Zaman 333, 347, 381
Sidwa, Bapsi 373
Simla Agreement 226
Singh, Manmohan 369
Singh, Ranjit 52–3
Sipah-e-Sahaba (SSP) (Shia-Sunni conflict) 285–8, 290, 366, 367
Sirhindi, Shaikh Ahmad 39, 40
Sirsukh 33
Sivapithecus 15
Siwalik Hills 14
Soomro, Illahi Bux 346
Sothi Siswal 17, 19
Sotkakoh 25
Soviet Union 223, 224, 240–41, 243, 258, 259, 260
    see also war, Soviet-Afghan
Sufism 14, 40
Suhrawardy, Hossain Shaheed 124, 171
Sulehri, Zia ud Din 373
Suleri, Sara 373
Sultan, Tipu 47
Sumerians 25
Surkotada 19
Sutkagen-dor 25
Swat Valley 392

Tagore, Rabindranath 63–4, 73
Talpur, Chulam Ali 140
Talukdar 50
Tanweer, Bilal 372
Tarar, Mustansar Hussain 374
Tarakai Qila 19
Tarar, Rafiq 264, 332–3, 334, 340
Taseer, Salman, assassination of 393–4
Tashkent Declaration 177, 184, 189–90, 224, 225
Taxila 13, 29, 30–33
    Dharmarajika 33
    stupa at Jaulian monastery 32
Tehreek-i- Laibaik-Ya-Rasool Allah 395
Tehrik-e-Nifaz-Shariat-Mohammadi (TNSM) 390, 391
Tehrik-e-Taliban Pakistan (TTP) 366–7, 390, 391, 392
Tehrik-i-Nifaz-i-Fiqa-i-Jafari (TNFJ) 285, 286, 290
Tilak, Gangadhar 44
Titu Mir 51–2
Tiwana, Khizr Hayat Khan 84–8, 100

Toynbee, Arnold 179
Truman, Harry S. *151*
Tughlaq dynasty 37
Turkmenistan 25

Umar, Ghulam 198, 202
Unionist Party 83, 84, 148
United States Agency for International Development (USAID) 116
Urdu–Hindi controversy 152–5

Vaishnavite 39, 41
Vedic tradition literature 27
viceregalism 105
Victoria, queen 60

Wahab, Muhammad bin Abdul 50
Walliullah, Shah 52
war
   Bangladesh Liberation War *see* Bangladesh
   civil war 198, 215
   Gulf War 296, 318, 321
   of Independence 57–8
   India–Pakistan war of 1965 183–4, 195, 224, 225, 249, 338
   India–Pakistan war of 1971 206–14, 338
   Soviet–Afghan 252, 258–61, 271–2, 290, 371
   'War on Terror' 368, 381, 387, 390, 425
   Yom Kippur War 239
Warsak Project 116
Wattoo, Mian Manzur Ahmed 322, 324, 327–8
Writer's Guild 175
Wyne, Ghulam Haider 313

Yousafzai Malala 393
yunani tibb 39

Zagros Mountains 16
Zakat and Ushr Ordinance 273, 276, 485
Zamir, Ehtesham 380
Zardari, Asif Ali 270, 298, 307, 309–11, 322, 335, 336, 359–64, 380–402, *383, 384*
Zardari, Hakim Ali 309, 311
zimmi 37